# THE VICE-PRESIDENTS AND CABINET MEMBERS

Biographies Arranged Chronologically
by Administration

## Volume II

*by*

**ROBERT I. VEXLER**

**1975**

**OCEANA PUBLICATIONS, INC.**
Dobbs Ferry, New York

Library of Congress Cataloging in Publication Data

Vexler, Robert I
    The Vice-Presidents and cabinet members.

    Includes index.
    1. Vice-Presidents--United States--Biography.
2. Cabinet officers--United States--Biography.
3. United States--Biography. I. Title.
E176.V48          973'.0992 [B]    75-28085
ISBN 0-379-12089-5 (v.1)
ISBN 0-379-12090-9 (v.2)

© Copyright 1975 by Oceana Publications, Inc.

Manufactured in the United States of America

# TABLE OF CONTENTS

## Volume I

## Volume II

VOLUME II

## ADMINISTRATION OF WILLIAM H. TAFT

### VICE PRESIDENT: JAMES SCHOOLCRAFT SHERMAN

James S. Sherman, Vice President in the Administration of President William Howard Taft, was born on October 24, 1855 in Utica, New York, the son of Richard Updike Sherman, a newspaper editor and state legislator, and Mary Frances (Sherman) Sherman. After being educated in the New Hartford public schools, Utica Academy and the Whitestown Seminary, James attended Hamilton College from which he was graduated with the Bachelor of Arts degree in 1878.

James studied law at Hamilton College and received his LL.B. degree in 1879. He was admitted to the bar in the same year and then began began his practice in his brother-in-law Henry J. Cookingham's law firm. James married Carrie Babcock on January 26, 1881. They had three children: Sherrill, Richard and Thomas. James soon became involved in politics as a Republican and business affairs. He was elected Republican Mayor of Utica in 1884 but did not run for reelection in 1886.

James S. Sherman was elected to the United States House of Representatives in 1886. He served in the Fifty-second through the Fifty-ninth Congresses from March 4, 1893 to March 3, 1909. He did not seek reelection in 1908. While in Congress he was head of the Indian Affairs Committee and was quite effective in his work. The Indian School at Riverside, California is called Sherman Institute in his honor. He often presided over the House when it was made into a committee of the whole. James also introduced the false branding bill protecting American cheese manufacturers. He presented a report advocating an interoceanic canal and urged construction of a cable to the Philippines. He also presided over three New York State Republican conventions.

Sherman became president of the New Hartford Canning Company when his father died in 1895. He was one of the founders of the Utica Trust and Deposit Company in 1899 and became its president in 1900. Hamilton College of which he was a trustee conferred upon him the LL.D. degree in 1905. He served as chairman of the Republican congressional campaign in 1900.

At the Republican National Convention in 1908 President Roosevelt had virtually dictated the nomination of William Howard Taft for President. The delegates balked at the proposal for Vice President and nominated James S. Sherman for Vice President. Taft and Sherman were elected in November 1908. They were inaugurated as President and Vice President respectively on March 4, 1909. Sherman was renominated in 1912 but died before the end of the campaign and his term of office on October 30, 1912 in Utica, New York. He was buried in Forest

Hill Cemetery.

Bibliography:
  Black, Gilbert J., ed.  William Howard Taft, 1857-
1930.  Dobbs Ferry, N.Y.: Oceana Publications, Inc.,
1970.
  Cookinham, Henry J.  History of Oneida County, New
York, from 1700 to the Present Time.  vol. I.  Chicago:
The S. J. Clarke Publishing Company, 1912.
  Kelly, Frank K.  The Fight for the White House; the
Story of 1912.  New York: Thomas Y. Crowell, 1961.
  Pringle, Henry F.  Life and Times of William H. Taft,
a Biography.  2 vols.  New York: Farrar and Rinehart,
Inc., 1939.
  Sherman, Frank D.  The Ancestry of John Taylor Sherman.
New York: Private Printing, 1918.

### SECRETARY OF STATE: PHILANDER CHASE KNOX

Refer to the biographical sketch of Philander C. Knox
under Attorney General in the Administration of William
McKinley, page 409.

### SECRETARY OF THE TREASURY: FRANKLIN MACVEAGH

Franklin MacVeagh, Secretary of the Treasury in the
Cabinet of President William H. Taft, was born on November 22, 1837 on a farm near Phoenixville, Pennsylvania, the son of Major John and Margaret (Lincoln)
MacVeagh.  After being educated by private tutors and
then at the Freeland Seminary, which later became Ur-
sinus College at Collegeville, Pennsylvania.  He then
went to Yale College from which he was graduated in
1862.

MacVeagh attended Columbia Law School, receiving the
LL.B. degree in 1864.  He next read law in Judge John
Worth Edmonds' office and was admitted to the bar in
the same year.  He practiced law with his brother Wayne
MacVeagh in Philadelphia.  Franklin had to leave his
practice because of poor health.  He moved to Chicago,
Illinois in 1866 and entered the firm of Whitaker and
Harmon, a wholesale grocery house.  Its name was soon
changed to Whitaker, Harmon and Company.  He married
Emily Eames on October 2, 1868.  They had five children.
The great fire at Chicago in 1871 destroyed MacVeagh's
firm.  He helped to feed the victims of the fire and
served on a relief committee.

MacVeagh went back into business as soon as he received the insurance funds.  He organized the wholesale
grocer firm of Franklin MacVeagh and Company which became one of the largest such firms in the United States.
Franklin also continued his civic responsibilities and
served on a Citizens; Committee Against Graft to elimi-

nate corruption from local government.  Among its suc-
cesses was the non-political reorganization of the fire
department, establishment of a responsible city government in place of the many offices and enlargement of
the water supply.  MacVeagh was also a member of the Civil Service Reform League of Chicago, serving as its
vice president during the years 1884 and 1885.  He became a director of the Commercial National Bank beginning in 1881 and continued for twenty-eight years.

Although MacVeagh was originally a Republican he joined
the Democrats and supported Grover Cleveland for President in 1884, 1888 and 1892.  He was the unsuccessful
Democratic candidate for Illinois Senator in 1894.  He
could not support the free silver platform of the Democrats in 1896 and returned to the Republican Party.  In
the same year he became president of the Chicago Bureau
of Charities and continued in that post until 1904.  He
published "A Program of Municipal Reform" in the American Journal of Sociology, March 1896.  He became a trustee of the University of Chicago in 1901 and continued
until 1913.

President William H. Taft named Fanklin MacVeagh Secretary of the Treasury on March 5, 1909.  He assumed
his office on March 8, 1909 and served until March 4,
1913.  He left the issue of currency reform to the national monetary commission.  He supported the proposal
for establishment of a central banking system.  He is
supposed to have suggested the concept of piecemeal
downward revision of tariffs to President Taft.  Mac-
Veagh helped to rehabilitate the customs service after
a Congressional committee report indicated frauds.  He
also modified old regulations in regard to payments to
the Treasury in certain kinds of currency.  In 1912
Franklin MacVeagh supported President Taft in his struggle against Theodore Roosevelt.

MacVeagh returned to business and philanthropic affairs
after leaving public office.  Among his activities during
his life were foundation of the Municipal Art League of
Chicago of which he was president.  This group was involved in furnishing designs for public improvements
and utilities.  He was a member of many academic organizations among which were the Chicago Historical Society,
the American Economic Association, the American Historical Association, the American Forestry Association, the
American Political Science Association, the American
Red Cross Association and the National Geographic Society.  Franklin MacVeagh died on July 6, 1934 in Chicago, Illinois.  He was buried in Graceland Cemetery.

Bibliography:
  Black, Gilbert J., ed.  William Howard Taft, 1857-1930.
Dobbs Ferry, N.Y.: Oceana Publications, Inc., 1970.
  Butt, Archibald W.  Taft and Roosevelt, the Intimate

Letters of Archie Butt.  Garden City, New York: Double-
day, Doran and Company, 1930.
    Duffy, Herbert S.  William Howard Taft.  New York:
Minton, Balch and Company, 1939.
    Gilbert, Paul T. and Bryson, C. L.  Chicago and Its
Makers. . .  Chicago: F. Mendelson, 1929.
    Pringle, Henry F.  The Life and Times of William Howard
Taft.  New York: Farrar and Rinehart, Inc, 1939.
    Wilensky, Norman M.  Conservatives in the Progressive
Era: The Taft Republicans of 1912.  Gainesville: Univer-
sity of Florida Press, 1965.

## SECRETARY OF WAR: JACOB MCGAVOCK DICKINSON

Jacob M. Dickinson, Secretary of War in the Cabinet
of President William H. Taft  was born on January 30,
1851 in Columbus, Mississippi, the son of Henry and
Anna (McGavock) Dickinson.  Jacob served as a volunteer
at the age of fourteen as a private in the Confederate
army under General Ruggles.  His family moved to Nashville, Tennessee after the Civil War.

After receiving a basic education in the private
schools Jacob went to the University of Nashville from
which he received the Bachelor of Arts degree in 1871
and the Masters degree in 1872.  He then studied law at
Columbia University after which he continued his legal
preparation in Leipzig and Paris.  Dickinson was admitted to the Tennessee bar in 1874, establishing his legal practice in Nashville.  Jacob married Martha Overton on April 20, 1876.  They had three sons: John Overton, Henry and Jacob McGavock, Jr.

Jacob Dickinson was president of the Tennessee Bar
Association in the years 1889 and 1890.  He also accepted temporary appointments on the Tennessee Supreme Court
in the years 1891, 1892 and 1893.  His next appointment
was that of United States assistant attorney general
from 1895 to 1897.  The Louisville and Nashville Railroad retained Dickinson as one of its attorneys.  He
became its general attorney in 1897 and continued until
1899.  He moved to Chicago, Illinois in that year.  He
was next retained as general solicitor of the Illinois
Central Railroad from 1899 to 1901 and was its general
counsel from 1901 to 1909.  During this period Jacob
was president of the American Bar Association during
1907 and 1908.

Dickinson also was in government service as a counsel
for the United States before the Alaskan Boundary Tribunal.  After this service Dickinson became interested
in international issues and helped to organize the American Society of International Law in 1906.  He was on
the executive council from 1907 to 1910 and was its
vice president beginning in 1910.

President William H. Taft appointed Jacob M. Dickinson

Secretary of War.  He served from March 5, 1909 until
his resignation in May 1911 because of financial re-
verses.  He returned to his private law practice.
Dickinson was called on to act as United States special
assistant attorney general in the prosecution of the
United States Steel Corporation in 1913.  Dickinson
was receiver of the Rock Island Lines from 1915 to 1917.
He also was involved in connection with prosecution of
the labor cases in 1922.

In the later 1920's Jacob Dickinson slowly began to
withdraw from legal affairs.  He was interested in
fishing and hunting which led to his belief in conservation.  He worked with the Izaak Walton League, serving
as its president from 1927 to 1928.  Jacob M. Dickinson
died on December 13, 1928 in Washington, D.C.  He was
buried in Nashville, Tennessee.

Bibliography:
  Black, Gilbert J., ed.  William Howard Taft, 1857-1930.
Dobbs Ferry, N.Y.: Oceana Publications, Inc., 1970.
  Butt, Archibald W.  Taft and Roosevelt, the Intimate
Letters of Archie Butt.  Garden City, N.Y.: Doubleday,
Doran and Company, 1930.
  Duffy, Herbert S.  William Howard Taft.  New York:
Minton Balch and Company, 1939.
  Lee, Blewett.  "Jacob McGavock Dickinson, 1851-1928,"
Journal of the American Bar Association (February, 1929),
69-71.
  Pringle, Henry F.  The Life and Times of William How-
ard Taft.  New York: Farrar and Rinehart, Inc., 1939.

## SECRETARY OF WAR: HENRY LEWIS STIMSON

Henry L. Stimson, Secretary of War in the Cabinet of
President William H. Taft, Secretary of State in the
Cabinet of President Herbert Hoover and again Secretary
of War in the Cabinets of Presidents Franklin D. Roosevelt and Harry S. Truman, was born on September 21, 1867
in New York, New York, the son of Lewis Atterbury Stimson, a surgeon, and Candace (Wheeler) Stimson.  Henry
attended Phillips Academy at Andover, Massachusetts and
then went to Yale University from which he was graduated
in 1888.  Stimson next studied at Harvard in 1888 and
1889, receiving the Master of Arts degree in the latter
year.

Stimson next went to Harvard Law School from 1889 to
1890.  He then studied and worked for the firm of Root
and Clark in 1890.  Henry was admitted to the bar in
1891 and began his legal practice in New York City by
continuing with the firm of Root and Clark.  He became
a partner in 1893.  Henry L. Stimson married Mabel
Wellington on July 6, 1893.  His law firm was reorganized
in 1897 as Root, Howard, Winthrop and Stimson.  It be-

became Winthrop and Stimson in 1901.

President Theodore Roosevelt appointed Henry L. Stimson United States district attorney for the Southern district of New York in 1906. He required Edward H. Harriman to testify in regard to his railroad operations and was successful in the prosecution of the sugar trust in regard to customs frauds. Although he resigned from the post in 1909 Stimson was appointed special counsel to serve in the federal antitrust suits. Stimson was defeated as the Republican candidate for Governor of New York in 1910 despite the strong backing of President Theodore Roosevelt.

President William H. Taft named Henry L. Stimson Secretary of War to succeed Jacob M. Dickinson. Stimson served at the War Department from May 16, 1911 until the end of the Taft administration on March 4, 1913. He supervised the reorganization of the army. After leaving the cabinet Stimson's next public service as a delegate to the New York State constitutional convention in 1915. He was chairman of the committee on state finances. He also participated in various military and civilian capacities during the First World War. He was a member of the cooperating home committee created by President Woodrow Wilson in 1914 to work with the Commission for Relief in Belgium.

Among his other activities during the War Henry L. Stimson was appointed a judge advocate with the rank of major in the United States army reserve. When the United States declared war Stimson was commissioned a lieutenant colonel in the 305th Field Artillery. He went to France in December 1917 and remained there until August 1918. In the latter month he was promoted to the rank of colonel in the 31st Field Artillery. He was commissioned a brigadier general in the army reserve corps.

Stimson returned to his law practice after the war. He still remained active in politics. President Calvin Coolidge named him a special peace envoy to Nicaragua in March 1927 to act as a mediator in the civil war which was raging over the presidential nomination there. He was able to arrange a settlement which was signed by both parties to the dispute on April 22, 1927. Stimson published <u>American Foreign Policy in Nicaragua</u> in 1927. After he returned from his mission President Coolidge named Henry Stimson governor general of the Philippine Islands in 1927. He succeeded General Leonard Wood.

Stimson served in the Philippines until March 1929. His administration was free from problems because of the diplomatic manner in which he handled problems. He convinced the natives that they should deal with their economic problems first and the concern themselves with independence. He received several honorary LL.D. degrees in 1929 from such institutions as Yale and New York Universities.

President Herbert Hoover appointed Henry L. Stimson Secretary of State in his Cabinet on March 4, 1929. He assumed his office on March 29 and served until the end of the administration on March 3, 1933. While at the State Department he headed the American delegation to the London Naval Conference in 1930. A treaty was arranged between the United States, Great Britain, Japan, France and Italy for limitation of naval armaments. Stimson also attended the seven power conference in 1931 at London to consider the financial problems in Germany and Central Europe. He was a delegate to the Geneva Disarmament Conference in 1932.

Stimson indicated his opposition to the Japanese occupation of Manchuria in 1931, supporting the League of Nations' sanction against the aggression. When President Franklin D. Roosevelt's administration was established in March 1933 Secretary of State Cordell asked Stimson for advice on foreign affairs. The University of Pennsylvania granted Henry L. Stimson the honorary LL.D. degree in 1930 as did Princeton in 1933.

Stimson returned to his legal practice in New York City and retained an interest in United States foreign policy. He published Democracy and Nationalism in 1934. In 1937 he urged that the government cooperate with the League of Nations in the efforts to stop Japanese aggression in China. President Franklin D. Roosevelt named Henry a member of the International Court of Arbitration at The Hague.

President Roosevelt appointed Henry L. Stimson Secretary of War although the latter had always been a Republican. He assumed his office on July 10, 1940 and continued to serve under President Harry S. Truman after President Roosevelt died on April 12, 1945. Stimson resigned on September 21, 1945. He supervised the recruitment and training of the nation's largest peacetime army prior to the United States' entrance into the Second World War. He also convinced Congress to pass the first draft law in peacetime in September 1940. Henry was responsible for creation of an independent air corps.

In his desire desire to support Britain and other states fighting the Axis powers Stimson strongly supported the lend lease law as well as the necessary legislation to provide the appropriations. He also wored to have merchant ships armed. President Roosevelt relied on him in discussions of strategy, and Stimson also participated in various allied conferences during the war. He reorganized the army command in order to provide for more effective operations. He served on various war boards during the war such as the Council of National Defense, the War Production Board, the Foreign Trade Zones Board, and the National Munitions Control Board. He was an adviser to Presidents Roosevelt and Truman on atomic energy.  He recommended to President Truman that the first atomic bomb be dropped on Japan.

After Stimson's retirement from the Cabinet President Truman awarded him the Distinguished Service Medal on September 28, 1945.  His autobiographical work entitled My Vacations appeared in 1949.  Stimson also served on the editorial advisory board of Foreign Affairs.  He died on October 20, 1950 in Huntington, New York.

Bibliography:
   Alperovitz, Gar.  Atomic Diplomacy: Hiroshima and Potsdam.  New York: Simon and Shuster, 1965.
   Black, Gilbert J., ed.  William Howard Taft, 1857-1930. Dobbs Ferry, N.Y.: Oceana Publications, Inc., 1970.
   Beard, Charles A.  President Roosevelt and the Coming of the War.  New Haven: Shoe String Press, 1948.
   Bremer, Howard F., ed.  Franklin D. Roosevelt, 1882-1945.  Dobbs Ferry, N.Y.: Oceana Publications, Inc., 1971.
   Butt, Archibald W.  Taft and Roosevelt, the Intimate Letters of Archie Butt.  Garden City, N.Y.: Doubleday, Doran and Company, 1930.
   Current, Richard N.  Secretary Stimson, A Study in Statecraft.  New Brunswick: Rutgers University Press, 1954.
   Duffy, Herbert S.  William Howard Taft.  New York: Minton Balch and Company, 1939.
   Ferrell, Robert H.  American Diplomacy in the Great Depression, Hoover-Stimson Foreign Policy, 1929-1933. New Haven: Yale University Press, 1957.
   Furer, Howard B., ed.  Harry S. Truman, 1884-1972. Dobbs Ferry, N.Y.: Oceana Publications, Inc., 1970.
   Lochner, Louis P.  Herbert Hoover and Germany.  New York: The Macmillan Company, 1960.
   Morison, Elting E.  Turmoil and Tradition: A Study of the Life and Times of Henry L. Stimson.  Boston: Houghton Mifflin Company, 1960.
   Perkins, Dexter.  The New Age of Franklin D. Roosevelt, 1932-1945.  Chicago: University of Chicago Press, 1957.
   Phillips, Cabell.  The Truman Presidency.  New York, 1966.
   Pringle, Henry F.  The Life and Times of William Howard Taft.  New York: Farrar and Rinehart, Inc., 1939.
   Rappaport, Armin.  Henry L. Stimson and Japan, 1931-1933.  Chicago: University of Chicago Press, 1963.
   Rice, Arnold, ed.  Herbert Hoover, 1874-1964.  Dobbs Ferry, N.Y.: Oceana Publications, Inc., 1971.
   Stimson, Henry L. (with McGeorge Bundy).  On Active Service in Peace and War.  New York, 1948.

## ATTORNEY GENERAL: GEORGE WOODWARD WICKERSHAM

George W. Wickersham, Attorney General in the Cabinet
of President William H. Taft, was born on September 19,
1858 in Pittsburgh, Pennsylvania, the son of Samuel
Morris Wickersham, an inventor in the iron and steel
industry, and Elizabeth Cox (Woodward) Wickersham.  After receiving his preparatory education George attended
Western University of Pennsylvania in Nazareth, Pennsylvania and then Lehigh University from 1873 to 1875 where
he studied civil engineering.  In 1878 Wickersham was a
private secretary to Matthew S. Quay who later became
a United States Senator.  George also studied law with
Robert H. McGrath and went to the University of Pennsylvania Law School from which he received the LL.B. degree
in 1880.

Wickersham established his law practice in Philadelphia
where he remained for two years.  He was also an editor
of "The Weekly Notes of Cases."  George moved to New
York City in 1882 and soon thereafter joined the firm
joined the firm of Strong and Cadwallader in 1883.  He
became a partner in 1887.  George married Mildred Wendell
on September 19, 1883.  They had five children: Cornelius,
Wendell, Mildred, Gwendolyn and Constance.

George Wickersham became active in Republican politics
in New York where he became acquainted with Elihu Root.
President William H. Taft appointed George W. Wickersham
Attorney General on March 5, 1909 in order to help enforce the Sherman anti-trust act.  He was highly active
in initiating many antitrust suits including those a-
gainst the Standard Oil Company, the United States Steel
Corporation and the International Harvester Company as
well as the meat-packing, sugar and cash register trusts.
He made many enemies in industrial and financial circles.
Wickersham proposed establishment of a body like the Interstate Commerce Commission which would regulate industry
involved in interstate commerce.  Out of his ideas grew
the Federal Trade Commission.  He drew up the original
Mann-Elkins Act, worked to create the corporation tax
provision of the Payne-Aldrich Tariff Act.  He served
until March 4, 1913.

After leaving office at the end of the Taft administration in March 1913 George Wickersham continued to
participate in public activities as well as maintaining
his legal practice.  He published The Changing Order
in 1914.  George served as chairman of the judiciary
committee of the New York State constitutional convention during the summer of 1915.  He was also a floor
leader in the convention.  In 1917 he published Some Legal Phases of Corporate Financing, Reorganization and
Reconstruction.

President Wilson named Wickersham a commissioner of

the War Trade Board to Cuba in which post he served from
August to September of 1918.  He investigated claimed
irregularities in purchasing supplies.  Wickersham went
to Paris to cover the Peace Conference in 1919 as a special correspondent for the New York Tribune.  In 1920
he supported Warren G. Harding for the Presidency.
Wickersham was a member of the commission to reorganize
the government of New York State.  In the interim he
served as the American delegate of the League of Nations committee working to codify international law.

President Herbert Hoover appointed George W. Wickersham
chairman of the newly established National Commission
on Law Observance and Enforcement.  The Commission analyzed many problems.  Its report on prohibition was con-
tradictory in that it urged retention of the Eighteenth
Amendment while presenting proof that the laws could
not truly be enforced.  George Wickersham died on January 26, 1936 in New York City.  He was buried in Rock-
side Cemetery in Englewood, New Jersey.

Bibliography:
Black, Gilbert J., ed.  William Howard Taft, 1857-1930.
Dobbs Ferry, N.Y.: Oceana Publications, Inc., 1970.
Butt, Archibald W.  Taft and Roosevelt, the Intimate
Letters of Archie Butt.  Garden City, N.Y.: Doubleday,
Doran and Company, 1930.
Duffy, Herbert S.  William Howard Taft.  New York:
Minton Balch and Company, 1939.
Jessup, Philip C.  Elihu Root. 2 vols.  New York:
Dodd, Mead and Company, 1938.
Pringle, Henry F.  The Life and Times of William How-
ard Taft.  New York: Farrar and Rinehart, Inc., 1939.
Report of the National Commission on Law Observance
and Enforcement.  Washington, D.C.: Government Printing
Office, 1929-31.
Wilensky, Norman M.  Conservatives in the Progressive
Era: The Taft Republicans of 1912.  Gainesville  Univer-
sity of Florida Press, 1965.

POSTMASTER GENERAL: FRANK HARRIS HITCHCOCK

Frank H. Hitchcock, Postmaster General in the Cabinet
of President William H. Taft  was born on October 5,
1847 in Amherst, Lorain County, Ohio, the son of Rev.
Henry Chapman and Mary Laurette (Harris) Hitchcock.
After receiving his basic education in the Boston public schools Hitchcock attended the Somerville Latin
School and then enrolled in Harvard in 1887.  He received
the Bachelor of Arts degree in 1891.  Frank had already
become interested in politics and worked for the local
Republican organization.

After graduating from Harvard Frank Hitchcock went to
Washington, D.C. where he worked for the Treasury De-

partment for a short period and then became a biologist
in the Department of Agriculture. After a year he
was transferred to the statistics division. He studied
law at the same time at Columbia University (now George
Washington University) from which he received the LL.B.
degree in 1894 and the LL.M. in 1895. Frank Hitchcock
was admitted to the bar in the District of Columbia in
1894. He continued to work for the Agriculture Department becoming chief of the foreign markets division in
1897. He was appointed chief clerk of the newly established Department of Commerce and Labor in February 1903
and continued to work in the department for about one
year. He reorganized the fur seal bureau in order to
give greater protection to the seals.

Hitchcock resigned from his position in the Department of Commerce when he was named assistant secretary
of the Republican National Committee in July 1904. He
was given direction over the eastern headquarters in
New York City. When George B. Cortelyou became Postmaster General on March 5, 1905 Hitchcock was appointed
first assistant postmaster general and continued in
that office until 1908. He effectively discharged his
duties.

President Theodore Roosevelt appointed Frank Hitchcock to the Keep Commission in 1905. It was assigned
the task of investigating the various governmental departments with an eye toward reorganization and modernization. Frank was also a member of the government exposition board which made arrangements for federal
exhibits at both the St. Louis and the Lewis and Clark
Expositions. He resigned from his position when President Roosevelt made him manager of the William Howard
Taft campaign early in 1908. When Taft was nominated
at the Republican National Convention in June, he named
Hitchcock chairman of the Republican National Committee.

President William H. Taft named Frank H. Hitchcock
Postmaster General. He assumed his office on March 5,
1909 and served until March 4, 1913. He was effective
in his administration of the Post Office Department.
Frank reduced the deficit and also managed to establish
a small surplus. He also supervised establishment of
the postal savings system and began an air mail service in 1911.

After leaving public office Hitchcock began to practice law in New York City in 1914. He remained active
in the Republican Party, managing the preconvention
campaigns of Charles Evans Hughes in 1916, Leonard
Wood in 1920 and Hiram Johnson in 1924. Hitchcock
then moved to Tuscon, Arizona in 1928 and became owner
and publisher of the Daily Citizen. He was named Republican national committeeman from Arizona in 1932
and 1933 and was also a colonel in the air corps reserve. He died on August 25, 1935 in Tuscon. He had

never married.

Bibliography:
  Black, Gilbert J., ed.  William Howard Taft, 1857-1930.
Dobbs Ferry, N.Y.: Oceana Publications, Inc., 1970.
  Butt, Archibald W.  Taft and Roosevelt, the Intimate
Letters of Archie Butt.  Garden City, N.Y.: Doubleday,
Doran and Company, 1930.
  Duffy, Herbert S.  William Howard Taft.  New York:
Minton Balch and Company, 1939.
  Hitchcock, Mary Lewis (Judson).  The Genealogy of the
Hitchcock Family.  Amherst, Mass.: Press of Carpenter
and Morehouse, 1895.
  Pringle, Henry F.  The Life and Times of William How-
ard Taft.  New York: Farrar and Rinehart, Inc., 1939.
  Wilensky, Norma M.  Conservatives in the Progressive
Era: The Taft Republicans of 1912.  Gainesville: Univer-
sity of Florida Press, 1965.
  Wright, G. F.  A Standard History of Lorain County,
Ohio. 2 vols.  Chicago and New York: The Lewis Publishing
Company, 1916.

## SECRETARY OF THE NAVY: GEORGE VON LENGERKE MEYER

Refer to the biographical sketch of George von L.
Meyer under Postmaster General in the Administration of
Theodore Roosevelt, page 439.

## SECRETARY OF THE INTERIOR:

## RICHARD ACHILLES BALLINGER

Richard A. Ballinger, Secretary of the Interior in the
Cabinet of President William H. Taft, was born on July
9, 1858 in Boonesboro, Boone County, Iowa, the son of
Richard H. and Mary E. (Norton) Ballinger.  His father
went into the cattle business in Kansas after the Civil
War.  Richard A. Ballinger was educated at the local
schools.  He then went to Kansas State University at
Lawrence, Washburn College in Topeka, Kansas and finally
Williams College in Williamstown, Massachusetts.  He was
graduated from Williams College in 1884.
  Richard Ballinger studied law with S. Corning Judd in
Chicago and was admitted to the bar in Springfield, Illinois in 1886.  He began his law practice in Kanakee, Illinois.  Richard married Julia A. Bradley on August 26,
1886.  They had two children, Edward S. and Richard T.
Ballinger became city attorney of Kanakee in 1888.  He
moved to New Decatur, Alabama where he was also city
attorney and finally to Port Townsend, Washington where
he established a law partnership with John N. Scott.
  Ballinger became active in local affairs and was elected judge of the Superior Court of Jefferson County in

1894, sitting on the bench until 1897. He compiled the Code of the State of Washington in 1897 which was known as <u>Ballinger's</u> <u>Annotated</u> <u>Codes</u> <u>and</u> <u>Statutes</u>. Richard eventually moved to Seattle where he served as mayor from 1904 to 1906. In the legal field he became a mining law expert and also wrote <u>A</u> <u>Treatise</u> <u>on</u> <u>the</u> <u>Property</u> <u>Rights</u> <u>of</u> <u>Husband</u> <u>and</u> <u>Wife</u> <u>Under</u> <u>the</u> <u>Community</u> <u>or</u> <u>Aranon-</u> <u>cial</u> <u>System</u> in 1895.

Secretary of the Interior James R. Garfield appointed Richard A. Ballinger Commissioner of the General Land Office in March 1907. He developed reforms in the land office. In the matter of gaining coal lands from the government Ballinger proclaimed that the right to mine should be separated from the ownership of the land above the coal deposits. After a year in office Ballinger returned to his law practice but continued to work for the Republican Party. He attended the Republican National Convention in 1908 and was active in campaigning for William Howard Taft.

President William H. Taft appointed Richard A. Ballinger Secretary of the Interior in which post he served from March 5, 1909 until his resignation on March 6, 1911. He almost immediately became involved in the issues surrounding conservation. President Theodore Roosevelt had launched his program in 1908. The point of dispute centered around coal mining claims in Alaska. Louis R. Glavis, a field man for the Land Office, encouraged by Gifford Pinchot, complained directly to President Taft that Ballinger was interfering with investigations which would show that certain coal land claims in Alaska were fraudulent. The President authorized Secretary of the Interior Ballinger to dismiss Glavis on September 13, 1909 because of insubordination. When the dispute was made public all the conservation policies of the Taft administration were openly discussed.

Congress also investigated the charges that Ballinger did not approve of the conservation program. Ballinger was charged with having opened the coal land in Alaska for private sale without consultation with the Department of Agriculture's Bureau of Forestry. This land had previously been removed from the market by Theodore Roosevelt. The Congresssional committee appointed to investigate the affair cleared Ballinger by a close vote in 1910. However, so much public criticism was raised against him that he had to resign within a year.

The issue of conservation contributed to the growing disagreement between Theodore Roosevelt and William H. Taft. Eventually Roosevelt formed the Progressive or Bull Moose Party in 1912 after he parted to gain the Republican nomination for President. After leaving office Ballinger returned to Seattle, Washington where he resumed his law practice. He died on June 6, 1922 in Seattle.

Bibliography:
Black, Gilbert J., ed. William Howard Taft, 1857-1930.
Dobbs Ferry, N.Y.: Oceana Publications, Inc., 1970.
   Butt, Archibald W. Taft and Roosevelt, the Intimate
Letters of Archie Butt. Garden City, N.Y.: Doubleday,
Doran and Company, 1930.
   Duffy, Herbert S. William Howard Taft. New York:
Minton Balch and Company, 1939.
   Penick, James L., Jr. Progressive Politics and Con-
servation, The Ballinger-Pinchot Affair. Chicago: Uni-
versity of Chicago Press, 1968.
   Pringle, Henry F. The Life and Times of William How-
ard Taft. New York: Farrar and Rinehart, Inc., 1939.
   Wilensky, Norma M. Conservatives in the Progressive
Era: The Taft Republicans of 1912. Gainesville: Univer-
sity of Florida Press, 1965.

SECRETARY OF THE INTERIOR: WALTER LOWRIE FISHER

Walter Lowrie Fisher, Secretary of the Interior in
the Cabinet of President William H. Taft, was born on
July 4, 1862 in Wheeling, West Virginia, the son of
Daniel Webster Fisher, a Presbyterian clergyman and
president of Hanover College, Hanover, Indiana, and Ar-
manda D. (Kouns) Fisher. After receiving his basic
education he studied at the preparatory department in
        College in Ohio and then went to Hanover Col-
lege from which he received the Bachelor of Arts degree
in 1883. He studied law with Wirt Dexter and was admitted to the bar in 1888.
   Walter Lowrie Fisher began his legal practice in Chicago as a member of the firm of Matz, Fisher and Boyden.
He continued with them until 1911. He became a special
assessment attorney for the city in 1889. He served
for about one year and then returned to continue his
legal practice. Walter Lowrie married Mable Taylor on
April 22, 1891. They had seven children: Walter Taylor,
Arthur, Thomas Hart, Frederick Taylor, Margaret, Howard
Taylor and Ruth Fisher.
   Fisher became an active member of the Municipal Voters' League of Chicago and was its secretary from
1901 to 1906. He became president of the organization
in 1906. He and the league attacked corrupt aldermen
and eventually helped to elect two-thirds of the city
council who pledged to support the intentions of the
Voters' League. Fisher was effective in attacking the
transit situation. When Edward F. Dunne was elected
mayor of Chicago in 1905 on a platform calling for immediate municipal ownership of the street railways, he
eventually appointed Fisher special transportation counsel in 1907. His plan was to grant franchises to the
companies subject to the condition that they could be
terminated if the municipal government could raise funds

to purchase the street railways.  The city council accepted the plan, and it was approved by the voters in
a referendum.  Fisher also served as attorney without
pay for the commission investigating fraud and excessive
expenditures of municipal funds.

Walter Lowrie Fisher became interested in various conservation measures.  He was elected president of the
Conservation League of America in 1908 and served until
1909.  In the latter year he and Gifford Pinchot helped
to found the National Conservation Association.  Fisher
became vice president in 1910.  President William H.
Taft appointed Fisher to the railroad securities commission in 1910, and he served until 1911.

President William H. Taft next appointed Walter Lowrie
Fisher Secretary of the Interior on March 13, 1911.  He
continued in office until the conclusion of the Taft administration on March 3, 1913.  He had been Gifford Pinchot's adviser in his dispute with Richard A. Ballinger.
He concerned himself with the Alaskan situation in regard to conservation.  In regard to the latter  he also
fostered concern for other parts of the United States
and encouraged development of the national parks.  Fisher
published Alaskan Coal Problems in 1911.

After leaving public office in 1913 Fisher returned
to his Chicago law practice.  In January 1916 his article
entitled "Preparations for Peace" was published in University Record.  He then published "A League to Enforce
Peace" in the July 1917 issue of the Annals of the American Academy of Political and Social Studies.  Fisher
continued his activities in support of municipal reform.
He was a special adviser to Judge H. Wilkerson and then
to the mayor concerning that railway plans from 1930
to 1932.  A federal court appointed him to direct the
merger of the surface and elevated transit lines in Chicago.  Walter Lowrie Fisher died on November 9, 1935
at his home in Winnetka, Illinois.

Bibliography:
  Black, Gilbert J., ed.  William Howard Taft, 1857-1930.
Dobbs Ferry, N.Y.: Oceana Publications, Inc., 1970.
  Butt, Archibald W.  Taft and Roosevelt, the Intimate
Letters of Archie Butt.  Garden City, N.Y.: Doubleday,
Doran and Company, 1930.
  Duffy, Herbert S.  William Howard Taft.  New York:
Minton Balch and Company, 1939.
  Fisher, Daniel W.  A Human Life; An Autobiography...
New York: F. H. Revell Company, 1909.
  King, Hoyt.  Citizen Cole of Chicago.  Chicago: Har-
der's, Inc., 1931.
  Penick, James L., Jr.  Progressive Politics and Con-
servation, The Ballinger-Pinchot Affair.  Chicago: Uni-
versity of Chicago Press, 1968.
  Pringle, Henry F.  The Life and Times of William How-

ard Taft.  New York: Farrar and Rinehart, Inc., 1939.
   Wilensky, Norma M.  Conservatives in the Progressive
Era: The Taft Republicans of 1912.  Gainesville: Univer-
sity of Florida Press, 1965.

### SECRETARY OF AGRICULTURE: JAMES WILSON

Refer to the biographical sketch of James Wilson under Secretary of Agriculture in the Administration of
Theodore Roosevelt, page 419.

### SECRETARY OF COMMERCE AND LABOR:

### CHARLES NAGEL

Charles Nagel, Secretary of Commerce and Labor in the
Cabinet of President William H. Taft, was born on August
9, 1849 on a farm in Colorado County, Texas, the son of
Dr. Hermann F. and Friedericke (Litzmann) Nagel.  Charles
worked on the family farm.  When the Civil War broke
out his father could not remain to support secession
and the Confederacy.  Dr. Nagel abandonned all his property and moved to St. Louis, Missouri through Mexico
then by sea to New York and then overland.  They arrived
in 1864.
   Charles Nagel went to a private boarding school and
a high school in St. Louis from which he graduated in
1868.  After a year of private study he enrolled in the
Washington University law department from which he was
graduated in 1872.  Nagel then went to Europe for a year
where he studied Roman civil law, medical jurisprudence
and political economy at the University of Berlin in
Germany.  He returned to St. Louis in 1873 and was admitted to the bar.  He then established his law practice.
He eventually became a member of the firm of Finkelnburg,
Nagel and Kirby.
   Charles Nagel married Fannie Brandeis on August 4,
1876.  They had one child, Hildegard.  His wife died
in 1889.  Charles was elected to the state legislature
in 1881 but found that he could not get constructive
legislation passed because the Republicans were in the
minority.  He was able, however, to block what he considered to be poor and unnecessary legislation.  Nagel
became a lecturer at the St. Louis Law School in 1886
and continued there until 1910.  He was an unsuccessful
candidate for councilman in St. Louis on the Independent
Municipal Party in 1891.  He was also defeated in his
bid as Republican candidate for judge of the supreme
court in 1892.
   Nagel was elected as Republican president of the city
council in 1893 and served for a four-year term.  He
was successful in preventing raids upon the treasury
and also convinced the municipal government to grant

franchises for public utilities with the provision that
the city be compensated.  He was concerned with maintenance and improvement of all agencies of the government.  Charles married Anne Shepley on May 5, 1895.
They had four children: Mary S., Edith, Charles and Anne
Dorothea.

Charles Nagel continued to be active in Republican
circles.  He was a member of the Republican National
Committee from 1908 to 1912.  President Taft appointed
him Secretary of Commerce and Labor on March 5, 1909.
He remained in office until the end of the administration on March 4, 1913.  He was successful in this post,
having had much experience in the various areas of industry, finance and transportation.

After leaving public office Charles Nagel returned to
his law practice as well as various other interests. He
was president of the Boy Scouts of St. Louis in 1918.
Among his other activities he served as a trustee of
Washington University, the St. Louis Medical School as
well as of the St. Louis Museum of Fine Arts.  Charles
Nagel died on June 5, 1940 in St. Louis, Missouri.

Bibliography:
   Black, Gilbert J., ed.  William Howard Taft, 1857-1930.
Dobbs Ferry, N.Y.: Oceana Publications, Inc., 1970.
   Butt, Archibald W.  Taft and Roosevelt, the Intimate
Letters of Archie Butt.  Garden City, N.Y.: Doubleday,
Doran and Company, 1930.
   Duffy, Herbert S.  William Howard Taft.  New York:
Minton Balch and Company, 1939.
   Pringle, Henry F.  The Life and Times of William How-
ard Taft.  New York: Farrar and Rinehart, Inc., 1939.
   Wilensky, Norma M.  Conservatives in the Progressive
Era: The Taft Republicans of 1912.  Gainesville: Univer-
sity of Florida Press, 1965.

## ADMINISTRATIONS OF WOODROW WILSON

### VICE PRESIDENT: THOMAS RILEY MARSHALL

Thomas R. Marshall, Vice President in the administration of President Woodrow Wilson, was born on March 14,
1854 in North Manchester, Massachusetts, the son of Dr.
Daniel Miller and Martha (Patterson) Marshall.  His
family moved when he was two years old to Illinois, then
to Kansas, LaGrange, Missouri and finally to Indiana.
He received his basic education at the local public
schools and then enrolled in Wabash College from which
he was graduated in 1873.

Marshall studied law in Judge Walter Olds' office in
Fort Wayne, Indiana and was admitted to the bar in Columbia City, Indiana in 1875.  He established a law partnership with William F. McNagny.  Thomas received the

Master of Arts degree in 1876 from Wabash College. Marshall ran unsuccessfully for prosecuting attorney of his county in 1880. He also taught Sunday school at the Presbyterian Church and was a member of the Columbia City School Board. He married Lois Irene Kimsey on October 2, 1895. They had no children.

Thomas R. Marshall was chairman of the Democratic committee of his congressional district from 1896 to 1898. He was nominated at the Democratic State convention in 1908 for Governor of Indiana and was elected. He was successful in gaining passage of various social reform measures such as a law prohibiting employment of children under fourteen, an employers' liability law, an act concerning corrupt practices in elections, a pure food law as well as taxation of various utilities. In addition a bill was passed for medical examination of school children and a minimum wage for teachers. He also tried to gain passage of the "Tom Marshall Constitution" which he supposedly wrote, but the state supreme court put a stop to the means to be used for its passage. He had been granted the honorary LL.D. degree by Wabash College in 1910 and the University of Pennsylvania in 1911.

Marshall was Indiana's favorite son candidate for the Presidency at the Democratic National Convention in 1912. After Woodrow Wilson was nominated for President Thomas Riley Marshall was named the Democratic nominee for Vice President. He and Wilson were elected in November 1912 and were reelected again in November 1912 serving two full terms from their inauguration on March 4, 1913 to March 3, 1921. Marshall was the first vice president to serve two successive terms since John C. Calhoun, who resigned during his second term and Daniel Tompkins.

As Vice President he carefully learned the rules of the Senate in order to act properly as its presiding officer. He often spoke out in regard to his own views. Marshall was ceremonial head of state during part of his second term when President Wilson was abroad at the Versailles Peace Conference and promoting the League of Nations as well as during his illness. Marshall welcomed many dignataries to the nation during this period. He coined the phrase "What this country needs is a really good five cent cigar." During his term in office Marshall was honored with the LL.D. degree by the following academic institutions: the University of North Carolina in 1913. the University of Maine in 1914 and Washington and Jefferson College in 1915.

After the end of his second term Thomas R. Marshall returned to his home in Indianapolis, Indiana in 1921. He was appointed a member of the Federal Coal Commission and served in 1922 and 1923. He was also a trustee of Wabash College. Thomas R. Marshall died on June 1, 1925 while on a business trip in Washington, D.C. He was buried in Indianapolis.

Bibliography:
  Blum, John Morton. Woodrow Wilson and the Politics of Morality. Boston: Little, Brown, 1936.
  Kettlebrough, Charles. Constitution Making in Indiana. vol. II. Indianapolis: Indiana Historical Commission, 1916.
  Levin, Norman G. Woodrow Wilson and World Politics: America's Response to War and Revolution. New York: Oxford University Press, 1968.
  Link, Arthur S. Woodrow Wilson and the Progressive Era, 1910-1917. New York: Harper, 1954.
  - - - -. Woodrow Wilson: Confusions and Crises, 1915-1916. Princeton: Princeton University Press, 1964.
  - - - -. Woodrow Wilson: The New Freedom. Princeton: Princeton University Press, 1956.
  - - - -. Woodrow Wilson: The Struggle for Neutrality, 1914-1915. Princeton: Princeton University Press, 1960.
  Recollections of Thomas R. Marshall, Vice President and Hoosier Philosopher -- A Hoosier Salad. Indianapolis: The Bobbs-Merrill Company, 1925.

## SECRETARY OF STATE: WILLIAM JENNINGS BRYAN

William Jennings Bryan, Secretary of State in the Cabinet of President Woodrow Wilson, was born in Salem, Morris County, Illinois on March 19, 1860, the son of Silas Lillard, a judge of the second judicial district of Illinois, and Mary Elizabeth (Jennings) Bryan. After receiving his basic education at the public schools he went to Whipple Academy in Jacksonville, Illinois. He enrolled at Illinois College in Jacksonville from which he was graduated in 1881. Bryan then studied law at Union College, receiving the LL.B. degree in 1883. He established his legal practice at Jacksonville while also studying for the Master of Arts degree in history and political science which he attained in 1884.

William Jennings Bryan married Mary Baird on October 1, 1884. They had three chidlren: William Jennings, Jr., Ruth and Grace. Bryan moved to Lincoln, Nebraska in 1887 where he continued his law practice in partnership with Adolphus A. Talbot. William also participated in politics, attending the Democratic state convention in 1888. He was elected as a Democrat to the United States House of Representatives in 1890 and served in the Fifty-second and Fifty-third Congresses from March 4, 1891 to March 3, 1895. He did not run for reelection in 1894. Bryan was a member of the Ways and Means Committee and worked with the silver men. He was an unsuccessful candidate for the United States Senate in 1894.

William Jennings Bryan became editor of the Omaha World-Herald, working for various political reforms, especially the free coinage of silver. He returned to political life as a delegate to the 1896 Democratic National Con-

vention in Chicago where he defended free silver and bi-
metallism in his "Cross of Gold Speech." His oratory
so moved the Convention that he was nominated to run for
President against William McKinley. The Populists and
Silver Republicans also supported him. Bryan conducted
a very active campaign but was defeated in the election
in November. When the Spanish-American War broke out
in 1898 he recruited the Third Nebraska Volunteer Infantry Regiment and was its colonel although he did not
see active duty. He was opposed to the acquisition of
the Philippine Islands.

Bryan was again nominated for President by the Democrats in 1900. He was also the candidate of the Popu-
list and the Silver Republican Parties. He campaigned
on a platform of anti-imperialism and was more soundly
defeated in this election. He continued his active public role by lecturing and also began publication of The
Commoner, a weekly political newspaper on January 23,
1901 in Lincoln, Nebraska. In 1904 the more moderate
and conservative Democrats controlled the convention at
St. Louis and nominated Judge Alton B. Parker to run a-
gainst President Theodore Roosevelt. The latter was reelected in November.

William Jennings Bryan made a tour around the world
in 1905 and 1906. He also continued to speak, delivering
many Chatauqua lectures. He was again nominated by the
Democrats in 1908 at their National Convention in Denver,
Colorado. Bryan's platform urged political reforms and
governmental regulation of business. He was defeated
by William Howard Taft who was strongly supported by
President Roosevelt. In 1912 Bryan eventually gave his
support to Woodrow Wilson. He was able to maintain
enough control and support within the party against the
conservatives to gain the nomination of Wilson over that
of Champ Clark of Missouri, Speaker of the House of Representatives.

Woodrow Wilson was elected President, and he named
William Jennings Bryan Secretary of State. Bryan served
in this office from March 5, 1913 until his resignation
on June 9, 1915. He served the President well both in
the State Department and through his political advice,
as evidenced in his helping to write and have passed the
act creating the Federal Reserve Bank and many other
political reforms. In the area of international relations Bryan was not able to prevent the California legislature from passing a bill in April 1913 aimed against
Japanese ownership of land. He was able to modify the
tone and severity of the bill.

Bryan supported the move to end "dollar diplomacy" as
a means of improving relations with South and Central
America. He also negotiated a treaty with Colombia in
April 1914 which ended the Panama dispute. He opposed
preferential treatment of American commerce through the

Panama Canal.  Bryan was dedicated to the concept of
world peace.  He negotiated and signed thirty arbitration treaties with foreign states in order to bring a-
bout peaceful settlements of any disputes.  Under these
agreements the aggrieved states were to wait for a year
while their disagreements were being investigated.  These
treaties did not prevent the outbreak of World War I in
1914.

Bryan urged that the United States remain neutral in
regard to the European conflict.  He soon ran into disagreement with President Wilson and the Cabinet when the
Lusitania was sunk on May 7, 1915.  The Secretary urged
investigation under the treaty system for a year, but
the other members of the administration did not agree.
In addition Bryan came to the conclusion that permitting
neutral ships to carry ammunition to belligerents was
against the spirit of neutrality.  He resigned rather
than sent the second Lusitania note with its strong
stand against Germany.  Bryan still remained loyal to
Wilson and supported him for reelection in 1916.

William Jennings Bryan returned to his lecturing and
writing.  He was elected president of the National Dry
Federation in 1918 and worked for adoption of the prohibition amendment.  He also supported the Women's
suffrage movement.  Bryan moved to Florida in 1921.  He
worked for the nomination of William G. McAdoo at the
Democratic National Convention in New York City in 1924.
He supported the nominee John W. Davis.

Bryan also became involved in the struggle against
evolution.  In 1924 he drafted the resolution which was
passed by the Florida legislature and declared it subversive to teach the concepts of Darwinism.  As a result
of his viewpoints he was appointed counsel for the state
of Tennessee in the prosecution of John Scopes, a high
school teacher in Dayton, Tennessee. who was indicted
for having taught the concept of evolution in violation
of a Tennessee statute in 1925.  Clarence Darrow was
defense attorney.  Bryan maintained the religious viewpoint against evolution.  Bryan won the "monkey trial."
He died shortly after the trial on July 26, 1925 at
Winchester, Tennessee near Dayton.  He was buried in
Arlington National Cemetery in Fort Meyer, Virginia.

Bibliography:
  Blum, John Morton.  Woodrow Wilson and the Politics
of Morality.  Boston: Little, Brown, 1936.
  Bryan, William Jennings.  The First Battle: A Story
of the Campaign of 1896.  Chicago: W. B. Conkey, 1896.
  - - - -.  A Tale of Two Conventions.  New York: Funk
and Wagnalls Company, 1912.
  Forbes, Genevieve, and Herrick, John O.  The Life of
William Jennings Bryan.  Chicago: Burton Publishing
House, 1925.

Fuller, Joseph. "William Jennings Bryan," in Bemis, Samuel Flagg, ed. The American Secretaries of State and Their Diplomacy. vol. 10. New York: A. A. Knopf, 1928.

Levin, Norman G. Woodrow Wilson and World Politics: America's Response to War and Revolution. New York: Oxford University Press, 1968.

Link, Arthur S. Woodrow Wilson and the Progressive Era, 1910-1917. New York: Harper, 1954.

- - - -. Woodrow Wilson: The New Freedom. Princeton: Princeton University Press, 1956.

- - - -. Woodrow Wilson: The Struggle for Neutrality, 1914-1915. Princeton: Princeton University Press, 1960.

The Memoirs of William Jennings Bryan. Philadelphia and Chicago: The John C. Winston Company, 1925.

Speeches of William Jennings Bryan. New York: Funk and Wagnalls Company, 1909.

Werner, Morris R. Bryan. New York : Harcourt, Brace and Company, 1929.

## SECRETARY OF STATE: ROBERT LANSING

Robert Lansing, Secretary of State in the Cabinet of President Woodrow Wilson, was born on October 17, 1864 in Watertown, New York, the son of John and Maria (Dodge) Lansing. After receiving his preparatory education Robert attended Amherst College from which he was graduated in 1886. He then read law in his father's office and was admitted to the bar in 1889. Robert Lansing became a member of the law firm of Lansing and Lansing in Watertown, New York where he remained until 1907.

Robert married Eleanor Foster, daughter of Secretary of State John W. Foster in President Benjamin Harrison's Cabinet on January 15, 1890. They had no children. Lansing helped to form the City National Bank of Watertown, New York in 1890. He had developed an interest and depth of knowledge of international law in part through his association with his father-in-law. As a result he was appointed associate counsel for the United States in the Bering Sea arbitration during 1892 to 1893. The tribunal sat in Paris.

Robert Lansing was also the counsel for the Mexican and Chinese legations in Washington, D.C. during the period 1894 to 1895. His previous work in regard to the Bering Sea issue was continued when he was appointed solicitor and counsel for the United States to the Bering Sea claims commission in 1896-97. His talents were further recognized when certain private individuals and groups retained him as counsel before the Canadian joint high commission during 1898 and 1899. He was again a counselor for the Mexican and Chinese legations in 1900 and 1901.

Lansing and Gary M. Jones wrote Government, Its Origin,

Growth and Form in the United States in 1902. Lansing's
talents in the international sphere were again called
upon when he was named solicitor and counsel for the
United States before the Alaskan boundary tribunal in
1903 and then in the North Atlantic coast fisheries arbitration at The Hague during the period 1908 to 1910.
He was next employed as a technical delegate for the
United States to the fur seal conference at Washington
in 1911 and was also United States counsel before the
Anglo-American claims arbitration.

Robert Lansing helped to establish the American Society
of International Law in 1906 as well as the magazine
called The American Journal of International Law in
1907.  He was appointed counselor for the State Department on March 20, 1914 and continued in that position
until June 26, 1915.  He was acting Secretary of State
when William Jennings Bryan was away and became Secretary
of State ad interim on June 9, 1915 after Bryan's resignation.

President Woodrow Wilson appointed Robert Lansing Secretary of State on June 23, 1915.  He served in this
office until his resignation on February 13, 1920.  Lansing found that President Wilson had Colonel House negotiate in matters of great delicacy.  The Secretary contributed to the development of many policies including
the recognition of Carranza and the arrangement of peaceful relations with Mexico.  He also protested the British blockade and contraband practices.  He was insistent
that strong language had to be used to protect the ex-
porting industries.  He also signed the "Sussex" notes
which forced the German government to promise to safe-
guard American citizens and ships on the high seas.  Amherst and Colgate granted Robert Lansing the honorary
LL.D. degree in 1915 as did Princeton University in 1917,
Columbia University and Union College in 1918.

As Secretary of State Lansing supervised the distribution of supplies to neutral states bordering on Germany,
enforcement of the Trading with the Enemy Act, aided the
Red Cross in Europe, and when the United States entered
the war Lansing took care of the interests and welfare
of American prisoners of war.  Lansing also negotiated
the treaty whereby the United States purchased the Danish
West Indies ratified by the Senate on February 20, 1917.
In addition he negotiated the Lansing-Ishii agreement
with Japan on November 2, 1917.  Under this arrangement
the United States recognized that Japan had special rights
in China.  The two states agreed not to seek special
privileges or infringe upon its sovereignty or territorial
integrity and opposing action by any other states.

President Wilson appointed Lansing a member of the
Peace Commission to the Versailles Peace Conference in
1918-19.  He helped to organize the administrative work,
serving as a member of the council of ten with President

Wilson and the heads of state and foreign ministers of
Great Britain, France and Italy as well as the two
Japanese ambassadors.  Lansing chaired the commission
investigating the responsibility of the belligerents and
blaming the central powers and their allies.  Lansing
signed the Versailles Treaty on June 28. 1919.

After President Wilson was stricken with a stroke Lansing held informal meetings of the Cabinet on various
pressing issues such as difficulties with Mexico as a
result of the kidnapping of the American consular agent
William O. Jenkins.  The latter was released but was
then arrested on the basis that his kidnapping was pre-
arranged.  The Secretary sent a note demanding Jenkins'
release on November 20.  Lansing also had the Cabinet
deal with a steel strike and a threatened coal strike.
When President Wilson recovered he insisted that Lansing
had been wrong in calling the Cabinet meetings, claiming
that this was the prerogative of the executive.

Lansing resigned as Secretary of State on February 13,
1920 at the request of the President.  Robert and Leser
H. Woolsey, solicitor of the State Department who also
resigned, formed the law firm of Lansing and Woolsey.
Robert involved himself in the practice of international
law.  He became an adviser of China, Finland and Persia.
His firm was retained in an advisory position to Chile
in April 1923 in settling its dispute with Peru.

Robert Lansing published The Big Four and Others of
the Peace Conference as well as Notes on Sovereignty
in 1921.  He also served as a trustee and vice president
of the Carnegie Endowment for International Peace,  In
addition he was president of the Archaelogical Society
of Washington.  Robert Lansing died on October 30, 1928
in Washington, D.C.


Bibliography:
Blum, John Morton.  Woodrow Wilson and the Politics
of Morality.  Boston: Little, Brown, 1936.
Levin, Norman G.  Woodrow Wilson and World Politics:
America's Response to War and Revolution.  New York:
Oxford University Press, 1968.
Link, Arthur S.  Woodrow Wilson and the Progressive
Era, 1910-1917.  New York: Harper, 1954.
- - - -.  Woodrow Wilson: Confusions and Crises, 1915-
1916.  Princeton: Princeton University Press, 1964.
- - - -.  Woodrow Wilson: The New Freedom.  Princeton:
Princeton University Press, 1956.
- - - -.  Woodrow Wilson: The Struggle for Neutrality,
1914-1915.  Princeton: Princeton University Press, 1960.
Pratt, Julius W.  "Robert Lansing," in Bemis, Samuel
Flagg, ed.  The American Secretaries of State and Their
Diplomacy.  vol. 10.  New York: A. A. Knopf, 1928.
Seymour, Charles, ed.  The Intimate Papers of Colonel
House.  4 vols.  Boston and New York: Houghton Mifflin

Company, 1926-1928.

Smith, Daniel M.  Robert Lansing and American Neutrality.  Berkeley: University of California Press, 1958.

## SECRETARY OF STATE: BAINBRIDGE COLBY

Bainbridge Colby, Secretary of State in the Cabinet of President Woodrow Wilson, was born on December 22, 1869 in St. Louis, Missouri, the son of John Peck Colby, a lawyer and civil war officer, and Frances (Bainbridge) Colby.  After receiving his preparatory education Bainbridge went to Williams College in Massachusetts from which he was graduated in 1890.  He studied law at Columbia University in 1890 and 1891 and then at New York Law School from which he received the LL.B. degree in 1892.  He was admitted to the bar in the same year and established his legal practice in New York City.

Colby developed a good practice and represented such clients as Samuel Clemens (Mark Twain) in the settlement of his affairs with his publishing house in 1894.  Bainbridge also became involved in Republican politics and was elected to the New York Assembly in 1901.  He served only one term and did not run for reelection.  He then returned to his law practice.  His activity in the Republican Party continued.  He supported Theodore Roosevelt in 1912 and broke with the Republican Party when it failed to nominate him.  Colby was a delegate to the Progressive or Bull Moose Party Convention which nominated Roosevelt for President in August 1912.  He campaigned for Roosevelt throughout the nation.  Bainbridge also ran unsuccessfully in New York as the Progressive Party Senatorial candidate in 1914 and 1916.

Colby fought the attempt to return the Progressives to the Republican fold in 1916.  He supported President Woodrow Wilson for reelection in 1916 and campaigned for him in a speaking tour throughout the nation.  After the election Colby returned to the practice of law and was retained in 1916 as counsel for a joint committee of the two branches of the New York legislature conducting an investigation of the public service commissions and public utility corporations in New York State.  He was next named special assistant to the United States attorney general in 1917 to investigate the News-Print Paper Association which was supposedly violating the Sherman Anti-Trust Law.  The directors and management were indicted.

After the United States entered the World War in 1917 President Woodrow Wilson named Colby a member of the United States shipping board.  He soon became a vice president and trustee of the Emergency Fleet Corporation and served from 1917 to 1919.  He was also a member of the American mission to the Inter-Allied Conference at Paris in November 1917.  After the signing of the armis-

tice in 1919 Colby resigned from the shipping board
to return to his law practice in New York.

President Woodrow Wilson named Bainbridge Colby Secretary of State to succeed Robert Lansing on March 22,
1920.  He continued in this post until the end of the
administration on March 4, 1921.  During his term of
office Bainbridge had to deal with the difficult problems concerning the opposition of Senators to the United
States entrance into the League of Nations.  He issued
a protest to the Japanese Government because of its
continued occupation of the northern half of Sakhalin
Island.  The Japanese government indicated that they
considered their position only temporary.

When the Russians invaded the newly created state of
Poland Secretary of State Colby issued a statement in
August 1920 expressing American support for Poland as
well as indicating the United States' attitude toward
the Bolshevik regime.  It remained the basis of American
attitudes toward Russia in which it was stated that the
United States could not recognize the Soviet Government.
As a result of Mexican attempts at reconciliation with
the United States Secretary Colby suggested that both
states name commissioners to conclude a treaty settling
many differences.  In the so-called "Mesopotamia Note"
of November 20, 1920 Secretary Colby maintained that
the United States had a right to involve itself in the
treatment and governance of mandates granted to the
allies under the terms of the peace treaties.  The League
of Nations did not have sole responsibility over them.
Colby's visits to Brazil, Uruguay and Argentina helped
to improve relations with Latin America.

After retiring from office Bainbridge Colby joined
President Wilson in a law partnership.  The firm continued until January 1, 1923 when Woodrow Wilson retired
because of his poor health.  Colby remained loyal to
the former president.  He was awarded the honorary LL.D.
degree by several colleges.  In addition Bainbridge
Colby was given an honorable mention from the Pulitzer
Prize Committee in 1934 for his editorial "Freedom
of the Press."  Colby died on April 11, 1920 in Bemus
Point, New York.

Bibliography:
   Blum, John Morton.  Woodrow Wilson and the Politics
of Morality.  Boston: Little, Brown, 1936.
   Levin, Norman G.  Woodrow Wilson and World Politics:
America's Response to War and Revolution.  New York:
Oxford University Press, 1968.
   Link, Arthur S.  Woodrow Wilson: The New Freedom.
Princeton: Princeton University Press, 1956.
   Spurgo, John.  "Bainbridge Colby," in Bemis, Samuel
Flagg, ed.  The American Secretaries of State and Their
Diplomacy.  vol. 10.  New York: A. A. Knopf, 1928.

Vexler, Robert I., ed. <u>Woodrow Wilson, 1856-1924</u>.
Dobbs Ferry, N.Y.: Oceana Publications, Inc., 1969.

SECRETARY OF THE TREASURY: WILLIAM GIBBS MCADOO

William G. McAdoo, Secretary of the Treasury in the
Cabinet of President Woodrow Wilson, was born on October
31, 1863 near Marietta, Georgia, the son of Judge
William Gibbs McAdoo and Mary Faith (Floyd) McAdoo.
His family lived under strict economic difficulties because of the loss of their slaves and the unprofitable
circumstances of their farm. William attended the University of Tennessee where his father was an adjunct
professor of English and History.
William G. McAdoo next obtained a position as a deputy clerk of the Sixth United States Circuit Court
of Appeals in Tennessee in May 1882. At the same time
he studied law at night and was admitted to the bar in
1885. He married Sarah Houston Fleming on November 18,
1885. They had five children: Harriet, Francis, Nona,
William and Sally. He practiced law in Chattanooga,
Tennessee until 1892 and then moved to New York City
where he became a partner of William McAdoo who was
not a relative. William Gibbs McAdoo also sold securities.
William G. McAdoo next became president of two companies involved in constructing the first tunnel under
the Hudson River which was completed on March 8, 1904.
The companies were eventually consolidated as the Hudson and Manhattan Railroad Company. William became
wealthy as a result of his business endeavors and then
became interested in politics as a Democrat. After
successfully helping Woodrow Wilson's campaign for the
governorship of New Jersey William McAdoo joined with
others to promote Wilson for the Presidency. He became
vice chairman of the Democratic National Committee in
1912. When William F. McCombs became ill McAdoo became
Wilson's acting campaign manager.
President Woodrow Wilson appointed William Gibbs Secretary of the Treasury on March 6, 1913. He served in
this office until his resignation on December 16, 1918.
While in office he helped to develop some form of central banking system which led in the end to passage
of the Federal Reserve Act in 1913. He served as
chairman of the Federal Reserve Board and also of the
Federal Farm Loan Board. His wife had died. He then
married Eleanor Randolph Wilson, daughter of the President, at the White House on May 7, 1914. They had two
daughters, Ellen and Mary.
President Wilson relied heavily on McAdoo's advice,
although it was sometimes unorthodox. William was one
of the advisers who urged war with Germany after resump-
tion of unrestricted submarine warfare. Once war with

Germany was declared McAdoo contributed a great deal
to the national effort.  He was chairman of the War
Finance Corporation.  When the railroads were taken over
by the government in 1917 William McAdoo was named director general of the railroads and served until January
10, 1919.  In addition he helped to finance the war effort by conducting four successful Liberty Bond campaigns
with patriotic publicity efforts.  The Secretary also
helped to institute the war risk insurance law.  This
was later expended to include life insurance for the
members of the armed forces.

McAdoo resigned from the Cabinet and returned to his
law practice in New York City.  William was considered
a strong candidate for the Democratic presidential nomination in 1920 but would not make an active campaign
without the approval and support of President Wilson
who delayed his decision concerning the possibility of
a third term.  William moved to Los Angeles, California
in 1922 to become associated with the western and southern wings of the Democratic Party.  He worked to improve his position in order to secure the Democratic
nomination in 1924.

McAdoo's candidacy was hurt when Edward L. Doheny,
who had bribed Secretary of the Interior Albert B. Fall
to secure a lease for the Elk Hills Oil reserve in California, indicated that McAdoo had served him in a legal
capacity in regard to oil and revenue cases.  McAdoo
was thus implicated in the Teapot Dome scandal.  William
fought the issue and remained a candidate.  The Democratic Convention was deadlocked for 103 ballots between
McAdoo and New York Governor Alfred E. Smith.  John W.
Davis was finally nominated.  In 1928 McAdoo wrote The
Challenge--Liquor and Lawlessness vs. Constitutional
Government.

McAdoo was chairman of the California delegation to
the Democratic National Convention in 1932 and announced
California's switch to Franklin D. Roosevelt.  William
was a member of the Democratic National Committee from
1932 to 1940.  He was elected to the United States
Senate from California in 1933, serving from March 4,
1933 until his resignation on November 8, 1928.  He had
not been renominated in 1938.  William divorced his
second wife Eleanor Wilson McAdoo in 1934 and the married Doris I. Cross on September14, 1935.

William G. McAdoo retired from public life in 1938
and returned to Los Angeles.  He served as chairman of
the board of directors of the American President Steamship Lines, continuing until he died in 1941.  He also
supported the League of Nations as well as women's
suffrage.  William G. McAdoo died on February 1, 1941.

Bibliography:
Blum, John Morton.  Woodrow Wilson and the Politics

of Morality. Boston: Little, Brown, 1936.
    Levin, Norman G. Woodrow Wilson and World Politics:
America's Response to War and Revolution. New York:
Oxford University Press, 1968.
    Link, Arthur S. Woodrow Wilson: Campaigns for Pro-
gressivism and Peace, 1916-1917. Princeton University
Press, 1963.
    - - - -. Woodrow Wilson: Confusions and Crises, 1915-
1916. Princeton: Princeton University Press, 1964.
    - - - -. Woodrow Wilson: The New Freedom. Princeton:
Princeton University Press, 1956.
    - - - -. Woodrow Wilson: The Struggle for Neutrality,
1914-1915. Princeton: Princeton University Press, 1960.
    Lippmann, Walter. Men of Destiny. New York: The
Macmillan Company, 1927.
    McAdoo, William Gibbs. Crowded Years, the Reminiscen-
ces of William G. McAdoo. Boston and New York: Houghton
Mifflin Company, 1931.
    Synon, Mary. McAdoo, The Man and His Times: A Panor-
ama in Democracy. Indianapolis: The Bobbs-Merrill
Company, 1924.

## SECRETARY OF THE TREASURY: CARTER GLASS

Carter Glass, Secretary of the Treasury in the Cabinet
of President Woodrow Wilson, was born on January 4, 1858
at Lynchburg, Virginia, the son of Robert Henry Glass,
a newspaper editor and postmaster at Lynchburg, and
Augusta (Christian) Glass. Carter received his basic
education in the public schools as well as private
schools until he was fourteen. He then began to work
for the Lynchburg Daily Republican of which his father
was editor. Carter was a printer's apprentice. He
next worked as a clerk in the office of the auditor of
the Atlantic, Mississippi and Ohio Railroad in Lynchburg
for three years.
    In 1880 Carter Glass became a reporter and editorial
writer for the Lynchburg News. He purchased the paper
in 1888 with two business friends supplying the major
part of the capital. Glass became active in politics
and was clerk of the Lynchburg city council from 1881
to 1901. In 1896 he purchased the Virginian and the
Evening Advance.
Carter Glass was active in the Democratic Party and
was elected state Senator in 1899. He was reelected
in 1901. He was also a delegate to the Virginia state
constitutional convention in 1901 and 1902 where he
helped to revise the suffrage laws of the state. Carter
was elected to the United States House of Representatives
to fill the vacancy caused by the death of Peter J.
Oley. Glass served in the Fifty-seventh to the Sixty-
fifth Congresses from November 4, 1902 until his resignation on December 16, 1918. He was a member of the

banking and currency committee and became very know-
ledgeable of financial matters.  He became chairman of
the committee after the Democrats gained control of the
House of Representatives in 1912.  Glass drew up the legislation which created the federal reserve system which
was finally adopted on December 23, 1913 and went into
operation on December 1, 1914.  While in Congress Glass
was also a member of the joint congressional committee
which created and was able to have passed the Federal
Farm Loan Act.  He also supported the war policies of
President Wilson.  Glass was a delegate to the Democratic National Convention in 1916, 1920, 1924 and 1928.
    President Woodrow Wilson appointed Carter Glass Sec-
retary of the Treasury on December 6, 1918.  He assumed
his duties on December 16, 1918.  He directed the post
war financial program of the government by setting up
a fund to help in paying off the war debt.  Glass resigned on February 2, 1920 after being appointed Senator
from Virginia by the Governor to fill the post left vacant when Thomas S. Martin died.  He was subsequently
elected to the office in 1924 and was reelected in 1930,
1936 and 1942.  The Virginia Democratic convention supported him for the presidential nomination in 1920 and
1924.
    While in the United States Senate in which he served
from February 2, 1920 until his death Glass was chairman of the appropriations committee and a member of the
Foreign Relations Committee.  He turned down President
Franklin D. Roosevelt's offer of the position of Secretary of the Treasury in 1933.  From 1941 to 1945 Carter
Glass was president pro tempore of the Senate.  Glass
died on May 28, 1946 in Washington, D.C.  He was buried
in Spring Hill Cemetery in Lynchburg, Virginia.

Bibliography:
    Blum, John Morton.  Woodrow Wilson and the Politics
of Morality.  Boston: Little, Brown, 1936.
    Canfield, Leon H.  The Presidency of Woodrow Wilson;
Prelude to a World in Crisis.  Rutherford, N.J.: Fair-
leigh Dickinson University Press, 1966.
    Levin, Norman G.  Woodrow Wilson and World Politics:
America's Response to War and Revolution.  New York:
Oxford University Press, 1968.
    Link, Arthur S.  Woodrow Wilson: Campaigns for Pro-
gressivism and Peace, 1916-1917.  Princeton University
Press, 1963.
    - - - -.  Woodrow Wilson: The New Freedom.  Princeton:
Princeton University Press, 1956
    Smith, Rixey, and Beasley, Norman.  Carter Glass.  A
Biography.  New York: Longmans, Green and Company, 1939.
    Vexler, Robert I., ed.  Woodrow Wilson, 1856-1924.
Dobbs Ferry, N.Y.: Oceana Publications, Inc., 1969.

## SECRETARY OF THE TREASURY: DAVID FRANKLIN HOUSTON

David F. Houston, Secretary of Agriculture and Secretary of the Treasury in the Cabinet of President Woodrow Wilson, was born on February 17, 1866 in Monroe,
Union County, North Carolina, the son of William Henry
Houston, a dealer in horses and mules as well as a grocer, and Pamela Anne (Stevens) Houston. David worked
in the country store run by his father and attended
school. He studied at the College of South Carolina
from which he was graduated in 1887. He remained there
for a year of graduate study and then was appointed superintendent of schools in Spartanburg, South Carolina,
retaining that post from 1888 to 1891.

David Houston next studied political science and economics at Harvard University beginning in the fall of
1891. He received the Master of Arts degree in 1892.
He soon obtained a position teaching political science
at the University of Texas in 1894 and continued until
1902. He published A Critical Study of Nullification
in South Carolina in 1896. He was dean of faculty from
1899 to 1902.

David Houston married Helen Beall on December 11, 1896.
They had five children: Duval, David, Elizabeth, Helen
and Lawrence. Houston was elected president of the
Agricultural and Mechanical College of Texas in 1902 and
remained in that position until 1905. He next became
president of the University of Texas, holding that office from 1905 to 1908. Houston's next administrative
post was that of chancellor at Washington and Lee University in St. Louis where he remained from 1908 to 1916.

David Houston's friendship with Colonel House led to
his introduction to Woodrow Wilson. Houston supported
him for President in 1912. President Wilson appointed
David Houston Secretary of Agriculture on March 5, 1913.
He prevented establishment of a federal system of long-
term rural credits until 1916. David agreed to passage
of the Federal Farm Loan Act in 1916 and then established
a good rural credit system. He also enlarged and reorganized the administrative structure of the department.
He in particular emphasized problems concerning marketing,
prices and distribution. In addition Houston helped to
establish a Cooperative Extension Service which provided
information for the farmers. In addition he worked to
develop an Office of Information and an Office of Markets.

President Wilson appointed David F. Houston Secretary
of the Treasury on January 31, 1920 to succeed Carter
Glass who had resigned. He assumed his duties on February
2. He was elected Chairman of the Federal Reserve Board.
He led the Board in its attempt to stop inflation. The
farmers blamed him and other Board members for bringing
about a decline in farm prices during 1920. Houston's

activities led to a controversy over federal fiscal
policies.  He left office at the end of the administration on March 4, 1921.

David Houston became president of Bell Telephone Securities Company shortly after leaving office.  In 1925
he was elected financial vice president of the American
Telephone and Telegraph Company.  Houston published
Eight Years with Wilson's Cabinet in 1926.  He became
president of the Mutual Life Insurance Company of New
York in 1927 and continued in that post until 1940.
David Houston died on September 2, 1940 and was buried
in Cold Spring Harbor Memorial Cemetery in New York.

Bibliography:
Blum, John Morton.  Woodrow Wilson and the Politics
of Morality.  Boston: Little, Brown, 1936.
Canfield, Leon H.  The Presidency of Woodrow Wilson;
Prelude to a World Crisis.  Rutherford, N.J.: Fair-
leigh Dickinson University Press, 1966.
Houston, David F.  Eight Years With Wilson's Cabinet.
Garden City, N.Y.: Doubleday, Page and Company, 1926.
Levin, Norman G.  Woodrow Wilson and World Politics:
America's Response to War and Revolution.  New York:
Oxford University Press, 1968.
Link, Arthur S.  Woodrow Wilson and the Progressive
Era, 1910-1917.  New York: Harper, 1954.
- - - -.  Woodrow Wilson: Campaigns for Progressivism
and Peace, 1916-1917.  Princeton: Princeton University
Press, 1963.
- - - -.  Woodrow Wilson: Confusions and Crises, 1915-
1916.  Princeton: Princeton University Press, 1964.
- - - -.  Woodrow Wilson: The New Freedom.  Princeton:
Princeton University Press, 1956.
- - - -.  Woodrow Wilson: The Struggle for Neutrality,
1914-1915. Princeton: Princeton University Press, 1960.
Payne, John W., Jr.  David F. Houston: A Biography.
New York, 1953.

SECRETARY OF WAR: LINDLEY MILLER GARRISON

Lindley M. Garrison, Secretary of War in the Cabinet
of President Woodrow Wilson, was born on November 28,
1864 in Camden, New Jersey, the son of Joseph Fithian
Garrison, a physician and minister who wrote The Formation of the Protestant Episcopal Church in the United
States and The American Prayer Book, and Elizabeth Van
Arsdale (Grant) Garrison.  After studying in the public
schools Lindley went to the Protestant Episcopal academy
of Philadelphia and then to Phillips Exeter Academy in
1884 and 1885.  He studied for one year at Harvard University after which he studied law in the office of
Redding, Jones and Carson of Philadelphia.  He attended
the University of Pennsylvania Law School from which he

was graduated in 1886.  He was admitted to the Pennsylvania bar in the same year.

Lindley Garrison began practicing law in the office of Redding, Jones and Carson in which he continued until 1888 when he moved to Camden, New Jersey.  In 1898 he became a member of Garrison, McManus and Enright in Jersey City.  Lindley married Margaret Hildeburn on June 30, 1900.  They had no children.  Garrison's legal talents were rewarded when he was appointed to the judiciary as vice-chancellor of New Jersey on June 15, 1904 and was reappointed in 1911.  He served with distinction until 1913.

President Woodrow Wilson appointed Lindley M. Secretary of War on March 5, 1913.  When the World War broke out in 1914 Garrison, who had no military training, urged that the United States increase the size of the army.  He wanted to provide the necessary officers and developed a system of military training camps for college students during the summer.  President Wilson at first approved enlargement of the army.  By July 1915 he revised his viewpoint and asked Garrison to prepare recommendations for strengthening the military establishment of a continental army of 400,000 with enlistments of six years.  President Wilson preferred to make use of the existing militia.

Among his other achievements Garrison wrote the legislation which provided for virtual autonomy of the Philippines with a legislature.  The bill was passed after he left office.  He also sent a large army force to patrol the border with Mexico which was wrecked by anarchy. New York University granted him the LL.D. degree in 1914. Rutgers did the same in 1915 and Kenyon College in 1916.

When Garrison and the President disagreed more openly concerning the best method to increase the size of the army and Congress rejected the Secretary's plan for expansion of the army, Garrison and assistant secretary Breckinridge resigned on February 11, 1916.

Lindley Garrison returned to the practice of law in New York City as a member of the firm of Hornblower, Miller, Garrison and Potter.  Brown University granted him the LL.D. degree in 1917.  On December 31, 1918 he was appointed receiver for the Brooklyn Rapid Transit Company.  Lindley Garrison died on October 19, 1932 in Seabright, New Jersey.

Bibliography:
 Baker, Ray Stannard, ed. Woodrow Wilson: Life and Letters. 8 vols.  Garden City, N.Y.: Doubleday Page, 1931-37.
 Blum, John Morton. Woodrow Wilson and the Politics of Morality.  Boston: Little, Brown, 1936.
 Canfield, Leon H. The Presidency of Woodrow Wilson; Prelude to a World Crisis.  Rutherford, N.J.: Fair-

leigh Dickinson University Press, 1966.

Levin, Norman G.  Woodrow Wilson and World Politics:
America's Response to War and Revolution.  New York:
Oxford University Press, 1968.

Link, Arthur S.  Woodrow Wilson and the Progressive
Era, 1910-1917.  New York: Harper, 1954.

- - - -.  Woodrow Wilson: Confusions and Crises, 1915-
1916.  Princeton: Princeton University Press, 1964.

- - - -.  Woodrow Wilson: The Struggle for Neutrality,
1914-1915.  Princeton: Princeton University Press, 1960.

Vexler, Robert I., ed.  Woodrow Wilson, 1856-1924.
Dobbs Ferry, N.Y.: Oceana Publications, 1969.

## SECRETARY OF WAR: NEWTON DIEHL BAKER

Newton D. Baker, Secretary of War in the Cabinet of
President Woodrow Wilson, was born on December 3, 1871
in Martinsburg, West Virginia, the son of Dr. Newton
Diehl Baker, who served in the Confederate Army, and
Mary (Dukehart) Baker.  After receiving his preparatory
education he entered Johns Hopkins University in 1888
and was graduated from there in 1892.  He then studied
law at Washington and Lee University from which he received the LL.B. degree in 1894.  He was admitted to
the bar in 1895 and practiced law in Martinsburg.

Baker was private secretary to Postmaster General William L. Wilson from 1896 to 1897.  At the end of the
Cleveland administration Newton traveled in Europe and
then began to practice law in Cleveland, Ohio as a member of Martin A. Foran's law firm.  He soon became acquainted with Mayor Tom Loftin Johnson who was trying
to reform the city government.  The mayor appointed him
assistant director of the Cleveland law department in
1902.  Newton married Mary Elizabeth Leopold on July 5,
1902.  They had three children: Elizabeth, Newton and
Margaret.

Newton D. Baker became Cleveland city solicitor in
January 1903 and was reelected to the post four times,
serving until 1912.  He was then elected Mayor of Cleveland in 1912.  He was highly successful in this office,
instituting a "home rule" charter.  In addition he supervised construction of a municipal electric power
plant and establishment of a municipal orchestra.  He
served in the office for two terms.

Baker attended the 1912 Democratic National Convention
as a supporter of Woodrow Wilson.  Newton's reputation
had grown and after his second term as Mayor, President
Wilson appointed Baker Secretary of War on March 6, 1916
to succeed Lindley M. Garrison.  Shortly after Baker's
appointment Pancho Villa made his raid across the American frontier from Mexico.  Secretary Baker ordered Brigadier General John J. Pershing to lead troops into
Mexico in pursuit of Villa.  In the interim between his

appointment and the American declaration of war against Germany in April 1917 Baker did not pursue the necessity of enlarging the army in light of President Wilson's views of neutrality and the divided feelings in the country.

Once the war began Baker, who at first opposed a general draft, efficiently administered the Conscription Act. He also reorganized the administrative structure of the War Department bringing effective civilians into the department. Baker was criticized by people and politicians of all viewpoints either because he did not go far enough in certain directions or went too far. He also was slow in removing those generals who were ineffective and inept until the Senate investigation beginning in December 1917 brought up this fact. The Secretary was somewhat unjustifiably blamed for the shortage of clothes, weapons and necessary facilities of the army camps.

Newton D. Baker retired from office on March 4, 1921 at the end of the administration and returned to Cleveland to practice law. He was counsel for many large corporations. In addition he served as director of the Cleveland Trust Company, the Baltimore and Ohio Railroad Company, as well as the Radio Corporation of America and Goodyear Tire and Rubber Company. He continued his interest in world peace and the League of Nations. President Calvin Coolidge appointed Baker a member of the Permanent Court of Arbitration at the Hague. President Franklin D. Roosevelt reappointed him in 1935.

Among his other activities Baker was the Protestant co-chairman of the National Conference of Christians and Jews from 1928 until his death in 1937. He was also a member of the National Commission on Law Enforcement and Observance in 1929 which was created by President Herbert Hoover. Baker also was president of the Woodrow Wilson Foundation from 1928 to 1931 and president of the American Judicature Society from 1930 to 1937. Newton D. Baker died on December 25, 1937 in Cleveland, Ohio and was buried in Lake View Cemetery.

Bibliography:
  Baker, Newton D. Why We Went to War. New York: Published by Harper and Brothers for Council on Foreign Relations, Inc., 1936.
  Baker, Ray Stannard, ed. Woodrow Wilson: Life and Letters. 8 vols. Garden City, N.Y.: Doubleday Page, 1931-37.
  Beaver, Daniel P. Newton D. Baker and the American War Effort, 1917-1919. Lincoln: University of Nebraska Press, 1960.
  Blum, John Morton. Woodrow Wilson and the Politics of Morality. Boston: Little, Brown, 1936.
  Cramer, Clarence H. Newton D. Baker: A Biography.

Cleveland: World Publishing Company, 1961.

    Hagedorn, Hermann. Leonard Wood, A Biography. 2 vols. New York: Harper and Brothers, 1931.

    Levin, Norman G. Woodrow Wilson and World Politics: America's Response to War and Revolution. New York: Oxford University Press, 1968.

    Link, Arthur S. Woodrow Wilson and the Progressive Era, 1910-1917. New York: Harper, 1954.

    - - - -. Woodrow Wilson: Campaigns for Progressivism and Peace, 1916-1917. Princeton: Princeton University Press, 1963.

    - - - -. Woodrow Wilson: The New Freedom. Princeton: Princeton University Press, 1956.

    - - - -. Woodrow Wilson: The Road to the White House. Princeton: Princeton University Press, 1947.

    Palmer, Frederick. Newton D. Baker--America at War, Based on the Personal Papers of the Secretary of War in the World War. . . New York: Dodd, Mead and Company, 1931.

    Pershing, John J. My Experiences in the World War. 2 vols. New York: Frederick A. Stokes Company, 1931.

    Vexler, Robert I., ed. Woodrow Wilson, 1856-1924. Dobbs Ferry, N.Y.: Oceana Publications, Inc., 1969.

    Villard, Oswald G. Fighting Years; Memoirs of a Liberal Editor. New York: Harcourt, Brace and Company, 1939.

## ATTORNEY GENERAL: JAMES CLARK MCREYNOLDS

James Clark McReynolds, Attorney General in the Cabinet of President Woodrow Wilson, was born on February 3, 1862 in Elkton, Kentucky, the son of Dr. John Oliver McReynolds, a surgeon and gynecologist, and Ellen (Reeves) McReynolds. After receiving his preparatory education James attended Vanderbilt University from which he was graduated in 1882. He then studied law at the University of Virginia, receiving his law degree in 1884. He was private secretary for a short period to United States Senator Howell E. Jackson who later became a Supreme Court Justice.

James Clark McReynolds the practiced law in Nashville, Tennessee. He became active in politics and was defeated as a gold Democratic candidate for Congress in 1896. His legal reputation grew as a result of which President Theodore Roosevelt appointed him assistant Attorney General on June 1, 1903 although James was a member of the opposing party. McReynolds continued in office until January 1, 1907. He shortly thereafter went to New York and joined the legal firm of Craveth, Henderson and deGersdorff.

Soon thereafter the Attorney General appointed James Clark McReynolds special counsel to prosecute the tobacco trust for alleged violation of the Sherman Anti-

trust Act.   James continued in this capacity until 1912
and then returned to private practice with the same firm
that he had joined in 1907.

President Woodrow Wilson named James Clark McReynolds
Attorney General on March 5, 1913.  James proceeded to
press the pending anti-trust prosecutions as well as
beginning new ones.  Among the important cases successfully completed were the dissolution of the Union Pa-
cific-Southern Pacific Railroad merger, the ending of
the wire communication monopoly by the American Telephone
and Telegraph Company, prohibition of price fixing by
the Elgin, Illinois Board of Trade, restraint of the National Wholesale Jewelers' Association from continuing
its conspiracy in restraint of trade.  In addition the
New York, New Haven and Hartford Railroad was required
to give up its monopoly of New England transportation
facilities.  McReynolds also cooperated in writing the
Covington Bill which established an Interstate Trade
Commission.

President Wilson next named James Clark McReynolds
an Associate Justice of the Supreme Court as successor
to Horace H. Lurton.  James took his seat on October 12,
1914.  After the beginning of the New Deal administration McReynolds stood with the majority in voiding much
of the legislation.  He dissented in such decisions as
those which upheld the constitutionality of the National
Labor Relations Board and the Social Security Act.  He
also defended states' rights in such cases as his dis-
sent in the case declaring a Pennsylvania registration
law unconstitutional.  He retired from the Supreme Court
on February 1, 1941.

In July 1941 James Clark McReynolds "adopted" some
thirty-three children who were victims of the German
bombings of England and contributed for their support.
Centre College granted him the honorary LL.D. degree
in 1941.  He never married.  James Clark McReynolds died
on August 24, 1946 in Washington, D.C.

Bibliography:
  Blum, John Morton.  Woodrow Wilson and the Politics
of Morality.  Boston: Little, Brown, 1936.
  Canfield, Leon H.  The Presidency of Woodrow Wilson;
Prelude to a World in Crisis.  Rutherford, N.J.: Fair-
leigh Dickinson University Press, 1966.
  Levin, Norman G.  Woodrow Wilson and World Politics:
America's Response to War and Revolution.  New York:
Oxford University Press, 1968.
  Link, Arthur S.  Woodrow Wilson and the Progressive
Era, 1910-1917.  New York: Harper, 1954.
  - - - -.  Woodrow Wilson: The New Freedom.  Princeton:
Princeton University Press, 1956.
  - - - -.  Woodrow Wilson: The Road to the White House.
Princeton: Princeton University Press, 1947.

- - - -. Woodrow Wilson: The Struggle for Neutrality,
1914-1915. Princeton: Princeton University Press, 1960.

## ATTORNEY GENERAL: THOMAS WATT GREGORY

Thomas Watt Gregory, Attorney General in the Cabinet
of President Woodrow Wilson, was born on November 6,
1861 in Crawfordsville, Mississippi, the son of Dr.
Francis Robert Gregory, a captain in the Confederate
army who was killed during the Civil War, and Mary C.
(Watt) Gregory. Thomas lived his early life in the home
of his maternal grandfather, Major Thomas Watt. After
receiving his preparatory education he went to Southwestern Presbyterian University in Clarksville, Tennessee
from which he was graduated in 1883. Thomas then studied
law at both the University of Virginia and the University of Texas, receiving the LL.B. degree from the last
in 1885.

Thomas Watt Gregory began his law practice in Austin,
Texas. He was assistant city attorney from 1891 to
1894. He turned down the offer of appointment as assistant attorney general of Texas in 1892 and a state
judgeship in 1896. Thomas married Julia Nalle on February 22, 1893. They had four children: Thomas Watt, Jr.,
Joseph, June and Cornelia.

Thomas Gregory was active in the Democratic Party,
attending the national conventions in 1904 and 1912. At
the 1912 convention in Baltimore Gregory strongly supported Woodrow Wilson's candidacy. The Texas delegation
was a major factor in gaining the nomination for Wilson.
After he was elected President, Wilson named Gregory
special assistant to Attorney General James Clark McReynolds. Thomas represented the Justice Department in a
suit against the New York, New Haven and Hartford Railroad Company for allegedly maintaining a monopoly of
transportation in New England. Gregory conducted the
negotiations whereby the company relinquished its control of the Boston and Maine and Boston and Albany Railroads as well as its steamship and traction lines.

President Woodrow Wilson next appointed Thomas Watt
Gregory Attorney General on August 29, 1914 to succeed
James Clark McReynolds who was named to the Supreme
Court. Gregory remained in office until his resignation
on March 4, 1919. Under his direction the Justice Department was involved in the prosecution of those people
who violated American neutrality in regard to the war
in Europe. A war emergency division was established
to help in this work. The Department also worked to
prevent sabotage on the part of Austrian and German
sympathizers to prevent production of arms for shipment
to the British, French and Russians.

After the nation entered the war in April 1917 Thomas
Watt Gregory was called upon to enforce the espionage,

sedition, sabotage and trading-with-the enemy acts as
well as to aid in administering the draft.  In addition
the department aided in drawing up the alien enemy act.
It also helped in the seizure of enemy owned property.  The
The Attorney General supervised the enlargement of the
Federal Bureau of Investigation and other investigatory
bodies.  He also organized the American Protective League
as a volunteer secret service group.

Gregory helped to protect civil rights by opposing legislation which would have given military tribunals rather than the courts the right to try civilians for espionage, sedition or violation of other emergency laws.
In addition to these activities Gregory also initiated
some anti-trust prosecutions and was able to achieve
federal prison administration.  Following Justice Hughes'
resignation from the Supreme Court in 1916 President
Wilson offered the seat to Thomas Watt Gregory who turned
it down because of his hearing loss.  Lincoln Memorial
University and Southwestern Presbyterian University
granted Gregory the honorary LL.D. degree.

Gregory was a clsoe adviser to the President urging
appointment of liberals to the Supreme Court and in-
clusion of Republicans in the peace delegation.  After
his resignation from the Cabinet he was an adviser to
the American delegation to the Peace Conference in Paris.
He then practiced law in Washington as a member of the
firm of Gregory and Todd.  He went to Houston, Texas
in 1923 where he practiced law until his death.  Among
his other activities Thomas was a regent of the University of Texas.  Thomas Watt Gregory died on February
26, 1933 in New York City.

Bibliography:
  Blum, John Morton.  Woodrow Wilson and the Politics
of Morality.  Boston: Little, Brown, 1936.
  Canfield, Leon H.  The Presidency of Woodrow Wilson;
Prelude to a World Crisis.  Rutherford, N.J.: Fair-
leigh Dickinson University Press, 1966.
  Levin, Norman G.  Woodrow Wilson and World Politics:
America's Response to War and Revolution.  New York:
Oxford University Press, 1968.
  Link, Arthur S.  Woodrow Wilson and the Progressive
Era, 1910-1917.  New York: Harper, 1954.
  - - - -.  Woodrow Wilson: Campaigns for Progressivism
and Peace, 1916-1917.  Princeton: Princeton University
Press, 1963.
  - - - -.  Woodrow Wilson: Confusions and Crises, 1915-
1916.  Princeton: Princeton University Press, 1964.
  - - - -.  Woodrow Wilson: The New Freedom.  Princeton:
Princeton University Press, 1956.
  - - - -.  Woodrow Wilson: The Road to the White House.
Princeton: Princeton University Press, 1947.

- - - -.  Woodrow Wilson: The Struggle for Neutrality,
1914-1915.  Princeton: Princeton University Press, 1960.
     Seymour, Charles.  The Intimate Papers of Colonel House.
4 vols.  Boston and New York: Houghton Mifflin Company,
1926-1928.
     Vexler, Robert I., ed.  Woodrow Wilson, 1856-1924.
Dobbs Ferry, N.Y.: Oceana Publications, Inc., 1969.
     White, William Allen.  Woodrow Wilson: The Man, His
Times and His Task.  Boston and New York: Houghton Mifflin Company, 1924.

## ATTORNEY GENERAL: ALEXANDER MITCHELL PALMER

A. Mitchell Palmer, Attorney General in the Cabinet
of President Woodrow Wilson, was born on May 4, 1872 in
Moosehead, Pennsylvania, the son of Samuel Bernard Palmer,
an engineer, and Caroline (Albert) Palmer.  A. Mitchell
Palmer attended the public schools and then studied at
the Moravian parochial school of Bethlehem, Pennsylvania.
He then went to Swarthmore College from which he was
graduated in 1891.  He next studied law for two years
with Judge John B. Strom in Stroudsburg and was admitted
to the Pennsylvania bar in 1893.

Palmer formed a legal partnership with Judge Strom.
Palmer was also appointed the official stenographer of
the 43rd judicial district district of Pennsylvania in
1892.  He married Roberta Bartlett Dixon on November 23,
1898.  They had one child, Mary.  Palmer soon became an
active member of the Democratic Party and was eventually
a member of the Pennsylvania State Democratic executive
committeee.  He was a successful Democratic candidate
to the United States House of Representatives and served
in the sixty-first, sixty-second and sixty-third Congresses from March 4, 1909 to March 3, 1915.  He did
not run for reelection in 1914.  Palmer was a cosponsor
of an anti-child labor bill.  He was a member of the
Ways and Means Committee.

A. Mitchell Palmer was a delegate to the Democratic
National Convention in 1912 in the role as National Committeeman from Pennsylvania.  He supported Woodrow Wilson
for the Presidential nomination.  He turned down the offer of the post of Secrtary of War because he was a Qua-
ker.  Palmer ran unsuccessfully for the United States
Senate against Boies Penrose.  Palmer then retired from
public life.  He remained a member of the Democratic National Committee from 1912 to 1920.  President Wilson
named Palmer Alien Property Custodian on October 22,
1917 in which post he remained until March 4, 1919.

President Wilson next appointed A. Mitchell Palmer
Attorney General in which post he served from March 5,
1919 until the end of the administration on March 4,
1921.  While in office he issued an injunction against
John L. Lewis' striking coal miners in 1919.  Palmer

fought inflation with the anti-trust laws, prosecuting
the "Beef Trust" for price fixing. The trust was dissolved. He attacked so-called radicals and anarchists
supporting government-sponsored raids on homes and offices. Palmer had been involved in many controversial
issues since his appointment to office and made many
enemies. He insisted upon elimination of any radical
group which he believed to be a threat to the war effort
and the government.

A. Mitchell Palmer was a leading candidate for the
1920 Democratic Presidential nomination at the Party's
Convention in San Francisco. After losing to Cox Palmer
retired to private life and his practice in Stroudsburg.
His wife died in 1922, and he married Margaret Fallon
Bunall on August 24, 1923. He continued to support the
Democratic Presidential candidates in 1924 and 1928.
He attended the 1932 Democratic National Convention in
Chicago where he was a member of the resolutions commit-
tee. He supported Franklin D. Roosevelt. A. Mitchell
Palmer died on May 11, 1936 in Washington, D.C. He was
buried in Laurelwood Cemetery in Stroudsburg, Pennsyl-
vania.

Bibliography:
  Blum, John Morton. Joe Tumulty and the Wilson Era.
Boston: Houghton Mifflin, 1951.
  - - - -. Woodrow Wilson and the Politics of Morality.
Boston: Little, Brown, 1936.
  Canfield, Leon H. The Presidency of Woodrow Wilson:
Prelude to a World Crisis. Rutherford, N.J.: Fair-
leigh Dickinson University Press, 1966.
  Levin, Norman G. Woodrow Wilson and World Politics:
America's Response to War and Revolution. New York:
Oxford University Press, 1968.
  Link, Arthur S. Woodrow Wilson and the Progressive
Era, 1910-1917. New York: Harper, 1954.
  - - - -. Woodrow Wilson: Campaigns for Progressivism
and Peace, 1916-1917. Princeton: Princeton University
Press, 1963.
  - - - -. Woodrow Wilson: The New Freedom. Princeton:
Princeton University Press, 1956.
  Vexler, Robert I., ed. Woodrow Wilson, 1856-1924.
Dobbs Ferry, N.Y.: Oceana Publications, Inc., 1969.
  White, William Allen. Woodrow Wilson: The Man, His
Times and His Task. Boston and New York: Houghton Miff-
lin Company, 1924.

POSTMASTER GENERAL: ALBERT SIDNEY BURLESON

Albert S. Burleson, Postmaster General in the Cabinet
of President Woodrow Wilson, was born on June 7, 1863
in San Marcos, Texas, the son of Edward Burleson, a
soldier in the Mexican War and a major in the Confederate

Army, and Emma (Kyle) Burleson.  After receiving his
basic education in the public schools Albert studied at
Texas Agricultural and Mechanical College in College
Station, Texas.  He then went to Baylor University at
Waco, Texas from which he received the Bachelor of Arts
degree.  He then studied law at the University of Texas
from which he received the LL.B. degree in 1884.  He
was admitted to the bar in 1885 and established his legal practice in Austin, Texas.

Burleson quickly entered public office, serving as
assistant city attorney from 1885 to 1890.  He married
Adele Steiner on December 22, 1889.  They had three
children: Laura, Lucy and Adele.  Albert's next public
position was that of district attorney for the twenty-
sixth judicial district in which office he served from
1891 to 1898.  He was elected as a Democrat to the United States House of Representatives, serving in the Fif-
ty-sixth to the Sixty-third Congresses from March 4,
1899 until his resignation on March 5, 1913.  While in
Congress he advocated policies which would aid the farmers and small businessmen.  He supported William Jennings Bryan for President.  In 1912 he supported Woodrow
Wilson helping to organize the campaign for his nomination.

President Woodrow Wilson named Albert S. Burleson
Postmaster General in which post he served from March
5, 1913 until the end of the administration on March 4,
1921.  While in office he helped to gain repeal of the
Panama Canal tolls exemption for United States ships.
Burleson was very effective in the administration of the
department, expanding the postal savings system as well
as the rural mail delivery and the newly established
parcel post system.  He also convinced President Wilson
to place all fourth-class postmasters under the civil
service.  Burleson supervised a readjustment of railway
mail rates based on the actual service.  He utilized
technical advances by motorizing many operations of the
postal service and introduced air mail service.

Albert S. Burleson also argued for public ownership
of both the telegraph and telephone.  During the war he
utilized the wartime statutes to ban publications from
the mail service which in any way criticized the government.  He continued to refuse mail privileges to certain
publications for a period of time after the war.  He
served as chairman of the United States Telegraph and
Telephone Administration in 1918, constantly opposing
the demands of labor for higher wages and collective
bargaining. Burleson was also chairman of the commission
attending the International Wire Communication Conference
in 1920.

After leaving office in 1921 Burleson returned to private life in Austin, Texas where he was involved in
banking as well as farming including the raising of live-

stock.  He opposed prohibition and indicated his concern
over the growth of the Ku Klux Klan.  He supported Alfred
E. Smith for the presidency in 1928.  Baylor University
conferred the honorary LL.D. degree upon him to 1930.
Albert S. Burleson died on November 24, 1937 in Austin,
Texas.  He was buried in Oakwood Cemetery.

Bibliography:
  Blum, John Morton.  Woodrow Wilson and the Politics
of Morality.  Boston: Little, Brown, 1936.
  Canfield, Leon H.  The Presidency of Woodrow Wilson:
Prelude to a World Crisis.  Rutherford, N.J.: Fair-
leigh Dickinson University Press, 1966.
  Levin, Norman G.  Woodrow Wilson and World Politics:
America's Response to War and Revolution.  New York:
Oxford University Press, 1968.
  Link, Arthur S.  Woodrow Wilson and the Progressive
Era, 1910-1917.  New York: Harper, 1954.
  - - - .  Woodrow Wilson: Campaigns for Progressivism
and Peace, 1916-1917.  Princeton: Princeton University
Press, 1963.
  - - - .  Woodrow Wilson: Confusions and Crises, 1915-
1916.  Princeton: Princeton University Press, 1964.
  - - - .  Woodrow Wilson: The New Freedom.  Princeton:
Princeton University Press, 1956.
  - - - .  Woodrow Wilson: The Road to the White House.
Princeton: Princeton University Press, 1947.
  - - - .  Woodrow Wilson: The Struggle for Neutrality,
1914-1915.  Princeton: Princeton University Press, 1960.
  Vexler, Robert I., ed.  Woodrow Wilson, 1856-1924.
Dobbs Ferry, N.Y.: Oceana Publications, Inc., 1969.

## SECRETARY OF THE NAVY: JOSEPHUS DANIELS

Josephus Daniels, Secretary of the Navy in the Cabinet
of President Woodrow Wilson, was born on May 18, 1862
in Washington, North Carolina, the son of Josephus
Daniels, a ship carpenter, and Mary Cleaves (Seabrook)
Daniels.  His mother moved to Wilson, North Carolina
where she was postmaster.  After receiving his preparatory education Josephus attended Wilson Collegiate Institute.  He ran a small newspaper The Cornucopia.  When
he was eighteen he became editor of the weekly Wilson
Advance.  He later bought the paper.
Josephus Daniels and his brother Charles began publication of the Kinston (North Carolina) Free Press in
1882.  In addition Josephus became one of the owners and
editor of the Rocky Mount Reporter.  He studied law at
the University of North Carolina during the year 1884-
1885 and was admitted to the bar in 1885.  He never
practiced law.  Josephus continued his newspaper career
the weekly Raleigh State Chronicle which he soon made
a daily.  He then sold the paper and edited The North

Carolina.

From 1887 to 1893 Josephus Daniels was state printer
of North Carolina. He married Addie Worth on May 2,
1888. They had six children: Adelaide, Josephus, Worth
Bagley, Jonathan Worth, Frank Arthur, and Addie. Daniels
was a chief clerk of the Department of the Interior from
1893 to 1895. During this period, in 1894, he became
owner of The News and Observer of Raleigh, North Carolina. He maintained control of the paper until his
death, supporting the Democratic Party. He was North
Carolina's representative on the Democratic National
Committee from 1896 to 1916, serving as chairman of the
publicity committee. He supported Woodrow Wilson's
candidacy in 1912.

President Woodrow Wilson appointed Josephus Daniels
Secretary of the Navy on March 5, 1913. He served in
this office during both terms until March 4, 1921.
Franklin D. Roosevelt was assistant Secretary of the
Navy during much of this period. Among Daniels' major
achievements was the establishment of schools on war-
ships as well as in the navy yards so that enlisted men
could take a variety of courses. Congress agreed to the
appointment of three to four hundred men each year from
the Navy and its Enlisted Reserve as well as the Marine
Corps and its Reserve Corps to the Naval Academy. He
prohibited intoxicants on naval vessels and shore es-
tablishments in 1914.

The Tampico incident occurred in 1914 when Mexican
officials arrested the paymaster and boat crew from the
USS Dolphin on April 9. The men were released although
Victoriana Huerta refused to permit a twenty-gun salute
to the American flag. In the midst of the Congressional
debate to determine whether arms should be used information was received concerning a German shipment of arms
to Mexico heading toward Vera Cruz. Secretary Daniels
ordered seizure of the city of Vera Cruz until the salute to the flag was made.

Josephus Daniels also instituted in 1915 a continuing
construction program for the navy after the outbreak of
the war in Europe. In July 1915 the Secretary appointed
a group of scientists to the newly organized Naval Consulting Board under Thomas A. Edison to help develop
new inventions. The navy performed well during the war.
Daniels published The Navy and the Nation in 1919.

At the end of the Wilson administration Josephus
Daniels retired to Raleigh where he continued publication
of The News and Observer. He wrote Our Navy at War
which was published in 1922 and the Life of Woodrow Wilson in 1924.

President Franklin D. Roosevelt named Josephus Daniels
Ambassador to Mexico in 1933 in which post he served for
eight years resigning in 1941. He greatly improved United States relations with Mexico. He began publication

of his five volume autobiography with Tar Heel Editor
in 1939.  The other volumes were The Editor in Politics
published in 1940, The Wilson Era: Years of Peace, 1910-
1917 published in 1947, The Wilson Era: Years of War and
After, 1917-1923 published in 1945 and Shirt Sleeve
Diplomat published in 1947.  Josephus Daniels died on
January 15, 1948 in Raleigh, North Carolina.

Bibliography:
   Blum, John Morton.  Woodrow Wilson and the Politics
of Morality.  Boston: Little, Brown, 1936.
   Canfield, Leon H.  The Presidency of Woodrow Wilson:
Prelude to a World Crisis.  Rutherford, N.J.: Fair-
leigh Dickinson University Press, 1966.
   Daniels, Josephus.  Tar Heel Editor.  Chapel Hill:
The University of North Carolina Press, 1939.
   - - - -.  The Editor in Politics.  Chapel Hill: The
University of North Carolina Press, 1940
   - - - -.  The Wilson Era: Years of Peace.  Chapel Hill:
The University of North Carolina Press, 1944.
   - - - -.  The Wilson Era: Years of War and After.
Chapel Hill: The University of North Carolina Press,
1946.
   - - - -.  Shirt Sleeve Diplomat.  Chapel Hill: The
University of North Carolina Press, 1947.
   Levin, Norman G.  Woodrow Wilson and World Politics:
America's Response to War and Revolution.  New York:
Oxford University Press, 1968.
   Link, Arthur S.  Woodrow Wilson and the Progressive
Era, 1910-1917.  New York: Harper, 1954.
   - - - -.  Woodrow Wilson: Campaigns for Progressivism
and Peace, 1916-1917.  Princeton: Princeton University
Press, 1963.
   - - - -.  Woodrow Wilson: Confusions and Crises, 1915-
1916.  Princeton: Princeton University Press, 1964.
   - - - -.  Woodrow Wilson: The New Freedom.  Princeton:
Princeton University Press, 1956.
   - - - -.  Woodrow Wilson: The Road to the White House.
Princeton: Princeton University Press, 1947.
   - - - -.  Woodrow Wilson: The Struggle for Neutrality,
1914-1915.  Princeton: Princeton University Press, 1960.
   Morrison, Joseph L.  Josephus Daniels, the Small-d
Democrat.  Chapel Hill: The University of North Carolina
Press, 1966.
   Vexler, Robert I., ed.  Woodrow Wilson, 1856-1924.
Dobbs Ferry, N.Y.: Oceana Publications, Inc., 1969.

SECRETARY OF THE INTERIOR: FRANKLIN KNIGHT LANE

Franklin K. Lane, Secretary of the Interior in the
Cabinet of President Woodrow Wilson, was born on July
15, 1864 near Charlottetown, Prince Edward Island, Canada, the son of Christopher Smith Lane, a Presbyterian

minister and dentist, and Caroline (Burns) Lane.  The
Lane family moved to Napa, California in 1871 where he
attended a grammar school and then an Oak Mound private
school.  When the family moved to Oakland, California
in 1876 he attended high school and then went to the University of California as a special student from 1884 to
1886 supporting himself working on a newspaper.

Franklin Lane studied law at Hastings Law School in
San Francisco and was admitted to the bar in 1888.  He
was a special correspondent for the San Francisco Chronicle in New York City.  He became part owner and editor
of the Tacoma, Washington Daily News in 1891, continuing
with the paper until 1895 when it became bankrupt and
was sold.  Franklin married Annie Claire Wintermute on
April 11, 1893.  They had two children: Franklin and
Nancy.  He began practicing law in San Francisco in 1895.

Lane soon entered politics as a member of the San Francisco charter committee in 1898.  In the same year he
was elected city and county as a Democrat and was reelected in 1901.  Lane was unsuccessful as the Democratic
candidate for Governor of California in 1902 and was defeated in the contest for mayor of San Francisco in 1903.

President Theodore Roosevelt nominated Lane to the Interstate Commerce Commission in December 1906, and he
was finally confirmed in that post of June 29, 1908.
He was elected as the American representative pf the
permanent International Railway Commission in 1910.
Lane became chairman of the Commission on January 1, 1913,
resigning in March 1913.

President Woodrow Wilson named Franklin K. Lane Secretary of the Interior on March 5, 1913.  He served until
his resignation on March 1, 1920.  Lane was a conserva-
tionist and worked to maintain the natural resources of
the West.  Among his contributions was his nomination
of an Alaskan as a governor of the Territory.  He also
recommended construction of a railway line from Seward
to Fairbanks, Alaska.  New York University conferred the
LL.D. degree upon Lane in 1915 and Brown University in
1916.  He also wrote a pamphlet called "Makers of the
Flag" in 1916.

Franklin K. Lane wrote a ritual for admitting Indians
to citizenship and thereby released many Indians from
government guardianship.  He urged establishment of national parks which led to the erection of the national
park service in 1916.  During the period of his service
seven national parks were established.  He also served
as chairman of the American delegation to the American-
Mexican joint commission.  As a result of the delibera-
tions an agreement was reached for withdrawal of General
Pershing's expedition from Mexico.

Secretary Lane originated a scheme to develop an electric power system from Portland, Maine to Richmond, Virginia.  He also had the Interior Department mobilize the

the nation's resources during the war, listing chemists
in the nation and establishing a chemical service to develop gases, gas masks, smoke streams and other instru-
ments of war. Lane also presented a program to deal
with unemployment at the end of the war. He helped to
develop plans for finding jobs for the millions of returning soldiers.

When the railroads were placed under government control Franklin K. Lane was appointed chairman of the railway wage commission. The result of the commission's
report was an increase in wages for the railroad workers.
He also instigated the calling of a national industrial
conference to develop a better policy for capital-labor
relations which failed to reach any solutions but prepared the way for a second conference which developed
concrete proposals. Lane published a group of his
speeches in the collection called The American Spirit
in 1918.

Franklin Lane was a supporter of the League of Nations.
The University of North Carolina granted him the LL.D.
in 1919 as did Williams College and Harvard University
in 1920. He shared the responsibility with Secretary
of State Robert Lansing for calling cabinet meetings
during President Wilson's illness. Lane resigned on
March 1, 1920 to become vice president of the Mexican
Petroleum Company. He died on May 18, 1921 in Rochester,
New York.

Bibliography:
Blum, John Morton. Woodrow Wilson and the Politics
of Morality. Boston: Little, Brown, 1936.
Canfield, Leon H. The Presidency of Woodrow Wilson:
Prelude to a World Crisis. Rutherford, N.J.: Fair-
leigh Dickinson University Press, 1966.
Lane, Franklin Knight. The Letters of Franklin K.
Lane, Personal and Political. Boston and New York:
Houghton Mifflin Company, 1924.
Levin, Norman G. Woodrow Wilson and World Politics:
America's Response to War and Revolution. New York:
Oxford University Press, 1968.
Link, Arthur S. Woodrow Wilson and the Progressive
Era, 1910-1917. New York: Harper, 1954.
- - - -. Woodrow Wilson: Campaigns for Progressivism
and Peace, 1916-1917. Princeton: Princeton University
Press, 1963.
- - - -. Woodrow Wilson: Confusions and Crises, 1915-
1916. Princeton: Princeton University Press, 1964.
- - - -. Woodrow Wilson: The New Freedom. Princeton:
Princeton University Press, 1956.
- - - -. Woodrow Wilson: The Road to the White House.
Princeton: Princeton University Press, 1947.
- - - -. Woodrow Wilson: The Struggle for Neutrality,
1914-1915. Princeton: Princeton University Press, 1960.

Vexler, Robert I., ed. <u>Woodrow Wilson, 1856-1924</u>.
Dobbs Ferry, N.Y.: Oceana Publications, Inc., 1969.

SECRETARY OF THE INTERIOR: JOHN BARTON PAYNE

John Barton Payne, Secretary of the Interior in the
Cabinet of President Woodrow Wilson, was born on January
4, 1855 in Pruntytown, Virginia (now West Virginia),
the son of Amos Payne, a physician and farmer, and Elizabeth Barton (Smith) Payne. At the beginning of the
Civil War the family moved to Orleans, Virginia. John
went to school there and studied under tutors. He became a clerk in the general store in Warrentown in 1870.
He was next employed by Major Robert F. Mason as a manager of the general store and freight and express office
in Thoroughfare Gap, Prince William County, Virginia,
remaining there for nine months.
John Barton Payne next worked for Adolphus Armstrong,
the clerk of the county and circuit courts in Pruntytown and studied law in the evenings. He was admitted
to the bar in 1876, establishing his practice in Kings-
wood, Preston County, West Virginia. In addition to
his legal practice he published the <u>West Virginia Argus</u>.
John married Kate Bunker on October 17, 1878. He entered politics as a Democrat serving as chairman of the
Preston County Democratic Committee. John was appointed
a special judge of the circuit court of Tucker County
in 1880 and was elected mayor of Kingwood in 1882.
Payne moved to Chicago in November 1882, where he
established his practice. The following year he was
elected a judge of the Cook County Superior Court. He
resigned in 1898 and returned to the practice of law
in partnership with        Walker. Payne was president
of the board of South Park Commissioners from 1911 to
1924 helping to develop a large playground system for
Chicago.
John Barton Payne turned down President Woodrow Wilson's offer of the position of solicitor general in
1913. After his wife died John married Jennie Byrd on
May 1, 1913. After the United States entered the war
in 1917, John accepted the position of arbitrator in
the ship building strikes on the West coast. Shortly
thereafter he moved to Washington. He was named general
counsel of the United States Shipping Board Emergency
Fleet Corporation in 1917 and became chairman of the
board in 1919. He drew up the legislation by which
the government took over the railroads. He was director
general of the railroads from May 1920 to April 1921.
President Wilson appointed John Barton Payne Secretary
of the Interior to replace Franklin K. Lane on February
28, 1920. He served in this post until March 4, 1921.
Payne continued the development of the national parks
and planned the methods of conserving the naval petro-

leum reserves.  President Warren G. Harding named John Barton Payne chairman of the American Red Cross on October 15, 1921 in which post he served without compensation as well as paying his traveling and other expenditures. He continued in this post under Presidents Calvin Coolidge, Herbert Hoover and Franklin D. Roosevelt.  He supervised the relief operations of many disasters. Payne also became chairman of the board of governors of the League of Red Cross Societies in 1922.  President Warren G. Harding also appointed Payne a commissioner to improve relations with Mexico in 1923.  He presided over the International Red Cross Conference in Tokyo, Japan in 1934.  John Barton Payne died on January 24, 1935 in Washington, D.C.

Bibliography:
  Blum, John Morton. _Woodrow Wilson and the Politics of Morality_.  Boston: Little, Brown, 1936.
  Canfield, Leon H.  _The Presidency of Woodrow Wilson: Prelude to a World Crisis_.  Rutherford, N.J.: Fairleigh Dickinson University Press, 1966.
  Levin, Norman G.  _Woodrow Wilson and World Politics: America's Response to War and Revolution_.  New York: Oxford University Press, 1968.
  Link, Arthur S.  _Woodrow Wilson: The New Freedom_. Princeton: Princeton University Press, 1956.
  Vexler, Robert I., ed.  _Woodrow Wilson, 1856-1924_. Dobbs Ferry, N.Y.: Oceana Publications, Inc., 1969.

## SECRETARY OF AGRICULTURE: DAVID FRANKLIN HOUSTON

Refer to the biographical sketch of David Franklin Houston under Secretary of the Treasury, page 482.

## SECRETARY OF AGRICULTURE: EDWIN THOMAS MEREDITH

Edwin T. Meredith, Secretary of Agriculture in the Cabinet of President Woodrow Wilson, was born on December 23, 1876 on a farm near Avoca, Iowa, the son of Thomas Oliver and Minerva Jane (Marsh) Meredith.  After receiving his basic education in the local country schools he went to the Highland Park College business school in Des Moines, Iowa in 1894.  The college later became Des Moines University Edwin left the school to take a position on the family-owned newspaper the _Farmer's Tribune_ which supported Populism.
Edwin Meredith married Edna C. Elliott on January 8, 1896.  They had two children: Edwin Thomas, Jr. and Mildred Marie.  His grandfather gave Edwin and Marie the _Farmer's Tribune_ as a wedding present.  Edwin soon expanded the paper's circulation to include the entire state.
Meredith established _Successful Farming_ in 1902 and

created it into a nation-wide journal. He eventually sold the _Farmer's Tribune_. Edwin initiated the concept of guaranteeing to repay his subscribers for any loss suffered as the result of false advertising in his journal.

After initially becoming a Republican Meredith switched to the Democratic Party. He was an unsuccessful candidate for United States Senator from Iowa in 1914 and then was defeated when he ran for governor of Iowa in 1916. Meredith was a director of the United States Chamber of Commerce from 1915 to 1919. Highland Park College conferred the LL.D. degree on Meredith in 1916. He served on a commission studying labor conditions in Britain, France and July in 1918.

Among his other activities Edwin T. Meredith was a member of the board of excess profits tax advisers which was created in November 1917 to help the internal revenue bureau in administering the war revenue tax law. He was also named director of the Chicago Federal Reserve Bank in 1918 and continued until 1920. He also worked to develop the concept of truth in advertising and served as president of the Associated Advertising Clubs of the World in 1919.

President Woodrow Wilson named Edwin T. Meredith Secretary of Agriculture on February 2, 1920 in which post he served until March 4, 1921. He was able to interest business firms in the problems and aspirations of the farmers. He urged relief for the farmers. Meredith also supported the League of Nations and the World Court. In addition he indicated his interest in tax and tariff reform.

After retiring from the Cabinet at the end of the Wilson administration Edwin Meredith returned to the publishing business. He bought the _Dairy Farmer_ in 1922 and founded the journal _Fruit, Garden and Home_ in the same year. The journal became _Better Homes and Gardens_ in August 1924. He was a director of the United States Chamber of Commerce again from 1923 until his death on June 17, 1928 in Des Moines, Iowa.

Bibliography:
    Blum, John Morton. _Woodrow Wilson and the Politics of Morality_. Boston: Little, Brown, 1936.
    Canfield, Leon H. _The Presidency of Woodrow Wilson: Prelude to a World Crisis_. Rutherford, N.J.: Fairleigh Dickinson University Press, 1966.
    Diamond, William. _The Economic Thought of Woodrow Wilson_. Baltimore: The Johns Hopkins Press, 1943.
    Levin, Norman G. _Woodrow Wilson and World Politics: America's Response to War and Revolution_. New York: Oxford University Press, 1968.
    Link, Arthur S. _Woodrow Wilson and the Progressive Era, 1910-1917_. New York: Harper, 1954.

- - - -.  Woodrow Wilson: Campaigns for Progressivism
and Peace, 1916-1917.  Princeton: Princeton University
Press, 1963.
- - - -.  Woodrow Wilson: Confusions and Crises, 1915-
1916.  Princeton: Princeton University Press, 1964.
- - - -.  Woodrow Wilson: The New Freedom.  Princeton:
Princeton University Press, 1956.
    Vexler, Robert I., ed.  Woodrow Wilson, 1856-1924.
Dobbs Ferry, N.Y.: Oceana Publications, Inc., 1969.

## SECRETARY OF COMMERCE: WILLIAM COX REDFIELD

William C. Redfield, Secretary of Commerce in the Cabinet of President Woodrow Wilson, was born on June 18,
1858 in Albany, New York, the son of Charles Bailey and
Mary (Wallace) Redfield.  His family moved to Pittsfield,
Massachusetts in 1867.  William received his basic education in the public schools of Pittsfield and more advanced instruction at home.  He worked in the Pittsfield
post office and as a travelling salesman for a paper
company.  He moved to New York City in 1877 and worked
for a blank-book manufacturer and wholesale stationer.
He began working for Rittoe and Company, printing press
manufacturers in 1879.
    Redfield next took a position with the Colwell Iron
Works in 1883.  He married Elise Mercein Fuller on
April 8, 1885.  They had two children: Elise and Humphrey.  William began working for S. H. Williams and Company of Brooklyn in 1885 which produced steel and iron
forgings.  He rose in the firm to become a partner in
1887 and then treasurer.  He became president in 1904.
    William C. Redfield became interested in politics in
1896, attending the Gold Democratic National Convention.
He was an unsuccessful Gold Democratic candidate for
Congress in the same year.  Mayor Seth Low appointed
Redfield commissioner of public works for the Borough
of Brooklyn.  William was also vice president and manager of the Warp Twisting-In Machine Company in New York.
He was elected a member of the board of the Equitable
Life Insurance Company in 1905 in part through the influence of Grover Cleveland.  He served as director until 1913.
    When Redfield retired from S. H. Williams and Company
he formed the Sirocco Engineering Company of Troy, New
York and New York City in 1907.  The company merged with
the American Blower Company of Detroit, Michigan.  William was vice president of the latter company from 1908
to 1913.  William C. Redfield was elected as a Democrat
to the United States House of Representatives in 1910.
He served in the Sixty-second Congress from March 4,
1911 to March 3, 1913.  He dealt with the issue of the
tariff, using his business experience.
William Redfield was president of the American Manu-

facturers Export Association in 1912. He wrote The New
Industrial Day in the same year. He was also a trustee
of the Long Island Savings and Trust Company and was
president of the National Society for the Promotion of
Industrial Education from 1912 to 1916. He was an unsuccessful candidate for the vice presidential nomination in 1912 and did not wish to run for a second term
in Congress.

President Woodrow Wilson named William C. Redfield
Secretary of Commerce in the newly organized Department
of Commerce when the Department of Commerce and Labor
was split into two Cabinet posts. He reorganized the
Bureau of Foreign and Domestic Commerce which was
involved in promoting and developing the United States
manufacturing industries as well as their domestic and
foreign markets. Branch offices were set up in the major cities of the nation. Redfield established the
commercial attache service.

Among the other offices in the Department of Commerce
under Redfield was the Bureau of Foreign and Domestic
Commerce which provided for the licensing of exports
necessary under war restrictions when the nation entered the World War. It provided information concerning
raw materials, trade and other statistics during the
war. The Bureau of Standards provided the necessary
optical glass needed by the armed forces, helped to solve
aeronautic problems and provided the figures needed for
various industries.

While in the Cabinet William C. Redfield served on the
federal Board for Vocational Education and was an ex-
officio member of the Council of National Defense and
the War Trade Board. He was also chairman of the Ameri-
can-Canadian Fisheries Conference whoch eventually produced a new fisheries treaty between the two nations.
He resigned his Cabinet post on November 1, 1919. He
was granted the honorary LL.D. degree by Amherst College
in 1913 and the University of North Carolina in 1914.

After leaving the Cabinet Redfield returned to his
business interests in New York City including banking,
insurance, and investment. He was also involved in
writing several books including With Congress and Cabinet in 1924, Dependent America in 1926 and We and the
World in 1927. He published several articles concerning
governmental activities in the Saturday Evening Post
from May 1924 to January 1925 entitled "Glimpses of Our
Government." William C. Redfield died on June 13, 1932
in New York City. He was buried in the Albany Rural
Cemetery in Albany, New York.

Bibliography:
   Baker, Ray S. and Dodd, E. E., eds. The Public Pa-
pers of Woodrow Wilson. vol. 2. New York: Harper and
Brothers, 1925.

Blum, John Morton. _Woodrow Wilson and the Politics of Morality_. Boston: Little, Brown, 1936.

Canfield, Leon H. _The Presidency of Woodrow Wilson: Prelude to a World Crisis_. Rutherford, N.J.: Fairleigh Dickinson University Press, 1966.

Levin, Norman G. _Woodrow Wilson and World Politics: America's Response to War and Revolution_. New York: Oxford University Press, 1968.

Link, Arthur S. _Woodrow Wilson and the Progressive Era, 1910-1917_. New York: Harper, 1954.

- - - -. _Woodrow Wilson: Campaigns for Progressivism and Peace, 1916-1917_. Princeton: Princeton University Press, 1963.

- - - -. _Woodrow Wilson: Confusions and Crises, 1915-1916_. Princeton: Princeton University Press, 1964.

- - - -. _Woodrow Wilson: The New Freedom._ Princeton: Princeton University Press, 1956.

- - - -. _Woodrow Wilson: The Struggle for Neutrality, 1914-1915_. Princeton: Princeton University Press, 1960.

Redfield, William C. _With Congress and Cabinet_  Garden City, N.Y.: Doubleday, Page and Company, 1924.

Vexler, Robert I., ed. _Woodrow Wilson, 1856-1924_. Dobbs Ferry, N.Y.: Oceana Publications, Inc., 1969.

## SECRETARY OF COMMERCE: JOSHUA WILLIS ALEXANDER

Joshua Willis Alexander, Secretary of Commerce in the Cabinet of President Woodrow Wilson, was born on January 22, 1852 in Cincinnati, Ohio, the son of Thomas W. and Jane (Robinson) Alexander. He and his mother moved to Canton, Davies County in 1863 where Joshua went to the public as well as private schools and then attended high school. He next studied at Christian University (later called Culver-Stockton College) in Canton, Missouri. He was graduated from the college in 1872.

Joshua Willis Alexander moved to Gallatin, Missouri in 1873 and studied law, being admitted to the bar in 1875. He then established his legal practice in Gallatin. Joshua married Roe Ann Richardson. They had eight children: Samuel Thomas, Julia, Frances, George Forrest, Rowena, Preston Carter, Walter Richardson, and Lawrence Woodward. Alexander became public administrator of Daviess County in 1877 and continued in that post until 1881. He served on the Gallatin board of education from 1882 to 1901 and was secretary as well as president of the board.

Joshua Alexander was elected a member of the Missouri House of Representatives and served in that body from 1883 to 1887, serving as speaker in the last year. He was next mayor of Gallatin in 1891 and 1892 and then a member of the board of managers of State Hospital No.2 from 1893 to 1896. He was appointed a judge of the

seventh judicial circuit of Missouri in 1900 and served
from January 1901 until February 1907.  Christian University granted him the A.M. degree in 1907.

Joshua Alexander was elected  to a six-year term as
judge but resigned in 1907 after being elected as a
Democrat to the United States House of Representatives.
He served in the Sixtieth through the Sixty-sixth Congresses from March 4, 1907 until his resignation on December 15, 1919.  He was a member and the chairman of
the merchant marine and fisheries committee.  After the
SS. Titanic was sunk Alexander introduced a joint resolution for an international conference to study the
issue of safety at sea.  He chaired the American commission to such a comference in London which met from
November 12, 1913 to January 20, 1914.  He also helped
to pass a series of laws regulating shipping while he
was in Congress.

President Woodrow Wilson appointed Joshua Willis
Alexander Secretary of Commerce on December 15, 1919
to succeed William C. Redfield.  He continued in this
office until the end of the administration on March 4,
1921.  Joshua then returned to Gallatin, Missouri where
he resumed his law practice.  He next served as a delegate-at-large in the Missouri constitutional convention
from May 1922 to November 1923.  He was a member of the
committee on taxation.  He received the LL.D. degree
from Christian University in 1923.  Joshua Alexander
died on February 27, 1936 in Gallatin, Missouri.  He
was buried in Brown Cemetery,

Bibliography:
  Blum, John Morton.  Woodrow Wilson and the Politics
of Morality.  Boston: Little, Brown, 1936.
  Canfield, Leon H.  The Presidency of Woodrow Wilson:
Prelude to a World Crisis.  Rutherford, N.J.: Fair-
leigh Dickinson University Press,1966.
  Levin, Norman G.  Woodrow Wilson and World Politics:
America's Response to War and Revolution.  New York:
Oxford University Press, 1968.
  Link, Arthur S.  Woodrow Wilson: Campaigns for Pro-
gressivism and Peace, 1916-1917.  Princeton: Princeton
University Press, 1963.
  - - - -.  Woodrow Wilson: Confusions and Crises, 1915-
1916.  Princeton: Princeton University Press, 1964.
  - - - -.  Woodrow Wilson: The New Freedom.  Princeton:
Princeton University Press, 1956.
  Vexler, Robert I., ed.  Woodrow Wilson, 1856-1924.
Dobbs Ferry, N.Y.: Oceana Publications, Inc., 1969.

SECRETARY OF LABOR: WILLIAM BAUCHOP WILSON

William B. Wilson, Secretary of Labor in the Cabinet
of President Woodrow Wilson, was born on April 2, 1862

in Blantyre, Scotland, the son of Adam Wilson, a miner, and Helen Nelson (Bauchop) Wilson. His parents emigrated to the United States where the family settled in Arnot, Pennsylvania. He received some education in the common schools until he was sent to work in the coal mines at the age of nine. He soon joined the mineworkers' union. William married Agnes Williamson June 7, 1883. They had nine children.

William B. Wilson became president of the district miners' union in 1888 and continued in the post until 1890. He was an unsuccessful candidate for the state legislature in 1888. William also served on the national executive board of the miners' union which organized the United Mine Workers of America in 1890. He became secretary treasurer of the union in 1900 and continued in that position for eight years. He was able to arrange conferences between coal miners and the owners which met biannually.

Wilson became active in the Democratic Party and was elected to the United States House of Representatives in 1906. He served in the Sixtieth through the Sixty-second Congresses from March 4, 1907 to March 3, 1913. He was defeated for reelection in 1912. While in the House he supported labor and helped to pass the law creating the Department of Labor.

President Woodrow Wilson appointed William B. Wilson first Secretary of Labor in his Cabinet on March 5, 1913. He continued to serve in that office until March 5, 1921. Among his accomplishments in the organization of the department was an overhaul of the Bureau of Immigration and Naturalization which he divided into two agencies. He also created offices to help mediate industrial disputes. William B. Wilson was a member of the Federal Board for Vocational Education from 1914 to 1921 and chairman during the last two years. He served on the Council of National Defense during the First World War. While in the Cabinet Wilson was elected president of the International Labor Conference of 1919. He helped to organize the United States Employment Service to find positions for returning veterans.

William B. Wilson was appointed a member of the International Joint Commission to prevent disputes in regard to the use of boundary waters between the United States and Canada, serving from March 4, 1921 until his resignation on March 21, 1921. He ran unsuccessfully for the United States Senate from Pennsylvania in 1926. He became involved in mining and agricultural disputes in Tioga County near Blassburg, Pennsylvania. William B. Wilson died on a train near Savannah, Georgia on May 25, 1934. He was buried in Blassburg, Pennsylvania.

Bibliography:
  Babson, Roger W. *William B. Wilson and the Department*

of Labor.  New York: Brentano's, 1919.

Baker, Ray S.  Woodrow Wilson, Life and Letters.  8 vols.  Garden City, N.Y.: Doubleday, Page, 1927-1939.

Blum, John Morton  Woodrow Wilson and the Politics of Morality.  Boston: Little, Brown, 1936.

Canfield, Leon H.  The Presidency of Woodrow Wilson: Prelude to a World Crisis.  Rutherford, N.J.: Fairleigh Dickinson University Press, 1966.

Evans, Chris.  History of the United Mine Workers of America.  2 vols.  Indianapolis, 1918-1920.

Levin, Norman G.  Woodrow Wilson and World Politics: America's Response to War and Revolution.  New York: Oxford University Press, 1968.

Link, Arthur S.  Woodrow Wilson and the Progressive Era, 1910-1917.  New York: Harper, 1954.

- - - -.  Woodrow Wilson: Campaigns for Progressivism and Peace, 1916-1917.  Princeton: Princeton University Press, 1963.

- - - -.  Woodrow Wilson: Confusions and Crises, 1915-1916.  Princeton: Princeton University Press, 1964.

- - - -.  Woodrow Wilson: The New Freedom.  Princeton: Princeton University Press, 1956.

- - - -.  Woodrow Wilson: The Road to the White House.  Princeton: Princeton University Press, 1947.

- - - -.  Woodrow Wilson: The Struggle for Neutrality, 1914-1915.  Princeton: Princeton University Press, 1960.

Vexler, Robert I., ed.  Woodrow Wilson, 1856-1924.  Dobbs Ferry, N.Y.: Oceana Publications, Inc., 1969.

## ADMINISTRATION OF WARREN GAMALIEL HARDING

### VICE PRESIDENT: CALVIN COOLIDGE

Calvin Coolidge, Vice President in the administration of President Warren G. Harding, was born on July 4, 1872 in Plymouth, Vermont, the son of John Calvin and Victoria Josephine (Moor) Coolidge.  Calvin began his education at Plymouth Notch and then attended Black River Academy in Ludlow, Vermont from 1887 until his graduation in 1890.  In the spring of 1891 he studied at St. Johnsburg Academy in Vermont where he received a college entrance certificate.  He began his studies at Amherst College in September 1891 and was graduated cum laude in June 1895.  He studied law with the firm of John C. Hammond and Henry P. Field in Northampton, being admitted to the bar in July 1897.

Calvin Coolidge had already become interested in politics when he supported Henry C. Field's successful bid for mayor of Northampton in the fall of 1895.  Coolidge became affiliated with the Republican Party.  He established his legal practice in Northampton, Massachusetts.  He continued his interest in politics, serving in many city offices.  He was elected to the city council in

1899 and then a city solicitor in 1900 and again in 1901. He was defeated for reelection in 1902.

Appointed temporary clerk of courts in June 1903, Calvin was elected for a full term in the fall of 1903. He married Grace Anna Goodhue on October 4, 1905. They had two children: John and Calvin, Jr. His next political success was his election to the Massachusetts House of Representatives in 1906 and was reelected in 1907. He then returned to his legal practice and was elected mayor of Northampton in 1909 serving two terms from 1906 through 1911. He was next elected a state senator, serving in the state legislature from 1912 to 1915. He was president of the Senate in 1914 and 1915.

Calvin Coolidge was elected Lieutenant-Governor of Massachusetts in 1915 and served from 1916 to 1918. In the last year he was elected governor on November 5. Coolidge was inaugurated on January 2, 1919. He helped to settle the Lawrence, Massachusetts textile strike on May 29. Following the outbreak of the Boston police strike on September 9, 1919 Coolidge took charge of the situation on September 11 at the request of Mayor Andrew J. Peters. When the Boston police commissioner Edwin V. Curtis dismissed all 1117 strikers Coolidge answered the request of  A F of L president Samuel Gompers that "There is no right to strike against the public safety by anybody, anywhere, any time. He was subsequently reelected governor of Massachusetts on November 4, 1919.

Calvin Coolidge was named the Republican Vice Presidential nominee at the Republican National Convention in Chicago in June 1920. Warren G. Harding and Calvin Coolidge were elected President and Vice President respectively in November 1920. They were inaugurated on March 4, 1921. Coolidge served as Vice President until August 3, 1923 when President Harding died and Coolidge became President. While he was Vice President Coolidge was elected a life trustee of Amherst College. He presided over the Senate during the period of the crises including the Teapot Dome and Veterans Bureaus scandals. He supported President Harding's proposal that the Senate agree to have the United States join the World Court. President Harding died in San Francisco, California on August 2, 1923. Calvin Coolidge took the oath of office as President at his family's farm house in Plymouth, Vermint at 2:47 A.M. on August 3. His father, a notary public, administered the oath. Coolidge served as President until March 3, 1929.

/For information concerning the period of Calvin Coolidge's Presidency, consult Philip R. Moran, ed. Calvin Coolidge, 1872-1933 in this series./

After retiring from office on March 4, 1929 Coolidge returned to Northampton, Massachusetts. His Autobiography began to appear in serial form in Cosmopolitan Maga-

zine in 1929.  He also wrote a syndicated newspaper
column.  Coolidge was invited to a luncheon at the
White House on July 24, 1929 by President Herbert Hoo-
ver to celebrate the signing of the Kellogg-Briand Peace
Pact which was negotiated during Coolidge's term in office.  Calvin was chairman of the Non-Partisan Railroad
Commission and was honorary president of the Foundation
of the Blind.  He became president of the American Antiquarian Society in May 1930.  Calvin Coolidge died on
January 5, 1933 at his home "The Beeches" in Northampton,
Massachusetts.  He was buried in the family plot in
Plymouth Cemetery, Plymouth Notch, Vermont on January 7,
1933.

Bibliography:
    Coolidge, Calvin.  The Autobiography of Calvin Coolidge.
New York: Cosmopolitan Book Corporation, 1929.
    Faulkner, Harold Underwood.  From Versailles to the
New Deal: A Chronicle of the Harding, Coolidge, Hoover
Era.  New Haven: Yale University Press, 1950.
    Fuess, Claude M.  Calvin Coolidge, Man from Vermont.
Boston: Little, Brown and Company, 1940.
    Latham, Edward C.  Meet Calvin Coolidge: The Man Behind
the Myth.  New York, 1960.
    McCoy, Donald R.  Calvin Coolidge.  The Quiet President.
New York: Macmillan, 1967.
    Moran, Philip R., ed.  Calvin Coolidge, 1872-1933.
Dobbs Ferry, N.Y.: Oceana Publications, Inc., 1970.
    - - - -.  Warren G. Harding, 1865-1923.  Dobbs Ferry,
N.Y.: Oceana Publications, Inc., 1970.
    White, William Allen.  A Puritan in Babylon: The Story
of Calvin Coolidge.  New York: The Macmillan Company,
1938.

## SECRETARY OF STATE: CHARLES EVANS HUGHES

Charles Evans Hughes, Secretary of State in the Cabinets of Presidents Warren G. Harding and Calvin Coolidge,
was born on April 11, 1862 in Glens Falls, New York, the
son of David Charles Hughes, a clergyman, and Mary Catherine (Connelly) Hughes.  After receiving his basic
education in the public schools of Newark, New Jersey
and New York City where the family had moved, Charles
attended Madison College which later became Colgate University.  He then studied at Brown University from which
he received the Bachelor of Arts degree in 1881.
    Hughes next accepted a position as professor of Greek
and mathematics at Delaware Academy in Delhi, New York
where he taught from 1881 to 1882.  He also studied law
with Judge William Gleason after which he read law at
the New York Law Institute and then went to Columbia
Law School, receiving the LL.B. degree in 1884.  He was
admitted to the bar in the same year and then served as

a clerk in the firm of Chamberlain, Carter and Hornblower in New York. At the same time he received a prize fellowship at Columbia University for the years 1884 to 1887.

Hughes became a partner in the firm which was renamed Carter, Hughes and Cravath in 1888. Charles married Antoinette Carter on December 15, 1888. They had four children: Charles, Helen, Catherine and Elizabeth. Hughes became a professor of law at Cornell University in 1891 and taught there until 1893. He returned to his law firm in New York which soon became Carter, Hughes and Dwight. In addition to his court duties Charles was also a special lecturer on general assignments and bankruptcy in New York law school. In June 1904 the firm was reorganized as Hughes, Rounds, Schurman and Dwight after Mr. Carter's death.

Charles Evans Hughes was named counsel for the state legislative committee investigating gas and electricity prices in 1905. His conduct of the investigation brought him fame. His work helped to form the New York State Commission of Gas and Electricity to regulate public utilities. Hughes was also a special counsel for New York State to study the conditions of the Equitable Life Assurance Society of New York. This expanded into a study of other companies during 1905 and 1906 and indicated flagrant abuses as well as indicating the reforms to be introduced.

Charles Evans Hughes turned down the Republican nomination for mayor of New York in 1905. His next public service was in 1906 when he was appointed a special assistant to the Attorney General in the investigation of the coal industry. In the fall of 1906 Hughes was elected Republican Governor of New York and was reelected in 1908, continuing in that office until his resignation on October 6, 1910. Among his achievements were the passage of legislation establishing a public service commission to supervise the utilities. He also investigated various departments and encouraged various reforms. Hughes also wrote Conditions of Progress in Democratic Government which were the Yale lectures in 1909.

President William Howard Taft nominated Charles Evans Hughes as an associate justice of the United States Supreme Court on May 2, 1910. He took his seat on October 10, 1910, continuing on the bench until his resignation on June 10, 1916 when he was nominated by the Republicans for President. He was defeated by President Woodrow Wilson in November 1916. Hughes then returned to New York City to practice law with his law firm.

When the crisis with Germany grew serious in 1917 Hughes supported President Wilson. Charles was appointed chairman of the New York City district board of draft appeals in 1917 and continued in this capacity until 1918. President Wilson next appointed Hughes

special assistant to the Attorney General to head the
investigation of the aircraft industry. Hughes supported Warren G. Harding for President in 1920.

President Warren G. Harding appointed Charles Evans
Hughes Secretary of State. He assumed his office on
March 4, 1921 and continued in office after the death of
Harding under President Calvin Coolidge. Hughes resigned
from the State Department on March 4, 1925. Among his
achievements were the acceptance of the right of the
United States to participate in the disposition of various former German territories. This involved the challenge of the government to Japanese control of the German cables at Yap which connected the United States with
the Far East.

Charles Evans Hughes also negotiated a treaty, signed
on August 25, 1921, which ended the technical state of
war between the United States and Germany, existing
since November 11, 1918 when the Armistice was arranged.
He also chaired the nine power international conference
in Washington, D.C. during 1921 and 1922 which dealt
with the limitation of arms. It was his proposal that
led to the treaty limiting capital tonnage for the United States, Great Britain and Japan in the ratio of
5:5:3. Hughes also arranged the four power treaty signed
by the United States, Great Britain, Japan and France,
which established an understanding on various issues
concerning the Pacific area as well as the nine-power
agreement concerning Chinese territorial integrity.

The United States also resumed diplomatic relations
with Mexico and improved relations with other Latin
American states during Hughes' term of office. He encouraged the creation of the commission headed by Charles
D. Dawes which helped to ease the burdens of reparations
payments for Germany. Hughes indicated that the United
States would insist upon maintaining the Monroe Doctrine
in opposition to any non-American nation attempting to
encroach upon the independence of American states. He
also maintained that the United States would continue
to withhold recognition of the Soviet Union.

After leaving the State Department in 1925 Hughes returned to his law practice in New York City. Governor
Al Smith of New York named him chairman of a state commission which studied the government of the state and
recommended that the 180 departments be reduced to
eighteen. He published The Pathway of Peace and Other
Lectures in 1925. On September 30, 1926 President
Calvin Coolidge appointed Hughes an American member of
the Permanent Court of International Justice at The
Hague in 1928 in which position he served until 1930.

Among his other activities Hughes was chairman of the
United States delegation to the Sixth Pan-American
Conference of the American States at Havanna, Cuba in
1928. His Columbia lectures of 1927 were published as

The Supreme Court of the United States.  In 1928 he delivered the Princeton University lectures which were
published as Our Relations with the Nations of the
Western Hemisphere.  He also gave the Yale University
lectures in 1929 which were published as Pan American
Peace Plans.

Charles Evans Hughes returned to the United States
Supreme Court when President Herbert Hoover named him
Chief Justice.  He took his seat as head of the Court
on February 13, 1930.  Among his other achievements he
maintained constitutional freedoms and helped to broaden
the power of Congress to regulate interstate commerce.

Hughes received the LL.D. degrees from Dartmouth and
Amherst Colleges as well as Yale and Princeton Universities.  He was also awarded the Roosevelt Memorial
Association medal in 1928.  Charles Evans Hughes died
on August 28, 1948 in Osterville, Massachusetts.

Bibliography:
Adams, Samuel Hopkins.  The Incredible Era; Life and
Times of Warren Gamaliel Harding.  Boston: Houghton
Mifflin, 1939.
Faulkner, Harold Underwood.  From Versailles to the
New Deal: A Chronicle of the Harding, Coolidge, Hoover
Era.  New Haven: Yale University Press, 1950.
Fuess, Claude M.  Calvin Coolidge, Man from Vermont.
Boston: Little, Brown and Company, 1940.
Glad, Betty.  Charles Evans Hughes and the Illusions
of Innocence: A Study in Diplomacy.  Urbana: University
of Illinois Press, 1966.
Moran, Philip R., ed.  Calvin Coolidge, 1872-1933.
Dobbs Ferry, N.Y.: Oceana Publications, Inc., 1970.
- - - -.  Warren G. Harding, 1865-1923.  Dobbs Ferry,
N.Y.: Oceana Publications, Inc., 1970.
Perkins, Dexter.  Charles Evans Hughes and American
Democratic Statesmanship.  Boston: Little, Brown, 1956.
Pusey, Merlo J.  Charles Evans Hughes.  New York:
Macmillan, 1951.
Sinclair, Andrew.  The Available Man; The Life Behind
the Mask of Warren Gamaliel Harding.  New York: Macmil-
lan, 1965.
Soule, George H.  Prosperity Decade: From War to De-
pression, 1917-1929.  New York: Rinehart, 1947.

SECRETARY OF THE TREASURY: ANDREW WILLIAM MELLON

Andrew W. Mellon, Secretary of the Treasury in the Cabinets of Presidents Warren G. Harding, Calvin Coolidge
and Herbert Hoover, was born on March 24, 1855 in
Pittsburgh, Pennsylvania, the son of Thomas Mellon, a
judge and banker, and Sara (Negley) Mellon.  After receiving his basic education in the public schools he went
to the Western University of Pennsylvania (later the Uni-

versity of Pittsburgh) leaving several months before
graduation in 1872 to open a lumber and building business
in Mansfield, Pennsylvania.

Andrew Mellon next entered his father's banking firm,
T. Mellon and Sons, in 1874. Thomas turned the firm over
to him in 1882. Andrew organized the Union Trust Company
in 1889. He purchased stock in 1890 in the company which
eventually became the Aluminum Company of America. It
was formed to develop Charles M. Hall's patent of 1889
for the manufacture of aluminum. Andrew became a director of the firm and was treasurer for a short period of
time. He also aided Edward Goodrich Acheson in stabilizing the Carborundum Company. During the 1890's he
organized several companies in the oil producing and re-
fining business. He helped to organize the Gulf Oil
Corporation as well as the Union Steel Company. In
addition he helped to establish coal and coke industries
including the Carborundum Company. Andrew married Nora
McMullen on September 12, 1900. They had two children:
Alisa and Paul.

Mellon achieved the incorporation of T. Mellon and
Sons as the Mellon National Bank in 1902. He wrote its
president. Eventually other banks in Pittsburgh merged
with the institution. Andrew involved himself in many
industrial enterprises, serving in an official capacity
in more than sixty companies. His marriage ended in
divorce in July 1912. In the meantime Mellon became active in Republican politics in Pennsylvania. He contributed to Charles Evans Hughes' campaign in 1916 and also
to a group opposed to the League of Nations.

President Warren G. Harding named Andrew Mellon Secretary of the Treasury on March 4, 1921. Andrew continued
in this post under President Coolidge after the death
of President Harding and also under President Herbert
Hoover until his resignation on February 12, 1932. Among
Mellon's accomplishments waas a tax plan known as the
"Mellon Plan" which carried out reductions in certain
personal income tax levels. He showed great ability in
dealing with government funds decreasing government expenditures. He was able to reduce the national debt by
almost eight billion dollars. Mellon opposed bonuses
for veterans as well as farm relief to be achieved
through the shipment of surplus agricultural products
abroad.

As chairman of the World Debt Commission Mellon reached
agreements in regard to the payment of war debts with
various European countries on the basis of "ability to
pay." He contributed to the government's policy of re-
fusing to recognize the connection between reparations
and war debts. As a result the United States had to
grant large loans to Germany in order for her to make
payments which were in turn used to pay war debts. Mellon
also supervised enforcement of Prohibition which was

initially handled by the Bureau of Internal Revenue and
later by a Bureau of Prohibition.  He also reorganized
the federal farm loan program in the early 1920's.  His
responsibility for purchasing property along Pennsylvania
Avenue in Washington, D.C. as part of Congress's program
to improve the avenue and the Mall as well as the construction of public buildings helped to beautify the
city.

Andrew Mellon wrote Taxation: The People's Business in
1929.  After the outbreak of the Depression in 1929 Mellon worked with President Herbert Hoover to develop a
policy of retrenchment.  He was in Europe with Secretary
of State Henry L. Stimson in June 1931 and sent warnings
of conditions in Germany which led to President Hoover's
proposal for a one-year moratorium on reparations payments.  Since Andrew Mellon's reputation had been hurt
by the Depression President Hoover convinced him to resign and accept the post of Ambassador to Great Britain
in February 1932.  He continued in the diplomatic post
until his resignation on March 7, 1933.  He then returned
to the Mellon National Bank.

Andrew Mellon was accused of having underpaid his income tax for 1931 because of an allegedly fraudulent
sale of stock.  The final decision of the Board of Tax
Appeals reached shortly after his death vindicated Mellon.

Andrew Mellon spent the remainder of his life involved
in his business career and philanthropic pursuits.  His
interest in art as evidenced in his large art collection
led him to help found the National Gallery of Art in
Washington, D.C. when in 1937 he offered his art collection to the federal government with securities for
construction of a building and establishment of a five
million dollar endowment.  Andrew Mellon died on August
26, 1937 in Southampton, Long Island, New York.  He
was buried in Allegheny Cemetery in Pittsburgh, Pennsylvania.

Bibliography:
  Adams, Samuel Hopkins.  The Incredible Era: Life and
Times of Warren Gamaliel Harding.  Boston: Houghton
Mifflin, 1939.
  Brandes, Joseph.  Herbert Hoover and Economic Diplomacy.
Pittsburgh: Pittsburgh University Press, 1962.
  Faulkner, Harold Underwood.  From Versailles to the
New Deal: A Chronicle of the Harding, Coolidge, Hoover
Era.  New Haven: Yale University Press, 1950.
  Fuess, Claude M.  Calvin Coolidge, The Man From Ver-
mont.  Boston: Little, Brown and Company, 1940.
  Galbraith, Kenneth J.  The Great Crash.  Boston: Hough-
ton Mifflin Company, 1954.
  Love, Philip H.  Andrew W. Mellon.  Baltimore: F. H.
Coggins and Company, 1929.
  Lyons, Eugene.  Herbert Hoover.  A Biography.  Garden

City, N.Y.: Doubleday and Company, Inc., 1964.
    Moran, Philip R., ed. Calvin Coolidge, 1872-1933.
Dobbs Ferry, N.Y.: Oceana Publications, Inc., 1970.
    - - - -. Warren G. Harding, 1865-1923. Dobbs Ferry,
N.Y.: Oceana Publications, Inc., 1970.
    O'Conner, Harvey. Mellon's Millions, the Biography
of a Fortune; the Life and Times of Andrew W. Mellon.
New York: The John Day Company, 1933.
    Prothro, James W. The Dollar Decade, Business Ideas
in the 1920's. Baton Rouge: Louisiana State University
Press, 1954.
    Rice, Arnold S., ed. Herbert Hoover, 1874-1964.
Dobbs Ferry, N.Y.: Oceana Publications, Inc., 1971.
    Romasco, Albert U. The Poverty of Abundance, Hoover,
the Nation, the Depression. New York: Oxford University
Press, 1965.
    Sinclair, Andrew. The Available Man; The Life Behind
the Mask of Warren Gamaliel Harding. New York: Macmillan, 1965.
    Soule, George H. Prosperity Decade: From War to De-
pression, 1917-1929. New York: Rinehart, 1947.

## SECRETARY OF WAR: JOHN WINGATE WEEKS

John W. Weeks, Secretary of War in the Cabinets of
Presidents Warren G. Harding and Calvin Coolidge, was
born on April 11, 1860 on a farm near Lancaster, New
Hampshire, the son of William Dennis Weeks, a probate
judge as well as a farmer, and Mary Helen (Fowler) Weeks.
After having received his education in the local schools
he began teaching and the received an appointment to the
United States Naval Academy in 1877 from which he was
graduated in 1881. He then served in the Navy as a
midshipman until his resignation on June 26, 1883. When
he left because there were not enough ships for all the
Annapolis graduates.
    John Weeks next was a civil engineer surveying land
in Florida. Soon after he became assistant land commissioner for the Florida Southern Railway in which position he remained until 1888. During this period John
married Martha A. Sinclair on October 7, 1885. They had
two children: Katherine and Charles Sinclair, who was to
serve as Secretary of Commerce in the Cabinet of President Dwight D. Eisenhower.
    John W. Weeks moved to Boston, Massachusetts in 1888
where he formed a banking and brokerage company with
Henry Hornblower, known as Hornblower and Weeks. He
continued with the firm until 1914. He was also a member of the Massachusetts Naval brigade from 1890 to
1900 and was its commander during the last six years.
In the meantime John and his family moved to Newton,
Massachusetts in 1893. Weeks became active in Republican politics and was chairman of the Republican state

convention in 1895.  John was also named a member of
the Board of Visitors to the United States Naval Academy
in 1896.

During the Spanish-American War he was a lieutenant
in the volunteer navy from April 23 to October 28, 1898.
He later was given a reserve commission as rear admiral.
He also was a rear admiral in the Massachusetts Naval
Reserve.  Weeks was an alderman of Newton, Massachusetts
from 1899 to 1902.  Elected mayor of Newton, he served
for two terms, 1902 and 1903.

John Weeks was elected as a Republican to the United
States House of Representatives.  He served in the Forty-
ninth to the Fifty-third Congresses from March 4, 1905
until his resignation on March 4, 1913.  He was elected
to the United States Senate by the Massachusetts legislature.  He served from March 4, 1913 to March 3, 1919.
While a member of Congress Weeks supported high tariffs.
He also voted for the Federal Reserve Act and fought
against both prohibition and women's suffrage.  John was
a candidate for the Republican Presidential nomination
in 1916.  He was defeated for reelection in 1918.  After leaving the Senate he continued his activities in
the Republican Party.  He supported Warren G. Harding
for President in 1920, heading the New York Republican
headquarters.

President Warren G. Harding appointed John W. Weeks
Secretary of War on March 4, 1921.  He continued in this
post after the death of Harding and served President
Calvin Coolidge until his resignation on October 13,
1925 because of poor health.  When Weeks entered office
he proceeded to continue the process of adjusting the
military to peace time conditions and to dispose of
huge amounts of war equipment.  Weeks also insisted that
a substantial standing army be maintained but was not
able to prevent the reduction to 125,000 men.  He supervised the work required under the national defense act
of 1920.  His appointment of the Wood-Forbes Commission
to investigate conditions in the Philippines was a con-
tributing factor to the appointment of Major General
Leonard Wood as governor general.

Before as well as after leaving the Cabinet John Weeks
indicated his opposition to the Volstead Act enforcing
the Prohibition Amendment because of the unrest caused
in the nation.  He also served during his life in such
organizations as the Society of the Cincinnat, the Sons
of the Revolution, the Society of the War of 1812, the
Military Order of Foreign Wars, and the Naval and Military Order of the Spanish-American War.  John W. Weeks
died on July 12, 1926 at Mount Prospect near Lancaster,
Mew Hampshire.  His body was cremated, and the ashes
were buried in Arlington National Cemetery in Fort Meyer,
Virginia.

Bibliography:
    Adams, Samuel Hopkins. The Incredible Era: Life and
Times of Warren Gamaliel Harding. Boston: Houghton
Mifflin, 1939.
    Faulkner, Harold Underwood. From Versailles to the
New Deal: A Chronicle of the Harding, Coolidge, Hoover
Era. New Haven: Yale University Press, 1950.
    Fuess, Claude M. Calvin Coolidge, the Man From Ver-
mont. Boston: Little, Brown and Company, 1940.
    Moran, Philip R., ed. Calvin Coolidge, 1872-1933.
Dobbs Ferry, N.Y.: Oceana Publications, Inc., 1970.
    - - - -. Warren G. Harding, 1865-1923. Dobbs Ferry,
N.Y.: Oceana Publications, Inc., 1970.
    Sinclair, Andrew. The Available Man; The Life Behind
the Mask of Warren Gamaliel Harding. New York: Macmillan, 1965.
    Soule, George H. Prosperity Decade: From War to De-
pression, 1917-1929. New York: Rinehart, 1947.

## ATTORNEY GENERAL: HARRY MICAJAH DAUGHERTY

   Harry M. Daugherty, Attorney General in the Cabinets
of Presidents Warren G. Harding and Calvin Coolidge,
was born on January 26, 1860 in Washington Court House,
Ohio, the son of John Harry Daugherty, a merchant tailor,
and Jane Amelia (Draper) Daugherty. Harry's father died
when he was four years old. He attended the local
schools and also worked at various jobs to help support
his family. He studied at the University of Michigan
Law School from which he received the LL.B. degree in
1881. He then began his law practice at Washington
Court House.
   Daugherty joined the Republican Party in 1881. He was
elected town clerk in 1882. Harry married Lucy Matilda
Walker on September 3, 1884. They had two children:
Emily Belle and Draper Mallie. Harry continued his law
practice while maintaining his interest and activities
in the Republican Party. He was elected to the Ohio
House of Representatives, serving two terms from 1890
to 1894. He tended to alienate members of his party.
He was defeated in his attempts to gain the Republican
nominations for state attorney general in 1895, United
States Congressman in 1896, governor in 1899 and United
States Senator in 1902, 1908 and 1916. He maintained
his active role in campaigning for Republican candidates.
   Daugherty was chairman of the Republican state executive committee in 1912. He supported Warren G. Harding
for the Republican Presidential nomination in 1920.
President Harding named Harry M. Daugherty Attorney
General on March 5, 1921. His conduct of investigations
concerning profiteering and frauds in regard to war contracts was often attacked. The special division established for this purpose did investigate many suits. In

addition settlements with private concerns brought several million dollars back to the Treasury.  Daugherty also intervened in the railroad shopmen's strike in 1922,
obtaining an injunction from the United States district
court in Chicago on August 31 which ended the strike
within thirty-six hours.  The action indicated that the
public interest was the deciding factor in all industrial
disputes.  As a result of a Congressional impeachment
resolution on September 9, 1922 an investigation of his
activities led to an exoneration concerning charges of
misconduct in October.

Daugherty was also involved in the Senate study of the
government oil leases arranged by former Secretary of
the Interior Albert B. Fall and Secretary of the Navy
Edwin B. Denby, but Daughtery was not implicated in these
actions.  Under Daugherty's leadership the Justice Department enforced prohibition legislation.  He also sponsored establishment of a federal prison for first offenders.  At the request of President Coolidge on March 24,
1924, Henry Daugherty resigned on March 25.  He claimed
that he was the scapegoat of the attacks against the
Republican Party.

Daugherty then returned to his law practice in Columbus, Ohio.  The Senate continued its attempt to uncover
evidence that he had conspired to defraud the government.
It investigated the Midland National Bank of Washington
Court House, Ohio of which his brother Mal S. Daugherty
was president.  Harry M. Daugherty was finally acquitted
in 1927.  Among his other activities he was a member of
the Masons, the Knights of Pythias and the Elks.  He retired from his law practice in 1932 and wrote The Inside
Story of the Harding Tragedy with Thomas Dixon in the
same year.  Harry M. Daugherty died on October 12, 1941
in Columbus, Ohio.

Bibliography:
  Adams, Samuel Hopkins.  The Incredible Era: Life and
Times of Warren Gamaliel Harding.  Boston: Houghton
Mifflin, 1939.
  Daugherty, Harry M.  The Inside Story of the Harding
Tragedy.  New York: The Churchill Company, 1932.
  Faulkner, Harold Underwood.  From Versailles to the
New Deal:  A Chronicle of the Harding, Coolidge, Hoover
Era.  New Haven: Yale University Press, 1950.
  Fuess, Claude M.  Calvin Coolidge, the Man From Ver-
mont.  Boston: Little, Brown and Company, 1940.
  Moran, Philip R., ed.  Calvin Coolidge, 1872-1933.
Dobbs Ferry, N.Y.: Oceana Publications, Inc., 1970.
  - - - -.  Warren G. Harding, 1865-1923.  Dobbs Ferry,
N.Y.: Oceana Publications, Inc., 1970.
  Sinclair, Andrew.  The Available Man: The Life Behind
the Mask of Warren Gamaliel Harding.  New York: Macmil-
  Soule, George H.  Prosperity Decade: From War to De-

pression, 1917-1929. New York: Rinehart, 1947.

## POSTMASTER GENERAL: WILLIAM HARRISON HAYS

William H. Hays, Postmaster General in the Cabinet of
President Warren G. Harding was born on November 5,
1879 in Sullivan, Indiana, the son of John Tennyson Hays,
a lawyer, and Mary (Cain) Hays. After receiving his basic education in the public schools William went to Wabash College from which he received the Bachelor of Arts
degree in 1900 and the Master of Arts degree in 1904.
He studied law with his father and was admitted to the
bar in 1900. He then entered his father's law firm.
William married Helen Louise Thomas on November 18, 1902.
They had one son: Will H. Hays, Jr.

William Hays soon became active in politics and joined
the Republican Party. He became chairman of the Sullivan County committee as well as a member of the party's
state advisory committee in 1904, continuing until 1908.
His activities led him to become chairman of the Republican state committee's speaker bureau in which position
he served from 1906 to 1908. He was elected city attorney for Sullivan County in 1908 and continued in that
office until 1913. At the same time Will served as
district chairman of the Republican state committee from
1910 to 1914. His rise in the Indiana Republican Party
continued when he became chairman of the state central
committee in 1914, continuing until 1918.

Will also served Indiana as a member of the state council of defense in 1917. He continued to serve the Republican Party as chairman of the national committee, continuing in that post from February 1918 to June 7, 1921.
He supported Warren G. Harding for President in 1920.

President Harding appointed William H. Hays Postmaster
General on March 5, 1921. While serving in that office
he contributed to the workings of post office affairs
in several ways by improving relations between the workers and the government including establishment of the
Post Office Welfare Department. In order to improve
mail delivery he initiated campaigns to encourage people
to mail early and to put complete addresses on all mail.
He was also successful in virtually stopping mail robberies by placing armed guards on trains and offering
large rewards. In addition Hays increased rural delivery
as well as the motor transport service and saved fifteen
million dollars. He also restored second-class mailing
privileges to newspapers.

William Hays resigned from his office on March 4, 1922
in order to assume the presidency of the Motion Picture
Producers and Distributors of America, Inc. This group
was established to improve the industry and increase its
educational and entertainment value. Among Hays' achievements were the establishment of a national arbitration

system to settle disputes within the motion picture business which eventually helped to improve relations and save a large sum of money. Hays helped to develop the production code for filmmakers in 1924. He also cooperated with the National Education Association to produce institutional films.

William H. Hays also continued his public services when he was appointed chairman of the coordinating committee of the American Red Cross and Near East Relief in October 1922 by President Harding. He was also a member of the National Council of the Boy Scouts of America. Among his other business activities Hays was a director of the Continental Banking Company and the Chicago and Eastern Illinois Railroad Company. He was elected national president of Phi Delta Theta Fraternity in 1920. William H. Hays died on March 7, 1954 in Sullivan, Indiana.

Bibliography:
  Adams, Samuel Hopkins. The Incredible Era: Life and Times of Warren Gamaliel Harding. Boston: Houghton Mifflin, 1939.
  Faulkner, Harold Underwood. From Versailles to the New Deal: A Chronicle of the Harding, Coolidge, Hoover Era. New Haven: Yale University Press, 1950.
  Moran, Philip R., ed. Warren G. Harding, 1865-1923. Dobbs Ferry, N.Y.: Oceana Publications, Inc., 1970.
  Russell, Francis. The Shadow of Blooming Grove: Warren G. Harding and His Times. New York: McGraw Hill, 1968.
  Sinclair, Andrew. The Available Man: The Life Behind the Mask of Warren Gamaliel Harding. New York: Macmillan, 1965.
  White, William Allen. Puritan in Babylon: The Story of Calvin Coolidge. New York: The Macmillan Company, 1938.

## POSTMASTER GENERAL: HUBERT WORK

Hubert Work, Postmaster General in the Cabinet of President Warren G. Harding and Secretary of the Interior in the Cabinets of Presidents Harding and Calvin Coolidge, was born on July 3, 1860 in Marion Center, Pennsylvania, the son of Moses Thompson and Tabitha Logan (Van Horn) Work. After receiving his basic education Hubert studied at the Pennsylvania State Normal School and the Medical Schools of the University of Michigan from 1882 to 1884 and the University of Pennsylvania from which he received the M.D. degree in 1885.

Hubert Work then moved to Greeley, Colorado where he established his medical practice. He married Laura M. Arbuckle in 1887. They had three children: Philip, Dorcas and Robert V. H. Work. He later moved to Pueblo

where he eventually founded the Woodcraft Hospital for
Mental and Nervous Diseases in 1896.  He was elected
president of the Colorado State Medical Society in 1896.
Work was elected president of the American Medico-Psy-
chological Society in 1911.

Hubert Work soon became active in the Republican Party and was chairman of the Colorado State Committee in
1912.  He was next the Colorado national committeeman
from 1913 to 1919.  When the United States entered World
War I he volunteered for the army.  Commissioned a major in the Army Medical Corps.  Dr. Work was assigned
to the staff of provost marshal General Crowder.  He was
eventually promoted to the rank of lieutenant colonel
and the colonel.  At the end of the war he became a
colonel in the officers reserve corps.

The Republican National Committee recognized his organizational talents and asked Hays to organize the farmers to organize the farmers to support Warren G. Harding in the 1920 election.  Dr. Work was elected president of the American Medical Association in the same
year.

President Warren G. Harding named Hubert Work first
assistant postmaster general on March 4, 1921.  He continued in that office until March 4, 1922 and then was
appointed Postmaster General.  He served in that post
until March 21, 1923.  While in office he instituted an
investigation which prepared for the reorganization of
the Post Office Department.  He also planned general improvements in the mail service.  The Treasury Department approved his suggestion that the government own the
post office buildings.  In addition he made arrangements
for regular transcontinental air mail service.

President Harding next appointed Dr. Hubert Work Secretary of the Interior following the resignation of
Albert B. Fall.  Work assumed the office on March 5,
1923.  Among his achievements were improvements in relations with the Indians as a result of meetings with
their representatives.  He also arranged for granting
citizenship to the American Indians born in the United
States.  He also investigated and subsequently restored
the oil leases of the Roxana Petroleum Company.

Work also reorganized the reclamation service.  In-
stead of a director to head it Work arranged for appointment of a commissioner, naming former Idaho Governor
David William Davis as the bureau chief.  Work was able
to reorganize other aspects of the Department and was
able to reduce its budget by $129,000,000.  Dr. Work was
present with President Harding on his trip to Alaska
during the summer of 1923 and was one of the attending
physicians at his last illness.  Work continued to serve
in the Interior Department under President Coolidge.
He resigned on July 24, 1928.

After leaving office Dr. Hubert Work continued his activities in the Republican Party, serving as chairman of the National Committee from 1928 to 1929. He continued to be active in many areas. Dr. Hubert Work died on December 14, 1942 in South Denver, Colorado.

Bibliography:
 Adams, Samuel Hopkins. The Incredible Era: Life and Times of Warren Gamaliel Harding. Boston: Houghton Mifflin, 1939.
 Faulkner, Harold Underwood. From Versailles to the New Deal: A Chronicle of the Harding, Coolidge, Hoover Era. New Haven: Yale University Press, 1950.
 Fuess, Claude M. Calvin Coolidge, the Man from Vermont. Boston: Little, Brown and Company, 1940.
 Moran, Philip R., ed. Calvin Coolidge, 1872-1933. Dobbs Ferry, N.Y.: Oceana Publications, Inc., 1970.
 - - - -. Warren G. Harding, 1865-1923. Dobbs Ferry, N.Y.: Oceana Publications, Inc., 1970.
 Russell, Francis. The Shadow of Blooming Grove: Warren G. Harding and His Times. New York: McGraw Hill, 1968.
 Sinclair, Andrew. The Available Man: The Life Behind the Mask of Warren Gamaliel Harding. New York: Macmillan, 1965.
 Soule, George H. Prosperity Decade: From War to Depression, 1917-1929. New York: Rinehart, 1947.
 White, William Allen. Puritan in Babylon: The Story of Calvin Coolidge. New York: The Macmillan Company, 1938.

## POSTMASTER GENERAL: HARRY STEWART NEW

Harry S. New, Postmaster General in the Cabinets of Presidents Warren G. Harding and Calvin Coolidge, was born on December 31, 1858 in Indianapolis, Indiana, the son of John Chalfont New, Treasurer of the United States under President Ulysses S. Grant, consul general at London under President Benjamin Harrison as well as a public servant during President Chester A. Arthur's administration, and Melissa New. After receiving his preparatory education in the public schools of Indianapolis Harry studied at Butler University in Indianapolis in 1880. He also was a reporter for the Indianapolis Journal beginning in 1878 and continuing to work for the paper in various positions including that of editor until 1903. He was also part owner and publisher with his father.
Harry S. New married Kathleen Virginia Mulligan on October 18, 1880. They had one daughter, Virginia, who died in infancy. After his first wife died Harry married Catherine McLaen on August 18, 1891. He was elected a state senator and remained in the Indiana legislature from 1896 to 1900. He was quite active in the Republican

Party.  Harry New was a volunteer in the army during the
Spanish-American War, serving as a captain and later
assistant adjutant general in the Third brigade, second
division of the Seventh Army Corps.  After the war he
returned to the newspaper and his political activities,
becoming a member of the Republican national committee
in 1900.  He remained on the committee until 1912, serving as vice chairman in 1906 and chairman from 1907 to
1908.  He declined President Theodore Roosevelt's offer
of the post of assistant postmaster general in 1906.

Harry New sold his interest in the Indianapolis Journal in 1903 and then became president of the Bedford
Stone and Construction Company.  He continued his political activities, being elected United States Senator
in 1916.  He served for one term from March 4, 1917 to
March 3, 1923.  He was not renominated in 1922.  New had
been the first political candidate to utilize the radio
as part of his campaign.  While in the Senate he was a
member of the committee on military affairs in which
capacity he served on the subcommittee on aviation and
helped to develop a great deal of the wartime legislation.  He also was a member of the committee on foreign
relations, opposing the League of Nations Covenant because of Article X which required every nation to help
preserve the territorial integrity of each member nation
against aggression.

After leaving the Senate Harry S. New continued to be
active in Republican affairs.  President Harding named
him Postmaster General on February 27, 1923 to succeed
Hubert Work.  He assumed his office on March 5, 1923
and continued under President Calvin Coolidge after
the assassination of Warren G. Harding until March 5,
1929.  New was able to use his political knowledge and
connections to gain the necessary appropriations for the
department.  After carefully investigating and then
planning air mail service he arranged for contracts with
private concerns rather than using government-owned
planes and was able to develop it to the point where
300,000 miles were covered daily.  He planned extension
of the system to Central and South America.

Harry S. New also created the government-owned and o-
perated system of motor service for the Post Office.
It was efficiently run to the point where New reduced
the cost per mile.  While he was in office he was granted
the honorary LL.D. degree in 1926 by Butler University.
After leaving office Harry S. New returned to his business career and shortly thereafter retired to live in
Washington, D.C.  He was United States commissioner to
the Century of Progress Exposition in Chicago in 1933
and 1934.

Among his various activities Harry S. New was a member
of the Masonic order and the Elks.  He was a co-founder
of the Columbia Club in Indianapolis.  Harry S. New

died on May 9, 1937 in Baltimore, Maryland.  He was
buried in the Crown Hill Cemetery of Indianapolis, Indiana

Bibliography:
  Adams, Samuel Hopkins.  The Incredible Era: Life and
Times of Warren Gamaliel Harding.  Boston: Houghton
Mifflin Company, 1939.
  Faulkner, Harold Underwood.  From Versailles to the
New Deal:  A Chronicle of the Harding, Coolidge, Hoover
Era.  New Haven: Yale University Press, 1950.
  Fuess, Claude M.  Calvin Coolidge, the Man from Ver-
mont.  Boston: Little, Brown and Company, 1940.
  Moran, Philip R., ed.  Calvin Coolidge, 1872-1933.
Dobbs Ferry, N.Y.: Oceana Publications, Inc., 1970.
  - - - -.  Warren G. Harding, 1865-1923.  Dobbs Ferry,
N.Y.: Oceana Publications, Inc., 1970.
  Russell, Francis.  The Shadow of Blooming Grove: War-
ren G. Harding and His Times.  New York: McGraw Hill,
1968.
  Sinclair, Andrew.  The Available Man: The Life Behind
the Mask of Warren Gamaliel Harding.  New York: Macmillan, 1965.
  Soule, George H. Prosperity Decade: From War to De-
pression, 1917-1929.  New York: Rinehart, 1947.
  White, William Allen.  Puritan in Babylon: The Story
of Calvin Coolidge.  New York: The Macmillan Company,
1938.

## SECRETARY OF THE NAVY: EDWIN DENBY

Edwin Denby, Secretary of the Navy in the Cabinets
of Presidents Warren G. Harding and Calvin Coolidge, was
born on February 18, 1870 in Evansville, Indiana, the
son of Charles Denby, a lawyer and United States minister to China, and Martha (Fitche) Denby.  After receiving
his basic education in the local schools of Evansville
Edwin moved to China with his parents in 1885.  He was
employed by the Chinese imperial maritime customs service from 1887 to 1894.
Returning to the United States in 1894 Edwin Denby
attended the law department of the University of Michigan from which he received the LL.B. degree in 1896 and
was admitted to the bar in the same year.  He then began
his legal practice in Detroit, Michigan.  He enlisted
in the navy during the Spanish-American War, serving
as a gunner's mate third class on board the Yosemite.
Edwin returned to his legal practice after the war and
then was elected to the Michigan House of Representatives,
serving there in 1903.  He was next a successful Republican candidate for the United States House of Representatives.  He was a member of the Fifty-ninth through the
Sixty-first Congresses from March 4, 1905 to March 3,

1911.

Denby was defeated in his campaign for reelection in 1910 and returned to his legal practice after the end of his term in Congress. He was also involved in banking and other business pursuits. He was involved in civic services as president of the Detroit Charter Commission in 1913 and 1914. He then became president of the Detroit Board of Commerce in 1916 and continued in that post in 1917. He enlisted as a private in the marine corps after the United States joined the war in 1917. He retired in 1919 with the rank of major in the United States marine corps reserve. He then returned to Detroit where he was named chief probation officer in the recorder's court of Detroit and then held the same position in 1920 in the Wayne County circuit court.

President Warren G. Harding appointed Edwin Denby Secretary of the Navy on March 4, 1921. He assumed his office on March 5 and continued to serve under President Calvin Coolidge after the death of Warren G. Harding Denby resigned on March 10, 1924. He does not appear to have had much influence in the conduct of naval affairs while in office. He became involved in the "Teapot Dome Affair" which involved the disposition of the naval reserves at Teapot Dome, Nevada and Elk Hills, California.

President Harding had ordered the transfer of the administration of the naval reserves from the Navy Department to the Department of the Interior on May 31, 1921 because the Interior Department had the necessary administration controls to handle oil leases. Secretary of the Interior Albert B. Fall made arrangements to lease the Teapot Dome area to Harry F. Sinclair and Elk Hills to Edward L. Doheny. Since Sinclair and Doheny insisted that Denby sign the leases, the latter became involved in the scandal surrounding the leases. Fall had accepted gifts and loans from Doheny and Sinclair. Denby insisted that the leases were legal when the Senate demanded that President Coolidge dismiss him from his post. Denby finally tendered his resignation on February 18, 1924, effective March 10. The Supreme Court later exonerated him in 1927.

Edwin Denby returned to his legal practice as well as his banking and business interests in Detroit. He died there on February 8, 1929. He was buried in Elmwood Cemetery in Detroit.

Bibliography:
    Adams, Samuel Hopkins. The Incredible Era: Life and Times of Warren Gamaliel Harding. Boston: Houghton Mifflin Company, 1939.
    Faulkner, Harold Underwood. From Versailles to the New Deal: A Chronicle of the Harding, Coolidge, Hoover Era. New Haven: Yale University Press, 1950.

Fuess, Claude M. Calvin Coolidge, the Man from Vermont. Boston: Little, Brown and Company, 1940.

Moran, Philip R., ed. Calvin Coolidge, 1872-1933. Dobbs Ferry, N.Y.: Oceana Publications, Inc., 1970.

- - - -. Warren G. Harding, 1865-1923. Dobbs Ferry, N.Y.: Oceana Publications, Inc.,1970.

Noggle, Burt. Teapot Dome: Oil and Politics in the 1920's. Baton Rouge: Louisiana State University Press, 1962.

Russell, Francis. The Shadow of Blooming Grove: Warren G. Harding and His Times. New York: McGraw Hill, 1968.

Sinclair, Andrew. The Available Man: The Life Behind the Mask of Warren Gamaliel Harding. New York: Macmillan, 1965.

Soule, George H. Prosperity Decade: From War to Depression, 1917-1929. New York: Rinehart, 1947.

## SECRETARY OF THE INTERIOR: ALBERT BACON FALL

Albert B. Fall, Secretary of the Interior in the Cabinet of President Warren G. Harding, was born on November 26, 1861 near Frankfort, Kentucky, the son of William R. and Edmonia (Taylor) Fall who were both teachers. He was sent to live with his grandfather Philip Slater Fall in Nashville, Tennessee while his father served in the Confederate Army. Albert studied in the Nashville public schools and began working at the age of eleven in a cotton factory in the city. He eventually taught school and studied law.

Albert B. Fall next moved to the West in 1881 seeking a milder climate because of his respiratory ailments. He was a cattle drover and a cowboy cook. Fall settled in Clarksville, Texas where he sold insurance and real estate as well as ran a grocery store. Albert married Emma Garland Morgan on May 7, 1883. They had four children: John Morgan, Alexina, Caroline and Jowett.

After several prospecting trips Fall completed his legal studies and was admitted to the bar in 1891. He established his legal practice in the same year in Las Cruces, New Mexico Territory where he made a specialty of Mexican law. Fall became a Democrat and was elected to the territorial house, serving from 1890 to 1892. He was next a member of the territorial council from 1892 to 1893. After serving as an associate justice of the New Mexico Supreme Court from 1893 to 1895 he returned to the territorial council from 1896 to 1897. He was then territorial attorney general in 1897.

During the Spanish-American War Fall served as a captain in the first Territorial Infantry. After the war Albert continued in public service. He was a member of the New Mexico territorial council from 1902 to 1904 and was attorney general in 1907. He was also a delegate to

the New Mexican constitutional convention in 1911 which
prepared the way for admission of the state in 1912.  In
the meantime Fall had gradually switched from the Democratic to the Republican Parties.

Albert B. Fall was elected to the United States Senate
in 1912 and was reelected in 1918.  While in the Senate
he was a strong supporter of American rights in Mexico
and advocated the United States entrance into the League
of Nations.  He had become friendly with Warren G. Harding.  He resigned his seat on March 4, 1921.

President Warren G. Harding named Albert B. Fall
Secretary of the Interior on March 4, 1921.  He became
involved in a scandal concerning the leasing of the government oil reserves in Teapot Dome, Wyoming to Harry
F. Sinclair and Elk Hills, California to Edward L. Doheny.  He was accused of accepting gifts and loans from
the individuals involved.

The oil reserve scandal first came to the surface in
April 1922.  As a result of continuing pressure Fall resigned on March 4, 1923.  The Senate continued its investigation of the affair leading to the charge of fraud
and corruption in regard to the execution of leases and
contracts with various private companies.  He was indicted
in June 1924 and was convicted of accepting a $100,000
bribe in October 1929.  Fall was fined $100,000 and sen-
tenced to one year imprisonment.  He was the first cabinet officer to be convicted for a serious crime and
served his term in 1931-1932.  In the meantime the
leases for the two areas were cancelled in 1927.

Albert B. Fall returned to his home and ranch in Three
Rivers, New Mexico.  He was ill during the last years
of his life and was hospitalized from 1942 to 1944.  He
died on November 30, 1942 in El Paso, Texas.  He was
buried in Evergreen Cemetery. He lived two yrs in
the hospital while dead!

Bibliography:
Adams, Samuel Hopkins.  The Incredible Era: Life and
Times of Warren Gamaliel Harding.  Boston: Houghton
Mifflin Company, 1939.
Bates, J. Leonard.  The Origins of Teapot Dome: Pro-
gressives, Parties and Petroleum, 1909-1921.  Urbana:
University of Illinois Press, 1963.
Fall, Albert Bacon.  The Memoirs of Albert B. Fall.
El Paso: Texas Western Press, 1966.
Faulkner, Harold Underwood.  From Versailles to the
New Deal: A Chronicle of the Harding, Coolidge, Hoover
Era.  New Haven: Yale University Press, 1950.
Moran, Philip R., ed.  Warren G. Harding, 1865-1923.
Dobbs Ferry, N.Y.: Oceana Publications, Inc., 1970.
Noggle, Burt.  Teapot Dome: Oil and Politics in the
1920's.  Baton Rouge: Louisiana State University Press,
1962.
Russell, Francis.  The Shadow of Blooming Grove: War-

ren G. Harding and His Times. New York: McGraw Hill, 1968.

Sinclair, Andrew. The Available Man: The Life Behind the Mask of Warren Gamaliel Harding. New York: Macmillan, 1965.

Werner, Morris Robert, and Starr, John. Teapot Dome. New York: Viking Press, 1959.

## SECRETARY OF THE INTERIOR: HUBERT WORK

Refer to the biographical sketch of Hubert Work under Postmaster General, page 520.

## SECRETARY OF AGRICULTURE:

## HENRY CANTWELL WALLACE

Henry C. Wallace, Secretary of Agriculture in the Cabinets of Presidents Warren G. Harding and Calvin Coolidge, was born on May 11, 1866 in Rock Island, Illinois, the son of Henry Wallace, a Presbyterian clergyman and later farmer and editor of Wallace's Farmer, and Nannie (Cantwell) Wallace. While receiving his education in the Rock Island public schools Henry worked on his father's farm. He then worked in the newspaper offices in Winterset where he learned the printer's trade. Henry attended Iowa State Agricultural College (now Iowa State College of Agriculture) from 1885 to 1887. He rented one of his father's farms in 1887 and married Carrie May Broadhead on November 29, 1887. They had six children: Henry A., who was to become Secretary of Agriculture, Vice President, and Secretary of Commerce in the administrations of President Franklin D. Roosevelt as well as Secretary of Commerce in the Cabinet of President Harry S. Truman, Annabelle J., John B., James W., Mary A., and Ruth E.

Henry C. Wallace returned to Iowa State Agricultural College in 1881 and graduated with the B.S.A. degree in 1892. He was then appointed assistant professor of agriculture in dairying. He became co-owner and publisher with Charles F. Curtis of Farm and Dairy in Ames, Iowa. Henry, his father and his brother John purchased the paper in 1895. They moved it to Des Moines, Iowa and changed its name to Wallace's Farmer which became one of the major agricultural journals in the nation.

Henry C. Wallace was secretary of the Cornbelt Meat Producers Association for fourteen years. He eventually became owner of five successful stock and dairy farms in Iowa and surrounding states. He was chairman of the Iowa executive committee of the Y.M.C.A. from 1914 to 1920. When his father died in 1916 Henry C. Wallace became editor-in-chief of Wallace's Farmer.

President Warren G. Harding appointed Henry C. Wallace

Secretary of Agriculture on March 5, 1921.  He continued
to serve under President Calvin Coolidge after the death
of President Harding.  While in office he urged relief
for the farmers who were suffering during the post war
period.  He reorganized the department for greater efficiency.  Wallace also supported various measures including the Agricultural Credits Act of 1923 which established federal land bank districts to provide the farmers
with personal and collateral credit for the intervals
between short-term commercial loans and long-term loans
based on farm lands.

The bills legalizing and regulating the cooperative
marketing associations and the measure providing for
addition of a farmer representative to the federal reserve board.  In addition Wallace worked to aid in the
establishment of improved efficiency of production and
marketing.  He urged that production be adjusted to consumption needs.  He also supported conservation through
retention of the forest service rather than having it
transferred to the Department of the Interior.

Secretary Wallace travelled to Alaska with President
Harding in 1923 to study the best methods of developing
and conserving natural resources.  He established the
Bureau of Agricultural Economics as well as the Bureau
of Home Economics.  Henry also utilized the newly developed radio for issuing market reports.  He wrote
Our Debt and Duties to the Farmers which was then published posthumously in 1925.  Wallace was awarded the
honorary LL.D. degree by Iowa State University in 1922
and the D.Agr. from the University of Maryland in the
same year as well as from the University of Arizona in
1923.  Henry C. Wallace died on October 24, 1924 in
Washington, D.C.  After funeral services were held at
the White House his body was brought to Des Moines, Iowa
for burial.

Bibliography:
  Adams, Samuel Hopkins.  The Incredible Era: Life and
Times of Warren Gamaliel Harding.  Boston: Houghton
Mifflin Company, 1939.
  Faulkner, Harold Underwood.  From Versailles to the
New Deal: A Chronicle of the Harding, Coolidge, Hoover
Era.  New Haven: Yale University Press, 1950.
  Fuess, Claude M.  Calvin Coolidge, the Man from Vermont.
Boston: Little, Brown and Company, 1940.
  Moran, Philip R., ed.  Calvin Coolidge, 1872-1933.
Dobbs Ferry, N.Y.: Oceana Publications, Inc., 1970.
  - - - -.  Warren G. Harding, 1865-1923.  Dobbs Ferry,
N.Y.: Oceana Publications, Inc., 1970.
  Russell, Francis.  The Shadow of Blooming Grove: War-
ren G. Harding and His Times.  New York: McGraw Hill,
1968.
  Sinclair, Andrew.  The Available Man: The Life Behind

the Mask of Warren Gamaliel Harding. New York: Macmillan, 1965.
     Soule, George H. Prosperity Decade: From War to De-
pression, 1917-1929. New York: Rinehart, 1947.

### SECRETARY OF COMMERCE: HERBERT HOOVER

Herbert Hoover, Secretary of Commerce in the Cabinets
of Presidents Warren G. Harding and Calvin Coolidge, was
born on August 10, 1874 in West Branch, Iowa, the son
of Jesse Hoover, a blacksmith and dealer in farm imple-
ments, and Hilda (Minthorn) Hoover, who was a teacher.
Herbert studied in the West Branch public school. His
father died in 1880 and his mother in 1883. Herbert then
moved to the farm of his uncle Allan Hoover near West
Branch. He then moved to Newberg, Oregon to live with
his uncle Dr. Henry J. Minthorn in September 1884. Herbert studied at the Friends' Pacific Academy. He next
moved to Salem, Oregon with the Minthorns in September
1888 where he worked as an office boy in his uncle's
land-settlement business.

Herbert Hoover next attended Leland Stanford Junior
University in Palo Alto, California beginning in October
1891. He studied geology there. After continuing his
studies including work on United States Geological Survey teams during the summers Herbert graduated from Stanford with the Bachelor of Arts degree on May 26, 1995.
Hoover worked for various mining firms in the west and
Australia. He married Lou Henry on February 10, 1899
and then went to China to work for its government. The
Hoovers had two children: Herbert Clark, Jr. and Allan
Henry. While in China Herbert helped to defend Tientsin
from June 10 to July 14, 1900 during the Boxer Rebellion.
He next became a partner in Bewick, Moreing and Company.
Herbert formed his consulting mining engineering firm
in 1908.

Hoover organized and directed the American Relief Commission in August 1914 to aid Americans stranded in
Europe at the outbreak of World War I. In November 1914
he developed a program for the relief of those Belgians
and Frenchmen whose lands had been taken over by the
German army. President Woodrow Wilson appointed Hoover
Food Administrator under the Lever Food and Fuel Control
Act. He effectively regulated many aspects of the American food program during the war. After the end of the
war President Wilson appointed Hoover Director General
of the American Relief Administration on March 2, 1919.
He supervised delivery of more than twenty-three million
tons of food to various European states for four months
and then was able to change the organization into a
private one.

After returning to the United States Hoover wrote articles, delivered various speeches, conducted public

meetings and testified at many Congressional hearings.
He supported American participation in the League of
Nations and tried to convince President Wilson to accept
the reservations proposed by the Senate.  Hoover became
active in the Republican Party and was even considered
for the Presidential nomination in 1920.  He supported
Warren G. Harding for President.  On September 27, 1920
Hoover was named chairman of the European Relief Council
which coordinated the work of various European relief
organizations.  He was elected president of the American
Engineering Council in November 1920.  He and his family
moved to Washington, D.C. in January 1921.

President Warren G. Harding named Herbert Hoover Secretary of Commerce on March 3, 1921.  He assumed his office on March 5, 1921 and continued to serve under President Calvin Coolidge after the death of Warren G. Harding
in 1923.  He resigned from the position on July 14, 1928
in order to campaign for the Presidency.  As Secretary
of Commerce he invited twenty-five business, labor and
farm leaders to serve on an advisory committee to aid
the Department of Commerce in March 1921.

Hoover was chairman of the Unemplyment Conference
called by President Harding on September 26, 1929.  He
also conducted the first national radio conference in
Washington, D.C. on February 27, 1922.  He published
American Individualism in 1922.  Hoover travelled with
President Harding to Alaska in 1923.  President Coolidge
appointed him chairman of the American St. Lawrence Commission on March 14, 1924.  The American and Canadian
commissions were to cooperate on the development of the
St. Lawrence River and Great Lakes systems.

Herbert Hoover recommended institution of a Bureau of
Civil Aviation in September 1925.  Congress approved its
establishment in May 1926.  Hoover participated in the
first telecast over a long distance on April 17, 1927.
When the Mississippi River flooded causing much damage
Hoover recommended revision of the federal government
control program.  He was chairman of the first international radio conference on October 4, 1927.

Hoover announced his intention to run for the Presidency on February 12, 1928 and was nominated by the Republican Party National Convention on June 14.  He was elected
President on November 6, 1928, defeating Alfred E. Smith,
Governor of New York.  Herbert Hoover was inaugurated
as the 31st President of the United States on March 4,
1929.

/For information concerning the period of Herbert
Hoover's Presidency, consult Arnold S. Rice, ed.  Herbert
Hoover, 1814-1964 in this series./

After retiring from the Presidency at the end of his
term of office on March 4, 1933, having been defeated
by the Democratic nominee Franklin D. Roosevelt on November 8, 1932, Hoover returned to his home in Palo Alto,

California.  He published <u>The</u> <u>Challenge</u> <u>to</u> <u>Liberty</u> in
1934.  During the late 1930's Hoover campaigned against
the New Deal.  He published <u>Forty</u> <u>Key</u> <u>Questions</u> about
<u>Our</u> <u>Foreign</u> <u>Policy</u> in 1940 and <u>America's</u> <u>First</u> <u>Crusade</u>
and <u>The</u> <u>Problems</u> <u>of</u> <u>Lasting</u> <u>Peace</u> in 1942.  He urged
development of a program for the care of the sick and
starving children of Europe in 1945.

President Harry S. Truman sent Hoover on a world wide
tour in 1946 to study famine conditions.  In February
1947 he went to Europe to study the postwar food programs for President Truman.  Hoover was next appointed
chairman of the Commission on Organization of the Executive Branch of the Government by President Truman on July
17, 1947.  The Hoover Commission made its report on June
17, 1949.  Many of its recommendations were accepted.
During the next few years he urged various programs for
the security of the United States.

President Dwight D. Eisenhower next appointed Herbert
Hoover chairman of the Commission on Organization of the
Executive Branch of the Government (the second Hoover
Commission) on September 29, 1953.  The Commission's re-
port, issued June 30, 1953, recommended various budget
savings.  Hoover remained active in Republican circles.
He addressed every Republican National Convention since
1936 and was consulted as an elder statesman.

Herbert Hoover published <u>The</u> <u>Ordeal</u> <u>of</u> <u>President</u> <u>Wilson</u>
in 1958.  He also wrote a three-volume work entitled  <u>An</u>
<u>American</u> <u>Epic</u> which was published from 1959 to 1961.  He
dedicated the Herbert Hoover Library at his birthplace,
West Branch, Iowa on August 10, 1962.  Herbert Hoover
died on October 20, 1964 in New York City.  After his
body had lain in state in the Capitol Rotunda in Washington, D.C. on October 23 and 24, he was buried in West
Branch, Iowa on October 25.

Bibliography:
  Adams, Samuel Hopkins.  <u>The</u> <u>Incredible</u> <u>Era</u>: <u>Life</u> <u>and</u>
<u>Times</u> <u>of</u> <u>Warren</u> <u>Gamaliel</u> <u>Harding.</u>  Boston: Houghton
Mifflin Company, 1939.
  Brandes, Joseph.  <u>Herbert</u> <u>Hoover</u> <u>and</u> <u>Economic</u> <u>Diploma-</u>
<u>cy</u>, <u>Department</u> <u>of</u> <u>Commerce</u> <u>Policy</u>, <u>1921-1928</u>.  Pittsburgh:
University of Pittsburgh Press, 1962.
  Faulkner, Harold Underwood.  <u>From</u> <u>Versailles</u> <u>to</u> <u>the</u>
<u>New</u> <u>Deal</u>: <u>A</u> <u>Chronicle</u> <u>of</u> <u>the</u> <u>Harding,</u> <u>Coolidge,</u> <u>Hoover</u>
<u>Era</u>.  New Haven: Yale University Press, 1950.
  Fuess, Claude M.  <u>Calvin</u> <u>Coolidge,</u> <u>the</u> <u>Man</u> <u>from</u> <u>Vermont</u>.
Boston: Little, Brown and Company, 1940.
  Lyons, Eugene.  <u>Herbert</u> <u>Hoover,</u> <u>A</u> <u>Biography</u>.  Garden
City, N.Y.: Doubleday and Company, Inc., 1964.
  Moran, Philip R., ed.  <u>Calvin</u> <u>Coolidge,</u> <u>1872-1933</u>.
Dobbs Ferry, N.Y.: Oceana Publications, Inc., 1970.
  - - - -.  <u>Warren</u> <u>G</u>. <u>Harding,</u> <u>1865-1923</u>.  Dobbs Ferry,
N.Y.: Oceana Publications, Inc., 1970.

Prothro, James W.  The Dollar Decade, Business Ideas
in the 1920's.  Baton Rouge: Louisiana State University
Press, 1954.
    Rice, Arnold S., ed.  Herbert Hoover, 1874-1964.  Dobbs
Ferry, N.Y.: Oceana Publications, Inc., 1971.
    Soule, George H.  Prosperity Decade: From War to De-
pression, 1917-1929.  New York: Rinehart, 1947.
    Tugwell, Rexford G.  Mr. Hoover's Economic Policy.
New York: The John Day Company, 1932.
    Wolfe, Harold.  Herbert Hoover, Public Servant and
Leader of the Loyal Opposition.  New York: Exposition
Press, 1956.

## SECRETARY OF LABOR: JAMES JOHN DAVIS

James J. Davis, Secretary of Labor in the Cabinets of
Presidents Warren G. Harding, Calvin Coolidge and Herbert
Hoover, was born on October 27, 1873 in Tredegon, South
Wales, the son of David James and Esther Ford (Nichols)
Davis.  He came to the United States with his parents in
1881.  They settled in Pittsburgh, Pennsylvania and
then moved to Sharon, Pennsylvania.  James attended the
public schools and then studied at Sharon Business College.  At the age of eleven he was apprenticed as a
puddler in the steel industry, working in Sharon and in
Birmingham, Alabama.  He moved to Elwood, Indiana in
1893 to work in the steel and tin-plate industry.  He
joined the Amalgamated Association of Iron, Steel and
Tin Workers, holding various offices and eventually
became president.

James J. Davis soon became involved in municipal affairs and was elected Elwood City clerk in 1898 and
continued in that post until 1902.  James was next elected recorder of Madison County and served in that office
from 1903 to 1907.  He joined the Loyal Order of Moose,
becoming general director in 1907.  He moved to Pittsburgh
in the same year.  James worked to increased the membership of the organization from a few hundred to three-
quarters of a million with branches throughout the world.

James Davis helped to establish various benefit organizations.  He married Jean Rodenbaugh on November 20, 1914.
They had five children: James John, Jane Elizabeth, Jean
Allys, Joan and Jewel.  During 1918-1919 he was chairman
of the Loyal Order of Moose War Relief Commission and
visited various army camps in the United States, Canada
and Europe.

President Warren G. Harding appointed James J. Davis
Secretary of Labor on March 5, 1921 in recognition of
his talents as evidenced in his union activities and
organizational work.  While in office Davis cooperated
with the President's Unemployment Conference chaired by
Herbert Hoover in September 1921 to find means of providing work for the unemployed including public works

construction.  He also worked to help settle many labor
disputes during the strikes of 1921 to 1923.

James J. Davis also arranged to have the many homes,
hotels and dormitories which were constructed during the
First World War throughout the country offered to tenant
workers.  He wrote his autobiography, The Iron Puddler
in 1922.  Bucknell University conferred the honorary
LL.D. degree upon him in 1924.  The Labor Department
under Davis' direction developed the machinery necessary
for the Bureau of Immigration to carry out the quotas
under the first law restricting immigration.  He traveled to Europe and South America to study the problems
of immigrants and economic conditions as a result of
which he created the Immigration Board of Review.

As a result of the passage of a maternity and infancy
act he supervised the work of the Children's Bureau of
the Department to provide federal aid for needy mothers
and babies. Davis also used his discretion in expanding
the scope of the law to cover such issues as mothers'
pensions, child dependency and juvenile delinquency.
The Children's Bureau was able to reduce the infant mor-
tality rate.  He continued to serve under both Presidents
Coolidge and Hoover.  James wrote Selective Immigration
in 1926 and coauthored You and Your Job in 1927 with John
C. Wright.  He received the honorary LL.D. degree from
Drake University in 1927.

James J. Davis was elected to the United States Senate
from Pennsylvania to fill the seat of William S. Vane
whom the Senate refused to seat.  He resigned his cabinet
post on December 9, 1930.  Davis was reelected in 1932
and 1938, serving from December 2, 1930 until January
3, 1945.  He was defeated in his reelection bid in 1944.
The University of Pittsburgh conferred the honorary LL.D.
degree upon him in 1932.

While in the Senate Davis cosponsored the Davis-Bacon
bill of 1930 which eventually culminated in the Walsh-
Healy Act establishing minimum wages for contractors on
federal jobs.  Vice President John Nance Garner named
Davis a member of the special Senate committee to inves-
tigate the Tennessee Valley Authority project.  Davis
was a member of many fraternal and service organizations.
James died on November 22, 1947 in Tacoma Park. Maryland.
He was buried in Uniondale Cemetery in Pittsburgh.
Pennsylvania.

Bibliography:
  Adams, Samuel Hopkins.  The Incredible Era: Life and
Times of Warren Gamaliel Harding.  Boston: Houghton
Mifflin Company, 1939.
  Davis, James J.  The Iron Puddler.  Indianapolis: The
Bobbs Merrill Company, 1922.
  Faulkner, Harold Underwood.  From Versailles to the
New Deal: A Chronicle of the Harding, Coolidge, Hoover

Era.   New Haven: Yale University Press, 1950.
   Fuess, Claude M.  Calvin Coolidge, the Man from Vermont.
Boston: Little, Brown and Company, 1940.
   Lyons, Eugene.  Herbert Hoover, A Biography.   Garden
City, N.Y.: Doubleday and Company, Inc., 1964.
   Moran, Philip R., ed.  Calvin Coolidge, 1872-1933.
Dobbs Ferry, N.Y.: Oceana Publications, Inc., 1970.
   - - - -.  Warren G. Harding, 1865-1923.  Dobbs Ferry,
N.Y.: Oceana Publications, Inc., 1970.
   Rice, Arnold S., ed.  Herbert Hoover, 1874-1964.  Dobbs
Ferry, N.Y.: Oceana Publications, Inc., 1971.
   Russell, Francis.  The Shadow of Blooming Grove: War-
ren G. Harding and His Times.  New York: McGraw Hill,
1968.
   Sinclair, Andrew.  The Available Man: The Life Behind
the Mask of Warren Gamaliel Harding.  New York: Mac-
millan, 1965.
   Soule, George H.  Prosperity Decade: From War to De-
pression, 1917-1929.  New York: Rinehart, 1947.

## ADMINISTRATIONS OF CALVIN COOLIDGE

### VICE PRESIDENT: CHARLES GATES DAWES

   Charles G. Dawes, Vice President in the second administration of President Calvin Coolidge, was born on August
27, 1865 in Marietta, Ohio, the son of Rufus R. Dawes,
a merchant and member of Congress, and Mary Berman
(Gates) Dawes.  After receiving his basic education at
Marietta Academy Charles attended Marietta College from
which he received the Bachelor of Arts degree in 1884.
He studied law at the Cincinnati Law School (which later
became associated with the University of Cincinnati),
receiving the LL.B. degree in 1886.  He was then admitted to the bar.  Dawes worked during the summers for the
Marietta, Columbus and Northern Ohio Railway Company as a
civil engineer.  He eventually became chief engineer
for construction.
   Charles G. Dawes moved to Lincoln, Nebraska where he
was admitted to the bar and began his legal practice
with the firm of Dawes, Coffroth and Cunningham.  His
involvement in the Nebraska rate cases which succeeded
in reducing the freight rates in the state.  In addition
to his legal practice Charles became involved in various
business enterprises.  He was a vice president of the
Lincoln Packing Company and a director of the American
Exchange National Bank.
   Charles Dawes married Carol D. Blymer on January 24,
1889.  They had two children: Rufus Fearing and Carolyn
and adopted two: Dena McCutcheon and Virginia.  Dawes
published The Banking System of the United States in 1892.
Among Dawes' other business interests he became president
of the Northwestern Gas Light and Coke Company of Evans-

ton, Illinois in 1893 and president of the La Cross,
Wisconsin Gas Light Company in 1894.  He was a Republican in politics and led the Illinois Republicans in support of William McKinley.  He was named a member of the
Republican National Executive Committee.

President McKinley appointed Dawes United States
Comptroller of the Currency in which position he served
from 1897 to 1901.  He proposed reforms in the banking
structure so that conditions which occurred during the
depression in the 1890's would not be repeated.  He was
also able to collect $25 million due to the government
from various national banks which had failed.

Dawes resigned from his post in October 1901 to campaign for the United States Senate.  After withdrawing
from the race in May 1902 Dawes became president of the
Central Trust Company of Chicago which he had just helped
to organize.  He continued in this post until 1921 and
then served as chairman of the board from 1921 to 1925.
In the interim Dawes published his Essays and Speeches
in 1915.  His son Rufus had been drowned in 1912, and
Dawes founded the Rufus Fearing Dawes Hotel for Desti-
tute Men in Chicago in Chicago and Boston.  He also established the Mary Dawes Hotel for Women in Chicago in
1920 in memory of his mother.

Shortly after the United States became involved in the
European War Dawes was commissioned a major in the 17th
Engineer Corps of the United States Army on June 11, 1917.
He was next promoted to lieutenant colonel in July and
went to France with one of the advance units of the
American Expeditionary Forces under the command of General John J. Pershing.  Commissioned a brigadier general
on October 15, 1918, Dawes carefully regulated purchases
to avoid inflated prices and duplications.  When the
allied forces were unified he was named United States
member of the Military Board of Allied Supply.  He was
awarded the Distinguished Service Medal and was granted
several foreign military medals.

At the end of the war in November 1918 he was named a
member of the Liquidation Commission.  He resigned from
the army on August 31, 1919 and urged ratification of
the Versailles Treaty and United States participation
in the League of Nations.  He ran unsuccessfully for
the Republican nomination for President in 1920.  Dawes
was named first director of the Bureau of the Budget
which was created by Congress in 1921.  He helped organize and coordinate all aspects of the bureau which
prepared appropriations bills for Congress.

In 1921 Dawes published A Journal of the Great War.
Charles resigned from the Bureau of the Budget in 1922
and published in 1923 The First Year of the Budget of the
United States which indicated his experiences.  Dawes
and Owen D. Young were appointed American members of the
committee of experts to suggest methods of balancing the

German budget and stabilizing its currency.  Charles was
selected chairman and helped formulate the Dawes Plan
which provided a program to create prder put of the German financial situation.  As a result of his work Charles
was awarded the Nobel Prize for peace along with Sir
Austen Chamberlain.

Charles G. Dawes was nominated for Vice President at
the Republican National Convention in Chicago in 1924
along with Calvin Coolidge the Presidential nominee.  They
were elected on November 4, 1924.  They were inaugurated
on March 4, 1925.  Dawes served as Vice President until
the end of his term on March 3, 1929.  While in office
he tried to convince the Senate to revise its rules,
especially the one which permitted a filibuster.  He also explained his proposals to the public.  Dawes was a
contender for the Republican nomination for President
in June 1928.

After leaving office in 1929 Charles Dawes served for
a period as chairman of a financial commission to the
Dominican Republic.  President Herbert Hoover appointed
him Ambassador to Great Britain in April 1929.  He was
involved in preliminary discussions for the London Conference on Naval Limitation in 1930.  After resigning
from his diplomatic post in 1932 Charles became chairman
of the National Economic League.

President Herbert Hoover convinced Charles G. Dawes
to accept the post of president of the Reconstruction
Finance Corporation in February 1932.  He helped to organize this group which was to aid American corporations
and then resigned in June 1932 when he returned to his
banking interests.  He continued to publish works concerning his experiences including Notes as Vice President
in 1935, A Journal of Reparations and A Journal as Ambassador to Great Britain in 1939.  He also continued to
serve in many charitable organizations.  In 1951 he published A Journal of the McKinley Years.  Charles G.
Dawes died on April 23, 1951.  He was buried in Chicago.

Bibliography:
    Dawes, Charles G.  Notes as Vice President.  Boston:
Little, Brown, and Company, 1935.
    Faulkner, Harold Underwood.  From Versailles to the
New Deal: A Chronicle of the Harding, Coolidge, Hoover
Era.  New Haven: Yale University Press, 1950.
    Fuess, Claude M.  Calvin Coolidge, the Man from Vermont.
Boston: Little, Brown and Company, 1940.
    McCoy, Donald R.  Calvin Coolidge.  New York: Macmil-
lan, 1967.
    Moran, Philip R., ed.  Calvin Coolidge, 1872-1933.
Dobbs Ferry, N.Y.: Oceana Publications, Inc., 1970.

SECRETARY OF STATE: CHARLES EVANS HUGHES

Refer to the biographical sketch of Charles Evans
Hughes under Secretary of State in the Administration
of Warren G. Harding, page 509.

SECRETARY OF STATE: FRANK BILLINGS KELLOGG

Frank B. Kellogg, Secretary of State in the Cabinet
of President Calvin Coolidge, was born on December 22,
1856 in Pottsdam, New York, the son of Asa Farnsworth
and Abigail (Billings) Kellogg.  The family moved to
Viola, Olmsted County, Minnesota in 1856 and later to
Elgin, Minnesota in 1872.  Frank was educated at the
public schools while working on the family farm.  Kellogg began reading law with the firm of H. A. Eckholdt
and R. A. Jones in Rochester, Minnesota in 1875, being
admitted to the bar in December 1877.
     Beginning his practice in Rochester in 1877 Kellogg
became city attorney in the following year, serving until 1881.  He formed a law partnership with Burt W. Eaton in 1880.  He was elected district attorney for
Olmstead County in 1881 and served in that office from
1882 to 1887.  Frank married Clara M. Cook on June 16,
1886.  They had no children.
     Kellogg eventually formed the firm of Davis, Kellogg
and Severance in St. Paul, Minnesota and eventually became connected with the leaders of the railroad industry.
He also served as a professor of equity at the Minnesota State University from 1890 to 1893.  He also became
active in the Republican Party, attending the national
conventions of 1904, 1908 and 1912.  Frank was also a
government delegate to the United States Congress of
Lawyers and Jurists at St. Louis in 1904.
     During President Theodore Roosevelt's administration
Kellogg served the Justice Department as a prosecutor of
corporations charged with violation of the Sherman Anti-
trust Act.  Among the companies tried under his supervision were the General Paper Company in 1905.  Frank
was a counsel for the Interstate Commerce Commission investigating Edward H. Harriman's railroad network.  The
subsequent prosecution led to the Supreme Court's ruling
that the Union Pacific's control of the Southern Pacific
was illegal.  He also served in the government's prosecution of the Standard Oil Trust which culminated in
a favorable ruling for the government in the United
States Circuit Court in 1909.
     Frank B. Kellogg was elected president of the Ameri-
can Bar Association in 1912 and served in that office
until 1913.  He supported Theodore Roosevelt as the Progressive candidate for President in 1912.  McGill University in Montreal awarded Kellogg the honorary LL.D. de-

gree in 1913.  In November 1916 Frank B. Kellogg was
elected United States Senator from Minnesota and served
in the Congress from March 4, 1917 until March 3, 1923.
Although he supported the concept of a League of Nations
he soon joined the opposition insisting upon mild reservations.  He was defeated in his bid for a second term.
    President Warren G. Harding named Frank B. Kellogg  a
delegate to the Fifth International Conference of American States in Santiago, Chile in 1923.  He then returned
to his law practice.  President Calvin Coolidge named
Kellogg ambassador to Great Britain on December 11, 1923.
He served in this post until his resignation on March 4,
1925.  He was able to gain support of the Dawes plan for
German reparations.
    President Calvin Coolidge named Frank B. Kellogg Sec-
retary of State on February 17, 1925.  He assumed his
office on March 5, 1925 and served until March 3, 1929.
While heading the State Department Kellogg was able to
reestablish friendly relations with Mexico.  His me-
diation of the border dispute between Chile and Peru led
to a renewal of relations between the two states leaving
the boundary settlement to be arranged in the future.
The final agreement was reached on May 14, 1929 with the
treaty signed on June 3, 1929 after Kellogg had left office.
    Kellogg negotiated many treaties which culminated in
the Kellogg-Briand Peace Pact, the Peace Pact of Paris,
which came about as a result of a proposal by M. Aristide
Briand, the French foreign minister.  The treaty, re-
nouncing war as an instrument of national policy and promising peaceful settlement of all disputes, was signed
on August 27, 1928.  The Senate ratified the treaty in
1929.  During his term of office Kellogg was awarded
the LL.D. degree by the University of Pennsylvania in
1926, New York University in 1927 and by Harvard and
Trinity in 1929.
    After leaving office Kellogg returned to the practice
of law in St. Paul, Minnesota.  He was awarded the Nobel
Peace Prize in 1930.  The League of Nations elected him
an associate judge of the Permanent Court for International Justice at The Hague in the same year.  He served
in this capacity until 1935 and then returned to St. Paul.
Frank B. Kellogg died on December 21, 1937 in St. Paul.
He was buried in the chapel of St. Joseph of Arimathea
in the Washington Cathedral in Washington, D.C.

Bibliography:
    Bryn-Jones, David.  Frank B. Kellogg: A Biography.
New York: G. P. Putnam's Sons, 1937.
    Ellis, Lewis E.  Frank B. Kellogg and American Foreign
Relations, 1925-1929.  New Brunswick, N.J.: Rutgers Uni-
versity Press, 1961.
    Faulkner, Harold Underwood.  From Versailles to the

New Deal: A Chronicle of the Harding, Coolidge, Hoover
Era. New Haven: Yale University Press, 1950.
     Ferrell, Robert H. Peace in Their Time: The Origins
of the Kellogg-Briand Pact. New Haven: Yale University
Press, 1952.
     Fuess, Claude M. Calvin Coolidge, the Man from Ver-
mont. Boston: Little, Brown and Company, 1940.
     McCoy, Donald R. Calvin Coolidge. New York: Macmil-
lan, 1967.
     Moran, Philip R., ed. Calvin Coolidge, 1872-1933.
Dobbs Ferry, N.Y.: Oceana Publications, Inc., 1970.

## SECRETARY OF THE TREASURY: ANDREW WILLIAM MELLON

Refer to the biographical sketch of Andrew W. Mellon
under Secretary of the Treasury in the Administration
of Warren G. Harding, page 512.

## SECRETARY OF WAR: JOHN WINGATE WEEKS

Refer to the biographical sketch of John W. Weeks under Secretary of War in the Administration of Warren G.
Harding, page 515.

## SECRETARY OF WAR: DWIGHT FILLEY DAVIS

Dwight F. Davis, Secretary of War in the Cabinet of
President Calvin Coolidge, was born on July 5, 1879 in
St. Louis, Missouri, the son of John Tilden Davis, a mer-
chant and banker, and Maria Jeanette (Filley) Davis.
After receiving his preparatory education at Smith Aca-
demy in St. Louis, Dwight went to Harvard from which he
was graduated in 1900. While at Harvard he played tennis. He donated the Davis Cup which became a symbol of
supremacy in international tennis in 1900. Dwight F.
Davis next attended Washington University Law School in
St. Louis, receiving the LL.B. degree in 1903.
     Dwight then began his business career in St. Louis.
He married Helen Bobbs on November 15, 1904. They had
four children: Dwight Filley, Alice Brooks, Cynthia and
Helen Brooks. Davis became interested in a variety of
civic affairs serving as a member of the public library
board from 1904 to 1907. During the same period he was
a member of the board of control of the Museum of Fine
Arts, serving again from 1911 to 1912. He was greatly
interested in public recreation facilities, serving as
recreation commissioner in 1906 and 1907. He was also
a member of the Public Paths Commission.
     Dwight F. Davis was also involved in city government
as a member of the house of delegates from 1907 to 1909
and the board of freeholders from 1909 to 1911. He was
chairman of the City Planning Commission as well as serving on the public improvements board from 1911 to 1915.

During the same years Dwight was city park commissioner.
He enlarged the recreational facilities including golf
courses, baseball fields and the establishment of the
first municipal tennis courts in the nation.  As a result
of his experience in municipal affairs he was appointed
to the executive committee of the National Municipal
League on which he served from 1908 to 1912.  He had also become active in Republican political affairs.

When the First World War broke out in Europe Davis advocated American preparedness.  He received military
training at the first Plattsburg Military Training Camp
in 1915.  He went to Europe for the Rockefeller War Relief Commission visiting Norway, Denmark, Sweden and
England during 1916 and 1917.  He then enlisted in the
army in 1917, receiving a commission in August 1917.
Davis was promoted to the rank of major and was chief
of staff of the 35th Army Division and fought in France.
He was awarded the Distinguished Service Cross.  Dwight
eventually rose to the rank of lieutenant colonel.  He
served as a colonel in the Officers' Reserve Corps.

Dwight F. Davis was unable to win the Republican nomination for United States Senator from Missouri in 1920.
Recognizing his experience and talents, President Warren
G. Harding appointed Davis a member of the War Finance
Corporation.  He was next named Assistant Secretary of
War in 1923.  During his term of service Davis defended
the Department against Colonel William Mitchell's charges
that aviation had been ignored.  Davis was instrumental
in establishing the Army Industrial College in 1923 which
was responsible for the preparation of officers in the
area of mobilization of industry during war time.  He
also supervised experimentation with a mechanized force
When John W. Weeks became ill Davis was appointed acting
Secretary of War in the spring of 1925.

President Calvin Coolidge appointed Dwight F. Davis
Secretary of War to succeed John W. Weeks on October 13,
1925.  Davis served in this post from October 14, 1925
to March 5, 1929.  He approved of the recommendations
of a Presidential board for the court martial of Colonel
Mitchell as well as development of military and commercial aviation.

President Herbert Hoover appointed Dwight Davis governor general of the Philippine Islands in 1929.  He worked
to improve the economic conditions, public works, and
the educational system.  Resigning in 1932, Davis traveled and develop a tung-oil plantation in Florida.  He
became a member of the board of trustees of the Brookings
Institution in 1935 and was chairman after 1939.  His
wife Helen died in 1932.  He married Pauline (Morton)
Sabin on May 8, 1936.  Among his other activities Dwight
was a director of the Lehman Corporation during 1941
and 1942.

Dwight F. Davis was named director general of the Army

Specialist Corps in June 1942, continuing until November when he became its advisor with the rank of major general. Among his other business activities Davis served as a director of the Security Building Company, the State National Bank and the Mortgage Trust Company. His social welfare activities included his directorship of the St. Louis Tenement House Association and the St. Louis Association for the Prevention of Tuberculosis. Dwight F. Davis died on November 28, 1945 in Washington, D.C. He was buried in Arlington National Cemetery.

Bibliography:
  Faulkner, Harold Underwood. From Versailles to the New Deal: A Chronicle of the Harding, Coolidge, Hoover Era. New Haven: Yale University Press, 1950.
  Fuess, Claude M. Calvin Coolidge, the Man from Vermont. Boston: Little, Brown and Company, 1940.
  McCoy, Donald R. Calvin Coolidge. New York: Macmillan, 1967.
  Moran, Philip R., ed. Calvin Coolidge, 1872-1933. Dobbs Ferry, N.Y.: Oceana Publications, Inc., 1970.
  Soule, George H. Prosperity Decade: From War to Depression, 1917-1929. New York: Rinehart, 1947.
  White, William Allen. Puritan in Babylon: The Story of Calvin Coolidge. New York: The Macmillan Company, 1938.

## ATTORNEY GENERAL: HARRY MICAJAH DAUGHERTY

Refer to the biographical sketch of Harry M. Daugherty under Attorney General in the Administration of Warren G. Harding, page 517.

## ATTORNEY GENERAL: HARLAN FISKE STONE

Harlan F. Stone, Attorney General in the Cabinet of President Calvin Coolidge, was born on October 11, 1872 in Chesterfield, New Hampshire, the son of Frederick Lauson and Ann Sophia (Butler) Stone. After studying in the local school and Amherst High School Harlan studied at the Massachusetts Agricultural College in Amherst. He then attended Amherst College, graduating with the Bachelor of Science degree in 1894. He then went to Columbia University Law School, receiving the LL.B. degree in 1898. He was admitted to the bar in New York in 1898. He had taught at Adelphi Academy.
Harlan F. Stone married Agnes Harvey on September 7, 1899. They had two children: Marshall Harvey and Lauson Harvey. Stone began his legal practice with the firm of Sullivan and Cromwell. While practicing law he was a lecturer on law at Columbia University from 1899 to 1902 and associate professor of law from 1902 to 1905. He became dean of the Columbia University School of Law

and served from 1910 until October 1923.  He insisted
upon raising the standards of law schools so that those
who were not truly qualified to study law would not be
admitted.  Stone served as president of the Association
of American Law Schools in 1919.

President Calvin Coolidge named Harlan F. Stone Attorney General on April 7, 1924 to replace Harry M. Daugherty who had been forced to resign.  Harlan Stone assumed
his office on April 9, 1924 and continued in that office
until March 2, 1925.  He established the precedent of
personally directing the more important cases.  Yale
University conferred the honorary LL.D. degree upon him
in 1924 as did Collumbia University and Williams College
in 1925.

President Coolidge next appointed Harlan F. Stone an
associate justice of the United States Supreme Court on
March 2, 1925.  While he was on the Supreme Court many
colleges and universities conferred the LL.D. degree
upon him including Harvard, Dartmouth and the Universities of Michigan, Pennsylvania and Chicago.  President
Franklin D. Roosevelt named Harlan F. Stone Chief Justice
of the Supreme Court on June 12, 1941.  He was confirmed
by the Senate on June 27, 1941.  In the same year he was
honorary president of the National Association of Legal
Aid Prganizations.

Among his other activities Harlan Stone served as a
vice president of the American Red Cross Society, as well
as the Washington Monument Society.  In addition he was
a trustee of Amherst College, chairman of the board of
trustees of the National Gallery of Art.  He was also
chancellor of the Smithsonian Institution and a fellow
of the American Academy of Arts and Sciences.  Harlan
F. Stone died on April 22, 1946 in Washington, D.C.

Bibliography:
  Baker, Leonard.  The Deal Between FDR and the Supreme
Court.  New York: Macmillan Company, 1967.
  Faulkner, Harold Underwood.  From Versailles to the
New Deal: A Chronicle of the Harding, Coolidge, Hoover
Era.  New Haven: Yale University Press, 1950.
  Fuess, Claude M.  Calvin Coolidge, the Man from Ver-
mont.  Boston: Little, Brown and Company, 1940.
  McCoy, Donald R.  Calvin Coolidge.  New York: Macmil-
lan, 1967.
  Moran. Philip R., ed.  Calvin Coolidge, 1872-1933.
Dobbs Ferry, N.Y.: Oceana Publications, Inc., 1970.
  White, William Allen.  Puritan in Babylon: The Story
of Calvin Coolidge.  New York: The Macmillan Company,
1938.

## ATTORNEY GENERAL: JOHN GARIBALDI SARGENT

John G. Sargent, Attorney General in the Cabinet of President Calvin Coolidge, was born on October 13, 1860 in Ludlow, Vermont, the son of John Henman and Ann Eliza (Harley) Sargent. After receiving his basic education at Vermont Liberal Institute in Plymouth, Vermont, John studied at the Black River Academy in Ludlow. He was graduated from the last in 1893. John Sargent then continued his education at Tufts College from 1883 to 1887, receiving the Bachelor of Arts degree in the latter year.

John G. Sargent married Mary Lorraine Garden on August 4, 1887. They had one daughter, Gladys Gordon. After studying law with William M. Stickney, John G. Sargent was admitted to the Vermont bar in 1890. He eventually became a partner with Mr. Stickney in Ludlow in the firm which eventually became Stickney, Sargent and Skeels. John became interested in politics and was elected as a Republican to a two-year term as state's attorney for Windsor County, Vermont in 1898. He served until 1900. His former law partner William M. Stickney, who had been elected Governor of Vermont, appointed Sargent secretary of civil and military affairs in 1900. After serving for two years he returned to his legal practice in 1902.

In 1907 John G. Sargent was a successful candidate for Vermont state attorney general, a position created in 1904. He served two terms from 1908 to 1912. After leaving office he returned to his private law practice. His firm became counsel for many large New England corporations.

President Calvin Coolidge named John G. Sargent Attorney General on March 17, 1925 to succeed Harlan F. Stone. Sargent assumed his office on March 18, 1925 and continued until the end of the administration on March 4, 1929. While in office he enforced Prohibition and maintained that evidenced secured by wiretapping was valid.

After leaving office John Sargent returned to his legal practice again. He was appointed a referee for the reorganization of the Vermont railroads in 1935. He became a director of both the Vermont Valley, Boston and Maine Railroad and the Central Vermont Railroad in 1935, remaining in these positions until his death. Among his other business interests Sargent was president of the Ludlow Savings Bank and Trust Company. His public service continued when he became chairman of the Vermont Commission on Uniform State Laws. He was interested in antiquarian and historical information and was a member of the Vermont Historical Society. He was a trustee of the Black River Academy. John G. Sargent died on March 5, 1939 in Ludlow, Vermont.

**Bibliography:**

Faulkner, Harold Underwood. From Versailles to the New Deal: A Chronicle of the Harding, Coolidge, Hoover Era. New Haven: Yale University Press, 1950.

Fuess, Claude M. Calvin Coolidge, the Man from Vermont. Boston: Little, Brown and Company. 1940.

McCoy, Donald R. Calvin Coolidge. New York: Macmillan, 1967.

Moran, Philip R., ed. Calvin Coolidge, 1872-1933. Dobbs Ferry, N.Y.: Oceana Publications, Inc., 1970.

White, William Allen. Puritan in Babylon: The Story of Calvin Coolidge. New York: The Macmillan Company, 1938.

## POSTMASTER GENERAL: HARRY STEWART NEW

Refer to the biographical sketch of Harry S. New under Postmaster General in the Administration of Warren G. Harding, page 522.

## SECRETARY OF THE NAVY: EDWIN DENBY

Refer to the biographical sketch of Edwin Denby under Secretary of the Navy in the Administration of Warren G. Harding, page 524.

## SECRETARY OF THE NAVY: CURTIS DWIGHT WILBUR

Curtis D. Wilbur, Secretary of the Navy in the Cabinet of President Calvin Coolidge, was born on May 10, 1867 in Boonesboro, Iowa, the son of Dwight Locke and Edna Maria (Lyman) Wilbur. After attending the rural schools in Boonesboro, Iowa and Jamestown, North Dakota Curtis went to the United States Naval Academy at Annapolis from which he was graduated in 1888. He almost immediately resigned his naval commission and moved to Los Angeles, California.

Curtis Wilbur taught school while studying law in Los Angeles. He was admitted to the bar in 1890 and established his legal practice in Los Angeles. Curtis married Ella T. Chilson on November 9, 1893. They had no children. His wife died several years later. Wilbur soon became active in the Republican Party. He married Olive Doolittle on January 13, 1898. They had four children: Edna May, Lyman Dwight, Paul Curtis, and Leonard Fiske.

Curtis Wilbur was named deputy district attorney of Los Angeles, serving from 1899 to 1903. He became acquainted with problems of juvenile laws and was instrumental in having the state pass laws for juveniles as well as having the juvenile court of Los Angeles created in 1903. Curtis Wilbur was elected judge of the superior court of Los Angeles in 1902 and was reelected in 1908 and 1914. He sat on the bench in the city until 1918

when California Governor Stephens named Wilbur an associate justice of the California Supreme Court to fill
an unexpired term.  He was then elected in the same year
to complete the unexpired term as well as for a full
twelve-year term.  He was elected chief justice of the
California Supreme Court in which post he remained until
his resignation in March 1924.

President Calvin Coolidge appointed Curtis D. Wilbur
Secretary of the Navy on March 18, 1924 to succeed
Edwin Denby.  He continued in office until March 4, 1929.
Secretary Wilbur began to reorganize the Naval Department
which had been seriously troubled by the scandal of the
oil leases and the forced resignation of his predecessor
Edwin Denby.  Wilbur also worked to increase the size
of the navy in line with the ratio of 5:5:3 for the
United States, Great Britain and Japan as established at
the Washington Conference on 1921.  He also urged greater
use and construction of air planes and air craft carriers.

After leaving the Naval Department in 1929 Curtis D.
Wilbur was appointed judge of the Ninth United States
Circuit Court of Appeals.  In 1931 he became senior circuit judge, continuing on the bench until 1945.  He then
retured to his estate in Los Altos, California called
"Pine Lane."  Curtis D. Wilbur died on September 8, 1954
in Los Altos, California.

Bibliography:
Faulkner, Harold Underwood. From Versailles to the
New Deal: A Chronicle of the Harding, Coolidge, Hoover
Era.  New Haven: Yale University Press, 1950.
Fuess, Claude M. Calvin Coolidge, the Man from Ver-
mont.  Boston: Little, Brown and Company, 1940.
McCoy, Donald R. Calvin Coolidge.  New York: Macmil-
lan, 1967.
Moran, Philip R., ed. Calvin Coolidge, 1872-1933.
Dobbs Ferry, N.Y.: Oceana Publications, Inc., 1970.
White, William Allen. Puritan in Babylon: The Story
of Calvin Coolidge.  New York: The Macmillan Company,
1938.

## SECRETARY OF THE INTERIOR: HUBERT WORK

Refer to the biographical sketch of Hubert Work under
under Postmaster General in the Administration of Warren
G. Harding, page 520.

## SECRETARY OF THE INTERIOR: ROY OWEN WEST

Roy O. West, Secretary of the Interior in the Cabinet
of President Calvin Coolidge, was born on October 27,
1868 in Georgetown, Illinois, the son of Pleasant West,
a merchant and banker, and Helen Anna (Yapp) West. After
receiving his basic education in the public schools in

Georgetown Roy then studied at De Pauw University from
which he received the Bachelor of Arts degree and then
the LL.B. degree in 1890.

Roy O. West was admitted to the Illinois bar in 1890.
He then established his legal practice in Chicago.  He
became active in the Republican Party.  West was assistant attorney of Cook County in 1893.  He was next given
charge of the county tax department.  Elected city attorney of Chicago in 1895 West served until 1897.  He
married Louisa Augustus on June 11, 1898.  They had one
son, Owen Augustus.  His wife Louisa died in 1901.

Roy West was elected to the Cook County Board of Review of Assessments in 1898 and served until 1914.  He
was a member of the Cook County Republican Committee from
1900 to 1928.  Roy West established the legal firm of
West and Eckhart with Percy B. Eckhart in 1902.  Roy
continued his political activities throughout his career,
serving as chairman of the Illinois Republican state central committee from 1904 to 1914.  Roy married Louise
McWilliams on June 8, 1904.  They had one daughter, Helen
Louise.  In state politics West managed the election
campaign for Governor Deneer in 1904 and his reelection
in 1908.  Roy became an alumni trustee of DePauw University in 1914.

Roy O. West was a delegate to the Republican National
Conventions in 1908, 1912 and 1916.  He was named a member of the Republican National Committee and served from
1912 to 1916.  He was secretary of the national committee
from 1924 to 1928 and western treasurer in 1928.  He attended the national convention of that year.  West successfully ran Mr. Deneen's campaign for United States
Senator in 1924.  West became president of the DePauw
University Board of Trustees in 1928 and continued in
that position until 1952.

President Calvin Coolidge named Roy O. West Secretary
of the Interior ad interim on July 25, 1928.  He was
appointed Secretary of the Interior on January 21, 1929
and served until the end of the administration on March
3, 1929.  After leaving office West headed a group of
conservative Republicans called the Rational Republican
Party.  They opposed the progressive faction in 1932.
West continued his law practice in Chicago.  DePauw University granted West the honorary LL.D. degree in 1938.

Roy O. West's next government post was that of special
assistant to the United States Attorney General in 1941,
continuing to serve during the Second World War and after.
He left the post in 1953.  West served as a hearing officer for conscientious objector cases under the Selective Service Act.  Roy O. West died on November 29, 1958
in Chicago, Illinois.

Bibliography:
Faulkner, Harold Underwood. From Versailles to the New Deal: A Chronicle of the Harding, Coolidge, Hoover Era. New Haven: Yale University Press, 1950.
Fuess, Claude M. Calvin Coolidge, the Man from Vermont. Boston: Little, Brown and Company, 1940.
McCoy, Donald R. Calvin Coolidge. New York: Macmillan, 1967.
Moran, Philip R., ed. Calvin Coolidge, 1872-1933. Dobbs Ferry, N.Y.: Oceana Publications, Inc., 1970.
White, William Allen. Puritan in Babylon: The Story of Calvin Coolidge. New York: The Macmillan Company, 1938.

## SECRETARY OF AGRICULTURE: HENRY CANTWELL WALLACE

Refer to the biographical sketch of Henry C. Wallace under Secretary of Agriculture in the Administration of Warren G. Harding, page 528.

## SECRETARY OF AGRICULTURE: HOWARD MASON GORE

Howard M. Gore, Secretary of Agriculture in the Cabinet of President Calvin Coolidge, was born on October 12, 1877 in Harrison County, West Virginia, the son of Solomon Deminion Gore, a farmer, and Marietta Payne (Rogers) Gore. Howard received his basic education in the local public schools while working on the family farm. He then attended the University of West Virginia from which he was graduated in 1900. Gore then became involved in farming enterprises as well as various aspects of merchandising and livestock breeding with his brothers. They formed the firms of Gore Brothers and H. M. Gore and Brothers. Howard married Roxalene Corder on September 30, 1906.

Howard Gore's interest in livestock and his leadership qualities were recognized when he was elected president of the West Virginia Livestock Association, serving in that office from 1912 to 1916. When the United States declared war on Germany in 1917 Gore was named assistant food administrator for West Virginia. He was eventually appointed assistant to the United States Food Administrator. Gore next served as a member of the West Virginia state board of education from 1920 to 1925.

At the request of the National Farm groups Howard M. Gore went to Washington to supervise their work in the Department of Agriculture. Recognizing his effective administrative talents, Secretary of Agriculture Henry C. Wallace named Gore Chief of Trade Practices in the division of the packers and stockyard administration. He supervised problems within the Department which arose as a result of the government suits against the packers in regard to stockyard marketing operations.

President Calvin Coolidge named Howard M. Gore assistant Secretary of Agriculture in 1923.  Henry C. Wallace died on October 25, 1924.  Howard M. Gore was named
Secretary of Agriculture ad interim on October 26, 1924
and served until November 22, 1924.  Gore had been elected Governor of West Virginia in November.  President
Coolidge then appointed him Secretary of Agriculture on
November 21, 1924.  He assumed his office on November 22.
Gore supported the livestock industry.  He resigned from
the Cabinet on March 4, 1925 to assume the office of Governor of West Virginia in which post he served until
1929.
    While Governor of West Virginia Howard M. Gore worked
to improve the tax and financial structure of the state.
He was an unsuccessful candidate for the United States
Senate in 1928.  Gore continued to serve West Virginia
after leaving the governor's office in 1929.  He was
named state Commissioner of Agriculture in 1931 and
continued in this post until 1933.  Beginning in the latter year Gore helped to develop and manage the livestock
auction markets.  He became a member of the West Virginia
Public Service Commission in 1941.  Among his other activities Gore helped to establish and was a member of the
first board of directors of the National Producers' Livestock Cooperative Association.  He also served on the
West Virginia Farm to Market Roads Administration.  Howard
M. Gore died on June 20, 1947 in West Virginia.

Bibliography:
    Faulkner, Harold Underwood.  From Versailles to the
New Deal: A Chronicle of the Harding, Coolidge, Hoover
Era.  New Haven: Yale University Press, 1950.
    Fuess, Claude M.  Calvin Coolidge, the Man from Ver-
mont.  Boston: Little, Brown and Company, 1940.
    McCoy, Donald R.  Calvin Coolidge.  New York: Macmil-
lan, 1967.
    Moran, Philip R., ed.  Calvin Coolidge, 1872-1933.
Dobbs Ferry, N.Y.: Oceana Publications, Inc., 1970.
    White, William Allen.  Puritan in Babylon: The Story
of Calvin Coolidge.  New York: The Macmillan Company,
1938.

SECRETARY OF AGRICULTURE: WILLIAM MARION JARDINE

    William M. Jardine, Secretary of Agriculture in the
Cabinet of President Calvin Coolidge, was born on January
16, 1879 in Oneida County, Idaho, the son of William
Jardine, a rancher and farmer, and Rebecca (Dudley) Jardine.  He spent most of his early life involved in various ranching activities.  He attended the district school
for three to four months every winter.  During 1896
William M. Jardine went to work in Big Hole, Montana.
    Jardine enrolled in the Agricultural College of Utah

in 1899.  While he pursued his studies he worked on his
father's farm and was a student assistant in the department of agronomy.  He received the Bachelor of Science
degree in 1904 and then became an instructor at the college.  He was also manager of the Utah Arid Farm Company.
William married Effie Nebeker on September 6, 1905.  They
had three children: William N., Marian, and Ruth.  Jardine continued his education at the graduate summer
school of the University of Illinois in 1906.  He was a
professor of the Agricultural College of Utah during
the 1905-1906 academic year.

William Jardine began to work for the United States
Department of Agriculture as an assistant cerealist in
1907, attempting to solve the problems of the farmers
of the Great Plains area where droughts ruined crops.
In July 1910 Jardine began working for the Kansas State
Agricultural College Experiment Station as an agronomist.
He was next appointed lecturer at the Michigan Agricul-
tural College in 1912.  William became dean of the Kansas
State Agricultural College and director of the experi-
mental station in 1913.

Jardine was president of the International Dry-Farming
Congress and Soil Products Exposition during the period
1915-1916 and then president of the American Society of
Agronomy during 1916-1917.  He was head of the Kansas
state council of defense and a member of the War Finance
Corporation during the First World War.  Jardine was
named president of the Kansas Agricultural College in
1918 and continued until 1925.  He was highly successful
in administering the college.

William M. Jardine opposed the McNary Haugen bill which
proposed to sell wheat in foreign markets, even at lower
prices than the domestic market.  The difference would
be made up with public funds.  Jardine believed that
price-fixing would harm the farmer in the long run.
President Coolidge appointed Jardine a member of the agricultural commission to investigate all aspects of agriculture.

President Calvin Coolidge appointed William M. Jardine
Secretary of Agriculture to succeed Howard M. Gore on
February 18, 1925.  Jardine served in the office until
March 4, 1929 at the end of the administration.  He
changed the Department's support of the McNary Haugen
bill.  Jardine proposed several remedies for agriculture
including elimination of waste in distribution overhead
so that the farmers would receive more for their product
without costing the consumer more.  He also toured the
country to study the department's field work and to
learn about agricultural conditions in all parts of the
nation.  The Agricultural College of Utah conferred the
honorary LL.D. degree upon Jardine in 1925.  Lafayette
College awarded him the same degree in 1927.

President Herbert Hoover named William M. Jardine his

envoy extraordinary and minister plenipotentiary to
Egypt in July 1930. Jardine continued in that post
until 1933. In the last year he became treasurer of Kansas and served until 1934. He was next appointed president of the Municipal University of Wichita in Kansas
in 1934, remaining in that office until 1939.

Among his other activities William Jardine served as
public interest director of the Federal Home Loan Bank
of Topeka, a member of the Federal Savings and Loan
Advisory Council and was also on the board of directors
of the National Safety Council. He was chairman of the
board of the Investment Corporation of America. He was
also a member of the executive board of the National Research Council. He served on the advisory council of the
Agricultural Commission of the American Bankers Association, the Rock Creek and Potomac Parkway Commission, the
federal board for vocational education and the federal
power commission. He was a consulting director of the
American Farm Bureau Federation and vice president of
the American Farming Association. William M. Jardine
died on January 17, 1955 in San Antonio, Texas.

Bibliography:
     Faulkner, Harold Underwood. From Versailles to the
New Deal: A Chronicle of the Harding, Coolidge, Hoover
Era. New Haven: Yale University Press, 1950.
     Fuess, Claude M. Calvin Coolidge, the Man from Ver-
mont. Boston: Little, Brown and Company, 1940.
     McCoy, Donald R. Calvin Coolidge. New York: Macmil-
lan, 1967.
     Moran, Philip R., ed. Calvin Coolidge, 1872-1933.
Dobbs Ferry, N.Y.: Oceana Publications, Inc., 1970.
     White, William Allen. Puritan in Babylon: The Story
of Calvin Coolidge. New York: The Macmillan Company,
1938.

## SECRETARY OF COMMERCE: HERBERT HOOVER

Refer to the biographical sketch of Herbert Hoover
under Secretary of Commerce in the Administration of
Warren G. Harding, page 530.

## SECRETARY OF COMMERCE: WILLIAM FAIRFIELD WHITING

William F. Whiting, Secretary of Commerce in the Cabinet of President Calvin Coolidge, was born on July 20,
1864 in Holyoke, Massachusetts, the son of William Whiting, a United States Congressman from 1883 to 1889 and
a paper manufacture, and Anna Maria (Fairfield) Whiting.
He received his basic education at the Holyoke public
schools and then studied at Williston Academy in East-
hampton, Massachusetts. Whiting then went to Amherst
College from which he received the Bachelor of Arts de-

gree in 1886.

William F. Whiting worked for his father in the Whiting Paper Company during his vacations and after completing his college work.  He soon became involved in the management of the company.  William married Anne Chapin on October 19, 1892.  They had four children: William, Edward. Fairfield and Ruth.  William F. became president of the Whiting Company in 1911 and helped to expand its operations until he resigned in 1928.  During this period he became active in several businesses and financial corporations.  Whiting had also been active in the Republican Party and attended the National Conventions in 1920, 1924 and 1928.

President Calvin Coolidge named William F. Whiting Secretary of Commerce on August 21, 1928 to fill the vacancy left when Herbert Hoover resigned to campaign for the Presidency.  Whiting continued in office until the end of the administration on March 3, 1929.  He was also chairman of the United States section of the inter-Americam High Commission, a member of the Federal Narcotics Control board as well as the federal oil conservation board, the United States Council of National Defense, the national board for vocational education and the foreign service buildings commission.

After leaving office William Whiting continued his activities in the Republican Party.  He attended the National Convention in 1932.  Whiting died on August 31, 1936 in Holyoke, Massachusetts.

Bibliography:

Faulkner, Harold Underwood.  From Versailles to the New Deal: A Chronicle of the Harding, Coolidge, Hoover Era.  New Haven: Yale University Press, 1950.

Fuess, Claude M.  Calvin Coolidge, the Man from Vermont.  Boston: Little, Brown and Company, 1940.

McCoy, Donald R.  Calvin Coolidge.  New York: Macmillan, 1967.

Moran, Philip R., ed.  Calvin Coolidge, 1872-1933. Dobbs Ferry, N.Y.: Oceana Publications, Inc., 1970.

White, William Allen.  Puritan in Babylon: The Story of Calvin Coolidge.  New York: The Macmillan Company, 1938.

## SECRETARY OF LABOR: JAMES JOHN DAVIS

Refer to the biographical sketch of James J. Davis under Secretary of Labor in the Administration of Warren G. Harding, page 533.

## ADMINISTRATION OF HERBERT HOOVER

## VICE PRESIDENT: CHARLES CURTIS

Charles Curtis, Vice President in the administration of President Herbert Hoover, was born on January 25, 1860 in Topeka, Kansas, the son of Oren A. and Ellen (Papan) Curtis. He received his basic education in the common schools of North Topeka. Charles was also a jockey during the summers. He studied law in Topeka and was admitted to the bar in Topeka in 1881. He established his legal practice in Topeka and soon became active in politics. Charles married Anna F. Baird on November 27, 1884. They had three children: Permelia, Hameking, and Leona.

Charles Curtis was prosecuting attorney of Shawnee County from 1885 to 1889. He was elected as a Republican to the United States House of Representatives in 1892. He served in the Fifty-third to the Fifty-ninth Congresses from March 4, 1893 until his resignation on January 28, 1907. He paid careful attention to the needs of his constituents. Charles was next elected to the United States Senate to fill the vacancy left by Joseph R. Burton's resignation. Curtis assumed his seat in the Senate on January 29, 1907. He had already been reelected to the House of Representatives in 1906. On March 3, 1907 Charles Curtis was reelected to the United States Senate for the term beginning March 4, 1907. He continued to serve until the end of his term on March 3, 1913. He was president pro tempore from December 4 to December 12, 1911. Charles was defeated for reelection in 1912.

Curtis headed the Kansas delegation to the Republican National Convention in 1908 at Chicago and also served as a delegate at various state conventions. He was elected to the Senate again beginning his term on March 4, 1915. Shortly after taking his seat he was elected Republican whip and continued in that post until 1924. He was reelected in 1920 and 1926. Charles was elected majoroty leader in 1924. He remained in the Senate until his resignation on March 3, 1929.

Charles Curtis was nominated for the Vice Presidency on the Republican ticket with Herbert Hoover on June 14, 1928. They were elected on November 6, 1928. Curtis was inaugurated as Vice President along with President Hoover on March 4, 1929. He served until the end of the administration on March 3, 1933. He was the candidate for Vice President on the unsuccessful Republican ticket in 1932. Charles then returned to his legal practice in Washington, D.C. Charles Curtis died on February 8, 1936 in Washington , D.C. His remains were taken to Topeka, Kansas where they were buried in the Topeka

Cemetery.

Bibliography:
  Lyons, Eugene. Herbert Hoover, A Biography. Garden
City, N.Y.: Doubleday amd Company, Inc., 1964.
  - - - -. Our Unknown Ex-President, A Portrait of
Herbert Hoover. Garden City, N.Y.: Doubleday and Com-
pany, Inc., 1948.
  McGee, Dorothy H. Herbert Hoover: Engineer, Humanitar-
ian, Statesman. New York: Dodd, Mead, 1965.
  Rice, Arnold S., ed. Herbert Hoover, 1874-1964.
Dobbs Ferry, N.Y.: Oceana Publications, Inc., 1971.
  Wilson, Carol. Herbert Hoover. A Challenge for To-
day. New York: Evans Publishing Company, 1968.

SECRETARY OF STATE: HENRY LEWIS STIMSON

Refer to the biographical sketch of Henry L. Stimson
under Secretary of War in the Administration of William
Howard Taft, page 456.

SECRETARY OF THE TREASURY: ANDREW WILLIAM MELLON

Refer to the biographical sketch of Andrew W. Mellon
under Secretary of the Treasury in the Administration
of Warren G. Harding, page 512.

SECRETARY OF THE TREASURY: OGDEN LIVINGSTON MILLS

Ogden L. Mills, Secretary of the Treasury in the Cabinet of President Herbert Hoover, was born on August
23, 1884 in Newport, Rhode Island, the son of Ogden and
Ruth Tiny (Livingston) Mills. He received his preparatory education at the Browning School of New York City
after which he studied at Harvard University, receiving
the Bachelor of Arts degree in 1905. Ogden next attended
Harvard Law School from 1904 to 1907, graduating with
the LL.B. degree in the latter year. He was admitted
to the New York bar in 1908 and began to practice law
in New York City with the firm of Stetson, Jennings and
Russell. Ogden married Margaret Stuyvesant Rutherford
on September 20, 1911. They had no children.
Ogden Mills soon became interested in politics and
was elected treasurer of the New York County Republican
committee, retaining that post until 1926. He attended
the Republican National Convention in 1912. Mills ran
unsuccessfully for the United States Congress in 1912.
He was elected to the New York Senate in 1914, serving
from 1914 to 1917 when he resigned. He was chairman of
the committee dealing with New York City affairs and
supported progressive social welfare and financial legislation. He attended the Republican National Convention
of 1916.

Ogden Mills entered the United States Army in 1917 when the United States entered the war against Germany. He served as a captain until the end of the war.  He was assigned to the Army War College in Washington.  He went overseas in 1918 and served in France.  When Mills returned to the United States he resumed his legal practice in New York City and also returned to his political activities and various business enterprises.  Ogden divorced his wife Margaret in 1919.   Ogden Mills was president of the New York State Tax Association.  He attended the Republican National Convention in 1920.

Mills was elected to the United States House of Representatives in 1920.  He served in the Sixty-seventh through the Sixty-ninth Congresses from March 4, 1921 to March 3, 1927.  He was appointed to the Ways and Means Committee in his first term.  He helped to pass the Mellon tax bill in 1926.  Ogden married Mrs. Dorothy (Randolph) Fell on September 2, 1924.  They had no children.  Mills was nominated in 1926 as the Republican candidate for Governor of New York but was defeated by Alfred E. Smith.  Ogden attended the Republican National Conventions of 1924 and 1928.

President Calvin Coolidge appointed Ogden Mills undersecretary of the Treasury on February 1, 1927.  He assumed his office on March 4, 1927 and continued to serve until February 11, 1932 when President Hoover appointed him Secretary of the Treasury.  He served in that post from February 13, 1932 until March 4, 1933. He was one of the major leaders  in the administration. He attended the Republican National Convention of 1932.

After leaving office Mills severely criticized the New Deal administration of Franklin D. Roosevelt.  Ogden mills became an author and lecturer.  He wrote What of Tomorrow? in 1935, Liberalism Fights On in 1936 and The Seventeen Million in 1937.  He also served as a director of many firms including the Atchison Topeka and Santa Fe Railroad, National Biscuit Company, Shredded Wheat Company, the Chase National Bank and the New York Tribune Company.  He also was involved in social welfare activities, serving as president of the Home for Incurables, a member of the executive committee of the Charity Organization and a director of the Tribune Fresh Air Fund. Ogden Mills died on October 11, 1937 in New York City. He was buried in St. James Churchyard in Staatsburg, New York.

Bibliography:
Lyons, Eugene.  Herbert Hoover, A Biography.  Garden City, N.Y.: Doubleday and Company, Inc., 1964.
- - - -.  Our Unknown Ex-President, A Portrait of Herbert Hoover.  Garden City, N.Y.: Doubleday and Company, Inc., 1948.

McGee, Dorothy H.  Herbert Hoover: Engineer, Humani-
tarian, Statesman.  New York: Dodd, Mead, 1965.
Prothro, James W.  The Dollar Decade, Business Ideas
in the 1920's.  Baton Rouge: Louisiana State University
Press, 1954.
Rice, Arnold S., ed.  Herbert Hoover, 1874-1964.
Dobbs Ferry, N.Y.: Oceana Publications, Inc., 1971.
Romasco, Albert U.  The Abundance, Hoover, the Nation,
the Depression.  New York: Oxford University Press, 1965.
Warren, Harris G.  Herbert Hoover and the Great De-
pression.  New York: Oxford University Press, 1959.
Wilson, Carol.  Herbert Hoover.  A Challenge for To-
day.  New York: Evans Publishing Company, 1968.

## SECRETARY OF WAR: JAMES WILLIAM GOOD

James W. Good, Secretary of War in the Cabinet of President Herbert Hoover, was born on September 24, 1866 in
Cedar Rapids, Linn County, Iowa, the son of Henry and
Margaret (Coombes) Good.  After receiving his basic education in the common schools James attended Coe College
in Cedar Rapids from which he received the Bachelor of
Science degree in 1892.  He then studied law at the University of Michigan Law School at Ann Arbor, receiving
the LL.B. degree in 1893.  He was admitted to the bar
in the same year and began the practice of law with Oliver H. Carson in the firm of Carson and Good in Indianapolis, Indiana.  James married Lucy Deacon on October 4,
1894.  They had two childrem: James William and Robert
William.
James Good returned to Cedar Rapids in 1896 where he
formed a law partnership with Charles J. Deacon.  He became active in politics as a Republican and was city
attorney from 1906 to 1908.  James was elected to the
United States House of Representatives in 1908.  He served
in the Sixty-first to the Sixty-seventh Congresses from
March 4, 1909 until his resignation on June 15, 1921.
While in the House James was one of the major promoters
of the establishment of the national budget system.
After resigning his seat Good moved to Evanston, Illinois where he continued the practice of law as a member
of the firm of Good, Childs, Bobb and Wescott.  He served
as western campaign manager of President Calvin Coolidge's
campaign in 1924.  He also helped to manage Herbert
Hoover's pre-nomination campaign.
President Hoover named James Good Secretary of War on
March 5, 1928 in which post he served until his death.
He served the administration well.  James Good died
on November 18, 1929 in Washington, D.C.  He was buried
in Oak Hill Cemetery, Cedar Rapids, Iowa.

Bibliography:
Lyons, Eugene.  Herbert Hoover, A Biography.  Garden

City, N.Y.: Doubleday and Company, Inc., 1964.
- - - -. Our Unknown Ex-President, A Portrait of
Herbert Hoover. Garden City, N.Y.: Doubleday and Com-
pany, Inc., 1948.
   McGee, Dorothy H. Herbert Hoover, Engineer, Humani-
tarian, Statesman. New York: Dodd, Mead, 1965.
   Prothro, James W. The Dollar Decade, Business Ideas
in the 1920's. Baton Rouge: Louisiana State University
Press, 1954.
   Rice, Arnold S., ed. Herbert Hoover, 1874-1964.
Dobbs Ferry, N.Y.: Oceana Publications, Inc., 1971.
   Warren, Harris G. Herbert Hoover and the Great De-
pression. New York: Oxford University Press, 1959.
   Willoughby, W. F. The National Budget System. Balti-
more: The Johns Hopkins Press, 1927.
   Wilson, Carol. Herbert Hoover. A Challenge for To-
day. New York: Evans Publishing Company, 1968.

## SECRETARY OF WAR: PATRICK JAY HURLEY

Patrick J. Hurley, Secretary of War in the Cabinet of
President Herbert Hoover, was born on January 8, 1883 in
Choctaw Indian Territory (now Lehigh) Oklahoma, the son
of Pierce and Mary (Kelly) Hurley. He had a minimal
amount of education, having to work first as a mule
driver in the Atoka Coal and Mining Company coal mines.
He eventually attended Baptist Indian University, which
later became Bacone Junior College, receiving the Bachelor of Arts degree in 1905. During this period he joined
the Indian Territory volunteer cavalry as a private in
1902, becoming a captain in 1907. In the same year he
joined the Oklahoma National Guard.
   Patrick Hurley studied law at the National University
in Washington, D.C., receiving the LL.B. degree in 1908.
He was admitted to the bar in the same year. He continued
his studies at George Washington University, receiving
the LL.D. degree in 1912. He established his legal practice in Tulsa, Oklahoma, acting as national attorney for
the Choctaw nation from 1912 to 1917.
   Since Patrick J. Hurley was a member of the Oklahoma
National Guard at the time of the United States' entry
into the war in 1917, he was commissioned a major in
the army and was sent to France as a judge advocate in
the first army. He was eventually promoted to the rank
of colonel. Hurley was awarded the Distinguished Service
Medal for the fine manner in which he arranged for United
States troops to march through the Duchy of Luxembourg
at the end of the war.
   After the war Patrick Hurley returned to Tulsa, Oklahoma and reopened his legal practice as well as becoming
involved in various business pursuits including banking,
oil and real estate. He was for a time president of the
First Trust and Savings Bank of Tulsa. He married Ruth

Wilson on December 5, 1919.  They had four children:
Patricia, Ruth, Wilson and Mary Hope.

Patrick Hurley became active in the Republican Party
and was a delegate to the National Convention in 1924.
He chaired the Oklahoma State Republican convention in
1926 and was active in Herbert Hoover's campaign for the
Presidency in 1928.  President Hoover appointed Hurley
assistant Secretary of War in 1929.

President Herbert Hoover named Patrick J. Hurley Secretary of War to succeed James Good after the latter's
death.  Patrick assumed his office on December 9, 1929
and served until the end of the administration on March
3, 1929.  While in office he was chairman of the war
policies commission which had been created by Congress
to prepare plans in the event of war.  He also worked
to develop the army air force and to provide additional
mechanization for the army.

After leaving public office Hurley became a corporation
attorney in Washington, D.C.  He was recalled to active
duty in the army during the fall of 1941.  After the Japanese attack on Pearl Harbor, December 7, 1941, Patrick
was soon promoted to the rank of brigadier general in
January 1942.  He was sent to the Pacific and was wounded
during the Japanese bonbing attack on Port Darwin, Australia on February 19, 1942.  President Franklin D.
Roosevelt appointed Patrick Hurley American minister to
New Zealand in 1942.  He was sent to the USSR on a
special mission to consult with Marshal Josef Stalin
in 1942.

After resigning his diplomatic post to New Zealand in
March 1943 Hurley was sent on several missions to the
Near East by President Roosevelt.  Patrick was awarded
the Distinguished Flying Cross for his hazardous air
missions.  He attended the Cairo and Teheran Conferences.
While attending the latter in Iran in December 1943 Hurley drafted the declaration which guaranteed Iranian
sovereignty after the war.  Patrick Hurley was promoted
to major general in December 1943.  He went to Chungking
in August 1944 to help prevent the collapse of the Chinese Nationalist government.  He received the Special
Grand Order medal of the Chinese National government.

Patrick J. Hurley was eventually appointed Ambassador
to China in which post he remained until November 1945
when he returned to denounce certain State Department
officials for their China policy.  Secretary of War Robert Patterson awarded Hurley the Medal for Merit in
1946 for his services to China.  Patrick J. Hurley died
on July 30, 1963 in Santa Fe, New Mexico.

Bibliography:
    Lohbeck, Don.  Patrick J. Hurley.  Chicago: H. Regnery,
1956.
    Lyons, Eugene.  Herbert Hoover. A Biography.  Garden

City, N.Y.: Doubleday and Company, Inc., 1964.

- - - -. Our Unknown Ex-President, A Portrait of
Herbert Hoover. Garden City, N.Y.: Doubleday and Company, Inc., 1948.

McGee, Dorothy H. Herbert Hoover, Engineer, Humanitarian, Statesman. New York: Dodd, Mead, 1965.

Prothro, James W. The Dollar Decade, Business Ideas
in the 1920's. Baton Rouge: Louisiana State University
Press, 1954.

Rice, Arnold S., ed. Herbert Hoover, 1874-1964.
Dobbs Ferry, N.Y.: Oceana Publications, Inc., 1971.

Warren, Harris G. Herbert Hoover and the Great Depression. New York: Oxford University Press, 1959.

Wilson, Carol. Herbert Hoover. A Challenge for Today. New York: Evans Publishing Company, 1968.

## ATTORNEY GENERAL: JAMES DEWITT MITCHELL

James DeWitt Mitchell, Attorney General in the Cabinet
of President Herbert Hoover, was born on September 9,
1874 in Winona, Minnesota, the son of William Mitchell,
an associate justice of the Minnesota supreme court, and
Frances (Meritt) Mitchell. After receiving his preparatory education at the Lawrenceville School in New Jersey,
James DeWitt Mitchell attended Yale University where he
studied electrical engineering in the Sheffield Scientific School. After two years he went to the University
of Minnesota and received the Bachelor of Arts degree
in 1895.

Mitchell also studied law at the University of Minnesota and received the Ll.B. degree in 1896. He was admitted to the bar in the same year and entered the firm
of Stringer and Seymour. At the outbreak of the Spanish-
American War in 1898 Mitchell joined the 15th Minnesota
Volunteer Infantry as a second lieutenant. He also became acting judge advocate of the Second United States
Army Corps. He was next appointed engineering officer
of the 3rd brigade, first division of the Second Army
Corps in 1899. After the war he was a captain and adjutant of the 4th regiment of the Minnesota National Guard
from 1899 to 1901.

James DeWitt Mitchell returned to St. Paul, Minnesota
and practiced law again, becoming a partner in the firm
of Butler, Mitchell and Doherty. James married Gertrude
Bancroft on June 27, 1901. They had two children: William and Bancroft. When the United States entered the
First World War in 1917 Mitchell helped to organize the
6th Minnesota infantry, serving as a colonel. This regiment was assigned home-guard duty. In 1918 James enlisted in the national army, training at Camp Taylor in
Kentucky.

After the end of the war Mitchell returned to his law
firm in 1919. He also was regional counsel for the Uni-

ted States Railroad administrator.  He headed the newly
organized legal firm of Mitchell, Doherty, Rumble, Bunn
and Butler in 1922.  He was a Democrat in his political
views.  President Calvin Coolidge named him solicitor
general on June 4, 1925 in which post he remained until
the end of the administration.

President Herbert Hoober named James DeWitt Mitchell
Attorney General on March 5, 1929.  While in that office
he successfully argued before the Supreme Court his con-
tention that the Jay Treaty of 1794 was abrogated by the
War of 1812 and that an alien who sought to enter the
United States to work for hire was not doing so for
business as interpreted in the Immigrant Act.  In the
Pocket Veto Case he successfully maintained that when
the Congress passed a bill less than ten days before its
adjournment, and the President did not sign or return
the same to the house of its origin it did not become
law.  In addition the ten days was meant to be ten calen-
dar rather than ten legislative days.  Mitchell served
until March 3, 1933 at the end of the Hoover administration.

After leaving public office Mitchell went to New York
City to practice law with the firm of Taylor, Capron and
Marsh in April 1933.  He was chief counsel in the Black
Tom and Kingsland sabotage cases against Germany in 1939.
James was appointed a special prosecutor in the federal
grand jury investigation concerning the publication of
supposedly confidential information.

Mitchell's next public appointment was in 1945 when
he became chief counsel to the Congressional Pearl Harbor investigating committee.  He was named a member of
a panel of jurists in December 1952 to study the firm
by the United Nations Secretary General of staff employees
who belonged to the American Communist Party.  The panel
upheld the right of the Secretary General to do so.
James DeWitt Mitchell died on August 24, 1955 in Syosset,
Long Island, New York.

Bibliography:
  Lyons, Eugene.  Herbert Hoover.  A Biography.  Garden
City, N.Y.: Doubleday and Company, Inc., 1964.
  - - - -.  Our Unknown Ex-President, A Portrait of
Herbert Hoover.  Garden City, N.Y.: Doubleday and Com-
  McGee, Dorothy H.  Herbert Hoover, Engineer, Humani-
tarian, Statesman.  New York: Dodd, Mead, 1965.
  Rice, Arnold S., ed.  Herbert Hoover, 1874-1964.
Dobbs Ferry, N.Y.: Oceana Publications, Inc., 1971.
  Romasco, Albert U.  Poverty of Abundance: Hoover, the
Nation, the Depression.  New York: Oxford University
Press, 1965.
  Warren, Harris G.  Herbert Hoover and the Great Depres-
sion.  New York: Oxford University Press, 1959.
  Wilson, Carol.  Herbert Hoover.  A Challenge for To-

<u>day</u>.  New York: Evans Publishing Company, 1968.

## POSTMASTER GENERAL:  WALTER FOLGER BROWN

Walter F. Brown, Postmaster General in the Cabinet of
President Herbert Hoover, was born on May 31, 1869 in
Massilon, Ohio, the son of James Marshall Brown, a law-
yer, and Lavinia (Folger) Brown.  After receiving his ba-
sic education at Western Reserve Academy in Hudson,
Ohio, Walter went to Harvard University from which he
was graduated with the Bachelor of Arts degree in 1892.
Brown then studied at Harvard Law School from which
he received the LL.B. degree in 1894.  He was admitted
to the bar and entered his father's law firm: James
M. and Walter F. Brown
Walter Brown joined the Republican Party, supporting
William McKinley in his successful campaign for governor
of Ohio in 1891.  Walter became a member of the Ohio
State Republican central committee in 1899 and was selected chairman in 1906.  He served in that last position
until 1912.  Walter married Katharin Hafer on September
10, 1903.  When James M. Folger retired, Walter founded
the firm of Brown, Hahn and Sanger.  He helped William
Howard Taft to gain the Republican presidential nomination in 1908.  He was a delegate to the Ohio constitutional convention of 1911-1912.  Brown supported Theodore Roosevelt in his campaign for the Presidency on
the Progressive Party ticket.
Walter F. Brown supported Warren G. Harding's campaign
for the Republican Presidential nomination in 1920.
Shortly after his inauguration in 1921 Harding named
Brown chairman of the Congressional Joint Committee on
Reorganization as the President's special representative.
The group examined the operation of the Federal Government and recommended establishment of a Department of
Education and Relief, transfer of certain agencies to
the Department of Commerce, reorganization of the Department of the Interior, establishment of a bureau of
purchase and supply for the Federal Government, transfer of various departmental solicitors from the Justice
Department to the department involved, and removal of
the bureau of the budget from the Treasury Department
to an independent agency directly under the President.
Brown resigned from the commission in 1924.  President
Coolidge named him assistant Secretary of Commerce under Herbert Hoover.  He supported Hoover for the Presidency in 1928.
President Herbert Hoover named Walter F. Brown Postmaster General on March 5, 1929.  He assumed his duties
on March 6 and continued until the end of the administration on March 3, 1933.  While in office Brown awarded
long-term mail contracts to efficient airlines and thus
helped to develop commercial aviation.

After leaving public office Walter Brown returned to
Toledo, Ohio where he again practiced law.  Among his
business interests he was a director of the Toledo
Trust Company and the National Can Company.  His interest
in social welfare was evidenced through his presidency
of the Toledo Humane Society and his service as a
trustee of the Lucas County Children's Home.  Walter F.
Brown died on January 26, 1961.

Bibliography:
  Lyons, Eugene.  Herbert Hoover.  A Biography.  Garden
City, N.Y.: Doubleday and Company, Inc., 1964.
  - - - -.  Our Unknown Ex-President, A Portrait of
Herbert Hoover.  Garden City, N.Y.: Doubleday and Com-
pany, Inc., 1948.
  McGee, Dorothy H.  Herbert Hoover, Engineer, Humani-
tarian, Statesman.  New York: Dodd, Mead, 1965.
  Rice, Arnold S., ed.  Herbert Hoover, 1874-1964.
Dobbs Ferry, N.Y.: Oceana Publications, Inc., 1971.
  Romasco, Albert U.  Poverty of Abundance: Hoover, the
Nation, the Depression.  New York: Oxford University
Press, 1965.
  Warren, Harris G.  Herbert Hoover and the Great De-
pression.  New York: Oxford University Press, 1959.
  Wilbur, Roy Lyman, and Hyde, Arthur Mastick.  The
Hoover Policies.  New York: C. Scribner's Sons, 1937.
  Wilson, Carol.  Herbert Hoover.  A Challenge for To-
day.  New York: Evans Publishing Company, 1968.

SECRETARY OF THE NAVY: CHARLES FRANCIS ADAMS

Charles F. Adams, Secretary of the Navy in the Cabinet
of President Herbert Hoover, was born on August 2, 1866
in Quincy, Massachusetts, the son of John Quincy Adams,
Jr., a lawyer, and Fanny (Crowninshield) Adams.  He
was the great great grandson of President John Adams
and the great grandson of President John Quincy Adams.
After receiving his basic education Charles went to Harvard from which he was graduated cum laude in 1888 with
the Bachelor of Arts degree.  He then studied at Harvard
Law School receiving the LL.B. degree in 1892.  Charles
toured Europe and then read law with Sigourey Butler in
Boston and was admitted to the bar in 1893.
Charles Adams first practiced law with Sigourney Butler
and the Judge Everett C. Bumpus.  He opened his own law
practice in Boston in 1894 after his father's death.  He
married Frances Lovering.  They had two children: Charles
Francis, Jr. and Catherine.  Charles was a member of the
Quincy City council from 1893 to 1895 and then was elected mayor, serving from 1896 to 1897.  Charles was elected treasurer of the corporation of Harvard College in
1898 and continued until 1929.
Charles F. Adams also became involved in a business

career and was associated with many firms.  He was a
trustee of the Boston Ground Rent Trust Company and the
Boston Real Estate Company as well as a director of the
Boston Consolidated Gas Company, the Edison Electric Il-
luminating Company of Boston and the New England Gas and
Coke Company.  Charles became involved in banking at an
early age and became a skilled yachtsman.  In 1920 he
captained the America Cup defender the Resolute which defeated the Shamrock IV.  He also was the pilot of the
Atlantic which won a race from America to New York in
1928.
     President Herbert Hoover appointed Charles Francis
Adams Secretary of the Navy in which post he served from
March 5, 1929 until the end of the administration on
March 3, 1933.  He was a member of the American delegation to the London Naval Conference in 1930 which agreed
to a naval treaty based on the ratio of 5:5:3:1.75:1.75
for the United States, Great Britain, Japan, France and
Italy.  Adams supervised the continued maintenance and
development of the navy during this period.
     Charles F. Adams was elected president of the Harvard
Board of Overseers in 1930 and continued in that office
until 1943.  Among his other activities Charles was
chairman of the Community Mobilization for Human Rights.
He became chairman of the board of the New York, New
Haven and Hartford Railroad in 1951.  Charles F. Adams
died on June 10, 1954 in Boston, Massachusetts.  He was
buried in Mount Wollaston Cemetery.

Bibliography:
  Lyons, Eugene.  Herbert Hoover.  A Biography.  Garden
City, N.Y.: Doubleday and Company, Inc., 1964.
  - - - -.  Our Unknown Ex-President, A Portrait of
Herbert Hoover.  Garden City, N.Y.: Doubleday and Com-
pany, Inc., 1948.
  McGee, Dorothy H.  Herbert Hoover, Engineer, Humani-
tarian, Statesman.  New York: Dodd, Mead, 1965.
  Rice, Arnold S., ed.  Herbert Hoover, 1874-1964.
Dobbs Ferry, N.Y.: Oceana Publications, Inc., 1971.
  Romasco, Albert U.  Poverty of Abundance, Hoover, the
Nation, the Depression.  New York: Oxford University
Press, 1965.
  Warren, Harris G.  Herbert Hoover and the Great Depres-
sion.  New York: Oxford University Press, 1959.
  Wilbur, Ray Lyman, and Hyde, Arthur Mastick.  The
Hoover Policies.  New York: C. Scribner's Sons, 1937.
  Wilson, Carol.  Herbert Hoover.  A Challenge for To-
day.  New York: Evans Publishing Company, 1968.

            SECRETARY OF THE INTERIOR: RAY LYMAN WILBUR

     Ray L. Wilbur, Secretary of the Interior in the Cabi-
net of President Herbert Hoover, was born on April 13,

1875 in Boonesboro, Iowa, the son of Dwight Locke and
Edna Maria (Lyman) Wilbur.  His brother Curtis Dwight
Wilbur was Secretary of the Navy in the Cabinet of Presi-
dent Calvin Coolidge.  Ray moved to Riverside, California
with his family.  He received his basic education in the
public schools and graduated from high school in 1892.
He the studied at Stanford University, receiving the
Bachelor of Arts degree in 1896 and then the Master of
Arts degree in 1897.  Ray attended Cooper Medical Col-
lege from which he received the M.D. degree in 1899.

Ray L. Wilbur was a lecturer and demonstrator in
physiology at Cooper Medical College from 1898 to 1900.
Ray married Marguerite May Blake on December 5, 1898.
They had five children: Jessica Foster, Blake Colborn,
Dwight Locke, Lois Proctor and Ray Lyman.  He was
next an assistant professor of physiology at Stanford
University from 1900 to 1903 after which he went to
Europe to follow special studies at Frankfort-Am-Main
and London during 1903 and 1904.  He was next involved
in a private practice at Palo Alto until 1909 when he
was appointed a professor of medicine at Palo Alto
University.  He also studied in Europe  at Munich and
Vienna during 1909 and 1910.

Dr. Ray L. Wilbur was appointed dean of the Stanford
University in 1911 and continued in that post until
1916.  He was elected president of Stanford University
in 1915 assuming the office in the same year and retaining it until 1943.  Wilbur was named chief of the
Conservation Division of the Food Administration in
1917 to aid Herbert Hoover.  Wilbur was next named regional educational director of students' army training
corps in 1918.  He then returned to his administrative
duties at Stanford.  He was president of the California
state conference of social agencies in 1919 and of the
council of social and health agencies of San Francisco
from 1922 to 1924.

In 1925 and again in 1927 Dr. Ray L. Wilbur was chairman of the Institute of Pacific Relations in Honolulu to
eliminate the racial tensions between the Orient and the
United States.  During this period he was awarded the
honorary LL.D. degree by the University of California
and the University of Pennsylvania in 1925 as well as
by the University of Arizona in 1929.  He was appointed
United States delegate to the Sixth Pan American Congress
in Havana, Cuba in 1928.  He chaired a committee on the
costs of medical care in the same year.

President Hoover named Dr. Roy L. Wilbur Secretary of
the Interior on March 5, 1929.  Wilbur was given a
sabbatical leave from Stanford for this reason.  He remained in office until March 4, 1933.  Wilbur examined
the natural resources including the policies concerning
oil leases on public land.  He determined that the Department would not award any additional leases for naval

oil reserves.  In discussing allocations for the proposed
Hoover Dam he successfully advocated that 36 per cent of
the power be granted to Arizona and 64 per cent to California during the period 1930 to 1980.

Dr. Wilbur urged that the bureau of Indian Affairs be
reorganized in a manner that would help to encourage
greater freedom for the Indians in regard to reservation
life in order to help develop more self-supporting and
responsible citizens.  In the spirit of decreasing federal government control he urged that public land be
returned to the states.  He created a national advisory
committee of fifty educators to study the nation's educational needs and to develop a federal policy.

Dr. Wilbur was appointed chairman of the White House
Conferences on Child Health and Protection during the
period 1929 to 1931.  Among his other duties he served
as chairman of the Oil Conservation Board from 1929 to
1933 and of the National Advisory Commission on Illi-
teracy in the period 1930 to 1931.  As part of the administration's response to the economic crisis Ray was
named co-chairman of the Conference on Home Building and
Home Ownership.

After leaving public office in 1933 Dr. Wilbur returned
to his post at Stanford University.  He retired from the
presidency of the institution in 1943 when he was elected lifetime chancellor of Stanford.  In the same year
he was awarded the Dr. William F. Snow medal for distinguished service to humanity.  Dr. Ray L. Wilbur died
on June 26, 1949 in Stanford, California.

Bibliography:
   Lyons, Eugene.  Herbert Hoover.  A Biography.  Garden
City, N.Y.: Doubleday and Company, Inc., 1964.
   - - - -.  Our Unknown Ex-President, A Portrait of
Herbert Hoover.  Garden City, N.Y.: Doubleday and Com-
pany, Inc., 1948.
   McGee, Dorothy H.  Herbert Hoover, Engineer, Humani-
tarian, Statesman.  New York: Dodd, Mead, 1965.
   Rice, Arnold S., ed.  Herbert Hoover, 1874-1964.
Dobbs Ferry, N.Y.: Oceana Publications, Inc., 1971.
   Robinson, Edgar E. and Edwards, Paul C.  Ray Lyman
Wilbur.  Memoirs.  Stanford, Calif.: Stanford University
Press, 1960.
   Romasco, Albert U.  Poverty of Abundance, Hoover, the
Nation, the Depression.  New York: Oxford University
Press, 1965.
   Warren, Harris G.  Herbert Hoover and the Great De-
pression.  New York: Oxford University Press, 1959.
   Wilbur, Ray Lyman and Hyde, Arthur Mastick.  The
Hoover Policies.  New York: C. Scribner's Sons, 1937.
   Wilson, Carol.  Herbert Hoover.  A Challenge for To-
day.  New York: Evans Publishing Company, 1968.

SECRETARY OF AGRICULTURE: ARTHUR MASTICK HYDE

Arthur M. Hyde, Secretary of Agriculture in the Cabinet of President Herbert Hoover, was born on July 12, 1877 in Princeton, Missouri, the son of Ira Barnes Hyde, a lawyer, judge and Congressman, and Caroline Emily (Mastick) Hyde. After receiving his basic education in the Princeton, Missouri public schools and Oberlin Academy in Ohio, Arthur attended the University of Michigan from which he was graduated with the Bachelor of Arts degree in 1899. He then studied law at the State University of Iowa, receiving the LL.B. degree in 1900.

Arthur M. Hyde was admitted to the Missouri bar in 1900 and then entered his father's law firm in which he continued until 1915. Arthur married Hortense Cullers on October 19, 1904. They had one daughter, Caroline Cullers. Hyde was a captain in the Missouri National Guard during the period 1904 to 1905. He early became involved in politics and served on the Republican county and district committees. He was elected mayor of Princeton for two terms, serving from 1908 to 1912. He was defeated as the Progressive Party candidate for state attorney general in 1912.

Arthur M. Hyde moved to Trenton, Missouri in 1915 where he established his own law firm. He also became involved in various loan and investment activities as well as sellin insurance. In addition Hyde was a director of a local bank and became a Buick distributor. Arthur returned to the Republican Party by 1916. He was elected governor of Missouri in 1920, serving one term from 1921 to 1925. He helped to improve the state's educational system, provided for the extension of education for farmers, developed financial stability for the state penal system and instituted a road building system. Park College granted Hyde the honorary LL.D. degree in 1922. The following year he was awarded the LL.D. degree by Drury, Westminster and Marshall Colleges. After leaving office Arthur became president of the Sentinel Life Insurance Company in 1927 and continued until 1928.

President Herbert Hoover appointed Arthur M. Hyde Secretary of Agriculture on March 5, 1929. He assumed his office on March 6, 1929. Hyde was made an ex-officio member of the Federal Farm Board established by the Agricultural Marketing Act. During his tenure as Secretary of Agriculture Hyde emphasized farm efficiency and the use of better machinery. He supported a research program for pest control. The University of Michigan granted him the honorary LL.D. degree in 1929. Hyde organized and chaired the Federal Drought Committee in 1930. He worked to encourage further road construction and other forms of unemployment relief. He served until March 3, 1933.

After leaving office in 1933 Arthur M. Hyde returned

to the practice of law in Kansas City, Missouri.  He
retired from his legal practice in 1934, returning to
Trenton where he concentrated on management of his farm
holdings.  He served as a trustee of Missouri Wesleyan
College and Southern Methodist University.  He organized
and was a member of the Conference of Methodist Laymen
during 1935 and 1936.  Arthur M. Hyde died on October
17, 1947 in New York City.

Bibliography:
  Lyons, Eugene.  Herbert Hoover.  A Biography.  Garden
City, N.Y.: Doubleday and Company, Inc., 1964.
  - - - -.  Our Unknown Ex-President, A Portrait of
Herbert Hoover.  Garden City, N.Y.: Doubleday and Com-
pany, Inc., 1948.
  McGee, Dorothy H.  Herbert Hoover, Engineer, Humani-
tarian, Statesman.  New York: Dodd, Mead, 1965.
  Rice, Arnold S., ed.  Herbert Hoover, 1874-1964.
Dobbs Ferry, N.Y.: Oceana Publications, Inc., 1971.
  Romasco, Albert U.  Poverty of Abundance, Hoover, the
Nation, the Depression.  New York: Oxford University
Press, 1965.
  Warren, Harris G.  Herbert Hoover and the Great De-
pression.  New York: Oxford University Press, 1959.
  Wilbur, Ray Lyman and Hyde, Arthur Mastick.  The
Hoover Policies.  New York: C. Scribner's Sons, 1937.
  Wilson, Carol.  Herbert Hoover.  A Challenge for To-
day.  New York: Evans Publishing Company, 1968.

## SECRETARY OF COMMERCE: ROBERT PATTERSON LAMONT

Robert P. Lamont, Secretary of Commerce in the Cabinet
of President Herbert Hoover, was born on December 1,
1867 in Detroit, Michigan, the son of Robert and Isabella
(Patterson) Lamont.  After receiving his basic education
in the Detroit public schools Lamont attended the University of Michigan where he studied civil engineering.
He was graduated with the Bachelor of Science degree in
1891.
Robert Lamont was first employed in 1891 as an engineer for the Chicago Columbian Exposition (the world's
fair) which was to open in 1893.  He began working for
the firm of Thailer and Schinglau in 1892 as secretary
and engineer, continuing with them until 1897.  Robert
married Helen Gertrude Trotter on October 24, 1894.  They
had three children: Robert Patterson, Gertrude and Dorothy.  Lamont became first vice president of the Simplex
Railway Appliance Company in which position he remained
from 1897 to 1905.  His next post was vice president of
the American Steel Foundries in Chicago.  He rose to the
presidency of the firm in 1912 and remained in that office until 1929.
During the First World War Robert P. Lamont entered

the army as a major.  He was eventually promoted to
colonel and served as chief of the Procurement Division
of the Army Ordnance Department in Washington, D.C.  At
the end of the war Robert remained on the board of claims
for a period of time, retiring as a colonel in 1919.
He was awarded the Distinguished Service medal.

Robert P. Lamont returned to his business career and
also was one of the leaders in the movement against the
Prohibition Amendment.  In 1927 after the Mississippi
flood the United States Chamber of Commerce appointed
him vice chairman of a committee of engineers, business
men, and lawyers to investigate and survey the disaster
areas.

President Herbert Hoover appointed Robert P. Lamont
Secretary of Commerce on March 5, 1929 and continued in
office until his resignation on August 7, 1932.  He then
returned to his business interests and became president
of the American Iron and Steel Institute.  Among his o-
ther activities Patterson was a trustee of the University of Chicago, the Art Institute of Chicago, the Newberry Library which specialized in the sciences, and the
Rosenwald Industrial Museum.  He also retained an interest in the University of Michigan and contributed to
its research projects, including the construction of
the University's observatory at Bloemfontein, South
Africa.  He also contributed to the support of the observatory.  Robert P. Lamont died on February 20, 1948 in
New York City.

Bibliography:
Brandes, Joseph.  Herbert Hoover and Economic Diplo-
macy: Department of Commerce Policy, 1921-1928.
Pittsburgh: University of Pittsburgh Press, 1962.
Lyons, Eugene.  Herbert Hoover.  A Biography.  Garden
City, N.Y.: Doubleday and Company, Inc., 1964.
- - - -.  Our Unknown Ex-President, A Portrait of
Herbert Hoover.  Garden City, N.Y.: Doubleday and Com-
pany, Inc., 1948.
McGee, Dorothy H.  Herbert Hoover, Engineer, Humani-
tarian, Statesman.  New York: Dodd, Mead, 1965.
Rice, Arnold S., ed.  Herbert Hoover, 1874-1964.
Dobbs Ferry, N.Y.: Oceana Publications, Inc., 1971.
Warren, Harris G.  Herbert Hoover and the Great De-
pression.  New York: Oxford University Press, 1959.
Wilbur, Ray Lyman and Hyde, Arthur Mastick.  The
Hoover Policies.  New York: C. Scribner's Sons, 1937.
Wilson, Carol.  Herbert Hoover.  A Challenge for To-
day.  New York: Evans Publishing Company, 1968.

SECERETARY OF COMMERCE: ROY DIKEMAN CHAPIN

Roy D. Chapin, Secretary of Commerce in the Cabinet
of President Herbert Hoover, was born on February 23,

1880 in Lansing, Michigan, the son of Edward Cornelius
and Ella (King) Chapin.  After receiving his education
in the Lansing public schools and graduating from Lansing High School Roy began his studies in the liberal
arts at the University of Michigan in 1899.  He left
the University in 1901, taking a job with the Olds Motor Works.  He drove an Oldsmobile from Detroit to New
York for the 1901 automobile show.

Roy Chapin became general sales manager of the Olds
company in 1904 and continued in this position until
1906.  He was appointed a delegate to the annual National
Good Roads Association at Seattle in 1905.  Roy Chapin
along with Howard Coffin, Frederick D. Beener, and James
J. Brady backed by Edwin R. Thomas formed the E. R.
Thomas-Detroit Company.  Chapin was treasurer and general
manager of the company from 1906 to 1908.  The company
was reorganized as the Chalmers-Detroit Motor Company
and produced the Chalmers-Detroit car.

The Hudson Motor Company was organized with Joseph L.
Hudson and Roscoe B. Jackson in February 1909, to produce a less expensive car, the Hudson.  Chapin became
secretary of the company.  He next became president of
the Hudson Motor Company in December 1909 and retained
the position until 1923 when he became chairman of the
board.  Roy married Inez Tiedeman on November 4, 1914.
They had six children: Roy Dikeman, Joan King, John Carsten, Sara Ann, Daniel and Marian.

During World War I Roy Chapin was chairman of the high-
ways transport committee of the Council of National Defense.  During the 1920's he served as a director of the
Michigan State Good Roads Association.  Chapin worked
to organize the Pan American Confederation for Highway
Education in 1924 and was made chairman of the newly
established World Transport Committee in Paris in 1927.
He was also involved in various other international conferences.

President Herbert Hoover named Roy Chapin interim Secretary of Commerce on August 8, 1932 and then appointed
him to the cabinet post on December 14, 1932 in which
post he served until March 3, 1933.  After leaving public office Chapin returned to his position as chairman
of the board of the Hudson Motor Car Company, becoming
president again in 1934.  He was also involved in various
other business corporations and banks as well as social
welfare agencies such as the Detroit Community Fund.
Roy D. Chapin died on February 16, 1936 in Detroit,
Michigan.  He was buried in Woodlawn Cemetery.

Bibliography:
  Brandes, Joseph.  Herbert Hoover and Economic Diplomacy: Department of Commerce Policy, 1921-1928.  Pittsburgh: Pittsburgh University Press, 1962.

Chapin, Gilbert D.  The Chapin Book of Genealogical Data. 2 vols.  Hartford, Conn.: Chapin Family Association, 1924.

Kennedy, Edward D.  The Automobile Industry; The Coming of Age of Capitalism's Favorite Child.  New York: Reynal and Hitchcock, 1941.

Lewis, Eugene W.  Motor Memories, A Saga of Whirling Gears.  Detroit: Alved, 1947.

Long, John C.  Roy D. Chapin.  Bethlehem, Pa., 1945.

Lyons, Eugene.  Herbert Hoover.  A Biography.  Garden City, N.Y.: Doubleday and Company, 1964.

- - - -.  Our Unknown Ex-President, A Portrait of Herbert Hoover.  Garden City, N.Y.: Doubleday and Company, Inc., 1948.

McGee, Dorothy H.  Herbert Hoover, Engineer, Humanitarian, Statesman.  New York: Dodd, Mead, 1965.

Rice, Arnold S., ed.  Herbert Hoover, 1874-1964. Dobbs Ferry, N.Y.: Oceana Publications, Inc., 1971.

Warren, Harris G.  Herbert Hoover and the Great Depression.  New York: Oxford University Press, 1959.

Wilbur, Ray Lyman and Hyde, Arthur Mastick.  The Hoover Policies.  New York: C. Scribner's Sons, 1937.

Wilson, Carol.  Herbert Hoover.  A Challenge for Today.  New York: Evans Publishing Company, 1968.

## SECRETARY OF LABOR: JAMES JOHN DAVIS

Refer to the biographical sketch of James J. Davis under Secretary of Labor in the Administration of Warren G. Harding, page 533.

## SECRETARY OF LABOR: WILLIAM NUCKLES DOAK

William N. Doak, Secretary of Labor in the Cabinet of President Herbert Hoover, was born on December 12, 1882 near Rural Retreat, Virginia, the son of Canaro Draton and Elizabeth (Dutton) Doak.  After receiving his basic education at the public schools near his home William studied at a business college in Bristol, Vermont.  He was employed by the Norfolk and Western Railroad at Bluefield, West Virginia in 1900.  William was elected a member of the Brotherhood of Railroad Trainmen in 1904.  He worked to encourage cooperation between the Norfolk and Western Railroad and its employees.

William N. Doak was general chairman of the brotherhood local for the Norfolk and Western system from 1908 to 1916.  He married Maria Cricher in 1908.  They had no children.  William was elected secretary-treasurer of the southern association of the general committees of the Order of Railroad Conductors and Brotherhood of Railroad Trainmen, serving from 1909 to 1916.  He was next elected general chairman of the brothergood for the Norfolk and Western Railroad systems for the period 1912

to 1916.  Doak was elected a vice president of the
brotherhood in 1916 and became its legislative representative in Washington, D.C.

In 1918 Doak became a member of the Railway Board of
Adjustment Number One to handle differences between the
four Brotherhoods and the railways.  He was placed in
charge of the brotherhood's national wage movement during
1919 and 1920.  William Doak was elected first vice
president of the brotherhood in 1922.  His next assignment was direction of the territorial wage movement during the periods 1923-24 and 1926-27.  He was a member
of various committees and boards of awards to bring
about labor settlements and wage awards.  He served on
the train service boards of adjustment for the southeastern and eastern territories from 1921 to 1928.

William N. Doak ran unsuccessfully for the Senatorial
nomination from Virginia in 1924, challenging Senator
Carter Glass.  Doak was chosen assistant president of
the brotherhood in 1927.  He was elected managing editor of The Railroad Trainmen as well as the national
legislative representative in 1928.

President Herbert Hoover named William N. Doak Secre-
tary of Labor on December 8, 1930 to succeed James J.
Davis.  Doak assumed his office cn December 9 and continued to serve until the end of the administration on
March 3, 1933.  William Green, president of the American
Federation of Labor, opposed the appointment because the
Secretary had traditionally come from the federation.
While in office Doak waged a battle to restrict immigration as a protection for American labor.  He supervised
strict enforcement of the immigration laws.  Doak ordered
the fingerprinting of all aliens to determine those who
had entered the country illegally.  As a result of his
activities the number of aliens departing from the United States exceeded those entering the country for the
first time in the history of the nation.

William N. Doak urged introduction of a six-hour work-
day and a five-day week for labor.  He convinced Congress to support the expansion of federal employment
services by establishing federal agencies in every state.
In addition he encouraged cooperation of the federal,
state and municipal employment agencies.  Lincoln Memorial University awarded Doak the honorary D.H.L. degree
in 1931.  After leaving office he retired to gardening.
William N. Doak died on October 23, 1933 in McLean,
Virginia.

Bibliography:
   Lyons, Eugene.  Herbert Hoover.  A Biography.  Garden
City, N.Y.: Doubleday and Company, 1964.
   - - - -.  Our Unknown Ex-President, A Portrait of
Herbert Hoover.  Garden City, N.Y.: Doubleday and Com-
pany, Inc., 1948.

McGee, Dorothy H.  Herbert Hoover, Engineer, Humanitarian, Statesman.  New York: Dodd, Mead, 1965.
    Rice, Arnold S., ed.  Herbert Hoover, 1874-1964.
Dobbs Ferry, N.Y.: Oceana Publications, Inc., 1971.
    Warren, Harris G.  Herbert Hoover and the Great Depression.  New York: Oxford University Press, 1959.
    Wilbur, Ray Lyman and Hyde, Arthur Mastick.  The Hoover Policies.  New York: C. Scribner's Sons, 1937.
    Wilson, Carol.  Herbert Hoover.  A Challenge for Today.  New York: Evans Publishing Company. 1968.

## ADMINISTRATIONS OF FRANKLIN DELANO ROOSEVELT

### VICE PRESIDENT: JOHN NANCE GARNER

John N. Garner, Vice President in the first two administrations of President Franklin Delano Roosevelt, was born on November 22, 1868 near Detroit, Red River County, Texas, the son of John Nance  a Confederate cavalry trooper, and Sarah (Guest) Garner.  After receiving his basic education in the public schools John went to Vanderbilt University at Nashville where he studied for one term.  He then studied law with the firm of Sims and Wright in Clarksville, Texas.  He was admitted to the bar in 1890 and established his practice in Uvalde, Texas with Tully Fuller.  The firm later became Clark, Fuller and Garner.  He also edited The Uvalde Leader, a weekly newspaper.
    Garner was elected a judge of Uvalde County, sitting on the bench from 1893 to 1896.  John married Ettie Rheiner on November 25, 1895.  They had one son, Tully Charles.  John N. Garner continued his activities and was not elected to the Texas House of Representatives, serving from 1898 to 1902.  He was a delegate to the Democratic National Convention in 1900.
    John Nance Garner was elected as a Democrat to the United States House of Representatives, serving in the Fifty-eighth through the Seventy-second Congresses from March 4, 1903 to March 3, 1933.  Garner opposed tariff reciprocity.  He was active in the campaign of 1910 which removed some of Speaker Joe Cannon's power by removing from the Speaker the chairmanship of the rules committee.
    Garner was appointed to the Ways and Means Committee in 1913, becoming the ranking Democratic member in 1923.  He was elected minority leader in 1928 for the Seventy-first Congress, holding that position until December 7, 1931 when his party had gained control of the House of Representatives, and Garner was elected Speaker.  While in the House Garner attended the 1916 and 1924 Democratic National Conventions as a delegate-at-large.
    James N. Garner was a candidate for the Democratic Presidential nomination in 1932.  He withdrew in favor of Franklin D. Roosevelt and was nominated for Vice

President on July 2, 1932. John N. Garner was reelected
to the Seventy-third Congress and was elected Vice President
dent on the ticket headed by Franklin Delano Roosevelt
on November 8, 1932. Garner resigned from the House of
Representatives on March 3, 1933. Franklin D. Roosevelt
and John N. Garner were inaugurated as President and
Vice President respectively on March 4, 1933. Garner
was reelected Vice President on November 3, 1936 along
with President Roosevelt. Garner served as Vice President
dent until the end of his second term on January 20,
1941. (The Twentieth Amendment to the Constitution
changing the date of inauguration of the President and
Vice President from March 4 to January 20 had been passed
and ratified in 1933.)

As a conservative Garner opposed President Roosevelt's
spending plans and other New Deal measures. When Roosevelt
velt reacted to the Supreme Court's decisions invalidating
ting much New Deal legislation by proposing his court
"packing" plan Vice President Garner indicated his opposition.
sition. Garner also opposed Roosevelt's attempt to gain
a third term nomination and was consequently dropped from
the Democratic ticket in 1940. After leaving public
life James N. Garner retired to private life in Texas
to become involved in real estate and banking as well
as ranching. He accumulated a large fortune, donating
$ 1 million to Southwest Texas Junior College in 1961.
James N. Garner died on November 7, 1967 in Uvalde,
Texas.

Bibliography:
  Bremer, Howard F., ed. Franklin D. Roosevelt, 1882-
1945. Dobbs Ferry, N.Y.: Oceana Publications, Inc.,
1969.
  Burns, James MacGregor. Roosevelt: The Lion and the
Fox. New York: Harcourt Brace Jovanovich, Inc., 1956.
  Conkin, Paul K. The New Deal. New York: Thomas Y.
Crowell Company, 1967.
  Schlesinger, Arthur M. The Coming of the New Deal.
Boston: Houghton Mifflin Company, 1959.
  - - - -. The Politics of Upheaval. Boston: Houghton
Mifflin Company, 1960.

## VICE PRESIDENT: HENRY AGARD WALLACE

Henry A. Wallace, Secretary of Agriculture in the Cabinet
binet of President Franklin D. Roosevelt, Vice President
in the third administration of Franklin D. Roosevelt,
and Secretary of Commerce in the Cabinets of Presidents
Franklin D. Roosevelt and Harry S. Truman, was born on
October 7, 1888 on a farm near Orient, Adair County,
Iowa, the son of Henry Cantwell Wallace, Secretary of
Agriculture in the Cabinets of Presidents Warren G. Harding
ding and Calvin Coolidge, and May (Broadhead) Wallace.

After receiving his education in the public schools he went to West Des Moines High School. He then studied at Iowa State College from which he received the B.S.A. degree in 1910. Henry A. became associate editor of Wallace's Farmer, serving on the editorial staff until 1924. Henry A. Wallace married Ilo Bowne on May 20, 1914. They had three children: Henry B., Robert B. and Jean B.

Henry A. Wallace became interested in breeding and hybridization of corn. He developed the first of a series of corn-hog ratios in 1915 which indicate the probable course of the markets. He published Agricultural Prices in 1919 and Corn and Corn Growing in 1923. When Henry A. Wallace's father died in 1924 he became editor of Wallace's Farmer, continuing until 1929. He became a respected agricultural economist and chaired the Agricultural Round Table at the International Institute of Politics at Williamstown, Massachusetts in 1927. Wallace was a delegate to the International Conference of Agricultural Economics at South Devon, England in 1929.

When the Republican administrations failed to help the farmer by helping to regulate agricultural production and provide necessary leadership Henry A. Wallace joined the Democratic Party and supported Alfred E. Smith for the Presidency in 1928. Wallace merged his paper with the Iowa Homestead and became editor of Wallace's Farmer and Iowa Homestead in 1929, continuing in that post until 1933. He became farm adviser to Franklin D. Roosevelt and supported him for the Presidency in 1932.

President Franklin D. Roosevelt named Henry A. Wallace Secretary of Agriculture on March 4, 1933. He remained in that post until his resignation on September 2, 1940 to campaign as Roosevelt's Vice Presidential running mate. While in office Wallace worked with the administration to provide farm relief. When the Agricultural Adjustment Act went into effect on May 12, 1933 Wallace established the Agricultural Adjustment Administration which was empowered to make contracts with individual farmers for crop adjustments and to help work out marketing arrangements.

Wallace proposed establishment of the "ever-normal granary" in June 1934. The drought of the same year in addition to the Supreme Court's declaration that the Agricultural Adjustment Act was unconstitutional enabled him to develop a broader program. The Soil Conservation and Domestic Allotment Act was passed in February 1936. This act was intended to have crops planted on certain lands to help prevent erosion. His ever-normal granary concept was enacted into law in 1938 as part of the Agricultural Adjustment Act. Loans were provided to help the farmers have a guaranteed return for their crops. They were also to hold crops off the market.

Among the other aspects of the aid to farmers was pro-

vision for wheat insurance whereby the farmers put wheat
into a fund in good years and withdrew it in bad.  Four
new regional laboratories were established to find industrial uses for agricultural produce.  Wallace wrote
America Must Choose, Statesmanship and Religions and
New Frontiers in 1934.  He also published Technology,
Corporations and the General Welfare in 1937 and Paths
to Plenty in 1938.

The Department of Agriculture worked with state
cies for better planning in the years of national and regional crop adjustment, better marketing arrangements,
improved farm living conditions, better care of the soil,
an improved tax structure for land, public land purchases,
and aid to citizens to put all resources to the best
use.  The Department also concerned itself with improving
the breeding of plants and animals as well as the establishment of family dietary needs on a national scale.
The various programs developed in the 1930's prepared
United States agriculture for its world role when war
broke out in Europe in 1939.

Henry A. Wallace attended the Democratic National Convention in Chicago in 1940 when President Roosevelt
was nominated for a third term.  Henry A. Wallace was
nominated for Vice President and was elected with Roosevelt on November 5, 1940.  They were inaugurated on
January 20, 1941.  The President appointed Wallace chairman of the newly created board of economic defense in
July 1941.  He was also named chairman of the supply,
priority and allocations board in August 1941.  When the
War Production Board was created in January 1942 Wallace
was named a member.  He visited the west coast of South
Africa in March and April 1943 and helped improve Latin
American relations.

When disagreements developed between Wallace, chairman
of the board of economic warfare, and Jesse Jones, head
of the Reconstruction Finance Corporation, concerning
the acquisition of war materials President Roosevelt a-
bolished the board of economic warfare on July 15, 1943
and created the office of economic warfare, headed by
Leo T. Crowley.  Wallace wrote The Century of the Common
Man in 1943.

Wallace visited China in May and June of 1944 to encourage the Chinese to continue the war effort against
the Japanese.  He reached an agreement concerning future
conditions in Asia.  President Roosevelt supported Wallace for the Vice Presidential nomination in 1944, but
opposition was expressed by some of the city political
machines and some Southern Democrats.  Roosevelt did not
want to create a rift in the Party.  Consequently Wallace
was defeated for the Vice Presidential nomination by
Senator Harry S. Truman of Missouri at the National Convention in July 1944.  Henry A. Wallace campaigned personally for President Roosevelt during the election.  He

also wrote Democracy Reborn in 1944.

President Franklin D. Roosevelt nominated Henry A. Wallace for the post of Secretary of Commerce in January 1945. Opposition grew to his appointment on the basis that he was not qualified to run the Reconstruction Finance Corporation. After the latter was removed from the Commerce Department by the George bill in March 1945, Wallace's nomination was confirmed by the Senate. He assumed his office on March 2, 1945 and continued to serve under President Harry S. Truman after the death of Franklin D. Roosevelt in April 1945. Wallace reorganized the Department of Commerce so that it could more effectively serve small business and the foreign trade community by establishing special offices for these fields. In addition he established a division for domestic trade and obtained Congressional approval for appointment of threeassistant secretaries of Commerce to head these areas.

In an address before a rally at Madison Square Garden in New York City on September 12, 1946 Henry A. Wallace commented on American foreign policy indicating conflicts with Secretary of State James F. Byrne's strong stand at Paris opposing the Soviet Union's expansion program. President Harry S. Truman requested Wallace's resignation on September 20, 1946. It was submitted and accepted the same day. Wallace became editor of the New Republic on December 16, 1946. He ran unsuccessfully as the Progressive candidate for President in 1948. He wrote The Century of the Common Man in the same year. He resided at South Salem, New York. Henry A. Wallace died on November 18, 1965 in Danbury, Connecticut.

Bibliography:
    Bremer, Howard F., ed. Franklin D. Roosevelt, 1882-1945. Dobbs Ferry, N.Y.: Oceana Publications, Inc., 1969.
    Burns, James MacGregor. Roosevelt: The Lion and the Fox. New York: Harcourt Brace Jovanovich, Inc., 1956.
    Conkin, Paul K. The New Deal. New York: Thomas Y. Crowell Company, 1967.
    Ekirch, Arthur. Ideologies and Utopias: The Impact of the New Deal on American Thought. Chicago: Quadrangle Books, 1969.
    MacDonald, Dwight. Henry Wallace, The Man and the Myth. New York: Vanguard Press, 1948.
    Schlesinger, Arthur M. The Coming of the New Deal. Boston: Houghton Mifflin Company, 1959.
    - - - -. The Politics of Upheaval. Boston: Houghton Mifflin Company, 1960.

## VICE PRESIDENT: HARRY S/HIPPE/ TRUMAN

Harry S. Truman, Vice President in the fourth Administration of President Franklin Delano Roosevelt, was born
on August 8, 1884 in Lamar, Missouri, the son of John
Anderson Truman, a farmer and livestock dealer, and Martha Ellen (Young) Truman. He moved with his family to
Cass County, Missouri on May 1, 1885. The family next
moved to a farm in Grandview, Jackson County, Missouri
in March 1887 and then to Independence, Missouri on December 12, 1890. Harry received his basic education in
the public schools of Independence, graduating from Central High School in June 1901. He worked at Clinton's
Drug Store.

Harry S. Truman worked as a timekeeper for the Santa
Fe Railroad beginning on September 15, 1901 and then obtained a position in the Kansas City Star mailroom beginning on August 10, 1902. His family moved to Kansas
City in 1904. At this time Harry decided to enter the
banking field, working for the National Bank of Commerce
and then the Union National Bank.

Truman joined the National Guard of Kansas City, Battery B as a private on February 16, 1905. He returned
to Grandview, Kansas in January 1906 to rejoin his family and worked on the farm until 1917. Shortly after his
father's death on November 5, 1914 Harry was given his
father's old post as road overseer of Washington Township
on November 15, 1914. He soon lost the post because of
an ambitious road-overhaul program. He was next named
postmaster of Grandview on April 1, 1915. Harry also
became involved in the Democratic Party, attending meetings of the Tenth Ward Democratic Club led by Michael
Pendergast, brother of Thomas, political boss of Kansas
City.

Harry S. Truman helped to organize Battery F of the
Second Missouri Field artillery and was elected a first
lieutenant on May 22, 1917. The unit was brought into
federal service as the 129th Field Artillery, 35th Division on August 5, 1917. Harry Truman and his troops
sailed for Paris on March 30, 1918 aboard the George
Washington. After attending the Second Corps Field
Artillery School at Montigny-sur-Aube from April 20
to June 18, 1918, he was next sent to Coetquidan at
Angers for additional training on July 4. Truman was
given command of Battery D, 129th Field Artillery on
July 11, 1918. He was promoted to captain in May although
he did not learn of it until October 6.

Truman left for the United States on April 9, 1919 and
arrived in New York on April 20. He was discharged from
the army on May 6, 1919. Harry married Elizabeth (Bess)
Virginia Wallace on June 28, 1919. They had one daughter,
Mary Margaret. Harry S. Truman and Eddie Jacobson opened
a haberdashery store on November 29, 1919. They closed

the store on April 21, 1922. Harry continued to pay his
creditors until the mid 1930's. He went into politics
and was elected county court judge of the Eastern District
of Jackson County on November 4, 1922, taking office on
January 15, 1923.

Truman entered Kansas City Law School in September 1923
and attended for two years until 1925 when he had to drop
out for personal reasons. He was defeated in his reelection bid on November 6, 1924. Harry next went to work
for the Automobile Club of Kansas City on January 7, 1925,
remaining with the organization until 1926. He was elected presiding judge of Jackson County on November 2,
1926, sitting on the bench until 1934.

Harrys S. Truman was elected as a Democrat from Missouri
to the United States Senate on November 5, 1934. He
served in the Senate from January 3, 1935 until his resignation on January 17, 1945. Truman was reelected in
1940. He was a member of the Interstate Commerce Committee of which he eventually became vice chairman, and
the Appropriations Committee. He supported most of the
New Deal legislation as well as President Roosevelt's
Supreme Court proposal.

Truman and Senator Warren Austin were mainly responsible for the Civil Aeronautics Act of 1938. He also cosponsored the Wheeler-Truman or Transportation Act of
1940. Harry S. Truman was a member of the Missouri delegation to the Democratic National Convention in Chicago
in July 1940. After having visited many army camps and
defense camps Harry Truman denounced the defense program.
He was appointed chairman of the Senate Special Committee
to Investigate the National Defense Program on February
17, 1941. He delivered the first annual report of the
Committee on January 15, 1942. The committee continued
to study the defense program and to present reports to
Congress. Truman headed the Missouri delegation to the
Democratic National Convention in Chicago in July 1944.

Harry S. Truman was nominated for Vice President, July
21, 1944 on the Democratic ticket headed by President
Franklin D. Roosevelt. Roosevelt and Truman were elected
on November 7, 1944. They were inaugurated on January
20, 1945. He was not assigned many duties by the President. Franklin D. Roosevelt died on April 12, 1945.
Harry S. Truman became the Thirty-third President of
the United States, taking the oath of office from Chief
Justice Harlan F. Stone.

/For details concerning the period of Harry S. Truman's
Presidency consult Howard B. Furer, ed. Harry S. Truman,
1884 - 1972) in this series./

After leaving office on January 20, 1953 Truman returned
to Missouri. He opened an office in the Federal Reserve
Building in Kansas City, Missouri in February 1953. Truman published the first volume of his Memoirs on August

5, 1955 and the second volume on January 22, 1956. He
attended the Democratic National Convention at Chicago
from August 13 to August 17, 1956 and backed the candidacy of W. Averell Harriman.   The Harry S. Truman Library was dedicated in Independence, Missouri on July 7,
1957 and was opened to the public on September 17, 1957.
     Harry S. Truman became a Chubb fellow at Yale on Febru-
ary 19, 1958.  He accepted a United States government
pension on September 17, 1958.  He published Truman
Speaks and Mr. Citizen in 1960.  Truman was named a delegate from Missouri to the Democratic National Convention in the same year but did not attend claiming that
the Convention was rigged.  He agreed to campaign for
John F. Kennedy after the latter was nominated and went
on a nationwide campaign tour in October 1960.  He received Medicare card number one from President Lyndon B.
Johnson in Independence on January 21, 1966.  President
Johnson briefed Truman on the proposed Vietnam Peace
Talks on May 4, 1968.  Harry S. Truman died on December
26, 1972 in Kansas City, Missouri.  He was buried on the
grounds of the Truman Library.

Bibliography:
     Bundschu, Harry A.   Harry S. Truman -- The Missourian.
New York, 1948.
     Daniels, Jonathan.  The Man of Independence.  Phila-
delphia: Lippincott, 1950.
     Furer, Howard B., ed.  Harry S. Truman, 1884-1972 .
Dobbs Ferry, N.Y.: Oceana Publications, Inc., 1970.
     Helm, William P.  Harry Truman, A Political Biography.
New York: Farrar, Strauss and Young, 1947.
     McNaughton, Frank and Hehmeyer, Walter.  This Man Tru-
man.  New York: McGraw Hill, 1945.
     Steinberg, Alfred.  The Man from Missouri: The Life and
Times of Harry S. Truman.  New York, 1962.
     Truman, Harry S.  Memoirs.  2 vols.  Garden City,
N.Y.: Doubleday, 1955.

## SECRETARY OF STATE: CORDELL HULL

     Cordell Hull, Secretary of State in the Cabinet of
President Franklin Delano Roosevelt, was born on October
2, 1871 in Olympus, Overton (now Pickett) County, Tennessee, the son of William Hull, a farmer, merchant and
lumberman, and Elizabeth (Riley) Hull.  He received his
basic education at a country school in Willow Grove and
Montvale Academy in Celina, Tennessee.  He next attended
the normal school at Bowling Green, Kentucky and National
Normal University at Lebanon, Ohio.  He studied law with
firms in Celina and Nashville after which he attended
the law department of Cumberland University in Lebanon,
Tennessee, receiving the LL.B. degree in 1891.  He was
admitted to the bar in the same year and established his

legal practice in Celina, Tennessee.

Cordell Hull soon became involved in politics, joining the Democratic Party. He attended the Democratic state convention in 1890. Cordell Hull was elected to the Tennessee House of Representatives in 1892 and served from 1893 to 1897. When the Spanish-American War broke out Hull helped to recruit the Fourth Regiment of the Tennessee Volunteer Infantry and was appointed captain. He served in Cuba during the winter of 1898-99 and was then inspector general of the city of Trinidad.

After the war Hull returned to his legal practice in Celina. He then moved to Gainsboro and later to Carthage, Tennessee. Governor James B. Frazier appointed Hull judge of the Fifth Judicial Circuit of Tennessee in 1903. He was later elected to the bench, sitting in all from 1903 to 1906. Cordell Hull was elected as a Democrat to the United States House of Representatives in 1906. He served in the Sixtieth through the Sixty-sixth Congresses from March 4, 1907 to March 3, 1921.

While in Congress Hull helped to obtain passage of the income tax and gained a national reputation as a tax and tariff expert. He also participated in the movement which reduced the powers of the Speaker of the House by depriving him of the right to make committee assignments and stripping him of the chairmanship of the Ways and Means Committee. Cordell married Rose Frances (Witz) Whitney on November 24, 1917. They had no children. Hull was defeated in his bid for reelection in 1920 as a result of the Republican landslide.

Hull became chairman of the Democratic national committee in 1921 and remained in that post until 1924. He was again elected to the United States House of Representatives in 1922 and served in the Sixty-eight through the Seventy-first Congresses from March 4, 1923 to March 3, 1931. His name was placed in nomination for President at the Democratic National Convention in 1928, and he ran second far behind Alfred E. Smith. Cordell Hull did not seek reelection to the House in 1930 but was a successful candidate for the United States Senate. He served from March 4, 1931 until his resignation on March 3, 1933.

President Franklin D. Roosevelt named Cordell Hull Secretary of State in which post he served from March 4, 1933 until his resignation because of ill health on November 29, 1944. Hull was responsible for the reciprocal trade program, trying to help restore the world's economic stability. The Trade Agreements Act of 1934 had been designed to win back the markets of South America. He worked to foster President Roosevelt's "Good Neighbor" policy with South America. He withdrew the marines from Haiti within two years of taking office.

The United States agreed at a conference at Montevideo in 1933 to refrain from intervention in the internal af-

fairs of other states.  At the Buenos Aires Conference
of 1936 the American Republics agreed to consult together should there be a threat to the Continent.  The government participated in various other conferences concerning the Continent and was able to gain the support
of most states in 1941 when the United States went to
war with Japan and Germany.

In July 1937 Cordell Hull issued a statement indicating
the willingness of the United States to work for world
peace.  He worked to find some means of cooperation between Japan and China after the outbreak of hostilities
between them in 1937.  He supported the League of Nations
during the 1930's.

Secretary Hull held informal discussions with the Japanese trying to find a peaceful settlement of differences between Japan and the United States but warned the
military and naval forces of a possible attack by the
Japanese  He was in conference with the Japanese envoys
while the attack was being made on Pearl Harbor on December 7, 1941.  Secretary Hull had arranged for the consolidation of the foreign commerce and foreign agricultural
services in 1939.  He established a board of economic
operations within the Department in 1941 to coordinate
economic activities against the Axis states.

Among other activities Hull came to an agreement with
Mexico settling the controversy with the latter concerning the Mexican government's seizure of United States
owned oil properties.  Among the honors he received while
at the State Department Hull was granted the honorary
LL.D. degrees from many colleges and universities, including the College of William and Mary and Williams College in 1934 and the Universities of Michigan and Wisconsin in 1935.  He resigned on November 29, 1944.

Cordell Hull had urged that international cooperation
continue after the war and was instrumental in helping
to develop the concepts which led to the establishment
of the United Nations.  President Harry S. Truman appointed him a delegate to the United Nations Conference
in San Francisco from April to June 1945.  Cordell Hull
died on July 23, 1955 in Bethesda, Maryland.  He was
buried in Washington Cathedral.  His Memoirs of Cordell
Hull were published posthumously in 1958.

Bibliography:
  Adler, Selig.  The Isolationist Impulse: Its Twentieth
Century Reaction.  New York: Macmillan Company, 1957.
  Beard, Charles A.  American Foreign Policy in the Ma-
king, 1932-1940.  New Haven: Shoe String Press, Inc.,
1946.
  Bremer, Howard F., ed.  Franklin D. Roosevelt, 1882-
1945.  Dobbs Ferry, N.Y.: Oceana Publications, Inc., 1971.
  Dallek, Robert.  Roosevelt Diplomacy and World War II.
New York: Holt, Rinehart and Winston, 1970.

Halasz, Nicholas. _Roosevelt Through Foreign Eyes_.
New York: Van Nostrand Reinhold Company, 1961.
Hull, Cordell. _Memoirs of Cordell Hull_. New York:
Macmillan Company, 1958.
Pratt, Julius W. _Cordell Hull, 1933-1944_. 2 vols.
New York: Cooper Square Publishers, 1964.
Rauch, Basil. _Roosevelt from Munich to Pearl Harbor_.
_A Study in the Creation of a Foreign Policy_. New York:
Creative Age Press, 1950.
Smith, Goddis. _American Diplomacy During the Second_
_World War, 1941-1945_. New York: John Wiley and Sons,
Inc., 1965.

## SECRETARY OF STATE:

### EDWARD REILLEY STETTINIUS, JR.

Edward R. Stettinius, Jr., Secretary of State in the
Cabinets of Presidents Franklin D. Roosevelt and Harry
S. Truman, was born on October 22, 1900 in Chicago, Illinois, the son of Edward Reilley Stettinius, a merchant,
banker and assistant Secretary of War in the administration of Woodrow Wilson, and Judith (Carrington) Stettinius. After receiving his preparatory education at the
Pomfret School in Connecticut from 1907 to 1919 Edward
Stettinius, Jr. went to the University of Virginia from
1919 where he considered a clerical calling and studied
law. While in College he was elected president of the
Young Men's Christian Society in 1921 and president of
his class.

Stettinius left the University of Virginia in 1924 to
become a stock clerk for the Hyatt Roller Bearing Works
of General Motors Corporation. Edward married Virginia
Gordon Wallace on May 15, 1926. They had three children:
Edward Reilley, III, Wallace and Joseph. Edward R.
Stettinius, Jr. rose in the ranks of General Motors, negotiating an insurance program for all the company's
employees. He was elected vice president in charge of
public and industrial relations in 1931. During the
economic crisis he became active as a government adviser.

Stettinius resigned from General Motors in 1934 and
became vice president of the United States Steel Corporation on April 1, 1934. In the fall of the same year he
became special adviser to the industrial advisory board.
He became chairman of the board of United States Steel
in April 1938, succeeding Myron C. Taylor.

President Franklin D. Roosevelt appointed Stettinius
chairman of the War Resources Board. Edward resigned
his position as chairman of United States Steel as well
as his connection with various aviation and air express
companies on May 28, 1940 to take charge of industrial
materials as a member of the advisory commission to the
council of national defense. He was next appointed

chairman of the priorities board and director of the Office of Production Management in January 1941, continuing until September 1943. He was given vast powers and responsibilities. He was a member of the Canadian-American joint defense committee and after the nation entered the war was a member of the United States Board of Economic Warfare.

President Franklin D. Roosevelt appointed Stettinius under Secretary of State to replace Sumner Welles on September 30, 1943. He remained in this post until November 30, 1944. Edward went on a mission to London from March to April 1944. He helped to organize the Dumbarton Oaks Conference held in Washington, D.C. during August and September 1944. He was the United States representative to the conference, cooperating with his fellow delegates from Great Britain, the U.S.S.R. and China in drafting various proposals for the United Nations.

President Franklin D. Roosevelt named Edward Stettinius Secretary of State on November 30, 1944 to succeed Cordell Hull. Stettinius assumed his office on December 1. He accompanied the President and was his chief adviser at the           Conference in the Crimea in February 1945. The decision to hold the United Nations Conference to organize the world security organization was made at this time. Stettinius was named chief United States representative to the conference. Various other agreements were made in regard to the disposition of territory in Europe and Asia at Yalta.

Secretary Stettinius next attended the Chapultepec Conference of American Republics in Mexico which dealt with the problems of war and peace. He helped to draft the Act of Chapultepec proposing a mutual defense system for the western hemisphere. He continued to serve under President Harry S. Truman after the death of Franklin D. Roosevelt on April 12, 1945. Stettinius presided over the first session of the United Nations Conference in San Francisco on April 25, 1945 and was elected one of the four rotating presidents as well as chairman of the executive and steering committee therefore having a major part in drafting the United Nations Charter

Stettinius was given charge of presenting the administration's case for ratification of the United Nations Charter before the Senate. The Senate accepted the Charter on August 8, 1945. The Secretary also represented the United States on the United Nations preparatory commission, attending its executive committee meeting in London during the fall of 1945. He was able to arrange a compromise between Great Britain and the Soviet Union over the presence of British troops in Greece.

Stettinius resigned his post on June 30, 1945 and was appointed premanent representative to the United Nations, remaining in this position until his resignation on June

3, 1946. He was next elected rector of the University
of Virginia on August 9, 1946. He was also a governor
of the Massachusetts Institute of Technology and a director of the following organizations: the Foreign Policy Administration, the Patrick Henry Memorial Organization, General Electric, and the Federal Reserve Bank
in Richmond, Virginia. Edward was also a member of the
board of the American Red Cross. Edward Stettinius died
on October 31, 1949 in Greenwich, Connecticut. He was
buried in Locust Valley Cemetery in Locust Valley, New
York.

Bibliography:
  Bremer, Howard F., ed. Franklin D. Roosevelt, 1882-
1945. Dobbs Ferry, N.Y.: Oceana Publications, Inc., 1971.
  Dallek, Robert. Roosevelt Diplomacy and World War II.
New York: Holt, Rinehart and Winston, 1970.
  Fearo, Richard F., Jr. The Yalta Conference. Indiana-
polis: D. C. Heath and Company, 1955.
  Furer, Howard B., ed. Harry S. Truman, 1884-1972.
Dobbs Ferry, N.Y.: Oceana Publications, Inc., 1970.
  Smith, Gaddis. American Diplomacy During the Second
World War, 1941-1945. New York: John Willey and Sons,
Inc., 1965.
  Stettinius, Edward R., Jr. Roosevelt and the Russians:
The Yalta Conference. Garden City, N.Y.: Greenwood Pub-
lishing Company, 1949.

SECRETARY OF THE TREASURY:

WILLIAM HARTMAN WOODIN

William H. Woodin, Secretary of the Treasury in the
Cabinet of President Franklin D. Roosevelt, was born on
May 27, 1868 in Berwick, Pennsylvania, the son of Clemuel
Ricketts and Mary Louisa (Dickerman) Woodin. After receiving his basic education at the New York Latin School
and the Woodbridge School, William entered the Columbia
University School of Mines. He began to work as a day
laborer in the plant of the Jackson and Woodin Manufacturing Company which produced railroad cars and equipment. He became general superintendent of the Company
in 1892, vice president in 1895, and succeeded his father as president in 1899.
William Woodin married Annie Jessup on October 9, 1899.
They had four children: Mary Anne, Jessup, William Hartman, Jr. and Elizabeth Foster. The Jackson and Woodin
Manufacturing Company was absorbed by The American Car
and Foundry Company in 1899. Woodin was district manager
of the Berwick plant. He soon went to the New York offices where he rose in the administrative ranks, becoming
president and member of the executive committee of the
American Car and Foundry Company in 1916. The Company

greatly expanded under Woodin's leadership. It greatly aided the war effort. William wrote The United States Pattern -- Trial and Experimental Pieces in 1913, which was a standard book on American coins.

Among his varied business interests and services Woodin was appointed New York State Fuel Administrator by Governor Miller. He was also president of the American Locomotive Company from 1925 to 1926 and again from 1927 to 1929. In addition he was president of the American Car and Foundry Export Company and the American Car and Foundry Securities Corporation. He was chairman of the board of the Brill Corporation, the Montreal Locomotive Works and the Railway Steel Spring Company. He was a director of the Cuba Company, the Cuba Railroad Company, the Consolidated Railroad of Cuba, the Remington Arms Company, Inc. and the Federal Reserve Bank of New York.

William H. Woodin was a Republican but supported New York Governor Alfred E. Smith for President in 1928 because of his stand against prohibition. New York Governor Franklin D. Roosevelt appointed William a member of a committee studying and revising the New York State banking laws. Woodin also became a member of the New York committee to deal with unemployment and the depression in 1931. He was chairman of the finance committee and a trustee of the Georgia Warm Springs Foundation. He was also treasurer of the Council on Adult Education for the Foreign Born and a trustee of Lafayette College. Woodin supported Roosevelt for President in 1932.

President Franklin D. Roosevelt appointed William H. Woodin Secretary of the Treasury on March 4, 1933. He immediately became involved in presenting programs to help recover from the economic crisis. He supervised the development of new banking regulations after President Roosevelt's bank holiday. He also worked to prevent the hoarding of gold. Pressure had developed for Woodin's resignation because he was listed as a preferred customer of J. P. Morgan and Company. Woodin soon became ill and received an indefinite leave of absence. President Roosevelt finally accepted his resignation effective January 1, 1934.

Woodin's other interest was music. He had studied music in Vienna, Berlin and Paris and became a composer. He published a book of children's songs in 1930 called Raggedy Ann's Sunny Songs and composed other pieces. He also wrote the "Franklin D. Roosevelt March" which was played at the President's inauguration in 1933. William H. Woodin died on May 3, 1934 in New York City.

Bibliography:
Bremer, Howard F., ed. Franklin D. Roosevelt, 1882-1945. Dobbs Ferry, N.Y.: Oceana Publications, Inc., 1971.
Burns, James MacGregor. Roosevelt: The Lion and the

Fox. New York: Harcourt Brace Jovanovich, Inc., 1956.
    Conkin, Paul K. The New Deal. New York: Thomas Y.
Crowell Company, 1967.
    Fasfeld, Daniel. The Economic Thought of Franklin D.
Roosevelt and the Origins of the New Deal. New York:
AMS Press, Inc., 1956.
    Schlesinger, Arthur M. The Coming of the New Deal.
Boston: Houghton Mifflin Company, 1959.
    - - - -. The Politics of Upheaval. Boston: Houghton
Mifflin Company, 1960.

## SECRETARY OF THE TREASURY: HENRY MORGENTHAU, JR.

Henry Morgenthau, Jr., Secretary of the Treasury in
the Cabinets of Presidents Franklin D. Roosevelt and
Harry S. Truman, was born on May 11, 1891 in New York
City, the son of Henry Morgenthau, ambassador to Turkey,
and Josephine (Sykes) Morgenthau. After receiving his
basic education at private schools including Phillips
Exeter Academy, he went to Cornell University to study
architecture but soon became interested in agriculture.
He studied at Cornell during the periods 1909-1910 and
1912-1913. Henry bought a farm in Duchess County, New
York. Henry married Elinor Fatman on April 17, 1916.
They had three children: Henry, Robert, and Joan.
    Henry Morgenthau served in the United States Navy during
the First World War as a lieutenant, junior grade. He
purchased the American Agriculturist in 1922 and published it in Poughkeepsie until 1933. Governor Franklin
D. Roosevelt of New York appointed Morgenthau chairman
of an agricultural advisory commission to recommend
changes in the state laws to benefit the rural areas.
Henry was named conservation commissioner of New York in
January 1931. He directed a reforestation program, reorganized the game protection program and increased the
number of campsites. Morgenthau helped Roosevelt to develop his agricultural program for his 1932 Presidential
campaign.
    President Roosevelt named Morgenthau chairman of the
federal farm board with instructions to reorganize the
government farm lending agencies. His work led to the
establishment of the farm credit administration on May
26, 1933. He was named governor of the administration.
President Roosevelt appointed Henry undersecretary of
the Treasury and acting secretary on November 17, 1933.
    When William Woodin became ill President Franklin D.
Roosevelt named Henry Morgenthau, Jr. Secretary of the
Treasury ad interim from January 1 to January 8, 1934.
He was then appointed Secretary of the Treasury on
January 8. Morgenthau continued to serve under President
Harry S. Truman after Franklin D. Roosevelt's death in
April 1945. Henry resigned on July 17, 1945. While in
office he dealt with problems concerning the domestic

and international economy caused by the depression.  He
faced the problem of low tax income at the same time that
expenditures were increasing for the public works program, aid to agriculture and housing, the social security and relief program, as well as the financial rehabilitation of business.

Morgenthau dealt  with problems coming from the defense
of devaluation of the dollar in regard to the reduction
of foreign currencies.  He also became involved in the
purchase and sale of foreign currency to help stabilize
the monetary situation.  He created a $2 billion stabi-
lization fund from the profits of devaluation.  He also
reduced the gold content of the dollar.

As business improved the Treasury Department received
additional tax revenues.  Morgenthau needed the additional funds beginning in 1939 when the war broke out in
Europe in order to support the defense program.  When
the United States entered the war in December 1941
Morgenthau was called on to deal with the immense problem of financing the war effort.  He also worked to encourage cooperation among the American nations in dealing
with assets of foreign enemies.

Henry Morgenthau, Jr. also supervised prosecution of
individuals and groups for income tax evasion and was
able to break up several criminal syndicates.  He also
successfully reduced the narcotic traffic.  While under
the Treasury Department the Coast Guard seized German
and Italian merchant vessels during the summer of 1941.
The Coast Guard was transferred to the Navy Department
in the fall of 1941.  Henry supervised construction of
gold storage vaults at Fort Knox, Kentucky and silver
bullion facilities at West Point, New York.  He also developed plans to transform Germany from an industrial
state to an agricultural county.  He resigned on July 17,
1945.

After leaving public office Henry Morgenthau, Jr. e-
ventually became general chairman of the United Jewish
Appeal in which post he served from 1947 to 1950.  He
was next a member of the American Financial and Development Corps for Israel from 1951 to 1954.  Henry Morgenthau, Jr. died on February 6, 1967.

Bibliography:
  Blum, John M.  From the Diaries of Henry Morgenthau,
Jr.  3 vols.  Boston: Houghton Mifflin, 1959-1967
  Bremer, Howard F., ed.  Franklin D. Roosevelt, 1882-
1945.  Dobbs Ferry, N.Y.: Oceana Publications, Inc., 1971.
  Burns, James MacGregor.  Roosevelt: The Lion and the
Fox.  New York: Harcourt Brace Jovanovich, Inc., 1956.
  - - - -.  Roosevelt: The Soldier of Freedom, 1940-1945.
New York: Harcourt Brace Jovanovich, 1956.
  Brown, Douglas V., et. al.  The Economics of the Reco-
very Program.  New York: Books for Libraries, Inc., 1968.

Conkin, Paul K.  The New Deal.  New York: Thomas Y. Crowell Company, 1967.
Ekirch, Arthur.  Ideologies and Utopias: The Impact of the New Deal on American Thought.  Chicago: Quadrangle Books, 1969.
Fasfeld, Daniel.  The Economic Thought of Franklin D. Roosevelt and the Origins of the New Deal.  New York: AMS Press, Inc., 1956.
Furer, Howard B., ed.  Harry S. Truman, 1884-1972. Dobbs Ferry, N.Y.: Oceana Publications, Inc., 1970.
Paris, James D.  Monetary Policies of the United States, 1932-1938.  New York: AMS Press, 1938.
Schlesinger, Arthur M.  The Coming of the New Deal. Boston: Houghton Mifflin Company, 1959.
- - - -.  The Politics of Upheaval.  Boston: Houghton Mifflin Company, 1960.

## SECRETARY OF WAR: GEORGE HENRY DERN

George H. Dern, Secretary of War in the Cabinet of President Franklin D. Roosevelt, was born on September 8, 1872 in Hooper, near Scribner, Dodge County, Nebraska, the son of John Dern, a rancher and businessman, and Elizabeth (Dern) Dern.  After receiving his basic education at the public schools he studied at Fremont Normal College (later Midland College) from which he was graduated in 1888.  He then studied at the University of Nebraska from 1893 to 1894 where he was captain of the football team.

George moved with his family to Salt Lake City, Utah in December 1894.  His father was president of the Mercur Gold Mining and Milling Company, and George was hired as a bookkeeper.  George married Lotte Brown on June 7, 1899.  They had seven children: Mary Joanna, John, William Brown, Elizabeth Ida, James George, and two girls who died early.

When a merger created the Consolidated Mercur Gold Mines Company in 1901 George Dern was appointed general manager.  He became involved with George Moore who developed the vacuum slime filtration process to separate impurities from the good ore abd helped to market this method.  He next worked with Theodore P. Holt and Neils C. Christensen in creating the Holt-Christensen chloridizing roasting process for treating low-grade silver ores.  Dern and Holt invented the Holt-Dern roaster to carry out thsi process.  This was widely adopted.  He became involved in various businesses including banking, power, as well as a creamery and a canning company.  He was also chosen grand master of the Masonic Order in Utah in 1913.

Dern soon became involved in politics and was elected state senator from Salt Lake County as a Democrat and Progressive in 1914.  He continued to serve in that body

until 1923.  He sponsored a great deal of beneficial
legislation including a workmen's compensation act, a
corrupt practices act, and an absentee voters law.  Dern
was next the successful Democratic nominee for governor
of Utah in 1924 and was reelected in 1928, serving until
1932.  He developed a tax revision program including a
state income tax, a corporation franchise act and creation of a school equalization fund.  Dern insisted upon
a states right position in regard to construction of the
dam in Boulder Canyon in regard to distribution of the
river's flow.  He also successfully led the fight against
President Hoover's proposal to grant states the surface
rights to federal lands but retaining mineral and other
rights for the national government.  Henry was chairman
of the National Governors' Conference in 1930.

President Franklin D. Roosevelt named George H. Dern
Secretary of War on March 4, 1933.  He served until his
death in 1936.  He insisted upon maintaining an efficient
army which could be easily expanded.  He also worked to
provide the military forces with better planes, tanks,
armored cars and arms.  He also developed a program for
a larger air force.  The army was called upon to provide
regular and reserve corps officers to run the Civilian
Conservation Corps camps.

Under Dern's administration the army Corps of Engineers
directed such public works projects as the Florida ship
canal, the Passamaquoddy dam on Maine's coast, the Bonneville Dam on the Columbia River, and the Peck Dam on
the Missouri River.  The dredging of the Mississippi
and Missouri River systems was also begun.  Dern represented President Roosevelt at the inauguration of
Philippine President Manuel Quezon, first president of
the Philippine Commonwealth in November 1935.  He also
visited Japan, China, Hawaii, as well as Guam, Wake and
Midway Islands.  George H. Dern died on August 27, 1936
in Washington, D.C.  He was buried in Mount Olivet Cemetery, Salt Lake City.

Bibliography:
  Bremer, Howard F., ed.  Franklin D. Roosevelt, 1882-
1945.  Dobbs Ferry, N.Y.: Oceana Publications, Inc.,
1971.
  Burns, James MacGregor.  Roosevelt: The Lion and the
Fox.  New York: Harcourt Brace Jovanovich, Inc., 1956.
  Conkin, Paul K.  The New Deal.  New York: Thomas Y.
Crowell Company, 1967.
  Moley, Raymond.  The First New Deal.  New York: Har-
court Brace Jovanovich, 1966.
  Schlesinger, Arthur M.  The Coming of the New Deal.
Boston: Houghton Mifflin Company, 1959.

## SECRETARY OF WAR: HARRY HINES WOODRING

Harry H. Woodring, Secretary of War in the Cabinet of President Franklin D. Roosevelt, was born on May 31, 1890 in Elk City, Kansas, the son of Hines Woodring, a farmer and Union soldier during the Civil War, and Melissa Jane (Cooper) Woodring. After receiving his basic education in the public schools and high school of Elk City as well as at the Montgomery County High School, he took a job in an Elk City bank. He also completed a one-year course of study in business and commerce at Lebanon University in Lebanon. He eventually moved to Neodesha, Kansas where he became a cashier in the First National Bank.

Harry H. Woodring entered the armed forces during the First World War, serving as a private and later second lieutenant in the United States Tank Corps. He then returned to his banking career, eventually obtaining a controlling interest in the First National Bank of Neshoda, Kansas. He sold his stock in 1929 and temporarily retired. He was state commander of the American Legion in the same year.

Woodring was the successful Democratic candidate for governor of Kansas in 1930. While in office he insisted upon economy and was able to save millions of dollars. He urged passage of a state income tax amendment and a budget law. President Franklin D. Roosevelt recognized Harry Woodring's talents and appointed him assistant Secretary of War on April 16, 1933. He also assumed the duties of assistant secretary of war for air when the post was eliminated. Harry married Helen Coolidge on July 25, 1933. They had three children: Marcus Coolidge, Melissa, and Cooper Coolidge.

President Franklin D. Roosevelt appointed Harry H. Woodring Secretary of War ad interim on September 25, 1936 following George H. Dern's death. President Roosevelt then named Woodring Secretary of War on May 6, 1937. Under his administration the army was modernized. An increase in strength was accompanied by improved weapons and equipment. He also emphasized improvements in aviation, especially the four-engine bombers called the "flying fortress." He instituted competitive bidding.

Recognizing the talents and abilities of General George C. Marshall, Woodring recommended his appointment as Army chief of staff in spite of the objections of several prominent Congressmen. He opposed institution of the draft and a commitment of United States troops to Europe. Woodring resigned his office on June 19, 1940. He opposed Roosevelt's campaign for a fourth term, and he headed the American Democratic National Committee. Harry Woodring died in retirement on September 9, 1967 in Topeka, Kansas.

Bibliography:
  Bremer, Howard F., ed.  Franklin D. Roosevelt, 1882-
1945.  Dobbs Ferry, N.Y.: Oceana Publications, Inc.,
1971.
  Burns, James MacGregor.  Roosevelt: The Lion and the
Fox.  New York: Harcourt Brace Jovanovich, Inc., 1956.
  Conkin, Paul K.  The New Deal.  New York: Thomas Y.
Crowell Company, 1967.
  Divine, Robert A.  Roosevelt and World War II.  Balti-
more: Johns Hopkins Press, 1969.
  Schlesinger, Arthur M.  The Coming of the New Deal.
Boston: Houghton Mifflin Company, 1959.
  Wann, A. J.  President as Chief Administrator: A Study
of Franklin D. Roosevelt.  Washington, D.C.: Public Af-
fairs Press, 1968.

## SECRETARY OF WAR: HENRY LEWIS STIMSON

Refer to the biographical sketch of Henry L. Stimson
under Secretary of War in the Administration of William
Howard Taft, page 515.

## ATTORNEY GENERAL: HOMER STILLE CUMMINGS

Homer S. Cummings, Attorney General in the Cabinet of
President Franklin D. Roosevelt, was born on April 30,
1870 in Chicago, Illinois, the son of Uriah Cummings,
an inventor and cement manufacturer, and Audie Schuyler
(Stillé) Cummings.  After receiving his preparatory education at the Heathcote School in Buffalo, New York.  Homer attended Sheffield Scientific School of Yale University, graduating with the Ph.B. degree in 1891.  He then
studied law at Yale University, receiving the LL.B. degree in 1893.
Homer Cummings was admitted to the bar in 1893 and established his legal practice in Stamford, Connecticut
in partnership with Samuel Fessenden and Galen A. Carter.
Homer married Helen Woodruff Smith on June 27, 1897.
Cummings' law firm was dissolved in 1900, and he practiced alone until 1909.  He became active in the Democratic Party.  He was elected mayor of Stamford in 1900 and
was reelected twice.  He served from 1900 to 1902 and
from 1904 to 1906.  Cummings was president of the Mayors'
Association of Connecticut from 1902 to 1903.  He also
served as president of the Stamford board of trade from
1903 to 1909.  He was also corporation counsel from 1908
to 1912.  His first wife died, and he married Marguerite
T. Owings in 1909.
Cummings continued his active work in the Democratic
Party.  He attended the Democratic National Conventions
beginning in 1900.  He became Democratic national committeeman from Connecticut in 1900 and continued to
serve until 1925.  He was elected vice chairman of the

national committee in 1913 and served until 1919. His
next public office was state attorney for Fairfield
County from July 1, 1914 to November 1, 1924. He was
an unsuccessful candidate for United States Senator in
1916.

During the First World War Homer Cummings served as a
member of the State Council of Defense in 1917. He was
chairman of the Democratic National Committee during
the period 1919-1920. He was one of the leaders of the
McAdoo forces and chairman of the resolutions committee
at the 1924 National Convention. Cummings was named
chairman of the Connecticut Commission on State Prison
Conditions in 1930. He turned down the offer of the
post of governor general of the Philippines. He married
Cecilia Waterbury on April 2, 1929. Homer was a delegate-at-large to the 1932 Democratic National Convention
at Chicago where he was a floor leader for Roosevelt.

President Franklin D. Roosevelt appointed Homer S.
Cummings Attorney General when Senator Thomas J. Walsh,
who had been selected, suddenly died. Homer Cummings
served from March 4, 1933 until his resignation on January 1, 1939. He sponsored several laws which were to
permit the federal government to help state and local
law officers in suppressing crime without usurping the
states' authority. He also worked to extend the right
of the Federal Bureau of Investigation to become involved
in bank robberies, kidnapping and other crimes.

Homer S. Cummings also helped to secure passage of the
Procedural Act of 1934 which granted the United States
Supreme Court the power to develop uniform rules of procedure in actions at law including the majority of civil
jury cases in the federal courts. He was active in the
establishment of Alcatraz Prison in San Francisco Bay
in 1934. During the same year he published Liberty Under Law and Administration. Lake Forest University, Rol-
lins College and Oglethorpe University granted him the
honorary LL.D. degree in 1934.

Attorney General Homer S. Cummings also defended the
constitutionality of the Securities and Exchange Commission, the Tennessee Valley Authority, the Agricultural
Adjustment Administration and the National Recovery Administration as well as other New Deal agencies. He published We Can Prevent Crime in 1937. After leaving office in 1939 Cummings returned to his legal practice.
He was a member of the American Judicature Society. Homer S. Cummings died on September 10, 1956 in Washington,
D.C.

Bibliography:
Bremer, Howard F. , ed. Franklin D. Roosevelt, 1882-
1945. Dobbs Ferry, N.Y.: Oceana Publications, Inc.,
1971.
Burns, James MacGregor. Roosevelt: The Lion and the

Fox.  New York: Harcourt Brace Jovanovich, Inc., 1956.
    Conkin, Paul K.  The New Deal.  New York: Thomas Y.
Crowell Company, 1967.
    Moley, Raymond.  The First New Deal.  New York:
Harcourt Brace Jovanovich, 1966.
    Schlesinger, Arthur M.  The Coming of the New Deal.
Boston: Houghton Mifflin Company, 1959.
    Wann, A. J.  President as Chief Administrator: A Study
of Franklin D. Roosevelt.  Washington, D.C.: Public Af-
fairs Press, 1968.

## ATTORNEY GENERAL: FRANK MURPHY

Frank Murphy, Attorney General in the Cabinet of President Franklin D. Roosevelt, was born on April 13, 1890
in Harbor Beach, Michigan, the son of John T. and Mary
(Brennan) Murphy.  After receiving his basic education
in the Harbor Beach public schools Frank went to the University of Michigan at Ann Arbor from which he was graduated in 1912.  He then studied law at the University of
Michigan, receiving the LL.B. degree in 1914.  He was
admitted to the bar in the same year.
    Frank Murphy became a clerk in the law firm of Monaghan
and Monaghan in Detroit.  When the United States entered
the war in 1917 Frank enlisted in the Army and was commissioned a first lieutenant and  was then promoted to
captain in the Fourth Division of the United States army.
He went to Europe during 1918-19 and served with the
army of occupation in Germany.  After leaving the army
he took graduate studies at Lincoln's Inn, London, England and Trinity College, Dublin, Ireland.
    Frank Murphy then returned to the practice of law in
Detroit.  He was appointed chief assistant United States
attorney for the eastern district of Michigan, serving
in 1919 and 1920.  He returned to his legal practice
and continued until 1923.  He became an instructor of
law at the University of Detroit in 1923 and taught there
until 1927.  At the same time he became involved in politics and was elected judge of the Recorder's Court of
Detroit in 1923, sitting on the bench until 1930.  Murphy won national attention when he created a sentencing
board, consisting of a psychaitrist, a probation officer
and himself.
    Murphy was elected mayor of Detroit in 1930.  He de-
veloped a work relief program.  He was reelected in 1932
but resigned his office on May 1, 1933 to become governor-
general of the Philippine Islands.  When the islands became a commonwealth in 1935 Frank Murphy was named the
first United States high commissioner.  He was instrumental in establishing several political and social reforms.  Returning to Michigan in 1936, Murphy was elected
Democratic governor of Michigan in which office he served
until January 1939.  He was defeated for reelection in

1938.

President Franklin D. Roosevelt named Frank Murphy
Attorney General on January 17, 1939.  He continued to
serve until January 17, 1940.  Murphy reorganized the
Justice Department so that there would be greater efficiency.  He created a civil liberties unit in the department's criminal division.  President Roosevelt next
appointed Murphy an associate justice of the Supreme
Court in January 1940.  He sat on the bench from January
17, 1940 until his death.  Frank won a reputation as a
champion of civil liberties.  Frank Murphy died on July
19, 1949 in Detroit, Michigan.

Bibliography:
  Baker, Leonard.  Back to Back: The Duel Between FDR
and the Supreme Court.  New York: Macmillan Company, 1967.
  Bremer, Howard F., ed.  Franklin D. Roosevelt, 1882-
1945.  Dobbs Ferry, N.Y.: Oceana Publications, Inc.,
1971.
  Burns, James MacGregor.  Roosevelt: The Lion and the
Fox.  New York: Harcourt Brace Jovanovich, Inc., 1956.
  - - - -.  Roosevelt: The Soldier of Freedom, 1940-1945.
New York: Harcourt Brace Jovanovich, Inc., 1970.
  Conkin, Paul K.  The New Deal.  New York Thomas Y.
Crowell Company, 1967.

## ATTORNEY GENERAL: ROBERT HOUGHWOUT JACKSON

Robert H. Jackson, Attorney General in the Cabinet of
President Franklin D. Roosevelt, was born on February
13, 1892 in Spring Creek, Pennsylvania, the son of William Eldred and Angelina (Houghwout) Jackson.  He received
his basic education in the Spring Creek public schools.
When his family moved to Jamestown, New York, Robert attended the Jamestown High School.  He next studied at
the Albany, New York Law School from 1912 to 1913, completing the two year program in one year.  He was admitted to the bar in 1913.

Robert H. Jackson established his law practice in Jamestown, New York in 1913.  He eventually became associated
for a time with Frank Molt and Benjamin S. Dean.  Robert
married Irene Alice Gerhardt on April 24, 1916.  They
had two children:  William Eldred and Mary Margaret.  He
became involved in a legal practice in Buffalo with the
firm of Penny, Kileen and Nye in 1919.  In the same year
he was corporation counsel for Jamestown.  Jackson was
counsel for various local business, banking and utility
firms.  He was senior partner of the firm of Jackson,
Herrick, Durkin and Leet in Jamestown from 1928 to 1934.

Robert H. Jackson served as president of the Federation of the Bar Association of Western New York from
1928-1932.  New York Governor Franklin D. Roosevelt appointed Robert to a special commission established by

the state legislature to investigate the administration of justice in the state. Jackson campaigned for Roosevelt in 1932. Robert H. Jackson was next appointed general counsel for the bureau of internal revenue of the Treasury Department in 1934. He tried the case against Andrew W. Mellon for alleged evasion of income tax payment. In 1935 Jackson was named special counsel for the Securities and Exchange Commission. He was taken named assistant attorney general in charge of the tax division in 1936. Among the cases he instituted were antitrust actions against the Aluminum Company of America and various automobile finance companies. President Roosevelt appointed Jackson solicitor general of the United States on March 4, 1938.

President Franklin D. Roosevelt next named Robert H. Jackson Attorney General on January 18, 1940 to succeed Frank Murphy. Jackson advised the President to negotiate the leasing of naval and air bases for fifty over-age destroyers with Great Britain. The President did not ask the Senate to ratify the arrangement. Jackson defended the international law aspects of the bases-for-destroyers deal at the Inter-American Bar Association in Havana, Cuba. He published The Struggle for Judicial Supremacy in June 1941. President Roosevelt named Robert H. Jackson an associate justice of the Supreme Court in June 1941. He assumed his seat on the bench on July 11, 1941.

President Harry S. Truman named Robert H. Jackson chief United States prosecutor charged with preparing and presenting the atrocity and war crimes charges against the German Nazi leaders on May 2, 1945. He met with representatives of Great Britain, the USSR and France and was able to convince them to agree to establish the four-member military tribunal on August 8, 1945. Jackson was instrumental in selecting Nuremberg as the site of the trial. He also was charged with the summary of the charges for the four powers.

Robert H. Jackson published Full Faith and Credit--The Lawyer's Clause of the Constitution in 1945. President Harry S. Truman awarded Jackson the Medal of Merit in 1946. The University of Brussels granted him the honorary LL.D. degree, as did the University of Buffalo and Western Maryland College in 1946. In the same year he published The Case Against the Nazi War Criminals. Jackson continued his services on the Supreme Court. He published The Nuremberg Case in 1947. His last judicial act in 1954 was his contribution to the unanimous decision of the court against racial segregation in the public schools. His book The Supreme Court in the American System of Government was published posthumously in 1955. Robert H. Jackson died on October 9, 1954 in Washington, D.C. He was buried in Trewsburg, New York.

Bibliography:
    Baker, Leonard. Back to Back. The Duel Between FDR
and the Supreme Court. New York: Macmillan Company, 1967.
    Bremer, Howard F., ed. Franklin D. Roosevelt, 1882-
1945. Dobbs Ferry, N.Y.: Oceana Publications, Inc.,
1971.
    Burns, James MacGregor. Roosevelt: The Lion and the
Fox. New York: Harcourt Brace Jovanovich, Inc., 1956.
    - - - -. Roosevelt: The Soldier of Freedom, 1940-1945.
New York: Harcourt Brace Jovanovich, Inc., 1970.
    Conkin, Paul K. The New Deal. New York: Thomas Y.
Crowell Company, 1967.

## ATTORNEY GENERAL: FRANCIS BEVERLY BIDDLE

Francis B. Biddle, Attorney General in the Cabinets of
Presidents Franklin D. Roosevelt and Harry S. Truman, was
born on May 9, 1886 in Paris, France, the son of Algernon
Sydney Biddle, a lawyer, and Frances (Robinson) Biddle.
He received his basic education at Haverford Academy in
Haverford, Pennsylvania from 1895 to 1899 and then attended Groton Academy in Groton, Massachusetts from 1899 to
1905. Francis went to Harvard from which he was graduated
with the Bachelor of Arts degree, cum laude, in 1909.
Biddle next studied law at Harvard Law School, receiving
the LL.B. degree in 1911.

Francis B. Biddle was private secretary to Supreme Court
Justice Oliver Wendell Holmes during the year 1911-1912.
He was admitted to the Pennsylvania bar in 1912 and joined
the law firm of Biddle, Paul and Jayne with which he remained until 1915. Francis was involved in the Progressive movement and campaigned for Theodore Roosevelt in
1912. Biddle was a delegate to the Progressive Convention in 1916. Francis was next a member of the firm of
Barnes, Biddle and Myers from 1917 to 1939. Francis married Katherine Garrison on April 27, 1918. They had two
children: Edmund Randolph and Garrison Chapin.

Biddle was a special assistant United States attorney
for the eastern district of Pennsylvania from 1922 to
1926. He had registered as a Republican but supported the
Democrats in the Presidential elections from 1928 to 1940.
Francis favored the New Deal proposals and served as
chairman of the National Labor Relations Board, created by
the National Recovery Act, during 1934 and 1935. He was
next appointed chief counsel to the joint Congressional
committee investigating the Tennessee Valley Authority
during 1938 and 1939.

President Franklin D. Roosevelt named Francis Biddle
a judge of the federal court of appeals for the third
circuit in March 1939. He continued on the bench until
January 1940 when he was appointed Solicitor General of
the United States. In the last position he pleaded
cases for the government before the Supreme Court in-

volving such issues as the validity of the wages and hour legislation, the Federal Power Act and the constitutionality of a state alien registration act.

President Franklin D. Roosevelt named Francis B. Biddle acting Attorney General when Robert H. Jackson was named an associate justice of the Supreme Court. President Roosevelt appointed Biddle Attorney General on August 25, 1941 and was confirmed in the post by the Senate on September 5. In this office Francis created the Interdepartmental Committee on Investigations which tried to establish procedures for loyalty investigations, presenting to it a list of allegedly subversive organizations compiled by the Federal Bureau of Investigation.

Francis Biddle continued to serve as Attorney General under President Harry S. Truman after the death of Franklin D. Roosevelt in April 1945. Biddle was a member of the International Military Tribunal in Nuremberg, Germany which was involved in the trials concerning the war guilt of the Nazi leaders. Brown University conferred the honorary LL.D. degree upon him in 1942. Biddle wrote Mr. Justice Holmes in 1942 and Democratic Thinking and the War in 1944. He retired from his post on June 30, 1945.

Biddle continued to write various works, publishing World's Best Hope in 1949 and The Fear of Freedom in 1951. He was elected chairman of the Americans for Democratic Action on June 4, 1951. Biddle was a delegate to the Democratic Convention in 1952. He was appointed a member of the Permanent Court of Arbotration at The Hague. In 1961 he wrote Natural Law and the Supreme Court. Francis B. Biddle died on October 4, 1968 at Cape Cod, Massachusetts.

Bibliography:
Bremer, Howard F., ed. Franklin D. Roosevelt, 1882-1945. Dobbs Ferry. N.Y.: Oceana Publications, Inc., 1971.
Burns, James MacGregor. Roosevelt: The Soldier of Freedom, 1940-1945. New York: Harcourt Brace Jovanovich, Inc., 1970.
Conkin, Paul K. The New Deal. New York: Thomas Y. Crowell Company, 1967.
Furer, Howard B., ed. Harry S. Truman, 1884-1972 Dobbs Ferry, N.Y.: Oceana Publications, Inc., 1970.
Phillips, Cabell B. H. The Truman Presidency: The History of a Triumphant Succession. New York: Macmillan, 1966.

## POSTMASTER GENERAL: JAMES ALOYSIUS FARLEY

James A. Farley, Postmaster General in the Cabinet of President Franklin D. Roosevelt, was born on May 30, 1888 in Grassy Point, New York, the son of James Farley,

a brick manufacturer, and Ellen (Goldrick) Farley.  James
attended the public schools and also had to work hard
to support his family after his father's death.  He ran
errands and sold papers.  He then cooperated in running
the family's growing stone and saloon.  He also worked
in Morrissey's brickyard.  James graduated from Stony
Point High School in 1905.  Farley then studied bookkeep-
ing at Packard Commercial School in New York City.  He
applied his studies when he worked for the Merlin, Ker-
holtz paper company as a bookkeeper.

James A. Farley began working for the Universal Gypsum
Company in 1906 as a sales manager, eventually becoming
a correspondent and salesman, remaining with the firm
until 1926.  James became interested in politics quite
early.  He worked to develop an effective Democratic organization in Rockland County and was then elected town
clerk of Stony Point in 1912, remaining in this office
until 1918.  In that year he was elected chairman of
the Rockland County Committee, continuing in that office
until 1929.  He was also a delegate to the Democratic
state convention.  Governor Smith appointed Farley port
warden of New York City in 1918.  He served from 1919
to 1920.

James A. Farley married Elizabeth Finnegan on April
28, 1920.  They had three children: Elizabeth, Ann and
James A.  He was elected supervisor of Rockland County
in 1920 and remained in this post until 1923.  James
was next elected to the New York Assembly in 1922.  He
was defeated for reelection in 1924 because he had voted
against the state prohibition enforcement law.  Farley
backed the nomination of Alfred Smith for governor of
New York in 1922.  Governor Smith appointed Farley New
York Athletic Commissioner in 1924.  He was a delegate
to the Democratic National Convention in 1924.

James established and became president of the James A.
Farley Company in 1926.  The company dealt in masons'
materials.  Farley merged his company with five others
as the General Builders' Supply Corporation in 1929 and
was president of the firm until 1933.  His political
career expanded when James became chairman of the New
York State Democratic committee in 1930.  He remained
in this post until 1944.  James supported Franklin D.
Roosevelt in his campaign for the Democratic nomination
for President and in the subsequent election in 1932.
Farley was elected chairman of the Democratic national
committee on July 2, 1932.  He played a major part in
the election campaign.

President Franklin D. Roosevelt appointed James A. Farley Postmaster General in which office he served from
March 4, 1933 to September 9, 1940.  He aided the President in developing the emergency legislation to help the
nation during the economic crisis, as well as in having
the necessary legislation passed.  This was accomplished

in part as a result of Farley's suggestion that political appointments be made after the emergency bills were
enacted.  As Postmaster General he carefully regulated
the activities of his department and was able to balance
the postal budget for the fiscal year ending June 30,
1934.  This was achieved even though the local letter
rate was reduced from three to two cents.

Farley also worked for repeal of the 18th (Prohibition)
Amendment.  In addition he cancelled the airmail contracts because they had been awarded without competitive bids.  He then arranged new contracts with reduced
rates and enlarged routes,  Farley was awarded the honorary D.C.L. degree by the University of the South in
1933 and the LL.D. degree by Canisius and Manhattan
Colleges as well as by John Marshall College of Law in
Jersey City in 1934.

After leaving public office in 1940 Farley returned
to the business world and became chairman of the board
of the Coca Cola Export Company.  He was reelected president of the General Builders' Supply Corporation in 1949.
Among his other activities he was appointed a trustee
of the Commission of Economic Development and the Cordell Hull Foundation.  He was also a director of the
Empire State Foundation.  He was also named a member of
the New York State Banking Board in 1955.  Farley is
a member of the following organizations: Elks, Redmen,
Eagles, and Knights of Columbus.

Bibliography:
  Bremer, Howard F., ed.  Franklin D. Roosevelt, 1882-
1945.  Dobbs Ferry, N.Y.: Oceana Publications, Inc.,
1971.
  Burns, James MacGregor.  Roosevelt: The Lion and the
Fox.  New York: Harcourt Brace Jovanovich, Inc., 1956.
  Conkin, Paul K.  The New Deal.  New York: Thomas Y.
Crowell Company, 1967.
  Ekirch, Arthur.  Ideologies and Utopias: The Impact
of the New Deal on American Thought.  Chicago: Quadrangle
Books, 1969.
  Farley, James A.  Jim Farley's Story; The Roosevelt
Years.  New York: Whittlesey House, 1948.
  Freidel, Frank.  Franklin D. Roosevelt: The Ordeal.
Boston: Little Brown and Company, 1952.
  - - - -.  Franklin D. Roosevelt: The Triumph.  Boston:
Little Brown and Company, 1956.
  Schlesinger, Arthur M.  The Coming of the New Deal.
Boston: Houghton Mifflin Company, 1959.
  - - - -.  The Politics of Upheaval.  Boston: Houghton
Mifflin Company, 1960.

POSTMASTER GENERAL: FRANK COMERFORD WALKER

Frank C. Walker, Postmaster General in the Cabinets
of Presidents Franklin D. Roosevelt and Harry S. Truman,
was born on May 30, 1886 in Plymouth, Pennsylvania, the
son of David Walker, a merchant and copper mine opera-
tor, and Ellen (Comerford) Walker.  Frank moved to Butte,
Montana with his family when he was a child.  He received his basic education in the parochial schools
there and then attended Gonzaga University from 1903 to
1906.  He next studied law at the University of Notre
Dame, receiving the LL.B. degree in 1909.

Frank was admitted to the bar in 1909 and established
a legal practice with his brother Thomas Joseph in the
firm of Walker and Walker.  He continued with this firm
until 1925.  Frank became interested in politics and
joined the Democratic Party.  He was assistant district
attorney for Silver Bow County from 1909 to 1912.  He
was then elected to the Montana legislature, serving in
that body in 1913.  Frank married Hallie Victoria Boucher
on November 11, 1914.  They had two children: Thomas
Joseph and Laura Hallie.  When the United States entered
the First World War Frank went into the army and served
as a first lieutenant.

Frank C. Walker moved to New York City in 1925 to become vice president and general counsel of the Comerford
Theaters, Inc., a chain of theaters in New York and
Pennsylvania.  He was also named general counsel for the
Mecco Realty Company and the Comerford Publix Corporation in Scranton, Pennsylvania.  He later became a director of the First National Bank of Scranton.  Walker
continued his political activities in the Democratic
Party, supporting Franklin D. Roosevelt for the Presidential nomination in 1932.  Frank was elected treasurer of the Democratic national committee after Roosevelt received the nomination.

President Franklin D. Roosevelt appointed Walker executive secretary of the President's executive council in
1933.  Frank was given the task of coordinating the
newly created government agencies.  President Roosevelt
then named Walker executive director of the national
emergency council which was a successor to the President's executive council.  Frank remained in that office
until July 1934.  He was reappointed to this position
in May 1935, continuing until his resignation in December 1935 to return to his business interests.  He became finance committee chairman for the Democratic
campaign in 1938.

President Franklin D. Roosevelt named Frank C. Walker
Postmaster General on September 10, 1940 to succeed
James A. Farley.  Walker continued in that post under
President Truman.  While in office he developed V-mail

in order to reduce the weight and bulk of mail addressed
to American servicemen abroad.  He also made innovations
such as helicopter and bus delivery of mail to rural
areas.  Frank was also chairman of the Democratic national committee during the period 1943-1944.  He
continued to serve as Postmaster General under President
Harry S. Truman after the death of Franklin D. Roosevelt.
Walker resigned on May 8, 1945.

President Truman appointed Frank Walker an alternate
United States delegate to the United Nations in 1946.
He attended the first session of the United Nations
General Assembly in that capacity and was the American
representative on the Assembly's legal committee.  Among
his business interests he was a director of the First
National Bank of Scranton and the Grace National Bank in
New York.  Frank Walker died on September 13, 1959 in
New York City.

Bibliography:
Bremer, Howard F., ed.  Franklin D. Roosevelt, 1882-
1945.  Dobbs Ferry,N.Y.: Oceana Publications, Inc.,
1971.
Burns, James MacGregor.  Roosevelt: The Soldier of
Freedom, 1940-1945.  New York: Harcourt Brace Jovano-
vich, Inc., 1970.
Conkin, Paul K.  The New Deal.  New York: Thomas Y.
Crowell Company, 1967.
Furer, Howard B., ed.  Harry S. Truman, 1884-1972.
Dobbs Ferry, N.Y.: Oceana Publications, Inc., 1970.
Tugwell, Rexford G.  FDR: Architect of an Era.  New
York: Macmillan Company, 1967.
Wann, A. J.  The President as Chief Administrator: A
Study of Franklin D. Roosevelt.  Washington, D.C.:
Public Affairs Press, 1968.

SECRETARY OF THE NAVY: CLAUDE AUGUSTUS SWANSON

Claude A. Swanson, Secretary of the Navy in the Cabinet of President Franklin D. Roosevelt, was born on
March 31, 1862 in Swansonville, Pittsylvania County,
near Danville, Virginia, the son of John M. Swanson, a
tobacco manufacturer, farmer and merchant, and Catherine
(Pritchett) Swanson.  Claude received his basic education in the public schools but had to interrupt it by
working as a farmer and teacher.  He was able to save
money to attend Virginia Polytechnic Institute for two
years.  He was a member of a local debating society which
helped him develop his speaking abilities.  While he was
working as a grocer's clerk, a group of Danville citizens heard him speak and offered to finance the rest of
his education.

Claude Swanson next attended Randolph-Macon College,
receiving the Bachelor of Arts degree in 1885.  He stu-

died law at the University of Virginia, completing the
two-year course of studies in one year and received the
LL.B. degree in 1886.  He was admitted to the bar in the
same year and established his practice in Chatham, Virginia.  He soon became active in politics as a Democrat.
Swanson was elected as a Democrat to the United States
House of Representatives in 1892.  He served in the Fifty-third to the Fifty-ninth Congresses from March 4, 1893
until his resignation, effective January 3, 1906.  He
served on the ways and means, post office and post-roads
committees.  Claude married Lizzie Deane Lyons on December 11, 1894.  They had no children.

Claude Swanson was a delegate-at-large to the 1896 Democratic national convention at Chicago.  He was defeated
in his campaign for governor of Virginia in 1901.  He
was successful in his gubernatorial campaign in 1905.
He began his term in January 1906 and served until 1910.
Swanson developed a progressive educational program for
the state.

After the end of his term on August 1, 1910 Swanson was
appointed to the United States Senate to fill the vacancy
caused by the death of John W. Daniel for the term ending
March 3, 1911.  The Virginia state legislature on February 28, 1911 again elected Swanson to the Senate for the
term beginning March 4, 1911.  Swanson was reelected in
1916, 1922 and 1928, serving from August 1, 1910 until
his resignation on March 3, 1933.  He was a member of
the naval affairs and foreign relations committees,
becoming chairman of the naval affairs committee in 1918.
He first met Franklin D. Roosevelt when the latter was
assistant Secretary of the Navy.  Claude's wife Elizabeth died in 1920.  He married Lulie (Lyons) Hall on
October 27, 1923.  They had no children.

While in the Senate Claude Swanson supported ratifica-
tion of the Versailles Treaty as well as the United
States membership in the League of Nations and member-
ship in the Permanent Court of International Justice at
The Hague.  President Hoover named him a delegate to the
Geneva Disarmament Conference in 1932.

President Franklin D. Roosevelt named Claude A. Swanson Secretary of the Navy on March 4, 1933.  He urged
an increase in the size of the navy, which had deteriorated, to the limits permitted by the London Naval Treaty
of 1930.  During the ensuing years he was mainly responsible for the inrease in the size and improvement of the
navy.  Congress had authorized construction of battleships and other vessels totalling $1.5 billion.
Claude A. Swanson died on July 7, 1939 while visiting
the President's camp on the Rapidan River in the Blue
Ridge Mountains near Crigilersville, Madison County,
Virginia.  Funeral services were held for him in the
United States Senate chamber.  He was buried in Holly-
wood Cemetery in Richmond, Virginia.

Bibliography:
  Bremer, Howard F., ed.  Franklin D. Roosevelt, 1882-
1945.  Dobbs Ferry, N.Y.: Oceana Publications, Inc.,
1971.
  Burns, James MacGregor.  Roosevelt: The Lion and the
Fox.  New York: Harcourt Brace Jovanovich, Inc., 1956.
  Conkin, Paul K.  The New Deal.  New York: Thomas Y.
Crowell Company, Inc., 1967.
  Freidel, Frank.  Franklin D. Roosevelt: The Ordeal.
Boston: Little Brown and Company, 1952.
  Furer, Howard B., ed.  Harry S. Truman, 1884-/1972/.
Dobbs Ferry, N.Y.: Oceana Publications, Inc., 1970.
  Hill, Charles P. Hill.  Franklin Roosevelt.  Fair
Saxon, N.J.: Oxford University Press, 1966.
  Schlesinger, Arthur M.  The Coming of the New Deal.
Boston: Houghton Mifflin Company, 1959.
  Wann, A. J.  The President as Chief Administrator: A
Study of Franklin D. Roosevelt.  Washington, D.C.: Pub-
lic Affairs Press, 1968.

## SECRETARY OF THE NAVY: CHARLES EDISON

  Charles Edison, Secretary of the Navy in the Cabinet
of President Franklin D. Roosevelt, was born on August
3, 1890 in Llewellyn Park, West Orange, New Jersey, the
son of Thomas Alva Edison, the inventor, and Mina (Miller) Edison.  After receiving his basic and preparatory
education at the Dearborn-Morgan School, the Cartaret
Academy, Orange, New Jersey, and the Hotchkiss School
in Lakeville, Connecticut, he went to the Massachusetts
Institute of Technology from 1909 to 1913.  He was
graduated in 1913 as an engineer.
  Charles Edison worked one year with the Edison Illu-
minating Company of Boston in 1914.  He returned to
Orange, New Jersey in 1915 to work with the Edison industries helping to organize and manage the  companies.
He became acting manager of the divisions of the Edison
plant which were temporarily without a manager.  He was
next appointed chairman of many directing boards of the
Edison industries.  Charles supervised production of materials of war during the First World War.  He was also
an assistant to his father.  Charles was chairman of the
West Orange Liberty Loan organization.  Charles married
Carolyn Hawkinson on March 27, 1918.  They had no children.
  Charles Edison became president and director of Thoms
A. Edison Company and its subsidiary firms in 1926.  He
was also involved in other business interests including
his position as president and director of the City View
Storage Corporation, the Metropolitan Current Corporation, the Pohatcong Railroad Company, and the E. K. Me-
dicinal Gas Laboratories, Inc.
  During the depression Charles Edison became concerned

with the serious conditions in the country and decided
to offer his services to the state and federal governments.  He was appointed to the New Jersey state recovery
board in 1933 and also was named a member of the regional
labor board which was provided for under the National
Industrial Recovery Act.  He soon became a compliance director for the National Recovery Administration and e-
ventually state director of the New Jersey division of
the National Emergency Council which was given the responsibility to coordinate the governmental agencies
and their activities.  He was called to Washington, D.C.
in 1934 and was named regional director of the Federal
Housing Administration,  He helped to draw up the regulations for New Jersey, Pennsylvania, Delaware and Maryland.  President Roosevelt named Edison to the National
Recovery Board in April 1935.

President Franklin D. Roosevelt appointed Edison assistant Secretary of the Navy on November 17, 1936.  When
Secretary of the Navy Claude A. Swanson became ill, Edison became acting secretary and continued after Swanson's
death on July 7, 1939.  President Roosevelt appointed
Edison Secretary of the Navy on December 30, 1939.  He
served in this office until July 10, 1940.  Edison carefully surveyed the needs, resources and materiel of
the Navy.  He opposed the scrapping of World War I destroyers which therefore made them available for the
bases-for-destroyers deal arranged by President Roosevelt with British Prime Minister Winston Churchill after
the outbreak of the Second World War.  Edison also continued the development of a larger navy through the construction of large numbers of ships.

Charles Edison resigned his Cabinet post shortly after being nominated by the Democrats for Governor of New
Jersey.  He was elected in November 1940 and served until
1944.  Charles maintained an independent stand and refused to work with Jersey City Mayor Frank Hague.  After
leaving public office Charles returned to his business
interests.  He was chairman of the board of McGraw-Edison
Company from 1957 to 1961.

Charles Edison soon became interested in the activities
of the New York Conservative Party, serving on the executive committee  and becoming a member of the party in
1963.  Charles Edison died on July 31, 1969 in New York
City.

Bibliography:
  Bremer, Howard F., ed.  Franklin D. Roosevelt, 1882-
1945.  Dobbs Ferry, N.Y.: Oceana Publications, Inc.,
1971.
  Burns, James MacGregor.  Roosevelt: The Lion and the
Fox.  New York: Harcourt Brace Jovanovich, Inc., 1956.
  - - - -.  Roosevelt: The Soldier of Freedom, 1940-1945.
New York: Harcourt Brace Jovanovich, Inc., 1970.

Conkin, Paul K.  The New Deal.  New York: Thomas Y.
Crowell Company, Inc., 1967.
Fehrenbech, T. R.  F. D. R's. Undeclared War, 1939-
1941.  New York: D. McKay Company, 1967.
Wann, A. J.  President as Chief Administrator: A
Study of Franklin D. Roosevelt.  Washington, D.C.: Pub-
lic Affairs Press, 1968.

## SECRETARY OF THE NAVY: (WILLIAM) FRANK(LIN) KNOX

Frank Knox, Secretary of the Navy in the Cabinet of
President Franklin D. Roosevelt, was born on January 1,
1874 in Boston, Massachusetts, the son of William Edwin
and Sarah Collins (Barnard) Knox.  He was christened
William Franklin but was known as Frank from his early
youth.  He began his education in the public schools of
Boston.  Frank moved with his family to Grand Rapids,
Michigan where he continued his education.  He left
school in his junior year to become a traveling salesman.
Frank lost his position during the depression of 1893
and then entered Alma College in Michigan, graduating
with the Bachelor of Arts degree in 1898.  He volunteered
for the army at the beginning of the Spanish-American
War in 1898 and was granted the degree in absentia.  He
was a member of Theodore Roosevelt's Rough Riders, joining
them at Tampa, Florida and fought in Cuba from April to
August 1898, including the battle of San Juan Hill.
Frank Knox married Annie Reid on December 28, 1898.
They had no children.  Frank became a reporter for the
Grand Rapids Herald.  He eventually rose to the positions
of city editor and circulation manager of the Herald.
Knox and John Adams Muehling purchased the Sault Ste. Marie Journal in 1901.  They made this weekly paper into
a daily and then merged it with the News.  Frank continued
to edit the paper until 1912, developing many campaigns
for city improvement and social reforms.  He became active in Republican affairs.  He was a major on the staff
of the governor of Michigan in 1908 and continued in that
post until 1910.
Frank Knox became a member of the Republican state committee in 1910.  President Taft appointed him to the
board of Indian commissioners in 1911.  Knox was the
western manager of Theodore Roosevelt's campaign as the
Progressive nominee for President in 1912.  Shortly
thereafter Knox and Muehling sold their paper which was
called the Evening News and moved to New Hampshire in October 1912.  They founded the Manchester Leader, a Progressive newspaper.  They were able to take over the Manchester Union in 1913.  Frank was appointed a major general on the staff of the Governor of New Hampshire.
Frank volunteered as a private in the first infantry
of the New Hampshire National Guard when the United
States declared war against Germany in 1917.  He was

sent to an officers' training school at Madison barracks, New York and was appointed captain of cavalry.  He became division personnel officer at Camp Dix, New Jersey. Frank Knox was promoted to the rank of major in December 1917, commanding an ammunition train.  He was sent to France where he remained from May 1918 to February 1919. He was commissioned a colonel in the reserve corps at the end of the war.

Knox returned to his newspapers in New Hampshire.  He organized the New Hampshire department of the American Legion, serving as its first commander.  He continued his active political work in the Republican Party.  Frank was a delegate-at-large and chairman of the New Hampshire delegation at the Republican National Convention in 1920. He supported Leonard Wood for the Presidential nomination. Knox was chairman of the New Hampshire Publicity Commission from 1922 to 1924.  He was an unsuccessful candidate for the Republican gubernatorial nomination in 1924.

In addition to his control of the two Manchester newspapers Frank Knox became publisher of the William Randolph Hearst newspapers in Boston in 1927.  He rose to the position of general manager of the Hearst newspaper chain in 1927, remaining in that position until 1931. In the latter year Knox  bought the controlling interest of the Chicago Daily News, an afternoon paper.  He was critical of the New Deal programs, especially after 1934.

Frank Knox was the favorite son candidate for president of the Illinois Republicans in 1936.  Knox won the vice presidential nomination in 1936, running with Alfred Landon of Kansas.  After the defeat of the Republican ticket in November Knox returned to his newspaper.  When World War II broke out in Europe in 1939, Knox became convinced that the United States would soon become involved and urged that the armed forces be expanded.

President Franklin D. Roosevelt appointed Frank Knox Secretary of the Navy in June 1940.  He accepted the position because of his concern with national security although he was a Republican.  Knox immediately began to work to increase the size and improve the efficiency of the Navy.  He was caught unaware by the Japanese attack on Pearl Harbor on December 7, 1941.  He flew to Hawaii and took charge of the investigation of the attack and the damage which was wrought.

Knox then speeded up the expansion of the navy as the United States became involved in the war effort.  He travelled to various naval bases in the Atlantic and Pacific.  He also worked to maintain civilian control over the Navy.  Frank Knox died on April 28. 1944 in Washington, D.C.

Bibliography:
    Beasley, Norman.  Frank Knox, American: A Short Biography.  New York: Doubleday, Doran and Company, 1936.

Bremer, Howard F., ed. Franklin D. Roosevelt, 1882-1945. Dobbs Ferry, N.Y.: Oceana Publications, Inc., 1971.

Burns, James MacGregor. Roosevelt: The Soldier of Freedom, 1940-1945. New York: Harcourt Brace Jovanovich, Inc., 1970.

Conkin, Paul K. The New Deal. New York: Thomas Y. Crowell Company, Inc., 1967.

Fehrenbech, T. R. F. D. R's. Undeclared War, 1939-1941. New York: D. McKay Company, 1967.

Knox, Frank. "We Planned It That Way." New York: Longmans, Green and Company, 1938.

- - - -. The United States Navy in National Defense. Washington, D.C.: American Council on Public Affairs, 1941.

Wann, A. J. President as Chief Administrator: A Study of Franklin D. Roosevelt. Washington, D.C.: Public Affairs Press, 1968.

Wohlsetter, Roberta. Pearl Harbor: Warning and Decision. Stanford: Stanford University Press, 1962.

## SECRETARY OF THE NAVY: JAMES VINCENT FORRESTAL

James V. Forrestal, Secretary of the Navy in the Cabinets of Presidents Franklin D. Roosevelt and Harry S. Truman and Secretary of Defense in the Cabinet of President Harry S. Truman, was born on February 15, 1892 in Beacon, New York, the son of James Forrestal, a builder and postmaster, and Mary A. (Toohey) Forrestal. He attended the public schools and Beacon high school, from which he was graduated in 1908.

James became involved in journalism. He was a reporter for the Journal, then working for the Mount Vernon Argus and the Poughkeepsie News Press. He went to Dartmouth College for one year from 1911 to 1912 following which he transferred to Princeton University, studying there from 1912 to 1915 when he was graduated. He was editor of the Daily Princetonian. Forrestal then went into the business world, working in the purchasing department of the New Jersey Zinc Company. He became a cigar salesman for the Tobacco Products Corporation. In January 1916 he joined the New York banking house of William A. Read and Company (later Dillon, Read and Company) as a bond salesman.

When the United States entered the First World War James V. Forrestal volunteered as a seaman second-class in the navy and was assigned to the aviation section. He was trained as a pilot with the Canadian Flying Corps and eventually rose to the rank of lieutenant (j.g.). He was discharged in 1919 and was then a lieutenant in the Naval Reserves. Forrestal then worked as a reporter on the New York World after which he returned to William A. Read and Company as the head of the bond department. He

was made a partner in 1923, a vice president in 1926 and
eventually president in January 1938, succeeding Clarence
Dillon.  He married Josephine Ogden on October 12, 1926.
They had two children: Michael and Peter.

President Franklin D. Roosevelt appointed James V. Forrestal his administrative assistant in 1940.  He was appointed to the newly established post of undersecretary
of the Navy in August 1940.  In this office James supervised problems concerning procurement and production
caused by the rapid growth of the Navy.  Forrestal became
acting Secretary of the Navy on May 10, 1944 following
the death of Secretary Knox in April.

President Roosevelt appointed James V. Forrestal Secretary of the Navy in which post he served from May 18,
1944 until September 17, 1947.  He continued under President Harry S. Truman after the death of Franklin D.
Roosevelt in April 1945.  Forrestal supervised the con-
tinuous growth of the Navy and urged American naval supremacy until establishment of an international organization to guarantee peace.  He also helped to reorganize
the armed forces.

Forrestal was appointed to the newly created post of
Secretary of Defense by President Harry S. Truman on
July 26, 1947.  He assumed this office on September 17,
1947, serving until his death.  He devoted his time to
aid in the efficient consolidation of the armed forces.
James V. Forrestal died on May 22, 1949 in Bethesda,
Maryland.

Bibliography:
  Albion, Robert G. and Connery, Robert H.  Forrestal
and the Navy.  New York: Columbia University Press, 1962.
  Bremer, Howard F., ed.  Franklin D. Roosevelt, 1882-
1945.  Dobbs Ferry, N.Y.: Oceana Publications, Inc.,
1971.
  Burns, James Macgregor.  Roosevelt: The Soldier of
Freedom, 1940-1945.  New York: Harcourt Brace Jovanovich,
Inc., 1970.
  Conkin, Paul K.  The New Deal.  New York: Thomas Y.
Crowell Company, Inc., 1967.
  Furer, Howard B., ed.  Harry S. Truman, 1884-1972.
Dobbs Ferry, N.Y.: Oceana Publications, Inc., 1970.
  Millis, Walter, ed.  The Forrestal Diaries.  New York:
Viking Press, 1951.
  Steinberg, Alfred.  The Man from Missouri: The Life and
Times of Harry S. Truman.  New York, 1962.
  Truman, Harry S.  Memoirs.  2 vols.  Garden City,
N.Y.: Doubleday, 1955.
  Wann, A. J.  President as Chief Administrator: A
Study of Franklin D. Roosevelt.  Washington, D.C.: Pub-
lic Affairs Press, 1968.

## SECRETARY OF THE INTERIOR:

## HAROLD LE CLAIR ICKES

Harold L. Ickes, Secretary of the Interior in the Cabinets of Presidents Franklin D. Roosevelt and Harry S. Truman, was born on March 15, 1874 in Frankstown township, Blair County, Pennsylvania, the son of Jesse Boone Williams and Martha Ann (McEwen) Ickes. He received his basic education in the public schools. Harold moved to Chicago in 1890 to live with an aunt when his mother died. He attended Englewood High School when he finished the four-year course in three years. He then went to work while he attended the University of Chicago, from which he was graduated with the Bachelor of Arts degree in 1897. Harold became interested in politics during this period.

During the next few years Harold L. Ickes worked as a reporter for the Chicago Tribune and the Chicago Chronicle. He attended both the Republican and the Democratic national conventions to report on them. Ickes soon attended the University of Chicago Law School from which he was graduated with the Doctor of Jurisprudence degree in 1907. After being admitted to the bar Harold began practicing law in Chicago. Harold married Anna Wilmarth Thompson on August 11, 1911. They had one child, Raymond.

Ickes also continued his interest in politics, although he never sought public office. He joined the Progressive Party and was elected chairman of the Cook County Progressive Committee in 1912. He eventually became a national committeeman and a member of the Progressive Party National Executive Committee. Ickes returned to the Republican Party and was a member of Charles Evans Hughes' campaign committee in 1916. He was a delegate-at-large to the Republican national convention in 1920 and opposed Warren G. Harding's nomination. He prevented passage of a motion to make the nomination unanimous.

Ickes broke with the Republicans and endorsed the Democratic nominees of Cox and Roosevelt in 1920. He managed Senator Hiram W. Johnson's campaign for the Republican nomination in 1924. Harold Ickes formed the People's Traction League to oppose Samuel Insull's plan to gain a perpetual railway franchise in 1930. The League was unsuccessful. Ickes also established the Utility Consumers' and Investors' League of Illinois to fight for reasonable utility rates. Harold organized the Progressive Republican League to support Franklin D. Roosevelt at the Democratic National Convention in 1932 and campaigned for Roosevelt in the ensuing election.

President Franklin D. Roosevelt appointed Harold L. Ickes Secretary of the Interior. He assumed his office on March 4, 1933 and continued in the administration of President Harry S. Truman after the death of Franklin D. Roosevelt in April 1945. Harold served until his resignation on March 17, 1946. Ickes began a reorganization of the Department and developed policies which set examples for other agencies. He was able to bring the bureau of mines back to the department from the Department of Commerce. He also consolidated the board of vocational education and the United States office of education.

Among Ickes' other achievements was the abolition of the Board of Indian Commissioners, creation of the soil erosion service and the subsistence homesteads division which was later transferred to the Department of Agriculture. He also created the office of adviser on the economic status of Negroes. Washington and Jefferson as well as Lake Forest Colleges awarded him the LL.D. degree in 1934. Tufts College and Northwestern University granted him the same in 1935.

Ickes led the Interior Department in the direction of complete dedication to conservation policies which involved preservation of natural resources. He supervised those projects which were involved in providing low-cost electric energy, including construction of Boulder, Shasta, Friant, Bonneville and Grand Coulee dams. He worked to have the national park service serve the recreational needs of all sections of the nation. The Taylor Grazing Act, passed in 1934, stabilized the use of the public ranges in the West.

The bituminous coal commission was brought to the department in 1939. At this time Ickes supervised the establishment of the fish and wild life service by merging the bureaus of fisheries and biological survey. Ickes also ordered an investigation of the activities of Richard A. Ballinger who had headed the Interior Department from 1909 to 1911. He was exonerated of certain charges.

Harold L. Ickes was named the first federal Public Works Administrator on July 8, 1933. In this post he supervised administration of $5 billion for federal and non-federal public works projects such as construction of many public schools, municipal buildings, water and sewage systems as well as highways and dams. He developed the first national low-cost housing program which helped to stimulate the nation's construction and materials industries. These projects employed large numbers of men who had been out of work because of the depression.

Among Harold L. Ickes' other responsibilities, he was federal oil administrator beginning in 1934, chairman of the natural resources committee from 1934 to 1939 when its functions were transferred to the executive offices of the President. Harold was also named National Recovery Administration administrator for the petroleum code in 1934. Harold Ickes' wife Anna died in 1935.

Ickes wrote The New Democracy in 1934, Back to Work in 1935, America's House of Lords in 1939 in addition to Third Term Bugaboo and Not Guilty in 1940.  Harold married Jane B. Dahlman on May 24, 1938 in Dublin, Ireland. They had two children: Harold McEwen and Jane.

President Roosevelt appointed Ickes solid fuels coordinator for national defense on November 5, 1941.  Ickes wrote Autobiography of a Curmudgeon in 1943.  He continued to serve under President Truman and helped to develop plans for return to a peacetime economy in the postwar period.  He left the Cabinet on March 17, 1946.  Harold wrote My Twelve Years with F.D.R. in 1948.  Ickes died on February 3, 1953 in Washington, D.C.  He was buried in Sandy Spring, Maryland.

Bibliography:
Bremer, Howard F., ed.  Franklin D. Roosevelt, 1882-1945.  Dobbs Ferry, N.Y.: Oceana Publications, Inc., 1971.
Burns, James MacGregor.  Roosevelt: The Lion and the Fox.  New York: Harcourt Brace Jovanovich, Inc., 1956.
- - - -.  Roosevelt: The Soldier of Freedom, 1940-1945. New York: Harcourt Brace Jovanovich, Inc., 1970.
Conkin, Paul K.  The New Deal.  New York: Thomas Y. Crowell Company, Inc., 1967.
Eccles, Marriner.  Beckoning Frontiers.  New York: Alfred A. Knopf, Inc., 1951.
Furer, Howard B., ed.  Harry S. Truman, 1884-1972. Dobbs Ferry, N.Y.: Oceana Publications, Inc., 1970.
Ickes, Harold.  The Autobiography of a Curmudgeon. New York: Random House, Inc., 1948.
- - - -.  My Twelve Years with F.D.R.  New York, 1948.
- - - -.  The Secret Diary of Harold Ickes.  3 vols. New York: Simon and Shuster, 1954.
Moley, Raymond.  The First New Deal.  New York: Harcourt Brace Jovanovich, 1966.
Wann, A. J.  President as Chief Administrator: A Study of Franklin D. Roosevelt.  Washington, D.C.: Public Affairs Press, 1968.

SECRETARY OF AGRICULTURE: HENRY AGARD WALLACE

Refer to the biographical sketch of Henry A. Wallace under Vice President, page 573.

SECRETARY OF AGRICULTURE: CLAUDE RAYMOND WICKARD

Claude R. Wickard, Secretary of Agriculture in the Cabinets of Presidents Franklin D. Roosevelt and Harry S. Turman, was born on February 28, 1893 on a farm in Carroll County, Indiana, the son of Andrew Jackson and Iva Leonora (Kirkpatrick) Wickard.  Claude received his basic education in the public schools and worked on the

family farm while in high school.  He then attended Purdue University Agricultural College, graduating with the
Bachelor of Science in Agriculture in 1915.  He then
took over the family farm.  Claude became interested in
soil-building as well as crop and live-stock production.
He married Louise Eckert in 1918.  They had two daughters:
Betty and Ann.

Wickard became active in the county and state farm organizations as well as politics.  He was elected state
senator in 1932.  Claude also represented the Indiana
farmers in advising the agricultural adjustment program
on swine production.  He became assistant chief of the
corn-hog division of the Agricultural Adjustment Administration in the Department of Agriculture.  He helped to
develop a program for stabilizing the production of corn
and hogs in relation to the demand in order to raise the
farmers' incomes.

In 1936 when the emphasis in the Agricultural Adjustment Administration was placed on geographical area rather than commodities Claude Wickard became assistant
director of the North Central region.  He was promoted
to director of the region in November 1936.  In 1939 he
became undersecretary of Agriculture.

President Franklin D. Roosevelt named Claude R. Wickard
Secretary of Agriculture on September 5, 1940 to succeed
Henry A. Wallace who became the Democratic nominee for
Vice President.  Wickard continued in office under President Harry S. Truman after the death of Franklin D.
Roosevelt in April 1945.  In analyzing the problems involved in the war in Europe and the development of the
defense program in the United States Wickard recognized
that there would be a rise in the demand for farm produce.
He suggested in December 1940 that there be an increase
in hog production at the very time when the hog farmers
were suffering from low prices.  He was proven correct
when shortly thereafter the increased demand nearly
doubled prices.

The Lend Lease Act of March 1941 added to the increased
demand to meet British needs.  Secretary Claude Wickard
devloped a program of price support for dairy products,
poultry and pork to help increase production.  The Agriculture Department was ordered to assemble food supplies
for shipment to Britain.  Wickard announced in September
1941 national goals for food production in 1942 with
three major objectives: to meet the needs of Americans,
Britain and her other allies, and to build up reserves
to feed the starving millions in Europe after the war.
He also had state and county agriculture defense boards
established.  Wickard proposed various measures for the
postwar era in terms of conservation as well as restoration of farm lands and forests.

Claude Wickard resigned from the Department of Agriculture on June 2, 1945.  President Harry S. Truman appointed

him administrator of the Rural Electrification Administration in which post he served until 1953.  After leaving public office for a period of time, he led an executive committee of farmers which supported Senator John
F. Kennedy in the 1960 Presidential campaign.  Among the
other activities in which Wickard participated were the
Indiana Farm Bureau Federation and the National Farm
Bureau Federation.  He was granted the Master Farmer of
Indiana award.  Claude Wickard was killed in an automobile accident on April 2, 1967 in Delphi, Indiana.  He
was buried in Deer Creek, Indiana.

Bibliography:
  Albertson, Dean.  Roosevelt's Farmer: Claude R. Wickard
in the New Deal.  New York: Columbia University Press,
1961.
  Bremer, Howard F., ed.  Franklin D. Roosevelt, 1882-
1945.  Dobbs Ferry, N.Y.: Oceana Publications, Inc.,
1971.
  Burns, James MacGregor.  Roosevelt: The Soldier of
Freedom, 1940-1945.  New York: Harcourt Brace Jovanovich,
Inc., 1970.
  Conkin, Paul K.  The New Deal.  New York: Thomas Y.
Crowell Company, Inc., 1967.
  Furer, Howard B., ed.  Harry S. Truman, 1884-/1972/.
Dobbs Ferry, N.Y.: Oceana Publications, Inc., 1970.
  Steinberg, Alfred.  The Man from Missouri: The Life and
Times of Harry S. Truman.  New York: Putnam, 1962.
  Wann, A. J.  President as Chief Administrator: A
Study of Franklin D. Roosevelt.  Washington, D.C.: Pub-
lic Affairs Press, 1968.

SECRETARY OF COMMERCE: DANIEL CALHOUN ROPER

  Daniel C. Roper, Secretary of Commerce in the Cabinet
of President Franklin D. Roosevelt, was born on April 1,
1867 in Marlboro County, South Carolina, the son of John
Wesley Roper, a farmer, merchant and Confederate officer
in the Civil War, and Henrietta Virginia (McLaurin) Roper.
He received his basic education in a one-room school and
then the high school in Laurinburg, North Carolina.  Roper next entered Wofford College in Spartanburg, South
Carolina, transferring after his sophomore year to Trinity College in Durham, North Carolina (now Duke University), graduating with the Bachelor of Arts degree in
1888.
  During the next four years Roper taught school, farmed
and sold insurance until 1892.  Daniel married Lou
McKenzie on December 25, 1889.  They had seven children:
Margaret May, James Hunter, Daniel Calhoun, Grace Henrietta, John Wesley, Harry McKenzie and Richard Frederick.
Daniel became involved in politics, joining the Farmers'
Alliance and supporting the Democrats.  He was elected

to the South Carolina House of Representatives in 1892
and  became a clerk of the United States Senate
Committee on Interstate Commerce in 1893
three years.  Roper moved to New York City where he entered the business world as an office manager from 1896
to 1898.  In the latter year he became a life insurance
agent.

Daniel C. Roper was next appointed an an enumerator of
cotton gins in the Bureau of Census in 1900, continuing
until 1911.  He learned a great deal about all aspects
of the cotton trade.  He studied law at the National
University, receiving the LL.B. degree in 1901.  Roper
was next appointed clerk of the House of Representatives
Ways and Means Committee in 1911.

Daniel supported Woodrow Wilson in the Presidential
election of 1912.  President Wilson appointed him assistant Postmaster General in 1913.  He remained in the
post until August 1916 when he resigned in order to work
in Wilson's reelection campaign.  While in the Post Office Department he developed and administered the parcel
post service.  Roper was appointed vice-chairman of the
United States Tariff Commission in March 1917.  He was
then named Commissioner of Internal Revenue in September
1917.  In this position he supervised the narcotic and
wartime prohibition laws and created an intelligence unit
for the investigation of tax frauds.

After resigning from his post on March 31, 1920 Daniel
Roper returned to New York and was president of the Mar-
lin Rockwell Corporation from 1920 to 1921.  He practiced
law in Washington from 1921 to 1933 with the firm of Roper, Hagerman, Hurren, and Parks.  Roper also continued
his political activities, supporting William Gibbs McAdoo
for the 1924 Democratic Presidential nomination,  He supported Franklin D. Roosevelt for the Democratic nomination in 1932.

President Franklin D. Roosevelt appointed Daniel C.
Roper Secretary of Commerce on March 4, 1933.  Roper
worked to reduce the budget of the Commerce Department.
He also established the Business Advisory Council in order to inform the Congress and the President of the attitude of business.  He served as chairman of the Cabinet committee to supervise the National Recovery Administration and also helped to organize and direct the early
New Deal programs.  He resigned from the Commerce Department on December 23, 1938 and returned to his law
practice in Washington, D.C.

President Roosevelt named Roper temporary minister to
Canada during King George IV's visit to the nation.
Daniel resigned after four months.  He next became a director of the Atlantic Coast Line Railroad.  Daniel Roper died on April 11, 1943 in Washington, D.C.

Bibliography:
   Bremer, Howard F., ed.  Franklin D. Roosevelt, 1882-
1945.  Dobbs Ferry, N.Y.: Oceana Publications, Inc.,
1971.
   Burns, James MacGregor.  Roosevelt: The Lion and the
Fox.  New York: Harcourt Brace Jovanovich, Inc., 1970.
   Conkin, Paul K.  The New Deal.  New York: Thomas Y.
Crowell Company, Inc., 1967.
   Karl, Barry.  Executive Reorganization and Reform in
the New Deal.  Cambridge: Harvard University Press, 1963.
   Moley, Raymond.  The First New Deal.  New York: Har-
court Brace Jovanovich, 1966.
   Roper, Daniel C.  Fifty Years of Public Life.  Durham,
N.C.: Duke University Press, 1941.
   Wann, A. J.  President as Chief Administrator: A
Study of Franklin D. Roosevelt.  Washington, D.C.: Pub-
lic Affairs Press, 1968.

## SECRETARY OF COMMERCE: HARRY LLOYD HOPKINS

Harry L. Hopkins, Secretary of Commerce in the Cabinet
of President Franklin D. Roosevelt, was born on August
17, 1890 in Sioux City, Iowa, the son of David Aldona
Hopkins, a harness maker and merchant, and Anna (Pickett)
Hopkins.  After receiving his basic education Harry attended Grinnell College from which he was graduated with
the Bachelor of Arts degree in 1912.  He began his career
as a social worker with a summer job as a counselor at
a camp at Round Brook, New Jersey run by Christodora
House for boys from New York's lower east side.
   Harry L. Hopkins next became an investigator and supervisor of case work for the Association for Improving
the Condition of the Poor in New York City.  Harry married Ethel Gross on October 21, 1913.  They had four
children: David Jerome, Barbara, Robert and Stephen Peter.
Hopkins was appointed executive secretary of the Board
of Child Welfare in the Public Charities Department of
New York in January 1914.  He introduced a system of
widows' pensions.
   Hopkins was turned down for military service in World
War I because of defective vision and then became general
manager of the American National Red Cross in Washington,
D.C. in January 1918 and continued in that position until
1922.  He was next appointed assistant director and then
director of the civilian relief division of the Red Cross.
He then became associate manager of the Gulf division
in New Orleans and manager of the Southern division with
its headquarters in Atlanta, Georgia.
   Harry returned to New York in 1922 to become assistant
director of the Association for the Improvement of the
Poor.  He was next appointed director of the New York
Tuberculosis Association in 1924 in which post he remained
until 1933.  He improved the organization and urged co-

operation with other groups.  Harry also increased the
Tuberculosis Association's income with the institution
of the annual sale of Christmas seals and began research on the disease called silicosis.

New York Governor Franklin D. Roosevelt recognized Hopkins' experience and appointed him deputy chairman of
the state Temporary Emergency Relief Administration in
1931.  This organization was to help those who were out
of work as a result of the depression.  He succeeded
Jesse Straus as chairman in 1932.  Harry Hopkins divorced
his first wife in 1931.  He next married Barbara Macpher-
son Duncan in the same year.  They had one daughter,
Diana.

President Roosevelt appointed Harry Hopkins administrator of the Federal Emergency Relief Administration
in May 1933.  He was given charge of the disbursement
of $500,000,000 to the states for the aid of the unem-
ployed in the nation.  In 1935 Hopkins was appointed head
of the Works Progress Administration in 1935 supervising
the expenditure of approximately $3 billion dollars Mayo
through 1938 for direct relief or more work projects. He
helped to remove 4,000,000 persons from the relief roles.
The various projects developed included improvement or
construction of facilities throughout the nation.  Grinnell College awarded Hopkins the honorary LL.D. degree
in 1935.

Although he became ill in 1936 Hopkins was able to
campaign for President Roosevelt.  He wrote Spending to
Save in the same year.  He underwent surgery at the
Clinic in Rochester, Minnesota in 1937 and then returned
to his Washington post.  Hopkins' second wife Barbara
died in 1937.  As threats to peace developed in 1938
President Roosevelt assigned Harry the task of investigating the capacity of the Pacific coast airplane manufacturing facilities.  He resigned his post in December 1938.  The University of South Carolina awarded him
the LL.D. degree in 1938.

President Franklin D. Roosevelt appointed Harry L. Hopkins Secretary of Commerce ad interim to succeed Daniel
C. Roper on December 24, 1938.  He was formally appointed
to the cabinet post on January 23, 1939.  He served until September 15, 1940.  Harry continued his active reform work for the government.  He was again ill during
part of 1939 and 1940.  He returned to Washington in
1940 and worked for Roosevelt's third term nomination.
President Roosevelt invited Hopkins to live at the White
House in May 1940.  He continued to reside there for
three and one-half years.

After resigning from the Cabinet on September 23, 1940
Harry worked in the campaign for President Roosevelt's
reelection.  President Roosevelt next sent Hopkins to
London to study the needs of the British.  He returned
to Washington in February 1941.  After the passage of

the Lend Lease Act in March 1941 President Roosevelt appointed Hopkins head of the Lend Lease Program.  He also became involved in the negotiations concerning the placement of United States' ships in the North Atlantic. Hopkins went to London again in July 1941 to view the new situation due to the entrance of Russia into the war. He also went to Moscow to discuss American aid to the Russians with Josef Stalin and V. M. Molotov.  He was also present at the Atlantic Conference in August 1941.

Harry Hopkins resigned as Lend Lease Administrator in October 1941 partly due to his poor health.  He continued to be involved in the Lend Lease Program, especially in regard to China.  Hopkins was a major figure in the Arcadia Conference which opened on December 22, 1941 in Washington, D.C. to plan war strategy.  Harry married Louise Gill (Macy) Brown on July 30, 1942.  Harry Hopkins was next appointed chairman of the Munitions Assignment Board.  He eventually was made a member of the Pacific War Council which sat in Washington to deal with the various problems in the Pacific.

Among Hopkins' other duties he was chairman of the President's Soviet Protocol Committee and a member of both the War Production Board from 1942 to 1944 and the War Resources Board from 1942 to 1945.  He was next sent to London for many important discussions and was present at most of the important conferences including Casablanca, Cairo, Teheran and Yalta.  He became ill during several periods of the war.  He was awarded the Distinguished Service medal in 1945.  Harry continued to serve President Harry S. Truman after the death of Franklin D. Roosevelt in April 1945.  Hopkins was sent to Russia to discuss the constitution of the Security Council of the United Nations with Marshall Stalin and V. M. Molotov. In July 1945 Hopkins resigned from his government posts and became the impartial chairman of the New York Women's Coat and Suit Industry in July 1945.  Harry L. Hopkins died on January 29, 1946 in New York City.

Bibliography:
   Bremer, Howard F., ed.  Franklin D. Roosevelt, 1882-1945.  Dobbs Ferry, N.Y.: Oceana Publications, Inc., 1971.
   Burns, James MacGregor.  Roosevelt: The Lion and the Fox.  New York: Harcourt Brace Jovanovich, Inc., 1956.
- - - -.  Roosevelt: The Soldier of Freedom, 1940-1945. New York: Harcourt Brace Jovanovich, Inc., 1970.
   Charles, Searle F.  Minister of Relief: Harry Hopkins and the Depression.  Syracuse, N.Y.: Syracuse University Press, 1963.
   Conkin, Paul K.  The New Deal.  New York: Thomas Y. Crowell Company, Inc., 1967.
   Eccles, Marriner.  Beckoning Frontiers.  New York: Alfred A. Knopf, Inc., 1951.

Moley, Raymond. The First New Deal. New York: Harcourt Brace Jovanovich, Inc., 1966.

Schlesinger, Arthur M. The Coming of the New Deal. Boston: Houghton Mifflin Company, 1959.

- - - -. The Politics of Upheaval. Boston: Houghton Mifflin Company, 1960.

Wann, A. J. President as Chief Administrator: A Study of Franklin D. Roosevelt. Washington, D.C.: Public Affairs Press, 1968.

## SECRETARY OF COMMERCE: JESSE HOLMAN JONES

Jesse H. Jones, Secretary of Commerce in the Cabinet of President Franklin D. Roosevelt, was born on April 5, 1874 in Robertson County, Texas, the son of William Hasque Jones, a tobacco merchant and farmer, and Anne (Holman) Jones. He received a basic education in a rural schoolhouse in Adairsville, Kentucky. Jesse worked for his uncle's firm, M. T. Jones Lumber Company, in Dallas, Texas beginning in 1894. He became manager in 1895 and general manager in 1898. He moved to Houston at the same time and continued with the firm until 1905.

Jesse H. Jones established the South Texas Lumber Company in 1902. In his position as president he supervised its growth into one of the major lumber yards in the Southwest. Jesse expanded his business interests in 1905 when he established the Southern Loan and Investment Company of which he was president. Its name was changed to Jesse H. Jones and Company in 1923. He next established the Texas Trust Company in 1909, merging it with the Bankers' Trust Company in 1911. He was chairman of the board of directors until 1920 when the bank became the Bankers; Mortgage Company. He was also an officer in various banks including vice president of the Lumberman's National Bank from 1907 to 1915 and the Union National Bank from 1910 to 1918, both in Houston.

Jesse also became interested in the building industry, organizing the Houston Hotel Association, Inc. in 1912. This company built hotels, apartment and office buildings. He also became owner of the Houston Chronicle in 1926. During the First World War Jones was director general of the department of military relief of the American Red Cross beginning in July 1917. He was a delegate to various Red Cross conferences during the spring of 1919. Jesse was director general of the Texas centennial celebration from 1926 to 1934.

Jesse Jones became interested in politics and a member of the Democratic Party. He was the director of finance for the Democratic national committee from 1924 to 1928. He was chairman of the advisory financial committee in 1928 and was able to have the national convention held in Houston in the same year. He was granted the honorary LL.D. degree by Southern University in 1925 and by Southern

Methodist University in 1927.  Jesse married Mary Gibbs
on December 15, 1929.  They had no children.

President Herbert Hoover named Jones to the Reconstruction Finance Corporation in 1932.  He was elected chairman on May 5, 1933 having continued under President
Franklin D. Roosevelt.  He also served as chairman of
the executive committee of the Export-Import Bank of
Washington, D.C.  When the Reconstruction Finance Corporation became a part of the newly established Federal
Loan Agency in 1939.  Jesse Jones was appointed head of
the agency on July 17, 1939, and he resigned the chairmanship of the Reconstruction Finance Corporation.  New
York and Temple Universities awarded Jones the LL.D.
degree in 1937.

President Franklin D. Roosevelt named Jesse Jones Secretary of Commerce on September 16, 1940.  He assumed
his office on September 19.  Among the posts which he
held in his capacity of Secretary of Commerce was chairman of the foreign trade zone board and a member of the
board of directors of the United States Textile Foundation, the council of national defense, the Smithsonian
Institution, the migratory bird conservation committee,
the rational munitions control board, the national emergency council and other organizations, totalling 39.
He added to his contributions to the rebuilding of American industry during the depression by coordinating all
elements for the war effort.  He resigned from office
in February 1945.

Jesse Jones resigned from the Commerce Department on
February 28, 1945.  He was involved in various philanthropic and educational activities.  He was treasurer of
the Will Rogers Memorial Commission and the Woodrow Wilson Birthplace Foundation and was later president of the
latter.  He was also a trustee of George Peabody College
for Teachers and the Tuskegee Institute.  In addition
Jesse Jones was chairman of the Texas Commission for the
United States Golden Gate Exposition in San Francisco
from 1937 to 1939 and for the New York World's Fair in
1939.  James returned to Texas after leaving public
office.  He wrote _Fifty Billion Dollars_ in 1951.  Jesse
Jones died on June 1, 1956 in Houston, Texas.

Bibliography:
  Bremer, Howard F., ed.  _Franklin D. Roosevelt, 1882-
1945_.  Dobbs Ferry, N.Y.: Oceana Publications, Inc.,
1971.
  Burns, James MacGregor.  _Roosevelt: The Soldier of
Freedom, 1940-1945_.  New York: Harcourt Brace Jovanovich,
Inc., 1970.
  Conkin, Paul K.  _The New Deal_.  New York: Thomas Y.
Crowell Company, Inc., 1967.
  Timmons, Bascom N.  _Jesse H. Jones: The Man and the
Statesman_.  New York, 1956.

Wann, A. J. *President as Chief Administrator: A Study of Franklin D. Roosevelt*. Washington, D.C.: Public Affairs Press, 1968.

## SECRETARY OF COMMERCE: HENRY AGARD WALLACE

Refer to the biographical sketch of Henry A. Wallace under Vice President, page 573.

## SECRETARY OF LABOR: FRANCES PERKINS

Frances Perkins, Secretary of Labor in the Cabinets of Presidents Franklin D. Roosevelt and Harry S. Truman, was born on April 10, 1882 in Boston, Massachusetts, the daughter of Winslow Perkins, a lawyer and merchant, and Susan (Wight) Perkins. After attending the local schools for her basic education, Frances went to Mount Holyoke College from which she was graduated in 1945. She pursued graduate studies in sociology and economics at the Universities of Chicago, Pennsylvania and Columbia. She received the Master of Arts degree from Columbia in 1910. While she was in Chicago Frances Perkins worked at Hull House. She was secretary of the Research and Protective Association in Philadelphia.

In New York City Miss Frances Perkins continued to work for reforms for the benefit of the working class. She was executive secretary of the Consumer's League from 1910 to 1912. His work led to the abolition of cellar bakeries. As a result of the Triangle Shirtwaist factory fire in 1911, a Commission of Safety was formed on which Frances served as executive secretary until 1917. Many bills were produced to prevent similar accidents. She wrote *Life Hazards from Fire in New York Factories* in 1912.

Miss Perkins participated in the movement which gained the nine-hour day for women in 1913. Frances was director of investigations for the New York State factory commission during 1912 and 1913. Frances married Paul Caldwell Wilson on September 26, 1913. They had one daughter, Susanna Winslow Perkins. Frances was next executive director of the New York Council of Organization for War Service from 1917 to 1919. She wrote *A Plan for Maternity Care* in 1918 and *Women As Employers* in 1919.

New York Governor Alfred E. Smith appointed Frances Perkins a member of the state industrial commission in 1919. She served on the commission until 1921. She was next director of the council of immigrant education from 1921 to 1923. Frances wrote *A Social Experiment Under the Workmen's Compensation Jurisdiction* in 1921. Governor Smith next appointed Miss Perkins to the New York State Industrial Board in 1922. She continued on the Board until 1933 and was chairman from 1926 to 1929.

Governor Franklin D. Roosevelt named Frances Perkins

head of the New York State Department of Labor in January 1929.  She supervised the administration of the labor law and workmen's compensation law.  She was also appointed an ex-officio member on the commission on unemployment problems in March, 1930.

President Franklin D. Roosevelt named Frances Perkins Secretary of Labor on March 4, 1933.  She was the first female member of a President's cabinet.  Frances continued in office under President Harry S. Truman after the death of Franklin D. Roosevelt in April 1945 until May 31, 1945. She initiated a program to aid the wage earning class. Among her activities as Secretary of Labor Miss Perkins participated in many of the New Deal measures.  She was granted the honorary LL.D. degree by the University of Wisconsin in 1933 and Amherst College in 1934.  The American Women's Association awarded Frances a medal for eminent achievement in 1933.  She wrote People at Work in 1934.

Under Frances Perkins' direction the Department of Labor recommended various relief concepts and public works projects.  Frances also participated in developing the necessary offices as required in the legislative measures of the New Deal, including creation of the public employment offices, the organization of the labor sections aiding the working class under the National Industrial Recovery Administration.  In addition she supervised establishment of minimum wages and maximum hours through the Wages and Hours Act.

Frances also directed such areas as the development of adult education, the investigation of unfavorable working conditions, and enforcement of the New Deal laws.  She also helped in the development and passage of such legislation as old age insurance and unemployment compensation.  Frances Perkins left the Truman administration in May 1945.

Among the organizations to which Frances Perkins belonged were the Maternity Center Association of which she was a director and founder.  She was also a director of the American Child Hygiene Association, the Consumers' League of New York and the New York child labor committee. Miss Perkins also served as Civil Service Commissioner from 1945 to 1953.  She wrote The Roosevelt I Knew in 1946.  Frances Perkins died on May 14, 1965 in New York City.  She was buried in Newcastle, Maine.

Bibliography:
Bernstein, Irving.  The New Deal and Collective Bargaining Policy.  Berkeley: University of California Press, 1950.
Bremer, Howard F., ed.  Franklin D. Roosevelt, 1882-1945.  Dobbs Ferry, N.Y.: Oceana Publications, Inc., 1971.
Conkin, Paul K.  The New Deal.  New York: Thomas Y.

Crowell Company, Inc., 1967.

Lawson, Don. <u>Frances</u> <u>Perkins</u>: <u>First</u> <u>Lady</u> <u>of</u> <u>the</u> <u>Ca-binet</u>. New York, 1960.

McFarland, Charles K. <u>Roosevelt</u>, <u>Lewis</u> <u>and</u> <u>the</u> <u>New</u> <u>Deal</u>. Fort Worth: Texas Christian University Press, 1970.

Moley, Raymond. <u>The</u> <u>First</u> <u>New</u> <u>Deal</u>. New York: Har-court Brace Jovanovich, 1966.

Wann, A. J. <u>President</u> <u>as</u> <u>Chief</u> <u>Administrator</u>: <u>A</u> <u>Study</u> <u>of</u> <u>Franklin</u> <u>D</u>. <u>Roosevelt</u>. Washington, D.C.: Public Affairs Press, 1968.

## ADMINISTRATIONS OF HARRY S. TRUMAN

### VICE PRESIDENT: ALBEN WILLIAM BARKLEY

Alben W. Barkley, Vice President in the second adminis-tration of President Harry S. Truman, was born on Novem-ber 24, 1877 near Lowes, Graves County, Kentucky. He was the son of John Wilson Barkley, a tobacco farmer and railroad section hand, and Electra (Smith) Barkley. Alben attended the public schools and worked on his fa-ther's farm. Alben next went to Marvin College in Clin-ton, Kentucky from which he received the Bachelor of Arts degree in 1897. He pursued graduate studies for one year at Emory College in Oxford, Georgia and then taught at Marvin College.

Alben Barkley studied law at the University of Virginia Law School and read law with Congressman John K. Wheeler, John K. Hendrick, and Judge William S. Bishop in Paducah, McCracken County, Kentucky. After being admitted to the bar in 1901. Alben established his law practice in Pa-ducah. He married Dorothy Brower on June 23, 1903. They had three children: David Murrell, Marian Frances, and Laura Louise. He soon became active in the Democratic Party.

Alben Barkley was elected prosecuting attorney for McCracken County, serving from 1905 to 1909. He was then elected judge of the McCracken County Court, sitting on the bench from 1909 to 1913. Alben Barkley was elected to the United States House of Representatives in 1912, serving in the Sixty-third through the Sixty-ninth Con-gresses from March 4, 1913 to March 3, 1927. He supported the Wilson administration's measures including the Fe-deral Reserve Act, the Farm Loan Act and the anti-trust legislation. He was chairman of the state Democratic conventions in 1919 and 1924. He attended his first na-tional convention in 1920 and was again a delegate in 1924.

Alben Barkley was next elected to the United States Senate in 1926 and was reelected in 1932, 1938 and 1944. He served from March 4, 1927 until his resignation on January 19, 1949 to become Vice President of the United

States.  Alben was elected Senate majority leader in 1938,
succeeding Joseph T. Robinson, and served in that post
until January 3, 1947 when he was elected minority leader
because the Republicans had a majority.  Barkley helped
to write the 21st Amendment to the Constitution which
repealed the 18th or Prohibition Amendment.  He served
on the foreign relations, banking and currency and interstate commerce committees.

Barkley continued his active interest in the Democratic
Party.  He attended the national conventions as a delegate-at-large while a Senator in 1928, 1932, 1936 and
1940.  He was permanent chairman of the 1944 Democratic
National Convention and placed Franklin D. Roosevelt's
name in nomination for a fourth term.  In 1948 Alben was
temporary chairman of the convention and was nominated
as the vice presidential running mate with Harry S. Truman.  They were elected on November 2, 1948.  Alben was
also head of the United States delegation to the Interparliamentary Union Conference at Rome in 1948.

Alben Barkley was inaugurated as Vice President on
January 20, 1949 along with President Harry S. Truman.
Barkley served until the end of the Administration on
January 20, 1953.  Alben married Jane (Mrs. Carleton S.)
Hadley on November 18, 1949.  After leaving office at
the end of his term Barkley was again elected to the Uni-
ted States Senate in 1954 and served from January 3, 1953
until his death on April 30, 1956 in Lexington, Virginia.
He was buried in Paducah, Kentucky.

Bibliography:
Barkley, Jane R. and Leighton, Frances S.  I married
the Veep.  New York: Vanguard Press, 1958.
Bernstein, Barton J. and Matusow, Allen F.  Truman
Administration: A Documentary History.  New York: Harper
and Row, 1966.
Furer, Howard B., ed.  Harry S. Truman, 1882-/1972/
Dobbs Ferry, N.Y.: Oceana Publications, Inc., 1970.
Philips, Cabell.  The Truman Presidency.  The History
of a Triumphant Succession.  New York: Macmillan, 1966.
Steinberg, Alfred.  The Man From Missouri: The Life
and Times of Harry S. Truman.  New York: Putnam, 1962.

SECRETARY OF STATE: EDWARD REILLEY STETTINIUS

Refer to the biographical sketch of Edward R. Stettinius
under Secretary of State in the Administration of Franklin D. Roosevelt, page 582.

SECRETARY OF STATE: JAMES FRANCIS BYRNES

James F. Byrnes, Secretary of State in the Cabinet of
President Harry S. Truman, was born on May 2, 1874 in

Charleston, South Carolina, the son of James F. Byrnes, a planter who died several months before his son was born, and Elizabeth E. (McSweeney) Byrnes. He attended the public schools and St. Patrick's Parochial School in Charleston and then went to work after studying stenography in 1891 as a clerk in the legal firm of Mordecai and Gadsden. He also studied with Judge Benjamin H. Rutledge.

James F. Byrnes was named official court stenographer for the second judicial circuit of South Carolina and moved to Aiken. He also studied law with James Aldrich and was admitted to the bar in 1903. He then established his law practice in Aiken and also became part owner and editor of the Aiken Journal and Review. He continued his work on the paper until 1947. James married Maud (Busch) Perkins on May 2, 1906. They had no children.

Byrnes was elected solicitor of the second judicial district of South Carolina in 1908, serving until 1910 when he was elected as a Democrat to the United States House of Representatives. He was a member of the Sixty-second through the Sixty-eighth Congresses from March 4, 1911 to March 3, 1925. He was a member of the appropriations committee. James was active in the Democratic Party and was a delegate-at-large to the Democratic National Convention in 1920. James ran unsuccessfully for the Senate in 1924. After leaving the House he returned to the practice of law with the firm of Nichols, Wyche and Byrnes in Spartanburg, South Carolina.

James F. Byrnes was elected to the United States Senate on November 4, 1930 and was reelected in 1936. He served until his resignation on July 8, 1941. He attended the Democratic National Conventions of 1932, 1936 and 1940. While in the Senate he supported Franklin D. Roosevelt's New Deal legislation. He was granted the honorary LL.D. degree by the College of Charleston in 1935, Presbyterian College in Clinton, South Carolina in 1937 and John Marshall College of Jersey City in 1939.

James F. Byrnes was appointed an associate justice of the Supreme Court in 1941 and continued on the bench until his resignation on October 3, 1942. President Franklin D. Roosevelt appointed Byrnes director of the wartime Office of Economic Stabilization in October 1942. He served in this office until May 27, 1943. He was next named director of the Office of War Mobilization on May 28, 1943 and remained in that post until April 2, 1945. He was a candidate for the Vice Presidential nomination in 1944. Byrnes accompanied President Roosevelt to the Yalta Conference in February 1945, where the President met with Prime Minister Winston Churchill of Great Britain and Premier Josef Stalin of the Soviet Union.

President Harry S. Truman, who had assumed the Presidency upon the death of Franklin D. Roosevelt in April 1945, named James F. Byrnes Secretary of State on July 2,

1945 to succeed Edward R. Stettinius.  James assumed the
office on July 3 and continued until January 7, 1947.
He traveled with President Truman to the Potsdam Conference in Berlin, attended by the heads of state and foreign
ministers of Great Britain and the Soviet Union.  Byrnes
helped to draft the Potsdam Declaration of August 2, 1945.
James next attended the London meeting of the Council of
Foreign Ministers of the United States, Great Britain,
France, the U.S.S.R. and China in September 1945.  Preliminary peace plans were developed there.  The conference became deadlocked over the question of which nations
should draft the peace treaties.

Byrnes declared on October 25, 1945 that the United
Nations Charter had come into force after twenty-nine
nations ratified it.  The Secretary urged Turkey in November 1945 to agree to a conference which would discuss
control of the Dardanelles.  As a result of disturbances
in Iran he sent a note to the Iranian Government on
December 7, 1945 stating that the United States stood
by the Teheran declaration of 1943 pledging the United
States, Great Britain and the Soviet Union to maintain
the sovereignty and territorial integrity of Iran.

Secretary Byrnes next issued a statement concerning
the rehabilitation of Germany as determined by the Potsdam declaration on December 11, 1945.  At Byrnes' urging
the Moscow Conference was held from December 16 to December 26, 1945 in which agreements were made on a wide range
of topics including peace treaties with various states
except Germany.  On February 28, 1946 he delivered a
speech in New York warning Russia not to try to force
its smaller neighbors into agreements and pledged United States support for the United Nations Charter.

In March 1946 Byrnes joined France and Great Britain
in condemning the Franco regime in Spain but would not
later join France in bringing the Spanish question before
the United Nations.  Byrnes pushed for United Nations
consideration of the Russo-Iranian dispute which eventually led to the withdrawal of Russian troops from Iran.
At the council of foreign ministers meeting in Paris during April and May 1946 Byrnes proposed a four-power military alliance for the purpose of keeping Germany dis-
armed for twenty-five years.  This was a reversal of
United States policy against formulation of such allian-
ces.

Byrnes delivered a statement at Stuttgart on September
6, 1946 indicating the American desire for development
of a democratic German state which would determine its
own affairs.  During the Council of foreign ministers
conference in New York James F. Byrnes won Russian agreement to complete peace treaties with Italy, Hungary, Rumania, Bulgaria and Finland which were to be signed by
agents of the ministers at a meeting in Paris in February
1947.

After retiring from public office Byrnes wrote Speaking Frankly in 1947. He practiced law in Washington, D.C. with the firm of Hogan and Hortson. James was elected governor of South Carolina and served from 1950 to 1955. Among his activities he is a member of the Masons, the Shriners and the Knights of Pythias.

Bibliography:
Bernstein, Barton J. and Matusow, Allen F. Truman Administration: A Documentary History, New York: Harper and Row, 1966.
Byrnes, James F. Speaking Frankly. New York: Harper and Row, 1947.
- - - -. All in One Lifetime. New York: Harper and Row, 1958.
Furer, Howard B., ed. Harry S. Truman, 1884-/1972/ Dobbs Ferry, N.Y.: Oceana Publications, Inc., 1970.
Philips, Cabell. The Truman Presidency. The History of a Triumphant Succession. New York: Macmillan, 1966.
Steinberg, Alfred. The Man from Missouri: The Life and Times of Harry S. Truman. New York: Putnam, 1962.

## SECRETARY OF STATE: GEORGE CATLETT MARSHALL

George C. Marshall, Secretary of State and Secretary of Defense in the Cabinet of President Harry S. Truman, was born on December 31, 1880 in Uniontown, Pennsylvania, the son of George Catlett and Laura (Bradford) Marshall. After receiving his basic education in the public and private schools of Uniontown he went to Virginia Military Institute in 1897 and was graduated in 1901 as senior first captain of the Corps of Cadets. He entered the United States Army as a second lieutenant of Infantry in February 1902. He married Elizabeth Carter Coles on February 11, 1902. They had no children.

Marshall was assigned to the 30th Infantry in the Philippines in May 1902 where he remained until November 1903. He then returned to the United States and was stationed at Fort Reno, Oklahoma, He next went to Fort Levenworth in 1907. George was promoted to first lieutenant in March 1907 and was graduated from the Army Staff College in 1908. He then became an instructor in the Army Service Schools department of military engineering from 1908 to 1910. He next served as inspector-instructor of the Massachusetts National Guard

George C. Marshall was made company commander in the 4th Infantry in September 1912 and served until June 1913 first at Fort Logan H. Roots, Arkansas and then at Galveston, Texas, He returned to the Philippines where he remained from 1913 to 1916. Marshall was promoted to captain in 1916. He returned to the United States in May 1916 as aide-de-camp to Major General James F. Bell in San Francisco.

George C. Marshall was assigned to the general staff of the First Division when the United States entered the First World War in 1917. He sailed for France in June 1917 with the first contingent of the Allied Expeditionary Force, where he served until 1919. George was awarded the Distinguished Service medal in 1919. He became aide-de-camp to General John J. Pershing in May 1919 and returned to the United States, remaining in that position until 1924. He was promoted during this period to the rank of lieutenant colonel in 1923.

Marshall's next assignment was with the 15th Infantry in Tientsin, China from 1924 to 1927. He returned to the United States in the last year where he taught at the Army War College in Washington, D.C. for several months and then went to Fort Benning Georgia where he was assistant commandant of the Infantry School for five years. He revolutionized infantry tactics. George's wife Elizabeth died in 1927. He next married Katherine Boyce (Tapper) Brown on October 15, 1930. They had no children. Marshall was commandant of the 8th Infantry at Fort Screven, Georgia from 1932 to 1933 and then commandant at Fort Moultrie, South Carolina. He was also commandant of District I of the Civilian Conservation Corps. His next assignment was senior instructor of the Illinois National Guard from 1933 to 1936. He was commanding general of the Fifth Brigade and Vancouver Barracks in the state of Washington from 1936 to 1938.

On July 1, 1939 Marshall was named acting chief of staff of the United States Army. He was promoted to the rank of general on September 1, 1939 and took office as chief of staff. He was able with difficulty to convince Congress to pass a peacetime Selective Service Act for one year service within the Western Hemisphere only after Germany had defeated France, the Netherlands and Belgium. After the Japanese attack on Pearl Harbor, December 7, 1941 and the United States declaration of war on Japan on December 8 and on the European Axis powers on December 11, President Franklin D. Roosevelt made Marshall directly responsible to him and appointed him to the Joint Chiefs of Staff.

In assuming leadership of the Combined Chiefs of Staff of the United States and the British Commonwealth of Nations forces Marshall helped to develop the long range plans for final victory. He was awarded the honorary LL.D. degree in 1941 by the College of William and Mary and Trinity College of Connecticut. During the war Marshall travelled with President Roosevelt to the August 1941 Atlantic Conference off the coast of Newfoundland with Prime Minister Winston Churchill. This meeting led to the formation of the Atlantic Charter. Marshall was a participant of the Conferences at Casablanca in January 1943, at Quebec, August 1943, at Cairo and Teheran, November 1943, at Quebec, September 1944, at Yalta, February 1945 and at Potsdam, July 1945.

George C. Marshall resigned as chief of staff on November 20, 1945. President Harry S. Truman appointed Marshall his special representative to China on November 26. When he arrived in December, George was able to convince the Communist and Nationalist leaders to sign a truce. He was not able to get them to make a lasting peace and returned to Washington in January 1947.

President Harry S. Truman appointed George C. Marshall Secretary of State to replace James F. Byrnes on January 8, 1947. He assumed his office on January 21, 1947 and served until January 20, 1949. He retired from the Army on February 28, 1947. Marshall was granted the honorary LL.D. degree in 1947 by Columbia, Princeton, Harvard, Brown and McGill Universities as well as by Amherst and Lafayette Colleges. As Secretary of State Marshall was able to gain ratification of the peace treaties with Bulgaria, Hungary, Italy, and Rumania.

Marshall reorganized the State Department for greater efficiency, establishing the post of assistant secretary for political affairs; instituting a policy-planning committee to organize the information necessary for long-term planning. He also centralized the intelligence service and improved the communications system. He was instrumental in obtaining Congressional approval for the Voice of America in the Information and Educational Exchange Act of 1948.

George C. Marshall attended the Council of Foreign Ministers Conference at Moscow in March 1947. He presented a plan to establish a German federal state on March 22. The conference adjourned on April 24, 1947 with the disparity of views between the United States and Russia quite evident. As a result of the pressure exerted by the Russians in Germany Secretary of State Marshall indicated in a speech at Washington on June 30, 1948 that the United States would not surrender its rights in Berlin. The Russians instituted a complete blockade of Berlin on June 24, 1947. Marshall conducted intensive negotiations with the Russians and also arranged to have the issue brought before the United Nations Security Council in September.

In addition to concern with Germany Secretary Marshall began to develop policies to increase America's commitment to other parts of Europe. As a result of his work with President Truman, the Truman Doctrine was developed and presented to the Congress by the President on March 17, 1947. He promised American aid to help nations maintain their freedom and independence. The President specifically asked for aid for Greece and Turkey. Marshall announced the outlines of a European recovery program later called the Marshall Plan or European Recovery Program in an address at Harvard University on June 5, 1947.

He thereby initiated a massive program involving self
help and American aid for many European states.  Marshall also pledged aid to Latin America after Europe got
on its feet.  He supported the work of the United Nations
while in the State Department.

After retiring from the State Department in January
1949 Marshall resumed his army duties.  He was president
of the American Red Cross from 1949 to 1950.  When hostilities broke out in Korea President Truman asked Marshall to take charge of the Defense Department.  Marshall
became Secretary of Defense on September 12, 1950.  He
indicated that he intended to create a defensive system
which would be able to handle any emergency.  On January
2, 1951 he ordered the establishment of an Armed Forces
Medical Policy Council in place of the various offices.
In addition Marshall reorganized the Munitions Board in
April 1951.

On April 2, 1951 Secretary of Defense Marshall ordered
that all men entering the armed services through enlist-
ment or the draft be divided proportionately among the
army, navy and air force.  Marshall was able to convince
Congress to pass the Universal Military Training and
Service Act in June 1951 which extended the Selective
Service System.  He ordered that all training be on an
integrated basis.  George Marshall also established the
management engineering staff under the Defense Management
Committee.  Marshall resigned from the Defense Department
on September 13, 1951.

George C. Marshall was given the Four Freedoms Award
in 1952.  His last public service was as chairman of the
United States delegation to the coronation of Queen
Elizabeth II of England in June 1953.  He was awarded
the Nobel Peace Prize in 1953 in recognition of the services he rendered as a result of the development of the
Marshall Plan.  In the same year the state of Virginia
chartered the George C. Marshall Research Foundation
to collect all materials relating to his life and public
services.  George C. Marshall died on October 16, 1959
in Washington, D.C.

Bibliography:
    Bernstein, Barton J. and Matusow, Allen F.  Truman
Administration: A Documentary History.  New York: Harper
and Row, 1966.
    Clay, Lucius.  Decision in Germany.  Garden City, N.Y.:
Doubleday, 1950.
    Furer, Howard B., ed.  Harry S. Truman, 1884-/1972/
Dobbs Ferry, N.Y.: Oceana Publications, Inc., 1970.
    Philips, Cabell.  The Truman Presidency.  The History
of a Triumphant Succession.  New York: Macmillan, 1966.
    Pogue, Forrest.  George Marshall.  New York: Viking
Press, 1963.
    Price, Harry B.  The Marshall Plan and Its Meaning.

Ithaca, N.Y.: Cornell University Press, 1955.
    Steinberg, Alfred. The Man from Missouri: The Life and Times of Harry S. Truman.    New York: Putnam, 1962.
    Wilson, Rose Page. General Marshall Remembered.   Englewood Cliff, N.J.: Prentice-Hall, 1968.

## SECRETARY OF STATE: DEAN GOODERHAM ACHESON

Dean G. Acheson, Secretary of State in the Cabinet of President Harry S. Truman, was born on April 11, 1893 in Middletown, Connecticut, the son of Edward Campion Acheson, Episcopal bishop of Connecticut, and Eleanor Gertrude (Gooderham) Acheson.  He received his preparatory education at the Groton School in Groton, Massachusetts and then studied at Yale University from which he received the Bachelor of Arts degree in 1917.  He nexte studied at Harvard University Law School where he received the LL.B. degree in 1918.  Dean married Alice Stanley on May 5, 1917.  They had three children: Jane, David Campion and Mary Eleanor.

After serving in the United States Navy as an ensign for six months in 1918 Acheson went to Washington, D.C. where he was private secretary to Louis Brandeis, associate justice of the United States Supreme Court.  Dean G. Acheson next entered the Washington law firm of Covington, Burling and Rublee in 1921, becoming a partner in 1926.  He continued with the firm which was eventually renamed Burling, Rublee, Acheson and Short until 1949. Acheson settled in Maryland and soon became active in Democratic politics.

President Franklin D. Roosevelt named Dean Acheson first undersecretary of the Treasury in May 1933.  Dean was acting secretary during the period of William Woodin's illness.  He resigned in November 1933 because of a serious difference with the President over monetary policies and the gold purchase plan.  Acheson returned to his legal practice.  He supported President Roosevelt in his reelection campaign in 1936.  Attorney General Frank Murphy appointed Acheson chairman of a committee to investigate and recommend improvements in the administrative procedure of the Executive Branch in February 1939. The committee's report was made to Congress in 1941, and some of the recommendations were incorporated in the Administrative Procedures Act in June 1946.  Acheson supported President Roosevelt for reelection in 1940.

President Roosevelt appointed Dean Acheson assistant Secretary of State in February 1941.  His specific duties involved the economic and commercial aspects of international relations.  He helped in arranging passage of the Lend-Lease Act in 1941.  Among his other assignments during this period Dean was chairman of the departmental Board of Economic Operations, the executive committee on

economic foreign policy and the policy and coordinating
committees of the Committee for Economic Policy in Liberated Areas.  He was director of the Office of Foreign
Economic Coordination and a member of the Frozen Funds
Committee, the Foreign Service Personnel Board, the Board
of Examiners for the Foreign Service and the Foreign Service School Board.

Among his other assignments Dean G. Acheson led the
American delegation and was permanent chairman of the
Atlantic City meeting in 1943 which created the United
Nations Relief and Rehabilitation Administration.  He was
a delegate to the United Nations Monetary Financial Conference at Bretton Woods, New Hampshire.  It was decided
to form the International Bank for Reconstruction and Development and the International Monetary Fund.

Dean G. Acheson was next appointed Undersecretary of
State on August 16, 1945, serving under James F. Byrne
and George C. Marshall in the Truman Administration.
Dean was acting Secretary of State while each was out
of the country on various missions.  He was a participant
in an Anglo-American financial and trade conference in
Washington from September to December 1945.  Acheson was
chairman of the Secretary of State's committee on atomic
energy in 1946.  In the Acheson-Lillienthal report the
committee recommended creation of an International Atomic
Development Authority which was approved by the United
Nations General Assembly on November 4, 1948.  Wesleyan
University awarded Acheson the honorary LL.D. degree in
1947.

Acheson resigned as Undersecretary of State in June
1947 and was awarded the United States Medal for Merit
by President Harry S. Truman.  Dean G. Acheson was a
member and chairman of the American Section of the United
States-Canadian Permanent Joint Defense Board during
1947 and 1948.  In addition in 1947 President Truman appointed Acheson a member and vice chairman of the Commission on Organization of the Executive Board of the
Government headed by Herbert Hoover.  The commission presented its report in May 1949.

President Harry S. Truman appointed Dean G. Acheson
Secretary of State on January 19, 1949.  He served in this
post until the end of the administration on January 19,
1953.  As Secretary Acheson worked to continue discussions
for the defense of the North Atlantic area which led to
the signing on April 4, 1949 of the North Atlantic Treaty,
creating the North Atlantic Treaty Organization.  Acheson
was chairman of the North Atlantic Council during 1949
and 1950.  After the fall of the Chinese Nationalist Government to the Communists, Republican criticism of Acheson's Far Eastern policy led him to issue a White Paper
on August 5, 1949 explaining how the weaknesses of Chiang
Kai-shek's troops and the failure of the Kuomintang government to act led to the loss of the people's support.

Secretary Acheson also reorganized the State Department in 1949.  He arranged an agreement with the Soviet Union for the ending of the latter's land blockade
of West Berlin which was lifted on May 12, 1949.  Acheson developed plans for the implementation of President
Truman's Point-Four program to aid the underdeveloped
parts of the world.  Acheson worked with the North Atlantic Treaty powers to provide the basis for establishment of a Western Europe military defense force during
1950.  In an address at the University of California
on March 16, 1950 Acheson presented a seven-point program as the basis for peaceful coexistence with the Soviet Union including the drafting of peace treaties with
Germany, Japan and Austria; withdrawal of Russian forces
from all satellite countries; ending of the obstruction
in the United Nations; a realistic atomic energy control
program; ending of Communist subversive activities out-
side of Russia; an end to the bad treatment of United
States diplomats in Russian-dominated countries; and
cessation of propaganda which distorted the views of
the United States.

When the North Korean Communist forces invaded South
Korea on June 25, 1950 Secretary of State Acheson was
able to arrange for United Nations intervention.  He
was later able to have Communist China declared an ag-
gressor in Korea after they had sent troops into Korea.
Acheson received the honorary LL.D. degree from Harvard
University in 1950 and was given the Freedom House Award
in the same year.  The Secretary gave John Foster Dulles
the assignment of negotiating a peace treaty with Japan.
Acheson presided over the San Francisco conference of
September 4-5 where a peace treaty was signed with Japan by the United States and forty-eight other nations.
He attended the North Atlantic Council meeting at Lis-
bon, Portugal where it was decided to build up a force
of fifty divisions; to approve establishment of a European Defense Community whereby Germany could contribute
to the defense of Western Europe; and to develop permanent headquarters for NATO in Paris.

After leaving the State Department Dean G. Acheson
wrote several books including A Democrat Looks at His
Party in 1955, A Citizen Looks at Congress in 1957,
Power and Diplomacy in 1958, Sketches of Men I Have
Known and Morning and Noon in 1965, as well as Present
at the Creation in 1969.  He is a member of the American
Bar Association.

Bibliography:
  Acheson, Dean G.  Morning and Noon.  Boston: Houghton
Mifflin, 1965.
  - - - -.  Power and Diplomacy.  New York: Atheneum,
1962.
  Bernstein, Barton J. and Matusow, Allen F.  Truman

Administration: A Documentary History. New York: Harper and Row, 1966.
    Davison, W. Phillips. The Berlin Blockade. Princeton: Princeton University Press, 1958.
    Furer, Howard B., ed. Harry S. Truman, 1884-/1972/ Dobbs Ferry, N.Y.: Oceana Publications, Inc., 1970.
    Neal, Fred W. United States Foreign Policy and the Soviet Union. Santa Barbara, Calif.: Center for the Study of Democratic Institutions, 1961.
    Philips, Cabell. The Truman Presidency. The History of a Triumphant Succession. New York: Macmillan, 1966.
    Schuman, Frederic L. The Cold War: Retrospect and Prospect. Baton Rouge: Louisiana State University Press, 1962.

## SECRETARY OF THE TREASURY:

### HENRY MORGENTHAU, JR.

Refer to the biographical sketch of Henry Morgenthau, Jr. under Secretary of the Treasury in the Administration of Franklin D. Roosevelt, page 586.

## SECRETARY OF THE TREASURY:

### FREDERICK MOORE VINSON

Frederick M. Vinson, Secretary of the Treasury in the Cabinet of President Harry S. Truman, was born on January 22, 1890 in Louisa, Kentucky, the son of James Vinson, county jailer, and Virginia (Ferguson) Vinson. After receiving his basic education in the local public schools and graduating from Louisa High School, Vinson attended Kentucky Normal College in Louisa. He was graduated in 1908 and then continued his studies at Centre College in Danville, receiving the Bachelor of Arts degree in 1909 and then studied law, receiving the LL.B. degree in 1911. He was admitted to the bar in the same year and established his practice in Louisa, Kentucky.

Frederick M. Vinson was city attorney of Louisa in 1914 and 1915. He also became involved in various business enterprises including banking, milling and wholesale grocery. After the United States entered the war Frederick joined the United States Army as a private. He was attending the central officers training school at Camp Pike, Arkansas when the armistice was signed. Vinson returned to his law practice and business interests. He was elected commonwealth attorney for the 32nd judicial district of Kentucky in 1921 and served until January 10, 1924. Frederick married Roberta Dixon on January 24, 1923. They had two sons: Frederick Moore and James Robert.

Frederick M. Vinson was elected as a Democrat to the
House of Representatives to fill the vacancy left by
resignation of William J. Fields. He served in the
Sixty-eighth through the Seventieth Congresses from January 12, 1924 to March 3, 1929 and was defeated for reelection in 1928. He returned to the practice of law
in Ashland, Kentucky. Frederick was again elected to
the House of Representatives in 1930 and served in the
Seventy-second to the Seventy-fifth Congresses from
March 4, 1931 to May 12, 1938 when he resigned. He was
a member of the House Ways and Means Committee and also
supported most of President Franklin D. Roosevelt's New
Deal measures. Vinson cosponsored a bill to stabilize
the soft coal industry. He supported Roosevelt's "court
packing" bill to reorganize the Supreme Court.
President Franklin D. Roosevelt appointed Frederick
M. Vinson an associate justice of the United States circuit court of appeals for the District of Columbia in
December 1937. He sat on the bench from May 1938 until
May 1943. Chief Justice Harlan Stone appointed Vinson
chief judge of the United States Emergency Court of Appeals, in which post he served until his resignation
on May 27, 1943. President Roosevelt appointed Vinson
director of the office of Economic Stabilization. He
was to stabilize prices in order to prevent runaway inflation. He also served as vice chairman of the United
States delegation to the United Nations Monetary and Financial Conference in July 1944 at Bretton Woods, New
Hampshire and served until March 5, 1945. He helped to
draw up the agreements to establish the International
Monetary Fund and the International Bank for Reconstruction and Development.
On March 5, 1945 President Roosevelt named Vinson federal loan administrator. He was charged with supervising the operations of the Reconstruction Finance Corporation. President Roosevelt next named Vinson Director
of War Mobilization and Reconversion in which post he
served from April 4, 1945 to July 22, 1945.
President Harry S. Truman appointed Frederick M. Vinson Secretary of the Treasury to succeed Henry Morgenthau,
Jr. He assumed his office on July 18, 1945. Vinson supervised the last war bond drive in November and December 1945. He recommended reductions in taxes in the
Revenue Act of 1945 to help relieve some of the heavy
tax burdens. He played a major role in the further development of the Bretton Woods agreements and in granting a $3.75 billion credit to Great Britain in order to
aid in the recovery and rehabilitation of the world's
economy.
Frederick M. Vinson was also named the United States'
member of the boards of governors of the International
Monetary Fund and the International Bank for Reconstruc-

tion and Development.  He became chairman of each of the
boards in March 1946.  In August 1945 Secretary of the
Treasury Vinson became chairman of the national advisory
council on international monetary and financial problems.
He urged increased credit for Great Britain and was instrumental in getting Congress to pass the necessary legislation on July 13, 1946.

President Truman named Frederick M. Vinson Chief Justice of the United States Supreme Court to succeed Harlan F, Stone on June 6, 1946.  Congress approved his nomination, and he was sworn in on June 24, 1946.  He was
awarded the Medal of Merit of the United States in 1947.
Vinson died on September 3, 1953 in Washington, D.C.

Bibliography:
  Bernstein, Barton J. and Matusow, Allen F.  Truman
Administration: A Documentary History.  New York: Harper
and Row, 1966.
  Furer, Howard B., ed.  Harry S. Truman, 1884-/1972/
Dobbs Ferry, N.Y.: Oceana Publications, Inc., 1970.
  Philips, Cabell.  The Truman Presidency.  The History
of a Triumphant Succession.  New York: Macmillan, 1966.
  Schubert, Glendon.  The Judicial Mind: The Attitudes
and Ideologies of Supreme Court Justices, 1946-1963.
Evanston, Ill.: Northwestern University Press, 1965.
  Steinberg, Alfred.  The Man from Missouri: The Life
and Times of Harry S. Truman.  New York: Putnam,

## SECRETARY OF THE TREASURY:

### JOHN WESLEY SNYDER

John W. Snyder, Secretary of the Treasury in the Cabinet of President Harry S. Truman, was born on June 21,
1895 in Jonesboro, Arkansas, the son of Jerre Hartwell
and Ellen (Hatcher) Snyder.  After receiving his basic
education in the public schools of Jonesboro, John went
to Vanderbilt University in 1914.  He enlisted in the
United States Army after the nation entered the First
World War.  He went to the officers' training camp at
Fort Logan H. Roots in Arkansas and was commissioned
a second lieutenant of field artillery.

John Snyder went to France in December 1917 with the
32nd division and attended the artillery school at
Coetquidan where he met Harry S. Truman.  Snyder was promoted to first lieutenant and then captain.  He fought
in France and served in the Army of Occupation in Germany
until June 1919.  After returning to the United States
Snyder became involved in the banking business, working
for the First National Bank of Forrest City, Arkansas.
He then went to the Bank of Steele in St. Louis, Missouri
and then to the First National Bank of Blytheville, Ar-

kansas.  John married Evlyn Cook on January 5, 1920.
They had one daughter, Edith Drucie.

John Snyder was appointed to the office of Comptroller
of Currency at Washington, D.C. in 1930.  He was involved in receiverships, liquidating the Missouri banks
which failed during the depression.  His next government
post was manager of the St. Louis branch of the Reconstruction Finance Corporation beginning in 1937 and continuing until 1943.  He was also named in 1940 special
assistant to the board of directors of the Reconstruction
Finance Corporation and a director and vice president of
the Defense Plants Corporation, which was established
as a subsidiary of the Reconstruction Finance Corporation to help finance development of plants and other
facilities for war production.  He continued in this capacity until December 31, 1942, although he did continue
for a time in an advisory capacity.  Snyder became vice
president of the First National Bank of St. Louis, Missouri in 1943.

President Truman next appointed John W, Snyder Federal
Loan Administrator in April 1945, succeeding Frederick
M. Vinson.  Snyder was appointed director of the Office
of War Mobilization and Reconversion in July 1945.  After
the victory over Japan Snyder played a major role in developing and administering plans for the transition of
the economy from a wartime to a peacetime basis.  He
worked diligently to convert plants to peacetime production, maintain price and rent controls, as well as to
effectively stabilize the labor situation.  He began to
encourage home building and convinced President Truman
to name a federal housing expediter.  Snyder also organized a massive program to help relieve the food and
fuel famine in liberated Europe in January 1946.

President Harry S. Truman appointed John W. Snyder Secretary of the Treasury to succeed Frederick M. Vinson on
June 12, 1946.  John assumed his office on June 25, 1946
and served until the end of the Truman administration
on January 20, 1953.  Among his achievements Secretary
Snyder was able to help reduce the national debt by about
$15 billion.  In order to strengthen the economy he in-
augurated a campaign for the sale of United States Savings bonds.

Among his other duties Snyder was chairman of the Library of Congress fund board and the National Advisory
Council on International Monetary and Financial Problems
as well as chairman of the board of trustees of the endowment fund of the American National Red Cross.  In addition Snyder was also United States governor of the International Monetary Fund and International Bank for
Reconstruction and Development.  In his official duties
he was also a trustee of the Federal Old Age and Survivors Insurance Trust Fund, the postal savings system,

the National Gallery of Art, and the National Archives
Council.  He was in addition a director of the Federal
Farm Mortgage Corporation and a member of the National
Park Trust Fund Board, the Defense Mobilization Board,
the Smithsonian Institution and the National Securities
Resources Board.

John W. Snyder left office at the end of the administration.  He is a colonel in the field artillery reserve and a member of the Missouri Reserve Officers Association.  He lives in retirement at his home in
Chevy Chase, Maryland.

Bibliography:
Bernstein, Barton J. and Matusow, Allen F.  Truman
Administration: A Documentary History.  New York: Harper
and Row, 1966.
Furer, Howard B., ed.  Harry S. Truman, 1884-/1972/
Dobbs Ferry, N.Y.: Oceana Publications, Inc., 1970.
Philips, Cabell.  The Truman Presidency.  The History
of a Triumphant Succession.  New York: Macmillan, 1966.
Steinberg, Alfred.  The Man from Missouri: The Life
and Times of Harry S. Truman.  New York: Putnam, 1962.

SECRETARY OF WAR: HENRY LEWIS STIMSON

Refer to the biographical sketch of Henry L. Stimson
under Secretary of War in the Administration of William
Howard Taft, page 456.

SECRETARY OF WAR: ROBERT PORTER PATTERSON

Robert Porter Patterson, Secretary of War in the Cabinet of President Harry S. Truman, was born on February
12, 1891 in Glens Falls, New York, the son of Charles
R. Patterson, an attorney and county district attorney,
and Lodice E. (Porter) Patterson.  After receiving his
preparatory and secondary education Robert attended Union
College from which he was graduated with the Bachelor
of Arts degree in 1912.  He then attended Harvard Law
School from which he received the LL.B. degree summa
cum laude in 1915.  He was president of the Harvard Law
Review in his last year.  He was admitted to the bar in
1915 and began to practice law in the same year in New
York with the firm of Root, Clark, Buckner and Howland.

Robert Porter Patterson joined the New York National
Guard as a private in the 7th Regiment at the time that
he began his practice of law.  He served on the Mexican
border for six months in 1916.  When the United States
entered World War I in 1917 Robert was commissioned a
second lieutenant in the officers reserve corps and was
sent to the Plattsburg, New York reserve officers training

camp. He was promoted to the rank of captain. Patterson went to France in April 1918 and was assigned to
Company F of the 306th Infantry in July. He was awarded
the Distinguished Service Cross for heroism in action
and received the Purple Heart after he was wounded on
August 16, 1918. He was promoted to major in March 1919.

Patterson returned to the United States in April 1919
and was mustered out of the army in May. He returned to
the practice of law with the firm of Root, Clark, Buckner
and Ballantine. Robert married Margaret Turleton Winchester on January 3, 1920. They had four children: Robert
Porter, Aileen W., Susan Hand, and Virginia D. Patterson
next became a partner in the legal firm of Webb and Patterson in 1922 and continued with the firm and its suc-
cessors until 1930.

President Herbert Hoover appointed Robert Patterson
United States district judge for the southern district
of New York in 1930. He remained on the bench until 1939.
He was elected president of the Harvard Law School Association in 1937 and continued in that position until
1949. In February 1939 President Franklin D. Roosevelt
named Patterson a judge of the United States circuit
court of appeals for the second circuit, including New
York, Connecticut and Vermont. He remained on the bench
until July 31, 1940.

President Franklin D. Roosevelt appointed Robert Patterson assistant Secretary of War in July 1940. He was
next named to the newly created post of Undersecretary
of War in December 1940. He had charge of procuring
munitions and all other supplies for the army and was
also the War Department's representative on many war
agencies including the war manpower commission and the
ward production board. He was also acting secretary when
the Secretary of War was away. He was awarded the nonor-
ary LL.D. degree by Rutgers University, the University
of Rochester and Montana School of Mines in 1941; by Bau-
dair College in 1942; and by Pennsylvania Military and
Washington and Jefferson Colleges in 1943.

President Harry S. Truman named Robert Porter Patterson Secretary of War on September 26, 1945 when Henry L.
Stimson resigned. Patterson assumed the office on September 27, 1945. President Truman also awarded him the
Distinguished Service Medal for his contributions during
the war. Robert served until his resignation on July 1,
1947. He continued to maintain the great degree of efficiency and energy in his direction of the Department
of War. He proceeded to tackle the demobilization problems and to maintain the army at a strength sufficient
to carry out its occupation tasks in Germany and Japan.

Secretary Patterson recommended extension of the selective service system and a 20 per cent pay increase
to stimulate enlistments. He recognized the problems

concerned with the housing shortage and established a
special army board to provide vacant housing facilities
for veterans and their families as well as single veterans attending educational institutions.

After leaving public office Patterson continued to be
active in various capacities.  He was president of Freedom House and chairman of the Commission on Organized
Crime.  Robert Porter Patterson died on January 22, 1952
in Elizabeth, New Jersey.  He was buried in Arlington
National Cemetery in Arlington, Virginia.

Bibliography:
   Bernstein, Barton J. and Matusow, Allen F.  Truman Ad-
ministration: A Documentary History.  New York: Harper
and Row, 1966.
   Furer, Howard B., ed.  Harry S. Truman, 1884-/1972/
Dobbs Ferry, N.Y.: Oceana Publications, Inc., 1970.
   Philips, Cabell.  The Truman Presidency.  The History
of a Triumphant Succession.  New York: Macmillan, 1966.
   Steinberg, Alfred.  The Man from Missouri: The Life
and Times of Harry S. Truman.  New York: Putnam, 1962.

### SECRETARY OF WAR: KENNETH CLAIBORNE ROYALL

Kenneth C. Royall, Secretary of War in the Cabinet of
President Harry S. Truman, was born on July 24, 1899 in
Goldsboro, North Carolina, the son of George Claiborne
Royall, a manufacturer, and Clara Howard (Jones) Royall.
After receiving his basic education in the public
schools of Goldsboro Kenneth studied at the Episcopal
High School in Alexandria, Virginia.  He next attended
the University of North Carolina from which he was graduated with the Bachelor of Arts degree in 1914.  He then
entered Harvard Law School, receiving the LL.B. degree
in 1917.  He was an associate editor of the Harvard Law
Review from 1915 to 1917.  Royall was admitted to the bar
in North Carolina in 1917.  Kenneth married Margaret Best
on August 18, 1917.  They had three children: Kenneth
Claiborne, Jr., Margaret, and George Pender.

Kenneth C. Royall served in the army as a second lieutenant of field artillery in the First World War.  He
was sent to France in 1918 where he became a first lieutenant.  He remained in Europe until 1919., serving with
the 317th Field Artillery, 81st Division.  After returning to the United States Royall began his legal practice
in Goldsboro.  He later practiced in Raleigh, North Carolina.  He also became involved in politics.  Kenneth was
elected to the North Carolina Senate in 1927 and was
chairman of the banking committee.  He wrote the state
bank liquidation law.  Kenneth was president of the North
Carolina Bar Association during 1929 and 1930.

Kenneth C. Royall was commissioned a colonel in the

United States Army in 1942, serving as chief of the legal section, Fiscal Division, Services of Supply.  He
was promoted in 1943 to the rank of brigadier general,
becoming deputy fiscal director of the Army Service Forces.  He served overseas in 1944 and 1945.  Royall became
special assistant to Secretary of War Henry L. Stimson
in April 1945.  He was awarded the Distinguished Service
Medal in 1945.  Kenneth C. Royall was named Undersecretary of War in November 1945, continuing in that office
until July 1947.
    President Harry S. Truman appointed Kenneth C. Royall
Secretary of War on July 21, 1947 after Robert Porter
Patterson's resignation.  He assumed his duties on July
25 and continued until September 17, 1947.  At that
time the armed services were unified under the Department of Defense.  Royall served as the first Secretary
of the Army until his resignation in April 1949.
    Kenneth C. Royall then returned to the practice of
law with the firm of Dwight, Royall, Harris, Koegel and
Caskey in New York City and Washington, D.C.  Among his
activities he has continued to serve as a member of the
General Alumni Association of the University of North
Carolina, having been president of the association in
1959 and 1960.  He served as a member of the Presidential
Racial Commission in Birmingham, Alabama in 1963.  He
has continued his political activities and was a delegate-at-large to the Democratic National Convention in
1964.  He was national chairman for the lawyer's commit
tee for the Lyndon B. Johnson-Hubert H. Humphrey ticket
in 1964.  Kenneth C. Royall is a trustee of the John
Fitzgerald Kennedy Memorial Library.  He lives in retirement in New York City.

Bibliography:
  Bernstein, Barton J. and Matusow, Allen F.  Truman
Administration: A Documentary History.  New York: Har-
per and Row, 1966.
  Furer, Howard B., ed.  Harry S. Truman, 1884-/1972/
Dobbs Ferry, N.Y.: Oceana Publications, Inc., 1970.
  Philips, Cabell.  The Truman Presidency.  The History
of a Triumphant Succession.  New York: Macmillan, 1966.
  Steinberg, Alfred.  The Man from Missouri: The Life
and Times of Harry S. Truman.  New York: Putnam, 1962.

       SECRETARY OF DEFENSE: JAMES VINCENT FORRESTAL

    Refer to the biographical sketch of James V. Forrestal
under Secretary of the Navy in the Administration of
Franklin D. Roosevelt, page 607.

## SECRETARY OF DEFENSE: LOUIS ARTHUR JOHNSON

Louis A. Johnson, Secretary of Defense in the Cabinet of President Harry S. Truman, was born on January 10, 1891 in Roanoke, Virginia, the son of Marcellus Alexander and Katherine Leftwich (Arthur) Johnson. Louis received his basic education in the public schools of Roanoke and then entered the University of Virginia, receiving the LL.B. degree in 1912. He was admitted to the West Virginia bar in the same year and established his legal practice in Clarksburg, West Virginia with John Strode Rixey in the firm of Rixey and Johnson.

Louis Johnson also became interested in politics and joined the Democratic Party. He was prosecuting attorney of Harrison County, West Virginia in 1912. Louis formed the firm of Stephoe and Johnson in 1913. Johnson was elected to the West Virginia House of Delegates in 1916. Louis was the majority floor leader in the 1917 and continued to serve in the legislature until 1924. He volunteered for the United States Army at the beginning of World War I. Louis went to officers' candidate school and was eventually sent to France to serve with the American Expeditionary Forces. He was discharged in June 1919, having been promoted to the rank of major.

Louis A. Johnson then returned to his legal practice. Louis married Ruth Frances Maxwell on February 7, 1920. They had two daughters: Lillian Maxwell and Ruth Katherine. Louis Johnson was a delegate to the Democratic national convention in 1924. His next public service occurred in 1933 when he was appointed a member of the federal advisory council for the employment service of the Department of Labor. He led a veteran's delegation to the 1936 Democratic national convention.

During the 1936 presidential campaign Johnson was chairman of the veteran's advisory committee of the Democratic national committee. He was also national chairman of the Democratic finance committee from 1936 to 1940. President Roosevelt named him assistant Secretary of War in June 1937. He worked to have the United States strengthen its armed forces in preparation for a possible war. He came into conflict with Secretary of War Harry Woodring. The nation had already begun its preparedness program when Johnson resigned his post in 1940. He was awarded the honorary LL.D. degree by Kenyon College in 1939.

President Roosevelt named Louis Johnson his special representative to India on March 16, 1942 in which post he remained until December 17, 1942. He had been negotiating with the Indian leaders for a supply depot for the Allied forces. Johnson returned to the United States and resumed his legal practice. Johnson was chairman of the Democratic finance committee again in 1948.

President Harry S. Truman named Louis A. Johnson Secretary of Defense on March 23, 1949 to succeed James V. Forrestal.  Johnson worked to complete the unification of the armed forces and to reduce expenditures while preserving the necessary military strength.  He strongly supported air power and ordered B-36 bombers to improve the Air Force's long-range intercontinental capability.  Charges concerning shady deals were investigated by a House committee which concluded in October 1949 that nothing illegal was involved in the contracts.  Charges were also made that the navy was not equally represented on the Joint Chiefs of Staff.  The Congressional investigating committee recommended in March 1950 that the Secretary of Defense begin a study in the National Security Council concerning the defensive plans including use of atomic weapons and the further definition and clarification of the intent of unification.

Secretary Johnson instituted the Weapons System Evaluation Group in 1949 for the purpose of analyzing the weapons development of the various services.  The Secretary was also criticized because of his continued economies which led to the closing of several military installations.  The criticism grew when United States forces were committed to the aid of South Korea in June 1950. Louis A. Johnson was awarded the honorary LL.D. degree in 1949 by Creighton, Villanova and Marietta Colleges and West Virginia University.  At the request of President Truman Johnson resigned his post on September 20, 1950.

Louis A. Johnson returned to his law practice, working mainly in the Washington office.  He was an officer in various businesses including president and director of the General Dyestuff Corporation and director of the Consolidated Vultee Aircraft Corporation.  He was also a director of the Union National Bank and the Community Savings and Loan Company of Clarksburg.  Louis A. Johnson died on April 24, 1956 in Washington, D.C.

Bibliography:
  Bernstein, Barton J. and Matusow, Allen F.  Truman Administration: A Documentary History.  New York: Harper and Row, 1966.
  Furer, Howard B., ed.  Harry S. Truman, 1884-/1972/ Dobbs Ferry, N.Y.: Oceana Publications, Inc., 1970.
  Philips, Cabell.  The Truman Presidency.  The History of a Triumphant Succession.  New York: Macmillan, 1966.
  Steinberg, Alfred.  The Man from Missouri: The Life and Times of Harry S. Truman.  New York: Putnam, 1962.

SECRETARY OF DEFENSE: GEORGE CATLETT MARSHALL

Refer to the biographical sketch of George C. Marshall under Secretary of State, page 626.

## SECRETARY OF DEFENSE

## ROBERT ABERCROMBIE LOVETT

Robert A. Lovett, Secretary of Defense in the Cabinet
of President Harry S. Truman, was born on September 14,
1895 in Huntsville, Texas, the son of Robert Scott Lovett,
a lawyer and railroad executive, and Lavinia Chilton
(Abercrombie) Lovett.  He received his preparatory education at the Hamilton Military Institute in New York
State and the Hill School in Pottstown, Pennsylvania.
Robert then attended Yale University.

Robert Lovett joined the Aerial Coast Patrol of the
Naval Reserve Group as a pilot.  When the United States
entered the First World War he became an ensign in the
Naval Air Service.  He was sent overseas and established
a United States Naval Air Service Transition Flying
School.  He was assigned to the Royal Navy Air Service
from November 1917 to January 1918, flying over the North
Sea in the submarine patrol.  He also bombed German submarine bases.  He was next assigned to command United
States Naval Squadron No. 1.  He was discharged in 1918
having been promoted to lieutenant.

Robert A. Lovett returned to the United States in January 1919 and completed his studies at Yale, graduating
with the Bachelor of Arts degree in the summer of 1919.
He married Adele Quarterly Brown on April 19, 1919.  They
had two children: Evelyn and Robert Scott.  Robert A.
Lovett then attended Harvard University Law School during
the academic year 1919-1920 and the Harvard Graduate
School of Business Administration from 1920 to 1921. He
then went to New York in 1921 to become a clerk in the
National Bank of Commerce.  He next joined the private
banking and investment firm Brown Brothers and Company
as a manager of the foreign department in 1923.  He became a partner in 1926.  In the same year he was elected
a director and member of the executive committee of the
Union Pacific Railroad Company.  He also served as a
director of various other railroads.

Robert A. Lovett was instrumental in effecting the
merger of Harriman and Company with Brown Brothers as
Brown Brothers Harriman and Company in 1931.  Lovett's
business acumen was recognized through his appointments
as director of the New York Trust Company, the Provident
Fire Insurance Company, the United States Guarantee Company, and the Columbia Broadcasting Company.

Lovett left Brown Brothers Harriman and Company in December 1940 to accept an appointment as special assistant
to the Secretary of War.  He was named assistant Secretary of War for air on April 10, 1941, assuming responsibility for increasing heavy bomber production from three
to four per month to 500.  President Harry S. Truman awar-

ded Lovett the Distinguished Service Medal for his service during the war on September 18, 1945.  Robert resigned from federal government service in December 1945
to return to Brown Brothers Harriman and Company.
President Harry S. Truman appointed Lovett Undersecretary
of Defense on July 1, 1947.  He became deputy Secretary
under General George C. Marshall in October 1950.

President Harry S. Truman appointed Robert A. Lovett
Secretary of Defense on September 14, 1951 to succeed
General Marshall.  Robert assumed his office on September
17, 1951.  As part of his duties he was chairman of the
Armed Forces Policy Council as well as a member of the
National Security Council, the Defense Mobilization Board
and the National Securities Board.  Lovett served in this
office until the end of the Truman Administration on January 20, 1953.

After leaving public office Robert A. Lovett returned
to his business interests.  He served as a consultant to
President John F. Kennedy from 1961 to 1963.  Lovett is
now living in retirement at his estate in Locust Valley,
Long Island, New York.

Bibliography:
Bernstein, Barton J. and Matusow, Allen F.  Truman Ad-
ministration: A Documentary History.  New York: Harper
and Row, 1966.
Furer, Howard B., ed. Harry S. Truman, 1884-/1972/
Dobbs Ferry, N.Y.: Oceana Publications, Inc., 1970.
Philips, Cabell.  The Truman Presidency.  The History
of a Triumphant Succession.  New York: Macmillan, 1966.
Steinberg, Alfred.  The Man from Missouri: The Life and
Times of Harry S. Truman.  New          Putnam, 1962.

## ATTORNEY GENERAL: FRANCIS BEVERLY BIDDLE

Refer to the biographical sketch of Francis B. Biddle
under Sttorney General in the Administration of Franklin
D. Roosevelt, page 596.

## ATTORNEY GENERAL: THOMAS CAMPBELL CLARK

Thomas C. Clark, Attorney General in the Cabinet of
President Harry S. Truman, was born on September 23, 1899
in Dallas, Texas, the son of William Henry Clark, a
lawyer, Texas public servant and member of the Democratic
Party, and Virginia Maxey (Falls) Clark.  After receiving
his basic education in the Dallas public schools and was
graduated from Bryan High School, where he edited the
school newspaper, in 1917, Thomas attended Virginia Military Institute from 1917 to 1918.  He joined a Texas National Guard regiment in 1918.  It was federalized as the
153rd Infantry.  Clark left the army at the end of the

---

war as a top sergent.

Thomas C. Clark then went to the University of Texas in January 1919 and received the Bachelor of Arts degree in 1921. He studied law and was graduated with the LL.B. degree in 1922. Admitted to the Texas bar in the same year he joined his father and brother in the law firm of Clark and Clark in Dallas. Thomas married Mary Jane Ramsey on November 8, 1924. They had three children: William Ramsey (Attorney General in the Cabinet of President Lyndon B. Johnson), Mildred, and Thomas Campbell.

Clark was appointed to head the civil division in the Dallas district attorney's office in 1927 and remained in that post until 1932. He formed a law partnership with the District Attorney William McGraw in 1932. Clark campaigned successfully for McGraw for the post of Texas attorney general in 1934 and then continued his practice alone from 1935 to 1937. He was also retained by the Texas Petroleum Council in January 1935.

In 1937 Thomas Clark was named special attorney for the Bureau of War Risk Litigation in the Department of Justice. He next became special assistant to the Attorney General, Homer S. Cummings, in 1938. Clark headed the Pacific coast office of the Anti-Trust Division from 1940 to 1942. In the latter year he served under Attorney General Francis Biddle as coordinator of enemy alien control and chief of the civilian staff which aided the army in removing people of Japanese origin from the West coast region.

Thomas C. Clark was appointed assistant Attorney General in charge of the Anti-Trust Division in March 1943. In August of the same year he was given charge of the criminal division. Clark was president of the Federal Bar Association for one term from 1944 to 1945. Bethany and Marshall Colleges awarded him the honorary LL.D. degree in 1945. President Harry S. Truman appointed Thomas C. Clark Attorney General to succeed Francis Biddle on June 15, 1945. Clark assumed his office on July 1, 1945. He launched prosecutions against black market operators. Among his other activities while in office Clark supervised antitrust cases against five major motion picture studios.

Thomas C. Clark also directed the prosecution of Judith Coplon, employed by the Justice Department; Alger Hiss, former State Department official; and Eugene Dennis, a Communist leader. He was given citations for his work against Communist infiltrators by such organizations as the Army and Navy Union and the American Legion. Clark also worked to reorganize the Justice Department into seven divisions and also contributed to the work of demobilization and reconversion to peace time industry.

President Truman named Thomas C. Clark an associate justice of the Supreme Court in 1949. He took the oath of office on August 24, 1949, remaining on the High Court

until 1967.  Clark was president of the Institute
Judicial Administration from 1966 to 1967.  He also
served as chairman of the National Collegiate State
Trial Judges association.  He lives in retirement.

Bibliography:
  Bernstein, Barton J. and Matusow, Allen F.  Truman
Administration: A Documentary History.  New York: Har-
per and Row, 1966.
  Furer, Howard B., ed.  Harry S. Truman, 1884-/1972/
Dobbs Ferry, N.Y.: Oceana Publications, Inc., 1970.
  Philips, Cabell.  The Truman Presidency.  The History
of a Triumphant Succession.  New York: Macmillan, 1966.
  Schubert, Glendon A.  The Judicial Mind: Attitudes and
Ideologies of the Supreme Court Justices, 1946-1963.
Evanston, Ill.: Northwestern University Press, 1965.
  Steinberg, Alfred.  The Man from Missouri: The Life and
Times of Harry S. Truman.  New York: Putnam, 1962.

## ATTORNEY GENERAL: JAMES HOWARD MCGRATH

J. Howard McGrath, Attorney General in the Cabinet of
President Harry S. Truman, was born on November 28,
1903 in Woonsocket, Rhode Island, the son of James J.
and Ida E. (May) McGrath.  He received his basic education at the Woonsocket parochial school and then attended LaSalle Academy in Providence, Rhode Island from
which he was graduated in 1922.  He studied at Providence
College, graduating with the Ph.B. and then went to Boston
University to study law.  He was graduated from the law
school in 1929.  He had joined the Young Men's Democratic League and was its president from 1924 to 1938.
J. Howard McGrath was admitted to the bar in 1929 and
established his legal practice in Providence.  He worked
as an assistant to Rhode Island Senator Gerry.  He continued his work in politics and was a member and vice
chairman of the Democratic state committee of Rhode
Island.  J. Howard married Estelle A. Cardonette on November 28, 1929.  They had one son, David.  J. Howard
McGrath became city solicitor of Central Falls, Rhode
Island in 1930, continuing in that post until 1934.  He
was also chairman of the Democratic state committee of
Rhode Island during the same period.  He was chairman of
the Rhode Island delegation to the Democratic national
convention in 1932.  In the same year he became a member of Senator Green's law firm.
McGrath was appointed United States district attorney
for Rhode Island in 1934 and remained in that office until 1934.  He was again a delegate to the Democratic national convention at Philadelphia in 1936.  J. Howard
then became associated with his father's real estate and
insurance firm, J. J. McGrath and Sons.  He was elected
governor of Rhode Island in 1940 and was reelected in

1943 and 1944. He served until his resignation in October 1945.

McGrath was a delegate to the Democratic national convention at Chicago in 1944 and was chairman of the committee on Permanent Organization. James was appointed United States solicitor general in October 1945 and served
until October 1946. He was the successful Democratic
candidate for United States Senator in 1946. He served
in the Senate from January 3, 1947 until he resigned on
August 23, 1949. He was also chairman of the Democratic
national committee from 1947 to 1949. McGrath wrote The
Power of the People and The Case for Truman in 1948.

President Harry S. Truman named J. Howard McGrath Attorney General on August 19, 1949 to succeed Tom C. Clark.
McGrath assumed his office on August 24 and continued in
office until his resignation on April 3, 1952. He continued to maintain and foster the high standards of the
office. McGrath was an unsuccessful candidate for the
Democratic nomination for United States Senator from
Rhode Island. J. Howard McGrath died on November 11,
1966.

Bibliography:
Bernstein, Barton J. and Matusow, Allen F. Truman
Administration: A Documentary History. New York: Har-
per and Row, 1966.
Furer, Howard B., ed. Harry S. Truman, 1884-/1972/
Dobbs Ferry, N.Y.: Oceana Publications, Inc., 1970.
Philips, Cabell. The Truman Presidency. The History
of a Triumphant Succession. New York: Macmillan, 1966.
Steinberg, Alfred. The Man from Missouri: The Life and
Times of Harry S. Truman. New York: Putnam, 1962.

### ATTORNEY GENERAL: JAMES PATRICK MCGRANERY

James P. McGranery, Attorney General in the Cabinet of
President Harry S. Truman, was born on July 8, 1895 in
Philadelphia, Pennsylvania, the son of Patrick and Brid-
get (Gallagher) McGranery. He received his basic education in the parochial schools of Philadelphia and Maher
Preparatory School. James enlisted in the Air Force
during the First World War and was an observation pilot
in the 111th Infantry Division. After the war James
went to Temple University where he eventually received
the LL.B. degree in 1928. He was admitted to the Pennsylvania bar in the same year and practice law in Philadelphia in the firm of Masterson and McGranery.

James P. McGranery was retained to represent the Philadelphia police and firmen's union. He also worked for
a short time for the Curtis Publishing Company. James
also became interested in politics and joined the Democratic Party. He was a member of the Pennsylvania state
committee from 1928 to 1932. He ran unsuccessfully for

district attorney of Philadelphia in 1931.  He also was
defeated in his bid for a Congressional seat in 1934.
McGranery served as chairman of the Philadelphia Registration Commission in 1935.

James P. McGranery was elected as a Democrat to the
United States House of Representatives in 1936.  He
served in the Seventy-fifth to the Seventy-eighth Congresses from January 3, 1937 until his resignation on
November 17, 1943.  He was a member of the ways and
means, banking and currency, and interstate and foreign
commerce committees.

President Franklin D. Roosevelt appointed James P.
McGranery assistant to the Attorney General (Francis
Biddle) in November 1943.  James was responsible for the
over-all administration of the Federal Bureau of Investigation, the Bureau of Immigration and Naturalization,
the Federal Bureau of Prisons, as well as the marshals
in the nation and territories.  He was also charged with
reviewing the findings of the boards of appeals under
the Selective Service Act.  McGranery resigned on October 9, 1946 to be sworn in as a judge of the United
States district court for Eastern Pennsylvania.  He
served until May 26, 1952.  He was awarded the honorary
LL.D. degree by Villanova College in 1949 and by National
University in 1952.

President Harry S. Truman named James P. McGranery
Attorney General on May 21, 1952 to succeed J. Howard
McGrath   McGranery assumed his office on May 27, 1952
in which post he remained until the end of the Truman
administration on January 20, 1953.  After retiring from
public office he returned to his law practice.  He was
interested in education and was a trustee of Immaculata
College in Pennsylvania as well as a member of the advisory council of Villanova College and a member of the
advisory board of Temple University Law School.  He was
also a member of the American Catholic Historical Society, the American Judicature Society, the American Legion
as well as the Philopatrian Literary Institute of Philadelphia.  James P. McGranery died on December 23, 1962.

Bibliography:
Bernstein, Barton J. and Matusow, Allen F.  Truman Ad-
ministration:  A Documentary History.  New York: Harper
and Row, 1966.
Furer, Howard B., ed.  Harry S. Truman, 1884-/1972/
Dobbs Ferry, N.Y.: Oceana Publications, Inc., 1970.
Philips, Cabell.  The Truman Presidency.  The History
of a Triumphant Succession.  New York: Macmillan, 1966.
Steinberg, Alfred.  The Man from Missouri: The Life
and Times of Harry S. Truman.  New York: Putnam, 1962.

## POSTMASTER GENERAL: FRANK COMERFORD WALKER

Refer to the biographical sketch of Frank C. Walker under Postmaster General in the Administration of Franklin D. Roosevelt, page 600.

## POSTMASTER GENERAL: ROBERT EMMET HANNEGAN

Robert E. Hannegan, Postmaster General in the Cabinet of President Harry S. Truman, was born on June 30, 1903 in St. Louis, Missouri, the son of John Patrick Hannegan, a police captain, and Anna (Holden) Hannegan. After receiving his basic education in the St. Louis public schools and attending Keatman High School, Robert studied at St. Louis University from 1921 to 1925, receiving the LL.B. degree in 1925. He was admitted to the bar in the same year and established his legal practice in St. Louis. Robert married Irma Protzmann on November 14, 1929. They had four children: Patricia, Robert Emmet, William Protzmann, and Sally Ann.

Robert E. Hannegan became active in the Democratic Party and was elected to the St. Louis Democratic committee from the 21st ward in 1933. He was able to swing his traditionally Republican ward to the Democratic forces in the election of the same year and became chairman of the committee in 1934. He was associated in his leadership of the St. Louis Democratic Party with Mayor Bernard F. Dickman during the next five years. After losing to Harry S. Truman in the Senatorial primary of 1934 Hannegan actively supported Truman in the campaign. Robert was the St. Louis representative to the Missouri General Assembly in 1935 and was again chairman of the St. Louis Democratic committee in 1936.

Hannegan successfully supported Senator Harry S. Truman's reelection campaign in 1940. The Democratic gubernatorial nominee was defeated in 1940, and the election was unsuccessfully fought in the Missouri assembly and supreme court. As a result of the unfavorable publicity, Mayor Dickman was defeated in his reelection bid in 1941. President Franklin D. Roosevelt appointed Robert E. Hannegan collector of internal revenue for the eastern district of Missouri in June 1942. He continued in this pots, greatly increasing the efficiency of collection until he was named commissioner of internal revenue in October 1943.

Robert E. Hannegan resigned his last post in January 1944 when he was elected chairman of the Democratic national committee, assuming the post on January 22. He was effective in strengthening the party which had declined after the resignation of James A. Farley in 1940. Hannegan helped to win the vice presidential nomination for Senator Harry S. Truman and to convince him to accept it.

President Harry S. Truman appointed Robert E. Hannegan
Postmaster General on May 8, 1945 after the resignation
of Frank C. Walker.  Robert assumed his office on July
1, 1945.  He supported President Truman in his Fair Deal
policies and urged that the United States share its knowledge of atomic energy with Great Britain and the Soviet
Union.  Hannegan resigned from his Cabinet post because
of ill health on December 15, 1947.  He then bought a
major interest in the St. Louis Cardinals baseball team,
selling it shortly before his death.  Robert E. Hannegan
died on October 6, 1949 in St. Louis.

Bibliography:
  Bernstein, Barton J. and Matusow, Allen F.  Truman
Administration: A Documentary History.  New York: Har-
per and Row, 1966.
  Furer, Howard B., ed.  Harry S. Truman, 1884-/19727
Dobbs Ferry, N.Y.: Oceana Publications, Inc., 1970.
  Helm, William P.  Harry Truman: A Political Biography.
New York: Duell, Sloan and Oearce, 1947.
  Philips, Cabell.  The Truman Presidency.  The History
of a Triumphant Succession.  New York: Macmillan, 1966.
  Steinberg, Alfred.  The Man from Missouri: The Life
and Times of Harry S. Truman.  New York: Putnam, 1962.
  Truman, Harry S.  Memoirs.  2 vols.  Garden City, N.Y.:
Doubleday, 1955.

## POSTMASTER GENERAL: JESSE MONROE DONALDSON

Jesse M. Donaldson, Postmaster General in the Cabinet
of President Harry S. Truman, was born on August 17, 1885
on a farm near Shelbyville, Illinois, the son of Moses
Martin Donaldson, a merchant and postmaster of Hanson,
Illinois, and Amanda Saletha (Little) Donaldson.  After
receiving his basic education in the Oconee, Illinois
public schools Jesse attended Shelbyville Normal School.
Donaldson then went to Teachers Normal College and
Sparks Business College in Shelbyville.  He taught school
in Shelby, Montgomery and Christian Counties from 1903
to 1908, aiding his father as a clerk in the post office
during his summer vacations.
Donaldson was appointed one of the first three letter-
carriers in Shelbyville on May 15, 1908 and gave up his
teaching career.  He continued in the postal service
until 1910 when he was appointed a clerk in the War Department.  He returned to the Post Office as a clerk and
supervisor in Muskogee, Oklahoma on July 1, 1911, continuing there for several years.  Jesse married Nell
Graybill on August 14, 1911.  They had three children:
Helen La Verne, Jesse Monroe and Doris Dee.
Jesse M. Donaldson was next appointed a postal inspector in the Kansas City, Missouri division on May 11,
1915, remaining there until 1932.  He was next made

postal inspector in charge of the Chattanooga, Tennessee division on August 1, 1932. Jesse was soon transferred to Washington, D.C. as a deputy second assistant postmaster general on June 12, 1933. He was promoted to first assistant postmaster general on April 11, 1936.

Jesse Donaldson continued to rise in the postal service when he was appointed chief post office inspector on March 1, 1945. He then became first assistant postmaster general on July 5, 1946. In this post he became chief legislative spokesman for the department before Congress.

President Harry S. Truman named Jesse M. Donaldson Postmaster General in November 1947 to succeed Robert E, Hannegan. He assumed his office on December 16, 1947. Jesse had the honor of becoming the first letter-carrier in history to rise to head the Post Office. Jesse worked to improve the efficiency of the department. He created the position of deputy postmaster general, appointed a seven-person advisory board from various areas of business, and established a research and development section. He also created a new money order system and set up new accounting procedures.

Among his other activities in the Post Office Department Donaldson established a highway post office service and expanded railway postal transportation as well as the development of air parcel post to 82 countries. Helicopter service was instituted in Los Angeles and Chicago. He also reduced home mail deliveries from two to one a day for greater economies. He resigned from the Cabinet at the end of the Truman Administration on January 20, 1953 and retired. Jesse M. Donaldson died in Kansas City, Missouri on March 25, 1970.

Bibliography:
    Bernstein, Barton J. and Matusow, Allen F. Truman Administration: A Documentary History. New York: Harper and Row, 1966.
    Daniels, Jonathan. The Man of Independence. Philadelphia: Lippincott, 1950.
    Furer, Howard B., ed. Harry S. Truman, 1884-/1972/ Dobbs Ferry, N.Y.: Oceana Publications, Inc., 1970.
    Philips, Cabell. The Truman Presidency. The History of a Triumphant Succession. New York: Macmillan, 1966.
    Steinberg, Alfred. The Man from Missouri: The Life and Times of Harry S. Truman. New York: Putnam, 1962.

SECRETARY OF THE NAVY: JAMES VINCENT FORRESTAL

Refer to the biographical sketch of James V. Forrestal under Secretary of the Navy in the Administration of Franklin D. Roosevelt, page 607.

SECRETARY OF THE INTERIOR: HAROLD LE CLAIR ICKES

Refer to the biographical sketch of Harold L. Ickes
under Secretary of the Interior in the Administration
of Franklin D. Roosevelt, page 609.

SECRETARY OF THE INTERIOR: JULIUS ALBERT KRUG

Julius A. Krug, Secretary of the Interior in the Cabinet of President Harry S. Truman, was born on November
23, 1907 in Madison, Wisconsin, the son of Julius John
Krug, a policeman, detective, sheriff and deputy state
fire marshal, and Emma (Korfmacher) Krug.  After receiving his basic education in the public schools of Madison, Julius attended the University of Wisconsin from
1925 to 1930, graduating with the Bachelor of Arts degree in 1929 and the Master of Arts degree in 1930 in
the field of utilities management and economics.  He married Margaret Catherine Dean while he was still in College on March 22, 1926.  They had two children: Marilyn
Ann and James Allan Krug.
     Julius A. Krug began to work as a business research
analyst for the Wisconsin Telephone Company in 1930.
He was next appointed chief of the depreciation section
of the Wisconsin Public Utilities Commission in 1932.
He was placed on assignment with the Federal Communications Commission in 1935 to aid it in investigating the
American Telephone and Telegraph Company.  He returned
to Wisconsin after a dispute over FCC policies.  In 1937
Julius A. Krug went to Kentucky to settle a utility rate
dispute, being appointed technical director of the Kentucky Public Service Commission.
     Julius Krug was appointed chief power engineer for the
Tennessee Valley Authority in December 1937.  He was
next appointed chief of the power branch of the office
of production management in June 1941.  When his office
was transferred to the Office of War Utilities he took
on additional duties.  Krug became vice chairman in
charge of materials distribution and chairman of the
War Production Board requirements committee, holding all
posts after March 3, 1943.  He was also program chief
of the War Production Board and head of the Office of
War Utilities.  He helped to provide all the necessary
power by supervision of the construction of new facilities and forming power pools.
     Julius Krug resigned his posts in April 1944 and ac-
cepted a commission as lieutenant commander in the Navy.
He was stationed in England and then at the advance headquarters in Normandy.  He was recalled to become acting
head of the War Production Board on August 24, 1944 when
the former chairman Donald M. Nelson was sent to China
to advise the government on industrial problems.  Julius
was appoined chairman of the War Production Board on

September 30, 1944. He supervised many aspects of industry to help bring the war to a successful conclusion, assigning priorities to plants in regard to materials and supervising production schedules. The War Production Board was closed on November 3, 1945. After leaving office, Krug became a consulting engineer.

President Harry S. Truman named Julius A. Krug Secretary of the Interior on March 6, 1946. He assumed his office on March 18. While in office he helped to negotiate contracts in the railroad and coal industries where strikes were taking place. Krug resigned from his post on November 30, 1949. Julius then became president of the Volunteer Asphalt Company in Brookside Mills. Julius A. Krug died on March 26, 1970 in Knoxville, Tennessee.

Bibliography:
    Bernstein, Barton J. and Matusow, Allen F.  Truman Administration: A Documentary History. New York: Harper and Row, 1966.
    Daniels, Jonathan. The Man of Independence. Philadelphia: Lippincott, 1950.
    Furer, Howard B., ed. Harry S. Truman, 1884-/1972/ Dobbs Ferry, N.Y.: Oceana Publications, Inc., 1970.
    Philips, Cabell. The Truman Presidency. The History of a Triumphant Succession. New York: Macmillan, 1966.
    Steinberg, Alfred. The Man from Missouri: The Life and Times of Harry S. Truman. New York: Putnam, 1962.
    Truman, Harry S.  Memoirs. 2 vols. Garden City, N.Y.: Doubleday, 1955.

## SECRETARY OF THE INTERIOR: OSCAR LITTLETON CHAPMAN

Oscar L. Chapman, Secretary of the Interior in the Cabinet of President Harry S. Truman, was born on October 22, 1896 in Omega, Virginia, the son of James Jackson Chapman, a farmer, and Rosa Archer (Blant) Chapman. After receiving his preparatory education Oscar attended Randolph Macon Academy in Bedford, Virginia. He joined the Navy during the First World War and was a pharmacist's mate. He served on hospital ships, crossing the Atlantic eighteen times in a three year period. At the end of the war Chapman, who was suffering from an illness he contracted while on duty, was sent to the Fort Lyon Hospital in Denver, Colorado. Oscar married Olga Pauline Edholm on December 21, 1920.

Oscar Chapman met Judge Robert B. Lindsey of the Juvenile Court of Denver. He appointed Oscar an assistant and later chief probation officer of the court in whicch post he served from 1921 to 1929. During this period Oscar studied at the University of Denver from 1922 to 1924 and the University of New Mexico from 1927 to 1928. He attended the Westminster Law School in Denver, Colorado, receiving the LL.B. degree in 1929. He was admitted to the Colorado bar in the same year. He established a law practice in Denver with Edward P. Costigan. He served as chairman for the Department of Colorado of the American Legion's state child committee. He was president of the state board of control of the Colorado Boy's Industrial School from 1930 to 1936. He was also president of the Council of Religious Education for Colorado. Oscar's wife died in 1930.

President Franklin D. Roosevelt appointed Oscar Chapman assistant Secretary of the Interior in May 1933. He remained in this post until 1946. Oscar also served as executive secretary to the Public Works Board and was a member of the Committee on Peace Relations of the District of Columbia in 1933. He also served as a member of the advisory board of the National Training School for Boys and headed the government division drives for the American Red Cross, the Community Fund and the War Fund.

In 1935 President Roosevelt appointed Chapman to the interdepartmental committee to coordinate health and welfare services of the government. He was next named a member of the committee on vocational education in 1936. Chapman was a delegate to the Inter-American Indian Congress in Mexico in 1940. Colorado State College of Education awarded Chapman the honorary LL.D. degree in 1940. Oscar married Ann Kendrick on February 24, 1940. They had one son, James Raleigh. Chapman served on the interdepartmental committee to review subversive activity charges against federal employees during 1941 and 1942. He was chairman of the personnel advisory board of the Office of the Provost Marshal General, United States Army from January to October 1943.

President Harry S. Truman appointed Oscar Chapman Undersecretary of the Interior in March 1946. He was vice chairman of the Inter-American Conference on Conservation of Renewable Natural Resources at Denver, Colorado in 1948. He was also appointed in the same year a member of the President's Advisory Committee on Management Improvement in Government. He travelled throughout the nation in 1948 campaigning for President Harry S. Truman and making advance arrangements for the President's speaking tour. Chapman was deputy chairman of the United States delegation to the United Nations Scientific Conference on Conservation and Utilization of Resources in 1949. Howard University awarded him the honorary LL.D. degree in 1949.

Oscar L. Chapman served as Secretary of the Interior ad interim from December 1, 1949 to January 19, 1950. President Harry S. Truman appointed Chapman Secretary of the Interior to succeed Julius A. Krug on January 19, 1950. He was a member of the National Issues Committee in 1953. Chapman retired from office at the end of the

Truman Administration on January 20, 1953. He continued his activities within the Democratic Party and
was a campaign aid to Lyndon B. Johnson in his bid for
the presidential nomination in 1960.

Bibliography:
  Bernstein, Barton J. and Matusow, Allen F. Truman
Administration: A Documentary History. New York: Har-
per and Row, 1966.
  Daniels, Jonathan. The Man of Independence. Phila-
delphia: Lippincott, 1950.
  Furer, Howard B., ed. Harry S. Truman, 1884-/1972/
Dobbs Ferry, N.Y.: Oceana Publications, Inc., 1970.
  Phillips, Cabell. The Truman Presidency. The History
of a Triumphant Succession. New York: Macmillan, 1966.
  Steinberg, Alfred. The Man from Missouri: The Life
and Times of Harry S. Truman. New York: Putnam, 1962.
  Truman, Harry S. Memoirs. 2 vols. Garden City, N.Y.:
Doubleday, 1955.

SECRETARY OF AGRICULTURE: CLAUDE RAYMOND WICKARD

Refer to the biographical sketch of Claude R. Wickard
under Secretary of Agriculture in the Administration of
Franklin D. Roosevelt, page 611.

SECRETARY OF AGRICULTURE: CLINTON PRESBA ANDERSON

Clinton P. Anderson, Secretary of Agriculture in the
Cabinet of President Harry S. Truman, was born on October 28, 1895 in Centerville, South Dakota, the son of
Andrew Jay and Hattie Belle (Presba) Anderson. After
receiving his basic education in the South Dakota
schools, Anderson attended Wesleyan University in Mitchell, South Dakota from 1913 to 1915 and then the University of Michigan at Ann Arbor from 1915 to 1916. He
became ill and moved to Albuquerque, New Mexico in 1917
and began working as a reporter and newspaper editor in
1918. He worked for the Albuquerque Journal during
1921 and 1922. Clinton married Henrietta McCartney on
June 22, 1921. They had two children: Sherburne Presba
and Nancy.
  In 1922 Anderson became manager of the insurance department of the New Mexico Loan and Mortgage Company in
Albuquerque. In 1924 he opened his own agency. He became active in politics and was appointed state treasurer on New Mexico in 1933, serving through 1934. He was
president of Rotary International in 1932 and 1933. He
was next appointed administrator of the New Mexico Relief Administration in 1935 and was also a field representative of the Federal Emergency Relief Administration
in 1935 and 1936. Clinton then became chairman and executive director of the Unemployment Compensation Commis-

sion of New Mexico, serving until 1938.

Clinton P. Anderson formed and was president of the
Mountain States Mutual Casualty Company in 1937.  During
1939 and 1940 he was managing director of the United
States Coronado Exposition Commission.  He was elected
as a Democrat to the United States House of Representatives in 1940.  He served in the Seventy-seventh, Seventy-eighth and Seventy-ninth Congresses from January 3,
1941 until his resignation on June 30, 1945.  He was
chairman of the committee investigating campaign expenditures for 1944.  In the Seventy-eighth Congress he was
chairman of a special committee appointed to investigate
food shortages.  Among the other committees on which he
served while in the House were census, Indian affairs,
irrigation and reclamation, and public lands and appropriations.

President Harry S. Truman named Clinton P. Anderson
Secretary of Agriculture on June 2, 1945.  He assumed
his office on June 30, 1945.  He was given sole control
of food production and marketing.  He encouraged the continued high production of food to meet the needs of the
world in the immediate period after the war.  In response
to President Truman's Nine Point Famine Relief Program
Anderson issued regulations for the conservation of
wheat, diminishing the consumption of grains and other
foods needed for export.  The Office of Emergency Food
Program was created on March 19, 1946 to coordinate all
parts of the program.  Through his work greater amounts
of food was produced.  He called for cultivation of additional farm land in 1947, further increasing the amount
of food produce.

Clinton P. Anderson was awarded the honorary LL.D. degree from the University of Michigan and St. Louis University as well as the honorary Agr. D. degree from
the New Mexico College of Agriculture and Mechanical
Arts in 1946.  Anderson resigned from the Department of
Agriculture on May 10, 1948 to successfully enter the
New Mexico Democratic primary for the Senate.  He was
elected to the Senate in November 1948 and was reelected
in 1954, 1960 and 1966.  He served from January 3, 1949
to January 2, 1973.  He served on various committees
including the committee on agriculture and forestry and
on interior and insular affairs.  He was also chairman
of the Joint Committee on Atomic Energy.

Bibliography:
Bernstein, Barton J. and Matusow, Allen F.  Truman
Administration: A Documentary History.  New York: Har-
per and Row, 1966.
Daniels, Jonathan.  The Man of Independence.  Phila-
delphia: Lippincott, 1950.
Furer, Howard B., ed.  Harry S. Truman, 1884-/1972/
Dobbs Ferry, N.Y.: Oceana Publications, Inc., 1970.

Phillips, Cabell. The Truman Presidency. The History of a Triumphant Succession. New York: Macmillan, 1966.
    Steinberg, Alfred. The Man from Missouri: The Life and Times of Harry S. Truman. New York: Putnam, 1962.
    Truman, Harry S. Memoirs. 2 vols. Garden City, N.Y.: Doubleday, 1955.

SECRETARY OF AGRICULTURE: CHARLES FRANKLIN BRANNAN

Charles F. Brannan, Secretary of Agriculture in the Cabinet of President Harry S. Truman, was born on August 23, 1903 in Denver, Colorado, the son of John Brannan, an electrical engineer, and Ella Louise (Street) Brannan. After receiving his basic education in the public schools, Charles was graduated from West High School in 1921. He then attended Regis College in Denver and the University of Denver, receiving his LL.B. degree from the latter in 1929. He was admitted to the bar in the same year and established his legal practice in Denver, continuing there until 1935. Charles married Eda V. Seltzer on June 29, 1932. They had no children.

In 1935 Charles F. Brannan was appointed assistant regional attorney of the Resettlement Administration of the United States Department of Agriculture in Denver. He was next named regional attorney in the department's office of solicitor in Denver in 1937. In 1940 Charles became half owner in a cattle ranch which he owned until 1948. He continued working for the government, being named regional director for Colorado, Wyoming and Montana of the Farm Security Administration which was the successor to the Resettlement Administration. He remained in this post until 1944.

Charles F. Brannan was appointed assistant Secretary of Agriculture in 1944 and served under Claude R. Wickard and Clinton P. Anderson. Charles was given responsibility for the long-term agricultural policy of the department and was vice-chairman of the policy and program committee which presented recommendations for Congressional action. In addition Brannan served as vice-chairman of the board of directors of the Community Credit Corporation and had the responsibility for directing water facilities and flood control as well as grazing and timberland management in the public land. In 1945 Brannan was the agricultural adviser to the American delegation at the United Nations Conference in San Francisco. He was also an adviser to the United Nations Economic and Social Council.

President Harry S. Truman named Charles F. Brannan Secretary of Agriculture on May 29, 1948 to succeed Clinton P. Anderson. Brannan assumed his office on June 2. Charles developed several recommendations for the agricultural price support program which became known as the Brannan plan. His intention was to change

the basis of the old support program from the old parity
idea to a formula for sustaining total farm income
perishable produce would be permitted to reach their own
price level, and the farmer would be paid the difference
between the average market level and the fair price support.  He was able to convince Congress to ratify the
International Wheat Agreement in 1950 which allocated
wheat supplies and production and determined world prices.  Brannan was chairman of the United States delegation to the Inter-American Conference on Agriculture at
Montevideo, Uruguay in December 1950.

Charles Brannan retired from office at the end of the
Truman Administration on January 20, 1953.  He had been
awarded the honorary LL.D. degree by the University of
Denver in 1948.  Charles returned to Denver to resume
his legal practice in 1953.  He continued his interest
in agriculture as a member of the Soil Conservation Society and as general counsel of the National Farmers
Union in 1953.  Among his other activities he is president of the University of Denver Alumni Association and
is a member of the Colorado Society.

Bibliography:
Bernstein, Barton J. and Matusow, Allen F.  Truman
Administration: A Documentary History.  New York: Har-
per and Row, 1966.
Daniels, Jonathan.  The Man of Independence.  Phila-
delphia: Lippincott, 1950.
Furer, Howard B., ed.  Harry S. Truman, 1884-/1972/
Dobbs Ferry, N.Y.: Oceana Publications, Inc., 1970.
Phillips, Cabell.  The Truman Presidency.  The History
of a Triumphant Succession.  New York: Macmillan, 1966.
Steinberg, Alfred.  The Man from Missouri: The Life
and Times of Harry S. Truman.  New York: Putnam, 1962.

SECRETARY OF COMMERCE: HENRY AGARD WALLACE

Refer to the biographical sketch of Henry A. Wallace
under Vice President in the Administration of Franklin
D. Roosevelt, page 573.

SECRETARY OF COMMERCE: WILLIAM AVERELL HARRIMAN

William Averell Harriman, Secretary of Commerce in
the Cabinet of President Harry S. Truman, was born on
November 15, 1891 in New York, New York, the son of
Edward Henry Harriman, financier and railroad builder,
and Mary W. (Averell) Harriman, philanthropist.  After
receiving his preparatory education at the Groton School
in Massachusetts, William Averell Harriman attended Yale
University from which he was graduated with the Bachelor
of Arts degree in 1912.

During his summer vacations William Averell worked as

a clerk and section hand in the Union Pacific Railroad
yards in Omaha, Nebraska.  He went to work for the Union
Pacific after graduating from college, moving into various positions of responsibility in transportation and
finance.  He became director of purchases and supplies,
remaining in that position until he resigned in 1917.
William first became active in various public service
areas in 1913 when he became a member of the Palisades
Park Commission formed by New York and New Jersey.  William was a member of the New York state fair commission
from 1915 to 1917.  He became a director of the Illinois
Central Railroad Company in 1915.  William Averell
Harriman married Kitty Lanier Lawrence on September 21,
1915.  They had two children: Mary and Kathleen.

Harriman became interested in shipping during the First
World War.  He bought a shipyard in Chester, Pennsylvania
in 1917 and organized the Merchant Shipbuilding Corporation.  He was chairman of the board from 1918 to 1927.
In the meantime he developed his interest in finance,
establishing the private banking firm of W. A. Harriman
and Company, Inc. in 1920.  He was chairman of the board
from 1920 to 1930.  The firm merged with Brown Brothers
and Company in 1931 to form Brown Brothers, Harriman and
Company in which William Averell was a partner.  He divorced his wife Kitty early in 1930 and married Mary
(Norton) Whitney on February 21, 1930.  They had no children.

Harriman also became involved with railroads again in
1931.  In June of that year he was appointed chairman
of the executive committee of the Illinois Central Railroad Company, continuing in that post until 1942.  He
became chairman of the board of the Union Pacific Railway in July 1932.  William was instrumental in developing
streamlined train service and low-cost dining car service.  He also was involved in creation of the Sun Valley, Idaho mountain resort.

While continuing his active business career William
also contributed his time to public service.  He was
named chairman of the New York State committee of the
government's employment campaign in 1933 and also a member of the Business Advisory Council for the Department
of Commerce, eventually becoming chairman in 1937.  He
served until 1940.  Harriman was appointed special assistant administrator of the National Recovery Administration in March 1934.  Later in the same year he succeeded Hugh R. Johnson as the administrative officer of
the NRA.

President Franklin D. Roosevelt called Mr. Harriman
to Washington, D.C. in June 1940 at the beginning of
the defense effort.  Shortly after the creation of the
Office of Production Management in January 1941, William
was named chief of the raw materials division.  The
President then sent Harriman to London as a minister in

March 1941 to coordinate effectively as well as to organize the shipment of American goods to Great Britain
under the lend-lease program. He also served as representative of the war shipping administration, the war
production board, the munitions assignment board and the
combined food board. He also attended the Atlantic Conference between British Prime Minister Churchill and
President Roosevelt where the Atlantic Charter was
signed in 1941.

President Roosevelt sent William A. Harriman as an ambassador to Moscow in September 1941 to arrange for aid
to Russia. He also represented the President in Moscow
at a meeting with Prime Minister Churchill and Premier
Stalin in August 1942. President Roosevelt named Harriman Ambassador to Russia on October 1, 1943 in which post
he remained until February 1946. Secretary of State
James F. Byrnes awarded Harriman the Medal for Merit
after he returned from Russia. Harriman returned to the
business world as director of the Illinois Central Railroad in 1946. President Harry S. Truman named Harriman
Ambassador to Great Britain in March 1946 in which post
he continued until September 1946.

President Truman next appointed William Averell Harriman Secretary of Commerce ad interim on September 28,
1946 in which office he continued until January 27, 1947
when he was formally appointed to the post. He served
until May 5, 1948, having succeeded Henry A. Wallace.
While in office Harriman worked to strengthen and improve
the operations of the Business Advisory Board. He also
contributed to the negotiations for a treaty with Rumania. In 1948 he was named United States representative
in Europe under the Economic Cooperative Act of 1948.
He continued his governmental service as ambassador extraordinary and plenipotentiary from 1948 to 1950 and
was then a special assistant to President Truman during
1950 and 1951.

William Averell Harriman was next the American representative of the NATO committee to study the western defense plans in 1951. He was then named director of the
Mutual Security Agency in which office he served from
1951 to 1953. Harriman was elected governor of New York
in 1954. He served from 1955 until the end of 1958. He
was defeated in his reelection bid by the Republican candidate Nelson A. Rockefeller.

William Averell Harriman continued his governmental
service as ambassador-at-large under President John F.
Kennedy in 1961. He became assistant Secretary of State
for political affairs from 1963 to 1965, serving under
President Lyndon B. Johnson. President Johnson named
Harriman Vietnamese peace talks representative on March
31, 1968. He served until January 5, 1969. Harriman
has also been a member of the Democratic policy council
and drafted a resolution urging withdrawal from Vietnam.

Harriman continues an active life in retirement.

Bibliography:
  Bernstein, Barton J. and Matusow, Allen F.  Truman
Administration: A Documentary History.  New York: Har-
per and Row, 1966.
  Daniels, Jonathan.  The Man of Independence.  Phila-
delphia: Lippincott, 1950.
  Furer, Howard B., ed.  Harry S. Truman, 1884-/1972/
Dobbs Ferry, N.Y.: Oceana Publications, Inc., 1970.
  Heller, Deane and Heller, David.  Kennedy Cabinet.
New York, 1961.
  Phillips, Cabell.  The Truman Presidency.  The History
of a Triumphant Succession.  New York: Macmillan, 1966.
  Steinberg, Alfred.  The Man from Missouri: The Life
and Times of Harry S. Truman.  New York: Putnam, 1962.

## SECRETARY OF COMMERCE: CHARLES SAWYER

Charles Sawyer, Secretary of Commerce in the Cabinet
of President Harry S. Truman, was born on February 10,
1887 in Cincinnati, Ohio, the son of Edward Milton and
Caroline (Butler) Sawyer.  Charles received his basic
education in the Cincinnati public schools and then went
to Oberlin College from which he was graduated with the
Bachelor of Arts degree in 1908.  He then pursued the
study of law at the University of Cincinnati, receiving
the LL.B. degree in 1911.  He was admitted to the bar
in the same year and established his legal practice in
Cincinnati.  He was also elected to the City Council in
1911.  Charles soon entered Judge Albert C. Shattuck's
firm.  He continued his political activities, serving
as a delegate to the Democratic National Convention in
Baltimore in 1912 and was reelected to the Cincinnati
City Council in 1913.
  When the United States entered the First World      in
1917 Sawyer enlisted in the army as a private.  He
trained at Fort Benjamin Harrison at Indianapolis, Indiana and was commissioned a captain of infantry.
Charles married Margaret Sterett on July 15, 1918.  They
had five children: Anne Johnston, Charles, Jean Johnston,
John and Edward.  He was later promoted to major and
sailed for France in July 1918.  He was stationed at the
Army General Staff College at Longres, France and was
then assigned to the 89th Division and later served in
the army of occupation in Germany.
  After returning to the United States Charles Sawyer
again practiced law and continued his active interest
in politics.  He was a delegate to the Democratic National Convention at Chicago in 1932, writing the prohibition repeal proposal which was eventually included in
the party platform.  Sawyer was elected lieutenant governor of Ohio, serving during 1933 and 1934.  He atten-

ded the 1936 convention at Philadelphia where he was
elected a national committeeman from Ohio.  Charles
was the unsuccessful Democratic candidate for governor
of Ohio in 1938.  Charles married Elizabeth De Veyrac
on June 10, 1942.  They had no children.  President
Franklin D. Roosevelt appointed Sawyer Ambassador to
Belgium and Luxembourg in 1944.  He remained in the post
until 1946 and then returned to his legal practice.
     President Harry S. Truman appointed Charles Sawyer
Secretary of Commerce on May 6, 1948.  He remained in
the office until the end of the Truman Administration
on January 20, 1953.  He was awarded the Freedom Federation Award in 1949.  While in office Sawyer took over
the Bureau of Public Roads.which had been transferred
from the Federal Works Agency in August 1949.  He also
supervised the establishment of the Maritime Administration which was created in May 1950 to assume the duties
of the United States Maritime Commission.  Among the
various duties of the last agency which he supervised
were letting contracts for construction of ships, making
up the difference between American and foreign costs,
and operation of the National Defense Reserve Fleet.
     Sawyer took on the additional responsibility for crea-
tion of the National Production Authority in September
1950, which was provided for under the Defense Production
Act of 1950.  It was to supervise acquisition of material
and equipment necessary for rearmament.  Among his other
duties Sawyer was chairman of the Foreign Trade Zones
Board, governor of the Inland Waterways Corporation,
as well as a member of the following organizations:
the Defense Mobilization Board, the National Munitions
Control Board and the National Security Resources Board.
     After leaving office in 1953 Sawyer continued his bu-
siness and legal work, resuming his legal practice in
Glendale, Ohio.  He is involved in several radio stations: WING of Dayton, Ohio and WIZE of Springfield,
Ohio.  He also owns the Lancaster, Ohio Eagle Gazette.
He held a minority interest in the Cincinnati baseball
team of the National League.  In the field of public
service Sawyer has been a trustee of Oberlin College
and is a member of the National Council of the Boy
Scouts of America.  He is presently living in retirement
at his home in Glendale, Ohio

Bibliography:
  Bernstein. Barton J. and Matusow, Allen F.  Truman
Administration: A Documentary History.  New York: Har-
per and Row, 1966.
  Daniels, Jonathan.  The Man of Independence.  Phila-
delphia: Lippincott, 1950.
  Furer, Howard B., ed.  Harry S. Truman, 1884-/1972/
Dobbs Ferry, N.Y.: Oceana Publications, Inc., 1970.
  Hillman, William.  Mr. President.  New York: Farrar,

Straus and Young, 1952.
    Phillips, Cabell. The Truman Presidency. The History
of a Triumphant Succession. New York: Macmillan, 1966.
    Steinberg, Alfred. The Man from Missouri: The Life
and Times of Harry S. Truman. New York: Putnam, 1962.

### SECRETARY OF LABOR: FRANCES PERKINS

Refer to the biographical sketch of Frances Perkins
under Secretary of Labor in the Administration of Franklin D. Roosevelt, page 620.

### SECRETARY OF LABOR: LEWIS BAXTER SCHWELLENBACH

Lewis B. Schwellenbach, Secretary of Labor in the Cabinet of President Harry S. Truman, was born on September
20, 1894 in Superior, Wisconsin, the son of Francis William and Martha (Baxter) Schwellenbach. Lewis moved to
Spokane, Washington with his parents in 1902. He studied
in the public schools of Spokane and then attended the
University of Washington at Seattle, graduating with the
LL.B. degree in 1917. He was also an assistant instructor at the University of Washington during 1916 and 1917.
    Lewis B. Schwellenbach served as a private during
World War I in the First Regiment, 12th Infantry and was
promoted to the rank of corporal. He was discharged on
February 2, 1919 and was admitted to the bar in the same
year. He established his legal practice in Seattle with
the firm of Roberts and Skevel. He then practiced law
alone beginning in 1921 and continued until 1924. He
was state commander of the American Legion in 1922.
    Schwellenbach early became interested in politics and
joined the Democratic Party. He was chairman of the
Washington Democratic convention in 1924. The following
year he joined the law firm of Schwellenbach, Merrick
and MacFarlane. He was chairman of the King County
Democratic committee from 1928 to 1930. In 1931 he again
practiced law alone. Lewis ran unsuccessfully for the
Democratic nomination for governor of Washington in 1932.
He was president of the board of regents of the University of Washington during 1933 and 1934.
    In 1934 Schwellenbach was elected to the United States
Senate. He assumed his seat on January 3, 1935 and continued until his resignation on December 6, 1940. Lewis
was a member of the agriculture and forestry, claims,
foreign relations, and immigration and pensions committees. In addition he served as chairman of the special
committee on conservation and utilization of aquatic
life and a member of the special committee investigating lobbying activities. Lewis married Anne Duffy on
December 30, 1935. They had no children.
    During this period Schwellenbach served as a delegate
to the Interparliamentary Union at The Hague in 1936.

He resigned from the Senate on December 6, 1940 to accept a judicial appointment as United States district
judge for the eastern district of Washington, remaining
on the bench until 1945.  He was also dean of the law
school of Gonzaga University during 1944 and 1945.

President Harry S. Truman named Lewis Schwellenbach
Secretary of Labor on June 1, 1945 to succeed Frances
Perkins.  Lewis assumed his office on July 1, 1945 and
served until his death.  He immediately began to reorganize the department and to centralize control of all
federal agencies dealing with labor in the department.
He was temporarily interrupted by a series of strikes
which broke out after the defeat of Japan.  Among the
organizations placed within the Department of Labor were
the United States Employment Service, the Apprentice
Training Service, the Retraining and Reemployment Administration, the Shipbuilding Stabilization Committee and
the National Wage Stabilization Board.

Schwellenbach also worked to end wartime regulation
of labor and to restore collective bargaining between
management and labor in part by strengthening the medication activities of the department.  He maintained that
labor unions have a responsibility for the public welfare
and sponsored measures to aid all workers including the
organized labor forces.  He supported and help draft such
measures as the full employment bill, women's equal pay
bill, extension of social security, increase benefits
and the national health act.  Lewis B. Schwellenbach
died on June 10, 1948 in Washington, D.C.  He was buried
in Washelli Cemetery in Seattle, Washington.

Bibliography:
Bernstein, Barton J. and Matusow, Allen F.  Truman
Administration: A Documentary History.  New York: Har-
per and Row, 1966.
Daniels, Jonathan.  The Man of Independence.  Phila-
delphia: Lippincott, 1950.
Furer, Howard B., ed.  Harry S. Truman, 1884-/1972/
Dobbs Ferry, N.Y.: Oceana Publications, Inc., 1970.
Hillman, William.  Mr. President.  New York: Farrar,
Straus and Young, 1952.
Phillips, Cabell.  The Truman Presidency.  The History
of a Triumphant Succession.  New York: Macmillan, 1966.
Steinberg, Alfred.  The Man from Missouri: The Life
and Times of Harry S. Truman.  New York: Putnam, 1962.

SECRETARY OF LABOR: MAURICE JOSEPH TOBIN

Maurice J. Tobin, Secretary of Labor in the Cabinet
of President Harry S, Truman, was born on May 22, 1901
in Boston, Massachusetts, the son of James Tobin, a carpenter, and Margaret M. (Daly) Tobin.  After receiving
his basic education at Our Lady of Perpetual Help Elemen-

tary School and the High School of Commerce in Boston
Tobin studied at Boston College. He also worked for the
Conway Leather Company from 1919 to 1922. He was next
employed by the New England Telephone and Telegraph Company, becoming district traffic manager in 1928 and
continuing until 1937.

Maurice J. Tobin early became interested in politics.
He was elected as a Democrat to the Massachusetts House
of Representatives in 1926, serving one two-year term.
He was next a member of the Boston School Committee from
1931 to 1934. Maurice married Helen M. Moran on November
19, 1932. They had three children: Helen Louise, Carol
Ann and Maurice Joseph. He was again a member of the
Boston School Committee from 1935 to 1937 and was chairman in 1935. In 1937 Tobin was elected mayor of Boston,
taking office in January 1938. He was elected for a
second term in 1942. He was granted the honorary LL.D.
degree by Boston University in 1940 and by Portia Law
School in 1941. He was next elected governor of Massachusetts in 1944, assuming office in January 1945. He
promoted passage of a law which provided for fair employment practice in Massachusetts which was passed in
1946.

President Harry S. Truman named Maurice J. Tobin Secretary of Labor ad interim on August 13, 1948. He was
formally appointed to the position on February 1, 1949
and continued to serve until the end of the Truman Administration on January 20, 1953. He was granted the
honorary LL.D. degree in 1949 by the University of
Massachusetts, Boston College, and John Carroll University and by St. John's University in 1950. Tobin helped
continue building of the department into an effective
organization. In 1949 the Bureau of Employment Security
was transferred to the Department from the Federal Security Agency.

As part of the reorganization scheme of the Department of Labor the post of assistant Secretary of Labor
was established in 1950. Maurice J. Tobin also took
on the responsibility of coordinating administration of
the laws in regard to wages and hours on federally financed or assisted construction projects. He supported
the Fair Labor Standards amendments of 1949 which came
into effect in 1950 providing for an increase in the
minimum wage to seventy-five cents an hour, extended
control over child labor and provided for departmental
supervision of wage payments. Maurice organized the
Federal Safety Council in 1950 within the Bureau of Labor Standards to promote safety conditions among federal
employees.

Secretary Tobin also sponsored various measures including extension of the Wagner-Peyser Act in 1950 to Puerto
Rico and the Virgin Islands in order to establish oublic
employment offices there. The Railway Labor Act was

amended in January 1951 permitting the roads and their
employees to bargain collectively for the union shop
as well as to check off union dues.  He also supported
measures in 1951 to provide better benefits through de-
ductions for seamen.  The Department of Labor recommended
increased benefits under the Federal Workmen's Compensation Act.

Secretary Tobin was given the added responsibility of
supervision over federal civilian manpower activities
after hostilities broke out in Korea.  He created rational, regional and area labor-management defense manpower committees as well as a woman's advisory committee
on defense manpower.  He also developed the Defense Man=
power Administration.  He also involved the Labor Department in various international activities.  Tobin attended and addressed the International Labor Conferences
in Geneva, Switzerland in 1950, 1951 and 1952.  Maurice
Tobin died shortly after leaving office on July 19, 1953
in Jamaica Plain, Massachusetts.  He was buried in Holy-
hood Cemetery.

Bibliography:
Bernstein, Barton J. and Matusow, Allen F.  Truman
Administration: A Documentary History.  New York: Har-
per and Row, 1966.
Daniels, Jonathan.  The Man of Independence.  Phila-
delphia: Lippincott, 1950.
Furer, Howard B., ed.  Harry S. Truman, 1884-/1972/
Dobbs Ferry, N.Y.: Oceana Publications, Inc., 1970.
Hillman, William.  Mr. President.  New York: Farrar,
Straus and Young, 1952.
Phillips, Cabell.  The Truman Presidency.  The History
of a Triumphant Succession.  New York: Macmillan, 1966.
Steinberg, Alfred.  The Man from Missouri: The Life
and Times of Harry S. Truman.  New York: Putnam, 1962.

## ADMINISTRATIONS OF DWIGHT D. EISENHOWER

### VICE PRESIDENT: RICHARD MILHOUS NIXON

Richard M. Nixon, Vice President in the Administrations of Dwight D. Eisenhower, was born on January 9,
1913 in Yorba Linda, California, the son of Francis Anthony Nixon, a citrus farmer and filling station and
grocery store owner, and Hannah (Milhous) Nixon.  He
attended the public schools and at the same time worked
in his father's gas station and delivered groceries.
Richard next attended Whittier College from which he
was graduated with the Bachelor of Arts degree in 1934.
He studied law at Duke University Law School and received
the LL.B. degree in 1937.  He was admitted to the bar
in the same year.
Richard M. Nixon began practicing law with the firm of

Wingert and Beasley in Whittier, California.  He was
next a member of the newly organized firm of Beasley,
Kroop and Nixon.  He married Thelma (Pat) Ryan on June
21, 1940.  They have two daughters: Patricia and Julie.
Richard Nixon was appointed an attorney in the Office of
Emergency Management in Washington, D.C. in January 1942
and remained in that post until August 1942.  He was then
commissioned a lieutenant j.g. in the United States Navy.
He served in the South Pacific and was discharged in
January 1946 with the rank of lieutenant commander.

Richard Nixon was elected as a Republican to represent
the 12th district from California in November 1946.  He
served in the Eightieth and Eighty-first Congresses from
January 3, 1947 to November 3, 1950.  Nixon was a member
of a Congressional committee which visited Europe to
study economic conditions.  He specifically studied
Greece, Italy and Trieste.  He then supported a bipartisan foreign policy.  While in Congress Nixon forced the
continuation of the investigation of the charges made by
Whitaker Chambers against Alger Hiss, former State Department official.  He had uncovered additional information, microfilms of state papers found in a pumpkin
on Chambers' farm in Maryland.  On this evidence Hiss
was convicted of perjury in a federal court in 1950.  He
also helped to draft the Taft-Hartley Labor Act.

Nixon was next elected to the United States Senate in
November 1950 for the term beginning January 3, 1951.
Governor Earl Warren appointed Nixon to fill the vacant
seat left by Sheridan Downey in December 1950.  Nixon
served in the Senate until January 20, 1953.  While
in that house Richard was a member of the government
operations and labor and public welfare committeees.
He was nominated as the Republican vice presidential
candidate at its national convention in July 1952 to run
with Dwight D. Eisenhower.  They were elected in November.

Dwight D. Eisenhower and Richard M. Nixon were inaugurated as President and Vice President respectively on
January 20, 1953.  Nixon acted as liason between the
executive and the Congress.  He also served as a spokesman for the administration in explaining administrative
programs to the public.  Richard also played an active
part in the Cabinet, even presiding in the absence of
the President.

Richard Nixon was also a member of the National Security Council as provided by the 1949 amendment to the National Security Act.  He was sent on several good will
missions throughout the world, including a 72-day trip
around the world in 1953 as well as visits to Latin
America in 1955, 1956 and 1958.  He also travelled to
Africa and Italy in 1957, to England in 1958 and to the
USSR in 1959.  Following President Eisenhower's illnesses
in 1955, 1956 and 1957, he and Nixon made an agreement
in March 1958 on the plans to be followed in the event

that the President not be able to carry out his duties.

Richard M. Nixon was awarded the honorary LL.D. degree by various colleges and universities including Bradley University in 1951, Teheran University, Iran in 1953, Whittier College in 1954, the University of Liberia, DePauw, Michigan State and Yeshiva Universities and Bethany College in 1957 as well as the University of San Diego and Fordham University in 1959. He served as Vice President until the end of the second Eisenhower Administration on January 20, 1961.

Richard M. Nixon was the unsuccessful Republican presidential candidate in 1960, being defeated by John F. Kennedy. Nixon then returned to private law practice with the firm of Adams, Duque and Hazeltine, remaining with them from 1961 to 1966. He was the unsuccessful Republican candidate for governor of California in 1962, claiming after the election that the press had badgered him throughout much of his political career. He wrote Six Crises in the same year. Richard Nixon then moved to New York City where he was associated with the legal firm of Mudge, Stern, Baldwin and Todd from 1963 to 1969. He was also a director of the Hosco Corporation.

Richard M. Nixon was nominated for the Presidency by the Republicans in 1968 and was elected in November. He was inaugurated on January 20, 1969. He was reelected in November 1972 in the midst of a growing crisis over a break-in at the Democratic National Headquarters in Washington, D.C. at the hotel-apartment-office complex called the Watergate.

/For information concerning the period of Richard M. Nixon's Presidency, consult Howard F. Bremer, ed. Richard M. Nixon, 1913- in this series./

As a result of the Senate investigation of the Watergate break-in and other related political activities, information eventually came to light that Nixon had tape recorded many conversations in the Oval Office of the White House. Information also came to the surface in the midst of the House of Representatives Judiciary Committee hearings concerning impeachment of the President which seemed to implicate Nixon and many of his close advisers in the attempt to cover up the Watergate break-in. Richard M. Nixon resigned the Presidency on August 9, 1974. He was the first President to do so since the Constitution came into effect in 1789. He retired to his home in San Clemente, California where his physical condition deteriorated as a result of flebitas. He was operated on to remove several blood clots from his leg and has since recuperated from the operation. He has been subponaed by several of his former aids to testify in the defense at the "Watergate" trial. President Gerald Ford, his successor, has pardoned Richard M. Nixon.

Bibliography:
   Brandon, Henry. The Retreat of American Power. Garden City, N.Y.: Doubleday, 1973.
   Bremer, Howard F., ed. Richard M. Nixon, 1913- Dobbs Ferry, N.Y.: Oceana Publications, Inc., 1975.
   De Toledano, Ralph. One Man Alone: Richard Nixon. New York: Funk and Wagnalls, Inc., 1969.
   Drury, Allen. Courage and Hesitation. Garden City: Doubleday, 1972.
   Evans, Rowland, and Novak, Robert P. Nixon in the White House: The Frustration of Power. New York: Random House, 1972.
   Hoyt, Edwin P. The Nixons: An American Family. New York: Random House, 1972.
   Lurie, Leonardo. The Running of Richard Nixon. New York: Coward, McCann and Gehegan, 1972.
   McCloskey, Paul W. Truth and Untruth: Political Deceit in America. New York: Simon and Schuster, Inc., 1972.
   Mazo, Earl, and Hess, Stephen. President Nixon: A Political Portrait. London: MacDonald and Company, 1968.
   Vexler, Robert I., ed. Dwight D. Eisenhower, 1890- 1969. Dobbs Ferry, N.Y.: Oceana Publications, Inc., 1970.
   Wills, Gary. Nixon Agonistes: The Crisis of the Self-Made Man. Boston: Houghton Mifflin Company, 1971.

## SECRETARY OF STATE: JOHN FOSTER DULLES

John Foster Dulles, Secretary of State in the Cabinet of President Dwight D. Eisenhower, was born on February 25, 1888 in Washington, D.C., the son of Allen Macy and Edith (Foster) Dulles. His family moved to Watertown where John Foster received his basic education in the public schools. He then attended Princeton University from which he received the Bachelor of Arts degree in 1908. While still at Princeton John went to the second Hague Peace conference in 1907 as his grandfather's secretary and also became secretary of the Chinese delegation. He then went to Paris, France to study at the Sorbonne during 1908 and 1909.

John Foster Dulles returned to the United States to study law at George Washington University law school in Washington, D.C. Dulles graduated with the LL.B. degree in 1911 and was admitted to the bar. He began to practice law in 1911 with the firm of Sullivan and Cromwell in New York City. John Foster married Janet Pomeroy Avery on June 26, 1912. They had three children: John Watson, Lilian Pomeroy and Avery.

President Woodrow Wilson sent John Foster Dulles on special diplomatic missions to Panama and Costa Rica in 1917. After the United States entered the Frist World War in 1917 Dulles was commissioned a captain in the

army in charge of the economic section of military intelligence and was later promoted to major. He was
next assigned as assistant to the chairman of the War
Trade Board in 1918. After the end of the war in 1918
John Foster Dulles was sent to Paris as a counsel to the
American Commission to Negotiate Peace and was named a
member of the Reparations Committee as well as the Supreme Economic Council in 1919. Dulles then returned
to his law practice becoming a partner in the firm of
Sullivan and Cromwell.

John Foster Dulles was appointed legal adviser to the
Bank of Poland concerning its plans for currency reforms
in 1927. He was next the American representative of
German bondholders at the Berlin Debt Conference in 1933.
He continued his legal practice and became more involved
in international law. He wrote War, Peace and Change in
1939. Dulles was foreign policy adviser to Governor
Thomas E. Dewey of New York, Republican nominee for the
presidency in 1944. He frequently consulted with Secretary of State Cordell Hull while serving in this capacity. Dulles also proposed citing concepts for the
United Nations and was named general adviser to the
United States delegation to the United Nations Conference at San Francisco from April to June 1945.

John Foster Dulles was next Republican adviser to Secretary of State James F. Byrnes at the London Conference
of the Council of Foreign Ministers in September 1945.
John was a member of the United States delegation to
the United Nations conference at London in January and
February 1946 and was a member of the steering committee
of the assembly. He continued as a member of the United States delegation from 1946 to 1950 and was chairman of the delegation at Paris in 1948. Among his other
activities Dulles was a trustee of the Rockefeller
Foundation, the Carnegie Endowment for International
Peace of which he was also chairman, the New York Public
Library and Union Theological Seminary. He was also a
member of the New York State Banking Board from 1946
to 1949.

John Foster Dulles was appointed to the United States
Senate to fill the vacancy left by the resignation of
Senator Robert F. Vacary. Dulles served from July 7,
1949 to November 8, 1949. He was also a consultant to
Secretary of State Dean Acheson in 1951 and 1952. President Harry S. Truman appointed Dulles as his special
representative with the rank of ambassador to negotiate
the Australian, New Zealand, Philippine and Japanese
security treaties during 1950 and 1951 as well as the
peace treaty with Japan in 1951.

President Dwight D. Eisenhower appointed John Foster
Dulles Secretary of State on January 20, 1953 in which
post he served until his illness brought about his resignation on April 15, 1959. While Secretary of State,

Dulles encouraged President Eisenhower to make his famous
announcement on February 25, 1953 that he would go to
any reasonable place to meet Russian Premier Josef Stalin
if it would help world peace.  Dulles was also involved
in decisions concerning national defense, anouncing on
January 12, 1954 that the nation would follow a policy
of "massive retaliation."  He also worked for world cooperation in regard to Indochina, attending the Geneva
Conference which began April 26, 1954.  Dulles withdrew
from the conference because he could not accept the
Russian and Chinese demands that the United States aban-
don its allies in Asia.  The government did not sign the
Geneva agreement on July 21, 1954.
    Secretary Dulles was involved in negotiations for arms
control with the Soviet Union.  He supervised negotiations which culminated in changing the Baghdad Pact into the Central Treaty Organization on August 18, 1957.
He urged on January 16, 1958 that an international commission be organized to guarantee that outer space would
be used for peaceful purposes.  He also helped President
Eisenhower in developing plans for peace in the Middle
East which the President proposed to the United Nations
on August 13, 1958.  Dulles resigned his post on April
15, 1959 because of the spread of cancer.  President
Eisenhower awarded Dulles the Medal of Freedom on May
20, 1959.  John Foster Dulles died on May 24, 1959.
After an official funeral he was buried in Arlington
National Cemetery.

Bibliography:
    Albertson, Dean, ed.  Eisenhower as President.  New
York: Hill and Wang, 1963.
    Beal, John R.  John Foster Dulles: A Biography.  New
York: Harper and Row, 1957.
    Donovan, Robert J.  Eisenhower, The Inside Story.  New
York: Harper and Row, 1956.
    Drummond, Roscoe.  Duel at the Brink: John Foster
Dulles' Command of American Power.  Garden City, N.Y.:
Doubleday, 1960.
    Hughes, Emmett J.  The Ordeal of Power: A Political
Memoir of the Eisenhower Years.  New York: Atheneum, 1963.
    Larson, Arthur.  Eisenhower: The President Nobody Knew.
New York: Scribner, 1968.
    Smith, A. Merriman.  Meet Mr. Eisenhower.  New York:
Harper and Row, 1955.
    Vexler, Robert I., ed.  Dwight D. Eisenhower, 1890-
1969.  Dobbs Ferry, N.Y.: Oceana Publications, Inc.,
1970.

## SECRETARY OF STATE: CHRISTIAN ARCHIBALD HERTER

    Christian A. Herter, Secretary of State in the Cabinet
of President Dwight D. Eisenhower, was born on March 25,

1895 in Paris, France, the son of Albert and Adele
(McGinnis) Herter, both artists.  Christian received
his basic education at the Ecole Alsatienne of Paris
from 1901 to 1904.  He then went to the Browning School
in New York City from 1904 to 1911 after which he went
to Harvard University, grdauating with the Bachelor of
Arts degree in 1915.  He then entered Columbia University School of Architecture in 1916.

Herter soon gave up his architectural studies to enter
the foreign service and was sent to the American Embassy
at Berlin in 1916.  He was appointed to head the American Legation at Brussels in 1917 after which he was a
special assistant in the State Department in Washington,
D.C. during 1917 and 1918.  Christian married Mary Caroline Pratt on August 25, 1917.  They had four children:
Christian Archibald, Frederic Pratt, Adele, and Eliot
Miles.  Herter was next appointed assistant commissioner
and secretary of the commission to negotiate a prisoner-
of-war agreement with Germany in 1918.  He was also secretary and staff member of the American Peace Commission
to negotiate peace in Paris during 1918 and 1919.

When Herbert Hoover was named director general of the
European Relief Council in 1919  Herter became his assistant as executive secretary of the Council during 1920
and 1921.  Christian then became personal assistant to
Secretary of Commerce Hoover in 1921 and continued in
this position until 1924.  Herter left government service in 1924 to be an editor and coowner of The Independent, a Boston weekly paper and continued with the paper
until 1928.  He also bought an interest in The Sportsman
and became its editor in 1927, remaining in that capacity until 1936.  He also lectured at Harvard University
on international relations from 1929 to 1930.

Christian A. Herter continued his involvement in politics when he was elected to the Massachusetts House
of Representatives, serving from 1931 to 1948.  He was
Speaker of the house from 1939 to 1943.  He was also an
overseer of Harvard from 1940 to 1944.  In February 1942
he became a member of a group of Americans and Canadians
working under a Carnegie Peace Foundation grant to plan
for a world organization of states.  Herter was next
elected to the United States House of Representatives
in 1942, serving in the Seventy-eighth to the Eighty-
third Congress from January 3, 1943 until 1953.  He proposed establishment of a Select Committee on European
Aid which was approved by the Congress after Secretary
of State George Marshall proposed his Marshall Plan.
Christian was a member of the committee which toured
eighteen European countries.  Herter was given the
Collier's Award for distinguished Congressional service
in 1948.

Christian A. Herter was elected governor of Massachusetts in 1952 and was reelected in 1954.  He did not

run for a third term.  He developed a program including
a merit system for compulsory automobile insurance, a
housing program and additional benefits for the elderly.
He was an overseer of Harvard University from 1950 to
1956.  Many colleges and universities granted Herter the
honorary LL.D. degree from 1954 to 1956.  Herter was
appointed Under Secretary of State in 1957, representing
the United States at the independence celebration of
Malaya.  He then visited the Philippines, Burma, Thai-
land, Formosa and Japan.  He was also chairman of the
Operations Coordinating Board.  Mr. Herter reorganized
the office which was involved in international cultural
affairs.
     President Dwight D. Eisenhower named Christian A. Her-
ter Secretary of State after the resignation of John
Foster Dulles on April 21, 1959.  Herter assumed his office on April 22 and continued to serve until January
19, 1961 at the end of the Eisenhower Administration.
Secretary Herter attended the Geneva Foreign Ministers
Conference in May and June 1959 as well as other succeeding conferences including the Paris summit conference
from December 19 to December 21, 1959.  Herter was able
to reduce some of the Russian pressure on West Berlin
and negotiated with the Russians over the issue of an
unarmed U-2 plane which was forced down in the Soviet
Union.  This led to a disruption of the December 1959
summit meeting in Paris.
     Among Herter's interests and activities after leaving
office in January 1961 he was a co-chairman of the United States Citizens Committee on NATO as well as chairman of the Atlantic Council of the United States Incorporated during 1961 and 1962.  Christian was named chief
planner and negotiator for American foreign trade in
November 1962.  In addition he has been a member of the
advisory council for the School of Advanced International
Studies and was chairman of the Boston branch of the
European Foreign Policy Association.  He was president
as well as chairman of the board of trustees of the
Foreign Service Educational Foundation.  Herter was also a director of the Commission for Relief of Belgium
Educational Foundation.  Among his other activities he
was a member of the international committee of the YMCA,
a trustee of the World Peace Foundation and the Boston
Library Society.  Christian A. Herter died on December
30, 1967 in Washington, D.C.

Bibliography:
     Albertson, Dean, ed.  Eisenhower as President.  New
York: Hill and Wang, 1963.
     Donovan, Robert J.  Eisenhower, The Inside Story.  New
York: Harper and Row, 1956.
     Drummond, Roscoe.  Duel at the Brink: John Foster
Dulles' Command of American Power.  Garden City, N.Y.:

Doubleday, 1960.

Hughes, Emmett J. The Ordeal of Power: A Political Memoir of the Eisenhower Years. New York: Atheneum, 1963.

Larson, Arthur. Eisenhower: The President Nobody Knew. New York: Scribner, 1968.

Vexler, Robert I., ed. Dwight D. Eisenhower, 1890-1969. Dobbs Ferry, N.Y.: Oceana Publications, Inc., 1970.

## SECRETARY OF THE TREASURY:

### GEORGE MAGOFFIN HUMPHREY

George M. Humphrey, Secretary of the Treasury in the Cabinet of President Dwight D. Eisenhower, was born on March 8. 1890 in Sheboygan, Michigan, the son of Watts Sherman and Caroline (Magoffin) Humphrey. George received his basic education in the public schools of Saginam, Michigan and then attended the University of Michigan from which he received the LL.B. degree in 1912 and was admitted to the bar in the same year. He then began practicing law with his father's firm, Humphrey, Grant and Humphrey in Saginaw. He remained with the firm until 1918. George married Pamela Sterk on January 15, 1913. They had three children: Cynthia Pamela, Gilbert Watts, and Caroline Helen.

George M. Humphrey became assistant general counsel for the M. A. Hanna Company of Cleveland, Ohio in 1918. He rose to become general counsel and then a junior partner in 1922. George was elected executive vice president in 1924 and president in 1929. He remained in this office until 1952 after which he was chairman of the board. Humphrey strengthened the company when in 1929 he merged the firm with the Weirton Steel Company and the Great Lakes Steel Company to form the National Steel Corporation of which he was chairman of the executive committee and a director. He continued to expand the company's holdings.

George M. Humphrey also had various other business interests and was an officer in many firms including president and director of the Producers Steamship Company, LaRue Mining Company, the Missouri Ore Company and many other firms. Humphrey was chairman of the Business Advisory Council to the United States Department of Commerce in 1946. He chaired a committee studying German industrial plants in 1948 in order to revise reparations. Western Reserve University granted him the honorary LL.D. degree in 1952 as did John Carroll University, Ohio Wesleyan University and the Universities of Michigan and Rochester in 1953.

President Dwight D. Eisenhower appointed George M. Humphrey Secretary of the Treasury on January 21, 1953.

At this time George resigned from the offices of the
many corporations in which he was interested.  When he
assumed office Humphrey immediately took action to place
the national debt on a longer term basis to avoid further inflation as well as to counteract competitive
private offerings necessary to finance large capital
outlays.  In order to attract investment by the public
in government securities he offered them for sale at
the prevailing rate of interest rather than that established by the Federal Reserve System.  This would also
reduce the amount of these securities held by the Federal Reserve banks.  As a result of Humphrey's program
50 per cent of new government securities were owned by
individuals.  The government was able to relax its
tight money policy, lower interest rates and borrow at
lower cost.

Under Humphrey's supervision the Treasury Department
kept a constant watch on the currency of the nation in
order to regulate credit and interest rates.  In his
capacity as Secretary of the Treasury George Humphrey
held several posts including honorary treasurer of the
American National Red Cross, chairman of the Library
of Congress Trust Fund, United States governor of the
International Monetary Fund and the International Bank
for Reconstruction and Development.  He was also a member of the board of trustees of the Postal Savings System, the Smithsonian Institution, the Foreign Service
Buildings Commission and the National Park Trust Fund
Board.  He services were also called on to be a trustee
of the National Gallery of Art, the National Munitions
Control Board, the Defense Mobilization Board and the
Small Business Loan Policy Board as well as a director
of the Federal Farm Mortgage Corporation.

During his term in office Humphrey was granted the
honorary LL.D. degree in 1954 by the University of
Pittsburgh and Brown and Lehigh Universities; in 1956
by Harvard University and the University of Notre Dame.
The National Association of Manufacturers named George
M. Humphrey Man of the Year in 1957.  He was named one
of the Fifty Foremost Leaders in the name year by Forbes
Magazine.  After Humphrey resigned from the Treasury
Department in July 1957 he resumed his business interests.
George remained honorary chairman of the board and a
director of the M. A. Hanna Company as well as a direc-
tor of the Canada and Dominion Sugar Company, Ltd., the
Consolidation Coal Company and the National City Bank.
Among his other activities he served as a trustee of
the American Assembly of Columbia University and the
Eisenhower Exchange Fellowships, Inc., an honorary
trustee of the Committee for Economic Development and
a member-at-large of the national board of directors
of Junior Achievement, Inc.

George M. Humphrey is a member of the Business Advisory

Council for the United States Department of Commerce
and a trustee of the Robert A. Taft Memorial Foundation,
Inc.  Humphrey has also continued to serve many groups
in the nation.  He received the National Human Relations
Award of the National Conference of Christian and Jews
in 1958.  He lives at present in retirement at his
"Holiday Hill Farm" in Mentor, Ohio.

Bibliography:
    Albertson, Dean, ed.  Eisenhower as President.  New
York: Hill and Wang, 1963.
    Donovan, Robert J.  Eisenhower, The Inside Story.  New
York: Harper and Row, 1956.
    Hughes, Emmett J.  The Ordeal of Power: A Political
Memoir of the Eisenhower Years.  New York: Atheneum,
1963.
    Larson, Arthur.  Eisenhower: The President Nobody Knew.
New York: Scribner, 1968.
    Vexler, Robert I., ed.  Dwight D. Eisenhower, 1890-
1969.  Dobbs Ferry, N.Y.: Oceana Publications, Inc.,
1970.

SECRETARY OF THE TREASURY:

ROBERT BERNARD ANDERSON

    Robert B. Anderson, Secretary of the Treasury in the
Cabinet of President Dwight D. Eisenhower, was born on
June 4, 1910 in Burleson, Texas, the son of Robert Lee
and Lizzie Ethel (Haskew) Anderson.  After receiving
his basic education in the public schools of Godley,
Texas, Robert studied at Weatherford College, a branch
of Southwestern University, receiving a teacher's certificate.  He then attended the University of Texas.
Robert taught Spanish, history and mathematics in 1928
and coached the football team in 1929 at Burleson High
School.
    Robert B. Anderson next entered the University of Texas
Law School in the summer of 1929, graduating with the
LL.B. degree in 1932.  He was elected to the Texas legislature in his last year of law school.  Robert was
admitted to the bar in 1932 and established his law
practice in Fort Worth, Texas.  He was named assistant
attorney general of Texas in 1933 while still serving
in the state legislature.  He also served as adjunct
professor or law at Texas University.  He was next appointed state tax commissioner in 1934.  In that capacity he was an ex-officio member of the State Racing
Commission and of the State Tax Board.  He was made
chairman and executive director of the Texas Unemployment Commission.
    Robert Anderson married Ollie May Rawlings on April
10, 1935.  They had two sons: Richard and Gerald Lee.

Robert was named general counsel of the Waggoner Estate
which was involved in ranching and oil.  He became general manager in 1941.  He continued his public service
as well and was a member of the Texas Economy Commission
in 1938 and also was appointed to the executive committee
of the Texas Research Council.  Anderson was also president of the Texas Mid-Continent Oil and Gas Association
from 1947 to 1951.  Among his other business activities
Anderson was vice president of Associated Refineries,
Inc.  He was a director of Northwest Broadcasting Company,
Inc., Southwestern Bell Telephone Company, the Vernon
Times Publishing Company and the Vernon Transit Company.
He was also a director and deputy chairman of the Federal
Reserve Bank in Dallas, Texas.  Robert served as a di-
rector of Texas Wesleyan College, chairman of the Texas
State Board of Education, president of the Vernon, Texas
School Board and a member of the national executive board
of the Boy Scouts of America.

Robert B. Anderson entered the service of the federal
government in the 1950's.  He was an aide to the secretary of the army in 1952.  President Dwight D. Eisenhower
named Anderson Secretary of the Navy in 1953.  He served
in this office until 1954.  He was next named deputy
Secretary of Defense, remaining in that post from 1954
to 1955.  He resigned from government office in 1955 to
accept the presidency of the Canadian oil and mining
compan, Ventures, Ltd.  Baylor and Long Island Universities awarded Robert B. Anderson the honorary LL.D. degree in 1953.  Illinois Wesleyan and Hanemann Medical
Colleges as well as Northwestern University granted him
the LL.D. degree in 1954 as did the University of Maine
in 1955.

President Dwight D. Eisenhower appointed Robert B. Anderson Secretary of the Treasury on July 2, 1957.  He
assumed his office on July 29, 1957 and served until the
end of the end of the Eisenhower Administration on January 20, 1961.  While in office he continued to develop
the financial strength and resources of the nation.

After retiring from public office in 1961 Robert
joined Carl M. Loeb, Rhoades and Company.  Among the o-
ther organizations of which he has been a member are the
Texas Bar Association, the United States, West Texas and
Vernon Chambers of Commerce, the Better Business Bureau
of Texas, the Texas Industrial Conference, the American
Petroleum Association of America and the Texas and Southwestern Cattle Raisers Association.

Bibliography:
  Albertson, Dean, ed. Eisenhower as President.  New
York: Hill and Wang, 1963.
  Donovan, Robert J.  Eisenhower, The Inside Story.  New
York: Harper and Row, 1956.
  Frier, David.  Conflict of Interest in the Eisenhower

Administration.  Ames: Iowa State University Press,
1969.
   Hughes, Emmett J.  The Ordeal of Power:  A Political
Memoir of the Eisenhower Years.  New York: Atheneum,
1963.
   Larson, Arthur.  Eisenhower: The President Nobody Knew.
New York: Scribner, 1968.
   Vexler, Robert I., ed.  Dwight D. Eisenhower, 1890-
1969.  Dobbs Ferry, N.Y.: Oceana Publications, Inc.,
1970.

## SECRETARY OF DEFENSE: CHARLES ERWIN WILSON

   Charles E. Wilson, Secretary of Defense in the Cabinet
of President Dwight D. Eisenhower, was born on July 18,
1890 in Minerva, Ohio, the son of Thomas E. Wilson, a
school principal, and Rosilynd (Untefer) Wilson.  Charles
moved with his family to Mineral City in 1894.  After
receiving his basic education in the local public schools
he attended Carnegie Institute of Technology from which
he was graduated in 1909 with a degree in Electrical
Engineering.  He then began working for Westinghouse
Corporation where he designed the first auto starter motor.  Charles married Jessie Ann Curtis in 1912.  They
had six children.
   During the First World War Charles E. Wilson was called
to Washington, D.C. to perform several special assignments for the Army, Navy and Air Corps.  He next became
chief engineer and factory manager for Remy Electric
Company.  Charles moved to Detroit, Michigan in 1919 and
eventually to Anderson, Indiana.  He rose within the
company and eventually became president of Delco-Remy
Corporation in 1926.  Wilson then became vice president
of General Motors Corporation in 1929, continuing in
that position until 1939.  He became a director of the
company in 1934.  Charles was executive vice president
from 1939 to 1940.  He was elected president of the
General Motors Corporation in 1941 and became chief executive officer in 1946.  He resigned from this position
in 1953.
   President Dwight D. Eisenhower named Charles E. Wilson
Secretary of Defense on January 21, 1953.  As Secretary
he developed narrow base defense plans and continued the
improvement of the defense establishment.  Wilson left
office on October 8, 1957 and returned to his business
activities.  He was a member of the board of trustees
of General Motors Corporation and a director of the
National Bank of Detroit.  He also served as chairman
of the Michigan advisory committee to the United States
Commission on Civil Rights.  He was a member of the Society of Automotive Engineers.  Charles E. Wilson died
on September 26, 1961 in Norwood, Louisiana.  He was
buried in Acadia Park Cemetery.

Bibliography:
    Albertson, Dean, ed. Eisenhower as President. New
York: Hill and Wang, 1963.
    Borklund, Carl W. Men of the Pentagon. New York:
F. A. Praeger, 1966.
    Donovan, Robert J. Eisenhower, The Inside Story. New
York: Harper and Row, 1956.
    Hughes, Emmett J. The Ordeal of Power: A Political
Memoir of the Eisenhower Years. New York: Atheneum,
1963.
    Larson, Arthur. Eisenhower: The President Nobody Knew.
New York: Scribner, 1968.
    Vexler, Robert I., ed. Dwight D. Eisenhower, 1890-
1969. Dobbs Ferry, N.Y.: Oceana Publications, Inc.,
1970.

## SECRETARY OF DEFENSE: NEIL HOSLER MCELROY

Neil H. McElroy, Secretary of Defense in the Cabinet
of President Dwight D. Eisenhower  was born on October
30, 1904 in Berea, Ohio, the son of Malcolm Ross McElroy,
a teacher and Susan Harriet (Hosler) McElroy.  He received
his basic education in the Berea and Cincinnati, Ohio
public schools and then went to Harvard University.  He
was graduated with the Bachelor of Arts degree in 1925.
He began working in the same year for the advertising
department of Proctor and Gamble Company in Cincinnati.
He became manager of the promotion department in 1929.
Neil married Mary Camilla Fry on June 29, 1929.  They
had three children: William Joseph, Hugh Leonard, and
Nancy Brennan.
    Neil McElroy continued to work with Proctor and Gamble
on an assignment to establish a new branch of the company in England in 1930.  Among his innovations were in-
tra-company competition of products and sponsorship of
the forerunners of the soap operas.  He became advertising and promotion manager of the company in 1940 and
then was elected to the board of directors and was made
vice president of advertising and production in 1943.
He became assistant to the president in 1946.  He was
director of the Cincinnati branch of the American Red
Cross from 1943 to 1946.  In 1946 McElroy became president of the Cincinnati Citizens Planning Board.  He was
elected president of Proctor and Gamble in October 1948,
and continued until October 1957.
    While head of Proctor and Gamble McElroy was also a
director of the Chrysler Corporation and the General
Electric Company.  He also was involved in many Cincinnati
institutions including chairman of the Cincinnati Community Chest in 1952, a trustee of the Cincinnati Institute
of Fine Arts, chairman of the advisory committee of the
the University of Cincinnati College of Medicine, director of the Cincinnati Chamber of Commerce and member

of the Citizens' Development Committee. In addition he was vice chairman of the United Community Campaigns of America as well as a member of the advisory board of the National Citizens Council for Better Schools. Miami University granted him the LL.D. degree in 1952 as did Kenyon and Baldwin-Wallace Colleges in 1955. McElroy served as chairman of the White House Conference on Education in 1955 and chairman of the National Industrial Conference Board in 1956. In the same year Xavier and Bradley Universities awarded the LL.D. degree.

President Dwight D. Eisenhower appointed Neil H. McElroy Secretary of Defense on October 9, 1957 to succeed Charles E. Wilson. He remained in this post until December 1, 1959. As part of his duties he was chairman of the Armed Forces Policy Council and the Joint Secretaries of the Armed Forces. McElroy was also a member of the National Security Council, the Defense Mobilization Board, the Council on Youth Fitness and the Smithsonian Institution. He stressed research and development which eventually included appointment of a director of guided missiles in November 1957 and creation of the Advanced Research Projects Agency for space programs in February 1958. The first American Satellite was launched on January 1, 1958.

Secretary McElroy supervised the reorganization of the Defense Department under the Department of Defense Reorganization Act of 1958. He intensified the use of modern weapons in the armed forces and worked to bring about the necessary adjustments in the organization of the services. He received the LL.D. degree from Harvard University in 1958.

After leaving public office in 1959 Neil H. McElroy returned to Proctor and Gamble as chairman of the Board in 1959. He was also a director of the Equitable Assurance Society and a member of the National Council of the United Negro College Fund. Among his other activities McElroy was at one time president of the Association of American Glycerine Producers, Inc., a member of the board of overseers of Harvard University, and president of Commonwealth Commercial Club during 1960 and 1961.

Bibliography:
    Albertson, Dean, ed. Eisenhower as President. New York: Hill and Wang, 1963.
    Borklund, Carl W. Men of the Pentagon. New York: F. A. Praeger, 1966.
    Donovan, Robert J. Eisenhower, The Inside Story. New York: Harper and Row, 1956.
    Frier, David. Conflict of Interest in the Eisenhower Administration. Ames: Iowa State University Press, 1969.
    Hughes, Emmett J. The Ordeal of Power: A Political Memoir of the Eisenhower Years. New York: Atheneum, 1963.

Larson, Arthur. Eisenhower: The President Nobody Knew. New York: Scribner, 1968.
Vexler, Robert I., ed. Dwight D. Eisenhower, 1890-1969. Dobbs Ferry, N.Y.: Oceana Publications, Inc., 1970.

SECRETARY OF DEFENSE:

THOMAS SOVEREIGN GATES, JR.

Thomas S. Gates, Jr. Secretary of Defense in the Cabinet of President Dwight D. Eisenhower, was born on April 10, 1906 in Philadelphia, Pennsylvania, the son of Thomas Sovereign Gates, a lawyer, banker and president of the University of Pennsylvania from 1930 to 1944, and Marie (Rogers) Gates. After receiving his basic education at Chestnut Hill Academy Thomas S. Gates, Jr. went to the University of Pennsylvania from which he received the Bachelor of Arts degree in 1928. He went to work selling securities for Drexel and Company, the Philadelphia investment banking firm. Thomas married Millicent Anne Brengle on September 29, 1928. They had four children: Millicent Anne, Patricia S., Thomas S. and Katherine Curtin.

Thomas Gates joined the United States Naval Reserve in 1935. He became a partner in Drexel and Company in 1940. Shortly after the United States entered the Second World War, Gates was commissioned a lieutenant in the Navy in April 1942. He studied at Quonset Point Air Intelligence School in Rhode Island. After graduating from the school Thomas was assigned to the staff of the commander-in-chief of the Atlantic Fleet to establish the Naval Air Intelligence Center. In 1943 he served on board the U.S.S. Monterey in the Pacific and was then assigned to Real Admiral C. T. Durgin's staff in 1944 in preparation for the invasion of France. He returned to the Pacific in 1945 and was involved in the campaign to liberate the Philippines, Iwo Jima and Okinawa. After the end of the war Gates was made a commander in the U.S. Naval Reserve in 1945.

Thomas Gates returned to Drexel and Company and became involved in several business pursuits. He became a director of the Beaver Coal Corporation in 1946 and was made vice president in 1948. He also became a director of the Scott Paper Company, International Basic Economy Corporation and John Wyner and Sons, Inc. President Eisenhower named Gates Undersecretary of the Navy in October 1953. During 1953 he worked with a navy reorganization committee to investigate any duplication of effort within the navy. He also developed the order which established the relationships between the various commands of the Navy and the Marine Corps. The University of Pennsylvania granted him the honorary LL.D. degree in

1956.

President Dwight D. Eisenhower named Thomas S. Gates, Jr. Secretary of the Navy in March 1957. He assumed his office on April 1. He maintained that aircraft carriers would be the primary striking force with atomic submarines armed with ballistic missiles as major deterrents. He worked to install guided-missile launchers on various ships and instituted the use of a new high altitude super-radar. He supervised retirement of the last of the battleships and the addition of many advanced atomic-powered submarines. While he was in office the Navy also tested high performance aircraft and was working on the development of various missiles. The Navy was also involved in the satellite program. While he was in office the United States Sixth Fleet at the request of Lebanese President Chamoun visited Lebanon on July 15, 1958. This was a result of disorders which had occurred there during June and July. President Eisenhower next named Gates deputy Secretary of Defense in May 1959.

President Dwight D. Eisenhower appointed Thomas S. Gates, Jr. Secretary of Defense ad interim on December 1, 1959. He continued until January 26, 1960 when he was formally appointed to the Cabinet post. He continued to serve until the end of the Eisenhower Administration on January 20, 1961. While in office he continued the development of American defenses and served as the National Security Council and the Defense Mobilization Committee.

After leaving public office Thomas S. Gates became president and a director of the Morgan Guaranty Trust Company in 1961 and continued in office until 1965 when he became chairman of the board. Among his other activities he was a trustee of the Foxcraft School, director of the Philadelphia Child Guidance Clinic, and a life trustee and member of the executive board of the University of Pennsylvania. He is also a member of the Academy of Political Science and the Council of Foreign Relations and served as a vice president of the Navy League of the United States.

Bibliography:
Albertson, Dean, ed. Eisenhower as President. New York: Hill and Wang, 1963.
Borklund, Carl W. Men of the Pentagon. New York: F. A. Praeger, 1966.
Donovan, Robert J. Eisenhower, The Inside Story. New York: Harper and Row, 1956.
Hughes, Emmett J. The Ordeal of Power: A Political Memoir of the Eisenhower Years. New York: Atheneum, 1963.
Larson, Arthur. Eisenhower: The President Nobody Knew. New York: Scribner, 1968.

Vexler, Robert I., ed.  Dwight David Eisenhower, 1890-
1960.  Dobbs Ferry, N.Y.: Oceana Publications, Inc., 1970.

ATTORNEY GENERAL: HERBERT BROWNELL, JR.

Herbert Brownell, Jr. Attorney General in the Cabinet
of President Dwight D. Eisenhower, was born on February
20, 1904 in Peru, Nebraska, the son of Herbert Brownell,
a college professor, and May Adeline (Miller) Brownell.
He received his basic education in the Lincoln, Nebraska
public schools and Lincoln High School from which he was
graduated in 1920.  Herbert then studied at the University of Nebraska, receiving the Bachelor of Arts degree
in 1924.  He taught journalism in 1924 at Dore College.
Herbert Brownell, Jr. next studied law at Yale University,
graduating with the LL.B. degree in 1927.
Herbert Brownell, Jr. was admitted to the New York bar
in 1928 and practiced law with the firm of Root, Clark,
Buckner and Ballantine from 1927 to 1929.  He then joined
the legal firm of Land, Day and Land of New York in 1929,
becoming a partner in 1932.  Brownell had also become active in politics as a Republican.  He ran unsuccessfully
for the state assembly in 1931.  He was elected to the
New York Assembly in 1932, representing the 10th district
in Manhattan from 1933 to 1937.  He was reelected five
times.  Herbert married Doris A. McCarter on June 16,
1934.  They had four children: Joan, Ann, Thomas McCarter,
and James Barker.
Brownell continued his legal practice while maintaining
an active interest in politics.  He managed Thomas E.
Dewey's successful campaign for governor of New York.
He was also manager of Dewey's unsuccessful campaigns
as the Republican candidate for President in 1944 and 1948.
Brownell was also Republican National chairman from 1944
to 1946.  He also had an important part as a strategist
in Dwight D. Eisenhower's presidential campaign in 1952.
President Dwight D. Eisenhower named Herbert Brownell,
Jr. Attorney General in November 1952,  Herbert served
in the office from January 21, 1953 until his resignation
on January 26, 1958.  He supervised reorganization of
the Justice Department as projected in the federal reorganization plan of 1953.  Among the various aspects the
duties of the solicitor general were indicated and that
a deputy attorney general was to serve as acting Attorney general when the Attorney General was away from
Washington.  All legal employees were to drop their private practices so that there would be no conflict of interest.
Mr. Brownell was also a member of the second Hoover
Commission, serving on its task force studying legal
procedures.  As a result of this work the government
launched two programs recruiting honor law graduates for
the Justice Department and creating an office of adminis-

trative procedures to simplify and modernize its practices.

Brownell also instituted a system whereby all nominees
for judicial positions would be made after they were
passed upon by the judicial selection committee of the
American Bar Association.  He also created a civil rights
division and an internal security division each run by
an assistant attorney general.  Brownell abolished employment of full-time witnesses.  The Justice Department
also worked to cut through the backlog of cases in the
courts and greatly reduced it.  As Attorney General he
also became involved in the discussion concerning the
drafting of a constitutional amendment concerning presidential diability.

After leaving public office in 1958 Herbert Brownell,
Jr. returned to his legal practice.  He had been honored
with the granting of the honorary LL.D. degree by various
academic institutions including Notre Dame, Fordham,
American and Brown Universities, Lafayette and Hamilton
Colleges and the National University of Ireland.  He
maintains membership in the American Bar Association,
the American Law Institute, the New York State Bar
Association and the Association of the Bar of the City
of New York.

Bibliography:
  Albertson, Dean, ed. Eisenhower as President.  New
York: Hill and Wang, 1963.
  Donovan, Robert J. Eisenhower, The Inside Story.  New
York: Harper and Row, 1956.
  Frier, David. Conflict of Interest in the Eisenhower
Administration.  Ames: Iowa State University Press, 1969.
  Hughes, Emmett J. The Ordeal of Power: A Political
Memoir of the Eisenhower Years.  New York: Atheneum,
1963.
  Larson, Arthur. Eisenhower: The President Nobody
Knew.  New York: Scribner, 1968.
  Vexler, Robert I., ed. Dwight D. Eisenhower, 1890-
1969.  Dobbs Ferry, N.Y.: Oceana Publications, Inc.,
1970.

### ATTORNEY GENERAL: WILLIAM PIERCE ROGERS

William P. Rogers, Attorney General in the Cabinet of
President Dwight D. Eisenhower and Secretary of State
in the Cabinet of President Richard M. Nixon, was born
on June 23, 1913 in Norfolk, New York, the son of Harrison Alexander Rogers, an insurance agent, and Myra (Bes-
wick) Rogers.  After receiving his basic education in
the Norfolk public schools, William completed his high
school education in Canton, New York where he and his
family had moved.  He then went to Colgate University,
receiving his Bachelor of Arts degree in 1934.  Rogers

then went to the Cornell University Law School, receiving the LL.B. degree in 1937. He edited the <u>Cornell</u> <u>Law</u> <u>Quarterly</u> from 1935 to 1937. He was admitted to the New York bar in the same year and began to practice law with the firm of Cadwalader, Wickersham and Taft. William married Adele Langston on June 27, 1936. They had four children: Dale, Anthony Wood, Jeffrey Langston, and Douglas Langston.

William P. Rogers became assistant district attorney of New York City, serving under District Attorney Thomas E. Dewey from January 1938 to August 1942. William entered the United States Navy in August 1942 as a lieutenant j.g. After receiving his training at Quonset Point, Rhode Island Rogers was stationed at the Naval Air Station at Anacostia in Washington, D.C. amd later served as an administrative officer of Carrier Group 10 aboard the USS <u>Intrepid</u> in the Pacific. He was released to inactive duty as a lieutenant commander in January 1946.

Rogers then returned to the New York District Attorney's office where he was named chief of the bureau of special sessions. He left the post in April 1947 when he was appointed counsel to the Senate's special committee investigating the national defense program. In March 1948 Rogers was asked to remain chief counsel of the Senate investigations subcommittee of the executive expenditures committee. Rogers resigned from the subcommittee in March 1950 to become a member of the Washington law office of the New York firm of Dwight, Royall, Harris, Koegel and Saskey. He was admitted to the Washington, D.C. bar in 1950. He was also involved in Republican activities and helped to convince the credentials committee at the 1952 Republican National Convention to seat the Eisenhower rather than the Taft delegates from Louisiana, Texas, Georgia and Florida. William also worked closely with Richard M. Nixon, the vice presidential candidate, during the campaign.

President Dwight D. Eisenhower named William P. Rogers deputy attorney general on January 27, 1953. Rogers was chief liason officer between the Justice Department and Congress as well as various federal agencies and departments. Rogers was charged with supervision of the drafting of all the department's legislative proposals, helping to have the 1957 Civil Rights Act passed. He also worked with Attorney General Herbert Brownell, Jr. to develop a program of recruitment of top law school graduates to work in the Department of Justice.

President Eisenhower named William P. Rogers Attorney General <u>ad</u> <u>interim</u> to replace Herbert Brownell, Jr. He served from November 8, 1957 to January 27, 1958 when he became Attorney General. He served until the end of the Administration on January 20, 1961. As Attorney General he promoted a constitutional amendment dealing

with presidential inability to perform his duties as
well as presidential disability.  Congress did not act
on this proposal.

As a result of the problems created by the beginning
of integration in Little Rock, Arkansas in 1957 Rogers
established in 1958 a Justice Department committee to
deal with federal aspects of integration.  He sent a
group of deputy United States marshals to Little Rock
to guarantee enforcement of orders of the federal courts.
He also instituted a special unit charged with fighting
syndicated crime in 1958 which intensified the anticrime
drive in 1959.

After leaving public office in 1961 he returned to his
private law practice.  He continued his work with the
Republican Party having supported Richard M. Nixon for
the Presidency in 1960.  He was a member of President
Lyndon B. Johnson's Commission on Law Enforcement from
1965 to 1967.  Rogers was a United States representative
to the twentieth session of the United Nations General
Assembly in 1967 and a member of the United Nations Ad
Hoc Committee on South Africa.  Rogers again supported
Nixon in the 1968 presidential campaign.

President Richard M. Nixon appointed William P. Rogers
Secretary of State on January 23, 1969.  One of his first
tasks even before assuming office was to help arrange
a new seating arrangement for the Vietnam peace talks.
William worked during 1970 to arrange for a hemispheric
agreement against terrorists, as well as an oil agreement with Canada.  He also began an internal reform of
the State Department and submitted a new peace plan for
the Middle East.  He signed treaties with Russia in 1971
to avoid nuclear accidents and to modernize the hot line.
President Nixon appointed him vice chairman of a Cabinet
level council on International Economic Policy.  He went
to China with President Nixon on the historic visit from
February 22 to 24, 1972.

During his term in office William P. Rogers attended
many conferences and travelled abroad.  Henry A. Kissinger conducted many of the crucial negotiations in international affairs including the arrangement for the visit
to China directly for the President.  He often bypassed
the State Department and reported to Rogers after the
fact.  Rogers resigned to make way for Kissinger's appointment on August 22, 1973.  William then returned to
his law practice.

Bibliography:
Albertson, Dean, ed. Eisenhower as President.  New
York: Hill and Wang, 1963.
Brandon, Henry. The Retreat of American Power.  Gar-
den City, N.Y.: Doubleday, 1973.
Bremer, Howard F., ed.  Richard M. Nixon, 1913-
Dobbs Ferry, N.Y.: Oceana Publications, Inc., 1975.

Donovan, Robert J. Eisenhower, The Inside Story. New York: Harper and Row, 1956.

Drury, Allen. Courage and Hesitation. Garden City, N.Y.: Doubleday, 1972.

Evans, Rowland, and Novak, Robert P. Nixon in the White House: The Frustration of Power. New York: Random House, 1972.

Hughes, Emmett J. The Ordeal of Power: A Political Memoir of the Eisenhower Years. New York: Atheneum, 1963.

Larson, Arthur. Eisenhower: The President Nobody Knew. New York: Scribner, 1968.

Mazo, Earl, and Hess, Stephen. President Nixon: A Political Portrait. London: MacDonald and Company, 1968.

Vexler, Robert I., ed. Dwight D. Eisenhower, 1890-1969. Dobbs Ferry, N.Y.: Oceana Publications, Inc., 1970.

Wills, Gary. Nixon Agonistes: The Crisis of the Self-Made Man. Boston: Houghton Mifflin Company, 1971.

## POSTMASTER GENERAL:

### ARTHUR ELLSWORTH SUMMERFIELD

Arthur E. Summerfield, Postmaster General in the Cabinet of President Dwight D. Eisenhower, was born on March 17, 1899 in Pinconning, Michigan, near Bay City, the son of William Henry Summerfield, an early rural mail carrier, and Cora Edith (Ellsworth) Summerfield. Arthur received his basic education in the local public schools, leaving at the age of thirteen to work for the Weston-Mott Company as a millboy and then in the production line. He then went to work for the Buick Motor Company in Flint, Michigan, remaining there until 1918 when he became chief inspector in the ammunition department of the Chevrolet plant in Flint. Arthur married Miriam W. Graim on July 22, 1918. They had three children: Gertrude, Miriam and Arthur E., Jr.

Summerfield went into the real estate business in 1919 becoming successful as the owner of the Summerfield Realty Company. In 1924 he also became a distributor for the Pure Oil Company in Flint. He then opened the Summerfield Chevrolet Company in Flint in September 1929. He eventually opened branches in Grand Rapids and Clio, Michigan. He ended his relationship with the Pure Oil Company in 1937 and became president of Bryant Properties Corporation in Flint.

Summerfield then became involved in politics, supporting Wendel Wilkie in the 1940 presidential campaign. Arthur became the Michigan director of the National Car Dealers Association in 1942 and continued in that capacity until 1949, serving for a period as regional vice president of the organization.

Arthur E. Summerfield made an unsuccessful attempt to gain the nomination for secretary of state of Michigan in 1942. He was chairman of the Postwar Planning Committee of the National Auto Dealers of America in 1943 and 1944. He was named finance director of the Republican state central committee in 1943 and was elected Republican national committeeman from Michigan at the 1944 national convention, serving in that post until 1952. During 1946 he was regional vice-chairman of the Republican national finance committee and also organized the Michigan Republicans for Vandenburg for President. In the same year Summerfield unsuccessfully sought the Republican nomination for governor of Michigan. He next became chairman of the Republican strategy committee in July 1949. Arthur was the Michigan director of the Boys Club of America in 1951 and 1952. He kept the Michigan delegation uncommitted at the 1952 Republican National Convention and eventually helped to gain the Presidential nomination for Dwight D. Eisenhower. Summerfield was named chairman of the Republican National Committee in 1952.

President Dwight D. Eisenhower named Arthur E. Summerfield Postmaster General on January 20, 1953. He assumed his office on January 21. Arthur had already resigned his chairmanship of the Republican National Committee because he did not believe that one man should hold both posts at the same time. While Postmaster General Summerfield extended rural free delivery and also gove door service to many rural areas. He replaced some 4,500 county post officers at a great saving, lengthened window service hours and increased the number of letter box collections. He also introduced next-day letter delivery in major metropolitan areas and promoted modernization and automation.

Summerfield developed the "air-lift" concept for first-class mail. He also worked to increase the wages of postal employees and to provide for a uniform benefit as well as low cost group life insurance and travel allowances for road clerks. The University of Michigan awarded Arthur E. Summerfield the honorary LL.D. degree in 1957, and Miami University granted him the same in 1959. He left office at the end of the Eisenhower Administration on January 20, 1961.

Arthur Summerfield returned to his automobile business after leaving government service. Among the other activities in which he became involved was his appointment as a director of the American Motorists' Insurance Company and the Lumbermen's Mutual Insurance Company. He was a member of the board of trustees of Cleary College in Ypsilanti, Michigan.

Bibliography:
    Albertson, Dean, ed.  Eisenhower as President.  New
York: Hill and Wang, 1963.
    Donovan, Robert J.  Eisenhower, The Inside Story.  New
York: Harper and Row, 1956.
    Hughes, Emmett J.  The Ordeal of Power: A Political
Memoir of the Eisenhower Years.  New York: Atheneum,
1963.
    Larson, Arthur.  Eisenhower: The President Nobody
Knew.  New York: Scribner, 1968.
    Vexler, Robert I., ed.  Dwight D. Eisenhower, 1890-
1969.  Dobbs Ferry, N.Y.: Oceana Publications, Inc.,
1970.

## SECRETARY OF THE INTERIOR: DOUGLAS JAMES MCKAY

    Douglas McKay, Secretary of the Interior in the Cabi-
net of President Dwight D. Eisenhower, was born on June
24, 1893 in Portland, Oregon, the son of Edwin Donald
McKay, a carpenter  and Minnie Abele (Musgrove) McKay.
Douglas received his basic education in the Portland
public schools and then went to Oregon State College
from which he was graduated with the Bachelor of Science
degree in 1917.  Douglas married Mabel Christine Hill on
March 31, 1917.  They had three children: Douglas, Shir-
ley, and Mary Lou.
    Douglas J. McKay began working for the Portland Ore-
gonian and the Daily News during college and continued
to work for them after graduation.  He served in the
army during the First World War as a first lieutenant
of the 361st Infantry Regiment, 91st Division.  He fought
in France and was wounded there.  Douglas became an insurance salesman in 1919 for Dooley and Company.  He
next worked for the Francie Motor Company in Portland
beginning in 1920 and was promoted to salesmanager in
1923.  He remained in that position until 1927 when he
moved to Salem, Oregon  There he opened the Douglas
McKay Chevrolet Company selling Chevrolets and Cadillacs.
He owned the company until 1955.  Douglas was at one
time president of the Oregon State Automobile Dealers
Association and a member of the Salem Chamber of
Commerce.
    Douglas McKay also became interested in politics.  He
joined the Republican Party.  Douglas was elected mayor
of Salem in 1932.  While in office he was able to have
the city purchase the Salem water system from the Oregon-
Washington Water Company and established the Salem Water
Bureau.  He was elected to the Oregon Senate in 1934
and served except for a period of time during the war.
McKay served as a captain in the army during the Second
World War and was promoted to the rank of major while
serving at Camp Adair, Oregon.  He continued to be a
member of the Oregon Senate until 1949 and was speaker

in 1947 and 1948.  He assumed the governorship when
Governor Earl Snell died in October 1947.  He was elected
governor of Oregon in November 1948 to complete the term
of Oregon in November 1948 to complete the term and was
elected for a regular four-year term in 1950.

President Dwight D. Eisenhower appointed Douglas Mckay
Secretary of the Interior on January 21, 1953.  While
in office he began a National Park Service Program called
"Mission 66" which was a ten-year development program
to expand the facilities of the National Parks so that
additional visitors could be accomodated.  He supervised
the addition of 400,000 acres to the parks.  Douglas
protected park lands against any type of encroachment,
explotation or reduction in size.  While he was in office
nine new wildlife areas were added.  He opposed transfer
of part of the Wichita Wildlife Refuge to the Army.

The Interior Department also began a long-range program to integrate Indians into American society by
improving their educational facilities and getting many
to voluntarily move to areas where additional jobs were
available.  McKay also had Indian health services transferred to the Department of Health, Education and Welfare.
The Department was also given the authority to regulate
mineral development by gas and oil leases on wild life
areas.  Douglas McKay was chairman of the President's
Mineral Policy Committee which made its final report
in 1954.  Its recommendations included regulation of
strategic and critical minerals and creation of the Office of Minerals Mobilization in the department.

Douglas McKay was chairman of the President's Committee
on Water Resources Policy.  He also supervised the development of a 20-year program for soil and moisture
conservation.  The Department also urged cooperation of
federal and nonfederal groups in development of hydroelectric power in the Northwest.  McKay instituted
economies through improvement of the management of agencies.  He resigned from the Department of the Interior
on June 8, 1956 in order to run unsuccessfully for the
United States Senate.  Douglas McKay died on July 22,
1959 in Salem, Oregon.

Bibliography:
  Albertson, Dean, ed.  Eisenhower as President.  New
York: Hill and Wang, 1963.
  Donovan, Robert J.  Eisenhower, The Inside Story.  New
York: Harper and Row, 1956.
  Hughes, Emmett J.  The Ordeal of Power: A Political
Memoir of the Eisenhower Years.  New York: Atheneum,
1963.
  Larson. Arthur.  Eisenhower: The President Nobody
Knew.  New York: Scribner, 1968.
  Vexler, Robert I., ed.  Dwight D. Eisenhower, 1890-
1969.  Dobbs Ferry, N.Y.: Oceana Publications, Inc., 1970.

## SECRETARY OF THE INTERIOR:

## FREDERICK ANDREW SEATON

Frederick A. Seaton, Secretary of the Interior in the Cabinet of President Dwight D. Eisenhower, was born on December 11, 1909 in Washington, D.C., the son of Fay Noble Seaton, a publisher, and Dorothea Elizabeth (Schmidt) Seaton. Frederick moved with his family to Manhattan, Kansas where he received his basic education in the public schools. He then studied at Kansas State College from 1927 to 1931, graduating in the latter year. He was director of sports activity while at college. Frederick also became a sports announcer for radio stations KSAC and WIBW of Manhattan, Kansas in 1929 and continued until 1937. In addition he was business manager for the Manhattan Little Theater during 1930 and 1931. Frederick married Gladys Hope Dowd on January 23, 1931. They had four children: Donald Richard, Johanna Christine, Monica Margaret, and Alfred Noble.

He began to work with his father's newspapers in 1931, becoming wire news editor for the Manhattan Morning Chronicle in 1932 and then city editor of the Evening Mercury in 1933. In the same year he became an associate editor of the Seaton Publications Company in Manhattan, continuing in that position until 1937. Frederick had become active in the Republican Party and was vice chairman of the Young Republican Club of Kansas from 1932 to 1934. He then was state chairman from 1934 to 1936 and was Young Republican national committeeman for Kansas in 1935. He was also vice chairman of the Kansas Republican state committee from 1934 to 1937.

Frederick Seaton was vice chairman of the Kansas delegation to the Republican National Convention in 1936 and became secretary to the Republican presidential nominee Alfred M. Landon in the same year. He was a member of the Republican National Speakers Bureau from 1936 to 1940. Seaton also expanded his business activities, and since 1937 was president of the Sheridan Newspapers, Inc. in Wyoming, the Seaton Publishing Company, Inc. in Kansas, the Manhattan Broadcasting Company, the Alliance Publishing Company in Nebraska, the Nebraska Broadcasting Company of Hastings, and the Western Farm Publishing Company.

Seaton moved to Hastings, Nebraska in 1937 and became publisher of the Seaton Publishing Company. He was made a director of the Nebraska State Grain Improvement Association in 1945. He also served two terms in the unicameral Nebraska legislature from 1945 to 1949. He was chairman of the Nebraska Legislative Council from 1947 to 1949 and a member of the Nebraska Judicial Council from 1948 to 1950. Frederick was vice president of the National Rivers and Harbors Congress in 1951.

Among his other activities Seaton was a trustee of the University of Nebraska Foundation and Hastings College.

On December 10, 1951 Seaton was appointed interim United States Senator from Nebraska to fill the vacancy caused by the death of Kenneth S. Sherry. Frederick remained in the Senate until January 3, 1953. He was a member of Dwight D. Eisenhower's personal advisory staff in 1952 during the presidential campaign. President Eisenhower named Frederick Seaton assistant Secretary of Defense for legislative and public affairs in September 1953 and continued until 1955 when on February 19 he was named presidential administrative assistant for Congressional liason. He was next promoted to deputy assistant on June 15, 1955.

President Dwight D. Eisenhower appointed Frederick A. Seaton Secretary of Defense on June 6, 1956. He assumed his office on June 8, 1956 and served until the end of the administration on January 20, 1961. He was the leader of the campaign for admission of Hawaii and Alaska to statehood. Frederick  endorsed the concept of federal, state and local government cooperation for the development of natural resources. He promoted various water supply and hydroelectric projects. He was also involved in a saline-water conversion program to produce fresh water from sea water. He was responsible for passage of legislation which provided loans for irrigation and reclamation projects.

Frederick A. Seaton helped to establish a 9,000,000-acre Arctic Wildlife Range and to institute a $3.00 duck stamp for the study of ducks which led to the passage of the Duck Stamp Act of 1958. He also arranged for the army at Fort Still to use part of the Wichita Mountains wildlife refuge for artillery practice without threatening the resources of the area. He carefully supervised Mission 66 which was aimed at improving, protecting and expanding the natural park system. President Eisenhower placed Seaton in charge of the program of adjusting and regulating crude oil imports.

After leaving government service Frederick Seaton returned to his work with the Seaton Publishing Company. Among the honors he received were the honorary LL.D. degrees from many colleges and universities including Kansas State College in 1955, the University of Alaska in 1958 and Miami University in Oxford, Ohio, Gettysburg College and the Universities of Hawaii and of the Redlands in 1959. He was also awarded the United States Medal of Freedom. Among the organizations in which he has been or is a member are the National Editorial Association and the American Academy of Political and Social Science.

Bibliography:
  Albertson, Dean, ed.   Eisenhower as President.   New

York: Hill and Wang, 1963.
    Donovan, Robert J. <u>Eisenhower</u>, <u>The</u> <u>Inside</u> <u>Story</u>.  New
York: Harper and Row, 1956.
    Hughes, Emmett J.  <u>The</u> <u>Ordeal</u> <u>of</u> <u>Power</u>: <u>A</u> <u>Political</u>
<u>Memoir</u> <u>of</u> <u>the</u> <u>Eisenhower</u> <u>Years</u>.  New York: Atheneum,
1963.
    Larson, Arthur.  <u>Eisenhower</u>: <u>The</u> <u>President</u> <u>Nobody</u> <u>Knew</u>.
New York: Scribner, 1968.
    Vexler, Robert I., ed.  <u>Dwight</u> <u>D.</u> <u>Eisenhower</u>, <u>1890-</u>
<u>1969</u>.  Dobbs Ferry, N.Y.: Oceana Publications, Inc.,
1970.

## SECRETARY OF AGRICULTURE: EZRA TAFT BENSON

Ezra Taft Benson, Secretary of Agriculture in the Cabinet of President Dwight D. Eisenhower, was born on
August 4, 1899 in Whitney, Idaho, the son of George Taft
Benson, a farmer, and Sarah (Dankley) Benson.  Ezra re-
ceived his basic education at the Whitney elementary
school and worked on the family farm.  He then attended
Oneida State Academy at Preston, Idaho from 1914 to 1918.
He also took a correspondence course and then studied
at Utah State Agricultural College from 1918 to 1921.
He was a Mormon missionary to Europe and Great Britain
from 1921 to 1923 and was president of the Newcastle
District for the Church of Jesus Christ of Latter-day
Saints.
    Ezra Taft Benson returned to Idaho where he ran his
own farm from 1923 to 1929.  He received the Bachelor
of Science degree from Brigham Young University in 1926
and then studied at Iowa State College, graduating with
the Master of Science degree in 1927.  Ezra married
Flora Smith Amussen on September 10, 1926.  They had
six children: Reed, Mark, Barbara, Beverly, Bonnie, and
Flora Ruth.  He was also a county agricultural agent for
the extension service of the University of Idaho in
Preston during 1929 and 1930.
    In 1930 Benson helped to establish the Idaho Corpora-
tive Council and was its secretary from 1933 to 1938.
He became a member of the Boy Scout Commission in 1930
and continued until 1933.  He also became an extension
economist and marketing specialist for the University
of Idaho in 1930 and continued until 1938.  Benson was
next executive secretary of the National Council of Farmer Cooperatives from 1939 to 1944.  He was a member of
the National Farm Credit Committee from 1940 to 1943
and a member of the National Agricultural Advisory Committee during World War II.
    Among his other activities Ezra Taft Benson was a mem-
ber of the executive committee of the board of trustees
of the American Institute of Cooperation in 1942 and
continued until 1952.  He was chairman of the board in
the last year.  He was a member of Region Twelve Execu-

tive Committee in 1945.  Benson represented the United
States at the first International Conference of Farm
Organizations in London in 1946.  During the same year
he was named director of the Farm Foundations and continued in that post until 1950.

President Dwight D. Eisenhower named Ezra Taft Benson
Secretary of Agriculture on November 24, 1952.  He toured
rural areas of the United States as preparation for his
post and took office on January 21, 1953.  He served until the end of the Eisenhower Administration on January
20, 1961.  Benson worked to reorganize the department.
He recommended that Congress introduce a degree of flexi-
bility in the price support program.  Under his direction
the Department of Agriculture developed a program of
moving surplus farm products from the warehouse for use
domestically and abroad.  He also used the soil bank
program to reduce production of surplus food products.

Ezra Taft Benson also further developed conservation
programs of soil and water.  In addition an experimental
program was begun to help develop more economic opportunities.  The University of Utah granted Benson the
honorary LL.D. degree in 1953 as did Bowdoin College in
1955 and the University of Maine in 1956.  Benson also
wrote Farmers at the Crossroads in 1956 as well as various
articles concerning agriculture.  He was granted the
LL.D. degree by the University of Hawaii in 1957 and by
Utah State University in 1958.

Among his other activities since Ezra Taft Benson left
public office in January 1961 has been his membership
on the board of trustees of Brigham Young University,
the American Marketing Association and the Farm Economics
Association.  He also remains an adviser on agricultural
matters.

Bibliography:
Albertson, Dean, ed. Eisenhower as President.  New
York: Hill and Wang, 1963.
Donovan, Robert J. Eisenhower, The Inside Story.  New
York: Harper and Row, 1956.
Hughes, Emmett J.  The Ordeal of Power: A Political
Memoir of the Eisenhower Years.  New York: Atheneum,
1963.
Larson, Arthur.  Eisenhower: The President Nobody
Knew.  New York: Scribner, 1968.
Vexler, Robert I., ed.  Dwight D. Eisenhower, 1890-
1969.  Dobbs Ferry, N.Y.: Oceana Publications, Inc.,
1970.

SECRETARY OF COMMERCE: (CHARLES) SINCLAIR WEEKS

Sinclair Weeks, Secretary of Commerce in the Cabinet
of President Dwight D. Eisenhower, was born on June 15,
1893 in West Newton, Massachusetts, the son of John

Wingate Weeks, Secretary of War in the Cabinets of Presidents Warren G. Harding and Calvin Coolidge, and Martha
Caroline (Sinclair) Weeks. Sinclair received his basic
education in the Newton public schools and then went
to Harvard University, graduating with the Bachelor of
Arts degree in 1914.

Sinclair Weeks then went to work as a clerk for the
First National Bank of Boston. He married Beatrice Dowse
on December 4, 1915. They had five children: Frances
Lee, John Wingate, Sinclair, Beatrice, and William Dowse.
Weeks joined the Massachusetts National Guard, serving
on the Mexican border in 1916. He entered the army during the First World War on July 25, 1917 as a second
lieutenant and was eventually promoted to the rank of
captain in Battery B of the 101st Field Artillery Regiment. He went to France where he fought in the 26th
Division.

After leaving the army at the end of the war on April
30, 1919 Sinclair Weeks continued to serve in the National Guard, eventually rising to the rank of lieutenant
colonel. He returned to the First National Bank of
Boston, remaining there until 1923 and eventually became
assistant cashier. He next joined Reed and Barton Corporation of Taunton, Massachusetts, manufacturer of metal products, in 1923, eventually becoming vice president, president and then chairman of the board. He left
the firm in 1953.

Sinclair Weeks also became interested in politics as
a Republican and was elected an alderman of Newton, serving from 1923 to 1929. He was next elected mayor, in
which office he served for three terms from 1930 to 1935.
Sinclair was chairman of Massachusetts Republican state
committee from 1936 to 1938 and was a member of the national committee from 1940 to 1953. Massachusetts Governor Leverett Saltonstall appointed Weeks to the United States Senate in February 1944 to fill the vacancy
left by the resignation of Henry Cabot Lodge, Jr. Sinclair Weeks served until December 1944. He did not
seek reelection to succeed himself. After his wife Beatrice's death he eventually married Jane (Tompkins)
Rankin on January 3, 1948.

Weeks returned to his business interests. He was
president and chairman of the board of United Carr Fas-
tener Corporation of Cambridge, Massachusetts and director of the Gilette Safety Razor Company, Pacific Mills,
the Pullman Company and the First National Bank of Boston. In the area of politics Weeks was chairman of the
finance committee of the Republican National Committee
from 1949 to 1953. He was also a member of the Board
of Overseers of Harvard University.

President Dwight D. Eisenhower named Sinclair Weeks
Secretary of Commerce in which post he served from January 21, 1953 until his resignation on November 12, 1958.

He produced a reduction in his departmental budget.  Sinclair also worked to promote greater efficiency and to reduce personnel by a policy of nonreplacement of vacant positions while expanding the services of the department. It encouraged the growth of business as well as transportation through expansion of the American highway system in the interest of defense.  Seaton also worked with the Maritime Administration in the largest shipbuilding program of merchant ships in peace time including construction of the world's first nuclear powered merchant vessel to be completed in 1959.

Weeks was able to gain a large appropriation for the Civil Aeronautics Administration to increase construction of airports and development of safety procedures for jet age travel.  The Commerce Department also improved its statistics services under his direction.  He also established or reorganized the Bureau of Foreign Commerce, Business and Defense Services Administration, Office of Area Development, and the Office of International Trade Fairs.  He was elected National Association of Manufacturers Man of the Year in 1954.  President Eisenhower accepted Weeks' resignation on October 24, 1958, effective November 10.

After leaving public office Weeks returned to his business interests.  He also serves as a director of the Wentworth Institute, a member of the corporation of Northeastern University, a trustee of New England Deaconess Hospital, a member of the board of overseers of the Boys Clubs of Boston.  He was also appointed a trustee of the Fessenden School in West Newton, Massachusetts and honorary vice president of the National Association of Manufacturers.

Bibliography:
Albertson, Dean, ed.  Eisenhower as President.  New York: Hill and Wang, 1963.
Donovan, Robert J.  Eisenhower, The Inside Story.  New York: Harper and Row, 1956.
Hughes, Emmett J.  The Ordeal of Power: A Political Memoir of the Eisenhower Years.  New York: Atheneum, 1963.
Larson, Arthur.  Eisenhower: The President Nobody Knew.  New York: Scribner, 1968.
Vexler, Robert I., ed.  Dwight D. Eisenhower, 1890-1969.  Dobbs Ferry, N.Y.: Oceana Publications, Inc., 1970.

SECRETARY OF COMMERCE:

## LEWIS LICHTENSTEIN STRAUSS

Lewis L. Strauss, Secretary of Commerce in the Cabinet of President Dwight D. Eisenhower, was born on January 31, 1896 in Charleston, West Virginia, the son of Lews S. Strauss, a businessman, and Rosa (Lichtenstein) Strauss. He received his basic education in the Charleston public schools and then attended John Marshall High School in Richmond, Virginia. Lewis became a travelling salesman after graduating from high school. He served as a volunteer staff member for Herbert Hoover who was chairman of the Commission for the Relief of Belgium, serving until 1919 without pay. He also became a personal secretary to Hoover when he was a head of the United States Food Administration.

Lewis Strauss was one of the four American delegates to the final Armistice Convention in 1919 at Brussels. He turned down the position of comptroller of the League of Nations in the summer. He became a member of the New York banking firm of Kuhn, Loeb and Company in 1919. In 1920 he was a member of the Belgian-American Educational Foundation. Among his other activities Strauss worked with George Sloan to raise funds to repatriate the 8,000 Austrian and Hungarian prisoners of war abandonned in Siberia. He helped Leopold Mannes and Leopold Godowsky, Jr. to develop their process for simple color photography which was sold by Eastman Kodak as Kodachrome in 1923. He also backed Edward H. Land who eventually invented the Land Polaroid camera.

Lewis Strauss married Alice Hanauer on March 5, 1925. They had two sons. Lewis was commissioned a lieutenant commander of the United States Naval Reserve in 1926. He became a partner of Kuhn Loeb and Company in 1928. During the same year he became active in Republican politics as vice treasurer of the Republican National Committee during Herbert Hoover's presidential campaign. He was called to active duty in the Navy in February 1941 and was assigned as a staff assistant to the chief of ordinance in which post he remained until 1943. He coordinated the navy's weapons inspection system and then represented his branch on the Interdepartmental Committee on Atomic Energy as well as on the Army and Navy Munitions Board. His next assignment was as special assistant to Secretary of the Navy James V. Forrestal in 1944.

Lewis L. Strauss was deputy chief of the Office of Navy Material and wrote the Strauss Draper report with William F. Draper which developed coordination for the Army and Navy to obtain supplies such as petroleum, clothing and food. He was given many service medals including the Navy Distinguished Service Medal and the Legion of Merit. President Harry S. Truman promoted Lewis L.

Strauss to the rank of rear admiral in November 1945. He
also served on the Navy's Civilian Research Advisory Committee after World War I.

Lewis Strauss returned to Kuhn, Loeb and Company but
was soon called back to government service in 1946 by
President Truman as a member of the Atomic Energy Commission. Strauss then resigned all his business posts.
He developed a monitoring system which enabled the United
States to detect the first Russian atomic bomb explosion
in 1949. He wanted the United States to develop a hy-
drogen bomb but met opposition from physicists and members
of the Commission. Strauss resigned from the Commission
in 1950 when his proposals were accepted in order to end
reminders of previous friction.

Lewis S. Straus next became a consultant and financial
adviser to the Rockefellers, retaining this post until
1953. President Dwight D. Eisenhower named Lewis Strauss
his special assistant on atomic energy matters in February 1953. The President next named him chairman of the
Atomic Energy Commission in which post he served from
July 2, 1953 until the end of his five year term on June
30, 1958. He then became a presidential assistant in the
Atoms for Peace program.

President Dwight D. Eisenhower appointed Lewis L.
Strauss Secretary of Commerce in October 1958. He served
on an _ad_ _interim_ basis from November 13, 1954 to June 27,
1959 when he resigned because the Senate had not confirmed
his appointment. He continued his active interest in
business and politics. He was asked to head a space study group for Senator Barry Goldwater during his presidential campaign of 1964 and then helped to establish the
Free Society Association which was chaired by Goldwater
in 1965.

Among Strauss' philanthropic activities he was a member
of and is still active in many organizations including
president of the trustees of the Institute for Advanced
Study in Princeton, New Jersey; a life trustee of Hampton
Institute and Sloan Kettering Institute. He has also
been involved as a trustee of Memorial Cancer Hospital,
the Institute for the Crippled and Disabled and the Bel-
gian Educational Foundation. He has been the recipient
of many honorary degrees by such higher institutions of
learning including Columbia, Tufts and New York Universities, the Jewish Theological Seminary, Union, Dickinson
and Hebrew Union Colleges, and the University of Pennsylvania.

Bibliography:
  Albertson, Dean, ed. _Eisenhower_ as _President_. New
York: Hill and Wang, 1963.
  Donovan, Robert J. _Eisenhower_, _The_ _Inside_ _Story_. New
York: Harper and Row, 1956.
  Frier, David. _Conflict_ _of_ _Interest_ _in_ _the_ _Eisenhower_

Administration. Ames: Iowa State University Press, 1969.
   Hughes, Emmett J. The Ordeal of Power: A Political
Memoir of the Eisenhower Years. New York: Atheneum,
1963.
   Larson, Arthur. Eisenhower: The President Nobody
Knew. New York: Scribner, 1968.
   Vexler, Robert I., ed. Dwight D. Eisenhower, 1890-
1969. Dobbs Ferry, N.Y.: Oceana Publications, Inc.,
1970.

SECRETARY OF COMMERCE: FREDERICK HENRY MUELLER

   Frederick H. Mueller, Secretary of Commerce in the Cabinet of President Dwight D. Eisenhower, was born on November 22, 1893 in Grand Rapids, Michigan, the son of
John Frederick Mueller, a furniture manufacturer, and
Emma Matilda (Oestenk) Mueller. Frederick received his
basic education in the Grand Rapids public schools. During this period he became an apprentice in his father's
furniture company at the age of 15. He next studied
mechanical engineering at Michigan State University
in East Lansing, graduating with the Bachelor of Science
degree in 1914.
   Frederick Mueller joined Mueller and Slack Company
which was discontinued as a corporation in 1919, becoming
a partnership as Mueller Furniture Company. Frederick
married Mary Darrah on November 6, 1915. They had two
children: Marcia Joan and Frederick Eugene.
   Frederick H. Mueller became general manager of Mueller
Furniture Company in 1922 and eventually was president,
remaining an officer until 1955. He helped to establish
the Grand Rapids Furniture Makers Guild in 1932 and was
its president until 1941. He was president of the National Association of Furniture Manufacturers in 1934
and continued as a member.
   Frederick became president in 1936 of the Furniture
Mutual Insurance Company of Grand Rapids, insuring the
stockholders for workmen's compensation as a result of
industrial accidents. He continued in this office until
1946. Mueller was also president and general manager of
Grand Rapids Industries, Inc. from 1941 to 1946. It
arranged for cooperation among all woodworking companies
in Grand Rapids to produce gliders for the United States
government during the Second World War. In addition he
organized and was group commander of the Cedar Rapids
Civil Air Patrol.
   Mueller was also president of the Butterworth Hospital from 1945 to 1955 as well as of the United Hospital
Fund, Inc. from 1948 to 1955. In addition he was a member of the governing board of Michigan State University
from 1945 to 1957. He was also a director of the Peoples
National Bank of Grand Rapids from 1949 to 1958. Mueller
was appointed assistant secretary for domestic affairs

in the Department of Commerce.  President Eisenhower next
named Mueller Undersecretary of Commerce on October 29,
1958.  The Senate confirmed his appointment on June 4,
1959.

President Dwight D. Eisenhower named Frederick H.
Mueller acting Secretary of Commerce on June 30, 1959.
He then appointed him Secretary of Commerce ad interim
on July 21, 1959 in which post Mueller served until August
6, 1959 when he became Secretary of Commerce.  Frederick
continued the important contributions of the department
to the economic growth of the nation.  After leaving
public office at the end of the administration on January 20, 1961 Frederick H. Mueller returned to Grand Rapids, Michigan where he lives in retirement with his
family.

Bibliography:
  Albertson, Dean.  Eisenhower as President.  New
York: Hill and Wang, 1963.
  Donovan, Robert J.  Eisenhower, The Inside Story.  New
York: Harper and Row, 1956.
  Frier, David.  Conflict of Interest in the Eisenhower
Administration.  Ames: Iowa State University Press, 1969.
  Hughes, Emmett J.  The Ordeal of Power: A Political
Memoir of the Eisenhower Years.  New York: Atheneum,
1963.
  Larson, Arthur.  Eisenhower: The President Nobody
Knew.  New York: Scribner, 1968.
  Vexler, Robert I., ed.  Dwight D. Eisenhower, 1890-
1969.  Dobbs Ferry, N.Y.: Oceana Publications, Inc.,
1970.

## SECRETARY OF LABOR: MARTIN PATRICK DURKIN

Martin P. Durkin, Secretary of Labor in the Cabinet of
President Dwight D. Eisenhower, was born on March 18,
1894 in Chicago, Illinois, the son of James J. Durkin,
a stationery engineer, and Mary Catherine (Higgins) Durkin.  After receiving his basic education in the parochial schools of Chicago Martin took courses in heating
and ventilation engineering and also worked in a packing
house.  Durkin became a steamfitter's helper in 1911 and
then a journeyman in the union in 1917.  When the United
States entered the First World War he served in the army
as a private and fought in France.

After returning to the United States Martin P. Durkin
returned to his work.  He was elected assistant business
agent of the Steamfitters Local 597 of the United Association of Journeymen and Apprentices of the Plumbing
and Pipe Fitting Industry of the United States and Canada,
serving from 1921 to 1937.  Martin married Anna H.
McNicholas on August 29, 1921.  They had three children:
Martin P., William J., and John F.

Durkin was elected vice president of the Chicago
Building Trades Council in which post he remained from
1927 to 1933.  His talents were recognized when he was
named state director of labor for Illinois from 1933 to
1941.  During this period Martin was also president of
the International Association of Governmental Labor Officials from 1933 to 1955.  He was national secretary-treasurer of the United Association of Plumbers and Steamfitters of the American Federation of Labor in 1941.  He was
elected president of the union in 1943, serving for the
next ten years.

President Dwight D. Eisenhower named Martin P. Durkin
Secretary of Labor.  He assumed his office on January 21,
1953.  He helped to institute legislation which created
unemployment compensation, a state employment service,
in addition to a state conciliation and medication service.  While in office Martin Durkin was also a member of the Defense Mobilization Board, the National Security Resources Board and the National War Labor Board.

Durkin was also a director of the Union Labor Life Insurance Company and the National Safety Council.  He was
granted the Rerum Novarum Award by St. Peter's College
in 1953.  Durkin resigned from his post as Secretary of
Labor on October 8, 1953 because of a disagreement over
the concepts involved in the Taft-Hartley Act.

Among his other activities Martin Durkin was vice
president of the Catholic Conference on Industrial Pat-
terns.  He also belonged to the Knights of Columbus and
the Holy Name Society.  Martin P. Durkin died on November
13, 1955 in Washington, D.C.

Bibliography:
Albertson, Dean. _Eisenhower as President_.  New
York: Hill and Wang, 1963.
Donovan. Robert J. _Eisenhower, The Inside Story_.  New
York: Harper and Row, 1956.
Frier, David. _Conflict of Interest in the Eisenhower
Administration_.  Ames: Iowa State University Press, 1969.
Hughes, Emmett J. _The Ordeal of Power: A Political
Memoir of the Eisenhower Years_.  New York: Atheneum,
1963.
Larson, Arthur. _Eisenhower: The President Nobody
Knew_.  New York: Scribner, 1968.
Vexler, Robert I., ed. _Dwight D. Eisenhower, 1890-
1969_.  Dobbs Ferry, N.Y.: Oceana Publications, Inc.,
1970.

### SECRETARY OF LABOR: JAMES PAUL MITCHELL

James P. Mitchell, Secretary of Labor in the Cabinet
of President Dwight D. Eisenhower, was born on November
12, 1900 in Elizabeth, New Jersey, the son of Peter J.
Mitchell, editor of a trade journal, and Anna C.

(Driscoll) Mitchell.  He received his basic education at
St. Patrick's parochial school and then attended Batten
High School in Elizabeth, graduating in 1917.  James then
worked in a local grocery store for a year, eventually
becoming manager.  He then opened his own store in Rahway,
New Jersey in 1918 and a second one in Elizabeth in 1921.

James P. Mitchell married Isabelle Nulton on January 22,
1923.  They had one daughter, Elizabeth.  After both of
Mitchell's stores failed in 1923 he worked as a truck
driver.  In 1926 he became an expediter in the Western
Electric Company plant in Kearny, New Jersey.  He then
worked in the personnell department until 1931 when he
was loaned by Western Electric to the New Jersey Relief
Administration to direct Union County relief and work
activities, continuing in that capacity until 1941.

James Mitchell left Western Electric in 1936 to supervise labor relations for the New York City division of
the Works Progress Administration.  He worked under
Brehan B. Somervell.  When Somervell went to Washington,
D.C. in 1940 to head the Army's construction Mitchell
joined him as head of the labor relations division.  In
1941 James P. Mitchell was appointed director of industrial personnell in the War Department.  He was responsible
for the labor problems involving production for the wartime army.  In addition he was a member of the National
Building Trades Stabilization Board and an alternate for
the Undersecretary of War on the War Manpower Commission.

At the end of the war in 1945 Mitchell returned to private business as director of personnel and industrial
relations for R. H. Macy and Company, in New York City.
He next became vice president in charge of labor relations for the New York firm of Bloomingdale Brothers in
1947.  He studied the military government's civilian employment program in Germany in 1948.  In the same year
he was a member of the personnel advisory board of the
Hoover Commission studying the organization of the Executive Branch of the government as well as chairman of the
employee relations committee of the National Retail Dry
Goods Association.

James P. Mitchell made a study of combat pay problems
for the Army in 1950 after the Korean War broke.  Among
his other activities he was a member of the executive
committee of the National Civil Service League and chairman of the executive committee of the Retail Labor
Standards Association of New York.  President Dwight D.
Eisenhower named Mitchell assistant secretary of the
army charged with manpower and reserve forces affairs
in April 1953.  He resigned from Bloomingdale's to assume
his post in July 1953, continuing in this office until
October 1953.

President Dwight D. Eisenhower appointed James P. Mitchell Secretary of Labor in which post he served on an
**ad interim** basis from October 9, 1954 until he was con-

firmed by the Senate and officially assumed his office
on January 20, 1954, serving until the end of the
administration on January 20, 1961.  He succeeded Martin P. Durkin.  While in office Mitchell insisted that
employers pay back-wages if they violated the minimum
wage and overtime regulations under the Fair Labor
Standards Act and the Walsh-Healey Public Contracts Act.
New industries were brought under the minimum wage regulations including the soft coal industry.

James P. Mitchell created several new positions including deputy undersecretary of labor and three deputy assistant secretaries of labor.  In addition he established
the Office of Research and Development.  Under his administration of the Department of Labor old age and survivors' insurance and unemployment insurance was extended
to millions of workers.  Congress passed a law on August
25, 1958 requiring reports of all employee welfare and
pensions plans which were supervised by the Secretary of
Labor.  In addition Mitchell instituted an evaluation of
the skilled and technical manpower of the nation as
well as developing a program to aid older workers in
finding positions.

While James P. Mitchell was in office he was granted
the honorary LL.D. degree by Fordham University in 1954
and was given a citation for outstanding service on behalf of labor by the Confederated Unions of America in
1956.  He was also given the 1956 America's Democratic
Legacy Silver Medallion by the Anti-Defamation League
of B'nai B'rith.  In 1957 he was given the National
Urban League's Equal Opportunity Day Award.  In the same
year Temple and Lehigh Universities granted Mitchell the
LL.D. degree.  Notre Dame and Fairleigh Dickinson Universities granted him the same in 1958.  He retired after leaving public office.  James P. Mitchell died on
October 19, 1964.

Bibliography:
  Albertson, Dean, ed.  Eisenhower as President.  New
York: Hill and Wang, 1963.
  Donovan, Robert J.  Eisenhower, The Inside Story.  New
York: Harper and Row, 1956.
  Frier, David.  Conflict of Interest in the Eisenhower
Administration.  Ames: Iowa State University Press, 1969.
  Hughes, Emmett J.  The Ordeal of Power: A Political
Memoir of the Eisenhower Years.  New York: Atheneum,
1963.
  Larson, Arthur.  Eisenhower: The President Nobody
Knew.  New York: Scribner, 1968.
  Vexler, Robert I., ed.  Dwight D. Eisenhower, 1890-
1969.  Dobbs Ferry, N.Y.: Oceana Publications, Inc.,
1970.

SECRETARY OF HEALTH, EDUCATION, AND WELFARE:

OVETA CULP HOBBY

Oveta Culp Hobby, first Secretary of Health, Education, and Welfare in the Cabinet of President Dwight D. Eisenhower, was born on January 19, 1905 in Killeen, Texas, the daughter of Isaac William Culp, a lawyer, and Emma (Hoover) Culp. After receiving her basic education in the Killeen public schools and from private tutors Oveta read law in her father's office. She next studied at Mary Hardin-Baylor College in Belton, Texas and then went to the University of Texas Law School in 1927. During this period she was parliamentarian of the Texas House of Representatives beginning in 1925 and continuing until 1931. She was also appointed a legal clerk in the Texas state Banking Department.

Oveta Culp became a member of the Democratic Party and attended the Democratic National Convention in 1928. She was appointed assistant to the Houston city attorney. She was an unsuccessful candidate for the state legislature in 1930. Oveta married William Pettus Hobby, who had been governor of Texas from 1917 to 1921 and was publisher of the Houston Post, on February 23, 1931. They had two children: William and Jessica.

Mrs. Hobby became a research editor on the Houston Post staff in 1931. She was next book editor for the paper from 1933 to 1936, becoming assistant editor in 1936. She remained in this position until 1938 when she was promoted to executive vice president. Oveta Culp Hobby wrote Mr. Chairman in 1937. She eventually became full-time manager of the Post. During this period Mrs. Hobby was also president of the Texas League of Women Voters and a director of the National Bank of Cleburne. She also became executive director of radio station KPRC. Her preeminence in the journalistic field was evidenced in her membership on the board of directors of the American Society of Newspaper Editors and the Texas Newspaper Publishers Association. Oveta was also a member of the Board of Regents of Texas State Teachers College and a director of Texas Medical College.

In July 1941 Oveta Culp Hobby was appointed head of the women's division of the Bureau of Public Relations in the War Department. She next was named director of the Women's Auxiliary Army Corps in May 1942 and was given the rank of major. She retired from this post in 1945 and returned to her journalistic career.

Mrs. Hobby served in 1948 as a consultant to the Hoover Commission for Organization of the Executive Branch of the Government. Her journalistic activities expanded when she was elected president of the Southern Newspaper Publishers in 1949. She became coeditor and publisher of the Houston Post in 1952. Oveta was an active suppor-

ter of Dwight D. Eisenhower during the 1952 presidential
campaign.  The President appointed her federal security
administrator in 1953.

On April 1, 1953 President Dwight D. Eisenhower signed
the law creating the new cabinet post, the Department
of Health, Education, and Welfare.  He named Oveta Culp
Hobby as the first Secretary of Health, Education, and
Welfare.  She assumed her office on April 11, 1953.
While in office Mrs. Hobby supervised the organization
of the department and coordination of the various agencies.  She urged adoption of various voluntary, nonprofit
insurance plans.  She resigned from her post on August
1, 1955.

After retiring from public office Mrs. Hobby returned
to her newspaper activities, becoming president of the
Houston Post Publishing Company in 1955.  She was also
named a trustee of the American Assembly in 1957 and
has continued on that board.  She became editor and
chairman of the Board of the Houston Post Company in
1965 and has continued to serve in that capacity.

Bibliography:
Albertson, Dean, ed.  Eisenhower as President.  New
York: Hill and Wang, 1963.
Donovan. Robert J.  Eisenhower, The Inside Story.  New
York: Harper and Row, 1956.
Frier, David.  Conflict of Interest in the Eisenhower
Administration.  Ames: Iowa State University Press, 1969.
Hughes, Emmett J.  The Ordeal of Power: A Political
Memoir of the Eisenhower Years.  New York: Atheneum,
1963.
Larson, Arthur.  Eisenhower: The President Nobody
Knew.  New York: Scribner, 1968.
Vexler, Robert I. , ed.  Dwight D. Eisenhower, 1890-
1969.  Dobbs Ferry, N.Y.: Oceana Publications, Inc.,
1970.

SECRETARY OF HEALTH, EDUCATION, AND WELFARE:

MARION BAYARD FOLSOM

Marion B. Folsom, Secretary of Health, Education, and
Welfare in the Cabinet of President Dwight D. Eisenhower,
was born on November 23, 1893 in McRae  Georgia, the son
of William Bryant and Margaret Jane (McRae) Folsom.
After receiving his basic education in the public schools,
Marion B. Folsom went to the University of Georgia from
which he was graduated with the Bachelor of Arts degree
in 1912.  He then attended Harvard University School of
Business Administration from which he received the Master of Business Administration degree in 1914.  In the
same year he was employed by the Eastman Kodak Company
of Rochester, New York.

Marion B. Folsom entered the United States Army during
the First World War as a captain in the quartermaster
corps.  Marion married Mary Davenport on November 16,
1918.  They had three children: Jane McRae, Marion Bayard, and Frances.  Mr. Folsom became an assistant to
the president of Eastman Kodak in 1921 and then assistant
to the chairman of the board in 1925.  Folsom became a
director of the Lincoln Rochester Trust Company in 1929,
remaining on the board until 1949.  He was promoted to
assistant treasurer of Eastman Kodak in 1930.  He was a
trustee of the Rochester Savings Bank from 1931 to 1944.
He served as a director of the Rochester Community Chest
since 1932.

President Franklin D. Roosevelt appointed Marion B.
Folsom to his Advisory Council on Economic Security in
1934 as a result of his development of the Rochester Unemployment Benefit Plan.  Marion served on the Council
until 1935.  He also served as president of the Rochester
Council of Social Agencies from 1934 to 1936.  In 1935
Folsom became treasurer of Eastman Kodak Company.  He remained in this post until 1953.  He also became a member
of the New York State Advisory Council on unemployment
in 1935 and continued until 1950.

Marion Folsom's next public service was as an employer
delegate of the United States to the Geneva International Labor Conference in 1936.  He was a member of the Federal Advisory Council on Social Security during 1937
and 1938.  Marion was next division executive of the
National Advisory Defense Commission from 1940 to 1941
and then a member of the Regional War Manpower Committee
from 1942 to 1945.  In 1942 he also became one of the
original trustees of the Committee for Economic Development, serving as chairman of the board from 1950 to 1953.
In addition in 1942 he became a director of the United
States Chamber of Commerce, serving until 1948.

Folsom continued to serve the Federal Government as
staff director of the House of Representatives special
committee on postwar economic policy and planning from
to 1944 to 1946.  The University of Rochester awarded
him the honorary LL.D. degree in 1945.  He was vice
chairman of the President's Advisory Committee on the
Merchant Marine from 1947 to 1948 and a member of the
National Industrial Conference Board from 1947 to 1953.
During this period Folsom was also president of the Eastman Savings and Loan Association in Rochester from 1947
to 1952.

Marion B. Folsom was a director of the Federal Reserve
Bank of New York from 1949 to 1953.  Hobart and William
Smith Colleges awarded him the honorary LL.D. degree in
1951.  Marion B. Folsom was appointed Undersecretary of
the Treasury in 1953 and served until 1955.  He was appointed to the Board of Governors of the American Red
Cross in 1953, continuing until 1958.  He worked with

the Department of Health, Education, and Welfare in 1954 to study old age and survivors insurance. He also aided in developing the group insurance program for federal employees which was enacted by Congress in 1954.

President Dwight D. Eisenhower named Marion B. Folsom Secretary of Health, Education, and Welfare on July 20, 1955. He assumed his office on August 1, 1955 and continued until August 1, 1958. Syracuse and Tufts Universities awarded him the LL.D. degree in 1955 as did Brown University and Swarthmore College in 1957. Marion B. Folsom worked to expand medical research activities, to train more public health personnel and nurses and to control water and air pollution. He was able to gain increased funds for the Office of Education and began a new program of educational research. He also prepared recommendations for the National Defense Act of 1958.

After leaving public office Marion Folsom was reelected to the board of directors of Eastman Kodak Company in August 1958 and has continued to work with the company. He was also reelected a trustee of the Rochester Savings Bank. Among his other activities he has served in various capacities including as a member of the Harvard College Board of Overseers, a trustee of the University of Rochester and of the Allendale School in Rochester. He has also been a director of the Rochester General Hospital.

Bibliography:
Albertson, Dean, ed. Eisenhower as President. New York: Hill and Wang, 1963.
Donovan, Robert J. Eisenhower, The Inside Story. New York: Harper and Row, 1956.
Frier, David. Conflict of Interest in the Eisenhower Administration. Ames: Iowa State University Press, 1969.
Hughes, Emmett J. The Ordeal of Power: A Political Memoir of the Eisenhower Years. New York: Atheneum, 1963.
Larson, Arthur. Eisenhower: The President Nobody Knew. New York: Scribner, 1968.
Vexler, Robert I., ed. Dwight D. Eisenhower, 1890-1969. Dobbs Ferry, N.Y.: Oceana Publications, Inc., 1970.

SECRETARY OF HEALTH, EDUCATION, AND WELFARE

ARTHUR SHERWOOD FLEMMING

Arthur S. Flemming, Secretary of Health, Education, and Welfare in the Cabinet of President Dwight D. Eisenhower, was born on June 12, 1905 in Kingston, New York, the son of Harvey Hardwick Flemming, judge of the Surrogate Court, and Harriet (Sherwood) Flemming. After receiving a

basic education in the Kingston public schools and graduating from Kingston High School Arthur attended Ohio
Wesleyan University, graduating with the Bachelor of Arts
degree in 1927.  Arthur then became an instructor in government and debate coach at American University, receiving his Master of Arts degree from the same institution
in 1928.  He studied law at George Washington University
and was graduated with the LL.B. degree in 1930.

Arthur S. Flemming became a member of the editorial
staff of the United States Daily (later U.S. News and
World Report) in 1930 and continued until 1934.  He was
also editor of Uncle Sam's Diary, a weekly presenting
current events for high school students, from 1932 to
1935. Arthur married Bernice Virginia Moler on December
14, 1934.  They had five children: Elizabeth Ann, Susan
Harriet, Harry Sherwood, Arthur Henry, and Thomas Madison.  Arthur S. Flemming became director of the School
of Public Affairs of American University in 1934, remaining in this capacity until 1938.  In the latter year he
became an executive officer of the University.

Flemming had already become involved in the Republican
Party and was named a Republican member of the Civil
Service Commission in 1939, remaining in that post until 1948.  During this period he was granted the honorary
LL.D. degree by Ohio Wesleyan University in 1941, American University in 1942, and Temple University in 1948.
Arthur became chief of labor supply in the Office of
Production Management in 1941 and served until 1942.  He
was next a member of the War Manpower Commission from
1942 to 1945.  He was also a member of the Manpower Supply Board of the Department of the Navy from 1943 to
1944.  He also became a trustee of Ohio Wesleyan University.

Arthur S.  Flemming was chosen one of the four members
of the Hoover Commission on July 17, 1947.  In June 1948
he was elected president of Ohio Wesleyan University and
took the office on July 31, 1948 and remained there until 1953.  Flemming was made chairman of the personnel
advisory board of the Atomic Energy Commission in September 1948.  He also served as vice-president of the
National Council of the Churches of Christ in America
from 1950 to 1954.  He was appointed a member of the International Civil Service Advisory Board in 1950.

Flemming's next public service position was as assistant to the Director of Defense Mobilization and chairman of the manpower policy committee of the Office of
Defense Mobilization beginning in February 1951.  He was
made acting head of the Office of Defense Mobilization
in January 1953.  He also became a member of President
Dwight D. Eisenhower's Advisory Committee on Government
Organization in 1953.  In June of the same year Arthur
became director of the Office of Defense Mobilization,
continuing until 1957.  He was on leave form Ohio Wes-

leyan University.  Arthur was also appointed a member of
the National Security Council in 1953.  He was again a
member of the Commission on Reorganization of the Executive Branch of the Government from 1953 to 1955.

President Dwight D. Eisenhower named Arthur S. Flemming
Secretary of Health, Education, and Welfare on July 9,
1958.  He assumed his duties on August 1, 1958 and continued until the end of the Eisenhower administration
on January 20, 1961.  He worked to maintain the social
welfare and medical services of the Department.  After
leaving public office in 1961 Arthur S. Flemming became
president of the University of Oregon.  He was also appointed a member of the National Advisory Commission of
the Peace Corps by President John F. Kennedy.

Bibliography:
    Albertson, Dean, ed.  Eisenhower as President.  New
York: Hill and Wang, 1963.
    Donovan, Robert J.  Eisenhower, The Inside Story.  New
York: Harper and Row, 1956.
    Frier, David.  Conflict of Interest in the Eisenhower
Administration.  Ames: Iowa State University Press, 1969.
    Hughes, Emmett J.  The Ordeal of Power: A Political
Memoir of the Eisenhower Years.  New York: Atheneum,
1963.
    Larson, Arthur.  Eisenhower: The President Nobody
Knew.  New York: Scribner, 1968.
    Vexler, Robert I., ed.  Dwight D. Eisenhower, 1890-
1969.  Dobbs Ferry, N.Y.: Oceana Publications, Inc.,
1970.

## ADMINISTRATION OF JOHN F. KENNEDY

### VICE PRESIDENT: LYNDON BAINES JOHNSON

Lyndon B. Johnson, Vice President in the Administration
of John F. Kennedy, was born on August 27, 1908 on a farm
near Stonewall, Texas, the son of Sam Early Johnson, a
rancher, school teacher and member of the state legislature, and Rebekah (Baines) Johnson.  He moved with
his family to Johnson City, Texas where Lyndon attended
the public schools.  When his family moved back to the
farm near Stonewall in January 1917 Lyndon went to the
one-room school at Junction.  After graduating from the
seventh grade in 1920 Johnson went to the school at Stonewall and then the Albert School.

When the Johnson family returned to Johnson City in
August 1923 Lyndon attended the Johnson City High School,
graduating in May 1924.  He and several friends went to
California in July 1924 and worked there for two years.
Lyndon returned to Texas in March 1926 and worked on a
road gang.  He then entered Southwest Texas State Teach-

ers  College in San Marcos, Texas on February 7, 1927.
He taught school from September 1, 1928 until the end
of May 1929 because of financial difficulties.  He returned to Southwest Texas State Teachers College on
June 1, 1929, graduating with the Bachelor of Science
degree on August 17, 1930.

Lyndon taught school Pearsall, Texas and then Sam
Houston High School in 1930 and 1931.  He was the debate
coach there.  He soon entered politics, working for
Richard M. Kleberg's successful campaign for Congress in
1931.  He was appointed Kleberg's secretary on November
29, 1931 accompanying the latter to Washington where he
advised him on many pieces of legislation.  Lyndon studied law at Georgetown University Law School in 1934 and
1935 finding it quite boring.  He married Claudia Alta
(Lady Bird) Taylor on November 17, 1924.  They had two
daughters: Lynda Bird and Lucy Baines.

President Franklin D. Roosevelt named Lyndon B. Johnson State Administrator of the National Youth Administration in Texas on July 1, 1936. He served until February 28, 1937. He was elected to the House of Representatives on April 10, 1937 to fill the vacancy left by the
death of J. P. Buchanan.  He served in the Seventy-fourth
through the Eightieth Congresses from May 18, 1937 to
January 3, 1949.  He was unsuccessful in his campaign
for the United States Senate in 1941 to fill the vacancy
left when Morris Sheppard died.

Lyndon B. Johnson was ordered to active duty by the
Navy on December 11, 1941.  He was already commissioned
as a lieutenant commander in the Naval Reserves.  President Roosevelt suggested that Johnson take a survey of
military supplies in the Australian combat zone on June
11, 1942.  Johnson arrived in New Zealand on May 21.
General Douglas McArthur awarded Johnson the Silver Star
Medal for gallantry in action.  In response to President
Roosevelt's directive of July 1, 1942 that all Congressmen leave the military service and return to their le-
gislatures, Johnson returned to Washington on July 15,
1942.  He was appointed chairman of the subcommittee in
vestigating Manpower Utilization in Naval Affairs on
October 16, 1942.

Lady Bird and Lyndon Johnson bought radio station KTBC
on December 27, 1942.  Johnson continued to serve in the
House of Representatives until the end of his term on
January 3, 1949.  He was elected to the United States
Senate on November 3, 1948.  The Democratic primary had
led to charges of fraud and was finally settled by the
courts.  Johnson served in the Senate from January 3,
1949 until January 3, 1961, having been reelected in
1954 and 1960.

While in the Senate Johnson frequently voted against
the Truman administration proposals.  He was elected
Majority Whip by the Democrats on January 2, 1951.  He

was elected Senate Minority Leader by the Democrats on
January 3, 1953.  Lyndon was elected Senate Majority Leader and Democratic Policy Committee Chairman on January
5, 1955.  He suffered a severe heart attack on July 2,
1955 and was released from Bethesda Naval Hospital on
August 7.  He had a checkup at the Mayo Clinic on December 24, 1955 where it was announced that he was completely recovered,
    Lyndon B. Johnson refused to agree to the Southern Mani-
festo pledge on March 11, 1956 to try to reverse the Supreme Court's 1954 decision prohibiting segregation in
the public schools.  Johnson attended the Democratic National Convention, August 13-17, 1956 as chairman of the
Texas delegation.  He was an unsuccessful candidate for
the presidential nomination.  President Dwight D. Eisenhower appointed Johnson to represent the United States
at the United Nations debate on outer space control on
November 10, 1958.
    Johnson was an unsuccessful candidate for the Democra-
tic presidential nomination against John F. Kennedy in
1960 after having run an ineffective campaign.  Johnson
was selected as the Democratic vice presidential nominee
on July 14, 1960.  John F. Kennedy and Lyndon B. Johnson
were elected President and Vice President respectively
on November 8, 1960.
    John F. Kennedy and Lyndon B. Johnson were inaugurated
as President and Vice President of the United States on
January 20, 1961.  Johnson now presided over the Senate
but did not have the power to control the political situation he had as Senate majority leader.  President Kennedy
appointed Johnson chairman of the Space Council in January 1961.  He was also named chairman of the President's
Committee on Equal Employment Opportunity for firms with
government contracts on March 6, 1961 and helped draft
a strong Executive order
    Lyndon B. Johnson made an official visit to Africa and
Europe from April 9 to 15, 1961 and a tour of Southwest
Asia and the Far East from May 5 to 19, 1961.  He made
a goodwill tour of the Mediterranean countries from
August 23 to September 22, 1962.  On June 17, 1963 Johnson attended Pope John XXIII's funeral in Rome as the
official United States representative.  He toured the Be-
nelux and Scandinavian countries from September 3 to
17, 1963.  He pledged continuation of American support
to the West European countries and to prowestern states
of Asia.  Lyndon B. Johnson was on a visit with President
John F. Kennedy to Dallas, Texas when Kennedy was assassinated.  Lyndon B. Johnson was sworn in as the Thirty-
sixth President of the United States by Judge Sarah T.
Hughes in Dallas, Texas.
    /For information concerning the period of Lyndon B.
Johnson's Presidency, consult Howard B. Furer, ed.  Lyndon B. Johnson, 1908-(1972) in this series./

As a result of pressure concerning the war in Vietnam
and a challenge for the Democratic presidential nomination from Robert Kennedy, President Lyndon Johnson
announced in a television address on March 31, 1968 that
he had ordered a halt to ninety percent of the bombing
in Vietnam.  In addition he launched a movement for peace
in South Vietnam.  President Johnson indicated that he
would neither seek nor accept the Democratic presidential
nomination.  Initial peace talks began in Paris, France
on May 12, 1968.  After leaving office at the end of his
administration on January 20, 1969 Lyndon B. Johnson returned to his ranch near Johnson City, Texas and worked
in his office at Austin, Texas.  Lyndon Johnson died on
January 22, 1973 in San Antonio, Texas.  He was buried
on his ranch.

Bibliography:
  Baker, Leonard.  The Johnson Eclipse: A President's
Vice Presidency.  New York: Macmillan, 1966.
  Evans, Rowland, and Novack, Robert.  Lyndon B. Johnson:
The Exercise of Power.  New York: New American Library,
1966.
  Furer, Howard B.  Lyndon B. Johnson, 1908-/1973/.
Dobbs Ferry, N.Y.: Oceana Publications, Inc., 1971.
  Goldman, Eric R.  The Tragedy of Lyndon B. Johnson.
New York: Knopf, 1969.
  Sidey, Hugh.  A Very Personal Presidency: Lyndon John-
son in the White House.  New York: Atheneum, 1968.
  Stone, Ralph A., ed.  John F. Kennedy, 1917-1963.
Dobbs Ferry, N.Y.: Oceana Publications, Inc., 1971.
  Zeiger, Henry A.  Lyndon B. Johnson. Man and President.
New York: Popular Library, 1965.

## SECRETARY OF STATE: DAVID DEAN RUSK

Dean Rusk, Secretary of State in the Cabinets of Presidents John F. Kennedy and Lyndon B. Johnson, was born on
February 9, 1909 in Cherokee County, Georgia, the son of
Robert Hugh Rusk, a farmer and mail carrier, and Frances
Elizabeth (Cloffeler) Rusk.  After receiving his basic
education in the Atlanta, Georgia public schools, Dean
worked in an Atlanta law office for two years to finance
his education.  He attended Davidson College, receiving
the Bachelor of Arts degree in 1931.
Dean Rusk became a reserve Infantry officer in 1931.
He then went to St. Johns College, Oxford University as
a Rhodes scholar receiving the Bachelor's degree in 1933
and the Master's in 1934.  He also studied at the University of Berlin and various other German colleges during
his vacations.  He returned to the United States in 1934
to take a position as an associate professor of government and international relations at Mills College in
Oakland, California.  Dean married Virginia Foisie on

June 19, 1937. They had three children: David Patrick, Richard Geary, and Margaret Elizabeth.

Dean Rusk began studying law at the University of California in 1937, continuing until 1940. He became dean of faculty at Mills College in 1938. Rusk was called to active duty in the army in 1941 first as a company commander at the Presidio in San Francisco and then at Fort Lewis, Washington where he was assistant operations officer in the Third Infantry Division. Later in 1941 he was sent to Washington, D.C. to serve in military intelligence. In 1943 after a staff course at Fort Leavenworth, Kansas, he went to the China-Burman-India Theater of operations. He was deputy chief of staff to General Joseph W. Stillwell. He returned to Washington where he served as assistant chief in the operations division of the United States War Department General Staff in June 1945, continuing until he was discharged from the army in February 1946 with the rank of colonel. He was awarded the Legion of Merit in 1945 and the Oak Leaf Cluster in 1946.

Dean Rusk then joined the State Department as assistant chief of the internal security affairs division. Secretary of War Robert Patterson appointed Rusk special assistant to coordinate joint foreign policy matters. Secretary of State George C. Marshall appointed Rusk director of the Office of United Nations Affairs in 1948. He was granted the LL.D. degree in the same year by Mills College and was awarded the same by many other colleges and universities during the next two decades.

Rusk was named assistant Secretary of State in February 1949. In May 1949 he was promoted to deputy under Secretary of State. He next accepted the post of assistant Secretary of State for Far Eastern affairs in March 1950 and served until 1951. He also was a delegate or alternate to the United Nations. Rusk urged United States military intervention under Korean auspices when the North Koreans invaded South Korea in June 1950. He also advised President Harry S. Truman to send the 7th Fleet to protect Formosa. Dean Rusk was next made president of the Rockefeller Foundation in 1952 in which post he remained until 1961. Under his direction the foundation made a commitment to aid the the underdeveloped areas of Asia, Africa and Latin America.

President John F. Kennedy appointed Dean Rusk Secretary of State in which office he served from January 21, 1961 and continued under President Lyndon B. Johnson until the end of his administration on January 21, 1969. He urged that the United States renew its efforts to arrange a nuclear test ban treaty and worked to arrange a nuclear test ban treaty and worked to arrange various conferences and other negotiations at which proposals were also made for disarmament at which proposals were also made for disarmament of conventional forces as well. He also attended conferences to deal with the serious situation concerning Berlin.

Dean Rusk urged the NATO countries to move quickly in the direction of European political and economic unity. He indicated support for the independence of Laos.  Secretary Rusk announced American support for United States action in the Congo in February 1961.  He also supported the decision of January 1961 to grant aid to the United Arab Republic to preserve the historic treasures of the Nile Valley.  In addition he made an agreement with Portugese Premier Antonio de Oliveira Salazar to extend American military rights to bases in the Azore Islands for five more years in 1961.

Secretary Rusk continued to work for closer cooperation between the United States and the Latin American nations.  He continued to serve at the State Department after the death of President John F. Kennedy on November 22, 1963.  He continued to back the policy of American intervention in South Vietnam and supported President Lyndon B. Johnson's policies in Southeast Asia.  Dean Rusk wrote The Winds of War in 1963.  After leaving office in January 1969 Rusk retired  and has continued his interest in world affairs.

Bibliography:

Fall, Bernard R.  Vietnam Witness, 1953-1966.  New York: Praeger, 1966.

Furer, Howard B., ed.  Lyndon B. Johnson, 1908-/1972/. Dobbs Ferry, N.Y.: Oceana Publications, Inc., 1971.

Geyelin, Philip L.  Lyndon B. Johnson and the World. New York: F. A. Praeger, 1966.

Rusk, Dean.  The Winds of War.  New York, 1963.

Schlesinger, Arthur M.  Jr.  The Bitter Heritage; Vietnam and American Democracy, 1941-1966.  Boston: Houghton Mifflin, 1967.

- - - -.  A Thousand Days: John F. Kennedy in the White House.  Boston: Houghton Mifflin, 1965.

Sidey, Hugh.  John F. Kennedy, President.  New York: Fawcett World Library, 1963.

Sorenson, Theodore C.  Decision Making in the White House: The Olive Branch or the Arrows.  New York: Columbia University Press, 1963.

- - - -.  Kennedy.  New York: Harper and Row, 1965.

Stone, Ralph A.  John F. Kennedy, 1917-1963.  Dobbs Ferry, N.Y.: Oceana Publications, Inc., 1971.

## SECRETARY OF THE TREASURY:

### CLARENCE DOUGLAS DILLON

Douglas Dillon, Secretary of the Treasury in the Cabinets of Presidents John F. Kennedy and Lyndon B. Johnson, was born on April 21, 1909 in Geneva, Switzerland,

the son of Clarence Dillon, an investment banker, and
Ann McEldin (Douglas) Dillon.  He received his basic
education at the Groton School and then went to Harvard
University, graduating with the Bachelor of Arts degree
in 1931.  Douglas married Phyllis Chess Ellsworth on
March 10, 1931.  They had two children: Phyllis Ellsworth
and Joan Douglas.  Dillon then entered his father's firm
in New York City, Dillon, Read and Company, in 1931 and
also became a member of the New York Stock Exchange.

Douglas Dillon became director of the United States
and Foreign Securities Corporation in 1937.  He was elected a vice-president and director of Dillon, Read and
Company in 1938.  He was called to Washington, D.C. to
serve the government in the fall of 1940 by working to
form a statistical control center for the Navy Department.  Shortly thereafter he was commissioned an ensign
in the United States Naval Reserve in October 1941.  He
was called to active duty in the spring of 1941 before
the attack on Pearl Harbor and the United States entrance
into the Second World War.  During the course of the war
he was assigned to Washington, D.C. and then to the Naval Air Station at Seattle, Washington after which he
served at sea in the Pacific with the carrier task forces
and then the 7th fleet for a total of eighteen months.
He was released from the Navy in 1945 having risen to
the rank of lieutenant commander.

Douglas Dillon then returned to Dillon, Reed and Company as chairman of the board from 1946 to 1953.  He was
also involved in politics as a Republican.  During this
period Dillon was president of the United States and
Foreign Securities Corporation from 1946 to 1953, president of the United States and International Securities
Corporation.  He was also a director of Amerada Petroleum Corporation from 1947 to 1953.  He became a member
of the Harvard Board of Overseers in 1952 and served
until 1958.

President Dwight D. Eisenhower appointed Douglas Dillon United States ambassador to France in which post he
served from February 1953 to March 1957.  He carefully
analyzed French politics and the potentiality for a
Franco-German agreement.  He was appointed deputy undersecretary of State for economic affairs in 1957 and
continued in office until 1958 when he was named undersecretary of state , serving until 1960.  He took charge
of the International Cooperation Administration and
helped to create the Inter-American Development Bank in
December 1959.

Douglas Dillon is also credited with having brought
together the six nations of the European Common Market
and the seven states of the European Free Trade Association along with other countries in the Organization
for Economic Cooperation and Development.  During this
period he received the honorary LL.D. degree from many

academic institutions including New York University in
1956, Columbia and Harvard Universities in 1959 and Williams College in 1960.

President John F. Kennedy named Douglas Dillon Secretary of the Treasury.  He assumed his office on January
21, 1961 and continued to serve under President Lyndon
B. Johnson after the assassination of John F. Kennedy.
Dillon remained in office until March 31, 1965.  Among
the other positions which he held in his capacity as
head of the Treasury Department was United States governor of the International Monetary Fund, the International
Bank for Reconstruction and Development and the Inter-
American Development Bank.  He also served as chairman
of the National Advisory Council on International Monetary and Financial Problems, managing trustee of the Federal Old-Age and Survivors Insurance Trust Fund, as well
as other posts including honorary treasurer of the American National Red Cross.

Dillon worked with the Administration to take the necessary steps which helped to change the financial condition of the nation from recession to recovery during
1961.  He also developed provisions granting tax credit
for depreciation of equipment and for investment in new
equipment which helped to increase exports and provide
additional employment.  During 1962 Secretary Dillon and
his Department developed a program of tax reduction which
President Kennedy submitted to Congress in January 1963.
Dillon also played a major role in helping to establish
the Alliance for Progress, a ten-year cooperative-aid
program.  He was awarded the LL.D. degree by many institutions including Princeton and Rutgers Universities in
1961 and the University of Pennsylvania in 1962.

After leaving public office Douglas Dillon returned
to his business interests.  He is also a trustee of
Groton School.  His cultural and philanthropic interests
are evident in the many posts which he held.  He was a
member of the boards of governors of the Metropolitan
Museum of Art and New York Hospital.  He is also a member of the Society of Cincinnati and the Society of Colo-
nial Wars.  He is a collector of art works, especially
the Impressionist and post-Impressionist schools.  He
breeds Guernsey cattle on his farm in Somerset County,
New Jersey.

Bibliography:
    Furer, Howard B., ed.  Lyndon B. Johnson, 1908-/1973/.
Dobbs Ferry, N.Y.: Oceana Publications, Inc., 1971.
    Harris, Seymour.  Economics of the Kennedy Years, and
a Look Ahead.  New York: Harper and Row, 1964.
    Heath, James.  The Kennedy Administration and the Busi-
ness Community.  New York: Harper and Row, 1969.
    Rowen, Hobart.  Free Enterprises: Kennedy, Johnson and
the Business Establishment.  New York: Putnam, 1964.

Schlesinger, Arthur M., Jr.  A Thousand Days: John F. Kennedy in the White House.  Boston: Houghton Mifflin, 1965.
   Sidey, Hugh.  John F. Kennedy, President.  New York: Fawcett World Library, 1963.
   Sorenson, Theodore C.  Kennedy.  New York: Harper and Row, 1965.
   Stone, Ralph A., ed.  John F. Kennedy, 1917-1963. Dobbs Ferry, N.Y.: Oceana Publications, Inc., 1971.
   Zeiger, Henry.  Lyndon B. Johnson, Man and President. New York: Popular Library, 1965.

### SECRETARY OF DEFENSE: ROBERT STRANGE MCNAMARA

Robert S. McNamara, Secretary of Defense in the Cabinets of Presidents John F. Kennedy and Lyndon B. Johnson, was born on June 9, 1916 in San Francisco, California, the son of Robert James McNamara, a shoe industry executive, and Clara Nell (Strange) McNamara.  After receiving his basic education in the Piedmont, California public schools Robert studied at the University of California at Berkeley from which he was graduated with the Bachelor of Arts degree in 1937.  He then went to Harvard University Graduate School of Business Administration where he received the Master of Business Administration degree in 1939.

Robert McNamara went to work in the same year for Price Waterhouse and Company in San Francisco.  He was appointed assistant professor of business administration of Harvard in 1940 and continued there until 1943.  Robert married Margaret Craig on August 13, 1940.  They had three children:Margaret Elizabeth, Kathleen, and Robert. In 1942 Robert S. McNamara became a consultant for the War Department to create a statistical control system for the United States Army Air Force.  He was sent to England as a civilian consultant in 1943.

McNamara was commissioned a captain in the Army Air Force in 1943, serving during the war in England, India, China and the Pacific area.  He was eventually promoted to lieutenant colonel in 1946 and was discharged in April.  He then became a colonel in the Air Force Reserve.  He was awarded the United States Legion of Merit in 1946.

Robert S.  McNamara formed a ten-man business management team in 1946.  It was employed by the Ford Motor Company with McNamara as manager of the planning and financial analysis offices.  He became comptroller in 1949 and then assistant general manager of the Ford division in 1953.  He was elected a vice-president and general manager of the division in 1955.  He then became vice-president and group executive of the car and truck divisions as well as a member of the board of directors in 1957.  McNamara became president of the Ford Motor

Company on November 9, 1960, succeeding Henry Ford II.
McNamara was also a director of the Scott Paper Company.
He resigned from both companies on January 17, 1961.

President John F. Kennedy named Robert S. McNamara
Secretary of Defense.  He assumed his office on January
21, 1961, continuing under President Johnson after the
assassination of President John F. Kennedy on November
22, 1963.  Robert served in office until February 29,
1968.  He reorganized the Defense Department for greater
efficiency in management.  He established a new post of
assistant secretary for installations and logistics in
February 1961.  This post combined several previous
offices.  He insisted upon various deterrents rather
than massive nuclear power.

Robert S. McNamara also developed a. planning-program-
ming-budgeting system and developed a five-year program.
He created the Office of Education and Manpower Resources
in May 1961.  McNamara appointed an assistant secretary
for civil defense.  To meet the crisis in Berlin during
August 1961 the Secretary ordered  activation of many
reservists.  He increased the strength of American troops
in Western Europe and ordered further training for
greater preparedness of the armed forces,  In September
1961 he created the United States Strike Command to coordinate activities of all armed forces.  He also established the Logistics Management Institute, a non-profit
fact-finding body as well as the Defense Supply Agency.

During the Cuban Missile crisis from October 22 to 28,
1962 Secretary McNamara activated elements of the Air
Force reserve.  During 1962 he had all language facilities consolidated into the Defense Language Institute.
The Secretary also created the Defense Supply Agency.
McNamara continued the increase of efficiency and improvement of weapons and equipment throughout his term
in office.  During the Johnson Administration the Secretary supervised the increase in the size of the armed
forces in Vietnam and the coordination of American activities there.  He also supervised creation of the Office
of Education and Manpower Resources under President
Johnson.  Following his five-day trip to Vietnam in July
1967 McNamara criticized General Westmoreland's handling
of the war, but because of presidential pressure he issued a statement that all was going well in Vietnam.

Robert McNamara accepted appointment as the president
of the International Bank for Reconstruction and Development on November 29, 1967.  He assumed this position
in March 1968 after leaving the Cabinet.  He has also
remained active in many service activities.

Bibliography:
  Art, Robert J.  TFX Decision: McNamara and the Mili-
tary.  Boston: Little Brown, 1968.
  Crown, James T.  Kennedy in Power.  New York: Ballan-

tine Books, 1961.

Furer, Howard F., ed. Lyndon B. Johnson, 1908-/1972/.
Dobbs Ferry, N.Y.: Oceana Publications, Inc., 1971.

Goldman, Eric R. The Tragedy of Lyndon B. Johnson.
New York: Knopf, 1969.

Kennedy, Robert F. Thirteen Days: A Memoir of the
Cuban Missile Crisis. New York: W. W. Norton, 1969.

Mollenhoff, Jack. The Pentagon: Politics, Profit and
Plunder. New York: Putnam, 1967.

Schlesinger, Arthur M., Jr. The Bitter Heritage; Vietnam and American Democracy, 1941-1966. Boston: Houghton
Mifflin, 1967.

- - - -. A Thousand Days: John F. Kennedy in the White
House. Boston: Houghton Mifflin Company, 1965.

Sidey, Hugh. John F. Kennedy, President. New York:
Fawcett World Library, 1963.

- - - -. A Very Personal Presidency: Lyndon Johnson
in the White House. New York: Atheneum, 1968.

Sorenson, Theodore C. Kennedy. New York: Harper and
Row, 1965.

Stone, Ralph A., ed. John F. Kennedy, 1917-1963.
Dobbs Ferry, N.Y.: Oceana Publications, Inc., 1971.

Zeiger, Henry. Lyndon B. Johnson, Man and President.
New York: Popular Library, 1965.

## ATTORNEY GENERAL: ROBERT FRANCIS KENNEDY

Robert F. Kennedy, Attorney General in the Cabinets
of Presidents John F. Kennedy and Lyndon B. Johnson, was
born on November 20, 1925 in Brookline, Massachusetts,
the son of Joseph Patrick Kennedy, a financier, business
executive and ambassador to Great Britain, and Rose
(Fitzgerald) Kennedy. He was the brother of John F. Kennedy, President of the United States, and Edward Kennedy,
United States Senator from Massachusetts.

Robert F. Kennedy received his basic education at the
Milton Academy in Massachusetts and then attended Harvard
University from which he was graduated in 1948. In 1944
while at Harvard Robert enlisted in the United States
Navy and was assigned as a seaman to the Joseph P. Kennedy, Jr., a destroyer named for his brother who had
been killed on a flying mission in Europe. Robert worked
for the Boston Post as a war correspondent in Palestine
during the summer of 1948. He then entered the University of Virginia Law School, receiving the LL.B. degree
in 1951. He was admitted to the Massachusetts bar in
the same year.

Robert F. Kennedy married Ethel Skakel on June 16, 1950.
They had eleven children: Kathleen Hartington, Joseph
Patrick, Robert Francis, Jr., David Anthony, Mary Court-
ney, Michael le Moyne, Mary Kerry, Christopher George,
Douglas, Rory Elizabeth, and Katherine. Robert F. Ken-
nedy became an attorney for the Justice Department in

the Criminal Division.  He resigned from this post in
1952 to manage John F. Kennedy's successful campaign
for the United States Senate from Massachusetts.

Robert returned to Washington in 1953 as assistant
counsel for the permanent subcommittee on investigations
of the Senate government operations committee.  He then
was an assistant counsel for the Hoover Commission on
Organization of the Executive Branch of the Government.
In January 1954 Kennedy returned to the Senate permanent
subcommittee on investigations, chaired by Senator Joseph
McCarthy, as chief counsel and staff director in January
1955 when Senator John L. McClellan, Democrat, became
chairman of the subcommittee.

Robert Kennedy was admitted to practice before the
United States Supreme Court in 1955.  He took a leave
of absence from the subcommittee legal staff in the
summer of 1955 to travel to the Soviet Republics in
Central Asia with Supreme Court Justice William O.
Douglas.  Kennedy was next employed as special assistant
to Adlai E. Stevenson's campaign manager in the presidential campaign of 1956.  Robert F. Kennedy was named
chief counsel of the Senate's select committee investigating improper activities in labor-management relations
in January 1957.  He continued until his resignation
in September 1959.

During the fall of 1959 Robert Kennedy began to work
for his brother John F. Kennedy who was formulating
plans to seek the Democratic nomination for President.
After John F. Kennedy was nominated for President by
the Democrats in July 1960, Robert became his campaign
manager.  Robert Kennedy wrote The Enemy Within in 1960.

President John F. Kennedy appointed his brother Robert
Attorney General.  Robert assumed his office on January
21, 1961 and continued to serve under President Lyndon
B. Johnson after his brother's assassination on November
22, 1963.  Robert resigned from his post on September
3, 1964.  He was active in leading the Department of
Justice in the prosecution of cases under the Civil
Rights Acts of 1957 and 1960, in particular protecting
the Black man's right to vote and other civil rights.

Robert also guided the Justice Department in enforcing
compliance with the 1954 school desegregation decision
by the Supreme Court.  He also increased departmental
efforts to end discrimination in employment and in
interstate transportation.  Attorney General Kennedy also directed the Department of Justice in an increased
campaign of prosecutions for violation of the antitrust
laws and had the Department investigate mergers, price
fixing, collusion on government contracts and other
issues.

Robert F. Kennedy launched an intensive campaign a-
gainst organized crime in various areas, including
gambling and narcotics.  He also directed operations

which led to investigations and prosecution of labor-management racketeering.  The Department also clamped down and prosecuted individuals for sending obscene materials through the mail.  A campaign was also carried out against the mislabeling and illegal sale of foods and drugs.  Kennedy directed the program to help state and local governments in combatting juvenile delinquency. as well as providing programs for rehabilitation of youthful offenders.  He also supported legislation for establishment of a broad-based private corporation to set up a global communications system using satellites. He sponsored various investigations including the New York City garbage collection industry.  He wrote Just Friends and Brave Enemies in 1962.  Various colleges and universities awarded him the honorary LL.D. degree.

Among his other activities Robert Kennedy was a member of the advisory council of the University of Notre Dame Law School.  After leaving the Cabinet in September 1964, Robert Kennedy successfully ran for the Democratic nomination for Senator of New York and was elected in November 1964, serving from January 3, 1965 until his death.  He announced his candidacy for the Democratic nomination for President on March 16, 1968 and won the primaries in Indiana, Nebraska, and California.  While on a campaign visit to Los Angeles, California Robert Kennedy was assassinated on June 5, 1968.  He was buried in Arlington National Cemetery on June 8, 1968.  His book Thirteen Days was published posthumously in 1969.

Bibliography:
  Crown, James T, Kennedy in Power.  New York: Ballantine Books, 1961.
  Furer, Howard F., ed.  Lyndon B. Johnson, 1908-/1972/ Dobbs Ferry, N.Y.: Oceana Publications, Inc., 1971.
  Goldman, Eric R.  The Tragedy of Lyndon B. Johnson. New York: Knopf, 1969.
  Jacobs, Jay, and Witken, Kristi N.  R. F. K.: His Life and Death.  New York, 1968.
  Kennedy, Robert F.  Thirteen Days: A Memoir of the Cuban Missile Crisis.  New York: W. W. Norton, 1969.
  Schlesinger, Arthur M., Jr. A Thousand Days: John F. Kennedy in The White House.  Boston: Houghton Mifflin Company, 1965.
  Sidey, Hugh.  John F. Kennedy, President.  New York: Fawcett World Library, 1963.
  - - - -.  A Very Personal Presidency: Lyndon Johnson in the White House.  New York: Atheneum, 1968.
  Sorenson, Theodore C.  Kennedy.  New York: Harper and Row, 1965.
  Stone, Ralph A., ed.  John F. Kennedy, 1917-1963. Dobbs Ferry, N.Y.: Oceana Publications, Inc., 1971.
  Westin, Alan F., ed.  Freedom Now!  The Civil Rights Struggle in America.  New York: Basic Books, 1964.

Zeiger, Henry A.  Robert F. Kennedy: A Biography.
New York: Meredith Press, 1969.

## POSTMASTER GENERAL: JAMES EDWARD DAY

James E. Day, Postmaster General in the Cabinet of
President John F. Kennedy, was born on October 11, 1914
in Jacksonville, Illinois, the son of James Allmond
Day, a surgeon, and Frances (Wilmot) Day.  James E. received his basic education in the public schools of
Springfield, Illinois and then went to the University
of Chicago, graduating with the Bachelor of Arts degree
in 1935.  He then went to Harvard University Law School
where he was treasurer of Lincoln's Inn Society from
1936 to 1937 and was legislative editor of the Harvard
Law Review.  He was graduated with the LL.B. degree in
1938.  James was admitted to the Illinois bar in the
same year.  He began to practice law in 1939 with the
Chicago firm of Sidley Austin, Burgess and Harper.
James E. Day trained as an officer in the United States
Naval Reserve during 1940 and 1941.  He married Mary
Louise Burgess on July 2, 1941.  They had three children:
Geraldine, Mary Louise, and James Edward.  Mr. Day was
commissioned as an ensign in the Navy in 1942.  He com-
manded the submarine chaser PC 597 in the South Pacific
and served on the destroyer escort Fowler in the Atlantic.  He rose to the rank of lieutenant by 1945 when he
was released from the Navy.  He then returned to his
legal practice with Sidley, Austin, Burgess and Harper,
continuing until 1949.
James E. Day wrote a novel, Bartholf Street, in 1947.
James supported Adlai Stevenson's campaign for governor
of Illinois.  In 1949 Day became legal and legislative
assistant to Adlai E. Stevenson who was elected governor
of Illinois.  He also served as a member of the Illinois
Commission on Intergovernmental Cooperation from 1949
to 1953.  Stevenson named Day state insurance commissioner in 1950.  He remained in this office until 1953.  Day
was also chairman of the midwestern zone committee of
the National Association of Insurance Commissioners.
He supported Stevenson's campaign for the Presidency in
1952.
James E. Day next became assistant general solicitor
of the Prudential Insurance Company of America of Newark,
New Jersey in 1953 and was promoted to associate general
counsel in 1956.  He was one of the major developers of
the variable insurance plan.  He moved to Los Angeles,
California as senior vice-president of the company's
western operations in 1957.  Day also became a member
of the California Democratic State Finance Committee
as well as the Chairman's Advisory Committee of the Los
Angeles County Democratic Central Committee from 1958

to 1966.

James E. Day was a vice-chairman of the California Governor's Commission on Metropolitan Area Problems from
1959 to 1961.   In addition he was chairman of the Southern California Research Council and treasurer of the
Statewide Water Development Committee.   He was a director
of one of the local chapters of the American National
Red Cross and the Arthritis and Rheumatism Foundation.
Day wrote a family genealogy in 1959 entitled Descendants
of Christopher Day of Bucks County, Pennsylvania.   He
was an early supporter of John F. Kennesy for the 1960
Democratic nomination and was a delegate to the Democratic National Convention from California in 1960.

President John F. Kennedy nominated James E. Day to
be Postmaster General on December 17, 1960.   Day assumed
his office on January 21, 1961 and served until September
29, 1963.   While he was in office the postal rates were
increased to meet the deficit.   He represented the President at the Osaka, Japan Trade Fair in April 1962.   Illinois College and the University of Nevada granted James
E. Day the honorary LL.D. degree in 1962.

James E. Day left the Cabinet to accept the position
as head of the Washington, D.C. branch of Sidley. Austin,
Burgess and Smith.   Among his other activities Day was
made director of various companies in the Zurich Insurance Group and was connected with the People's Life
Insurance Company.   He is a member of the board of fel-
lows of Claremont College in California.   He was also
president of the National Civil Service League from
1964 to 1966 and helped to establish Democratic Associates, Incorporated of which he was chairman.   He is a member of the American Bar Association.

Bibliography:
Crown, James T.   Kennedy in Power.   New York: Ballan-
tine Books, 1961.
Schlesinger, Arthur M., Jr.   A Thousand Days: John F.
Kennedy in the White House.   Boston: Houghton Mifflin
Company, 1965.
Sidey, Hugh.   John F. Kennedy, President.   New York:
Fawcett World Library, 1963.
Sorenson, Theodore C.   Kennedy.   New York: Harper and
Row, 1965.
Stone, Ralph A., ed.   John F. Kennedy, 1917-1963.
Dobbs Ferry, N.Y.: Oceana Publications, Inc., 1971.

POSTMASTER GENERAL: JOHN A. GRONOUSKI

John A. Gronouski, Postmaster General in the Cabinets
of President John F. Kennedy and Lyndon B. Johnson, was
born on October 26, 1919 in Dunbar, Wisconsin, the son
of John Austin and Mary (Riley) Gronouski.   After re-

ceiving his basic education at St. Peter's School in Oshkosh, Wisconsin John Gronouski entered Oshkosh Teachers College and eventually received the Bachelor of Arts degree from the University of Wisconsin in January 1942. During World War II Gronouski served in the Army Air Corps, entering as a private in April 1942. He was a navigator with the 8th Air Force and was eventually promoted to the rank of first lieutenant. He was discharged in October 1945.

John A. Gronouski next pursued graduate studies in the business and finance fields at the University of Wisconsin from which he was graduated in 1947 with the Master of Arts degree. John married Mary Louise Metz on January 24, 1948. They have two children: Stacey and Julie. John Gronouski took a position lecturing on public financing and banking at the University of Maine from 1948 to 1956. He pursued further graduate work at the University of Wisconsin and then moved to Chicago where he became a research associate for the Federation of Tax Administrators in November 1952 and continued until August 1956. During this period John also taught statistics at the Roosevelt College evening school in 1953.

John A. Gronouski received his Ph.D. from the University of Wisconsin in 1955. He became a research associate for the University of Wisconsin for one year in 1956. Gronouski was appointed professor of finance at Wayne State University at Detroit in 1957 where he taught for two years. He was named research director of the Wisconsin Department of Taxation in 1959 and in the same year also became executive director of the Revenue Survey Commission. In 1960 he was appointed Wisconsin state commissioner of taxation.

President John F. Kennedy appointed John A. Gronouski Postmaster General to succeed J. Edward Day on September 9, 1963. He assumed his post on September 30, 1963, continuing under President Johnson after the assassination of John F. Kennedy on November 22, 1963 until his resignation on November 2, 1965. Gronouski coordinated the efforts that went into the use of the zip code. He also was able to develop a vertical improved mail delivery system. He suggested that airmail postage be eliminated and that first class mail be moved under priority class.

President Johnson next appointed John A. Gronouski Ambassador to Poland in which post he served from 1965 to 1968. Since leaving office Gronouski has been active in various areas. He is a trustee of the John F. Kennedy Library and a member of the board of trustees of the Pulaski Foundation. In addition Gronouski is a member of the editorial advisory board of <u>National Tax Journal</u> as well as a member of the American Economic Association and the National Tax Association. He is

honorary co-chairman of the committee for the endowed
chair of Polish studies at the University of Chicago
and a member of the Polish Institute of Arts and
Sciences. He was awarded the honorary LL.D. degree
from Alliance College.

Bibliography:
   Burns, James MacGregor. John Kennedy: A Political
Profile. New York: Harcourt, Brace, 1960.
   Crown, James T. Kennedy in Power. New York: Ballan-
tine Books, 1961.
   Donald, Aida Dipace, ed. John F. Kennedy and the New
Frontier. New York: Hill and Wang, 1966.
   Furer, Howard F., ed. Lyndon B. Johnson, 1908-/1972/.
Dobbs Ferry, N.Y.: Oceana Publications, Inc., 1971.
   Goldman, Eric R. The Tragedy of Lyndon B. Johnson.
New York: Knopf, 1969.
   Schlesinger, Arthur M., Jr. A Thousand Days: John F.
Kennedy in The White House. Boston: Houghton Mifflin
Company, 1965.
   Sidey, Hugh. John F. Kennedy, President. New York:
Fawcett World Library, 1963.
   - - - -. A Very Personal Presidency: Lyndon Johnson
in the White House. New York: Atheneum, 1968.
   Sorenson, Theodore C. Kennedy. New York: Harper and
Row, 1965.
   Stone, Ralph A., ed. John F. Kennedy, 1917-1963.
Dobbs Ferry, N.Y.: Oceana Publications, Inc., 1971.

## SECRETARY OF THE INTERIOR: STEWART LEE UDALL

   Stewart L. Udall, Secretary of the Interior in the
Cabinets of Presidents John F. Kennedy and Lyndon B.
Johnson, was born on January 31, 1920 in Saint Johns,
Arizona, the son of Levi Stuart Udall, chief justice
of the Arizona Supreme Court, and Louise (Lee) Udall.
After receiving his basic education in the St. Johns
public schools Stewart went to Eastern Arizona Junior
College. During the Second World War he served in the
United States Army Air Force as a gunner in a B-24 in
Italy. He then completed his college education, recei-
ving the LL.B. degree in 1948 from the University of
Arizona Law School. He was admitted to the bar in the
same year.
   Stewart Udall married Ermalee Webb on August 1, 1947.
They have six children: Thomas, Scott, Lynn, Lori,
Dennis and James. Udall began the practice of law with
his brother Morris in Tuscon where he continued from
1948 to 1954. In the latter year he was elected to
the United States House of Representatives, representing
the Second District of Arizona in the Eighty-fourth
through the Eighty-seventh Congresses from January 3,
1955 to January 1961. While in Congress he was a member

of the committees on interior and insular affairs, education and labor and the Joint Committee on Navajo-Hopi Indian Administration. He urged repurchase and return to the Cocominno and Sitryreaves national forests of approximately 100,000 acres originally detached from them by court order in 1955. He urged that federal assistance be given to producers of asbestos, copper, flourite, lead, tungsten and zinc. Stewart Udall supported Senator John F. Kennedy's labor reform legislation in 1959. He also supported civil-rights legislation.

President John F. Kennedy named Stewart L. Udall Secretary of the Interior. Udall assumed his post on January 21, 1961 and continued under President Lyndon B. Johnson after the assassination of President John F. Kennedy on November 22, 1963. He left office on January 23, 1969. Udall almost immediately proclaimed an eighteen-month moratorium on the sale of public lands in order to prevent additional abuses as a result of outmoded land policies. He also tried to eliminate undesirable land programs.

Stewart L. Udall established a four-man task force to analyze the work of the Bureau of Indian Affairs. The report called for development of human and natural resources on the Indian reservations. The Bureau instituted a long-range construction program for providing additional school facilities for the Indians and also helped to establish new manufacturing plants for employment of the Indians. Mr. Udall also developed a five-point program aimed at development of public power facilities.

Secretary Udall initiated a series of contracts in 1961 for building plants to save helium. The Office of Coal Research was also created to indicate more effective use of coal. He supervised creation of new National Wildlife Refuges and National Wildlife Ranges. As Secretary of the Interior Udall was also chairman of the Migratory Bird Conservation Commission and a member of the National Forest Reservation Commission, the National Park Trust Fund Board and the President's Council on Physical Fitness. He worked throughout his term in office to improve the land programs of the nation and to preserve the natural resources.

After leaving public office in 1969 Stewart L. Udall was appointed to lead an Overseer Group at the New School for Social Research in New York City. He has also been writing articles on various aspects of government for some journals.

Bibliography:
  Burns, James MacGregor. John Kennedy: A Political Profile. New York: Harcourt Brace, 1960.
  Crown, James T. Kennedy in Power. New York: Ballan-

tine Books, 1961.

Donald, Aida Dipace, ed.  John F. Kennedy and the New
Frontier.  New York: Hill and Wang, 1966.

Furer, Howard B., ed.  Lyndon B. Johnson, 1908-/1972/.
Dobbs Ferry, N.Y.: Oceana Publications, Inc., 1971.

Goldman, Eric R.  The Tragedy of Lyndon B. Johnson.
New York: Knopf, 1969.

Schlesinger, Arthur M., Jr.  A Thousand Days: John F.
Kennedy in The White House.  Boston: Houghton Mifflin
Company, 1965.

Sidey, Hugh.  John F. Kennedy, President.  New York:
Fawcett World Library, 1963.

- - - -.  A Very Personal Presidency: Lyndon Johnson
in the White House.  New York: Atheneum, 1968.

Sorenson, Theodore C.  Kennedy.  New York: Harper and
Row, 1965.

Stone, Ralph A., ed.  John F. Kennedy, 1917-1963.
Dobbs Ferry, N.Y.: Oceana Publications, Inc., 1971.

## SECRETARY OF AGRICULTURE:

## ORVILLE LOTHORP FREEMAN

Orville L. Freeman, Secretary of Agriculture in the
Cabinets of Presidents John F. Kennedy and Lyndon B.
Johnson, was born on May 9, 1918 in Minneapolis, Minnesota, the son of Orville Freeman, a merchant, and
Frances (Schroeder) Freeman.  After receiving a basic
education in the Minneapolis public schools Orville
went to the University of Minnesota from which he was
graduated with the Bachelor of Arts degree in 1940.  He
then began studying law at the University of Minnesota
but was called into military service in 1941 as a 2nd
lieutenant, serving with the United States Marine Corps
Reserve throughout the war.  He fought on Guadacanal
and Bougainville Islands with the Third Marine Division.
He was wounded.  Freeman was next sent to Washington
D.C. where he helped to create and administer a Marine
Corps veterans rehabilitation program, continuing until
1945 when he was discharged with the rank of major.

Orville L. Freeman married Jane Charlotte Shields on
May 2, 1942.  They have two children: Constance Jane and
Michael Orville.  Orville continued with the Marine Corps
Reserve after the war, eventually rising to the rank of
lieutenant colonel.  He returned to the University of
Minnesota Law School in 1945 to complete his studies and
was graduated in 1946 with the LL.B. degree.  He had
already become active in politics and was a leader in
the Democratic-Farmer-Labor Party which had been created
in 1944 as a result of the merger of the Democratic and
Farmer-Labor Parties.  He was a member of the Hennepin
County Central Committee in 1945.

In 1946 Orville L. Freeman was appointed assistant in

charge of veterans' affairs to Minneapolis Mayor Hubert
H. Humphrey.  Orville continued in this post until 1949.
He became secretary of the Minnesota State Central Committee of the Democratic-Farmer-Labor Party in 1946 and
served until 1948.  During this period he was also a
member of the Minneapolis Civil Service Commission from
1946 to 1949.  He was admitted to the Minnesota bar in
1947.  Freeman began his legal practice with the firm of
Larson, Loevinger, Lindquist, Freeman and Fraser in 1947
and continued with it until 1955.

Freeman was elected state chairman of the Democratic-
Farmer-Labor Party in 1948 and remained in that capacity
until 1950.  He was also chairman of the Minnesota delegation to the Democratic National Convention in 1948.
He managed Hubert H. Humphrey's successful campaign for
the United States Senate in the same year.  Orville was
an unsuccessful candidate for state attorney general in
1950.  In the same year he was president of the Minnesota Association of Claimants Compensation Attorney's
Cooperation Services, Incorporated.

Orville L. Freeman ran unsuccessfully for governor of
Minnesota in 1952.  He was elected governor in 1954 and
was reelected in 1956 and 1958.  He instituted a ten
year program for development of Minnesota's schools,
higher educational institutions and hospitals in 1955.
During the next few years he developed various tax reforms and conservation programs.  He supported John F.
Kennedy's candidacy for the Democratic Presidential nomination in 1960.  Freeman was defeated in his reelection bid in 1960.

President John F. Kennedy named Orville L. Freeman Secretary of Agriculture.  He assumed his office on January
21, 1961 and continued to serve under President Lyndon
B. Johnson after the assassination of John F. Kennedy
on November 22, 1963.  Freeman continued in the office
until January 21, 1969.  He immediately began a study
of a program to bring about a stabilization and equalization of farm production and demand in order to stop the
huge buildup in grain storage.  This was accomplished
through special legislation which helped to reduce the
surplus grain.  He helped to gain an extension of the
Agricultural Trade Development and Assistance Act which
permitted the government to sell or give a large amount
of the surplus produce.  He supervised an increase in
the agricultural credit services of the Farmers Home Administration.

Freeman supervised research for elimination of animal
diseases and improvement of food.  Secretary Freeman
worked to increase protection of fish and wildlife.  In
addition studies were made to determine safe food supplies after a nuclear attack.  Freeman worked to make
his department more effective in improvement of food
production and to bring the best available research in-

formation to the attention of farmers and the public
at large.
   Among his activities after leaving office at the end
of the Johnson Administration Orville L. Freeman con-
tinued his interest in political affairs and in advising
agricultural groups.  He is a member of the American
Judicature Society and the American Civil Liberties
Union.  He continues as a member of the Marine Corps
Reserve and is also a member of the Marine Corps League
American Veterans Committee, the Veterans of Foreign
Wars, the American Legion and the Disabled Veterans of
America.

Bibliography:
   Burns, James MacGregor.  John Kennedy: A Political
Profile.  New York: Harcourt, Brace, 1960.
   Crown, James T.  Kennedy in Power.  New York: Ballan-
tine Books, 1961.
   Donald, Aida Dipace, ed.  John F. Kennedy and the New
Frontier.  New York: Hill and Wang, 1966.
   Furer, Howard B., ed.  Lyndon B. Johnson, 1908-/1972/.
Dobbs Ferry, N.Y.: Oceana Publications, Inc., 1971.
   Goldman, Eric R.  The Tragedy of Lyndon B. Johnson.
New York: Knopf, 1969.
   Schlesinger, Arthur M., Jr.  A Thousand Days: John F.
Kennedy in the White House.  Boston: Houghton Mifflin
Company, 1965.
   Sidey, Hugh.  John F. Kennedy, President.  New York:
Fawcett World Library, 1963.
   - - - -.  A Very Personal Presidency: Lyndon Johnson
in the White House.  New York: Atheneum, 1968.
   Sorenson, Theodore C.  Kennedy.  New York: Harper and
Row, 1965.
   Stone, Ralph A., ed.  John F. Kennedy, 1917-1963.
Dobbs Ferry, N.Y.: Oceana Publications, Inc., 1971.

   SECRETARY OF COMMERCE: LUTHER HARTWELL HODGES

   Luther H. Hodges, Secretary of Commerce in the Cabinets of Presidents John F. Kennedy and Lyndon B. John-
son, was born on March 9, 1898 in Pittsylvania County,
Virginia, the son of John James Hodges, a farmer. and
Lovicia (Gammon) Hodges.  After receiving his basic
education in the public schools of Spray and Leaksville,
North Carolina, Luther went to the University of North
Carolina from which he received the Bachelor of Arts degree in 1919.  He joined the Student Army Training Corps
in 1918 and was commissioned a second lieutenant in the
United States Army, serving at Camp Grant, Illinois.
   After graduating from college in 1919 Luther Hodges
became secretary to the general manager of Marshal
Field and Company's textile mills in the Leaksvill-Spray
area.  Luther married Martha Elizabeth Blakeney on June

22, 1922.  They have three children: Betsy, Nancy and
Luther Hartwell, Jr.  In 1927 Hodges became manager of
the Marshall Field  blanket mill in Spray.  During this
period he was a member of the North Carolina Vocational
Board from 1929 to 1933 and a member of the State Highway Commission from 1933 to 1937.  Hodges was promoted
to production manager of the Marshall Field mills in
the territory around Leaksville in 1934 and general manager of the same in 1939.  In 1940 he became general
manager of all Marshall Field mills in the United States
and abroad.  Luther was elected vice president in charge
of mills and sales in 1943.  He was chairman of the
Rotary International postwar committee from 1943 to
1945.

Hodges served the federal government during the Second
World War when he took charge of the textile pricing program of the Office of Price Administration in 1944.  He
next became special consultant to the Secretary of Agriculture in 1945.  In the same year he was the Rotary
consultant to the United Nations Conference on International organization at San Francisco.  He was later representative of Rotary International to the United Nations
Security Council.  He was chairman of the Rotary Convention in Rio de Janeiro, Brazil in 1948.  Luther Hodges
was appointed head of the industry division of the Economic Cooperation Administration and went to the Federal
Republic of Germany in 1950.  Hodges retired from Marshall
Field and Company in the same year.  He then became a
consultant to the Department of State in regard to the
International Management Conference in 1951.

Luther Hodges had become active in the Democratic Party and was elected lieutenant governor of North Carolina
in November 1952.  He became governor of the state when
Governor William B. Ulmstead died in November 1954.
Hodges was elected governor of North Carolina in 1956
for the four-year term ending in January 1961.  He was
able to have legislation passed increasing money for
education and stimulating the growth of industry.  He
also was able to establish a research park in the area
bounded by the communities housing the University of
North Carolina at Chapel Hill, North Carolina State College at Raleigh and Duke University at Durham.  In 1959
Hodges was one of nine American governors who toured the
Soviet Union.

President John F. Kennedy named Luther Hodges Secretary of Commerce.  He assumed his office on January 21,
1961 and continued to serve under President Lyndon B.
Johnson after the assassination of John F. Kennedy in
November 1963.  He left office on January 17, 1965.  Luther worked to help revitalize the nation's economy.  He
established the Area Redevelopment Administration under
the Area Redevelopment Act of 1961 to help redevelop urban and rural areas.  Hodges reorganized the Bureau of

Public Roads, replacing the Commissioner with the Office
of Deputy Federal Highway Administrator.  He also supervised establishment of the United States Travel Service
under the International Service Act of 1961.

Hodges merged supervision of domestic and foreign business activities in 1962 under an assistant secretary who
was placed in charge of the Bureaus of International Commerce and the Business and Defense Services Administration.  He appointed a group to study the nation's transportation study which led to the creation of the Office
of Emergency Transportation  Hodges also helped to create the new post of assistant secretary of commerce for
science and technology.  He also stimulated the expansion of the United States Coast and Geodetic Survey's
work.

After leaving public office Luther Hodges returned to
various business and philanthropic activities, including
directorships of Drexel Industries Incorporated, Servo-
mation Corporation, Williams Brothers, Gulf and Western
Industries and Glen Alden Corporation.  He remained active in Rotary International, serving as its president
during 1967 and 1968.  He also published several works:
Businessman in the State House and The Business Con-
science.  He was also granted the honorary LL.D. degree
by the University of North Carolina and North Carolina
State College as well as other academic institutions.

Bibliography:
Burns, James MacGregor.  John Kennedy: A Political
Profile.  New York: Harcourt, Brace, 1960.
Crown, James T.  Kennedy in Power.  New York: Ballan-
tine Books, 1961.
Donald, Aida Dipace, ed.  John F. Kennedy and the New
Frontier.  New York: Hill and Wang, 1966.
Furer, Howard B., ed.  Lyndon B. Johnson, 1908-/1972/
Dobbs Ferry, N.Y.: Oceana Publications, Inc., 1971.
Goldman, Eric R.  The Tragedy of Lyndon B. Johnson.
New York: Knopf, 1969.
Harris, Seymour E.  Economics of the Kennedy Years,
and a Look Ahead.  New York: Harper and Row, 1964.
Heath, James F.  The Kennedy Administration and the
Business Community.  Chicago: University of Chicago Press,
1969.
Rowen, Hobart.  Free Enterprises: Kennedy, Johnson and
the Business Establishment.  New York: Putnam, 1964.
Schlesinger, Arthur M., Jr.  A Thousand Days: John F.
Kennedy in the White House.  Boston: Houghton Mifflin
Company, 1965.
Sidey, Hugh.  John F. Kennedy, President.  New York:
Fawcett World Library, 1963.
- - - -.  A Very Personal Presidency: Lyndon Johnson
in the White House.  New York: Atheneum, 1968.
Sorenson, Theodore C.  Kennedy.  New York: Harper and

Row, 1965.
  Stone, Ralph A., ed.  John F. Kennedy, 1917-1963.
Dobbs Ferry, N.Y.: Oceana Publications, Inc., 1971.

SECRETARY OF LABOR: ARTHUR JOSEPH GOLDBERG

Arthur J. Goldberg, Secretary of Labor in the Cabinet
of President John F. Kennedy, was born on August 8, 1908
in Chicago, Illinois, the son of Joseph and Rebecca
(Perlstein) Goldberg.  While receiving his basic education in the Chicago public schools.  Arthur worked as a
delivery boy for a Chicago shoe factory.  He went to
Crane Junior College from 1924 to 1926, working in the
post office and on construction gangs.  He next studied
law at Northwestern University from which he was graduated with the B.S.L. degree in 1929.  He was admitted to
the Illinois bar in the same year.
  Arthur Goldberg had begun working as a clerk for the
legal firm of Kornfrer, Horwitz, Halligan and Dennis of
Chicago in 1927 and began to practice law with the firm
in 1929.  He was next associated with the firm of Pritzker and Pritzker from 1931 to 1933.  Arthur married
Dorothy Kargans on July 18, 1931.  They have two children:
Barbara and Robert Michael.  Arthur next began his own
legal practice in Chicago in 1933 and continued until
1945.  During the Second World War Arthur was a special
assistant with the Office of Strategic Services in 1942.
  Goldberg was commissioned a captain in the United States
Army in 1943 and was soon promoted to major.  He continued
working with the Office of Strategic Services, being appointed chief of the labor division and went to Europe
several times to work with trade unionists to get them
involved in undercover work behind the enemy lines.
  In 1945 Arthur Goldberg became a partner in the Chicago
law firm of Goldberg and Devoe, continuing until 1947
when he became senior member of the firm of Goldberg,
Devoe, Shadar and Mikva.  He was professor of law at John
Marshall Law School from 1945 to 1948 and also represented various international unions.  He became general
counsel for the Congress of Industrial Organizations (CIO)
and the United Steelworkers of America in 1948.  In the
same year he established a  second law firm in Washington, D.C.: Goldberg, Feller and Bredhoff.
  Arthur Goldberg was a director of the Amalgamted Trust
and Savings Bank and of the Amalgamated Life and Insurance Company from 1946 to 1959.  During this period
Goldberg also lectured at the Chicago School of Industrial
Relations.  He helped to arrange the merger of the American Federation of Labor and the Congress of Industrial
Organizations  and suggested the name AFL-CIO in December
1955.  Since 1952 he has been a member of the American
Committee for a United Europe.  Goldberg was named a
trustee and director of the Philip Murray Memorial Foun-

dation of 1955 and has continued in this capacity.  He
wrote AFL-CIO: Labor United in 1956.  In 1957 he began
his services for the Carnegie Endowment for International
Peace and the National Legal Aid Association.  He became
a member of the board of governors of the American Red
Cross in 1960.

President John F. Kennedy named Arthur Goldberg Secretary of Labor in which post he served from January 21,
1961 to September 24, 1962.  Arthur almost immediately
helped to settle the New York tugboat strike.  He recommended that the federal government develop a long-range
program for creation of the additional jobs needed.  He
also urged that the government expand its program of retraining workers in areas where industry had been reduced
or withdrawn.  This led to passage of legislation creating the Area Redevelopment Administration for retraining
of workers.  In order to dael with the problem of unemployment he urged passage of legislation temporarily
extending unemployment insurance.  Goldberg also reorganized the office of Manpower Administration.  He worked
to increase the minimum wage.

Arthur Goldberg influenced the passage of the Man Power
Development and Retraining Program Act in 1962.  He began an experimental project for training and pacement
for training young men in Newark, New Jersey.  Arthur
helped to establish the President's Advisory Committee
on Labor-Management Policies and also the President's
Committee on Equal Opportunity.  He was vice chairman
of the latter and aimed at eliminating racial discrimination in employment.  He suggested that President Kennedy
call the White House Conference on National Economic Issues on 1962.  He also mediated in several strikes although he thought that the Labor Department should act
only when the national interest was involved.

Among his awards Arthur Goldberg was named outstanding
labor personality of the year by the New York  Newspaper
Guild.  He received the honorary LL.D. degree from Hebrew
Union College and Roosevelt University in 1961 from the
University of Portland and Dropsie College in 1962.  He
received the same from Amherst and Boston Colleges as
well as Northwestern and Yeshiva Universities in 1963.
President John F. Kennedy appointed Arthur Goldberg an
associate justice of the United States Supreme Court in
1962.  He remained on the bench until 1965 when President
Lyndon B. Johnson named him United States Ambassador to
the United Nations.  Goldberg continued in that position
until 1968 when he returned to his private legal practice
He wrote Defenses of Freedom in 1966.  Arthur Goldberg
ran unsuccessfully as the Democratic candidate for governor of New York against Nelson Rockefeller in 1970.  Goldberg continues as a member of the American, Illinois and
Chicago Bar associations.  He is still involved in his
legal practice in Washington, D.C.

Bibliography:
   Burns, James MacGregor.  John Kennedy: A Political Pro-
file.  New York: Harcourt, Brace, 1960.
   Crown, James T.  Kennedy in Power.  New York: Ballan-
tine Books, 1961.
   Donald, Aida Dipace, ed.  John F. Kennedy and the New
Frontier.  New York: Hill and Wang, 1966.
   Furer, Howard B., ed.  Lyndon B. Johnson, 1908-/1972/
Dobbs Ferry, N.Y.: Oceana Publications, Inc., 1971.
   Goldman, Eric R.  The Tragedy of Lyndon B. Johnson.
New York: Knopf, 1969.
   Rowen, Hobart.  Free Enterprises: Kennedy, Johnson and
the Business Establishment.  New York: Putnam, 1964.
   Schlesinger, Arthur M., Jr.  A Thousand Days: John F.
Kennedy in the White House.  Boston: Houghton Mifflin
Company, 1965.
   Sidey, Hugh.  John F. Kennedy, President.  New York:
Fawcett World Library, 1963.
   Sorenson, Theodore C.  Kennedy.  New York: Harper and
Row, 1965.
   Stone, Ralph A., ed.  John F. Kennedy, 1917-1963.
Dobbs Ferry, N.Y.: Oceana Publications, Inc., 1971.

## SECRETARY OF LABOR: W/ILLIAM/ WILLARD WIRTZ

W. Willard Wirtz, Secretary of Labor in the Cabinets
of Presidents John F. Kennedy and Lyndon B. Johnson, was
born on March 14, 1912 in Dekalb, Illinois, the son of
William Willard Wirtz, an educator and businessman, and
Alpha Belle (White) Wirtz.  After receiving his basic
education in the Dekalb public schools he studied at
Northern Illinois State Teachers College from 1928 to
1930 and then transferred to the University of California,
attending from 1930 to 1931.  He then went to Beloit College from which he was graduated with the Bachelor of
Arts degree in 1933.

W. Willard Wirtz then taught at the Kewanee, Illinois
High School during the academic year 1933-34 after which
he went to Harvard University Law School, receiving the
LL.B. degree in 1937.  Willard married Mary Jane Quisen-
berry on September 8, 1936.  They have two sons: Richard
and Philip.  He was next an assistant professor of law
at the State University of Iowa from 1937 to 1939 and
was admitted to the Iowa bar in 1939.  He then taught
at the Northwestern University School of Law from 1939
to 1942 and in the latter year was appointed assistant
general counsel for the Board of Economic Warfare, serving until 1943 when Wirtz became general counsel as
well as public member of the War Labor Board, remaining
in that capacity until 1945.  He was next chairman of
National Wage Stabilization Board in 1946.

Mr. Wirtz then returned to the Northwestern University
School of Law as a full professor, remaining on the

faculty from 1946 to 1954. He was named a member of the
Illinois Liquor Control Commission in 1950 and served
until 1956. He supported Adlai E. Stevenson in the latter's 1952 presidential campaign and was one of his ad-
visors. Wirtz was admitted to the Illinois bar in 1955
and in the same year formed the Chicago law firm of
Stevenson and Wirtz. The firm merged with that of Paul,
Weiss, Rifkind, Wharton and Garrison of New York in 1957.

President John F. Kennedy named W. Willard Wirtz Undersecretary of Labor in 1961. The President appointed him
Secretary of Labor to succeed Arthur Goldberg in 1962.
Wirtz assumed his office on August 30, 1962 and continued
to serve under President Lyndon B. Johnson after the
assassination of John F. Kennedy in November 1963. He
remained at his post until the end of the Johnson administration on January 20, 1969. Wirtz guided the Department in the direction of taking responsibility for
mediating in strikes which harmed the crucial interests
of the nation. In addition Mr. Wirtz investigated the
various problems caused by greater technological developments and proposed methods for solving them through retraining and other aids for those who were unemployed,
including alerting the American people to be more concerned.

Secretary Wirtz also supported the trade expansion bill
and carefully administered the operations required under
the Manpower Development and Training Act. After leaving
public office W. Willard Wirtz returned to the practice
of law. He is a member of the National Academy of Arbi-
trators as well as the American, Illinois and Chicago
bar associations. He has been a trustee of the Penn-
Central Railroad.

Bibliography:
Burns, James MacGregor. John Kennedy: A Political
Profile. New York: Harcourt, Brace, 1960.
Crown, James T. Kennedy in Power. New York: Ballan-
tine Books, 1961.
Donald, Aida Dipace, ed. John F. Kennedy and the New
Frontier. New York: Hill and Wang, 1966.
Furer, Howard B., ed. Lyndon B. Johnson, 1908-/1972/.
Dobbs Ferry, N.Y.: Oceana Publications, Inc., 1971.
Goldman, Eric. The Tragedy of Lyndon B. Johnson. New
York: Knopf, 1969.
Rowen, Hobart. Free Enterprises: Kennedy, Johnson and
the Business Establishment. New York: Putnam, 1964.
Schlesinger, Arthur M., Jr. A Thousand Days: John F.
Kennedy in the White House. Boston: Houghton Mifflin
Company, 1965.
Sidey, Hugh. John F. Kennedy, President. New York:
Fawcett World Library, 1963.
- - - -. A Very Personal Presidency: Lyndon Johnson
in the White House. New York: Atheneum, 1968.

Sorenson, Theodore C. <u>Kennedy</u>. New York: Harper and
Row, 1965.
Stone, Ralph A., ed. <u>John F. Kennedy, 1917-1963</u>.
Dobbs Ferry, N.Y.: Oceana Publications, Inc., 1971.

## SECRETARY OF HEALTH, EDUCATION, AND WELFARE:

### ABRAHAM ALEXANDER RIBICOFF

Abraham A. Ribicoff, Secretary of Health, Education,
and Welfare in the Cabinet of President John F. Kennedy,
was born on April 9, 1910 in New Britain, Connecticut,
the son of Samuel Ribicoff,a factory worker, and Rose
(Sable) Ribicoff. After receiving his basic education
in the New Britain public schools he worked one year
for G. E. Prentice Company of New Britain and then studied at New York University from 1928 to 1929. He then
studied law at the University of Chicago and headed the
Chicago office of G. E. Prentice Company from 1929 to
1931. Abraham married Ruth Siegel on June 28, 1931.
They have two children: Peter and Jane.
Abraham Ribicoff received the LL.B. degree from the
University of Chicago in 1933 and was admitted to the
Connecticut bar in the same year. He began to practice
law in Hartford with A. S. Bordon and became a partner
in the firm of Bordon and Ribicoff in 1938. He became
active in the Democratic Party and was elected to the
lower house of the Connecticut legislature in 1938, serving until 1942. He formed a new law firm in Hartford
with his brother Irving and David Kotkin: Ribicoff,
Ribicoff and Kotkin in 1941. During the same year he
became a member of the American Arbitration Association.
Abraham Ribicoff was a judge of the Hartford municipal
court from 1941 to 1943 and chairman of the Connecticut
addembly of municipal court judges from 1941 to 1942. He
was appointed chairman of the Commission for the Study
of Alcoholism and Crime in 1943. He again sat on the
bench as a judge of the Hartford Municipal Court from
1945 to 1947. During the same period he was a member
of the bipartisan Hartford Charter Revision Committee.
He was next named a hearing examiner on the Connecticut
Interracial Commission from 1947 to 1948.
Abraham Ribicoff was elected to the United States House
of Representatives in 1948. He served in the Eighty-
first and Eighty-second Congresses from January 3, 1949
to January 3, 1953. He was a member of the foreign affairs committee and sponsored an amendment protecting
American investors abroad in the bill providing for a
second year of Marshall Plan aid. He also supported a
Pacific pact and aid for recovery in the Far East. He
was a delegate to the San Francisco Peace Conference in
September 1951. Abraham Ribicoff was also named a member of the group working on the United States-Australia-

New Zealand mutual defense pact and the Philippine Security Treaty.

Abraham Ribicoff was elected governor of Connecticut in 1954 and was reelected in 1958, serving from 1955 to January 1961. While governor he worked with the legislature to reform the state's legal code, helped provide for a simpler means of amending the state constitution and worked to institute the primary system in Connecticut. Ribicoff tightened motor vehicle enforcement, reducing Connecticut's death rate considerably. In addition a State Board of Mental Health was created while he was in office.

President John F. Kennedy appointed Abraham Ribicoff Secretary of Health, Education, and Welfare in which post he served from January 21, 1961 to July 30, 1962. He recommended that Congress provide funds to colleges and universities to improve teacher training and other educational programs as well as to offer opportunities for education to a greater number of people. He supervised the additional responsibilities of the Office of Education in developing retraining programs for unemployed people under the Area Redevelopment Act of 1961. He also obtained funds for dental research.

Under Ribicoff's direction the United States Public Health Service licensed Types I and II of the Sabin oral live-virus poliomyelitis vaccine in 1961 and supervised its use. The Health Service also increased its radiation scanning of milk, foodstuffs, water, and air. Abraham appointed a 16-member Citizens Advisory Committee to investigate how the Food and Drug Administration could offer greater consumer protection. He established a Committee for Consumer Protection in July 1962.

Secretary Ribicoff recommended protection for children of families receiving public assistance, recommending that the Bureau of Asssistance be renamed the Bureau of Family Services. As a result of his proposals Congress passed a welfare reform bill in 1962. Abraham Ribicoff and President Kennedy tried in vain to have Congress pass a medicare program for the aged. Ribicoff has been awarded many honorary degrees from such institutions of higher learning as Amherst, Trinity and Hebrew Union Colleges as well as New York and Yeshiva Universities. He resigned from the Cabinet to run for the United States Senate from Connecticut. He was elected in November 1962 and reelected in 1968 and 1974. He has served in the Senate since January 3, 1963 and has been instrumental in securing passage of many important social welfare measures.

Bibliography:
 Burns, James MacGregor. John Kennedy: A Political Profile. New York: Harcourt, Brace, 1960.
 Crown, James T. Kennedy in Power. New York: Ballan-

tine Books, 1961.
    Donald, Aida Dipace, ed.  John F. Kennedy and the New
Frontier.  New York: Hill and Wang, 1966.
    Schlesinger, Arthur M., Jr.  A Thousand Days: John F.
Kennedy in the White House.  Boston: Houghton Mifflin
Company, 1965.
    Sidey, Hugh.  John F. Kennedy, President.  New York:
Fawcett World Library, 1963.
    Sorenson, Theodore C. Kennedy.  New York: Harper and
Row, 1965.
    Stone, Ralph A., ed.  John F. Kennedy, 1917-1963.
Dobbs Ferry, N.Y.: Oceana Publications, Inc., 1971.

## SECRETARY OF HEALTH, EDUCATION, AND WELFARE

### ANTHONY JOSEPH CELEBREZZE

Anthony J. Celebrezze, Secretary of Health, Education,
and Welfare in the Cabinets of Presidents John F. Kennedy
and Lyndon B. Johnson, was born on September 4, 1910 in
Anzi, Italy, the son of Rocco Celebrezze, a railroad
worker, and Dorothy (Marcugusieppe) Celebrezze.  They
were visiting Italy at the time of Anthony's birth.
Anthony and his mother remained in Italy until 1912 when
they rejoined his father Rocco in Cleveland, Ohio.  After
receiving his basic education in the Cleveland public
schools Anthony studied at John Carroll University during
1930 and 1931.  He worked at many jobs in order to finance
his education.  Celebrezze studied law at Ohio Northern
University, receiving the LL.B. degree in 1936.
    Anthony J. Celebrezze was admitted to the Ohio bar in
1938 and began working for the legal department of the
Ohio State Bureau of Unemployment in the same year.  Anthony married Anne Marco on May 7, 1938.  They have
three children: Anthony Joseph, Jean Anne, and Susan Marie.  Celebrezze resigned from the Ohio State Bureau of
Unemployment in 1939 and began his legal practice in
Cleveland.  During World War II he served as a seaman in
the Navy.
    After the war Anthony Celebrezze continued his practice
and also became involved in politics.  He was elected
as a Democrat to the Ohio Senate in 1950 and was reelected in 1952.  The following year, 1953, he was elected
mayor of Cleveland and was highly successful, being reelected four time in 1955, 1957, 1959 and 1961.  He was
awarded the Brotherhood Award.  Mayor Celebrezze was a
director of the United States Conference of Mayors.
During 1958 and 1959 he was president of the American
Municipal Association.
    President Dwight D. Eisenhower recognized his talents
and named Celebrezze a member of the Advisory Commission
on Intergovernmental Relations in 1959.  President John
F. Kennedy reappointed him to the commission in October

1962.  Celebrezze was elected president of the United
States Conference of Mayors in 1962.  He was given the
National Fiorello La Guardia Award in 1961.

President John F. Kennedy named Anthony J. Celebrezze
Secretary of Health, Education, and Welfare to succeed
Abraham Ribicoff.  Celebrezze assumed his office on
July 31, 1962 and continued to serve under President
Lyndon B. Johnson until August 17, 1965.  During 1962
Mr. Celebrezze was given the National Conference of
Christian and Jews National Human Relations Award, the
National Award of the Catholic Resettlement Council, the
Public Service Award of the National Council of the YMCA
and the Camp Fire Girls Gulick Award.  He received honor-
ary degrees from several colleges and universities.  As
Secretary of Health, Education, and Welfare he supported
the medicare program for the aged.  Mr. Celebrezze refused to give financial aid to the parochial schools
on the grounds that it was unconstitutional.

Anthony J. Celebrezze left the post of Secretary of
Health, Education, and Welfare in 1965 when he was appointed a member of the Sixth Circuit Court of Appeals
and has continued on the bench since that time.

Bibliography:
Burns, James MacGregor.  John Kennedy: A Political
Profile.  New York: Harcourt, Brace, 1960.
Crown, James T.  Kennedy in Power.  New York: Ballan-
tine Books, 1961.
Donald, Aida Dipace, ed.  John F. Kennedy and the New
Frontier.  New York: Hill and Wang, 1966.
Furer, Howard B., ed.  Lyndon B. Johnson, 1908-/1972/.
Dobbs Ferry, N.Y.: Oceana Publications, Inc., 1971.
Goldman, Eric.  The Tragedy of Lyndon B. Johnson.  New
York: Knopf, 1969.
Schlesinger, Arthur M., Jr.  A Thousand Days: John F.
Kennedy in the White House.  Boston: Houghton Mifflin
Company, 1965.
Sidey, Hugh.  John F. Kennedy, President.  New York:
Fawcett World Library, 1963.
- - - -.  A Very Personal Presidency: Lyndon Johnson
in the White House.  New York: Atheneum, 1968.
Sorenson, Theodore C.  Kennedy.  New York: Harper and
Row, 1965.
Stone, Ralph A., ed.  John F. Kennedy, 1917-1963.
Dobbs Ferry, N.Y.: Oceana Publications, Inc., 1971.

## ADMINISTRATIONS OF LYNDON B. JOHNSON

### VICE PRESIDENT: HUBERT HORATIO HUMPHREY, JR.

Hubert H. Humphrey, Vice President in the second administration of President Lyndon B. Johnson, was born on May 27, 1911 in Wallace, South Dakota, the son of Hubert Horatio Humphrey, a pharmacist, and Christine (Sannes) Humphrey. After receiving his basic education in the Doland public schools and graduating from Doland High School in 1929, Hubert went to the University of Minnesota and then worked with his father. Hubert then attended the Denver College of Pharmacy from 1932 to 1933 and worked for the Humphrey Drug Company from 1933 to 1937.

Hubert H. Humphrey married Muriel Fay Buck on September 3, 1936. They have four children: Nancy Faye, Hubert Horatio III, Robert Andrew and Douglas Sannes. Hubert Humphrey returned to the University of Minnesota and received the Bachelor of Arts degree in 1939. He then studied political science and was an assistant instructor in political science at the University of Louisiana from 1939 to 1940, receiving the Master of Arts degree in the latter year. Hubert then returned to the University of Minnesota to pursue additional graduate work from 1940 to 1941 and was also an assistant instructor of political science.

In 1941 Hubert H. Humphrey became a member of the administrative staff of the Works Progress Administration and was later head of the state division. He also served as assistant state supervisor of adult education, chief of the war services section and director of the training reemployment division during this period until 1943. In the latter year Humphrey was appointed assistant regional director of the War Manpower Commission. He was also a visiting professor of political science at Macalaster College in St. Paul during the 1943-44 academic year.

Humphrey maintained an interest in Democratic politics and was active in fusing the Democratic and Farmer Labor Parties in Minnesota during the 1940's. He was named state campaign manager for the Roosevelt-Truman ticket in 1944. Humphrey was next elected mayor of Minneapolis in which post he served from 1945 to 1948. He was awarded the Association of Commerce award for the Outstanding Minneapolitan as well as the Outstanding Young Man in the state by the Minnesota Junior Association of Commerce in 1945.

Hubert H. Humphrey was elected as a Democrat to the United States Senate from Minnesota in 1948 and was reelected in 1954 and 1960. He was a United States delegate to the United Nations from 1956 to 1958 and a delegate to the UNESCO Conference at Paris in the latter year. He was elected majority whip in 1961. President Lyndon

B. Johnson chose Humphrey as his Vice-Presidential running mate in 1964, and he was subsequently nominated by
the Democrats and elected in November.  He wrote The
Cause Program for America and War on Poverty in 1964.
He also edited Integration vs Segregation in the same
year.

Hubert H. Humphrey was sworn in as Vice President with
President Lyndon B. Johnson on January 20, 1965, serving
until the end of the administration on January 20, 1969.
While in office he was honorary chairman of the President's Council on Equal Opportunity, the National Aeronautics and Space Council and the Peace Corps Advisory
Council.  In addition he was a member of the National
Security Council and the Board of Regents of the Smithsonian Institution.  Humphrey helped to coordinate the
civil rights work of the various federal agencies and
was the liason of the administration with the nation's
mayors.

Hubert H. Humphrey was the unsuccessful Democratic
candidate for President in 1968.  After leaving public
office Hubert returned to teaching at Macalaster College
and the University of Minnesota,  He was also associated
with the educational enterprises of the Encyclopedia
Britannica.  Humphrey was again elected United States
Senator from Minnesota on November 3, 1970 and has continued to serve in the upper house since January 1971.
He is a member of the American Political Science Association and the American Academy of Arts and Sciences.

Bibliography:
Evans, Rowland, and Novack, Robert.  Lyndon B. Johnson:
The Exercise of Power; A Political Biography.  New York:
New American Library, 1966.
Furer, Howard B., ed.  Lyndon B. Johnson, 1908-/1973/
Dobbs Ferry, N.Y.: Oceana Publications, Inc., 1971.
Goldman, Eric.  The Tragedy of Lyndon Johnson.  New
York: Knopf, 1969.
Griffith, Winthrop.  Humphrey.  New York: Morrow,
1965.
Humphrey, Hubert H.  The War on Poverty.  New York:
McGraw Hill, 1964.
Sherrill, Robert, and Ernst, Harry W.  Drugstore Li-
beral.  New York: Grossman Publishers, 1968.
Zeiger, Henry A.  Lyndon B. Johnson.  Man and Presi-
dent.  New York: Popular Library, 1965.

## SECRETARY OF STATE: DAVID DEAN RUSK

Refer to the biographical sketch of David Dean Rusk
under Secretary of State in the Administration of John
F. Kennedy, page 712.

SECRETARY OF THE TREASURY: CLARENCE DOUGLAS DILLON

Refer to the biographical sketch of Douglas Dillon under Secretary of the Treasury in the Administration of John F. Kennedy, page 714.

SECRETARY OF THE TREASURY: HENRY HAMILL FOWLER

Henry H. Fowler, Secretary of the Treasury in the Cabinet of President Lyndon B. Johnson, was born on September 5, 1908 in Roanoke, Virginia, the son of Mack Johnson and Bertha (Browning) Fowler. After receiving his basic education, Henry went to Roanoke College from which he was graduated in 1929 with the Bachelor of Arts degree. He then went to Yale University Law School, receiving the LL.B. degree in 1952. He continued his education to receive the J.S.D. degree in 1933. Fowler was admitted to the Virginia bar in 1933 and became counsel for the Tennessee Valley Authority in 1934, remaining in that post until 1938 when he was appointed assistant general counsel in 1939.

Henry H. Fowler married Trudye Pamela Hathcote on October 19, 1938. They have three children: Mary, Susan, and Henry Hamill. Fowler's next appointment was that of special assistant to the Attorney General as chief counsel to the subcommittee of the Senate Committee on Education and Labor from 1939 to 1940. In 1941 he was named special counsel to the Federal Power Commission. Later in the same year he became assistant general counsel for the Office of Production Management. During the Second World War Fowler was a member of the War Production Board from 1942 to 1944 and in the latter year became economic advisor to the United States Mission of Economic Affairs in London, England. He continued to serve the federal government in 1945 as a special assistant to the administrator of the Foreign Economic Administration.

Henry H. Fowler left governmeny service after the war to form the firm of Fowler, Leva, Hawes and Symington in 1946. He remained with the firm until 1951 when he returned to public office under President Dwight D. Eisenhower as deputy administrator of the National Production Authority, becoming its administrator in 1952. During the latter year he next became head of the Defense Production Administration, continuing until 1953. Fowler then returned to his law practice, continuing until 1961. He was president of the Yale Law School Association of Washington in 1955. He attended the Democratic National Convention in 1956.

President John F. Kennedy named Henry H. Fowler undersecretary of the Treasury in 1961. He remained in this post under President Johnson after the assassination of John F. Kennedy until 1964. He resigned to return to his law firm in 1964. Yale University awarded Fowler the

honorary LL.D. degree in 1962.  President Lyndon B. Johnson appointed Henry H. Fowler Secretary of the Treasury
to succeed Douglas Dillon in 1965.  Fowler served from
April 1, 1965 until December 20, 1968.  As part of his
duties Fowler was the United States representative to the
International Monetary Fund as well as the World Bank and
the International American Development Bank.  While in
office he was able to achieve a reduction in the silver
content of coins in order to preserve the national silver
reserves.  He also served on the Intergovernmental Relations Advisory Committee.  Fowler was awarded honorary
LL.D. degrees in 1966 by William and Mary College and
Wesleyan University.

    After leaving office in 1969 Henry H. Fowler became a
general partner in Goldman, Sachs and Company of New
York City and is still a member of the firm.  Among his
other business activities Mr. Fowler is a director of the
following corporations: the Corning Glass Works, U. S.
Industries, Inc., the United States and Foreign Securities
Corporation, and Deveco, Inc.  In addition he contributes
much of his time as a trustee of the Alfred P. Sloan
Foundation, the Carnegie Endowment for Peace, and Roanoke
College.  He is chairman of the Institute for International Education, and a member of the Council on Foreign Relations, the Foreign Policy Association of which he was
a director, and the national committee on money and
credit.

Bibliography:
    Evans, Rowland, and Novak, Robert.  Lyndon B. Johnson:
The Exercise of Power; A Political Biography.  New York:
New American Library, 1966.
    Furer, Howard B., ed.  Lyndon B. Johnson, 1908-/1973/.
Dobbs Ferry, N.Y.: Oceana Publications, Inc., 1971.
    Goldman, Eric.  The Tragedy of Lyndon Johnson.  New
York: Knopf, 1969.
    Rowen, Hobart.  Free Enterprises: Kennedy, Johnson and
the Business Establishment.  New York: Putnam, 1964.
    Sidey, Hugh.  A Very Personal Presidency: Lyndon John-
son in the White House.  New York: Atheneum, 1968.
    Zeiger, Henry A.  Lyndon B. Johnson.  Man and Presi-
dent.  New York: Popular Library, 1965.

## SECRETARY OF THE TREASURY: JOSEPH WALKER BARR

    Joseph W. Barr, Secretary of the Treasury in the Ca-
binet of President Lyndon B. Johnson, was born on January 17, 1918 in Vincennes, Indiana, the son of Oscar
Lynn and Shella Florence (Walker) Barr.  After receiving
his basic education in the public schools Joseph went to
Depauw University from which he received the Bachelor
of Arts degree in 1939.  Joseph married Beth Williston
on September 3, 1939.  They have five children: Bonnie,

Cherry, Joseph Williston, Elizabeth Eugenia, and Lynn Hamilton.

Joseph W. Barr next studied at Harvard University for two years, receiving the Master of Arts degree in 1941. During World War II he was a lieutenant commander in the United States Navy from 1942 to 1945. He was awarded the Bronze Star. After the end of the war Joseph became treasurer of his father's company, the O. L. Barr Grain Company, in 1946. He was elected to the United States House of Representatives from the 11th Indiana District, serving in the Eighty-sixth Congress from January 3, 1959 to January 3, 1961.

President John F. Kennedy appointed Joseph W. Barr assistant to the Secretary of the Treasury in 1961. He remained in this post until 1964 when he was named chairman of the Federal Deposit Insurance Corporation, serving until 1965. He was next appointed undersecretary of the Treasury, remaining in that office from 1965 to 1968.

President Lyndon B. Johnson named Joseph W. Barr Secretary of the Treasury as a recess appointment to succeed Harry H. Fowler on December 21, 1968. He was confirmed by the Senate on January 9, 1969, serving until the end of the administration on January 20, 1969. After leaving public office Barr was president of the American Security and Trust Company in Washington, D.C. from 1969 to 1972, becoming chairman of the board in 1972. He has continued to serve in that capacity. Among his other business activities Joseph Barr is a director of the 3M Company, the Commercial Credit Company, the Burlington Industries and the Washington Gas Light Company. He is a trustee of DePauw University and a member of the Board of Regents of Georgetown University.

Bibliography:
  Evans, Rowland, and Novack, Robert. Lyndon B. Johnson: The Exercise of Power; A Political Biography. New York: The American Library, 1966.
  Furer, Howard B., ed. Lyndon B. Johnson, 1908-/1973/. Dobbs Ferry, N.Y.: Oceana Publications, Inc., 1971.
  Goldman, Eric. The Tragedy of Lyndon Johnson. New York: Knopf, 1969.
  Rowen, Hobart. Free Enterprises: Kennedy, Johnson and the Business Establishment. New York: Putnam, 1964.
  Zeiger, Henry A. Lyndon B. Johnson. Man and President. New York: Popular Library, 1965.

SECRETARY OF DEFENSE: ROBERT STRANGE MACNAMARA

Refer to the biographical sketch of Robert S. McNamara under Secretary of Defense in the Administration of John F. Kennedy, page 717.

SECRETARY OF DEFENSE: CLARK MCADAMS CLIFFORD

Clark M. Clifford, Secretary of Defense in the Cabinet of President Lyndon B. Johnson, was born on December 25, 1906 in Fort Scott, Kansas, the son of Frank Andrew Clifford, an official of the Missouri Pacific Railway and Georgia (McAdams) Clifford. Clark moved to St. Louis with his family and received his basic education in the public schools of the city. Clifford was gradua- ted from Soldan High School and then attended Washing- ton University of St. Louis from which he received the LL.B. degree in 1928.

Clark Clifford was admitted to the bar in 1928 and prac- ticed law as a member of the legal firm of Holland, Lashly and Donnell until 1933. Clark married Margery Pepperell Kimball on October 3, 1931. They had three children: Margery Pepperell, Joyce Carter, and Randall. Mr. Clifford next became a partner in the firm of Hol- land, Lashly and Lashly in 1933, remaining with the firm until 1937. It then became Lashly, Lashly, Miller and Clifford in 1938. He was a partner in the firm un- til 1950. He also taught trial psychology at Washington University.

During World War II Clark M. Clifford was commissioned a lieutenant j.g. in the United States Naval Reserve in 1944. He was stationed at the Pacific Naval Supply Of- fices in San Francisco and was eventually made an assis- tant to the director of the logistics division. He was promoted to the rank of lieutenant commander in July 1945 and was sent to Washington as an assistant to the President's naval aide. In 1946 Clifford was made a captain and became President Harry S. Truman's naval aide.

Clark Clifford was next appointed special counsel to President Truman in 1946 and served in this capacity until 1950. He aided in the formulation of the Truman Doctrine to defend countries threatened by insurgents. In February 1950 he became a senior partner in the Washington, D.C. law firm of Clifford and Miller and continued his legal practice until 1968. During this period he supported John F. Kennedy for the Presidency in 1960. He was named a member of President-elect Ken- nedy's Committee on the Establishment in 1960. Clark became a member of President Kennedy's Foreign Advisory Board on May 16, 1961. He helped to settle the steel industry problems in New York City in 1962. President Kennedy appointed Clark Clifford Chairman of the Foreign Intelligence Advisory Board on April 23, 1963 in which post he served until 1968.

President Lyndon B. Johnson asked Clark M. Clifford to serve as his adviser. In this capacity he went to Asia for the President in 1965 on a fact-finding mission. In June 1967 Clark was appointed to a committee to study

the Middle East crisis.  President Johnson appointed
Clark M. Clifford Secretary of Defense to succeed Robert
S. McNamara on January 18, 1968.  Clark assumed his office on March 1 and served until the end of the Johnson
administration on January 20, 1969.  Among his activities
while in office, Clifford worked out the limitation of
the bombing of North Vietnam.  He also continued the
peace negotiations without the South Vietnamese representatives.  Secretary Clifford made strenuous efforts
to convince North Korea to release the Pueblo and its
crew.  In addition he worked to eliminate racial discrimination in military housing.
   After leaving public office in 1969 Clark M. Clifford
became a senior partner in the Washington, D.C. law firm
of Clifford, Warnke, Glass, McIlwain and Finney.  Among
his other business activities he is a director of the
National Bank of Washington, the Sheraton Corporation
and the General Aniline and Film Corporation.  He is
also a trustee of Washington University.  Clark was
awarded the Medal of Freedom.

Bibliography:
   Anderson, Patrick.  President's Men.  Garden City,
N.Y.: Doubleday, 1968.
   Evans, Rowland, and Novack, Robert.  Lyndon B. Johnson:
The Exercise of Power; A Political Biography.  New York:
New American Library, 1966.
   Furer, Howard B., ed.  Lyndon B. Johnson, 1908-/1973/.
Dobbs Ferry, N.Y.: Oceana Publications, Inc., 1971.
   Geyelin, Philip L.  Lyndon B. Johnson and the World.
New York: F. A. Praeger, 1966.
   Goldman, Eric.  The Tragedy of Lyndon Johnson.  New
York: Knopf, 1969.
   Horowitz, D., and Welsh, D.  "Clark Clifford, Attorney
of Law,"  Ramparts, vol. 7.  August 24, 1968.
   Sidey, Hugh.  A Very Personal Presidency: Lyndon John-
son in the White House.  New York: Atheneum, 1968.
   Zeiger, Henry A.  Lyndon B. Johnson.  Man and Presi-
dent.  New York: Popular Library, 1965.

ATTORNEY GENERAL: ROBERT FRANCIS KENNEDY

   Refer to the biographical sketch of Robert F. Kennedy
under Attorney General in the Administration of John
F. Kennedy, page 719.

ATTORNEY GENERAL:

NICHOLAS DEBELLEVILLE KATZENBACH

   Nicholas deB. Katzenbach, Attorney General in the Cabinet of President Lyndon B. Johnson, was born on January
17, 1922 in Philadelphia, Pennsylvania, the son of Edward

Lawrence Katzenbach, a corporation lawyer who was New
Jersey attorney-general from 1924 to 1929, and Maria
Louise (Hilson) Katzenbach, a member of the New Jersey
state board of education for 44 years. After receiving
his preparatory education at Philips Exeter Academy from
which he was graduated in 1939, Nicholas went to Princeton University.

Nicholas Katzenbach enlisted in the United States Army
Air Force in 1941 and was commissioned a second lieutenant. He became a navigator. Nicholas was captured by
the Italians in 1943. He was released from the Air
Force as a first lieutenant in 1945, having been decorated with the Air Medal with three clusters. He returned
to Princeton from which he was graduated with the Bachelor of Arts degree in 1945. He entered Yale Law School
in 1945.

Nicholas married Lydia King Phelps Stokes on June 8,
1946. They have four children: Christopher Wolcott,
John Strong Minor, Maria Louise and Anne de Belleville.
While at Yale. Nicholas was editor in charge of the Yale
Law Journal. He went to England to study at Balliol College of Oxford University from 1947 to 1949. He returned
to the United States and was admitted to the New Jersey
bar in 1950. He joined the firm of Katzenbach, Gildea
and        in Trenton, New Jersey in 1950. In the same
year he became a part time consultant as an attorney
advisor to the secretary of the air force at the Pentagon, continuing until 1956. During this period he was
an associate professor of law at Yale University from
1952 to 1956. He was next appointed a full professor of
Law at the University of Chicago Law School in 1956 and
continued to teach there until 1960.

In 1961 Nicholas Katzenbach was appointed assistant
attorney general in charge of the Office of Legal Counsel. In the same year he wrote The Political Founders
of International Law with Morton A. Kaplan. Nicholas
became deputy attorney general in April 1962, remaining
in that office until 1964 when he became acting Attorney
General.

President Lyndon B. Johnson appointed Nicholas deB.
Katzenbach Attorney General to succeed Robert F. Kennedy
in 1965. He served in this post from February 13, 1965
until October 3, 1966. Nicholas was awarded the Woodrow
Wilson Award by Princeton University on February 20,
1965. While in office Katzenbach helped to gain passage
of the Civil Rights Bill and also was able to settle the
General Aniline and Film Corporation controversy. President Johnson next named Katzenbach undersecretary of
state in October 1966. He continued in this office until the end of the Johnson administration in January
1969.

After leaving public office in 1969 Nicholas Katzenbach
became a vice president, general counsel, and director

of the IBM Corporation and is still with the firm.  He
became a member of the New York bar in 1972.  Nicholas
Katzenbach is a member of the American Judicature Society and the American Bar Association.

Bibliography:
  Evans, Rowland, and Novack, Robert.  Lyndon B. Johnson:
The Exercise of Power; A Political Biography.  New York:
New American Library, 1966.
  Furer, Howard B., ed.  Lyndon B. Johnson, 1908-/1973/.
Dobbs Ferry, N.Y.: Oceana Publications, Inc., 1971.
  Goldman, Eric.  The Tragedy of Lyndon Johnson.  New
York: Knopf, 1969.
  Sidey, Hugh.  A Very Personal Presidency: Lyndon
Johnson in the White House.  New York: Atheneum, 1968.

ATTORNEY GENERAL: /WILLIAM/ RAMSEY CLARK

Ramsey Clark, Attorney General in the Cabinet of President Lyndon B. Johnson, was born on December 18, 1927 in
Dallas, Texas, the son of Tom C. Clark, United States
Attorney General under President Harry S. Truman and
Associate Justice of the United States Supreme Court
from 1946 to 1967, and Mary Jane (Ramsey) Clark.  After
receiving his basic education in the public schools of
Dallas, Texas and Los Angeles, California, Ramsey attended Woodrow Wilson High School in Washington, D.C.,
graduating in 1945.  He enlisted in the United States
Marine Corps in the same year and was discharged in 1945.
Ramsey Clark then attended the University of Texas
from which he was graduated with the Bachelor of Arts degree in June 1949.  Ramsey married Georgia Welch on
April 16, 1949.  They have two children: Ronda Kathleen
and Thomas Campbell.  Ramsey went to the University of
Chicago from which he received the Master of Arts degree in American History and the J.D. degree in December
1950.  He was admitted to the Texas bar in 1951 and
joined the Dallas law firm of Clark, Coan, Holt and Tish.
Ramsey later became a partner in the firm which was renamed Clark, West Keller, Clark and Ginsberg.  He was
then admitted to practice before the United States Supreme Court in 1956.  Ramsey had also become active in
the Democratic Party and supported Adlai Stevenson for
the presidency in 1956 and John F. Kennedy in 1960.
Ramsey Clark was appointed assistant attorney general
in charge of litigation of federal lands in the Kennedy
administration.  He served in this capacity capacity from
February 16, 1961 until February 13, 1965.  While in
this office he took charge of the federal civil forces
at the University of Mississippi riots in 1962 and also
was involved in the problems at Birmingham, Alabama in
1963.  During 1963 he became director of the American
Judicature Society.  Ramsey was elected president of

the American Bar Association and the Southwest Legal Foundation in 1964. He served until 1965.

Ramsey Clark became acting Attorney General on October 13, 1966. President Lyndon B. Johnson named Ramsey Clark Attorney General in which office he remained from March 10, 1967 until the end of the administration on January 20, 1969. Ramsey was granted the honorary LL.D. degree by Loyola University in 1967. While in office Clark acted against segregation in the southern schools. He also urged passage of the bill which outlawed wire tapping in cases which did not affect the national security. He also supported the Supreme Court ruling in the case of Miranda vs. Arizona and was opposed to capital punishment.

After leaving public office Ramsey Clark returned to his law practice. He was also adjunct professor at Howard University from 1969 to 1972 and at the Brooklyn Law School. He wrote Crime in America. Clark took a strong stand against the Vietnamese war. He became a member of the New York bar in 1970. Ramsey Clark ran unsuccessfully for the United States Senate from New York in 1974 against Jacob Javits, Ramsey is a member of the Federal, American and Dallas Bar Association.

Bibliography:
    Furer, Howard B., ed. Lyndon B. Johnson, 1908-/1973/. Dobbs Ferry, N.Y.: Oceana Publications, Inc., 1971.
    Goldman, Eric. The Tragedy of Lyndon Johnson. New York: Knopf, 1969.
    Schlesinger, Arthur M., Jr. A Thousand Days: John F. Kennedy in the White House. Boston: Houghton Mifflin Company, 1965.
    Sidey, Hugh. John F. Kennedy, President. New York: Fawcett World Library, 1963.
    - - - -. A Very Personal Presidency: Lyndon Johnson in the White House. New York: Atheneum, 1968.
    Sorenson, Theodore C. Kennedy. New York: Harper and Row, 1965.
    "Watch on the Attorney General," Harper's, vol. 235. November, 1967.

## POSTMASTER GENERAL: JOHN A. GRONOUSKI

Refer to the biographical sketch of John A. Gronouski under Postmaster General in the Administration of John F. Kennedy, page 723.

## POSTMASTER GENERAL: LAWRENCE FRANCIS O'BRIEN

Lawrence F. O'Brien, Postmaster General in the Cabinet of President Lyndon B. Johnson, was born on July 7, 1917 in Springfield, Massachusetts, the son of Lawrence F. O'Brien, Sr., a hotel owner and real estate dealer, and

Myra (Sweeney) O'Brien.  After receiving his basic education in the local schools and Cathedral High School
Lawrence became interested in politics and worked for the
Springfield Democrats, organizing political campaigns as
early as 1938.  He worked as a bar tender and became
active in the Hotel and Restaurant Employees Union.  He
also continued to pursue his education, studying at
Northeastern University in Boston, and was graduated with
the LL.B. degree in 1942.

Lawrence F. O'Brien entered the United States Army
during World War II and served as a sergeant from 1943 to
1945.  Lawrence married Elva I. Brassard on May 30, 1944.
They have one son, Lawrence Francis III.  After the war
Lawrence managed O'Brien Realty Company.  He ran the
Congressional campaigns for Democrat Foster Furcolo in
1946 and 1948, going to Washington, D.C. in the latter
year as Congressman Furcolo's assistant in which post
he served until 1950.

O'Brien worked for John F. Kennedy's senatorial campaigns in 1952 and 1958.  He was a member of the Massachusetts Democratic Committee during 1956 and 1957.  In
1959 O'Brien became director of organization for the Kennedy team in planning for the 1960 presidential contest.
He was then appointed the Democratic national committee's
national director of organization in 1960 in order to coordinate John F. Kennedy's presidential campaign.  On
January 2, 1961 President Kennedy appointed him special
White House assistant for Congressional relations and
personnell in which position he continued to serve under
President Lyndon B. Johnson until 1965.  Lawrence received
the honorary LL.D. degree from Western New England College in 1962.  He helped to manage President Johnson's
campaign for the Presidency in 1964.

President Lyndon B. Johnson named Lawrence O'Brien
Postmaster General in which post he served from November
3, 1965 until April 1968.  While in office he suggested
that a non profit government corporation be established
to replace the postal department.  He received the LL.D.
degree from Villanova University in 1966 and Loyola University in 1967.  After leaving the cabinet Lawrence
O'Brien managed Hubert Humphrey's presidential campaign
in 1968.  O'Brien served as chairman of the Democratic
National Committee from 1968 to 1969.

Mr. O'Brien became president of McDonald and Company,
Inc. on January 7, 1969.  In September of that same year
he joined a citizens' group for postal reform.  He again
became Democratic national chairman on March 5, 1970 and
continued in that capacity until 1972.  He received the
honorary LL.D. degree from Xavier University and the
L.H.D. from American International and Wheeling Colleges
in 1971.

Bibliography:
   Evans, Rowland, and Novack, Robert. Lyndon B. Johnson:
The Exercise of Power. New York: New American Library,
1966.
   Furer, Howard B., ed. Lyndon B. Johnson, 1908-/1973/.
Dobbs Ferry, N.Y.: Oceana Publications, Inc., 1971.
   Goldman, Eric. The Tragedy of Lyndon Johnson. New
York: Knopf, 1969.
   Schlesinger, Arthur M., Jr. A Thousand Days: John F.
Kennedy in the White House. Boston: Houghton Mifflin,
1965.
   Sidey, Hugh. A Very Personal Presidency: Lyndon John-
son in the White House. New York: Atheneum, 1968.
   Zeiger, Henry A. Lyndon B. Johnson. Man and Presi-
dent. New York: Popular Library, 1965.

## POSTMASTER GENERAL: WILLIAM MARVIN WATSON, JR.

W. Marvin Watson, Postmaster General in the Cabinet of
President Lyndon B. Johnson, was born on June 6, 1924
in Oakharst, Texas, the son of William Marvin Watson,
Sr. and Lillie Mae (Anderson) Watson.  After receiving a
basic education in the local public schools W. Marvin became a private in the United States Marine Corps in
1943.  He was discharged in 1946 as a sergeant.  He attended Baylor University and was graduated with the B.B.A.
degree in 1949 and the Master of Arts degree in 1950.
W. Marvin married Marion Baugh November 29, 1950.  They
have three children: Winston Lee, Kimberly Baugh, and
William Marvin, III.
   W. Marvin Watson, Jr. became manager of the Dainger-
field, Texas Chamber of Commerce.  He was secretary of
the North East Texas Municipal Water District from 1951
to 1954 and president from 1954 to 1965.  He was Dainger-
field city secretary in 1954, continuing until 1958 when
he became a city judge.  He was employed as an executive
assistant to the president of the Lone Star Steel Company
in 1956 and continued in that post until 1965.  Among
his other activities he was vice president for the Texas
Red River Valley Association.
   Watson became interested in Democratic politics and was
a member of the Texas state Democratic executive committee
of which he was chosen chairman and served from 1964 to
1965.  President Lyndon B. Johnson named Watson as one
of his special assistants in 1965 in which position he remained until 1968.
   President Lyndon B. Johnson appointed W. Marvin Watson,
Jr. Postmaster General to succeed Lawrence F. O'Brien.
Watson assumed his office on April 10, 1968 and served
until the end of the administration on January 21, 1969.
Ouachita Baptist University granted Watson the honorary
L.H.D. degree in 1968.  He continued the effective management of the Post Office Department.  After leaving public

office in 1969 Mr. Watson became president of the Occidental Interest Corporation.  He was senior vice president of the Occidental Petroleum Corporation during 1971 and 1972.  Since the latter year he has served as executive vice president of corporate affairs.  He is also an officer and is director of various subsidiary firms and is also a director of the Sulphur Export Corporation and the National Liberty Corporation.  He is also a member of the Fleet Admiral Chester W. Nimitz Commission and of the council for institutional development of Baylor University.  In addition he serves on the board of directors of the Billy Graham Evangelistic Association and is also on the board of development of Hardin Simmons University.

Bibliography:
   Evans, Rowland, and Novack, Robert. Lyndon B. Johnson: The Exercise of Power.  New York: New American Library, 1965.
   Furer, Howard B., ed.  Lyndon B. Johnson, 1908-/1973/. Dobbs Ferry, N.Y.: Oceana Publications, Inc., 1971.
   Goldman, Eric.  The Tragedy of Lyndon Johnson.  New York: Knopf, 1969.
   Sidey, Hugh.  A Very Personal Presidency: Lyndon Johnson in the White House.  New York: Atheneum, 1968.
   Zeiger, Henry A.  Lyndon B. Johnson.  Man and President. New York: Popular Library, 1965.

#### SECRETARY OF THE INTERIOR: STEWART LEE UDALL

Refer to the biographical sketch of Stewart L. Udall under Secretary of the Interior in the Administration of John F. Kennedy, page 725.

#### SECRETARY OF AGRICULTURE:

#### ORVILLE LOTHORP FREEMAN

Refer to the biographical sketch of Orville L. Freeman under Secretary of Agriculture in the Administration of John F. Kennedy, page 727.

#### SECRETARY OF COMMERCE: LUTHER HARTWELL HODGES

Refer to the biographical sketch of Luther H. Hodges under Secretary of Commerce in the Administration of John F. Kennedy, page 729.

#### SECRETARY OF COMMERCE: JOHN THOMAS CONNOR

John T. Connor, Secretary of Commerce in the Cabinet of President Lyndon B. Johnson, was born on November 3, 1914 in Syracuse, New York, the son of Michael J. and

Mary V. (Sullivan) Connor.  After receiving his preliminary education in the Syracuse public schools John went
to Syracuse University from which he was graduated with
the Bachelor of Arts degree in 1936.  He then studied at
Harvard Law School, receiving the J.D. degree in 1939.
He was admitted to the New York bar in the same year.
He began practicing law with the New York legal firm of
Cravath de Gorsdorff, Swaine and Wood.  He continued
with the firm until 1942.

John T. Connor married Mary O'Boyle on June 22, 1940.
They have three children: John Thomas, Jr., Geoffrey,
and Lisa Forrestal.  John was appointed general counsel
for the office of Scientific Research and Development
in Washington in 1942, continuing until 1944 when he was
a special assistant to the Secretary of the Navy from
1945 to 1947.  During this period he was for a time counsel to the Office of Naval Research in 1946.  Connor became general attorney for Merck and Company in 1947,
eventually becoming secretary and counsel, continuing
until 1953.  He was awarded the Presidential Certificate
of Merit in 1948.

John T. Connor was next elected vice president of
Merck and Company in 1950.  He became director and president in 1955 and continued until 1965.  During this
period he was granted the Brotherhood Award by the National Conference of Christians and Jews in 1959.  During 1962 he was given the New Jersey Patent Law Association's Jefferson Medal and the Harvard Business Club
Award.

President Lyndon B. Johnson appointed John T. Connor
Secretary of Commerce to succeed Luther H. Hodges in
1965.  Connor assumed his office on January 18, 1965.
While in office he urged that the Departments of Labor
and Commerce be united.  He was named New Jersey Business
Statesman of the year in 1965.  John resigned from office
on January 18, 1967.  After leaving office Mr. Commor
became president of Allied Chemical Corporation in which
post he remained until 1968.  He has been a director of
the company since 1967, chief executive officer since
1968 and chairman of the board since 1969.  In addition
he is a director of the General Motors Corporation, the
General Foods Corporation and Chase Manhattan Bank.

Among his other activities John T. Connor has been
chairman and director of the Manufacturing Chemists Association.  He became a trustee of the Committee for Economic Development.  He is also a member of the American
Management Association's advisory committee for training
government executives.  He is also chairman of the New
Jersey Committee for Improving Science and Mathematics
in the Secondary Schools and a member of the New Jersey
State Water Resources Advisory Committee.  Among his
philanthropic activities he helped to raise money for
the New Jersey Association for Mental Health as well as

Seton Hall College of Medicine and Dentistry.  In addi-
tion he is chairman of the Council for Financial Aid to
Education and chairman of the board of trustees of the
National Symphony Orchestra.

Bibliography:
  Evans, Rowland, and Novack, Robert.  Lyndon B. Johnson:
The Exercise of Power.  New York: New American Library,
1966.
  Furer, Howard B., ed.  Lyndon B. Johnson, 1908-/1973/.
Dobbs Ferry, N.Y.: Oceana Publications, Inc., 1971.
  Goldman, Eric.  The Tragedy of Lyndon Johnson.  New
York: Knopf, 1969.
  Sidey, Hugh.  A Very Personal Presidency: Lyndon John-
son in the White House.  New York: Atheneum, 1968.
  Zeiger, Henry A.  Lyndon B. Johnson.  Man and President.
New York: Popular Library, 1967.

### SECRETARY OF COMMERCE:

### ALEXANDER BUEL TROWBRIDGE, JR.

Alexander B. Trowbridge, Jr., Secretary of Commerce in
the Cabinet of President Lyndon B. Johnson, was born on
December 12, 1929 in Englewood, New Jersey, the son of
Alexander Buel Trowbridge, a college history professor,
and Julia (Chamberlain) Trowbridge.  Alexander received
his basic education at Phillips Academy in Andover,
Massachusetts, graduating in 1947.  He then entered
Princeton University from which he was graduated in 1951
with the Bachelor of Arts degree.  He volunteered for
reconstruction work in western Europe and was a member of
the International Intern Program of the United Nations
headquarters at Lake Success, New York in 1948.  Alexander was also an assistant to Congressman Franklin D.
Roosevelt, Jr. in 1950.
  After graduating from Princeton in 1951 Alexander B.
Trowbridge, Jr. went to work for the Central Intelli-
gence Agency.  In the same year he joined the Marine
Corps and was commissioned a second lieutenant.  He
served in Korea until 1953 with the First Division.  He
was decorated with the Bronze Star with the Combat V.
After being discharged he eventually went to work for the
California Texas Oil Company and was marketing assistant
for petroleum from 1954 to 1958.  Alexander married Nancy
Herst on July 2, 1955.  They have three children: Stephen:
Scott, and Kimberley.
  Alexander Trowbridge, Jr. next accepted a position with
Esso Standard Oil, S.A., Ltd. in Cuba from 1959 to 1960
after which he went to San Salvador as division manager
for Standard Oil from 1961 to 1963.  He wrote The Over-
seas Americans with H. Cleveland and others in 1960.  He
helped to write Spearheads of Democracy--Labor in the

Developing Countries in 1962.  Alexander Trowbridge was
sent to San Juan, Puerto Rico to become president and
division manager of Esso Standard Oil Company in 1963 and
continued in these positions until 1965.  During this period he was also a director of the Federation of the YMCA
and of the Better Business Bureau.  Trowbridge was named
assistant secretary of commerce for domestic and international business on May 6, 1965 in which post he served
until becoming Secretary of Commerce on February 1, 1967.

President Lyndon B. Johnson appointed Alexander B. Trowbridge, Jr. Secretary of Commerce on June 8, 1967.  He
assumed his office on June 14, 1967 and continued until
March 1, 1968.  While in office he supported the merger
of the Department with the Department of Labor.  He also
established the office of foreign investment to help stem
the balance of payments deficit.  He was awarded the
President's E. certificate for export service in 1968.

After leaving office Alexander Trowbridge, Jr. became
president and chief executive officer in the American
Management Association in New York City in May 1968
and continued in that post until 1970.  In the latter
year he became president of The Conference Board, Inc. in
New York City.  Among his other business associations
Trowbridge is a director of Allied Chemical Corporation,
American Motors Corporation, Gannett Co., Inc., Pet, Inc.
and the Bowery Savings Bank.  He is also a member of the
National Export Expansion Council.  He is vice chairman
of the Atlantic Council of the United States.  Alexander
B. Trowbridge, Jr. is also on the National Planning Asso-
ciation and the United States-Korea Economic Council.  In
addition he is a trustee of the Frank E. Gannett Newspaper
Foundation and of the Aspen Institute for Humanistic
Studies.

Bibliography:
Evans, Rowland, and Novack, Robert.  Lyndon B. Johnson:
The Exercise of Power.  New York: New American Library,
1966.
Furer, Howard B., ed.  Lyndon B. Johnson, 1908-/1973/.
Dobbs Ferry, N.Y.: Oceana Publications, Inc., 1971.
Goldman, Eric.  The Tragedy of Lyndon Johnson.  New
York: Knopf, 1969.
Sidey, Hugh.  A Very Personal Presidency: Lyndon John-
son in the White House.  New York: Atheneum, 1968.
Zeiger, Henry A.  Lyndon B. Johnson.  Man and President.
New York: Popular Library, 1967.

## SECRETARY OF COMMERCE: CYRUS ROWLETT SMITH

Cyrus R. Smith, Secretary of Commerce in the Cabinet
of President Lyndon B. Johnson, was born on September 9,
1899 in Minerva, Texas, the son of Ray Edgerton and Marion
(Burck) Smith.  After receiving his basic education Cyrus

went to the University of Texas from 1920 t0 1924, graduating in the last year with the Bachelor of Arts degree.
At the same time he began working for Peat, Marwick, Mitchell and Company in 1921, continuing with them until
1926.  He next was assistant treasurer of the Texas-Loui-
siana Power Company from 1926 to 1928.  He was vice president of Texas Air Transport, Inc. at Fort Worth from 1929
to 1930.

Cyrus Smith was next made vice president of American
Airlines, Inc. in 1930 and continued in that post until
1933.  He was elected president and chief executive in
1934, continuing until April 1942 when he resigned to enter the United States Army Air Forces and was commissioned as a colonel.  Smith was promoted to brigadier
general and then major general.  He was deputy commander
of the Air Transport Command from 1942 to 1945.  Cyrus was
awarded the Distinguished Service Medal, the Air Service
Medal and the Legion of Merit.  He returned to American
Airlines as chairman of the board in 1946 and continued
in that post until 1968.

President Lyndon B. Johnson named Cyrus R. Smith Secretary of Commerce to succeed Alexander B. Trowbridge,
Jr. on March 1, 1968.  Smith assumed his office on March
6, 1968 and continued to serve until the end of the administration on January 20, 1969.  Cyrus continued the
policies aimed at improving the United States balance of
payments and improving the domestic business pursuits.
After leaving office Smith became a partner in Lazard
Freres and Son, an investment house.  He remained with
the firm until 1973.  Cyrus Smith returned to American
Airlines in 1973 as chief executive officer and is still
serving in that capacity.

Bibliography:
   "Commerce's Rugged New Pilot," Chemical Week, vol. 102,
March 2, 1968.
   Furer, Howard B., ed.  Lyndon B. Johnson, 1908-/1973/.
Dobbs Ferry, N.Y.: Oceana Publications, Inc., 1971.
   Goldman, Eric F.  The Tragedy of Lyndon Johnson.  New
York: Knopf, 1969.

SECRETARY OF LABOR: W/ILLIAM/ WILLARD WIRTZ

Refer to the biographical sketch of W/illiam/ Willard
Wirtz under Secretary of Labor in the Administration of
John F. Kennedy, page 734.

SECRETARY OF HEALTH, EDUCATION, AND WELFARE:

ANTHONY JOSEPH CELEBREZZE

Refer to the biographical sketch of Anthony J. Celebrezze under Secretary of Health, Education, and Welfare

in the Administration of John F. Kennedy, page 738.

SECRETARY OF HEALTH, EDUCATION, AND WELFARE:

JOHN WILLIAM GARDNER

John W. Gardner, Secretary of Health, Education, and Welfare in the Cabinet of President Lyndon B. Johnson, was born on October 8, 1912 in Los Angeles, California, the son of William Frederick and Marie (Flora) Gardner. After receiving his preliminary education John Gardner went to Stanford University from which he was graduated with the Bachelor of Arts degree in 1935. John married Aida Marroquin. They have two children: Stephanie and Francesca. John continued his studies at Stanford and received the Master of Arts degree in 1936. He then became a teaching assistant of psychology at the University of California where he also studied for his doctorate which he earned in 1938.

John W. Gardner was appointed an instructor of psychology at Connecticut College for Women in New London. He next became an assistant professor of psychology at Mount Holyoke College in South Hadley, Massachusetts in 1940. John Gardner was named head of the Latin American Section of the Foreign Broadcast Intelligence Service of the Federal Communications Commission in 1942, continuing until 1943 when he enlisted in the United States Marine Corps. He was assigned to the Office of Strategic Services in Europe and was eventually discharged in 1946 with the rank of captain.

In 1946 John W. Gardner became a consultant to the United States Air Force and the Department of Defense. He also became a member of the staff of the Carnegie Foundation in 1946 and was made an executive associate in 1947 and a vice president in 1949, continuing until 1955. Gardner became vice chairman of the board of trustees of the New York School of Social Work in 1949, remaining in that capacity until 1955. He was also chairman of the social science panel of the Science Advisory Board of the United States AirForce from 1951 to 1955. He next became president of the Carnegie Foundation for the Advancement of Learning in 1955, remaining in that office until 1965. John was awarded the honorary LL.D. degree by the University of California in 1959. He was also awarded the Air Forces Exceptional Services Award.

Among his other activities John Gardner was a trustee of the Metropolitan Museum of Art from 1957 to 1965. In addition he was a member of the advisory committee on the social sciences of the National Science Foundation from 1959 to 1962 and a director of the Woodrow Wilson Foundation from 1960 to 1963. Mr. Gardner wrote Excellence: Can We Be Equal and Excellent Too? in 1961. He was also chairman of the United States Advisory Commission on In-

ternational Educational and Cultural Affairs from 1962
to 1964.  John wrote <u>Self</u> <u>Renewal</u> in 1963.  President Lyndon B. Johnson awarded Gardner the Presidential Medal of
Freedom in 1964.  Gardner was also appointed chairman of
the White House Conference on Education in 1965.

President Lyndon B. Johnson named John W. Gardner Secretary of Health, Education, and Welfare to succeed Anthony J. Celebrezze on August 11, 1965.  Gardner assumed
his office on August 18, 1965 and served until March
1968.  While in office he sponsored the enforcement of
civil rights in any programs developed by the department
and urged that the states and local organizations do like-
wise.  He was awarded the Public Welfare Medal and the
Family of Man education award in 1966.  Gardner also received the United Auto Workers Social Justice Award and
the Anti-Defamation League's Democratic Legacy award in
1968.

After leaving public office in 1968 John W. Gardner became chairman of the Urban Coalition and continued until
1970.  He was a visiting professor at Harvard University
from 1968 to 1969.  Gardner also became a counsellor for
the Carnegie Foundation in 1968 and has continued since
then.  He directed a special study of problems of urban
areas for the Carnegie Corporation of New York.  He became a trustee of Stanford University in 1968.  In the
same year he wrote <u>The</u> <u>Recovery</u> <u>of</u> <u>Confidence</u>.  Gardner
began to serve as chairman of Common Cause in 1970.  Dur-
ing the same year he was granted the AFL-CIO Murray Green
medal.  He published <u>In</u> <u>Common</u> <u>Cause</u> in 1972.  John W.
Gardner received the American Institute of Public Ser-
vice award for distinguished service in 1973.

Bibliography:
  Evans, Rowland, and Novack, Robert.  <u>Lyndon</u> <u>B</u>. <u>Johnson</u>:
<u>The</u> <u>Exercise</u> <u>of</u> <u>Power</u>.  New York: New American Library,
1966.
  Furer, Howard B., ed.  <u>Lyndon</u> <u>B</u>. <u>Johnson</u>, <u>1908-/1973/</u>.
Dobbs Ferry, N.Y.: Oceana Publications, Inc., 1971.
  Goldman, Eric.  <u>The</u> <u>Tragedy</u> <u>of</u> <u>Lyndon</u> <u>Johnson</u>.  New
York: Knopf, 1969.
  Sidey, Hugh.  <u>A</u> <u>Very</u> <u>Personal</u> <u>Presidency</u>: <u>Lyndon</u> <u>Johnson</u>
<u>in</u> <u>the</u> <u>White</u> <u>House</u>.  New York: Atheneum, 1968.
  Zeiger, Henry A.  <u>Lyndon</u> <u>B</u>. <u>Johnson</u>.  <u>Man</u> <u>and</u> <u>President</u>.
New York: Popular Library, 1967.

SECRETARY OF HEALTH, EDUCATION, AND WELFARE:

WILBUR JOSEPH COHEN

Wilbur J. Cohen, Secretary of Health, Education, and
Welfare in the Cabinet of President Lyndon B. Johnson,
was born on June 10, 1913, in Milwaukee, Wisconsin, the
son of Aaron Cohen, a store owner, and Bessie (Ruben-
stein) Cohen.  After receiving his basic education

in the public schools of Milwaukee Wilbur attended Lincoln
High School from which he was graduated in 1930.  He went
to the University of Wisconsin from which he received the
Ph.B. degree in 1934.  In the same year he became a member of the Committee on Economic Security,serving until
1935.

Wilbur Cohen cooperated in the drafting of the Social
Security Act in 1935.  He then began serving with the
Social Security Administration.  He was technical advisor
to the chairman of the Social Security Board. Mr. Alt-
meyer, from 1936 to 1952.  Wilbur married Eloise Bittel
on April 8, 1938.  They have three sons: Christopher,
Bruce, and Stuart.  Wilbur Cohen became director of the
division of research and statistices of the Social Security Administration in 1953, serving in that capacity until
1956.  He was appointed professor of public welfare administration at the University of Michigan in 1956, holding
the chair until 1969.

In 1956 Wilbur Cohen became a consultant on aging for
the Senate Committee on Labor and Public Welfare, serving
until 1957 and again in 1959.  He received the Distinguished Service award of the Department of Health, Education, and Welfare in 1956.  He was also a consultant to
the United Nations from 1956 to 1957.  In the latter year
he was also a visiting professor at the University of
California of Los Angeles.  He wrote Retirement Policies
Under Social Security with William Haber in 1957.  He was
next chairman of the Advisory Council for Retirement Ad-
visors, Inc.  from 1959 to 1960.  In 1959 he became a
member of the Public Assistance Advisory Council and also
a consultant to the White House Conference on Aging, continuing in the latter post until 1960.  He became a counsel
to Senator John F. Kennedy in 1960.  He was also chairman of the President's Task Force on Health and Social
Security in 1960.

President John F. Kennedy appointed Wilbur J. Cohen
assistant secretary of Health, Education, and Welfare for
legislation in 1961.  He remained in this post until 1965.
Wilbur was a delegate to the General Assembly International Social Security Association in Turkey in 1961.  During
the same year he collaborated in the writing of Social
Security Programs, Problems, and Policies.  In 1962 he
contributed to Income and Welfare in the United States.
Cohen was a director of the American Public Welfare Association from 1962 to 1965.

President Lyndon B. Johnson named Wilbur Cohen undersecretary of Health, Education, and Welfare in 1965.  He
remained in this post until 1968.  In 1965 Wilbur was
granted an award by the National Association for Mentally
Retarded Children and by the Association of Physical
Medicine.  In 1967 he received the Rockefeller Public
Service award.  The following year he received the Wilbur
award of the Golden Ring Council of Senior Citizens.  He

was acting Secretary of Health, Education, and Welfare from March 1 to March 22, 1968.

President Lyndon B. Johnson appointed Wilbur J. Cohen Secretary of Health, Education, and Welfare in which office he served from March 22, 1968 until the end of the administration on January 20, 1969.  He represented the United States at various conferences including the International Conferences on Social Security, as well as the International Conference on Social Work and the International Labor Conference.  He was chairman of the President's Committee on Mental Retardation in 1968. During the same year he was also a trustee of the John F. Kennedy Center for the Performing Arts.  Secretary Cohen was able to obtain addition funds to increase the medical research of the National Institute of Health.  He also worked to establish community health programs.  He also had the department provide training for administrators and teachers so that they could teach skills to uneducated adults.

After leaving public office in 1969 Wilbur Cohen became a consultant to the Ford Foundation.  He was also appointed Dean of the University of Michigan School of Education.  He is a member of many organizations among which are the International Association of Gerontology, the National Conference of Social Welfare of which he was president in 1969, the Council of Social Work Education, the American Public Health Association, and the American Association of Higher Education.

Bibliography:
  Evans, Rowland, and Novack, Robert.  Lyndon B. Johnson: The Exercise of Power.  New York: New American Library, 1968.
  Furer, Howard B., ed.  Lyndon B. Johnson, 1908-/1973/. Dobbs Ferry, N.Y.: Oceana Publications, Inc., 1971.
  Goldman, Eric.  The Tragedy of Lyndon B. Johnson.  New York: Knopf, 1969.
  Sidey, Hugh.  A Very Personal Presidency: Lyndon Johnson in the White House.  New York: Atheneum, 1968.

SECRETARY OF HOUSING AND URBAN DEVELOPMENT:

ROBERT CLIFTON WEAVER

Robert C. Weaver, first Secretary of Housing and Urban Development in the Cabinet of President Lyndon B. Johnson, was born on December 29, 1907 in Washington, D.C., the son of Mortimer G. and Florence (Freeman) Weaver.  After receiving his basic education in the Washington, D.C. public schools Robert went to Harvard University from which he was graduated with the Bachelor of Arts degree in 1929.  He then continued his studies, receiving the Master of Arts degree in 1931 and the Doctor of Philosophy degree in 1934.

Robert Weaver began to work for the Department of the Interior as an advisor concerning Negro affairs in 1933, continuing until 1937.  Robert married Ella V. Heath on July 19, 1935.  They have one son, Robert.  Mr. Weaver was next appointed a special assistant to the United States Housing Authority administrator in 1937 and remained in that post until 1940.  In the latter year he became an administrative assistant in the Office of Production Management and the WPF, remaining until 1942.  He served the government in various capacities during and immediately after the war.  He wrote Negro Labor: A National Problem in 1946.

Robert C. Weaver became a visiting professor at Columbia Teachers College in 1947 and also taught at the New York University School of Education from 1947 to 1949.  He published The Negro Ghetto in 1948.  Weaver was next employed by the J. H. Whitney Foundation from 1949 to 1954 as director of opportunity fellowships.

Robert Weaver returned to public office in 1954 when he became deputy commissioner of the New York State Division of Housing, continuing in that post until 1955 when he was appointed New York State rent administrator.  He remained in that office until 1959.  He was next a consultant for the Ford Foundation from 1959 to 1960, and then served as vice-chairman of Housing and Redevelopment of Roads during the period 1960-1961.  He returned to federal government service as administrator of the Federal Highway and Home Finance Agency from 1961 to 1966.  He was also chairman of the NAACP.  Weaver was awarded the NAACP Springorn Medal in 1962.  During this period he wrote The Urban Complex in 1964 and Dilemma of Urban America in 1965.

President Lyndon B. Johnson signed the bill creating the Department of Housing and Urban Development on September 9, 1965.  The President appointed Robert C. Weaver first Secretary of Housing and Urban Development.  Weaver was the first black to serve in the Cabinet.  Robert C. Weaver assumed his office on January 18, 1966 and remained in the post until January 1, 1969.  He worked to help convince Congress to pass the Demonstration Cities program announced by President Johnson.

After leaving public office in 1969 Robert Weaver became president of Bernard M. Baruch College, continuing until 1970.  He was next appointed professor of urban affairs at Hunter College in 1970.  Among his other activities he is a trustee of the Bowery Savings Bank and the Metropolitan Life Insurance Company.

Bibliography:
    Evans, Rowland, and Novack, Robert.  Lyndon B. Johnson: The Exercise of Power.  New York: New American Library, 1966.
    Furer, Howard B., ed.  Lyndon B. Johnson, 1908-/1973/.

Dobbs Ferry, N.Y.: Oceana Publications, Inc., 1971.
    Goldman, Eric. The Tragedy of Lyndon Johnson. New
York: Knopf, 1969.
    Sidey, Hugh. A Very Personal Presidency: Lyndon John-
son in the White House. New York: Atheneum, 1968.
    Zeiger, Henry A. Lyndon B. Johnson.     and President.
New York: Popular Library, 1967.

SECRETARY OF HOUSING AND URBAN DEVELOPMENT:

ROBERT COLDWELL WOOD

   Robert C. Wood, Secretary of Housing and Urban Development in the Cabinet of President Lyndon B. Johnson, was
born on September 16, 1923 in Saint Louis, Missouri, the
son of Thomas Frank and Mary (Bradshaw) Wood. After receiving his basic education in the Saint Louis public
schools Robert entered the United States Army during
World War II, serving with the Infantry. He received the
Bronze Star. Robert Wood then studied at Princeton
University, receiving the Bachelor of Arts degree in
1946. He then went to Harvard University from which he
received the Master of Arts degree in 1947, the Master
of Business Administration degree in 1948 and the Doctor
of Philosophy degree in 1950.
   Robert C. Wood was appointed an associate director of
the Florida Legislative Bureau in 1949 and continued in
that post until 1951 when he received an appointment in
the Bureau of the Budget as a management organization
expert. He remained with the organization until 1953.
He was appointed a lecturer and then an assistant professor at Harvard University from 1953 to 1957. In the
last year Wood became an assistant professor of political
science at Massachusetts Institute of Technology. He
wrote Suburbia, Its People and Their Politics in 1958 and
Metropolis Against Itself in 1959. He was promoted to
associate professor in 1959 and full professor in 1962.
   Robert C. Wood wrote 1400 Governments, The Political
Economy of the New York Region in 1960 and collaborated
with others in Schoolmen and Politics in 1962. He also
contributed to Government and Politics of the United
States in 1965. He became head of the Political Science
Department at Massachusetts Institute of Technology in
1965, continuing in that capacity until 1966.
   President Lyndon B. Johnson named Robert C. Wood under-
secretary of Housing and Urban Development when the
department was created. Wood remained in the post until
1968. President Johnson appointed Robert Wood Secretary
of Housing and Urban Development to succeed Robert C.
Weaver. Robert C. Wood served in the office from
January 2, 1969 until the end of the administration on
January 20, 1969.
   After leaving public office Robert Wood returned to the

Massachusetts Institute of Technology as professor and
chairman of the Political Science Department, serving
from 1969 to 1970. He became president of the University
of Massachusetts in 1970. Robert Wood continued his
research and published The Necessary Majority -- Middle
America and the Urban Crisis in 1972.

Bibliography:
  Evans, Rowland, and Novack, Robert. Lyndon B. Johnson:
The Exercise of Power. New York: New American Library,
1968.
  Furer, Howard B., ed. Lyndon B. Johnson, 1908-/1973/.
Dobbs Ferry, N.Y.: Oceana Publications, Inc., 1971.
  Goldman, Eric. The Tragedy of Lyndon Johnson. New
York: Knopf, 1969.
  Sidey, Hugh. A Very Personal Presidency: Lyndon Johnson
in the White House. New York: Atheneum, 1968.

SECRETARY OF TRANSPORTATION: ALAN STEPHENSON BOYD

    Alan S. Boyd, first Secretary of Transportation in the
Cabinet of President Lyndon B. Johnson, was born on January 20, 1922 in Jacksonville, Florida, the son of Clarence
and Elizabeth (Stephenson) Boyd. After receiving his basic education at the Jacksonville public schools he went
to the University of Florida from 1939 to 1941. During
the Second World War Boyd became a pilot with the United
States troop transport command, serving from 1942 to 1945.
He was promoted to the rank of major.
    Alan Boyd married Flavil Juanita Townsend on April 3,
1943. They have one son, Mark Townsend. After the war
Alan went to the University of Virginia Law School and was
graduated with the LL.B. degree in 1948. He was admitted
to the Virginia bar in 1947. Alan was next admitted to
the Florida bar in 1948 and established his legal practice
there, continuing until 1957. During this period Boyd
was appointed chairman of the civilian committee for the
development of aviation in Florida in 1954.
    Alan S. Boyd was named general counsel for the Florida
State Turnpike Authority in 1955. During the same year
he became a member of the Florida Railroad, serving until
1959. He also was a member of the Public Utilities Commission in Tallahassee and was chairman of the board
during 1957 and 1958. President Dwight D. Eisenhower
appointed Alan S. Boyd to the Civil Aeronautics Board on
November 11, 1959. President John F. Kennedy reappointed
Boyd in 1961. He remained on the board until 1965 when
he was named undersecretary of Commerce in charge of
transportation in 1965 and continued in that post until
1967.
    President Lyndon B. Johnson signed the bill creating
the Department of Transportation on October 15, 1966. He
named Alan S. Boyd the first Secretary of Transportation

in which post he served from January 16, 1967 until the
end of the administration on January 20, 1969.  Alan
Boyd organized the department and then ordered a study of
oil pollution.  He also developed highway safety rules and
suggested action on a railroad strike bill.

After leaving public office in 1969, Alan Boyd became
president of the Illinois Central Railroad.  Among his
other business activities he is a director of the Parke-
Davis Company and the Deposit Guaranty National Bank.
He is a member of the American Bar Association as well as
the Bar Associations of Virginia, Florida and Dade County.
He is also a member of the National Association of Railroad and Utilities Commissioners.

Bibliography:
   Evans, Rowland, and Novack, Robert.  Lyndon B. Johnson:
The Exercise of Power.  New York: New American Library,
1968.
   Furer, Howard B., ed.  Lyndon B. Johnson, 1908-/1973/.
Dobbs Ferry, N.Y.: Oceana Publications, Inc., 1971.
   Goldman, Eric.  The Tragedy of Lyndon Johnson.  New
York: Knopf, 1969.
   Sidey, Hugh.  A Very Personal Presidency: Lyndon Johnson
in the White House.  New York: Atheneum, 1968.

ADMINISTRATIONS OF RICHARD M. NIXON

VICE PRESIDENT: SPIRO THEODORE AGNEW

Spiro T. Agnew, Vice President in the administrations
of President Richard M. Nixon, was born on November 9,
1918 in Baltimore, Maryland, the son of Theodore S. Agnew,
owner of a restaurant, and Margarete (Akers) Agnew.  He
received his basic education in the Baltimore public
schools and then went to Johns Hopkins University from
1937 to 1940 after which he attended Baltimore Law School.
At the same time he worked as a clerk at the Maryland
Casualty Company and then as a manager of a supermarket,
a claims adjuster and personnell director for the Lumberman's Mutual Casualty Company, and then for Schreiber
Food Stores.

Mr. Agnew was a member of the United States Army during
the Second World War from 1941 to 1945.  Spiro married
Elinor Isabel Judefind on May 27, 1942.  They have four
children: James Rand, Pamela Lee, Susan Scott and Elinor
Kimberly.  While in the army he fought in France and Germany with the 10th Armored Division.  At the end of the
war in 1945 Agnew returned to Baltimore Law School and
received the LL.B. degree in 1947.  He was admitted to
the bar in 1949.  He worked for Karl F. Steinmann's legal firm and then established his legal practice in

Towson, a suburb of Baltimore.

Spiro T. Agnew had originally been a Democrat but soon became a member of the Republican Party.  In 1957 he was named to the Baltimore County Zoning Board of Appeals and was its chairman from 1958 to 1961.  In the latter year Agnew was elected chief executive of Baltimore County in 1961, serving in that post from 1962 to 1967.  He was elected Governor of Maryland in 1966 and served from 1967 to 1969.  Spiro T. Agnew was nominated as the Republican vice-presidential candidate, August 8, 1968, on the ticket with the presidential nominee Richard M. Nixon. They were elected on November 5, 1968.

Spiro T. Agnew was sworn in as Vice President of the United States along with Richard M. Nixon as President on January 20, 1969.  Agnew was a major spokesman for the administration, criticizing the news media claiming that it was not completely objective in covering the administration.  Vice President Agnew travelled on behalf of the administration to Asia, Africa, and Europe during 1970 and 1971.  The conservatives welcomed his methods, but critics claimed that his attacks on the dissenting youth of the nation were further dividing the company.

During the 1972 election campaign Spiro T. Agnew spoke throughout the country but softened his attacks.  He was reelected with President Nixon in November 1972.  They took the oath of office for a second term on January 20, 1973.  Agnew served as chairman of a Cabinet level task force to aid school districts in desegregation in 1970. As a result of investigations of Agnew's activities while an official in Maryland and his use of certain campaign funds, he faced an income tax charge.  He resigned from the Vice Presidency on October 10, 1973 and pleaded "no contest" in court to the charge.  He was given a suspended prison sentence and a $10,000 fine.  He has since been involved in various activities including the writing of a book.

Bibliography:
Bremer, Howard F., ed.  Richard M. Nixon, 1913-    . Dobbs Ferry, N.Y.: Oceana Publications, Inc., 1975.
Drury, Allen.  Courage and Hesitation.  Garden City, N.Y.: Doubleday, 1972.
Evans, Rowland, and Novack, Robert.  Nixon in the White House: The Frustration of Power.  New York: Random House, 1972.
Keogh, James.  President Nixon and the Press.  New York: Funk and Wagnalls, 1972.
Mankiewicz, Frank.  Perfectly Clear.  New York: Quadrangle, 1974.
Mazo, Earl, and Hess, Stephen.  Nixon: A Political Portrait.  New York, 1969.
Pinchot, Ann, et. al.  Where He Stands: The Life and Convictions of Spiro T. Agnew.  New York, 1968.

## VICE PRESIDENT: GERALD RUDOLPH FORD

Gerald R. Ford, Vice President in the second administration of President Richard M. Nixon, was born on July
14, 1913 in Omaha, Nebraska, the son of Mr. King and Mrs.
Dorothy (Gardner) King. His parents were divorced in
1915. When his mother married Gerald R. Ford, her young
son adopted his stepfather's name. He was raised in
Grand Rapids, Michigan and received his basic education
in the local public schools. Gerald then went to the
University of Michigan where he played football. He was
named most valuable player of 1934. Ford was graduated
with the Bachelor of Arts degree in 1935 and eventually
went to Yale Law School. He supported himself by working
as a part time football coach. Gerald Ford received the
LL.B. degree in 1941 and was admitted to the bar in the
same year. He began to practice law with the firm of
Busten and Ford.

Gerald Ford entered the United States Navy in 1942 during World War II, serving as an aviation operations officer. When he was discharged in 1946 Ford had been promoted to the rank of lieutenant commander. He then returned to the practice of law with his law firm and continued until 1949. Gerald married Elizabeth Bloomer on
October 15, 1948. They have four children: Michael,
John, Steven, and Susan.

Gerald R. Ford was elected as a Republican to the United
States House of Representatives from the Fifth Michigan
district in 1948. He served in the Eighty-first to the
Ninety-third Congresses from January 3, 1949 until his
resignation on December 6, 1973. He received the Junior
Chamber of Commerce Award as one of the ten outstanding
young men in the United States in 1950. Gerald was a delegate to the Interparliamentary Union at Warsaw, Poland
in 1959 and in Belgium in 1961. He was also a delegate
to the Bilderberg Group Conference in 1962.

Gerald Ford was given the Distinguished Congressional
Service Award by the American Political Science Association in 1961. He was elected House Minority Leader by
the Republicans in 1965 and retained this post until 1973.
Gerald Ford was chairman of the Republican National Convention in 1968 and helped Richard M. Nixon to win the
Presidential nomination. Ford led an unsuccessful move
to impeach Supreme Court Justice William O. Douglas in
1970.

After the resignation of Vice President Spiro T. Agnew
in October 1973, President Richard M. Nixon nominated
Gerald R. Ford for Vice President under the provisions
of the Twenty-fifth Amendment to the Constitution on
October 12, 1973. After an intensive investigation by
both Houses of Congress Mr. Ford was confirmed as Vice
President and sworn in December 6, 1973. While

Vice President, Ford supported President Nixon in his
defense concerning the crisis over the break-in at Democratic headquarters at the Watergate in Washington, D.C.
and the subsequent coverup.  President Nixon announced
his resignation on August 8, 1974, effective August 9.
   As a result of this unprecedented resignation of a
President of the United States, Mr. Ford, who was the
first Vice President selected under the procedures of the
Twenty-fifth Amendment to the Constitution, became President of the United States on August 9, 1974   Upon becoming President, Mr. Ford aksed for the cooperation of
Congress.  He urged reduction of government expenditures
and cautiously began to tackle the problems of inflation
and a growing unemployment rate.  In addition he has been
faced with the energy crisis and problems concerning the
use of oil as well as the Arab insistence upon increasing
the price of crude oil.  Mr. Ford nominated Nelson A.
Rockefeller for Vice President under the provisions of
the Twenty-fifth Amendment on August 20, 1974.  Rockefeller was sworn in as Vice President on December 19,
1974.

Bibliography:
   Bremer, Howard F., ed.  Richard M. Nixon, 1913-    .
Dobbs Ferry, N.Y.: Oceana Publications, Inc., 1975.
   Mankiewicz, Frank.  Perfectly Clear.  New York:
Quadrangle, 1974.
   Rather, Dan.  The Palace Guard.  New York: Harper,
1974.

### SECRETARY OF STATE: WILLIAM PIERCE ROGERS

   Refer to the biographical sketch of William P. Rogers
under Attorney General in the Administration of Dwight
D. Eisenhower, page 684.

### SECRETARY OF STATE: HENRY ALFRED KISSINGER

   Henry A. Kissinger, Secretary of State in the Cabinets of Presidents Richard M. Nixon and Gerald R. Ford,
was born on May 27, 1923 in Fuerth, Germany, the son
of Louis and Paula (Stern) Kissinger.  After receiving
part of his basic education in Germany, Henry and his
family came to the United States in 1938.  He became a
naturalized citizen in 1943.  He served in the United
States Army from 1943 to 1946.  Henry then studied at
Harvard University, receiving the Bachelor of Arts degree in 1950.  Henry married Ann Fleisher on February
6, 1949.  They had two children and were divorced in
1964.
   Henry Kissinger became executive director of the Harvard international seminar in 1951 and continued in
that post until 1959.  Among his other activities Henry

was a consultant to the operations research office from 1950 to 1961, a consultant to the director of psychology of the strategy board in 1952 and study director of nuclear weapons and foreign policy of the Council of Foreign Relations from 1955 to 1956. He was next a director of the special studies project for the Rockefeller Brothers Fund, Inc. from 1956 to 1958.

Henry A. Kissinger published Nuclear Weapons and Foreign Policy as well as A World Restored; Castlereagh, Metternich and the Restoration of Peace in 1957. Henry became a consultant to the government weapons systems evaluation group from 1959 to 1960. During this period Kissinger was a lecturer in the government department at Harvard from 1957 to 1959. He became an associate professor in 1959 and professor in 1962, continuing until 1969. From 1960 to 1969 he was a member of the faculty of the Harvard Center for International Affairs. Kissinger was given a citation by the Overseas Press Club and the Woodrow Wilson Prize for the best book in the fields of government, politics and international affairs in 1958.

Henry Kissinger was a consultant to the National Security Council from 1961 to 1962 and to the United States Arms Control and Disarmament Agency from 1961 to 1968. He published The Necessity for Choice: Prospects of American Foreign Policy in 1961. He was appointed a consultant to the State Department and continued until 1969. He also edited Problems of National Strategy: A Book of Readings in 1965.

President Richard M. Nixon appointed Henry Kissinger an assistant on national security affairs in 1969. In this capacity Kissinger was able to meet with various world leaders. He met with Premier Chou-en-Lai of the Peoples Republic of China on July 9, 1971 to arrange for President Nixon's visit to China. Kissinger was also President Nixon's representative to the Paris peace talks on Vietnam. Kissinger signed the cease fire agreement on January 27, 1973 and a subsequent agreement on June 13 to stop all truce violations.

President Richard M. Nixon nominated Henry A. Kissinger as Secretary of State to succeed William P. Rogers on August 22, 1973. In this capacity Kissinger helped to end the Middle East War of September 1973 and also began to get the two sides to begin negotiations. As provided by law he received Vice President Spiro T. Agnew's resignation on October 10, 1973. Secretary Kissinger was awarded the Nobel Peace Prize on October 16, 1973. He was able to arrange a pact between Israel and Syria in 1974. He was also named to the Economic Policy Board.

Henry married Nancy Maginnes on March 30, 1974. He continued to travel extensively for the President. Under the provisions of the law Secretary of State Kissinger received President Richard M. Nixon's resignation on

August 9, 1974. Kissinger has continued to serve under President Gerald R. Ford.

Bibliography:
  Brandon, Harry. The Retreat of American Power. Garden City, N.Y.: Doubleday, 1973.
  Bremer, Howard F., ed. Richard M. Nixon, 1913-____. Dobbs Ferry, N.Y.: Oceana Publications, Inc., 1975.
  Drury, Allen. Courage and Hesitation. Garden City, N.Y.: Doubleday, 1972.
  Graubard, Stephen. Kissinger: Portrait of a Mind. New York: Norton, 1973.
  Kalb, Marvin, and Kalb, Bernard. Kissinger. New York: Little, Brown and Company, 1974.
  Van der Linden, Frank. Nixon's Quest for Peace. Washington, D.C.: Robert B. Luce, Inc., 1972.

## SECRETARY OF THE TREASURY: DAVID M. KENNEDY

David M. Kennedy, Secretary of the Treasury in the Cabinet of President Richard M. Nixon, was born on July 21, 1905 in Randolph, Utah, the son of George and Katherine (Johnson) Kennedy. David received his basic education in the local public schools. He went to Weber College in Ogden, Utah and was graduated with the Bachelor of Arts degree in 1928. David married Lenora Bingham om November 4, 1925 while in college. They have four children: Marilyn Ann, Barbara Ann, Carol Joice, and Patricia Lenore. After graduating from college David M. Kennedy served as a Mormon missionary in England for two years.

After returning to the United States David Kennedy began working as a staff member of the board of governors of the Federal Reserve System in 1930 and continued with the Federal Reserve until 1946. He was a technical assistant in the division of bank operations, then an economist in the division of research and statistics and also a special assistant to the chairman of the board of governors. During the period that he worked for the Federal Reserve System David Kennedy studied at Georgetown University, receiving the Master of Arts degree in 1935. He then attended the George Washington University Law School, graduating with the LL.B. degree in 1937. He next attended Stonier School of Banking at Rutgers University and was graduated in 1939.

In 1946 Mr. Kennedy left the Federal Reserve System to become a member of the bond department of the Continental Illinois Bank and Trust Company in Chicago. He became a second vice president in 1948 and a vice president in 1951, continuing in that capacity until 1953. In October 1953 David M. Kennedy was appointed special assistant to Secretary of the Treasury George M. Humphrey in which post he served until December 1954. He then

returned to the Continental Illinois National Bank and
Trust Company as a vice president, serving until 1958.
He next became director and president of the bank, serving until 1959 when he became chairman of the board and
chief executive officer.  He continued utnil 1969.

Among his other activities David Kennedy was appointed
with twelve other citizens to form the Communications
Satellite Corporation by President John F. Kennedy in
1962.  David M. Kennedy was elected a member of the
permanent board of directors of the corporation in 1964.
President Lyndon B. Johnson named Kennedy chairman of a
commission studying means of improving the federal budget drafting methods in 1967.

President Richard M. Nixon appointed David M. Kennedy
Secretary of the Treasury on December 11, 1968.  Kennedy
assumed his office on January 22, 1969, serving until
his resignation on December 14, 1970.  While in office
he proposed that the administration institute a tight
budget and a restrictive monetary policy.  He also urged
that there be a temporary maintenance of high interest
rates in order to curb inflation.  In addition he insisted that the government maintain the official United
States price of gold.  Secretary Kennedy also held the
following official positions while serving in the Treasury Department: United States Governor of the International Monetary Fund, the International Bank for Reconstruction and Development as well as the Inter-American
Development Bank and the Asian Development Bank.  President Nixon also appointed him a member of the National
Commission on Productivity.

President Richard M. Nixon named David M. Kennedy Ambassador-at-Large with cabinet rank and Ambassador to
NATO on December 14, 1971.  Kennedy served in this capacity until 1973.  Among his other public service activities David Kennedy has been a member of various committees and still continues to serve on some of them.
These include the national public advisory committee on
Regional Economic Development and the Federal Advisory
Committee on Financial Assets.  His experience with the
Federal Reserve System was put to use when he became a
member of the federal advisory council of the Federal
Reserve Board.  He has also been chairman of the President's Commission on Budgetary Concepts and the national
advisory council on International Monetary and Financial
Policies.  He has also served various academic and cultural institutions as a member of the citizens committee
of the University of Illinois, the board of associates
of Depaul University, the Library of Congress Trust Fund
and the board of directors of the Chicago Foundation for
Cultural Development as well as chairman of the executive committee of the development council of Brigham
University.

Bibliography:
    Bremer, Howard F., ed.  Richard M. Nixon, 1913-____.
Dobbs Ferry, N.Y.: Oceana Publications, Inc., 1975.
    Drury, Allen.  Courage and Hesitation.  Garden City,
N.Y.: Doubleday, 1972.
    Evans, Rowland, and Novack, Robert.  Nixon in the White
House: The Frustration of Power.  New York: Random House,
1972.
    Mazo, Earl, and Hess, Stephan.  Nixon: A Political
Portrait.  New York, 1969.

## SECRETARY OF THE TREASURY: JOHN BOWDEN CONNALLY

John B. Connally, Secretary of the Treasury in the Cabinet of President Richard M. Nixon, was born on February 27, 1917 in Floresville, Texas, the son of John Bowden
and Lea Wright Connally.  After receiving his basic education in the public schools of San Antonio and Floresville, Texas from September 1923 to June 1933, John went
to the University of Texas from which he was eventually
graduated with the LL.B. degree in 1941.  He was admitted
to the Texas bar in September 1941.  John married Ida Nell
Brill on December 21, 1940.  They have three children:
John Bowden III, Sharon, and Mark.
    John Connally became a member of the Naval Reserve as
an ensign on June 11, 1941 and served in the Navy during
the Second World War.  He was discharged in January 1946.
Connally then returned to Texas where he was one of the
organizers of radio station KVET in 1946.  He was president and general manager of the station from 1946 to 1949.
Connally became a special assistant to Senator Lyndon B.
Johnson in 1949.  John began his legal practice with the
firm of Powell, Wirtz and Rauhat in Austin, Texas during
1949 and continued until 1952 when he joined the oil
firm of Richardson and Bass in Fort Worth as its attorney.
    President John F. Kennedy appointed John B. Connally
Secretary of the Navy which office he assumed on January
25, 1961.  He received the Distinguished Alumnus Board
of the University of Texas Ex-students Association in
1961.  Connally was next elected Governor of Texas on
November 3, 1962.  He took office in 1963 and served until 1969.  John Connally was with President John F. Kennedy in Dallas, Texas when the latter was assassinated
on November 22, 1963.  Governor Connally was seriously
wounded at the same time but eventually recovered.
    After leaving the governor's office in 1969 John Connal-
ly became a partner in the law firm of Vinson, Elkins,
Searles and Connally in Houston and continued with the
firm until December 1971.  He also was a member of the
United States Advisory Council on Executive Organization
from 1969 to 1970.
    President Richard M. Nixon appointed John B. Connally
Secretary of the Treasury on December 9, 1970.  He assumed

his office on February 11, 1971 and continued until May 16, 1972.  While in office he was a member of the President's Foreign Intelligence Advisory Board, the Advisory Committee on the Reform of the International Monetary System, and the Cost of Living Council.  As Secretary of the Treasury Connally continued to work to curb the inflationary trend of the economy.  While in office he urged bsuiness tax relief.  He was helpful in lobbying with Congress to have administration bills passed.  John Connally also aided in preparation of the dollar devaluation bill.  He was a major advisor in regard to Vietnamese policy including the mining of North Vietnamese harbors in 1972.

President Richard M. Nixon appointed John Connally a special advisor to the President in 1973.  He went on a tour of Latin America and Asia in June and July 1972.  He then headed a Democrats for Nixon Committee beginning on August 19, 1972.  John Connally announced in 1973 that he had become a Republican.

Bibliography:

Bremer, Howard F., ed.  Richard M. Nixon, 1913-____.  Dobbs Ferry, N.Y.: Oceana Publications, Inc., 1975.

Drury, Allen.  Courage and Hesitation.  Garden City, New York: Doubleday, 1972.

Evans, Rowland, and Novack, Robert.  Nixon in the White House: The Frustration of Power.  New York: Random House, 1972.

## SECRETARY OF THE TREASURY: GEORGE PRATT SHULTZ

George P. Shultz, Secretary of Labor and Secretary of the Treasury in the Cabinet of President Richard M. Nixon, was born on December 13, 1920 in New York City, the son of Birl E. Shultz, personnel director and founder of the New York Stock Exchange Institute, and Margaret Lennox (Pratt) Shultz.  After receiving his basic education at the Loomis Institute in Windsor, Connecticut from which he was graduated in 1938 George Pratt went to Princeton University where he studied economics.  He was graduated with the Bachelor of Arts degree in 1942.

George Shultz entered the United States Marine Corps in 1942 and served until 1945 when he was discharged with the rank of captain.  Shultz then went to Massachusetts Institute of Technology for graduate work.  He was a teaching assistant in economics from 1946 to 1947.  George married Helena Maria O'Brien on February 16, 1946.  They have five children: Margaret Ann, Kathleen Pratt, Peter Milton, Barbara Lennox, and Alexander George.  Shultz became an instructor of economics at Massachusetts Institute in 1948 and continued until 1949 when he received the Doctor of Philosophy in that year.

George Shultz was next appointed assistant professor of industrial relations in 1949 and continued until 1954. He wrote The Dynamics of a Labor Market with Charles A. Myers in 1951. He was first named to arbitration panels for labor management disputes in 1953. George was acting director of industrial relations at Massachusetts Institute of Technology from 1954 to 1955 and was promoted in the latter year to associate professor. He was senior staff economist for President Eisenhower's Council of Economic Advisers from 1955 to 1956.

George P. Shultz resigned from Massachusetts Institute of Technology to become professor of industrial relations at the University of Chicago Graduate School of Business in 1957. He became a consultant to Secretary of Labor James P. Mitchell in 1959 and continued until 1960. In the latter year Shultz and Thomas L. Whisler wrote Management and the Computer. President John F. Kennedy appointed Shultz a consultant to the President's Advisory Committee on Labor-Management Policy. He remained on the committee until 1962.

George Shultz was a member of the Illinois Governor's Committee on Unemployment during 1961 and 1962. He was a staff director of the national labor policy study committee on economic development. In 1962 George Shultz was appointed dean of the University of Chicago Graduate School of Business. He remained in this post until 1968. He also became co-chairman of the Automation Fund Committee and a member of the Grantee Ford Foundation in 1962. Among his other activities Shultz became a member of the National Manpower Policy Task Force in 1963. He was chairman of the National Manpower Policy Task Force in 1963 and chairman of the task force to review the United States Employment Service programs in 1965. During this period George Shultz coauthored Strategies for the Displaced Worker with Arnold A. Weber in 1966. In the same year he and Robert Z. Aliber coedited Guidelines, Informed Controls, and the Market Place.

George Shultz was a fellow of the Center for Advanced Studies in the Behavioral Sciences located in Stratford, Connecticut during 1968 and 1969. In addition he was president of the Industrial Relations Association. He was also involved in various businesses as a director of Borg-Warner Corporation, Stein, Roe, and Farnham and the General Transportation Company.

President-elect Richard M. Nixon named George P. Shultz chairman of a task force to study manpower, labor-management relations, and wage price policy in 1968. Mr. Nixon named Shultz Secretary of Labor on December 11, 1968. George assumed his office on January 22, 1969. He helped to avoid a national railroad strike in April 1969 and developed a program to train some hard-core unemployed people in July 1969.

President Nixon appointed George P. Shultz head of
the Construction Industry Collective Bargaining Commission on September 22, 1969.  Among his other responsibilities Mr. Shultz was appointed to the Cabinet level
committee to aid school districts in desegrgation and to
the National Commission on Productivity.  He helped to
prevent a postal strike in 1970 and also began planning
the establishment of postal academies.  George Shultz
left the Labor Department in 1970 to become director of
the Office of Management and Budget in 1970, continuing
in that post until 1972.

President Richard M. Nixon appointed George P. Shultz
Secretary of the Treasury on May 16, 1972 and assumed
his duties on June 12.  He was appointed an assistant
to the President and head of the new Cabinet level Council on Economic Policy in December 1972.  He announced
the beginning of Phase 3 of the wage-price control program in January 1973.  He was appointed the chief United
States representative on the United States-Soviet Joint
Commercial Commission and head of the East-West Trade
Policy Committee on March 6, 1973.  He urged an end to
wage and price controls in February 1974.  Shultz resigned from the Treasury Department on March 14, 1974.

Bibliography:
   Bremer, Howard F., ed.  Richard M. Nixon, 1913-     .
Dobbs Ferry, N.Y.: Oceana Publications, Inc., 1975.
   Drury, Allen.  Courage and Hesitation.  Garden City,
New York: Doubleday, 1972.
   Evans, Rowland, and Novack, Robert.  Nixon in the White
House: The Frustration of Power.  New York: Random House,
1972.

SECRETARY OF THE TREASURY: WILLIAM EDWARD SIMON

William E. Simon, Secretary of the Treasury in the Cabinets of Presidents Richard M. Nixon and Gerald R. Ford,
was born on November 27, 1927 in Paterson, New Jersey,
the son of an insurance broker.  His mother died when
he was eight.  William grew up in Spring Lake, New Jersey.  After receiving his basic education William E.
Simon attended Blair Academy and then Newark Academy
from which he was graduated in 1946.  William joined the
United States Army in 1946 and served in Japan.  He
swam with  the Army team in the Pacific Olympics.  He
was discharged in 1948 and then went to Lafayette College in Easton, Pennsylvania.  He was graduated from
Lafayette College in 1952.  William married Carol Girard
in 1949.  They have seven children.

William E. Simon began working for the Union Securities
Company in New York City in 1952.  He was involved in
trading municipal bonds and remained with the company until 1957.  Simon then became vice president of Weeden

and Company, continuing until 1963. He became a member
of the firm of Salomon Brothers in January 1964 and was
made a partner in October. He was in charge of federal
bonds and securities. He helped the company to greatly
expand its business. William E. Simon was elected the
first president of the Association of Primary Dealers in
United States government securities.

President Richard M. Nixon nominated William E. Simon
as deputy secretary of the Treasury on December 6, 1972.
He was confirmed by the Senate and assumed his office in
January 1973. William managed the daily operations of the
Treasury Department and was chairman of the Interagency
Oil Policy Committee charged with dealing with the national energy crisis. President Nixon appointed Simon administrator of the Federal Energy Office to succeed John
Love on December 4, 1973. Simon developed an allocation
program which he presented on December 12, 1973 providing
the necessary fuel for industry and then for home heating.
He insisted that the oil companies reduce their production
of gasoline by five percent. He used his authority to
insist upon adherence to his allocation program to meet
the energy needs of the nation.

President Richard M. Nixon named William E. Simon Secretary of the Treasury to succeed George P. Shultz on April
17, 1974. Simon was confirmed by the Senate and assumed
his office on April 30. He called for fiscal restraint
in order to curb the national inflation rate on May 27,
1974. He indicated to Congress on June 11, 1974 that
he was in favor of ending the forty-year ban which prohibited United States citizens from owning gold. President Nixon sent Secretary Simon on a visit to the Middle
East which included Egypt and Israel from July 14 to 18,
1974. He discussed financial investments as well as
trade and oil developments.

Mr. Simon continued to serve as Secretary of the Treasury under President Gerald R. Ford after the resignation
of Richard M. Nixon on August 9, 1974. On August 20
President Ford named Simon to an eight-member steering
committee to plan for an economic summit conference in
the fall. He was also named a member of the new Council
on Wage and Price Stability on August 29. He attended an
economic conference at Paris with the finance ministers
of Great Britain, France, West Germany and Japan on September 7 and 8, 1974. President Ford appointed Simon
head of a 14-member Economic Policy Board on September
28, 1974. Simon attended the second meeting of the U.S.-
U.S.S.R. Economic and Trade Council from October 13-16,
1974 in Moscow. He indicated in November that he was
against price controls.

Bibliography:
  Bremer, Howard F., ed. Richard M. Nixon, 1913-____.
Dobbs Ferry, N.Y.: Oceana Publications, Inc., 1975.

Drury, Allen. Courage and Hesitation. Garden City,
N.Y.: Doubleday, 1972.

Evans, Rowland, and Novack, Robert. Nixon in the White
House: The Frustration of Power. New York: Random House,
1972.

New York Times. December 17, 1972, Section VI, p. 5.
New York Times. December 5, 1973, p. 35.

## SECRETARY OF DEFENSE: MELVIN R. LAIRD

Melvin R. Laird, Secretary of Defense in the Cabinet
of President Richard M. Nixon, was born on September 1,
1922 in Omaha, Nebraska, the son of Rev. Melvin R. Laird,
a clergyman and Wisconsin state senator, and Helen (Connor) Laird. Melvin moved with his parents to Marshfield,
Wood County, Wisconsin where he received his basic education in the public schools and Marshfield High School.
Melvin then went to Carleton College in Northfield, Minnesota from which he was graduated in 1942. During the
same year Laird enlisted in the United States Navy, obtaining a commission in 1944. He served on the Maddox,
a destroyer in Task Force 58 and the Pacific Third Fleet.
He was wounded in battle and given the Purple Heart.

Melvin R. Laird married Barbara Masters on October 15,
1945. They have three children: John Osborne, Alison,
and David. Melvin Laird was elected to the Wisconsin
State Senate in 1946 to fill the vacancy left by the
death of his father. He was the youngest state senator
in the United States and was reelected in 1948 without
opposition. During the same year Laird attended the
Republican National Convention. He studied at the University of Wisconsin Law School while he was a state
senator. In the Wisconsin Senate Laird was chairman of
the military and veterans affairs committee, the legislative council and the tax committee. He was also a
member of the Wisconsin Educational Commissioner. He
was also secretary-treasurer of the family-owned Connor
Builder Supply Company.

In 1950 and 1952 Melvin Laird was chairman of the state
Republican Party platform committee, and in the latter
year was a delegate to the Republican National Convention. Laird was elected to the United States House of
Representatives on November 4, 1952, serving in the
Eighty-third to the Ninety-first Congresses from January
3, 1953 until his resignation on January 21, 1969. He
was a member of the following committees: Agriculture and
House Appropriations, as well as the defense, health,
education, and welfare, and labor subcommittees.

Melvin R. Laird was a United States delegate to the
World Health Organization at Geneva in 1959 and again in
1963 and 1965. He wrote A House Divided: America's
Strategy Gap in 1962 and was editor of The Conservative
Papers in 1964. Laird was chairman of the Republican

Conference in the Eighty-ninth and Ninetieth Congresses
from 1965 to 1969.  During the Eighty-ninth Congress,
1965-1967, Melvin Laird was chairman of the Joint Senate-
House Committee on the statement of Republican principles.
He edited The Republican Papers in 1968.
  President Richard M. Nixon appointed Melvin R. Laird
Secretary of Defense.  Laird assumed his office on January
22, 1969.  While in office he helped to develop the Sentinel anti-ballistic missile system.  In order to achieve
economies in the operation of the Defense Department
Secretary Laird ordered that some military bases and installations be closed.  He also helped to increase the
efficiency of the military establishment through improved
weapons and cooperated in directing the necessary actions
in South East Asia.
  Secretary of Defense Laird opposed establishing a de-
finite date for withdrawal of troops from South Vietnam
and announced the ending of all student and occupational
deferments for the draft as of January 1, 1971.  He also
developed a program for improvement of race relations in
the armed forces in 1971.  He resigned from the Defense
Department on November 27, 1972 and then became a domestic adviser of President Nixon during 1973 and 1974.
In the latter year he became a senior counsellor for Rea-
der's Digest.  Melvin Laird received recognition for his
public services including the 15th Annual Albert Lasker
medical award and the American Cancer Society--National
Association of Mental Health Man of the Year Award.

Bibliography:
  Bremer, Howard, ed.  Richard M. Nixon, 1913-    .
Dobbs Ferry, N.Y.: Oceana Publications, Inc., 1975.
  Drury, Allen.  Courage and Hesitation.  Garden City,
N.Y.: Doubleday, 1972.
  Evans, Rowland, and Novack, Robert.  Nixon in the White
House: The Frustration of Power.  New York: Random House,
1972.
  Time,  August 29, 1969. vol. 94, pp. 13-15.

SECRETARY OF DEFENSE: ELLIOT LEE RICHARDSON

  Elliot L. Richardson, Secretary of Health, Education,
and Welfare, Secretary of Defense, and Attorney General
in the Cabinet of President Richard M. Nixon, was born on
July 20, 1920 in Boston, Massachusetts, the son of Dr.
Edward P. and Clara (Shattuck) Richardson.  After receiving his basic education Eliot went to Harvard College from which he was graduated with the Bachelor of
Arts degree in 1942.  He then entered the United States
Army in 1942, serving as a first lieutenant in the 4th
Infantry Division until 1945.  He was decorated with
the Bronze Star and the Purple Heart with the oak leaf
cluster.

Elliot L. Richardson went to Harvard Law School after the war and received the LL.B. degree in 1947. He was a law clerk for United States Court of Appeals Judge Learned Hand from 1947 to 1948 and then a clerk for United States Supreme Court Justice Felix Frankfurter from 1948 to 1949. Elliot Richardson then joined the legal firm of Gray, Best, Coolidge and Rugg in 1949, continuing until 1953. He was admitted to the Massachusetts bar in 1950. Elliot was a lecturer of law at Harvard in 1952. He married Anne Francis Hazard on August 2, 1952. They have three children: Henry, Anne, and Michael.

Richardson served as an assistant to Senator Leverett Saltonstall from 1953 to 1954 and then returned to the practice of law with the firm of Ropes, Gray, Best, Coolidge and Rugg from 1954 to 1956. In 1957 Richardson was named assistant secretary for legislation of the Department of Health, Education, and Welfare, continuing until 1959. During this period he was acting Secretary of Health, Education, and Welfare from April to July 1958.

Elliot Richardson continued his public service as United States Attorney for Massachusetts from 1959 to 1961. In the latter year he was appointed special assistant to the United States Attorney General. He then became a partner in the Boston firm of Ropes and Gray, remaining in private practice from 1961 to 1964. Richardson was elected lieutenant governor of Massachusetts in 1964, serving from 1965 to 1967 and then was state attorney general from 1967 to 1969.

Among his other activities Elliot L. Richardson was a vice president and director of the Massachusetts Bay United Fund, a president and director of the World Affairs Council of Boston, a director of the United Community Services of Metropolitan Boston, and chairman of the Greater Boston United Fund Campaign. In addition he served on the board of Overseers of Harvard College.

President Richard M. Nixon named Elliot L. Richardson undersecretary of State on January 4, 1969. He served until 1970. President Nixon appointed Elliot Richardson Secretary of Health, Education, and Welfare on June 15, 1970 to fill the post left vacant when Robert Finch resigned. Richardson assumed his office on June 24. He supported the proposed model cities plan and indicated his opposition to a welfare test bill. He developed a northern school integration drive and suggested a six percent rise in social security payments in 1971. He also ordered medicaid child care. He wrote an introduction to the report issued by a special task force which was published in 1973 called Work in America.

President Nixon nominated Elliot Richardson as Secretary of Defense in 1972. He was confirmed on January 29, 1973. He worked to reduce military expenditures.

Elliot L. Richardson was next appointed Attorney General
on April 30, 1973 and assumed his office on May 25, 1973.
He supported the work of special Watergate Prosecutor
Archibald Cox, who had been named on May 18.  Richardson
insisted that Cox be given the logs which recorded the
times and dates of the Nixon-Dean meetings.  When Cox
ran into disagreements with President Nixon concerning
the use of White House tape recordings Cox was dismissed
on October 20, 1973.  Richardson resigned as Attorney
General at the same time.  He had previously made arrangements for Vice President Agnew's resignation and
the disposition of the income tax case against him.
Richardson was granted the honorary LL.D. degree by many
institutions including Emerson and Springfield Colleges,
the University of Pittsburgh and Yeshiva, Ohio State,
Temple, and Michigan State Universities.

Bibliography:
    Bremer, Howard F., ed.  Richard M. Nixon, 1913-____ .
Dobbs Ferry, N.Y.: Oceana Publications, Inc., 1975.
    Drury, Allen.  Courage and Hesitation.  Garden City,
N.Y.: Doubleday, 1972.
    Evans, Rowland, and Novack, Robert.  Nixon in the
White House: The Frustration of Power.  New York: Ran-
dom House, 1972.
    McCloskey, Paul W.  Truth and Untruth: Political De-
ceit in America.  New York: Simon and Schuster, Inc.,
1972.
    Spalding, Henry D.  The Nixon Nobody Knows.  New York:
Jonathan David, Pubs., Inc., 1972.
    Wills, Gary.  Nixon Agonistes: The Crisis of the Self-
Made Man.  New York: Houghton, 1971.

### SECRETARY OF DEFENSE: JAMES RODNEY SCHLESINGER

    James R. Schlesinger, Secretary of Defense in the Ca-
binets of Presidents Richard M. Nixon and Gerald R. Ford,
was born on February 15, 1929 in New York City, the son
of Julius and Rhea (Rogen) Schlesinger.  After receiving
his basic education James went to Harvard University from
which he was graduated with the Bachelor of Arts degree
summa cum laude in 1950.  He went on to graduate studies
at Harvard, earning the Master of Arts degree in 1952.
He was a Frederick Sheldon prize fellow at Harvard from
1950 to 1951.
    While studying for his doctorate James married Rachel
Mellinger on June 19, 1954.  They have eight children:
Cora K., Charles L., Anne R., William F., Emily, Thomas
S., Clara, and James Rodney.  He received the Ph.D. from
Harvard in 1956.  James Schlesinger was appointed an
assistant professor at the University of Virginia in 1955.
He was eventually promoted to associate professor and
continued on the faculty until 1963.  During this period

he was a member of the board of associates of the Foreign Policy Research Institute at the University of Pennsylvania from 1962 to 1963. James wrote The Political Economy of National Security in 1966.

James R. Schlesinger next served as a senior member of the RAND Corporation from 1963 to 1967. He was editor of the Journal of Finance in 1964 and 1965. In 1967 Schlesinger collaborated in writing Issues in Defense Economics. He was then a director of strategic studies from 1967 to 1969. Appointed assistant director of the Federal Bureau of the Budget in 1969 Dr. Schlesinger also served as acting deputy director during 1969 and 1970. He continued his public service as assistant director of the Office of Management and Budget from 1970 to 1971.

President Richard M. Nixon named James R. Schlesinger chairman of the Atomic Energy Commission in 1971. He continued in this post until February 1973. James was then named director of the CIA (Central Intelligence Agency), serving from February to July 1973. James R. Schlesinger was named Secretary of Defense to succeed Elliot L. Richardson on May 10, 1973 and was confirmed on June 28. He continued to serve under President Gerald R. Ford after the resignation of Richard M. Nixon on August 9, 1974. He is a member of the National Security Council. Schlesinger has consistently supported the arms policy as established by the administration.

Bibliography:
  Bremer, Howard F., ed. Richard M. Nixon, 1913-    .
Dobbs Ferry, N.Y.: Oceana Publications, Inc., 1975.
  Mankiewicz, Frank. Perfectly Clear. New York: Quadrangle, 1974.
  Rather, Dan. The Palace Guard. New York: Harper, 1974.

### ATTORNEY GENERAL: JOHN NEWTON MITCHELL

John N. Mitchell, Attorney General in the Cabinet of President Richard M. Nixon, was born on September 5, 1913 in Detroit, Michigan, the son of Joseph Charles and Margaret Agnes (McMahon) Mitchell. He moved with his family to Long Island, New York when he was a child and received his basic education at the Blue Point and Patchogue public schools. John went to Jamaica High School in Queens, New York and then studied at Fordham University. He was admitted to the Fordham Law School before he completed the Bachelor of Arts degree and was graduated with the LL.B. degree in 1938.

John N. Mitchell was admitted to the New York bar in 1938. He began his legal practice with the firm of Caldwell and Raymond, continuing until 1942. He also pursued post graduate work during 1938 and 1939. John married Martha around this time. They have two children: John

Newton, III, and Jill Elizabeth.  John Mitchell became
a partner in the firm of Caldwell, Trimble, and Mitchell
in 1942.  John entered the United States Navy during the
Second World War and was a commander of several squadrons
of torpedo boats.  He served from 1943 to 1946.  Mitchell
then returned to his law firm.  In 1967 his firm merged
with that of Richard Nixon to become Nixon, Mudge, Rose,
Guthrie, Alexander, and Mitchell.
    President-elect Richard M. Nixon named John N. Mitchell
Attorney General on December 11, 1968.  He assumed his
office on January 21, 1969.  While in office John urged
that there be an expansion of wiretapping in criminal
cases.  He suggested legislation for extension of the
Voting Rights Act of 1965.  In addition he supervised
action for the states to enforce the registration of
eighteen year olds under the Voting Rights Act of 1970.
As a result of disagreements concerning Supreme Court
nominations Mitchell indicated that all future choices
would be cleared first with the American Bar Association.
He proposed strong narcotics legislation and insisted
on law enforcement on college campuses.  In 1971 Mitchell
was involved in action to stop publication of the Pentagon Papers on Vietnam from being published by the New
York Times.  He was a member of the cabinet level task
force to aid school districts in developing desegregation plans.
    John N. Mitchell resigned his post as Attorney General
on February 15, 1972 in order to become Richard Nixon's
campaign manager.  Then on June 18, 1972 a break-in at
the Democratic headquarters at the Watergate office
building-apartment complex was foiled.  As information
began to come out, it was alleged that certain Republican officials were involved.  Mitchell quit his post
as campaign manager on July 1, 1972 in part as a result
of his wife's pressure.  He was eventually linked with
a secret GOP fund.  John N. Mitchell was brought to
trial with others in 1974 for alleged involvement in the
coverup of the Watergate break in and was found guilty
in December 1974.

Bibliography:
    Bremer, Howard F., ed.  Richard M. Nixon, 1913-    .
Dobbs Ferry, N.Y.: Oceana Publications, Inc., 1975.
    Drury, Allen.  Courage and Hesitation.  Garden City,
N.Y.: Doubleday, 1972.
    Evans, Rowland, and Novack, Robert.  Nixon in the
White House: The Frustration of Power.  New York: Ran-
dom House. 1972.
    McCloskey, Paul W.  Truth and Untruth: Political De-
ceit in America.  New York: Simon and Shuster,, Inc.,
1972.
    Spalding, Henry D. The Nixon Nobody Knows.  New York:
Jonathan David, Pubs., Inc., 1972.

Wills, Gary. Nixon Agonistes: The Crisis of the Self-Made Man. Boston: Houghton Mifflin, 1971.
Witcover, Jules. The Resurrection of Richard Nixon. New York: Putnam. 1970.

ATTORNEY GENERAL: RICHARD GORDON KLEINDIENST

Richard G. Kleindienst, Attorney General in the Cabinet of President Richard M. Nixon, was born in August 1923 in Winslow, Arizona, the son of Alfred and Gladys (Love) Kleindienst. After receiving his basic education in the local schools Richard went to Harvard University from which he was graduated with the Bachelor of Arts degree in 1947. He next studied law at Harvard and received the LL.B. degree in 1950. He was admitted to the Arizona bar in the same year. Richard married Margaret Dunbar on September 3, 1948. They have four children: Alfred Dunbar, Wallace Heath, Anne Lucille, and Carolyn Love.
Richard G. Kleindienst began practicing law with the firm of Jennings, Strauss, Salmon and Trask in Phoenix, eventually becoming a partner. Richard was elected to the Arizona House of Representatives and served from 1953 to 1954. He was chairman of the Arizona Young Republican League in 1953. He became a member of the Republican National Committee in 1956, serving until 1960. In 1958 Kleindienst became a senior partner in the firm of Shimmel, Hill, Kleindienst and Bishop in Phoenix, remaining with the firm until 1969.
Kleindienst also continued his involvement in Republican politics. He was chairman of the Arizona Republican committee from 1956 to 1960 and again from 1961 to 1963. He was a member of the Republican National Commitee for a second time in 1961 and again in 1963. Richard became national director of field operations for the Goldwater Presidential committee in 1964. Kleindienst was the unsuccessful Republican candidate for governor of Arizona in the same year. He was national director of operations for the Nixon for President Committee in 1968. During the same year he was general counsel of the Republican National Committee. Among his other activities Kleindienst was a member of the Urban League, Goodwill Industries, the Arizona and American Heart Associations.
President Richard M. Nixon appointed Richard G. Kleindienst deputy attorney general in 1969. He remained in this post until 1972. President Nixon appointed Richard Kleindienst Attorney General to succeed John Mitchell on February 15, 1972. He was sworn in on June 12, 1972. Richard approved of wiretaps against organized crime and also proposed tougher drug laws. He soon became involved in the problems surrounding the Watergate investigation. He resigned on April 30, 1973 because he would have to prosecute people with whom he had a professional asso-

ciation.    Richard G. Kleindienst then returned to his
legal practice.

Bibliography:
  Bremer, Howard F., ed.   Richard M. Nixon, 1913-____.
Dobbs Ferry, N.Y.: Oceana Publications, Inc., 1975.
  Drury, Allen.  Courage and Hesitation.  Garden City,
N.Y.: Doubleday, 1972.
  Evans, Rowland, and Novack, Robert.  Nixon in the
White House: The Frustration of Power.  New York: Ran-
dom House, 1972.
  McCloskey, Paul W.  Truth and Untruth: Political Deceit
in America.  New York: Simon and Shuster, Inc., 1972.
  McGinnis, Joe.  The Selling of the President, 1968.
New York: Trident Press, 1969.
  Spalding, Henry D.  The Nixon Nobody Knows.  New York:
Jonathan David, Pubs., Inc., 1972.
  Wills, Gary.  Nixon Agonistes: The Crisis of the Self-
Made Man.  Boston: Houghton Mifflin, 1971.
  Witcover, Jules.  The Resurrection of Richard Nixon.
New York: Putnam, 1970.

## ATTORNEY GENERAL: ELLIOT LEE RICHARDSON

Refer to the biographical sketch of Elliot L. Richardson under Secretary of Defense, page 777.

## ATTORNEY GENERAL: WILLIAM B. SAXBE

William B. Saxbe, Attorney General in the Cabinets of
Presidents Richard M. Nixon and Gerald R. Ford, was born
on June 24, 1916 in Mechanicsburg, Ohio, the son of Bart
Rockwell and Faye Henry (Carey) Saxbe.  After receiving
his basic education William studied at Ohio State University from which he received the Bachelor of Arts degree in 1940.  William married Ardath Louise Kleinhans on
September 14, 1940.  They have three children: William
Bart, Juliet Louise, and Charles Rockwell.
  William Saxbe entered the United States Army, serving
with the 107th cavalry from 1940 to 1942.  He then transferred to the United States Army Air Force in 1942 and
continued until he was discharged in 1945.  He next attended the Ohio State University Law School, graduating
with the LL.B. degree in 1948 and was admitted to the
Ohio bar.  He established his law practice in Mechanicsburg where he continued until 1955.  William was elected
to the Ohio General Assembly and served from 1947 to 1948
and again from 1949 to 1950.  He was elected to the Ohio
House of Representatives and served as majority leader
from 1951 to 1952 and then its speaker from 1953 to 1954.
  William Saxbe became attorney general of Ohio in 1957
and served until 1960.  He was a partner in Dargusch, Saxbe and Dargusch from 1960 to 1963 and then became Ohio

attorney general again from 1963 to 1968.  In the last
year he was elected to the United States Senate, serving
from January 3, 1969 until his resignation on January 4,
1974.  He was also granted honorary degrees by various
institutions including Central State University, Ohio
Wesleyan University and Wilmington College.  He announced
on October 9, 1973 that he was going to return to his
law practice.
    President Richard M. Nixon nominated William B. Saxbe
for the post of Attorney General to succeed Elliot L.
Richardson on November 1, 1973.  Following the settlement
of the constitutional problem which prohibited a Congressman from taking a government post for which he had voted
to raise the salary by reducing the salary, President
Nixon formally submitted Saxbe's name in December.  He
was confirmed by the Senate and assumed his office on
January 4, 1974.  Mr. Saxbe supported Leon Jaworski, the
special Watergate prosecutor, in the matter of receiving
the White House tape recordings.
    On June 4, 1974 President Richard Nixon abolished the
Attorney General's list of subversive organizations.  After Richard Nixon's resignation on August 9, 1974 Attorney General William B. Saxbe continued to serve under
President Gerald R. Ford.  As Attorney General he supported Richard Nixon's rights to the White House tapes.
William Saxbe resigned on December 13, 1974 and was nominated by President Ford as Ambassador to India.

Bibliography:
    Bremer, Howard F., ed.  Richard M. Nixon, 1913-____.
Dobbs Ferry, N.Y.: Oceana Publications, Inc., 1975.
    Mankiewicz, Frank.  Perfectly Clear.  New York: Quad-
rangle, 1974.
    Rather, Dan.  The Palace Guard.  New York: Harper, 1974.

## POSTMASTER GENERAL: WINTON MALCOLM BLOUNT

    Winton M. Blount, Postmaster General in the Cabinet
of President Richard M. Nixon, was born on February 1,
1921 in Union Springs, Alabama, the son of Winton Blount,
owner of a short-line railroad and a construction materials business, and Clara Belle (Chalker) Blount.  After receiving his basic education in the public schools
of Union Springs Winton went to Staunton Military Academy in Virginia.  Winton next attended the University
of Alabama from 1939 to 1941, receiving the Bachelor of
Arts degree in the latter year.
    During World War II he was a lieutenant in the United
States Army Air Force from 1942 to 1945.  Winton married
Mary Katherine Archibald on September 2, 1942.  They have
five children: Winton M., III, Thomas A., S. Roberts,
Katherine, and Joseph W.  After the war Winton Blount
established Blount Brothers, Corporation, a general con-

tracting firm in 1946 of which he was president and
chairman of the Board until December 1968. He was also
a director of other business concerns including Gulf
American Fire and Casualty Company, the First National
Bank of Montgomery, Alabama, the Kershaw Manufacturing
Company and Jackson-Atlantin, Inc.

In connection with his business activities Mr. Blount
has also been president of the Alabama State Chamber of
Commerce, director of the Southern States Industrial
Council, and the National Association of Manufacturers.
He is a life member of the Southern Research Institute.
Mr. Blount has also been a director, chairman of the
executive committee and treasurer of the Young Presi-
dents' organization.

Winton M. Blount also became interested in Republican
politics. He was chairman of the Alabama Citizens for
Eisenhower in 1952 and southeastern director of the
Nixon-Lodge campaign in 1960. Among his philanthropic
activities he has been a member of the board of directors
of the United Appeal of Montgomery and of the Montgomery
YMCA. He was named one of four Outstanding Young Men of
Alabama in 1956 and the Man of the Year of Montgomery in
1961. He also received a citation for distinguished
service to Montgomery in 1966. Mr. Blount was elected
president of the United States Chamber of Commerce in
1968.

President Richard M. Nixon nominated Winton M. Blount
Postmaster General on December 11, 1968. After being
confirmed by the United States Senate on January 20,
1969 Mr. Blount assumed his office on January 22, 1969.
Among his duties as Postmaster General he was a member
of the President's Domestic Affairs Council, the Cabinet
Committee on Construction, the Cabinet Committee to pro-
vide aid to school districts for desegregation, the
President's Committee on Vietnam Veterans, the Presi-
dent's Committee on Employment of the Handicapped, the
National Council on Organized Crime, the President's
Council on Youth Opportunity, the Cabinet Committee on
Education, and the national advisory Committee for Jobs
for Veterans Program. During this period he was given
the Brotherhood Award of the National Conference of
Christians and Jews.

While in office Postmaster General Blount filled all
postmaster vacancies through merit and thus worked to
end patronage. He insisted on the development of efficient management operations on the regional level. When
the nation's first strike of postal workers broke out in
March 1970 Mr. Blount helped to begin negotiations. He
was named director of the new Office of Management and
Budget on June 10, 1970. He worked to have legislation
passed creating a Postal Corporation to handle the nation's mail service as a result of which the Cabinet
post was abolished on July 1, 1971. Winton M. Blount

became head of the United States Postal Service on July 1, 1971, continuing in that capacity until December 7, 1971. He was given the Silver Quill Award of the American Business Press in 1971.

After leaving public office Winton Blount returned to his business life and is at present chairman of the executive committee of Blount, Inc. He is a member of the National Association of Manufacturers and the United States and Alabama Chambers of Commerce.

Bibliography:
Bremer, Howard F., ed. Richard M. Nixon, 1913-____. Dobbs Ferry, N.Y.: Oceana Publications, Inc., 1975.
Drury, Allen. Courage and Hesitation. Garden City, N.Y.: Doubleday, 1972.
Evans, Rowland, and Novack, Robert. Nixon in the White House: The Frustration of Power. New York: Random House, 1972.
Spalding, Henry D. The Nixon Nobody Knows. New York: Jonathan David, Pubs., Inc., 1972.
Wills, Gary. Nixon Agonistes: The Crisis of the Self-Made Man. Boston: Houghton Mifflin, 1971.
Witcover, Jules. The Resurrection of Richard Nixon. New York: Putnam, 1970.

## SECRETARY OF THE INTERIOR:

### WALTER JOSEPH HICKEL

Walter J. Hickel, Secretary of the Interior in the Cabinet of President Richard M. Nixon, was born on August 18, 1919 in Ellinwood, Kansas, the son of Robert A. Hickel, a farmer, and Emma (Zecha) Hickel. After receiving his basic education in the public schools of Clafin, Kansas until the age of 16, Walter moved to California. He worked as a carpenter until 1940 when he moved to Alaska. Walter married Janice Cannon on September 22, 1941. They had one son, Theodore. His wife died in August 1943.

While in Alaska Walter Hickel was a bar tender and worked for the Alaska Railroad and as a construction worker. He soon began building homes on his own and then eventually constructed and managed rental units as well as residential areas and hotels. Walter married Ermalee Stratz on November 22, 1945. They have five children: Robert, Walter, John, Joseph, and Karl.

Walter Hickel founded the Hickel Construction Company in Anchorage, Alaska in 1947. He built and owned the Traveler's Inn in Anchorage in 1953 and still manages it. He became involved in Republican politics and was Alaskan Republican national committeeman from 1954 to 1964. He also built and has continued to operate the Traveler's Inn of Fairbanks, Alaska. Among his other major enter-

prises were the construction of Hotel Captain Cook and
the Northern Lights Shopping Center, both in Anchorage.

Mr. Hickel was also chairman of the board of the Hickel
Investment Company and of the Anchorage Natural Gas Company. He helped to lead the struggle for Alaskan statehood, and after admission he became the first elected
Republican governor of Alaska on December 5, 1966, serving until 1969.

President-elect Richard M. Nixon nominated Walter
Hickel as Secretary of the Interior on December 11, 1968.
The Senate Committee on Interior and Insular Affairs seriously investigated his nomination because of concern for
his views in regard to conservation. He was finally confirmed on January 23, 1969 and assumed his office on
January 25. He was a member of the anti-pollution panel.
He backed a bill which required oil companies to clean
up offshore oil spills. In addition he wanted to have
pollution legislation for regulation of detergents, ve-
getable oils and other chemicals.

Secretary of the Interior Hickel also supported construction of the Alaska pipeline. He differed with some
aspects of President Richard Nixon's attitude with regard
to his relations with the youth. Hickel sent President
Nixon a letter on May 6, 1970 urging that he establish
communication with the youth. President Nixon asked for
Hickel's resignation on November 25, 1970. Walter was
named Alaskan of the Year in 1969 and received the DeSmet
medal from Gonzaga University.

Among his other activities since leaving the Cabinet
Walter Hickel has been a director of Western Airlines, a
member of the world advisory council of the International
Design Science Institute and a member of the committee on
scientific freedom and responsibility. He is also a
member of the Pioneers of Alaska and the Alaska Chamber
of Commerce. He received the Horatio Alger award in
1972.

Bibliography:
  Bremer, Howard F., ed. Richard M. Nixon, 1913-    .
Dobbs Ferry, N.Y.: Oceana Publications, Inc., 1975.
  Drury, Allen. Courage and Hesitation. Garden City,
N.Y.: Doubleday, 1972.
  Evans, Rowland, and Novack, Robert. Nixon in the
White House: The Frustration of Power. New York: Ran-
dom House, 1972.
  Spalding, Henry D. The Nixon Nobody Knows. New York:
Jonathan David, Pubs., Inc., 1972.
  Wills, Gary. Nixon Agonistes: The Crisis of the Self-
Made Man. Boston: Houghton Mifflin, 1971.

SECRETARY OF THE INTERIOR:

ROGERS CLARK BALLARD MORTON

Rogers C. B. Morton, Secretary of the Interior in the Cabinets of Presidents Richard M. Nixon and Gerald R. Ford, was born on September 14, 1914 in Louisville, Kentucky, the son of David C. and Mary (Ballard) Morton. He received his preliminary education at the Woodbury Fo Forest Preparatory School and then went to Yale University from which he was graduated with the Bachelor of Arts degree in political science and business in June 1937. Rogers worked for his father's milling business. He was married to Anne Jones on May 27, 1939. They have two children: David and Anne.

Rogers C. B. Morton joined the United States Army in 1941 as a private. He was eventually promoted to captain and served until the end of the Second World War in 1945. He then returned to Ballard and Ballard, his father's milling company, to help supervise its operations. He became president in October 1947, continuing until June 1951. The company then merged with Pillsbury in July 1951 and Rogers Morton became vice president of Pillsbury.

Rogers Morton was elected as a Republican to the United States House of Representatives from Maryland in 1962, serving in the Eighty-eighth to the Ninety-first Congresses from January 3, 1963 to January 3, 1971. He attended the 1968 Republican National Convention and supported Richard M. Nixon for President. Morton was elected chairman of the Republican National Committee in 1969 and continued in that capacity until 1971. He was also a member of the board of governors and the board of visitors of Washington College in Chestertown, Maryland. Morton has also been a director and member of the executive committee of the Civil Advisory Board Air Training command of the Air Force and director of Atlas Chemical Industries, Inc.

President Richard M. Nixon nominated Rogers C. B. Morton for the post of Secretary of the Interior to succeed Walter Hickel on December 11, 1970. Morton assumed his office on January 29, 1971. He delayed the decision to construct the Alaskan pipeline until further information concerning effects on the environment could be gathered. Morton eventually granted the permit for construction on May 11, 1972. When a federal court barred construction he appealed the decision in 1973. As the concern for oil grew, Secretary Morton promised that the Atlantic states would be consulted and given a role in deciding upon off-shore oil drilling.

Rogers C. B. Morton reorganized the Interior Department at the beginning of the second Nixon administration. He continued to serve under President Gerald R. Ford after the resignation of Richard M. Nixon on August 9, 1974. President Ford named Morton a member of the Economic Policy Board and the National Energy Board. In 1974 he urged decontrol of oil prices and supported an increase in the gasoline tax.

Bibliography:
   Bremer, Howard F., ed. Richard M. Nixon, 1913-____. Dobbs Ferry, N.Y.: Oceana Publications, Inc., 1975.
   Drury, Allen. Courage and Hesitation. Garden City, N.Y.: Doubleday, 1972.
   Evans, Rowland, and Novack, Robert. Nixon in the White House: The Frustration of Power. New York: Random House, 1972.
   Mankiewicz, Frank. Perfectly Clear. New York: Quadrangle, 1974.
   Rather, Dan. The Palace Guard. New York: Harper, 1974.
   Spalding, Henry D. The Nixon Nobody Knows. New York: Jonathan David, Pubs., Inc., 1972.
   Wills, Gary. Nixon Agonistes: The Crisis of the Self-Made Man. Boston: Houghton Mifflin, 1971.
   Witcover, Jules. The Resurrection of Richard Nixon. New York: Putnam, 1970.

## SECRETARY OF AGRICULTURE: CLIFFORD MORRIS HARDIN

Clifford M. Hardin, Secretary of Agriculture in the Cabinet of President Richard M. Nixon, was born on October 9, 1915 in Knightstown, Indiana, the son of James Alvin Hardin, a farmer, and Mabel (Macy) Hardin. After receiving his basic education in the local public schools Clifford went to Purdue University from which he was graduated with the Bachelor of Science degree in 1937. He was a teaching assistant at Purdue from 1933 to 1939 while studying for the Master of Science degree in agricultural economics which he received in 1939.

Clifford Hardin married Martha Love Wood on June 28, 1939. They have five children: Susan Carol, Clifford Wood, Cynthia Wood, Nancy Ann, and James Alvin. Clifford Hardin next attended the University of Chicago from 1939 to 1940 and then returned to Purdue University as a graduate assistant, receiving the Doctor of Philosophy degree in 1941.

Dr. Hardin was appointed an instructor at the University of Wisconsin in 1941 and was promoted to assistant professor of agricultural economics in 1942. He next went to Michigan State University in 1944 and was promoted to full professor as well as becoming chairman of the agricultural economics department in 1946. During the following year, 1947, Dr. Hardin was a member of the United States delegation to the International Conference of Agricultural Economists in England.

In 1948 Clifford M. Hardin was appointed assistant director of the agricultural experimental station at Nebraska University and then was its director from 1949 to 1953. In the latter year he was appointed dean of the Agricultural School, continuing until 1954 when he became chancellor of the University of Nebraska in which position he served until 1969. He became a trustee of Bankers Life Insurance Company of Nebraska in 1958. He became president of the American Association of State Universities and Land Grant Colleges in 1960 and was next chairman of the executive committee in 1961.

Dr. Clifford Hardin was named a trustee of the Rockefeller Foundation in 1961. He became chairman of the Omaha branch of the Federal Reserve Bank of Kansas City in 1962. President John F. Kennedy appointed Clifford Hardin a committee member to review the United States foreign aid program in December 1962. In 1963 he was a member of the President's Committee to Strengthen the Security of the Free World. He also served as a member of the Council of Higher Education in American Republics from 1963 to 1969. In addition he was appointed to the National Science Board in 1966 and continued until 1970. Hardin was also co-chairman of the Agriculture Department's task force assigned with the duty improving federal-state experimental relationships during 1968.

President-elect Richard M. Nixon nominated Dr. Clifford M. Hardin Secretary of Agriculture on December 11, 1968. Hardin assumed his office on January 22, 1969. He introduced food stamp reforms. Clifford also opposed a total ban on DDT. Hardin resigned from his office on November 11, 1971.

After leaving public office Dr. Clifford Hardin became vice chairman of the board of directors of Ralston-Purina Company of St. Louis, serving from 1969 to 1971. He became chairman of the board in the latter year. He also has been a chairman of the board of Ralston-Purina of Canada Ltd and Don Mills of Ontario, Canada since 1971. Among his other activities he has been a director of Bethlen Manufacturing Company and a member of the educational advisory committee of the W. K. Kellogg Foundation. He has also contributed his time as a member of International Volunteer Services, Inc. and the Overseas Development Council.

Bibliography:
Bremer, Howard F., ed. Richard M. Nixon, 1913-____. Dobbs Ferry, N.Y.: Oceana Publications, Inc., 1975.
Drury, Allen. Courage and Hesitation. Garden City, N.Y.: Doubleday, 1972.
Evans, Rowland, and Novack, Robert. Nixon in the White House: The Frustration of Power. New York: Random House, 1972.
Spalding, Henry D. The Nixon Nobody Knows. New York: Jonathan David, Pubs., Inc., 1972.

Wills, Gary. <u>Nixon</u> <u>Agonistes</u>: <u>The</u> <u>Crisis</u> <u>of</u> <u>the</u> <u>Self-</u>
<u>Made</u> <u>Man</u>.  Boston: Houghton Mifflin 1971.

SECRETARY OF AGRICULTURE: EARL LAUER BUTZ

Earl L. Butz, Secretary of Agriculture in the Cabinets
of Presidents Richard M. Nixon and Gerald R. Ford, was
born on July 3, 1909 in Albion, Indiana, the son of Herman Lee and Ada Tillie (Lauer) Butz.  After receiving
his basic education in the local schools Earl Butz went
to Purdue University from which he was graduated with
the Bachelor of Science in Agriculture degree in 1932.
He was a farmer during 1933.  He continued his studies
at Purdue and spent the summer of 1936 studying at the
University of Chicago.

Butz was a graduate research assistant in agricultural
economics at Purdue from 1934 to 1935.  He was next a research economist for the Federal Land Bank in Louisville
from 1935 to 1936.  Earl Butz received the Doctor of
Philosophy degree in 1937.  Earl married Mary Emma Powell
on December 22, 1937.  They have two children: William
Powell and Thomas Earl.

After receiving his doctorate Earl Butz became an instructor in agricultural economics at Purdue University
in 1937, continuing until 1939 when he was promoted to
assistant professor.  He was next an associate professor
from 1943 to 1946.  Butz also served on the research
staff of the National Bureau of Economic Research during
1944 and 1945.  In addition he was a research economist
for the Brookings Institute in 1944.  Butz was appointed
professor and chairman of the agricultural economics department at Purdue in 1946 and continued until 1954.

Among his other academic activities Earl Butz was a
lecturer at the School of Banking of the University of
the University of Wisconsin from 1946 to 1965.  He was also a lecturer at Rutgers University from 1950 to 1958.
In addition Earl Butz became a director of Standard Life
Insurance Company in 1951 and continued until 1971.  He
was appointed chairman of the United States delegation to
the FAO in Rome in 1955 and again in 1957.

Dr. Butz was selected dean of the Agricultural College
at Purdue in 1957, continuing in this post until 1967.
He became a trustee for the Foundation of American Agriculture in 1957 and remained on the board until 1971.
He was also a director of Ralston Purina Company of St.
Louis from 1958 to 1971.  In addition in 1960 he became
a director of International Minerals and Chemical Corporation of Chicago, continuing until 1971.  He was also a
member of the board of directors of the Farm Foundation
in Chicago and remained until 1970.  Butz served as a
trustee of the Nutrition Foundation beginning in 1967
and continuing until 1971.  He was made a director of
Stokely Van Camp Company in 1969 and continued until 1971.

Dr. Butz was a member of the White House Task Force on Foreign economic development from 1969 to 1970.

President Richard M. Nixon named Earl L. Butz Secretary of Agriculture to succeed Clifford M. Hardin on November 11, 1971. He assumed his office and was sworn in on December 2, 1971. He supported farm aid cuts and tried to work for a rollback in agricultural prices. He signed a United States-Soviet agricultural pact on June 19, 1973. Earl Butz continued in office under President Gerald R. Ford after the resignation of President Richard M. Nixon on August 9, 1974. President Ford named Earl Butz a member of the Economic Policy Board in 1974. Among his other duties the Secretary was named a member of the Council on Wage and Price Stability. He has been a controversial member of the administration, maintaining that prices will eventually find their own level.

Bibliography:
Bremer, Howard F., ed. Richard M. Nixon, 1913-    . Dobbs Ferry, N.Y.: Oceana Publications, Inc., 1975.
Evans, Rowland, and Novack, Robert. Nixon in the White House: The Frustration of Power. New York: Random House, 1972.
Mankiewicz, Frank. Perfectly Clear. New York: Quadrangle, 1974.

SECRETARY OF COMMERCE: MAURICE HOBART STANS

Maurice H. Stans, Secretary of Commerce in the Cabinet of President Richard M. Nixon, was born on March 22, 1908 in Shakopee, Minnesota, the son of J. Hubert and Mathilda (Nyssen) Stans. After receiving his basic education in the local public schools and at Shakopee High School Maurice moved to Chicago where he worked as a stenographer to support himself while studying at Northwestern University from 1925 to 1928. He then moved to New York and attended Columbia University from 1928 to 1930. He also became an office boy in the accounting firm of Alexander Grant and Company in 1928. He rose to become a partner in 1931, remaining until 1945. He became an executive partner in 1940 and continued with the company until 1955.

Maurice married Kathleen Carmody on September 7, 1933. They have four children: Steven, Maureen, Theodore, and Terrell. Maurice Stans became a treasurer and director of Moore Corporation, a manufacturer of stoves, in 1938. He was chairman of the board from 1942 to 1945. Among his other activities Maurice Stans founded the Stans Foundation in 1940 to aid charitable institutions. He became a consultant for the United States House of Representatives appropriations committee in 1953 and in the same year was appointed financial consultant to Postmaster General Arthur Summerfield. continuing in this post until

1955.
President Dwight D. Eisenhower appointed Maurice Stans
deputy postmaster general in September 1955. He remained
in this post until 1957. He next became deputy director
of the Bureau of the Budget in 1957 and was appointed its
director on March 13, 1958. He served with the Bureau until 1961.

Mr. Stans left public office at the end of the Eisenhower administration to become president of the Western
Bank Corporation in Los Angeles, continuing with the
company until 1962. During these two years Maurice was
also a syndicated columnist. The United States Chamber
of Commerce granted Stans its Great Living American Award
in 1961. He continued his business career as senior
partner of William R. Staats and Company from 1963 to 1964
and was next president of William R. Staats Co., Inc.
during 1964 and 1965. In the latter year Maurice Stans
became president of Glore Forgan, William R. Staats, Inc.
of New York, continuing until 1969. He was chairman of
the Nixon Finance Committee in 1968 and chairman of the
Republican National Finance Committee during 1968 and
1969. Stans was also a director of the National Association of Manufacturers from 1968 to 1969.

President-elect Richard M. Nixon named Maurice H. Stans
Secretary of Commerce on December 11, 1968. He was sworn
in and assumed his office on January 22, 1969. He headed
a United States trade commission to Europe in April 1969.
Stans made plans for federal aid to businessmen and development of a model cities program. He also defended
the Alaskan pipeline. As head of the Commerce Department
Stans was a member of the National Commission on Productivity. In July 1971 he issued a report which favored
adoption of the metric system.

Maurice Stans resigned from his post at the Commerce
Department on January 27, 1972 to aid in the reelection
campaign of President Richard M. Nixon. As a result of
his campaign work he was linked to the raid on the Democratic Headquarters in the Watergate complex. The charges
were made, and Stans denied GOP funding. Maurice was
named a defendant in the Democratic suit relating to the
break-in and was connected with a secret Republican fund
on October 26, 1972 by Clark MacGregor. Stans was subsequently indicted on charges of involvement in the coverup
of the Watergate break-in and found guilty in December
1974.

Bibliography:
Bremer, Howard F., ed. Richard M. Nixon, 1913-____.
Dobbs Ferry, N.Y.: Oceana Publications, Inc., 1975.
Drury, Allen. Courage and Hesitation. Garden City,
N.Y.: Doubleday, 1972.
Evans, Rowland, and Novack, Robert. Nixon in the
White House: The Frustration of Power. New York: Ran-

dom House, 1972.

McCloskey, Paul W.  Truth and Untruth: Political Deceit in America.  New York: Simon and Shuster, Inc., 1972.

Mankiewicz, Frank.  Perfectly Clear.  New York: Quadrangle, 1974.

Rather, Dan.  The Palace Guard.  New York: Harper, 1974.

Spalding, Henry D.  The Nixon Nobody Knows.  New York: Jonathan David, Pubs., Inc., 1972.

Wills, Gary.  Nixon Agonistes: The Crisis of the Self-Made Man.  Boston: Houghton Mifflin, 1971.

Witcover, Jules.  The Ressurection of Richard Nixon.  New York: Putnam, 1970.

## SECRETARY OF COMMERCE: PETER G. PETERSON

Peter G. Peterson, Secretary of Commerce in the Cabinet of President Richard M. Nixon, was born on June 5, 1926 in Kearney, Nebraska, the son of George and Venet (Paul) Peterson.  After receiving his basic education Peter studied at the Massachusetts Institute of Technology during 1944 and 1945.  He then went to Northwestern University from which he was graduated with the Bachelor of Science degree in 1947.  He worked for Market Facts, Inc. in Chicago as a market analyst from 1947 to 1949 and was promoted to associate director in 1949.  He continued in this position until 1951.  In the latter year Mr. Peterson received the Master of Business Administration degree from the University of Chicago.  He became an executive vice president of Market Facts, Inc., remaining in this post until 1953.

Peter G. Peterson married Sally Hornbogen in May 1953.  They have four children: John Scott, James S., David, and Holly.  He also served on the Citizens for Eisenhower Committee in 1952.  Mr. Peterson was appointed a director of marketing services of McCann-Erickson in 1953 and was promoted to vice president in 1954.  He was general manager of the Chicago office from 1955 to 1957 and then a director and assistant to the president, charged with coordinating the services of the regional offices from 1957 to 1958.  He was named Outstanding Young Man of Chicago in 1955 by the Junior Chamber of Commerce.

Peter Peterson became a vice president and director of Bell and Howell Company, continuing until 1961 when he was elected president.  In the same year he was named Outstanding Young Man of the Year by the United States Junior Chamber of Commerce.  Mr. Peterson became president and chief executive officer of the Bell and Howell Company in 1963, remaining in these positions until 1968 when he was named chairman of the board and chief executive officer.  He resigned his position in 1970.

Among his other business activities Mr. Peterson has been a director of the First National Bank of Chicago and

the Illinois Bell Telephone Company.  He was also involved in various public services as chairman of the
Illinois Planning Committee, a trustee of the Cancer Research Foundation, the Salk Institute for Biological
Research, the Brookings Institution, and the Committee
for Economic Development.  He has also been on the board
of Directors of National Educational Television, chairman
of the council of medical and biological research and a
member of the board of trustees of the University of
Chicago.

Peter G. Peterson was appointed an assistant to President Richard M. Nixon for foreign economic policy in 1970
and continued in this post until 1972.  He was also executive director of the Council on International Economic
Policy in 1972.  President Richard M. Nixon nominated
Peter G. Peterson as Secretary of Commerce on January 27,
1972.  He was confirmed and assumed his office on February 21.  Among his activities as head of the Commerce
Department Mr. Peterson signed the United States-Soviet
grain agreement on July 8, 1972 and the Soviet Trade
Pact on October 18, 1972.  He was named to the newly established Council on Economic Policy on December 1, 1972.

President Richard M. Nixon replaced Peter G. Peterson
as Secretary of Commerce on December 6, 1972 and gave
him a special assignment to investigate how the United
States could improve coordination of its economic policy
with the major trading partners in Europe and Asia.  He
has returned to his business interests.

Bibliography:
Bremer, Howard F., ed.  Richard M. Nixon, 1913-    .
Dobbs Ferry, N.Y.: Oceana Publications, Inc., 1975.
Drury, Allen.  Courage and Hesitation.  Garden City,
N.Y.: Doubleday, 1972.
Evans, Rowland, and Novack, Robert.  Nixon in the
White House: The Frustration of Power.  New York: Ran-
dom House, 1972.
Mazo, Earl, and Hess, Stephan.  Nixon: A Political Por-
trait.  New York, 1969.
Spalding, Henry D.  The Nixon Nobody Knows.  New York:
Jonathan David, Pubs., Inc., 1972.

SECRETARY OF COMMERCE: FREDERICK BAILY DENT

Frederick B. Dent, Secretary of Commerce in the Cabinets of Presidents Richard M. Nixon and Gerald R. Ford,
was born on August 17, 1922 in Cape May, New Jersey, the
son of Magruder and Edith (Baily) Dent.  He received his
basic education at St. Paul's School from which he was
graduated in 1940.  He then went to Yale University,
graduating with the Bachelor of Arts degree in 1943.
Frederick married Mildred C. Harrison on March 11, 1944.
They have five children: Frederick Baily, Mildred Hutche-

son, Pauline Harrison, Diana Gwynn, and Magruder Harrison.

After graduating from college Frederick Dent entered the United States Naval Reserve in 1943 and served until 1946. He then became a director of Joshua L. Baily and Company, Inc. of New York City in 1946, continuing with the firm until 1947. He next became president of Mayfair Mills in Arcadia, South Carolina in 1947 and remained with the firm until 1972. Among his other business activities Mr. Dent was a director of the General Electric Company, the South Carolina National Bank, the Crompton Company, Scott Paper Company, the Mutual Life Insurance Company of New York.

Mr. Dent is also a member of and a director of the South Carolina Textile Manufacturers Association and the American Textile Manufacturers Institute. He was also involved in various public service activities such as the Spartanburg County Planning and Development Commission and a trustee of the Institute of Textile Technology and the Spartanburg Day School. In addition he was a member of the Business Council from 1960 to 1972.

President Richard M. Nixon appointed Frederick B. Dent Secretary of Commerce to replace Peter G. Peterson on December 6, 1972. He was confirmed by the United States Senate and assumed his office on January 18, 1973. As head of the Commerce Department Mr. Peterson is a member of the Council on Economic Policy. He developed and instituted the "SavEnergy" plan in October 1973. Secretary Dent continued to serve under President Gerald R. Ford after the resignation of Richard M. Nixon on August 9, 1974. President Ford appointed Frederick B. Dent a member of the Council of Wage and Price Stability in August 1974 and a member of the Economic Policy Board in September. He still continues to be active in commercial activities of the nation.

Bibliography:
  Bremer, Howard F., ed. Richard M. Nixon, 1913-____.
Dobbs Ferry, N.Y.: Oceana Publications, Inc., 1975.
  Mankiewicz, Frank. Perfectly Clear. New York: Quadrangle, 1974.

## SECRETARY OF LABOR: GEORGE PRATT SHULTZ

Refer to the biographical sketch of George P. Shultz under Secretary of the Treasury, page 772.

## SECRETARY OF LABOR: JAMES DAY HODGSON

James D. Hodgson, Secretary of Labor in the Cabinet of President Richard M. Nixon, was born on December 3, 1915 in Dawson, Minnesota, the son of Fred Arthur Hodgson, a lumberyard owner, and Casahora M. (Day) Hodgson. After receiving his basic education James went to the University of Minnesota and was graduated with the Bachelor of Arts degree in 1938. He then pursued graduate studies at the University of Minnesota from 1938 to 1940. At the same time he became an employment supervisor for the Minnesota Department of Employment, serving from 1938 to 1941. Mr. Hodgson then went to work as a personnel clerk for Lockheed Aircraft Corporation in 1941.

James D. Hodgson joined the United States Navy during the Second World War as an intelligence officer in the Pacific, serving as a lieutenant from 1943 to 1946. James married Maria Derend on August 24, 1943. They have two children: Nancy Ruth and Frederick Jesse. At the end of World War II James Hodgson returned to Lockheed Aircraft, continuing with the firm until 1969. He eventually became corporate vice president for industrial relations in 1968. He also served as a member of the Los Angeles Labor-Management Executive Committee and from 1965 to 1967 as community adviser for the Industrial Relations Institute of the University of California.

President Richard M. Nixon named James V. Hodgson undersecretary of Labor in January 1969. When George Shultz resigned President Nixon appointed James D. Hodgson Secretary of Labor on June 10, 1970. Shultz was a member of the National Commission on Productivity. In April 1971 he announced establishment of a White House Stabilization Committee and also developed a job drive for Vietnam Veterans in June. Mr. Hodgson resigned from his position on November 29, 1972, indicating that he might consider an international post. In 1973 he became chairman of the Presidential Committee on National Health Costs and Policy.

Bibliography:
Bremer, Howard F., ed. Richard M. Nixon, 1913-____. Dobbs Ferry, N.Y.: Oceana Publications, Inc., 1975.
Drury, Allen. Courage and Hesitation. Garden City, N.Y.: Doubleday, 1972.
Evans, Rowland, and Novack, Robert. Nixon in the White House: The Frustration of Power. New York: Random House, 1972.
Mankiewicz, Frank. Perfectly Clear. New York: Quadrangle, 1974.
Spalding, Henry D. The Nixon Nobody Knows. New York: Jonathan David, Pubs., Inc., 1972.

## SECRETARY OF LABOR: PETER JOSEPH BRENNAN

Peter J. Brennan, Secretary of Labor in the Cabinets of Presidents Richard M. Nixon and Gerald R. Ford, was born on May 24, 1918 in New York City, the son of John J. Brennan, an iron worker, and Agnes (Moore) Brennan. His father died in 1921, and his mother raised the family

by working in a factory. Peter received his basic education in the New York public schools and was graduated
from Commerce High School. While attending City College
on a part time basis Peter J. Brennan worked as an apprentice painter. He worked for Macy's Department Store
for several years, applying the finishing touches to
display rooms. Peter married Josephine Brickley in 1940.
They have three children: Peter J., Jr., Joan, and Peggy.
    Peter Brennan was a member of Local 1456 of the Pain-
ters, Decorators, and Paperhangers of America. He became
a journeyman painter in 1944. Peter joined the United
States Navy in 1944, serving on a submarine in the Pacific. He was discharged with the rank of petty officer
second class. After the war Peter Brennan returned to
his painting work. He was also acting business agent
of Local 1456. He was officially appointed to the post
when his predecessor died in 1947.
    Peter J. Brennan continued his work in union affairs
and indicated a desire to rise in administrative rank.
Peter became maintenance chairman of the Building Construction Trades Council of Greater New York in 1951.
He was able to gain a reputation and influence by volun-
teering for many assignements. Peter was elected president of the Building and Construction Trades Council in
1957 when the former president Howard M. Spedon died.
Peter Brennan continued in this post until 1973. He was
elected president of the New York State Building and
Construction Trades Council in 1958 and served until
1973.
    Peter Brennan gained a reputation during the 1960's
for his opposition to the hiring of blacks and Puerto
Ricans in the building trades, which he denied. As a
result of attacks by various civil rights organizations
including the National Association for the Advancement
of Colored People, Brennan began to work to end discrimination in the building trades in 1963. He became
ex-officio head of a committee to screen black appli-
cants. The committee was not as successful as many had
hoped.
    In May 1970 when students throughout the country were
demonstrating against American involvement in Cambodia
and the deaths of several protesting students at Kent
State University in Ohio, Peter Brennan organized his
"hard hats" to march to New York City Hall in opposition
to the student demonstrators. Brennan and other prowar
labor leaders were invited to the White House by President Richard M. Nixon. Mr. Brennan began to support
the President and urged labor to vote for Nixon's reelection in 1972.
    Among his other activities Mr. Brennan has been a for-
mer vice-president of the New York State AFL-CIO. He was
a member of the National Advisory Committee for the Education of Disadvantaged Children, the New York State Job

Development Advisory Committee, and the Advisory Board
on Prevailing Wages for Public Works in New York State.
He has received many awards in recognition of his services.

President Richard M. Nixon appointed Peter J. Brennan
Secretary of Labor to succeed James D. Hodgson on November 29, 1972.  Before he officially assumed his post
Mr. Brennan was able to gain a 90-day cooling-off period
in the six-week strike against the Long Island Railroad
which he announced on January 17, 1973.  The United States
Senate confirmed his nomination on January 31, 1973, and
he assumed his office.  In April 1973 Secretary Brennan
indicated his approval of the railroad industry's 18-
month contract.  On April 10, 1973 Mr. Brennan presented
the Administration proposals to raise the federal minimum wage, while setting a lower minimum for youth.  This
las was attacked by other labor leaders.

Although he had urged President Nixon to sign the minimum wage bill, he defended the President's veto in
September 1973.  He criticized the AFL-CIO support of
impeachment of the President on November 22, 1973.  In
February 1974 Secretary Brennan promised that federal
money would be available for summer jobs for youth.  He
also indicated that some compromise on a minimum wage
bill was possible.  Mr. Brennan has continued to serve
under President Gerald Ford after the resignation of
Richard M. Nixon on August 9, 1974.

President Gerald Ford named Peter J. Brennan a member
of the new Council on Wage and Price Stability on August
29, 1974, and the Economic Policy Board on September 28.
Secretary Brennan presented plans for development of a
public service job program on September 1.  He has
continued to work to aid in management of labor affairs.

Bibliography:
  Bremer, Howard F., ed.  Richard M. Nixon, 1913-____ .
Dobbs Ferry, N.Y.: Oceana Publications, Inc., 1975.
  Mankiewicz, Frank.  Perfectly Clear.  New York: Quad-
rangle, 1974.
  New York Times. November 30, 1972, page 37.
  Time. December 11, 1972. vol. 100, page 20.

SECRETARY OF HEALTH, EDUCATION, AND WELFARE:

ROBERT HUTCHINSON FINCH

Robert H. Finch, Secretary of Health, Education, and
Welfare in the Cabinet of President Rochard M. Nixon,
was born on October 9, 1925 in Tempe, Arizona, the son
of Robert L. Finch, member of the State Legislature, and
Gladys (Hutchinson) Finch.  He moved with his family when
he was young to Inglewood, California.  He attended the
public schools there, receiving his basic education.

Robert joined the United States Marine Corps during
World War II and became a first lieutenant.  He then went
to Occidental College in Los Angeles from which he was
graduated with the Bachelor of Arts degree in Political
Science in 1947.

Robert Finch married Carol Crothers on February 14,
1946.  They have four children: Maureen, Kevin, Priscilla,
and Cathleen.  Robert soon became interested in politics
and went to Washington where he served as an administrative aid to Representative Poulson.  In 1948 Robert Finch
edited the National Young Republican Federation newspaper
and attended the Republican National Convention.  Robert
Finch went to the University of South California law
school from which he received the LL.B. degree in 1951
and was admitted to the bar in the same year.

Robert H. Finch began practicing law in 1951 with the
law firm which eventually became Finch, Bell, Duitsman
and Margulis and continued with the firm until 1966.  Robert also served as a first lieutenant during the Korean
War from 1951 to 1953.  He was unsuccessful as a Republican candidate for Congress during both 1952 and 1954.
He returned to his law practice after having served in
the Korean War.  Finch served as a trustee and counsel
of Palos Verdes College from 1953 to 1956 and as a member
of the board of directors of the Centinela Valley YMCA
from 1954 to 1958.

Robert H. Finch was vice chairman of the Republican
Central Committee of Los Angeles County from 1954 to 1956
and chairman of the committee from 1956 to 1958.  He attended the Republican National Convention in 1956.  During
the same year Finch helped to establish and was first
president of the Palos Verdes Savings and Loan Association, remaining in that capacity until 1958.  Robert
Finch served as administrative assistant to Vice President Richard M. Nixon from 1958 to 1960.  Finch attended
the Republican National Convention in 1960 and served as
campaign director for Richard Nixon's presidential campaign.  He returned to his legal practice.

Among his other activities Robert Finch was a member of
the advisory board of Marymount College from 1960 to 1963.
He also served on the advisory committee of the Caro
Foundation from 1962 to 1968.  He continued his political
activities as chairman of George Murphy's campaign for
the United States Senate in 1964.  Finch became a trustee
of Occidental College in 1965, serving until 1969.  Mr.
Finch was elected lieutenant governor of California on
November 8, 1966 and served from 1967 to 1969.  He was
president of the California Senate, a trustee of the
California State Colleges and a regent of the University
of California while serving in the state government.
Finch was granted the honorary LL.D. degree by Occidental
College in 1967, Lincoln University in 1968, and the Uni-
versity of California at Los Angeles in 1967.

President-elect Richard M. Nixon appointed Robert H.
Finch Secretary of Health, Education, and Welfare on
December 11, 1968.  He assumed his office on January 23,
1969.  Secretary Finch cut off aid to several Southern
school districts which had failed to comply with desegregation decisions, promising also to end segregation
throughout the nation.  He was a member of the Cabinet
level task force to aid school districts in desegregation.
Mr. Finch announced establishment of a commission to study pesticides and their effects on humans.  In addition
he became a member of the Richard Nixon Foundation in
1969.
On June 9, 1969 Secretary Robert Finch announced the
licensing of the manufacture and distribution of the
vaccine against rubella.  He also set up strict anti-
pollution regulations.  In addition Secretary Finch recommended that an optional preventive care program for persons covered by medicare and medicaid.  As Secretary of
Health, Education, and Welfare Robert Finch was a member
of the Domestic Council, the Advisory committee on Intergovernmental Relations, the Cabinet Committees on Education and on Voluntary Action.  In addition he was
chairman of the President's Committee on Children and
Youth as well as the Air Quality Advisory Board, and the
Federal Radiation Council.
Robert H. Finch resigned his post as Secretary of
Health, Education, and Welfare on June 6, 1970 because of
various physical strains.  He was then appointed a counselor to the President and served in that capacity until
1972.  He returned to private life and the practice of
law as a partner in the firm of McKenna, Fitting, and
Finch in 1972 and has continued in that capacity since
that time.

Bibliography:
    Bremer, Howard F., ed.  Richard M. Nixon, 1913-____.
Dobbs Ferry, N.Y.: Oceana Publications, Inc., 1975.
    Drury, Allen.  Courage and Hesitation.  Garden City,
N.Y.: Doubleday, 1972.
    Evans, Rowland, and Novack, Robert.  Nixon in the
White House: The Frustration of Power.  New York: Ran-
dom House, 1972.
    McGinnis, Joe.  The Selling of the President, 1968.
New York: Trident Press, 1969.
    Mankiewicz, Frank.  Perfectly Clear.  New York: Quad-
rangle, 1974.
    Spalding, Henry D.  The Nixon Nobody Knows.  New York:
Jonathan David, Pubs., Inc., 1972.
    Time.  December 13, 1968.  vol. 92.
    Wills, Gary.  Nixon Agonistes: The Crisis of the Self-
Made Man.  Boston: Houghton Mifflin, 1971.

SECRETARY OF HEALTH, EDUCATION, AND WELFARE:

ELLIOT LEE RICHARDSON

Refer to the biographical sketch of Elliot L. Richardson under Secretary of Defense, page 777.

SECRETARY OF HEALTH, EDUCATION, AND WELFARE:

CASPAR WILLARD WEINBERGER

Caspar W. Weinberger, Secretary of Health, Education, and Welfare in the Cabinets of Presidents Richard M. Nixon and Gerald R. Ford, was born on August 18, 1917 in San Francisco, California, the son of Herman and Cerise Carpenter (Hampson) Weinberger. After receiving his basic education Caspar went to Harvard University from which he was graduated with the Bachelor of Arts degree summa cum laude. He then went to Harvard Law School, receiving the LL.B. degree in 1941. Caspar married Jane Dalton on August 16, 1942. They have three children: Arlin, Cerise, and Caspar Willard, Jr.

Caspar W. Weinberger entered the United States Army as a private in the infantry in 1941 and served for the duration of the war until 1945, having risen to the rank of captain. He was decorated with the Bronze Star. After being discharged from the Army Caspar Weinberger became a law clerk for United States Judge William E. Orr in which capacity he served from 1945 to 1947. Caspar began practicing law with the legal firm of Heller, Ehrman, White and McAuliffe in 1947.

Caspar soon became active in Republican political activities. He was elected to the California legislature from the 21st District, serving from 1952 to 1958. He became vice chairman of the California Republican Committee in 1960 and continued until 1962 when he became chairman. He remained in that capcity until 1964. He continued his public service in 1967 as chairman of the Committee on California Government Organization and Economics, serving until 1968. Caspar was next director of finance of California from 1968 to 1969.

President Richard M. Nixon appointed Caspar Weinberger chairman of the Federal Trade Commission in 1970 and then deputy director of the Office of Management and the Budget. He remained in that post from 1970 to 1972 when he became director of the Office of Management and the Budget in May. President Richard Nixon nominated Caspar W. Weinberger for the post of Secretary of Health, Education, and Welfare on November 28, 1972. He was confirmed by the United States Senate on February 8, 1973 and then assumed his office. He continued to serve under President Gerald R. Ford after the resignation of Richard M. Nixon on August 9, 1974. Secretary Weinberger urged de-

velopment of reforms in the welfare structure and opposed
gas rationing.  He vigorously supported the Nixon Administration health bill and further integration of
schools in the North.  President Gerald Ford named Caspar
Weinberger a member of the Economic Policy Board on
September 28, 1974.  The Secretary is still continuing
his active leadership of the Department of Health, Education, and Welfare.

Bibliography:
    Bremer, Howard F., ed.  Richard M. Nixon, 1913-    .
Dobbs Ferry, N.Y.: Oceana Publications, Inc., 1975.
    Drury, Allen.  Courage and Hesitation.  Garden City,
N.Y.: Doubleday, 1972.
    Evans, Rowland, and Novack, Robert.  Nixon in the
White House: The Frustration of Power.  New York: Ran-
dom House, 1972.
    Mankiewicz, Frank.  Perfectly Clear.  New York: Quad-
rangle, 1974.
    New York Times.

SECRETARY OF HOUSING AND URBAN DEVELOPMENT:

GEORGE WILCKEN ROMNEY

    George W. Romney, Secretary of Housing and Urban De-
velopment in the Cabinet of President Richard M. Nixon,
was born on July 8, 1907 in Chihuahua, Mexico, the son of
Gaskell Romney, a contractor, and Anna (Pratt) Romney.
While receiving his basic education he began working at
the age of 11 as a sugar harvester and later found employment as a lath and plaster workman.  He then studied at
Latter Day Saints University in Salt Lake City from 1922
to 1926.  Romney was a Mormon missionary in Scotland and
England from 1927 to 1928.  When he returned to the United States George went to the University of Utah in 1929
and then to George Washington University from 1929 to
1930 while he was a tariff specialist for United States
Senator David I. Walsh.
    George W. Romney became an apprentice of the Aluminum
Company of America in 1930 and then a salesman in Los
Angeles in 1931.  George married Lenore La Fount on July
2, 1931.  They have four children: Lynn, Jane, Scott,
and Willard.  Mr. Romney next became the Washington representative of the Aluminum Company of America and the
Aluminum Ware Association in 1932, continuing until 1938.
During this period he was also a member of the Labor-
Management Commission.  In addition he was president of
the Washington Trade Associations Executives during 1937
and 1938.
    In 1939 George Romney became Detroit manager of the Auto-
mobile Manufacturers Association and continued in this

capacity until 1941.  He was then general manager of the
association from 1942 to 1948.  He was also president of
the Detroit Trade Association in 1941.  George Romney
was also active in government service during the Second
World War, serving as a management member of the War
Manpower Commission and was the managing director of the
Automotive Council War Production Board from 1942 to
1945.  In addition from 1944 to 1947 Mr. Romney was director of the American Trade Association Executives, and
was also a managing director of the National Automobile
Golden Jubilee Committee in 1946.  He was named United
States employer delegate to the Metal Trades Industry
Conferences in 1946, continuing until 1949.

George W. Romney became vice president of the Nash-
Kelvinator Corporation in 1950 and served until 1953 when
he became executive vice president for the year 1953-54
and director of the company from 1953 to 1955.  He was
president, chairman of the board, and general manager
of American Motors Corporation from 1954 to 1962.  Romney
was elected Republican governor of Michigan in 1962 and
served in that office from 1963 to 1968.  In the latter
year he was for a while a candidate for the Republican
nomination for President but withdrew before the convention.

President-elect Richard M. Nixon named George Romney
Secretary of Housing and Urban Development on December
11, 1968.  Romney assumed his office on January 22, 1969.
As Secretary Mr. Romney revised and reorganized the Model
Cities program giving additional power to the mayors and
encouraging the involvement of state governments and private interests.  In addition he developed a program
called "Operation Breakthrough" for additional low cost
housing for the poor in 1969 and continued to foster this
program during 1970.  Among other problems which Mr.
Romney faced was the rising home mortgage interest rates.

George Romney resigned from his post as Secretary of
Housing and Urban Development on November 27, 1972.  After leaving the Cabinet in 1972 Mr. Romney became chairman and cief executive officer of the National Center
for Voluntary Action and has continued to serve in this
capacity.

Bibliography:
   Angel, D. Duane. <u>Romney: A Political Biography</u>.  Jeri-
cho, N.Y.: The Exposition Press, 1967.
   Bremer, Howard F., ed. <u>Richard M. Nixon, 1913-    </u>.
Dobbs Ferry, N.Y.: Oceana Publications, Inc., 1975.
   Drury, Allen. <u>Courage and Hesitation.</u>  Garden City,
N.Y.: Doubleday, 1972.
   Evans, Rowland, and Novack, Robert. <u>Nixon in the
White House: The Frustration of Power.</u>  New York: Ran-
dom House, 1972.
   Gollan, Antoni E.  <u>Romney Behind the Image</u>.  Arling-

lington, Va.: Crestwood Books, 1967.

Harris, T. George. Romney's Way; A Man and an Idea. Englewood Cliffs, N.J.: Prentice-Hall, 1967.

Mollenhoff, Clara R. George Romney: Mormon in Politics. Des Moines, Iowa: Meredith Press, 1967.

Mankiewicz, Frank. Perfectly Clear. New York: Quadrangle, 1974.

## SECRETARY OF HOUSING AND URBAN DEVELOPMENT:

### JAMES THOMAS LYNN

James T. Lynn, Secretary of Housing and Urban Development in the Cabinets of Presidents Richard M. Nixon and Gerald R. Ford, was born on February 27, 1927 in Cleveland, Ohio, the son of Fred R. and Dorothea Estelle (Petersen) Lynn. James received his basic education in the Euclid, Ohio public schools and was graduated from Euclid Central High School in 1944. He next attended Adelbert College of Western Reserve University (now Case Western Reserve University).

James entered the United States Naval Reserve in 1945 as a seaman first class. He was discharged in 1946 with the specialist rank of ETM2C. James then returned to college where he majored in economics and received the Bachelor of Arts degree summa cum laude in 1948. He next studied at Harvard Law School from which he was graduated with the LL.B. degree magna cum laude in 1951. He was admitted to the bar and began his legal practice with the Cleveland firm of Jones, Day, Cockley and Revevis. James dealt with various aspects of corporate and business law, becoming a partner in 1960. James married Joan Miller on June 5, 1954. They have three children: Marjorie, Peter, and Sarah.

President Richard M. Nixon learned of James' interest in government service and appointed James T. Lynn general counsel to the Department of Commerce in which post he served from March 1969 to April 1971. At that time he was appointed Undersecretary of Commerce. James accompanied Secretary of Commerce Peter G. Peterson to Moscow in July 1972 to negotiate the United States-Soviet trade agreement which the Soviet Union signed in October 1972.

President Richard M. Nixon nominated James T. Lynn as Secretary of Housing and Urban Development to succeed George Romney on December 5, 1972. The United States Senate confirmed his appointment on January 31, 1973, and he assumed his office. Secretary Lynn helped to draft the five-year "Better Communities" bill which President Nixon submitted to Congress on April 19, 1973. The bill called for revenue sharing of funds beginning with $2.3 billion under a formula which favored small cities and suburban

counties. It replaced the departments various grants
with block grants to communities for programs of their
own choice. Reaction to this proposal was mixed.

On November 2, 1973 Secretary of Housing and Urban Development James T. Lynn announced that his department
would approve funding for 70,000 new apartments. He indicated that this was only an interim step and was not
a retreat from the administration's intention to phase
out many programs. In order to stimulate the housing
industry Secretary Lynn announced in early 1974 that the
government would reduce the allowable interest rate
on Federal Housing Authority (FHA) and Veterans Administration (VA) mortgages from 8.50 to 8.25 percent. In
addition the government was committing $6.6 billion
dollars for construction of 200,000 units in order
to push down mortgage interest rates. The mortgage interest rate was eventually put back to 8.50 percent.

James T. Lynn continued to serve as Secretary of Housing and Urban Development under President Gerald R.
Ford after the resignation of Richard M. Nixon on August
9, 1974. President Ford named Lynn a member of the
Economic Policy Board on September 28, 1974.

Bibliography:
Bremer, Howard F., ed. Richard M. Nixon, 1913-____.
Dobbs Ferry, N.Y.: Oceana Publications, Inc., 1975.
Evans, Rowland, and Novack, Robert. Nixon in the
White House: The Frustration of Power. New York: Ran-
dom House, 1972.
Mankiewicz, Frank. Perfectly Clear. New York: Quad-
rangle, 1974.
New York Times. December 6, 1972, p. 28.

### SECRETARY OF TRANSPORTATION: JOHN ANTHONY VOLPE

John A. Volpe, Secretary of Transportation in the Cabinet of President Richard M. Nixon, was born on December 8, 1908 in Wakefield, Massachusetts, the son of Vito
and Filomena (Benedetto) Volpe. After receiving his
basic education he went to Malden High School in Boston.
John A. Volpe was employed as a journeyman plastere from
1926 to 1928. In the latter year he began his studies
at the Wentworth Institute. After graduating from the
school in 1930 John became a timekeeper of a residential
and commercial construction firm, eventually becoming
assistant superintendent of construction.

John Volpe established the John A. Volpe Construction
Company in March 1933 and served as its president until
1960. John married Jennie Benedetto on June 18, 1934.
They have two children: Jean and John Anthony, Jr. During the Second World War John Volpe served in the United
States Navy as a lieutenant with the Civil Engineer Corps
from 1943 to 1945.

After the war Volpe became active in the Republican
Party.  In 1950 he was elected deputy chairman of the
Massachusetts Republican Committee, continuing until
1953.  He was an alternate delegate to the 1952 Republican National Convention.  John A. Volpe was appointed
to the Massachusetts Commission of Public Works in 1953
and served in this capacity until 1956.  President Dwight
D. Eisenhower named Volpe the first federal highway administrator in 1956.  He remained in this office until
1957.  In 1960 he became chairman of the board of the
John A. Volpe Construction Company and remained in that
post until 1969.

John Volpe was elected governor of Massachusetts in
1960.  He served one term from 1961 to 1963 and was defeated for reelection in 1962.  He successfully ran for
the post of governor again in 1966 and served from 1967
to 1969.  Volpe was chairman of the National Governors
Conference from 1967 to 1968.

President-elect Richard M. Nixon nominated John A.
Volpe for the post of Secretary of Transportation on
December 11, 1968.  Volpe assumed his office on January
22, 1969.  While in the Cabinet he proposed a mass transit program to be financed by Congressional authoriza-
tions for a five-year period.  He was a supporter of
Vice President Spiro T. Agnew's criticism of dissenters.
During the 1971 controversy over the supersonic transport plane Secretary of Transportation Volpe insisted
upon its value and feasibility, urging that it be developed and put into commercial operation.  He supported
state no-fault automobile insurance programs.  In 1969
John Volpe was decorated with the Knight of Malta and
the Italian Knight of the Grand Cross Order of Merit.
John A. Volpe resigned from his office on December 7,
1972 and was named Ambassador to Italy.  He remains in
this diplomatic post.

Bibliography:
  Bremer, Howard F., ed.  Richard M. Nixon, 1913-____.
Dobbs Ferry, N.Y.: Oceana Publications, Inc., 1975.
  Drury, Allen.  Courage and Hesitation.  Garden City,
N.Y.: Doubleday, 1972.
  Evans, Rowland, and Novack, Robert.  Nixon in the
White House: The Frustration of Power.  New York: Ran-
dom House, 1972.
  Mankiewicz, Frank.  Perfectly Clear.  New York: Quad-
rangle, 1974.
  Mazo, Earl, and Hess, Stephan.  Nixon: A Political
Portrait.  New York, 1969.
  New York Times.

SECRETARY OF TRANSPORTATION:

CLAUDE STOUT BRINEGAR

Claude S. Brinegar, Secretary of Transportation in
the Cabinets of Presidents Richard M. Nixon and
Gerald R. Ford, was born on December 16, 1926, the son
of Claude Leroy and Lyle (Rawies) Stout Brinegar. After
receiving his basic education Claude Brinegar entered
the United States Army Air Force in 1945 and served until 1947. He then studied at Stanford University from
which he was graduated with the Bachelor of Arts degree
in economics in 1950. Claude married Elva Jackson on
July 1, 1950. They have two children: Claudia Meredith
and Thomas.

From 1950 to 1953 Claude S. Brinegar was a research
assistant at the Food Research Institute in Stanford,
California and an economic consultant for the Emporium-
Capwell Corporation in San Francisco. He also continued
his education, receiving the Master of Science degree in
mathematics and statistics in 1951 and the Doctor of
Philosophy degree in economics in 1954.

Claude Brinegar began working for the Union Oil Company in 1953. He became manager for economics and corporation planning in 1962, continuing in that position
until 1965. He was vice president for economics and
corporation planning from 1965 to 1966. Claude S. Brinegar was also president of the Pure Oil Company division
from 1965 to 1968 and president of the Pure Transportation Company from 1966 to 1972. During this period
Brinegar was also director of the International Speed-
way Corporation of Daytona Beach, Florida from 1966 to
1973. He was also president of the Union 76 division
of Union Oil in Los Angeles and also senior vice president, director, and member of the executive committee
of Union Oil Company from 1968 to 1973.

President Richard M. Nixon nominated Claude S. Brinegar
Secretary of Transportation to succeed John A. Volpe on
December 7, 1972. Brinegar was confirmed on January 18,
1973 and assumed his office. He continued to serve
under President Gerald R. Ford after the resignation of
Richard M. Nixon on August 9, 1974. Secretary Brinegar
supported establishment of a road fund for improvement
and expansion of mass transit. He signed an Air Service
agreement with the Soviet Union on June 23, 1973.

At the end of 1973 Dr. Brinegar tried to settle the
problems of the truckers concerning the rising fuel costs.
He supported the administration's stand in 1974 that the
federal government pay one-third rather than one-half
of transit aids. President Ford named Claude A. Brinegar
a member of the Economic Policy Board in September 1974.
Brinegar tendered his resignation on December 18, 1974,

effective February 1, 1975.

Bibliography:
  Bremer, Howard F., ed.  Richard M. Nixon, 1913-____.
Dobbs Ferry, N.Y.: Oceana Publications, Inc., 1975.
  Mankiewicz, Frank. Perfectly Clear.  New York: Quad-
rangle, 1974.
  New York Times.

## ADMINISTRATION OF GERALD R. FORD

### VICE PRESIDENT: NELSON ALDRICH ROCKEFELLER

Nelson A. Rockefeller, Vice President in the Administration of President Gerald R. Ford, was born on July
8, 1908 in Bar Harbor, Maine, the son of John Davison
Rockefeller, Jr. and Abby Greene (Aldrich) Rockefeller.
He is a member of the Rockefeller family whose fortune
was founded by John D. Rockefeller, Sr. in the oil industry.  Nelson received his basic education at the Lincoln School of Teachers College in New York City from
1917 to 1926.  He then studied at Dartmouth from which
he was graduated with the Bachelor of Arts degree in
1930.  Nelson married Mary Todhunter Clark on June 23,
1930.   They had four children: Rodman, Ann and Steven
who are twins, and Mary.  A fifth child, Michael, died.
  Nelson Rockefeller became a director of Rockefeller
Center, Inc. in 1931 and continued in this capacity until 1958.  He was president of Rockefeller Center from
1938 to 1945.  He has been a trustee of the Museum of
Modern Art since 1932.  He was treasurer from 1935 to
1939 and president from 1939 to 1941 and again from 1946
to 1953.  Rockefeller was also a founder of the Museum
of Primitive Art and then served as trustee and president.
  Nelson A. Rockefeller soon became involved in public
affairs.  From 1940 to 1944 he was coordinator of Inter-
American affairs for the State Department.  He was next
assistant Secretary of State from 1944 to 1945.  Nelson
was awarded the Order of Merit of Chile in 1945 as well
as the Brazilian National Order of the Southern Cross in
1946 and the Mexican Order of the Aztec Eagle in 1949.
  Nelson next became chairman of Rockefeller Center, Inc.
in 1945 and continued until 1953.  In the latter year
he became Undersecretary of Health, Education, and Welfare.  He remained in this post until 1954.  Mr. Rockefeller was next appointed special assistant to President
Dwight D. Eisenhower, serving in this capacity from 1954
to 1955.
  Nelson A. Rockefeller was elected governor of New York
State in 1958.  He served from 1959 until his resignation

in 1973.  He was reelected in 1962, 1966, and 1970.  During his term in office Nelson Rockefeller worked to further develop and improve the organization and management of the State.  He wrote <u>The Future of Federalism</u> in 1962, <u>Unity, Freedom and Peace</u> in 1968, and <u>Our Environment Can Be Saved</u> in 1970.  He was given the Gold Medal award of the National Institute of the Social Sciences in 1967 and the Conservation and Water Management award of the Great Lakes Commission in 1970 as well as many others. Nelson divorced his first wife Mary in 1962.  He married Margaretta ("Happy") Fitler Murphy on May 4, 1963. They have two children: Nelson A. and Mark F.  Governor Rockefeller was a candidate for the Republican nomination for President in 1960, 1964 and 1968.

Nelson Rockefeller became chairman of the Commission on Water Quality in 1972.  He established the Commission on Critical Choices for Americans, becoming chairman chairman after his resignation as governor in 1973.  As a result of President Richard M. Nixon's resignation on August 9, 1974 and the succession to the Presidency of Gerald R. Ford, the latter was required by the provisions of the Twenty-fifth Amendment to the Constitution to nominate a Vice President.  On August 20, 1974 President Gerald R. Ford nominated Nelson A. Rockefeller for Vice President.  Mr. Rockefeller supported President Ford's pardon of Richard M. Nixon on September 8, 1974.

As a result of the Congressional investigation concerning his nomination information was released that he had made over $500,000 in gifts to many associates and officials.  Much of this was in the form of loans which were eventually made permanent gifts.  Nelson Rockefeller and his family revealed their total worth.  The United States Senate confirmed Rockefeller's nomination on December 10, and the House of Representatives did the same on December 19.  Nelson A. Rockefeller was sworn in as the forty-first Vice President of the United States on December 19, 1974.

<u>Bibliography</u>:
    Abels, Jules.  <u>The Rockefeller Millions</u>.  New York: Macmillan, 1965.
    Alsop, Stewart J. O.  <u>Nixon and Rockefeller, A Double Portrait</u>.  Garden City, N.Y.: Doubleday, 1960.
    Courtney, Kent.  <u>Nelson Rockefeller's Candidacy</u>.  New Orleans: Conservtaive Society of America, 1963.
    Desmond, James.  <u>Nelson Rockefeller; A Political Biography</u>.  New York: Macmillan, 1964.
    Gervasi, Frank.  <u>The Real Rockefeller</u>.  New York: Atheneum Publishers, 1964.
    Katz, Myer.  <u>Rockefeller Power</u>.  New York: Simon and Shuster, 1974.

SECRETARY OF STATE: HENRY ALFRED KISSINGER

Refer to the biographical sketch of Henry A. Kissinger under Secretary of State in the Administration of Richard M. Nixon, page 767.

SECRETARY OF THE TREASURY: WILLIAM EDWARD SIMON

Refer to the biographical sketch of William E. Simon under Secretary of the Treasury in the Administration of Richard M. Nixon, page 774.

SECRETARY OF DEFENSE: JAMES RODNEY SCHLESINGER

Refer to the biographical sketch of James R. Schlesinger under Secretary of Defense in the Administration of Richard M. Nixon, page 779.

ATTORNEY GENERAL: WILLIAM BART SAXBE

Refer to the biographical sketch of William B. Saxbe under Attorney General in the Administration of Richard M. Nixon, page 783.

SECRETARY OF THE INTERIOR:

ROGERS CLARK BALLARD MORTON

Refer to the biographical sketch of Rogers C. B. Morton under Secretary of the Interior in the Administration of Richard M. Nixon, page 788.

SECRETARY OF AGRICULTURE: EARL LAUER BUTZ

Refer to the biographical sketch of Earl L. Butz under Secretary of Agriculture in the Administration of Richard M. Nixon, page 791.

SECRETARY OF COMMERCE: FREDERICK BAILY DENT

Refer to the biographical sketch of Frederick B. Dent under Secretary of Commerce in the Administration of Richard M. Nixon, page 795.

SECRETARY OF LABOR: PETER JOSEPH BRENNAN

Refer to the biographical sketch of Peter J. Brennan under Secretary of Labor in the Administration of Richard M. Nixon, page 797.

SECRETARY OF HEALTH, EDUCATION, AND WELFARE:

CASPAR WILLARD WEINBERGER

Refer to the biographical sketch of Caspar W. Weinberger under Secretary of Health, Education, and Welfare in the Administration of Richard M. Nixon, page 802.

SECRETARY OF HOUSING AND URBAN DEVELOPMENT:

JAMES THOMAS LYNN

Refer to the biographical sketch of James T. Lynn under Secretary of Housing and Urban Development in the Administration of Richard M. Nixon, page 805.

SECRETARY OF TRANSPORTATION:

CLAUDE STOUT BRINEGAR

Refer to the biographical sketch of Claude S. Brinegar under Secretary of Transportation in the Administration of Richard M. Nixon, page 808.

APPENDIX: PRESIDENTIAL ADMINISTRATIONS

# EXECUTIVE OFFICERS, 1789–1971

### First Administration of GEORGE WASHINGTON

#### APRIL 30, 1789, TO MARCH 3, 1793

PRESIDENT OF THE UNITED STATES—GEORGE WASHINGTON, of Virginia.

VICE PRESIDENT OF THE UNITED STATES—JOHN ADAMS, of Massachusetts.

SECRETARY OF STATE—JOHN JAY, of New York, was Secretary for Foreign Affairs under the Confederation, and continued to act, at the request of Washington, until Jefferson took office. THOMAS JEFFERSON, of Virginia, September 26, 1789; entered upon duties March 22, 1790.

SECRETARY OF THE TREASURY—ALEXANDER HAMILTON, of New York, September 11, 1789.

SECRETARY OF WAR—HENRY KNOX, of Massachusetts, September 12, 1789.

ATTORNEY GENERAL—EDMUND RANDOLPH, of Virginia, September 26, 1789; entered upon duties February 2, 1790.

POSTMASTER GENERAL—SAMUEL OSGOOD, of Massachusetts, September 26, 1789. TIMOTHY PICKERING, of Pennsy v: nia, August 12, 1791; entered upon duties August 19, 1791.

### Second Administration of GEORGE WASHINGTON

#### MARCH 4, 1793, TO MARCH 3, 1797

PRESIDENT OF THE UNITED STATES—GEORGE WASHINGTON, of Virginia.

VICE PRESIDENT OF THE UNITED STATES—JOHN ADAMS, of Massachusetts.

SECRETARY OF STATE—THOMAS JEFFERSON, of Virginia, continued from preceding administration. EDMUND RANDOLPH, of Virginia, January 2, 1794. TIMOTHY PICKERING, of Pennsylvania (Secretary of War), ad interim, August 20, 1795. TIMOTHY PICKERING, of Pennsylvania, December 10, 1795.

SECRETARY OF THE TREASURY—ALEXANDER HAMILTON, of New York, continued from preceding administration. OLIVER WOLCOTT, Jr., of Connecticut, February 2, 1795.

SECRETARY OF WAR—HENRY KNOX, of Massachusetts, continued from preceding administration. TIMOTHY PICKERING, of Pennsylvania, January 2, 1795. TIMOTHY PICKERING, of Pennsylvania (Secretary of State), ad interim, December 10, 1795, to February 5, 1796. JAMES McHENRY, of Maryland, January 27, 1796; entered upon duties February 6, 1796.

ATTORNEY GENERAL—EDMUND RANDOLPH, of Virginia, continued from preceding administration. WILLIAM BRADFORD, of Pennsylvania, January 27, 1794; entered upon duties January 29, 1794. CHARLES LEE, of Virginia, December 10, 1795.

POSTMASTER GENERAL—TIMOTHY PICKERING, of Pennsylvania, continued from preceding administration. TIMOTHY PICKERING, of Pennsylvania, recommissioned June 1, 1794. JOSEPH HABERSHAM, of Georgia, February 25, 1795.

### Administration of JOHN ADAMS

#### MARCH 4, 1797, TO MARCH 3, 1801

PRESIDENT OF THE UNITED STATES—JOHN ADAMS, of Massachusetts.

VICE PRESIDENT OF THE UNITED STATES—THOMAS JEFFERSON, of Virginia.

SECRETARY OF STATE—TIMOTHY PICKERING, of Pennsylvania, continued from preceding administration; resignation requested May 10, 1800, but declining to resign, he was dismissed May 12, 1800. CHARLES LEE, of Virginia (Attorney General), ad interim, May 13, 1800. JOHN MARSHALL, of Virginia, May 13, 1800; entered upon duties June 6, 1800. JOHN MARSHALL, of Virginia (Chief Justice of the United States), ad interim, February 4, 1801, to March 3, 1801.

SECRETARY OF THE TREASURY—OLIVER WOLCOTT, Jr., of Connecticut, continued from preceding adminstration. SAMUEL DEXTER, of Massachusetts, January 1, 1801.

SECRETARY OF WAR—JAMES McHENRY, of Maryland, continued from preceding administration. BENJAMIN STODDERT, of Maryland (Secretary of the Navy), ad interim, June 1, 1800, to June 12, 1800. SAMUEL DEXTER, of Massachusetts, May 13, 1800; entered upon duties June 12, 1800. SAMUEL DEXTER, of Massachusetts (Secretary of the Treasury), ad interim, January 1, 1801.

ATTORNEY GENERAL—CHARLES LEE, of Virginia, continued from preceding administration.

POSTMASTER GENERAL—JOSEPH HABERSHAM, of Georgia, continued from preceding administration.

SECRETARY OF THE NAVY—BENJAMIN STODDERT, of Maryland, May 21, 1798; entered upon duties June 18. 1798.

## First Administration of THOMAS JEFFERSON

### MARCH 4, 1801, TO MARCH 3, 1805

PRESIDENT OF THE UNITED STATES—THOMAS JEFFERSON, of Virginia.

VICE PRESIDENT OF THE UNITED STATES—AARON BURR, of New York.

SECRETARY OF STATE—JOHN MARSHALL, of Virginia (Chief Justice of the United States), for one day (March 4, 1801), and for a special purpose. LEVI LINCOLN, of Massachusetts (Attorney General), ad interim, March 5, 1801. JAMES MADISON, of, Virginia, March 5, 1801; entered upon duties May 2, 1801.

SECRETARY OF THE TREASURY—SAMUEL DEXTER, of Massachusetts, continued from preceding administration to May 6, 1801. ALBERT GALLATIN, of Pennsylvania, May 14, 1801.

SECRETARY OF WAR—HENRY DEARBORN, of Massachusetts, March 5, 1801.

ATTORNEY GENERAL—LEVI LINCOLN, of Massachusetts, March 5, 1801, to December 31, 1804.

POSTMASTER GENERAL—JOSEPH HABERSHAM, of Georgia, continued from preceding administration. GIDEON GRANGER, of Connecticut, November 28, 1801.

SECRETARY OF THE NAVY—BENJAMIN STODDERT, of Maryland, continued from preceding administration. (Temp) HENRY DEARBORN, of Massachusetts (Secretary of War), ad interim, April 1, 1801. ROBERT SMITH, of Maryland, July 15, 1801; entered upon duties July 27, 1801.

---

## Second Administration of THOMAS JEFFERSON

### MARCH 4, 1805, TO MARCH 3, 1809

PRESIDENT OF THE UNITED STATES—THOMAS JEFFERSON, of Virginia.

VICE PRESIDENT OF THE UNITED STATES—GEORGE CLINTON, of New York.

SECRETARY OF STATE—JAMES MADISON, of Virginia, continued from preceding administration.

SECRETARY OF THE TREASURY—ALBERT GALLATIN, of Pennsylvania, continued from preceding administration.

SECRETARY OF WAR—HENRY DEARBORN, of Massachusetts, continued from preceding administration. JOHN SMITH (chief clerk), ad interim, February 17, 1809.

ATTORNEY GENERAL—JOHN BRECKENRIDGE, of Kentucky, August 7, 1805 (died December 14, 1806). CÆSAR A. RODNEY, of Delaware, January 20, 1807.

POSTMASTER GENERAL—GIDEON GRANGER, of Connecticut, continued from preceding administration.

SECRETARY OF THE NAVY—ROBERT SMITH, of Maryland, continued from preceding administration.

---

## First Administration of JAMES MADISON

### MARCH 4, 1809, TO MARCH 3, 1813

PRESIDENT OF THE UNITED STATES—JAMES MADISON, of Virginia.

VICE PRESIDENT OF THE UNITED STATES—GEORGE CLINTON, of New York. (Died April 20, 1812.)

PRESIDENT PRO TEMPORE OF THE SENATE—WILLIAM H. CRAWFORD, of Georgia.

SECRETARY OF STATE—ROBERT SMITH, of Maryland, March 6, 1809. JAMES MONROE, of Virginia, April 2, 1811; entered upon duties April 6, 1811.

SECRETARY OF THE TREASURY—ALBERT GALLATIN, of Pennsylvania, continued from preceding administration.

SECRETARY OF WAR—JOHN SMITH (chief clerk), ad interim, continued from preceding administration. WILLIAM EUSTIS, of Massachusetts, March 7, 1809; entered upon duties April 8, 1809; served to December 31, 1812. JAMES MONROE, of Virginia (Secretary of State), ad interim, January 1, 1813. JOHN ARMSTRONG, of New York, January 13, 1813; entered upon duties February 5, 1813.

ATTORNEY GENERAL—CÆSAR A. RODNEY, of Delaware, continued from preceding administration; resigned December 5, 1811. WILLIAM PINKNEY, of Maryland, December 11, 1811; entered upon duties January 6, 1812.

POSTMASTER GENERAL—GIDEON GRANGER, of Connecticut, continued from preceding administration.

SECRETARY OF THE NAVY—ROBERT SMITH, of Maryland, continued from preceding administration. CHARLES W. GOLDSBOROUGH (chief clerk), ad interim, March 8, 1809. PAUL HAMILTON, of South Carolina, March 7, 1809; entered upon duties May 15, 1809; served to December 31, 1812. CHARLES W. GOLDSBOROUGH (chief clerk), ad interim, January 7, 1813, to January 18, 1813. WILLIAM JONES, of Pennsylvania, January 12, 1813; entered upon duties January 19, 1813.

## Second Administration of JAMES MADISON

### MARCH 4, 1813, TO MARCH 3, 1817

PRESIDENT OF THE UNITED STATES—JAMES MADISON, of Virginia.

VICE PRESIDENT OF THE UNITED STATES—ELBRIDGE GERRY, of Massachusetts. (Died November 23, 1814.)

PRESIDENT PRO TEMPORE OF THE SENATE—JOHN GAILLARD, of South Carolina.

SECRETARY OF STATE—JAMES MONROE, of Virginia, continued from preceding administration. JAMES MONROE, of Virginia (Secretary of War), ad interim, October 1, 1814. JAMES MONROE, of Virginia, February 28, 1815.

SECRETARY OF THE TREASURY—ALBERT GALLATIN, of Pennsylvania, continued from preceding administration. WILLIAM JONES, of Pennsylvania (Secretary of the Navy), performed the duties of the Secretary of the Treasury during the absence of Mr. Gallatin in Europe (April 21, 1813, to February 9, 1814). GEORGE W. CAMPBELL, of Tennessee, February 9, 1814. ALEXANDER J. DALLAS, of Pennsylvania, October 6, 1814; entered upon duties October 14, 1814. WILLIAM H. CRAWFORD, of Georgia, October 22, 1816.

SECRETARY OF WAR—JOHN ARMSTRONG, of New York, continued from preceding administration. JAMES MONROE, of Virginia (Secretary of State), ad interim, August 30, 1814. JAMES MONROE, of Virginia, September 27, 1814; entered upon duties October 1, 1814. JAMES MONROE, of Virginia (Secretary of State), ad interim, March 1, 1815. ALEXANDER J. DALLAS, of Pennsylvania (Secretary of the Treasury), ad interim, March 14, 1815, to August 8, 1815. WILLIAM H. CRAWFORD, of Georgia, August 1, 1815; entered upon duties August 8, 1815. GEORGE GRAHAM (chief clerk), ad interim, October 22, 1816, to close of administration.

ATTORNEY GENERAL—WILLIAM PINKNEY, of Maryland, continued from preceding administration. RICHARD RUSH, of Pennsylvania, February 10, 1814; entered upon duties the day following.

POSTMASTER GENERAL—GIDEON GRANGER, of Connecticut, continued from preceding administration. RETURN J. MEIGS, Jr., of Ohio, March 17, 1814; entered upon duties April 11, 1814.

SECRETARY OF THE NAVY—WILLIAM JONES, of Pennsylvania, continued from preceding administration. BENJAMIN HOMANS (chief clerk), ad interim, December 2, 1814. BENJAMIN W. CROWNINSHIELD, of Massachusetts, December 19, 1814; entered upon duties January 16, 1815.

---

## First Administration of JAMES MONROE

### MARCH 4, 1817, TO MARCH 3, 1821

PRESIDENT OF THE UNITED STATES—JAMES MONROE, of Virginia.

VICE PRESIDENT OF THE UNITED STATES—DANIEL D. TOMPKINS, of New York.

SECRETARY OF STATE—JOHN GRAHAM (chief clerk), ad interim, March 4, 1817. RICHARD RUSH, of Pennsylvania (Attorney General), ad interim, March 10, 1817. JOHN QUINCY ADAMS, of Massachusetts, March 5, 1817; entered upon duties September 22, 1817.

SECRETARY OF THE TREASURY—WILLIAM H. CRAWFORD, of Georgia, continued from preceding administration. WILLIAM H. CRAWFORD, of Georgia, recommissioned March 5, 1817.

SECRETARY OF WAR—GEORGE GRAHAM (chief clerk), ad interim, March 4, 1817. JOHN C. CALHOUN, of South Carolina, October 8, 1817; entered upon duties December 10, 1817.

ATTORNEY GENERAL—RICHARD RUSH, of Pennsylvania, continued from preceding administration to October 30, 1817. WILLIAM WIRT, of Virginia, November 13, 1817; entered upon duties November 15, 1817.

POSTMASTER GENERAL—RETURN J. MEIGS, Jr., of Ohio, continued from preceding administration.

SECRETARY OF THE NAVY—BENJAMIN W. CROWNINSHIELD, of Massachusetts, continued from preceding administration. JOHN C. CALHOUN, of South Carolina (Secretary of War), ad interim, October 1, 1818. SMITH THOMPSON, of New York, November 9, 1818; entered upon duties January 1, 1819.

---

## Second Administration of JAMES MONROE

### MARCH 4, 1821, TO MARCH 3, 1825

PRESIDENT OF THE UNITED STATES—JAMES MONROE, of Virginia.

VICE PRESIDENT OF THE UNITED STATES—DANIEL D. TOMPKINS, of New York.

SECRETARY OF STATE—JOHN QUINCY ADAMS, of Massachusetts, continued from preceding administration.

SECRETARY OF THE TREASURY—WILLIAM H. CRAWFORD, of Georgia, continued from preceding administration.

SECRETARY OF WAR—JOHN C. CALHOUN, of South Carolina, continued from preceding administration.

ATTORNEY GENERAL—WILLIAM WIRT, of Virginia, continued from preceding administration.

POSTMASTER GENERAL—RETURN J. MEIGS, Jr., of Ohio, continued from preceding administration. JOHN McLEAN, of Ohio, commissioned June 26, 1823, to take effect July 1, 1823.

SECRETARY OF THE NAVY—SMITH THOMPSON, of New York, continued from preceding administration. JOHN RODGERS (commodore, United States Navy, and President of the Board of Navy Commissioners), ad interim, September 1, 1823. SAMUEL L. SOUTHARD, of New Jersey, September 16, 1823.

## Administration of JOHN QUINCY ADAMS

### MARCH 4, 1825, TO MARCH 3, 1829

PRESIDENT OF THE UNITED STATES—John Quincy Adams, of Massachusetts.
VICE PRESIDENT OF THE UNITED STATES—John C. Calhoun, of South Carolina.
SECRETARY OF STATE—Daniel Brent (chief clerk), ad interim, March 4 1825. Henry Clay, of Kentucky, March 7, 1825.
SECRETARY OF THE TREASURY—Samuel L. Southard, of New Jersey (Secretary of the Navy), ad interim, March 7, 1825. Richard Rush, of Pennsylvania, March 7, 1825; entered upon duties August 1, 1825.
SECRETARY OF WAR—James Barbour, of Virginia, March 7, 1825. Samuel L. Southard, of New Jersey (Secretary of the Navy), ad interim, May 26. 1828. Peter B. Porter, of New York, May 26, 1828; entered upon duties June 21. 1828.
ATTORNEY GENERAL—William Wirt, of Virginia, continued from preceding administration.
POSTMASTER GENERAL—John McLean, of Ohio, continued from preceding administration.
SECRETARY OF THE NAVY—Samuel L. Southard, of New Jersey, continued from preceding administration.

## First Administration of ANDREW JACKSON

### MARCH 4, 1829, TO MARCH 3, 1833

PRESIDENT OF THE UNITED STATES—Andrew Jackson, of Tennessee.
VICE PRESIDENT OF THE UNITED STATES—John C. Calhoun, of South Carolina.   (Resigned December 28, 1832.)
PRESIDENT PRO TEMPORE OF THE SENATE—Hugh Lawson White, of Tennessee.
SECRETARY OF STATE—James A. Hamilton, of New York, ad interim, March 4, 1829. Martin Van Buren, of New York, March 6, 1829; entered upon duties March 28, 1829. Edward Livingston, of Louisiana, May 24, 1831.
SECRETARY OF THE TREASURY—Samuel D. Ingham, of Pennsylvania, March 6, 1829. Asbury Dickins (chief clerk), ad interim, June 21, 1831. Louis McLane, of Delaware, August 8, 1831.
SECRETARY OF WAR—John H. Eaton, of Tennessee, March 9, 1829. Philip G. Randolph (chief clerk), ad interim, June 20, 1831. Roger B. Taney, of Maryland (Attorney General), ad interim, July 21, 1831. Lewis Cass, of Ohio, August 1, 1831; entered upon duties August 8, 1831.
ATTORNEY GENERAL—John M. Berrien, of Georgia, March 9, 1829, to June 22, 1831. Roger B. Taney, of Maryland, July 20, 1831.
POSTMASTER GENERAL—John McLean, of Ohio, continued from preceding administration. William T. Barry, of Kentucky, March 9, 1829; entered upon duties April 6, 1829.
SECRETARY OF THE NAVY—Charles Hay (chief clerk), ad interim, March 4, 1829. John Branch, of North Carolina March 9, 1829. John Boyle (chief clerk), ad interim, May 12, 1831. Levi Woodbury, of New Hampshire, May 23, 1831.

## Second Administration of ANDREW JACKSON

### MARCH 4, 1833, TO MARCH 3, 1837

PRESIDENT OF THE UNITED STATES—Andrew Jackson, of Tennessee.
VICE PRESIDENT OF THE UNITED STATES—Martin Van Buren, of New York.
SECRETARY OF STATE—Edward Livingston, of Louisiana, continued from preceding administration. Louis McLane, of Delaware, May 29, 1833. John Forsyth, of Georgia, June 27, 1834; entered upon duties July 1, 1834.
SECRETARY OF THE TREASURY—Louis McLane, of Delaware, continued from preceding administration. William J. Duane, of Pennsylvania, May 29, 1833; entered upon duties June 1, 1833. Roger B. Taney, of Maryland, September 23, 1833. McClintock Young (chief clerk), ad interim, June 25, 1834. Levi Woodbury, of New Hampshire, June 27, 1834; entered upon duties July 1, 1834.
SECRETARY OF WAR—Lewis Cass, of Ohio, continued from preceding administration. Carey A. Harris, of Tennessee (Commissioner of Indian Affairs), ad interim, October 5, 1836. Benjamin F. Butler, of New York (Attorney General), ad interim, October 26, 1836. Benjamin F. Butler, of New York, commissioned March 3, 1837, ad interim, "during the pleasure of the President, until a successor, duly appointed, shall accept such office and enter upon the duties thereof."
ATTORNEY GENERAL—Roger B. Taney, of Maryland, continued from preceding administration to September 23, 1833. Benjamin F. Butler, of New York, November 15, 1833; entered upon duties November 18, 1833.
POSTMASTER GENERAL—William T. Barry, of Kentucky, continued from preceding administration. Amos Kendall, of Kentucky. May 1, 1835.
SECRETARY OF THE NAVY—Levi Woodbury, of New Hampshire, continued from preceding administration. Mahlon Dickerson, of New Jersey, June 30, 1834.

## Administration of MARTIN VAN BUREN

### MARCH 4, 1837, TO MARCH 3, 1841

PRESIDENT OF THE UNITED STATES—MARTIN VAN BUREN, of New York.

VICE PRESIDENT OF THE UNITED STATES—RICHARD M. JOHNSON, of Kentucky.

SECRETARY OF STATE—JOHN FORSYTH, of Georgia, continued from preceding administration.

SECRETARY OF THE TREASURY—LEVI WOODBURY, of New Hampshire, continued from preceding administration.

SECRETARY OF WAR—BENJAMIN F. BUTLER, of New York, ad interim, continued from preceding administration. JOEL R. POINSETT, of South Carolina, March 7, 1837; entered upon duties March 14, 1837.

ATTORNEY GENERAL—BENJAMIN F. BUTLER, of New York, continued from preceding administration. FELIX GRUNDY, of Tennessee, July 5, 1838, to take effect September 1, 1838. HENRY D. GILPIN, of Pennsylvania, January 11, 1840.

POSTMASTER GENERAL—AMOS KENDALL, of Kentucky, continued from preceding administration. JOHN M. NILES, of Connecticut, May 19, 1840, to take effect May 25, 1840; entered upon duties May 26, 1840.

SECRETARY OF THE NAVY—MAHLON DICKERSON, of New Jersey, continued from preceding administration. JAMES K. PAULDING, of New York, June 25, 1838, to take effect "after the 30th instant"; entered upon duties July 1, 1838.

---

## Administration of WILLIAM HENRY HARRISON

### MARCH 4, 1841, TO APRIL 4, 1841

PRESIDENT OF THE UNITED STATES—WILLIAM HENRY HARRISON, of Ohio.   (Died April 4, 1841.)

VICE PRESIDENT OF THE UNITED STATES—JOHN TYLER, of Virginia.

SECRETARY OF STATE—J. L. MARTIN (chief clerk), ad interim, March 4, 1841.   DANIEL WEBSTER, of Massachusetts, March 5, 1841.

SECRETARY OF THE TREASURY—McCLINTOCK YOUNG (chief clerk), ad interim, March 4, 1841.   THOMAS EWING, of Ohio, March 5, 1841.

SECRETARY OF WAR—JOHN BELL, of Tennessee, March 5, 1841.

ATTORNEY GENERAL—JOHN J. CRITTENDEN, of Kentucky, March 5, 1841.

POSTMASTER GENERAL—SELAH R. HOBBIE, of New York (First Assistant Postmaster General), ad interim, March 4, 1841. FRANCIS GRANGER, of New York, March 6, 1841; entered upon duties March 8, 1841.

SECRETARY OF THE NAVY—JOHN D. SIMMS (chief clerk), ad interim, March 4, 1841.   GEORGE E. BADGER, of North Carolina, March 5, 1841.

---

## Administration of JOHN TYLER

### APRIL 6, 1841, TO MARCH 3, 1845

PRESIDENT OF THE UNITED STATES—JOHN TYLER, of Virginia.

PRESIDENT PRO TEMPORE OF THE SENATE—SAMUEL L. SOUTHARD, of New Jersey; WILLIE P. MANGUM, of North Carolina.

SECRETARY OF STATE—DANIEL WEBSTER, of Massachusetts, continued from preceding administration. HUGH S. LEGARÉ, of South Carolina (Attorney General), ad interim, May 9, 1843.   WILLIAM S. DERRICK (chief clerk), ad interim, June 21, 1843. ABEL P. UPSHUR, of Virginia (Secretary of the Navy), ad interim, June 24, 1843.   ABEL P. UPSHUR, of Virginia, July 24, 1843 (killed by the explosion of a gun on the U. S. S. *Princeton* February 28, 1844).   JOHN NELSON, of Maryland (Attorney General), ad interim, February 29, 1844.   JOHN C. CALHOUN, of South Carolina, March 6, 1844; entered upon duties April 1, 1844.

SECRETARY OF THE TREASURY—THOMAS EWING, of Ohio, continued from preceding administration. McCLINTOCK YOUNG (chief clerk), ad interim, September 13, 1841.   WALTER FORWARD, of Pennsylvania, September 13, 1841.   McCLINTOCK YOUNG (chief clerk), ad interim, March 1, 1843.   JOHN C. SPENCER, of New York, March 3, 1843?   entered upon duties March 8, 1843. McCLINTOCK YOUNG (chief clerk), ad interim, May 2, 1844.   GEORGE M. BIBB, of Kentucky, June 15, 1844; entered upon duties July 4, 1844.

SECRETARY OF WAR—JOHN BELL, of Tennessee, continued from preceding administration. ALBERT M. LEA, of Maryland (chief clerk), ad interim, September 12, 1841.   JOHN C. SPENCER, of New York, October 12, 1841.   JAMES M. PORTER, of Pennsylvania, March 8, 1843.   WILLIAM WILKINS, of Pennsylvania, February 15, 1844; entered upon duties February 20, 1844.

ATTORNEY GENERAL—JOHN J. CRITTENDEN, of Kentucky, continued from preceding administration. HUGH S. LEGARÉ, of South Carolina, September 13, 1841; entered upon duties September 20, 1841 (died June 20, 1843).   JOHN NELSON, of Maryland, July 1, 1843.

POSTMASTER GENERAL—FRANCIS GRANGER, of New York, continued from preceding administration. SELAH R. HOBBIE, of New York (First Assistant Postmaster General), ad interim, September 14, 1841.   CHARLES A. WICKLIFFE, of Kentucky, September 13, 1841; entered upon duties October 13, 1841.

SECRETARY OF THE NAVY—GEORGE E. BADGER, of North Carolina, continued from preceding administration. JOHN D. SIMMS (chief clerk), ad interim, September 11, 1841.   ABEL P. UPSHUR, of Virginia, September 13, 1841; entered upon duties October 11, 1841.   DAVID HENSHAW, of Massachusetts, July 24, 1843.   THOMAS W. GILMER, of Virginia, February 15, 1844; entered upon duties February 19, 1844 (killed by the explosion of a gun on the U. S. S. *Princeton* February 28, 1844).   LEWIS WARRINGTON (captain, United States Navy), ad interim, February 29, 1844.   JOHN Y. MASON, of Virginia, March 14, 1844; entered upon duties March 26, 1844.

## Administration of JAMES K. POLK

### MARCH 4, 1845, TO MARCH 3, 1849

PRESIDENT OF THE UNITED STATES—JAMES K. POLK, of Tennessee.
VICE PRESIDENT OF THE UNITED STATES—GEORGE M. DALLAS, of Pennsylvania.
SECRETARY OF STATE—JOHN C. CALHOUN, of South Carolina, continued from preceding administration. JAMES BUCHANAN,
of Pennsylvania, March 6, 1845; entered upon duties March 10, 1845.
SECRETARY OF THE TREASURY—GEORGE M. BIBB, of Kentucky, continued from preceding administration. ROBERT J.
WALKER, of Mississippi, March 6, 1845; entered upon duties March 8, 1845.
SECRETARY OF WAR—WILLIAM WILKINS, of Pennsylvania, continued from preceding administration. WILLIAM L. MARCY,
of New York, March 6, 1845; entered upon duties March 8, 1845.
ATTORNEY GENERAL—JOHN NELSON, of Maryland, continued from preceding administration. JOHN Y. MASON, of Virginia,
March 6, 1845; entered upon duties March 11, 1845. NATHAN CLIFFORD, of Maine, October 17, 1846, to March 18, 1848,
when he resigned. ISAAC TOUCEY, of Connecticut, June 21, 1848; entered upon duties June 29, 1848.
POSTMASTER GENERAL—CHARLES A. WICKLIFFE, of Kentucky, continued from preceding administration. CAVE JOHNSON,
of Tennessee, March 6, 1845.
SECRETARY OF THE NAVY—JOHN Y. MASON, of Virginia, continued from preceding administration. GEORGE BANCROFT,
of Massachusetts, March 10, 1845. JOHN Y. MASON, of Virginia, September 9, 1846.

---

## Administration of ZACHARY TAYLOR

### MARCH 4, 1849, TO JULY 9, 1850

PRESIDENT OF THE UNITED STATES—ZACHARY TAYLOR, of Louisiana. (Oath administered March 5, 1849. Died
July 9, 1850.)
VICE PRESIDENT OF THE UNITED STATES—MILLARD FILLMORE, of New York.
SECRETARY OF STATE—JAMES BUCHANAN, of Pennsylvania, continued from preceding administration. JOHN M. CLAYTON,
of Delaware, March 7, 1849.
SECRETARY OF THE TREASURY—ROBERT J. WALKER, of Mississippi, continued from preceding administration.
McCLINTOCK YOUNG (chief clerk), ad interim, March 6, 1849. WILLIAM M. MEREDITH, of Pennsylvania, March 8, 1849.
SECRETARY OF WAR—WILLIAM L. MARCY, of New York, continued from preceding administration. REVERDY JOHNSON,
of Maryland (Attorney General), ad interim, March 8, 1849. GEORGE W. CRAWFORD, of Georgia, March 8, 1849; entered
upon duties March 14, 1849.
ATTORNEY GENERAL—ISAAC TOUCEY, of Connecticut, continued from preceding administration. REVERDY JOHNSON, of
Maryland, March 8, 1849.
POSTMASTER GENERAL—CAVE JOHNSON, of Tennessee, continued from preceding administration. SELAH R. HOBBIE, of
New York (First Assistant Postmaster General), ad interim, March 6, 1849. JACOB COLLAMER, of Vermont, March 8, 1849.
SECRETARY OF THE NAVY—JOHN Y. MASON, of Virginia, continued from preceding administration. WILLIAM B. PRESTON,
of Virginia, March 8, 1849.
SECRETARY OF THE INTERIOR—THOMAS EWING, of Ohio, March 8, 1849.

---

## Administration of MILLARD FILLMORE

### JULY 10, 1850, TO MARCH 3, 1853

PRESIDENT OF THE UNITED STATES—MILLARD FILLMORE, of New York.
PRESIDENT PRO TEMPORE OF THE SENATE—WILLIAM R. KING, of Alabama; DAVID R. ATCHISON, of Missouri.
SECRETARY OF STATE—JOHN M. CLAYTON, of Delaware, continued from preceding administration. DANIEL WEBSTER, of
Massachusetts, July 22, 1850 (died October 24, 1852). CHARLES M. CONRAD, of Louisiana (Secretary of War), ad interim,
October 25, 1852. EDWARD EVERETT, of Massachusetts, November 6, 1852.
SECRETARY OF THE TREASURY—WILLIAM M. MEREDITH, of Pennsylvania, continued from preceding administration.
THOMAS CORWIN, of Ohio, July 23, 1850.
SECRETARY OF WAR—GEORGE W. CRAWFORD, of Georgia, continued from preceding administration. SAMUEL J. ANDERSON
(chief clerk), ad interim, July 23, 1850. WINFIELD SCOTT (major general, U. S. Army), ad interim, July 24, 1850. CHARLES
M. CONRAD, of Louisiana, August 15, 1850.
ATTORNEY GENERAL—REVERDY JOHNSON, of Maryland, continued from preceding administration, served to July 22, 1850.
JOHN J. CRITTENDEN, of Kentucky, July 22, 1850; entered upon duties August 14, 1850.
POSTMASTER GENERAL—JACOB COLLAMER, of Vermont, continued from preceding administration. NATHAN K. HALL, of
New York, July 23, 1850. SAMUEL D. HUBBARD, of Connecticut, August 31, 1852; entered upon duties September 14, 1852.
SECRETARY OF THE NAVY—WILLIAM B. PRESTON, of Virginia, continued from preceding administration. LEWIS WARRINGTON
(captain, U. S. Navy), ad interim, July 23, 1850. WILLIAM A. GRAHAM, of North Carolina, July 22, 1850; entered upon duties
August 2, 1850. JOHN P. KENNEDY, of Maryland, July 22, 1852; entered upon duties July 26, 1852.
SECRETARY OF THE INTERIOR—THOMAS EWING, of Ohio, continued from preceding administration. DANIEL C. GODDARD
(chief clerk), ad interim, July 23, 1850. THOMAS M. T. McKENNAN, of Pennsylvania, August 15, 1850. DANIEL C. GODDARD
(chief clerk), ad interim, August 27, 1850. ALEXANDER H. H. STUART, of Virginia, September 12, 1850; entered upon duties
September 16, 1850.

## Administration of FRANKLIN PIERCE

### MARCH 4, 1853, TO MARCH 3, 1857

PRESIDENT OF THE UNITED STATES—FRANKLIN PIERCE, of New Hampshire.

VICE PRESIDENT OF THE UNITED STATES—WILLIAM R. KING, of Alabama. (Died April 18, 1853.)

PRESIDENT PRO TEMPORE OF THE SENATE—DAVID R. ATCHISON, of Missouri; LEWIS CASS, of Michigan; JESSE D. BRIGHT, of Indiana; CHARLES E. STUART, of Michigan; JAMES M. MASON, of Virginia.

SECRETARY OF STATE—WILLIAM HUNTER (chief clerk), ad interim, March 4, 1853. WILLIAM L. MARCY, of New York, March 7, 1853.

SECRETARY OF THE TREASURY—THOMAS CORWIN, of Ohio, continued from preceding administration. JAMES GUTHRIE, of Kentucky, March 7, 1853.

SECRETARY OF WAR—CHARLES M. CONRAD, of Louisiana, continued from preceding administration. JEFFERSON DAVIS, of Mississippi, March 7, 1853. SAMUEL COOPER (Adjutant General, U. S. Army), ad interim, March 3, 1857.

ATTORNEY GENERAL—JOHN J. CRITTENDEN, of Kentucky, continued from preceding administration. CALEB CUSHING, of Massachusetts, March 7, 1853.

POSTMASTER GENERAL—SAMUEL D. HUBBARD, of Connecticut, continued from preceding administration. JAMES CAMPBELL, of Pennsylvania, March 7, 1853.

SECRETARY OF THE NAVY—JOHN P. KENNEDY, of Maryland, continued from preceding administration. JAMES C. DOBBIN, of North Carolina, March 7, 1853.

SECRETARY OF THE INTERIOR—ALEXANDER H. H. STUART, of Virginia, continued from preceding administration. ROBERT MCCLELLAND, of Michigan, March 7, 1853.

---

## Administration of JAMES BUCHANAN

### MARCH 4, 1857, TO MARCH 3, 1861

PRESIDENT OF THE UNITED STATES—JAMES BUCHANAN, of Pennsylvania.

VICE PRESIDENT OF THE UNITED STATES—JOHN C. BRECKINRIDGE, of Kentucky.

SECRETARY OF STATE—WILLIAM L. MARCY, of New York, continued from preceding administration. LEWIS CASS, of Michigan, March 6, 1857. WILLIAM HUNTER (chief clerk), ad interim, December 15, 1860. JEREMIAH S. BLACK, of Pennsylvania, December 17, 1860.

SECRETARY OF THE TREASURY—JAMES GUTHRIE, of Kentucky, continued from preceding administration. HOWELL COBB, of Georgia, March 6, 1857. ISAAC TOUCEY, of Connecticut (Secretary of the Navy), ad interim, December 10, 1860. PHILIP F. THOMAS, of Maryland, December 12, 1860. JOHN A. DIX, of New York, January 11, 1861; entered upon duties January 15, 1861.

SECRETARY OF WAR—SAMUEL COOPER (Adjutant General, U. S. Army), ad interim, March 4, 1857. JOHN B. FLOYD, of Virginia, March 6, 1857. JOSEPH HOLT, of Kentucky (Postmaster General), ad interim, January 1, 1861. JOSEPH HOLT, of Kentucky, January 18, 1861.

ATTORNEY GENERAL—CALEB CUSHING, of Massachusetts, continued from preceding administration. JEREMIAH S. BLACK, of Pennsylvania, March 6, 1857; entered upon duties March 11, 1857. EDWIN M. STANTON, of Pennsylvania, December 20, 1860; entered upon duties December 22, 1860.

POSTMASTER GENERAL—JAMES CAMPBELL, of Pennsylvania, continued from preceding administration. AARON V. BROWN, of Tennessee, March 6, 1857 (died March 8, 1859). HORATIO KING, of Maine (First Assistant Postmaster General), ad interim, March 9, 1859. JOSEPH HOLT, of Kentucky, March 14, 1859. HORATIO KING, of Maine (First Assistant Postmaster General), ad interim, January 1, 1861. HORATIO KING, of Maine, February 12, 1861.

SECRETARY OF THE NAVY—JAMES C. DOBBIN, of North Carolina, continued from preceding administration. ISAAC TOUCEY, of Connecticut, March 6, 1857.

SECRETARY OF THE INTERIOR—ROBERT MCCLELLAND, of Michigan, continued from preceding administration. JACOB THOMPSON, of Mississippi, March 6, 1857; entered upon duties March 10, 1857. MOSES KELLY (chief clerk), ad interim, January 10, 1861.

## First Administration of ABRAHAM LINCOLN

### MARCH 4, 1861, TO MARCH 3, 1865

PRESIDENT OF THE UNITED STATES—ABRAHAM LINCOLN, of Illinois.

VICE PRESIDENT OF THE UNITED STATES—HANNIBAL HAMLIN, of Maine.

SECRETARY OF STATE—JEREMIAH S. BLACK, of Pennsylvania, continued from preceding administration. WILLIAM H. SEWARD, of New York, March 5, 1861.

SECRETARY OF THE TREASURY—JOHN A. DIX, of New York, continued from preceding administration. SALMON P. CHASE, of Ohio, March 5, 1861; entered upon duties March 7, 1861. GEORGE HARRINGTON, of the District of Columbia (Assistant Secretary), ad interim, July 1, 1864. WILLIAM P. FESSENDEN, of Maine, July 1, 1864; entered upon duties July 5, 1864.

SECRETARY OF WAR—JOSEPH HOLT, of Kentucky, continued from preceding administration. SIMON CAMERON, of Pennsylvania, March 5, 1861; entered upon duties March 11, 1861. EDWIN M. STANTON, of Pennsylvania, January 15, 1862; entered upon duties January 20, 1862.

ATTORNEY GENERAL—EDWIN M. STANTON, of Pennsylvania, continued from preceding administration. EDWARD BATES, of Missouri, March 5, 1861. JAMES SPEED, of Kentucky, December 2, 1864; entered upon duties December 5, 1864.

POSTMASTER GENERAL—HORATIO KING, of Maine, continued from preceding administration. MONTGOMERY BLAIR, of the District of Columbia, March 5, 1861; entered upon duties March 9, 1861. WILLIAM DENNISON, of Ohio, September 24, 1864; entered upon duties October 1, 1864.

SECRETARY OF THE NAVY—ISAAC TOUCEY, of Connecticut, continued from preceding administration. GIDEON WELLES, of Connecticut, March 5, 1861; entered upon duties March 7, 1861.

SECRETARY OF THE INTERIOR—MOSES KELLY (chief clerk), ad interim, March 4, 1861. CALEB B. SMITH, of Indiana, March 5, 1861. JOHN P. USHER, of Indiana (Assistant Secretary), ad interim, January 1, 1863. JOHN P. USHER, of Indiana, January 8, 1863.

------

## Second Administration of ABRAHAM LINCOLN

### MARCH 4, 1865, TO APRIL 15, 1865

PRESIDENT OF THE UNITED STATES—ABRAHAM LINCOLN, of Illinois.   (Died April 15, 1865.)

VICE PRESIDENT OF THE UNITED STATES—ANDREW JOHNSON, of Tennessee.

SECRETARY OF STATE—WILLIAM H. SEWARD, of New York, continued from preceding administration.

SECRETARY OF THE TREASURY—GEORGE HARRINGTON, of the District of Columbia (Assistant Secretary), ad interim, March 4, 1865. HUGH McCULLOCH, of Indiana, March 7, 1865; entered upon duties March 9, 1865.

SECRETARY OF WAR—EDWIN M. STANTON, of Pennsylvania, continued from preceding administration.

ATTORNEY GENERAL—JAMES SPEED, of Kentucky, continued from preceding administration.

POSTMASTER GENERAL—WILLIAM DENNISON, of Ohio, continued from preceding administration.

SECRETARY OF THE NAVY—GIDEON WELLES, of Connecticut, continued from preceding administration.

SECRETARY OF THE INTERIOR—JOHN P. USHER, of Indiana, continued from preceding administration.

------

## Administration of ANDREW JOHNSON

### APRIL 15, 1865, TO MARCH 3, 1869

PRESIDENT OF THE UNITED STATES—ANDREW JOHNSON, of Tennessee.

PRESIDENT PRO TEMPORE OF THE SENATE—LAFAYETTE S. FOSTER, of Connecticut; BENJAMIN F. WADE, of Ohio.

SECRETARY OF STATE—WILLIAM H. SEWARD, of New York, continued from preceding administration.

SECRETARY OF THE TREASURY—HUGH McCULLOCH, of Indiana, continued from preceding administration.

SECRETARY OF WAR—EDWIN M. STANTON, of Pennsylvania, continued from preceding administration; suspended August 12, 1867. ULYSSES S. GRANT (General of the Army), ad interim, August 12, 1867. EDWIN M. STANTON, of Pennsylvania, reinstated January 13, 1868, to May 26, 1868. JOHN M. SCHOFIELD, of Illinois, May 28, 1868; entered upon duties June 1, 1868.

ATTORNEY GENERAL—JAMES SPEED, of Kentucky, continued from preceding administration. J. HUBLEY ASHTON, of Pennsylvania (Assistant Attorney General), acting, July 17, 1866. HENRY STANBERY, of Ohio, July 23, 1866. ORVILLE H. BROWNING, of Illinois (Secretary of the Interior), ad interim, March 13, 1868. WILLIAM M. EVARTS, of New York, July 15, 1868; entered upon duties July 20, 1868.

POSTMASTER GENERAL—WILLIAM DENNISON, of Ohio, continued from preceding administration. ALEXANDER W. RANDALL, of Wisconsin (First Assistant Postmaster General), ad interim, July 17, 1866. ALEXANDER W. RANDALL, of Wisconsin, July 25, 1866.

SECRETARY OF THE NAVY—GIDEON WELLES, of Connecticut, continued from preceding administration.

SECRETARY OF THE INTERIOR—JOHN P. USHER, of Indiana, continued from preceding administration. JAMES HARLAN, of Iowa, May 15, 1865. ORVILLE H. BROWNING, of Illinois, July 27, 1866, to take effect September 1, 1866.

### First Administration of ULYSSES S. GRANT

#### MARCH 4, 1869, TO MARCH 3, 1873

PRESIDENT OF THE UNITED STATES—ULYSSES S. GRANT, of Illinois.

VICE PRESIDENT OF THE UNITED STATES—SCHUYLER COLFAX, of Indiana.

SECRETARY OF STATE—WILLIAM H. SEWARD, of New York, continued from preceding administration. ELIHU B. WASH-BURNE, of Illinois, March 5, 1869. HAMILTON FISH, of New York, March 11, 1869; entered upon duties March 17, 1869.

SECRETARY OF THE TREASURY—HUGH MCCULLOCH, of Indiana, continued from preceding administration. JOHN F. HARTLEY, of Maine (Assistant Secretary), ad interim, March 5, 1869. GEORGE S. BOUTWELL, of Massachusetts, March 11, 1869.

SECRETARY OF WAR—JOHN M. SCHOFIELD, of Illinois, continued from preceding administration. JOHN A. RAWLINS, of Illinois, March 11, 1869. WILLIAM T. SHERMAN, of Ohio, September 9, 1869; entered upon duties September 11, 1869. WILLIAM W. BELKNAP, of Iowa, October 25, 1869; entered upon duties November 1, 1869.

ATTORNEY GENERAL—WILLIAM M. EVARTS, of New York, continued from preceding administration. J. HUBLEY ASHTON, of Pennsylvania (Assistant Attorney General), acting, March 5, 1869. EBENEZER R. HOAR, of Massachusetts, March 5, 1869; entered upon duties March 11, 1869. AMOS T. AKERMAN, of Georgia, June 23, 1870; entered upon duties July 8, 1870. GEORGE H. WILLIAMS, of Oregon, December 14, 1871, to take effect January 10, 1872.

POSTMASTER GENERAL—ST. JOHN B. L. SKINNER, of New York (First Assistant Postmaster General), ad interim, March 4, 1869. JOHN A. J. CRESWELL, of Maryland, March 5, 1869.

SECRETARY OF THE NAVY—WILLIAM FAXON, of Connecticut (Assistant Secretary), ad interim, March 4, 1869. ADOLPH E. BORIE, of Pennsylvania, March 5, 1869; entered upon duties March 9, 1869. GEORGE M. ROBESON, of New Jersey, June 25, 1869.

SECRETARY OF THE INTERIOR—WILLIAM T. OTTO, of Indiana (Assistant Secretary), ad interim, March 4, 1869. JACOB D. COX, of Ohio, March 5, 1869; entered upon duties March 9, 1869. COLUMBUS DELANO, of Ohio, November 1, 1870.

---

### Second Administration of ULYSSES S. GRANT

#### MARCH 4, 1873, TO MARCH 3, 1877

PRESIDENT OF THE UNITED STATES—ULYSSES S. GRANT, of Illinois.

VICE PRESIDENT OF THE UNITED STATES—HENRY WILSON, of Massachusetts. (Died November 22, 1875.)

PRESIDENT PRO TEMPORE OF THE SENATE—THOMAS W. FERRY, of Michigan.

SECRETARY OF STATE—HAMILTON FISH, of New York, continued from preceding administration. HAMILTON FISH, of New York, recommissioned March 17, 1873.

SECRETARY OF THE TREASURY—GEORGE S. BOUTWELL, of Massachusetts, continued from preceding administration. WILLIAM A. RICHARDSON, of Massachusetts, March 17, 1873. BENJAMIN H. BRISTOW, of Kentucky, June 2, 1874; entered upon duties June 4, 1874. CHARLES F. CONANT, of New Hampshire (Assistant Secretary), ad interim, June 21, 1876, to June 30, 1876. LOT M. MORRILL, of Maine, June 21, 1876; entered upon duties July 7, 1876.

SECRETARY OF WAR—WILLIAM W. BELKNAP, of Iowa, continued from preceding administration. WILLIAM W. BELKNAP, of Iowa, recommissioned March 17, 1873. GEORGE M. ROBESON, of New Jersey (Secretary of the Navy), ad interim, March 2, 1876. ALPHONSO TAFT, of Ohio, March 8, 1876; entered upon duties March 11, 1876. JAMES D. CAMERON, of Pennsylvania, May 22, 1876; entered upon duties June 1, 1876.

ATTORNEY GENERAL—GEORGE H. WILLIAMS, of Oregon, continued from preceding administration. GEORGE H. WILLIAMS, of Oregon, recommissioned March 17, 1873. EDWARDS PIERREPONT, of New York, April 26, 1875, to take effect May 15, 1875. ALPHONSO TAFT, of Ohio, May 22, 1876; entered upon duties June 1, 1876.

POSTMASTER GENERAL—JOHN A. J. CRESWELL, of Maryland, continued from preceding administration. JOHN A. J. CRES-WELL, of Maryland, recommissioned March 17, 1873. JAMES W. MARSHALL, of Virginia, July 3, 1874; entered upon duties July 7, 1874. MARSHALL JEWELL, of Connecticut, August 24, 1874; entered upon duties September 1, 1874. JAMES N. TYNER, of Indiana, July 12, 1876.

SECRETARY OF THE NAVY—GEORGE M. ROBESON, of New Jersey, continued from preceding administration. GEORGE M. ROBESON, of New Jersey, recommissioned March 17, 1873.

SECRETARY OF THE INTERIOR—COLUMBUS DELANO, of Ohio, continued from preceding administration. COLUMBUS DELANO, of Ohio, recommissioned March 17, 1873. BENJAMIN R. COWEN, of Ohio (Assistant Secretary), ad interim, October 1, 1875. ZACHARIAH CHANDLER, of Michigan, October 19, 1875.

## Administration of RUTHERFORD B. HAYES

### MARCH 4, 1877, TO MARCH 3, 1881

PRESIDENT OF THE UNITED STATES—RUTHERFORD B. HAYES, of Ohio.  (Oath administered March 5, 1877.)

VICE PRESIDENT OF THE UNITED STATES—WILLIAM A. WHEELER, of New York.

SECRETARY OF STATE—HAMILTON FISH, of New York, continued from preceding administration.  WILLIAM M. EVARTS, of New York, March 12, 1877.

SECRETARY OF THE TREASURY—LOT M. MORRILL, of Maine, continued from preceding administration.  JOHN SHERMAN, of Ohio, March 8, 1877; entered upon duties March 10, 1877.

SECRETARY OF WAR—JAMES D. CAMERON, of Pennsylvania, continued from preceding administration.  GEORGE W. McCRARY, of Iowa, March 12, 1877.  ALEXANDER RAMSEY, of Minnesota, December 10, 1879; entered upon duties December 12, 1879.

ATTORNEY GENERAL—ALPHONSO TAFT, of Ohio, continued from preceding administration.  CHARLES DEVENS, of Massachusetts, March 12, 1877.

POSTMASTER GENERAL—JAMES N. TYNER, of Indiana, continued from preceding administration.  DAVID M. KEY, of Tennessee, March 12, 1877; resigned June 1, 1880; served to August 24, 1880.  HORACE MAYNARD, of Tennessee, June 2, 1880; entered upon duties August 25, 1880.

SECRETARY OF THE NAVY—GEORGE M. ROBESON, of New Jersey, continued from preceding administration.  RICHARD W. THOMPSON, of Indiana, March 12, 1877.  ALEXANDER RAMSEY, of Minnesota (Secretary of War), ad interim, December 20, 1880.  NATHAN GOFF, Jr., of West Virginia, January 6, 1881.

SECRETARY OF THE INTERIOR—ZACHARIAH CHANDLER, of Michigan, continued from preceding administration.  CARL SCHURZ, of Missouri, March 12, 1877.

———

## Administration of JAMES A. GARFIELD

### MARCH 4, 1881, TO SEPTEMBER 19, 1881

PRESIDENT OF THE UNITED STATES—JAMES A. GARFIELD, of Ohio.  (Died September 19, 1881.)

VICE PRESIDENT OF THE UNITED STATES—CHESTER A. ARTHUR, of New York.

SECRETARY OF STATE—WILLIAM M. EVARTS, of New York, continued from preceding administration.  JAMES G. BLAINE, of Maine, March 5, 1881; entered upon duties March 7, 1881.

SECRETARY OF THE TREASURY—HENRY F. FRENCH, of Massachusetts (Assistant Secretary), ad interim, March 4, 1881.  WILLIAM WINDOM, of Minnesota, March 5, 1881; entered upon duties March 8, 1881.

SECRETARY OF WAR—ALEXANDER RAMSEY, of Minnesota, continued from preceding administration.  ROBERT T. LINCOLN, of Illinois, March 5, 1881; entered upon duties March 11, 1881.

ATTORNEY GENERAL—CHARLES DEVENS, of Massachusetts, continued from preceding administration.  WAYNE MacVEAGH, of Pennsylvania, March 5, 1881; entered upon duties March 7, 1881.

POSTMASTER GENERAL—HORACE MAYNARD, of Tennessee, continued from preceding administration.  THOMAS L. JAMES, of New York, March 5, 1881; entered upon duties March 8, 1881.

SECRETARY OF THE NAVY—NATHAN GOFF, Jr., of West Virginia, continued from preceding administration.  WILLIAM H. HUNT, of Louisiana, March 5, 1881; entered upon duties March 7, 1881.

SECRETARY OF THE INTERIOR—CARL SCHURZ, of Missouri, continued from preceding administration.  SAMUEL J. KIRKWOOD, of Iowa, March 5, 1881; entered upon duties March 8, 1881.

## Administration of CHESTER A. ARTHUR

### SEPTEMBER 20, 1881, TO MARCH 3, 1885

PRESIDENT OF THE UNITED STATES—Chester A. Arthur, of New York.

PRESIDENT PRO TEMPORE OF THE SENATE—Thomas F. Bayard, of Delaware; David Davis, of Illinois; George F. Edmunds, of Vermont.

SECRETARY OF STATE—James G. Blaine, of Maine, continued from preceding administration. Frederick T. Frelinghuysen, of New Jersey, December 12, 1881; entered upon duties December 19, 1881.

SECRETARY OF THE TREASURY—William Windom, of Minnesota, continued from preceding administration. Charles J. Folger, of New York, October 27, 1881; entered upon duties November 14, 1881 (died September 4, 1884). Charles E. Coon, of New York (Assistant Secretary), ad interim, September 4, 1884. Henry F. French, of Massachusetts (Assistant Secretary), ad interim, September 8, 1884. Charles E. Coon, of New York (Assistant Secretary), ad interim, September 15, 1884. Walter Q. Gresham, of Indiana, September 24, 1884. Henry F. French, of Massachusetts (Assistant Secretary), ad interim, October 29, 1884. Hugh McCulloch, of Indiana, October 28, 1884; entered upon duties October 31, 1884.

SECRETARY OF WAR—Robert T. Lincoln, of Illinois, continued from preceding administration.

ATTORNEY GENERAL—Wayne MacVeagh, of Pennsylvania, continued from preceding administration. Samuel F. Phillips, of North Carolina (Solicitor General), ad interim, November 14, 1881. Benjamin H. Brewster, of Pennsylvania, December 19, 1881; entered upon duties January 3, 1882.

POSTMASTER GENERAL—Thomas L. James, of New York, continued from preceding administration. Thomas L. James, of New York, recommissioned October 27, 1881. Timothy O. Howe, of Wisconsin, December 20, 1881; entered upon duties January 5, 1882 (died March 25, 1883). Frank Hatton, of Iowa (First Assistant Postmaster General), ad interim, March 26, 1883. Walter Q. Gresham, of Indiana, April 3, 1883; entered upon duties April 11, 1883. Frank Hatton, of Iowa (First Assistant Postmaster General), ad interim, September 25, 1884. Frank Hatton, of Iowa, October 14, 1884.

SECRETARY OF THE NAVY—William H. Hunt, of Louisiana, continued from preceding administration. William E. Chandler, of New Hampshire, April 12, 1882; entered upon duties April 17, 1882.

SECRETARY OF THE INTERIOR—Samuel J. Kirkwood, of Iowa, continued from preceding administration. Henry M. Teller, of Colorado, April 6, 1882; entered upon duties April 17, 1882.

---

## First Administration of GROVER CLEVELAND

### MARCH 4, 1885, TO MARCH 3, 1889

PRESIDENT OF THE UNITED STATES—Grover Cleveland, of New York.

VICE PRESIDENT OF THE UNITED STATES—Thomas A. Hendricks, of Indiana. (Died November 25, 1885.)

PRESIDENT PRO TEMPORE OF THE SENATE—John Sherman, of Ohio; John J. Ingalls, of Kansas.

SECRETARY OF STATE—Frederick T. Frelinghuysen, of New Jersey, continued from preceding administration. Thomas F. Bayard, of Delaware, March 6, 1885.

SECRETARY OF THE TREASURY—Hugh McCulloch, of Indiana, continued from preceding administration. Daniel Manning, of New York, March 6, 1885; entered upon duties March 8, 1885. Charles S. Fairchild, of New York, April 1, 1887.

SECRETARY OF WAR—Robert T. Lincoln, of Illinois, continued from preceding administration. William C. Endicott, of Massachusetts, March 6, 1885.

ATTORNEY GENERAL—Benjamin H. Brewster, of Pennsylvania, continued from preceding administration. Augustus H. Garland, of Arkansas, March 6, 1885; entered upon duties March 9, 1885.

POSTMASTER GENERAL—Frank Hatton, of Iowa, continued from preceding administration. William F. Vilas, of Wisconsin, March 6, 1885. Don M. Dickinson, of Michigan, January 16, 1888.

SECRETARY OF THE NAVY—William E. Chandler, of New Hampshire, continued from preceding administration. William C. Whitney, of New York, March 6, 1885.

SECRETARY OF THE INTERIOR—Merritt L. Joslyn, of Illinois (Assistant Secretary), ad interim, March 4, 1885. Lucius Q. C. Lamar, of Mississippi, March 6, 1885. Henry L. Muldrow, of Mississippi (First Assistant Secretary), ad interim, January 11, 1888. William F. Vilas, of Wisconsin, January 16, 1888.

SECRGTARY OF AGRICULTURE—Norman J. Colman, of Missouri, February 13, 1889.

## Administration of BENJAMIN HARRISON

### MARCH 4, 1889, TO MARCH 3, 1893

PRESIDENT OF THE UNITED STATES—BENJAMIN HARRISON, of Indiana.

VICE PRESIDENT OF THE UNITED STATES—LEVI P. MORTON, of New York.

SECRETARY OF STATE—THOMAS F. BAYARD, of Delaware, continued from preceding administration. JAMES G. BLAINE, of Maine, March 5, 1889; entered upon duties March 7, 1889. WILLIAM F. WHARTON, of Massachusetts (Assistant Secretary), ad interim, June 4, 1892. JOHN W. FOSTER, of Indiana, June 29, 1892. WILLIAM F. WHARTON, of Massachusetts (Assistant Secretary), ad interim, February 23, 1893.

SECRETARY OF THE TREASURY—CHARLES S. FAIRCHILD, of New York, continued from preceding administration. WILLIAM WINDOM, of Minnesota, March 5, 1889; entered upon duties March 7, 1889 (died January 29, 1891). ALLURED B. NETTLETON, of Minnesota (Assistant Secretary), ad interim, January 30, 1891. CHARLES FOSTER, of Ohio, February 24, 1891.

SECRETARY OF WAR—WILLIAM C. ENDICOTT, of Massachusetts, continued from preceding administration. REDFIELD PROCTOR, of Vermont, March 5, 1889. LEWIS A. GRANT, of Minnesota (Assistant Secretary), ad interim, December 6, 1891. STEPHEN B. ELKINS, of West Virginia, December 22, 1891; entered upon duties December 24, 1891.

ATTORNEY GENERAL—AUGUSTUS H. GARLAND, of Arkansas, continued from preceding administration. WILLIAM H. H. MILLER, of Indiana, March 5, 1889.

POSTMASTER GENERAL—DON M. DICKINSON, of Michigan, continued from preceding administration. JOHN WANAMAKER, of Pennsylvania, March 5, 1889.

SECRETARY OF THE NAVY—WILLIAM C. WHITNEY, of New York, continued from preceding administration. BENJAMIN F. TRACY, of New York, March 5, 1889.

SECRETARY OF THE INTERIOR—WILLIAM F. VILAS, of Wisconsin, continued from preceding administration. JOHN W. NOBLE, of Missouri, March 5, 1889; entered upon duties March 7, 1889.

SECRETARY OF AGRICULTURE—NORMAN J. COLMAN, of Missouri, continued from preceding administration. JEREMIAH M. RUSK, of Wisconsin, March 5, 1889; entered upon duties March 7, 1889.

---

## Second Administration of GROVER CLEVELAND

### MARCH 4, 1893, TO MARCH 3, 1897

PRESIDENT OF THE UNITED STATES—GROVER CLEVELAND, of New York.

VICE PRESIDENT OF THE UNITED STATES—ADLAI E. STEVENSON, of Illinois.

SECRETARY OF STATE—WILLIAM F. WHARTON, of Massachusetts (Assistant Secretary), ad interim, continued from preceding administration. WALTER Q. GRESHAM, of Illinois, March 6, 1893 (died May 28, 1895). EDWIN F. UHL, of Michigan (Assistant Secretary), ad interim, May 28, 1895. ALVEY A. ADEE, of the District of Columbia (Second Assistant Secretary), ad interim, May 31, 1895. EDWIN F. UHL, of Michigan (Assistant Secretary), ad interim, June 1, 1895. RICHARD OLNEY, of Massachusetts, June 8, 1895; entered upon duties June 10, 1895.

SECRETARY OF THE TREASURY—CHARLES FOSTER, of Ohio, continued from preceding administration. JOHN G. CARLISLE, of Kentucky, March 6, 1893.

SECRETARY OF WAR—STEPHEN B. ELKINS, of West Virginia, continued from preceding administration. DANIEL S. LAMONT, of New York, March 6, 1893.

ATTORNEY GENERAL—WILLIAM H. H. MILLER, of Indiana, continued from preceding administration. RICHARD OLNEY, of Massachusetts, March 6, 1893. JUDSON HARMON, of Ohio, June 8, 1895; entered upon duties June 11, 1895.

POSTMASTER GENERAL—JOHN WANAMAKER, of Pennsylvania, continued from preceding administration. WILSON S. BISSELL, of New York, March 6, 1893. WILLIAM L. WILSON, of West Virginia, March 1, 1895; entered upon duties April 4, 1895.

SECRETARY OF THE NAVY—BENJAMIN F. TRACY, of New York, continued from preceding administration. HILARY A. HERBERT, of Alabama, March 6, 1893.

SECRETARY OF THE INTERIOR—JOHN W. NOBLE, of Missouri, continued from preceding administration. HOKE SMITH, of Georgia, March 6, 1893. JOHN M. REYNOLDS, of Pennsylvania (Assistant Secretary), ad interim, September 1, 1896. DAVID R. FRANCIS, of Missouri, September 1, 1896; entered upon duties September 4, 1896.

SECRETARY OF AGRICULTURE—JEREMIAH M. RUSK, of Wisconsin, continued from preceding administration. JULIUS STERLING MORTON, of Nebraska, March 6, 1893.

## First Administration of WILLIAM McKINLEY

### MARCH 4, 1897, TO MARCH 3, 1901

PRESIDENT OF THE UNITED STATES—WILLIAM McKINLEY, of Ohio.

VICE PRESIDENT OF THE UNITED STATES—GARRET A. HOBART, of New Jersey. (Died November 21, 1899.)

PRESIDENT PRO TEMPORE OF THE SENATE—WILLIAM P. FRYE, of Maine.

SECRETARY OF STATE—RICHARD OLNEY, of Massachusetts, continued from preceding administration. JOHN SHERMAN, of Ohio, March 5, 1897. WILLIAM R. DAY, of Ohio, April 26, 1898; entered upon duties April 28, 1898. ALVEY A. ADEE (Second Assistant Secretary), ad interim, September 17, 1898. JOHN HAY, of the District of Columbia, September 20, 1898; entered upon duties September 30, 1898.

SECRETARY OF THE TREASURY—JOHN G. CARLISLE, of Kentucky, continued from preceding administration. LYMAN J. GAGE, of Illinois, March 5, 1897.

SECRETARY OF WAR—DANIEL S. LAMONT, of New York, continued from preceding administration. RUSSELL A. ALGER, of Michigan, March 5, 1897. ELIHU ROOT, of New York, August 1, 1899.

ATTORNEY GENERAL—JUDSON HARMON, of Ohio, continued from preceding administration. JOSEPH McKENNA, of California, March 5, 1897; entered upon duties March 7, 1897. JOHN K. RICHARDS, of Ohio (Solicitor General), ad interim, January 26, 1898. JOHN W. GRIGGS, of New Jersey, January 25, 1898; entered upon duties February 1, 1898.

POSTMASTER GENERAL—WILLIAM L. WILSON, of West Virginia, continued from preceding administration. JAMES A. GARY, of Maryland, March 5, 1897. CHARLES EMORY SMITH, of Pennsylvania, April 21, 1898.

SECRETARY OF THE NAVY—HILARY A. HERBERT, of Alabama, continued from preceding administration. JOHN D. LONG, of Massachusetts, March 5, 1897.

SECRETARY OF THE INTERIOR—DAVID R. FRANCIS, of Missouri, continued from preceding administration. CORNELIUS N. BLISS, of New York, March 5, 1897. ETHAN A. HITCHCOCK, of Missouri, December 21, 1898; entered upon duties February 20, 1899.

SECRETARY OF AGRICULTURE—JULIUS STERLING MORTON, of Nebraska, continued from preceding administration. JAMES WILSON, of Iowa, March 5, 1897.

---

## Second Administration of WILLIAM McKINLEY

### MARCH 4, 1901, TO SEPTEMBER 14, 1901

PRESIDENT OF THE UNITED STATES—WILLIAM McKINLEY, of Ohio. (Died September 14, 1901.)

VICE PRESIDENT OF THE UNITED STATES—THEODORE ROOSEVELT, of New York.

SECRETARY OF STATE—JOHN HAY, of the District of Columbia, continued from preceding administration. JOHN HAY, of the District of Columbia, recommissioned March 5, 1901.

SECRETARY OF THE TREASURY—LYMAN J. GAGE, of Illinois, continued from preceding administration. LYMAN J. GAGE, of Illinois, recommissioned March 5, 1901.

SECRETARY OF WAR—ELIHU ROOT, of New York, continued from preceding administration. ELIHU ROOT, of New York, recommissioned March 5, 1901.

ATTORNEY GENERAL—JOHN W. GRIGGS, of New Jersey, continued from preceding administration. JOHN W. GRIGGS, of New Jersey, recommissioned March 5, 1901. JOHN K. RICHARDS, of Ohio (Solicitor General), ad interim, April 1, 1901. PHILANDER C. KNOX, of Pennsylvania, April 5, 1901; entered upon duties April 10, 1901.

POSTMASTER GENERAL—CHARLES EMORY SMITH, of Pennsylvania, continued from preceding administration. CHARLES EMORY SMITH, of Pennsylvania, recommissioned March 5, 1901.

SECRETARY OF THE NAVY—JOHN D. LONG, of Massachusetts, continued from preceding administration. JOHN D. LONG, of Massachusetts, recommissioned March 5, 1901.

SECRETARY OF THE INTERIOR—ETHAN A. HITCHCOCK, of Missouri, continued from preceding administration. ETHAN A. HITCHCOCK, of Missouri, recommissioned March 5, 1901.

SECRETARY OF AGRICULTURE—JAMES WILSON, of Iowa, continued from preceding administration. JAMES WILSON, of Iowa, recommissioned March 5, 1901.

## First Administration of THEODORE ROOSEVELT

### SEPTEMBER 14, 1901, TO MARCH 3, 1905

PRESIDENT OF THE UNITED STATES—THEODORE ROOSEVELT, of New York.

PRESIDENT PRO TEMPORE OF THE SENATE—WILLIAM P. FRYE, of Maine.

SECRETARY OF STATE—JOHN HAY, of the District of Columbia, continued from preceding administration.

SECRETARY OF THE TREASURY—LYMAN J. GAGE, of Illinois, continued from preceding administration. LESLIE M. SHAW, of Iowa, January 9, 1902; entered upon duties February 1, 1902.

SECRETARY OF WAR—ELIHU ROOT, of New York, continued from preceding administration. WILLIAM H. TAFT, of Ohio, January 11, 1904, to take effect February 1, 1904.

ATTORNEY GENERAL—PHILANDER C. KNOX, of Pennsylvania, continued from preceding administration. PHILANDER C. KNOX, of Pennsylvania, recommissioned December 16, 1901. WILLIAM H. MOODY, of Massachusetts, July 1, 1904.

POSTMASTER GENERAL—CHARLES EMORY SMITH, of Pennsylvania, continued from preceding administration. HENRY C. PAYNE, of Wisconsin, January 9, 1902. ROBERT J. WYNNE, of Pennsylvania, October 10, 1904.

SECRETARY OF THE NAVY—JOHN D. LONG, of Massachusetts, continued from preceding administration. WILLIAM H. MOODY, of Massachusetts, April 29, 1902; entered upon duties May 1, 1902. PAUL MORTON, of Illinois, July 1, 1904.

SECRETARY OF THE INTERIOR—ETHAN A. HITCHCOCK, of Missouri, continued from preceding administration.

SECRETARY OF AGRICULTURE—JAMES WILSON, of Iowa, continued from preceding administration.

SECRETARY OF COMMERCE AND LABOR—GEORGE B. CORTELYOU, of New York, February 16, 1903. VICTOR H. METCALF, of California, July 1, 1904.

---

## Second Administration of THEODORE ROOSEVELT

### MARCH 4, 1905, TO MARCH 3, 1909

PRESIDENT OF THE UNITED STATES—THEODORE ROOSEVELT, of New York.

VICE PRESIDENT OF THE UNITED STATES—CHARLES WARREN FAIRBANKS, of Indiana.

SECRETARY OF STATE—JOHN HAY, of the District of Columbia, continued from preceding administration. JOHN HAY, of the District of Columbia, recommissioned March 6, 1905 (died July 1, 1905). FRANCIS B. LOOMIS, of Ohio (Assistant Secretary), ad interim, July 1, 1905, to July 18, 1905. ELIHU ROOT, of New York, July 7, 1905; entered upon duties July 19, 1905. ROBERT BACON, of New York, January 27, 1909.

SECRETARY OF THE TREASURY—LESLIE M. SHAW, of Iowa, continued from preceding administration. LESLIE M. SHAW, of Iowa, recommissioned March 6, 1905. GEORGE B. CORTELYOU, of New York, January 15, 1907, to take effect March 4, 1907.

SECRETARY OF WAR—WILLIAM H. TAFT, of Ohio, continued from preceding administration. WILLIAM H. TAFT, of Ohio, recommissioned March 6, 1905. LUKE E. WRIGHT, of Tennessee, June 29, 1908; entered upon duties July 1, 1908.

ATTORNEY GENERAL—WILLIAM H. MOODY, of Massachusetts, continued from preceding administration. WILLIAM H. MOODY, of Massachusetts, recommissioned March 6, 1905. CHARLES J. BONAPARTE, of Maryland, December 12, 1906; entered upon duties December 17, 1906.

POSTMASTER GENERAL—ROBERT J. WYNNE, of Pennsylvania, continued from preceding administration. GEORGE B. CORTELYOU, of New York, March 6, 1905. GEORGE VON L. MEYER, of Massachusetts, January 15, 1907, to take effect March 4, 1907.

SECRETARY OF THE NAVY—PAUL MORTON, of Illinois, continued from preceding administration. PAUL MORTON, of Illinois, recommissioned March 6, 1905. CHARLES J. BONAPARTE, of Maryland, July 1, 1905. VICTOR H. METCALF, of California, December 12, 1906; entered upon duties December 17, 1906. TRUMAN H. NEWBERRY, of Michigan, December 1, 1908.

SECRETARY OF THE INTERIOR—ETHAN A. HITCHCOCK, of Missouri, continued from preceding administration. ETHAN A. HITCHCOCK, of Missouri, recommissioned March 6, 1905. JAMES R. GARFIELD, of Ohio, January 15, 1907, to take effect March 4, 1907.

SECRETARY OF AGRICULTURE—JAMES WILSON, of Iowa, continued from preceding administration. JAMES WILSON, of Iowa, recommissioned March 6, 1905.

SECRETARY OF COMMERCE AND LABOR—VICTOR H. METCALF, of California, continued from preceding administration. VICTOR H. METCALF, of California, recommissioned March 6, 1905. OSCAR S. STRAUS, of New York, December 12, 1906; entered upon duties December 17, 1906.

## Administration of WILLIAM H. TAFT

### MARCH 4, 1909, TO MARCH 3, 1913

PRESIDENT OF THE UNITED STATES—WILLIAM H. TAFT, of Ohio.

VICE PRESIDENT OF THE UNITED STATES—JAMES S. SHERMAN, of New York. (Died October 30, 1912.)

PRESIDENT PRO TEMPORE OF THE SENATE—WILLIAM P. FRYE, of Maine (resigned April 27, 1911). JACOB H. GALLINGER, of New Hampshire, and AUGUSTUS O. BACON, of Georgia, alternating.

SECRETARY OF STATE—ROBERT BACON, of New York, continued from preceding administration. PHILANDER C. KNOX, of Pennsylvania, March 5, 1909.

SECRETARY OF THE TREASURY—GEORGE B. CORTELYOU, of New York, continued from preceding administration. FRANKLIN MacVEAGH, of Illinois, March 5, 1909; entered upon duties March 8, 1909.

SECRETARY OF WAR—LUKE E. WRIGHT, of Tennessee, continued from preceding administration. JACOB M. DICKINSON, of Tennessee, March 5, 1909; entered upon duties March 12, 1909. HENRY L. STIMSON, of New York, May 16, 1911; entered upon duties May 22, 1911.

ATTORNEY GENERAL—CHARLES J. BONAPARTE, of Maryland, continued from preceding administration. GEORGE W. WICKERSHAM, of New York, March 5, 1909.

POSTMASTER GENERAL—GEORGE VON L. MEYER, of Massachusetts, continued from preceding administration. FRANK H. HITCHCOCK, of Massachusetts, March 5, 1909.

SECRETARY OF THE NAVY—TRUMAN H. NEWBERRY, of Michigan, continued from preceding administration. GEORGE VON L. MEYER, of Massachusetts, March 5, 1909.

SECRETARY OF THE INTERIOR—JAMES R. GARFIELD, of Ohio, continued from preceding administration. RICHARD A. BALLINGER, of Washington, March 5, 1909. WALTER LOWRIE FISHER, of Illinois, March 7, 1911.

SECRETARY OF AGRICULTURE—JAMES WILSON, of Iowa, continued from preceding administration. JAMES WILSON, of Iowa, recommissioned March 5, 1909.

SECRETARY OF COMMERCE AND LABOR—OSCAR S. STRAUS, of New York, continued from preceding administration CHARLES NAGEL, of Missouri, March 5, 1909.

---

## First Administration of WOODROW WILSON

### MARCH 4, 1913, TO MARCH 3, 1917

PRESIDENT OF THE UNITED STATES—WOODROW WILSON, of New Jersey.

VICE PRESIDENT OF THE UNITED STATES—THOMAS R. MARSHALL, of Indiana.

SECRETARY OF STATE—PHILANDER C. KNOX, of Pennsylvania, continued from preceding administration. WILLIAM JENNINGS BRYAN, of Nebraska, March 5, 1913. ROBERT LANSING, of New York (counselor), ad interim, June 9, 1915. ROBERT LANSING, of New York, June 23, 1915.

SECRETARY OF THE TREASURY—FRANKLIN MacVEAGH, of Illinois, continued from preceding administration. WILLIAM GIBBS McADOO, of New York, March 5, 1913; entered upon duties March 6, 1913.

SECRETARY OF WAR—HENRY L. STIMSON, of New York, continued from preceding administration. LINDLEY M. GARRISON, of New Jersey, March 5, 1913. HUGH L. SCOTT (United States Army), ad interim, February 12, 1916; served from February 11 to March 8, 1916. NEWTON D. BAKER, of Ohio, March 7, 1916; entered upon duties March 9, 1916.

ATTORNEY GENERAL—GEORGE W. WICKERSHAM, of New York, continued from preceding administration. JAMES CLARK McREYNOLDS, of Tennessee, March 5, 1913; entered upon duties March 6, 1913. THOMAS WATT GREGORY, of Texas, August 29, 1914; entered upon duties September 3, 1914.

POSTMASTER GENERAL—FRANK H. HITCHCOCK, of Massachusetts, continued from preceding administration. ALBERT SIDNEY BURLESON, of Texas, March 5, 1913.

SECRETARY OF THE NAVY—GEORGE VON L. MEYER, of Massachusetts, continued from preceding administration. JOSEPHUS DANIELS, of North Carolina, March 5, 1913.

SECRETARY OF THE INTERIOR—WALTER LOWRIE FISHER, of Illinois, continued from preceding administration. FRANKLIN KNIGHT LANE, of California, March 5, 1913.

SECRETARY OF AGRICULTURE—JAMES WILSON, of Iowa, continued from preceding administration. DAVID FRANKLIN HOUSTON, of Missouri, March 5, 1913; entered upon duties March 6, 1913.

SECRETARY OF COMMERCE—CHARLES NAGEL, of Missouri (Secretary of Commerce and Labor), continued from preceding administration. WILLIAM C. REDFIELD, of New York, March 5, 1913.

SECRETARY OF LABOR—CHARLES NAGEL, of Missouri (Secretary of Commerce and Labor), continued from preceding administration. WILLIAM BAUCHOP WILSON, of Pennsylvania, March 5, 1913.

## Second Administration of WOODROW WILSON

### MARCH 4, 1917, TO MARCH 3, 1921

PRESIDENT OF THE UNITED STATES—WOODROW WILSON, of New Jersey.  (Oath administered March 5, 1917.)

VICE PRESIDENT OF THE UNITED STATES—THOMAS R. MARSHALL, of Indiana.

SECRETARY OF STATE—ROBERT LANSING, of New York, continued from preceding administration.  FRANK L. POLK, of New York (Under Secretary), ad interim, February 14, 1920, to March 13, 1920.  BAINBRIDGE COLBY, of New York, March 22, 1920; entered upon duties March 23, 1920.

SECRETARY OF THE TREASURY—WILLIAM GIBBS McADOO, of New York, continued from preceding administration.  CARTER GLASS, of Virginia, December 6, 1918; entered upon duties December 16, 1918.  DAVID F. HOUSTON, of Missouri, January 31, 1920; entered upon duties February 2, 1920.

SECRETARY OF WAR—NEWTON D. BAKER, of Ohio, continued from preceding administration.

ATTORNEY GENERAL—THOMAS WATT GREGORY, of Texas, continued from preceding administration.  A. MITCHELL PALMER, of Pennsylvania, March 5, 1919.

POSTMASTER GENERAL—ALBERT SIDNEY BURLESON, of Texas, continued from preceding administration.  ALBERT SIDNEY BURLESON, of Texas, recommissioned January 24, 1918.

SECRETARY OF THE NAVY—JOSEPHUS DANIELS, of North Carolina, continued from preceding administration.

SECRETARY OF THE INTERIOR—FRANKLIN KNIGHT LANE, of California, continued from preceding administration.  JOHN BARTON PAYNE, of Illinois, February 28, 1920; entered upon duties March 13, 1920.

SECRETARY OF AGRICULTURE—DAVID FRANKLIN HOUSTON, of Missouri, continued from preceding administration.  EDWIN T. MEREDITH, of Iowa, January 31, 1920; entered upon duties February 2, 1920.

SECRETARY OF COMMERCE—WILLIAM C. REDFIELD, of New York, continued from preceding administration.  JOSHUA WILLIS ALEXANDER, of Missouri, December 11, 1919; entered upon duties December 16, 1919.

SECRETARY OF LABOR—WILLIAM BAUCHOP WILSON, of Pennsylvania, continued from preceding administration.

---

## Administration of WARREN G. HARDING

### MARCH 4, 1921, TO AUGUST 2, 1923

PRESIDENT OF THE UNITED STATES—WARREN G. HARDING, of Ohio.  (Died August 2, 1923.)

VICE PRESIDENT OF THE UNITED STATES—CALVIN COOLIDGE, of Massachusetts.

SECRETARY OF STATE—BAINBRIDGE COLBY, of New York, continued from preceding administration.  CHARLES EVANS HUGHES, of New York, March 4, 1921; entered upon duties March 5, 1921.

SECRETARY OF THE TREASURY—DAVID F. HOUSTON, of Missouri, continued from preceding administration.  ANDREW W. MELLON, of Pennsylvania, March 4, 1921; entered upon duties March 5, 1921.

SECRETARY OF WAR—NEWTON D. BAKER, of Ohio, continued from preceding administration.  JOHN W. WEEKS, of Massachusetts, March 5, 1921.

ATTORNEY GENERAL—A. MITCHELL PALMER, of Pennsylvania, continued from preceding administration.  HARRY M. DAUGHERTY, of Ohio, March 5, 1921.

POSTMASTER GENERAL—ALBERT SIDNEY BURLESON, of Texas, continued from preceding administration.  WILL H. HAYS, of Indiana, March 5, 1921.  HUBERT WORK, of Colorado, March 4, 1922.  HARRY S. NEW, of Indiana, February 27, 1923; entered upon duties March 5, 1923.

SECRETARY OF THE NAVY—JOSEPHUS DANIELS, of North Carolina, continued from preceding administration.  EDWIN DENBY, of Michigan, March 5, 1921.

SECRETARY OF THE INTERIOR—JOHN BARTON PAYNE, of Illinois, continued from preceding administration.  ALBERT B. FALL, of New Mexico, March 5, 1921.  HUBERT WORK, of Colorado, February 27, 1923; entered upon duties March 5, 1923.

SECRETARY OF AGRICULTURE—EDWIN T. MEREDITH, of Iowa, continued from preceding administration.  HENRY C. WALLACE, of Iowa, March 5, 1921.

SECRETARY OF COMMERCE—JOSHUA WILLIS ALEXANDER, of Missouri, continued from preceding administration.  HERBERT C. HOOVER, of California, March 5, 1921.

SECRETARY OF LABOR—WILLIAM BAUCHOP WILSON, of Pennsylvania, continued from preceding administration.  JAMES J. DAVIS, of Pennsylvania, March 5, 1921.

## First Administration of CALVIN COOLIDGE

### AUGUST 3, 1923, TO MARCH 3, 1925

PRESIDENT OF THE UNITED STATES—Calvin Coolidge, of Massachusetts.

PRESIDENT PRO TEMPORE OF THE SENATE—Albert B. Cummins, of Iowa.

SECRETARY OF STATE—Charles Evans Hughes, of New York, continued from preceding administration.

SECRETARY OF THE TREASURY—Andrew W. Mellon, of Pennsylvania, continued from preceding administration.

SECRETARY OF WAR—John W. Weeks, of Massachusetts, continued from preceding administration.

ATTORNEY GENERAL—Harry M. Daugherty, of Ohio, continued from preceding administration. Harlan F. Stone, of New York, April 7, 1924; entered upon duties April 9, 1924.

POSTMASTER GENERAL—Harry S. New, of Indiana, continued from preceding administration.

SECRETARY OF THE NAVY—Edwin Denby, of Michigan, continued from preceding administration. Curtis D. Wilbur, of California, March 18, 1924.

SECRETARY OF THE INTERIOR—Hubert Work, of Colorado, continued from preceding administration.

SECRETARY OF AGRICULTURE—Henry C. Wallace, of Iowa, continued from preceding administration (died October 25, 1924). Howard M. Gore, of West Virginia (Assistant Secretary), ad interim, October 26, 1924, to November 22, 1924. Howard M. Gore, of West Virginia, November 21, 1924; entered upon duties November 22, 1924.

SECRETARY OF COMMERCE—Herbert C. Hoover, of California, continued from preceding administration.

SECRETARY OF LABOR—James J. Davis, of Pennsylvania, continued from preceding administration.

———

## Second Administration of CALVIN COOLIDGE

### MARCH 4, 1925, TO MARCH 3, 1929

PRESIDENT OF THE UNITED STATES—Calvin Coolidge, of Massachusetts.

VICE PRESIDENT OF THE UNITED STATES—Charles G. Dawes, of Illinois.

SECRETARY OF STATE—Charles Evans Hughes, of New York, continued from preceding administration. Frank B. Kellogg, of Minnesota, February 16, 1925; entered upon duties March 5, 1925.

SECRETARY OF THE TREASURY—Andrew W. Mellon, of Pennsylvania, continued from preceding administration.

SECRETARY OF WAR—John W. Weeks, of Massachusetts, continued from preceding administration. Dwight F. Davis, of Missouri, October 13, 1925; entered upon duties October 14, 1925.

ATTORNEY GENERAL—James M. Beck, of Pennsylvania (Solicitor General), ad interim, March 4, 1925, to March 16, 1925. John G. Sargent, of Vermont, March 17, 1925; entered upon duties March 18, 1925.

POSTMASTER GENERAL—Harry S. New, of Indiana, continued from preceding administration. Harry S. New, of Indiana, recommissioned March 5, 1925.

SECRETARY OF THE NAVY—Curtis D. Wilbur, of California, continued from preceding administration.

SECRETARY OF THE INTERIOR—Hubert Work, of Colorado, continued from preceding administration. Roy O. West, of Illinois, ad interim, July 25, 1928, to January 21, 1929. Roy O. West, January 21, 1929.

SECRETARY OF AGRICULTURE—Howard M. Gore, of West Virginia, continued from preceding administration. William M. Jardine, of Kansas, February 18, 1925; entered upon duties March 5, 1925.

SECRETARY OF COMMERCE—Herbert C. Hoover, of California, continued from preceding administration. William F. Whiting, of Massachusetts, ad interim, August 21, 1928, to December 11, 1928. William F. Whiting, December 11, 1928.

SECRETARY OF LABOR—James J. Davis, of Pennsylvania, continued from preceding administration.

## Administration of HERBERT C. HOOVER

### MARCH 4, 1929, TO MARCH 3, 1933

PRESIDENT OF THE UNITED STATES—HERBERT C. HOOVER, of California.

VICE PRESIDENT OF THE UNITED STATES—CHARLES CURTIS, of Kansas.

SECRETARY OF STATE—FRANK B. KELLOGG, of Minnesota, continued from preceding administration. HENRY L. STIMSON, of New York, March 4, 1929; entered upon duties March 29, 1929.

SECRETARY OF THE TREASURY—ANDREW W. MELLON, of Pennsylvania, continued from preceding administration. OGDEN L. MILLS, of New York, February 10, 1932; entered upon duties February 13, 1932.

SECRETARY OF WAR—DWIGHT F. DAVIS, of Missouri, continued from preceding administration. JAMES W. GOOD, of Illinois, March 5, 1929; entered upon duties March 6, 1929. PATRICK J. HURLEY, of Oklahoma, December 9, 1929.

ATTORNEY GENERAL—JOHN G. SARGENT, of Vermont, continued from preceding administration. JAMES DEWITT MITCHELL, of Minnesota, March 5, 1929; entered upon duties March 6, 1929.

POSTMASTER GENERAL—HARRY S. NEW, of Indiana, continued from preceding administration. WALTER F. BROWN, of Ohio, March 5, 1929; entered upon duties March 6, 1929.

SECRETARY OF THE NAVY—CURTIS D. WILBUR, of California, continued from preceding administration. CHARLES F. ADAMS, of Massachusetts, March 5, 1929.

SECRETARY OF THE INTERIOR—ROY O. WEST, of Illinois, continued from preceding administration. RAY L. WILBUR, of California, March 5, 1929.

SECRETARY OF AGRICULTURE—WILLIAM M. JARDINE, of Kansas, continued from preceding administration. ARTHUR M. HYDE, of Missouri, March 5, 1929; entered upon duties March 6, 1929.

SECRETARY OF COMMERCE—WILLIAM F. WHITING, of Massachusetts, continued from preceding administration. ROBERT P. LAMONT, of Illinois, March 5, 1929. ROY D. CHAPIN, of Michigan, ad interim, August 8, 1932, to December 14, 1932. ROY D. CHAPIN, of Michigan, December 14, 1932.

SECRETARY OF LABOR—JAMES J. DAVIS, of Pennsylvania, continued from preceding administration. WILLIAM N. DOAK, of Virginia, December 8, 1930; entered upon duties December 9, 1930.

---

## First Administration of FRANKLIN DELANO ROOSEVELT

### MARCH 4, 1933, TO JANUARY 20, 1937

PRESIDENT OF THE UNITED STATES—FRANKLIN DELANO ROOSEVELT, of New York.

VICE PRESIDENT OF THE UNITED STATES—JOHN N. GARNER, of Texas.

SECRETARY OF STATE—CORDELL HULL, of Tennessee, March 4, 1933

SECRETARY OF THE TREASURY—WILLIAM H. WOODIN, of New York, March 4, 1933. HENRY MORGENTHAU, Jr., of New York (Under Secretary), ad interim, January 1, 1934, to January 8, 1934. HENRY MORGENTHAU, Jr., of New York, January 8, 1934.

SECRETARY OF WAR—GEORGE H. DERN, of Utah, March 4, 1933. *died 8/27/36*

ATTORNEY GENERAL—HOMER S. CUMMINGS, of Connecticut, March 4, 1933.

POSTMASTER GENERAL—JAMES A. FARLEY, of New York, March 4, 1933.

SECRETARY OF THE NAVY—CLAUDE A. SWANSON, of Virginia, March 4, 1933.

SECRETARY OF THE INTERIOR—HAROLD L. ICKES, of Illinois, March 4, 1933.

SECRETARY OF AGRICULTURE—HENRY A. WALLACE, of Iowa, March 4, 1933.

SECRETARY OF COMMERCE—DANIEL C. ROPER, of South Carolina, March 4, 1933.

SECRETARY OF LABOR—FRANCES PERKINS, of New York, March 4, 1933.

## Second Administration of FRANKLIN DELANO ROOSEVELT

### JANUARY 20, 1937, TO JANUARY 20, 1941

PRESIDENT OF THE UNITED STATES—FRANKLIN DELANO ROOSEVELT, of New York.

VICE PRESIDENT OF THE UNITED STATES—JOHN N. GARNER, of Texas.

SECRETARY OF STATE—CORDELL HULL, of Tennessee, continued from preceding administration.

SECRETARY OF THE TREASURY—HENRY MORGENTHAU, Jr., of New York, continued from preceding administration.

SECRETARY OF WAR—GEORGE H. DERN, of Utah, continued from preceding administration (died August 27, 1936). HARRY H. WOODRING, of Kansas (Assistant Secretary), ad interim, September 25, 1936, to May 6, 1937. HARRY H. WOODRING, of Kansas, May 6, 1937. HENRY L. STIMSON, of New York, July 10, 1940.

ATTORNEY GENERAL—HOMER S. CUMMINGS, of Connecticut, continued from preceding administration. FRANK MURPHY, of Michigan, ad interim, January 2, 1939, to January 17, 1939. FRANK MURPHY, of Michigan, January 17, 1939. ROBERT H. JACKSON, of New York, January 18, 1940.

POSTMASTER GENERAL—JAMES A. FARLEY, of New York, continued from preceding administration. JAMES A. FARLEY, of New York, recommissioned January 22, 1937. FRANK C. WALKER, of Pennsylvania, September 10, 1940.

SECRETARY OF THE NAVY—CLAUDE A. SWANSON, of Virginia, continued from preceding administration (died July 7, 1939). CHARLES EDISON, of New Jersey, Acting Secretary from August 5, 1939, to December 30, 1939. CHARLES EDISON, of New Jersey (Assistant Secretary), ad interim, December 30, 1939, to January 11, 1940. CHARLES EDISON, of New Jersey, January 11, 1940. FRANK KNOX, of Illinois, July 10, 1940.

SECRETARY OF THE INTERIOR—HAROLD L. ICKES, of Illinois, continued from preceding administration.

SECRETARY OF AGRICULTURE—HENRY A. WALLACE, of Iowa, continued from preceding administration. CLAUDE R. WICKARD, of Indiana, August 27, 1940; entered upon duties September 5, 1940.

SECRETARY OF COMMERCE—DANIEL C. ROPER, of South Carolina, continued from preceding administration. HARRY L. HOPKINS, of New York, ad interim, December 24, 1938, to January 23, 1939. HARRY L. HOPKINS, of New York, January 23, 1939. JESSE H. JONES, of Texas, September 16, 1940; entered upon duties September 19, 1940.

SECRETARY OF LABOR—FRANCES PERKINS, of New York, continued from preceding administration.

---

## Third Administration of FRANKLIN DELANO ROOSEVELT

### JANUARY 20, 1941, TO JANUARY 20, 1945

PRESIDENT OF THE UNITED STATES—FRANKLIN DELANO ROOSEVELT, of New York.

VICE PRESIDENT OF THE UNITED STATES—HENRY A. WALLACE, of Iowa.

SECRETARY OF STATE—CORDELL HULL, of Tennessee, continued from preceding administration. EDWARD R. STETTINIUS, of Virginia, November 30, 1944; entered upon duties December 1, 1944.

SECRETARY OF THE TREASURY—HENRY MORGENTHAU, Jr., of New York, continued from preceding administration.

SECRETARY OF WAR—HENRY L. STIMSON, of New York, continued from preceding administration.

ATTORNEY GENERAL—ROBERT H. JACKSON, of New York, continued from preceding administration. FRANCIS BIDDLE, of Pennsylvania, September 5, 1941.

POSTMASTER GENERAL—FRANK C. WALKER, of Pennsylvania, continued from preceding administration. FRANK C. WALKER, of Pennsylvania, recommissioned January 27, 1941.

SECRETARY OF THE NAVY—FRANK KNOX, of Illinois, continued from preceding administration (died April 28, 1944). JAMES V. FORRESTAL, of New York, May 18, 1944.

SECRETARY OF THE INTERIOR—HAROLD L. ICKES, of Illinois, continued from preceding administration.

SECRETARY OF AGRICULTURE—CLAUDE R. WICKARD, of Indiana, continued from preceding administration.

SECRETARY OF COMMERCE—JESSE H. JONES, of Texas, continued from preceding administration.

SECRETARY OF LABOR—FRANCES PERKINS, of New York, continued from preceding administration.

## Fourth Administration of FRANKLIN DELANO ROOSEVELT

### JANUARY 20, 1945, TO APRIL 12, 1945

PRESIDENT OF THE UNITED STATES—Franklin Delano Roosevelt, of New York.  (Died April 12, 1945.)

VICE PRESIDENT OF THE UNITED STATES—Harry S. Truman, of Missouri.

SECRETARY OF STATE—Edward R. Stettinius, of Virginia, continued from preceding administration.

SECRETARY OF THE TREASURY—Henry Morgenthau, Jr., of New York, continued from preceding administration.

SECRETARY OF WAR—Henry L: Stimson, of New York, continued from preceding administration.

ATTORNEY GENERAL—Francis Biddle, of Pennsylvania, continued from preceding administration.

POSTMASTER GENERAL—Frank C. Walker, of Pennsylvania, continued from preceding administration.  Frank C. Walker, of Pennsylvania, recommissioned February 6, 1945.

SECRETARY OF THE NAVY—James V. Forrestal, of New York, continued from preceding administration.

SECRETARY OF THE INTERIOR—Harold L. Ickes, of Illinois, continued from preceding administration.

SECRETARY OF AGRICULTURE—Claude R. Wickard, of Indiana, continued from preceding administration.

SECRETARY OF COMMERCE—Jesse H. Jones, of Texas, continued from preceding administration.  Henry A. Wallace, of Iowa, March 1, 1945; entered upon duties March 2, 1945.

SECRETARY OF LABOR—Frances Perkins, of New York, continued from preceding administration.

———

## First Administration of HARRY S. TRUMAN

### APRIL 12, 1945, TO JANUARY 20, 1949

PRESIDENT OF THE UNITED STATES— Harry S. Truman, of Missouri.

PRESIDENT PRO TEMPORE OF THE SENATE—Kenneth McKellar, of Tennessee.  Arthur S. Vandenberg, of Michigan, January 4, 1947.

SECRETARY OF STATE—Edward R. Stettinius, of Virginia, continued from preceding administration.  James F. Byrnes, of South Carolina, July 2, 1945; entered upon duties July 3, 1945.  George C. Marshall, of Pennsylvania, January 8, 1947; entered upon duties January 21, 1947.

SECRETARY OF THE TREASURY—Henry Morgenthau, Jr., of New York, continued from preceding administration.  Fred M. Vinson, of Kentucky, July 18, 1945; entered upon duties July 23, 1945.  John W. Snyder, of Missouri, June 12, 1946; entered upon duties June 25, 1946.

SECRETARY OF DEFENSE—James Forrestal, of New York, July 26, 1947; entered upon duties September 17, 1947.

SECRETARY OF WAR—Henry L. Stimson, of New York, continued from preceding administration.  Robert Porter Patterson, of New York, September 26, 1945; entered upon duties September 27, 1945.  Kenneth C. Royall, of North Carolina, July 21, 1947; entered upon duties July 25, 1947, and served until September 17, 1947.

ATTORNEY GENERAL—Francis Biddle, of Pennsylvania, continued from preceding administration.  Tom C. Clark, of Texas, June 15, 1945; entered upon duties July 1, 1945.

POSTMASTER GENERAL—Frank C. Walker, of Pennsylvania, continued from preceding administration.  Robert E. Hannegan, of Missouri, May 8, 1945; entered upon duties July 1, 1945.  Jesse M. Donaldson, of Missouri, December 16, 1947.

SECRETARY OF THE NAVY—James V. Forrestal, of New York, continued from preceding administration; served until September 17, 1947.

SECRETARY OF THE INTERIOR—Harold L. Ickes, of Illinois, continued from preceding administration.  Julius A. Krug, of Wisconsin, March 6, 1946; entered upon duties March 18, 1946.

SECRETARY OF AGRICULTURE—Claude R. Wickard, of Indiana, continued from preceding administration.  Clinton P. Anderson, of New Mexico, June 2, 1945; entered upon duties June 30, 1945.  Charles F. Brannan, of Colorado, May 29, 1948; entered upon duties June 2, 1948.

SECRETARY OF COMMERCE—Henry A. Wallace, of Iowa, continued from preceding administration.  William Averell Harriman, of New York, ad interim, September 28, 1946, to January 28, 1947.  William Averell Harriman, of New York, January 28, 1947.  Charles Sawyer, of Ohio, May 6, 1948.

SECRETARY OF LABOR—Frances Perkins, of New York, continued from preceding administration.  Lewis B. Schwellenbach, of Washington, June 1, 1945; entered upon duties July 1, 1945 (died June 10. 1948).  Maurice J. Tobin, of Massachusetts, ad interim, August 13, 1948.

## Second Administration of HARRY S. TRUMAN

### JANUARY 20, 1949, TO JANUARY 20, 1953

PRESIDENT OF THE UNITED STATES—Harry S. Truman, of Missouri.

VICE PRESIDENT OF THE UNITED STATES—Alben W. Barkley, of Kentucky.

SECRETARY OF STATE—Dean G. Acheson, of Connecticut, January 19, 1949; entered upon duties January 21, 1949.

SECRETARY OF THE TREASURY—John W. Snyder, of Missouri, continued from preceding administration.

SECRETARY OF DEFENSE—James Forrestal, of New York, continued from preceding administration. Louis A. Johnson, of West Virginia, March 23, 1949; entered upon duties March 28, 1949. George C. Marshall, of Pennsylvania, September 20, 1950; entered upon duties September 21, 1950. Robert A. Lovett, of New York, September 14, 1951; entered upon duties September 17, 1951.

ATTORNEY GENERAL—Tom C. Clark, of Texas, continued from preceding administration. J. Howard McGrath, of Rhode Island, August 19, 1949; entered upon duties August 24, 1949. James P. McGranery, of Pennsylvania, May 21, 1952; entered upon duties May 27, 1952.

POSTMASTER GENERAL—Jesse M. Donaldson, of Missouri, continued from preceding administration. Jesse M. Donaldson, of Missouri, recommissioned February 8, 1949.

SECRETARY OF THE INTERIOR—Julius A. Krug, of Wisconsin, continued from preceding administration. Oscar L. Chapman, of Colorado (Under Secretary), ad interim, December 1, 1949, to January 19, 1950. Oscar L. Chapman, of Colorado, January 19, 1950.

SECRETARY OF AGRICULTURE—Charles F. Brannan, of Colorado, continued from preceding administration.

SECRETARY OF COMMERCE—Charles Sawyer, of Ohio, continued from preceding administration.

SECRETARY OF LABOR—Maurice J. Tobin, of Massachusetts, ad interim, continued from preceding administration. Maurice J. Tobin, of Massachusetts, February 1, 1949.

---

## First Administration of DWIGHT D. EISENHOWER

### JANUARY 20, 1953, TO JANUARY 20, 1957

PRESIDENT OF THE UNITED STATES—Dwight D. Eisenhower, of New York.

VICE PRESIDENT OF THE UNITED STATES—Richard M. Nixon, of California.

SECRETARY OF STATE—John Foster Dulles, of New York, January 21, 1953.

SECRETARY OF THE TREASURY—George M. Humphrey, of Ohio, January 21, 1953.

SECRETARY OF DEFENSE—Charles E. Wilson, of Michigan, January 26, 1953; entered upon duties January 28, 1953.

ATTORNEY GENERAL—Herbert Brownell, Jr., of New York, January 21, 1953.

POSTMASTER GENERAL—Arthur E. Summerfield, of Michigan, January 21, 1953.

SECRETARY OF THE INTERIOR—Douglas McKay, of Oregon, January 21, 1953. Frederick A. Seaton, of Nebraska, June 6, 1956; entered upon duties June 8, 1956.

SECRETARY OF AGRICULTURE—Ezra Taft Benson, of Utah, January 21, 1953.

SECRETARY OF COMMERCE—Sinclair Weeks, of Massachusetts, January 21, 1953.

SECRETARY OF LABOR—Martin P. Durkin, of Maryland, January 21, 1953. James P. Mitchell, of New Jersey, ad interim, October 9, 1953, to January 19, 1954. James P. Mitchell, of New Jersey, January 19, 1954.

SECRETARY OF HEALTH, EDUCATION, AND WELFARE—Oveta Culp Hobby, of Texas, April 10, 1953; entered upon duties April 11, 1953. Marion B. Folsom, of New York, July 20, 1955; entered upon duties August 1, 1955.

## Second Administration of DWIGHT D. EISENHOWER

### JANUARY 20, 1957, TO JANUARY 20, 1961

PRESIDENT OF THE UNITED STATES—DWIGHT D. EISENHOWER, of Pennsylvania.

VICE PRESIDENT OF THE UNITED STATES—RICHARD M. NIXON, of California.

SECRETARY OF STATE—JOHN FOSTER DULLES, of New York, continued from preceding administration. CHRISTIAN A. HERTER, of Massachusetts, April 21, 1959; entered upon duties April 22, 1959.

SECRETARY OF THE TREASURY—GEORGE M. HUMPHREY, of Ohio, continued from preceding administration. ROBERT BERNERD ANDERSON, of Connecticut, July 2, 1957; entered upon duties July 29, 1957.

SECRETARY OF DEFENSE—CHARLES E. WILSON, of Michigan, continued from preceding administration. NEIL H. McELROY, of Ohio, August 19, 1957; entered upon duties October 9, 1957. THOMAS S. GATES, Jr., of Pennsylvania, ad interim, December 1, 1959, to January 26, 1960. THOMAS S. GATES, Jr., of Pennsylvania, January 26, 1960.

ATTORNEY GENERAL—HERBERT BROWNELL, Jr., of New York, continued from preceding administration. WILLIAM P. ROGERS, of Maryland, ad interim, November 8, 1957, to January 27, 1958. WILLIAM P. ROGERS, of Maryland, January 27, 1958.

POSTMASTER GENERAL—ARTHUR E. SUMMERFIELD, of Michigan, continued from preceding administration. ARTHUR E. SUMMERFIELD, of Michigan, recommissioned February 4, 1957.

SECRETARY OF THE INTERIOR—FREDERICK A. SEATON, of Nebraska, continued from preceding administration.

SECRETARY OF AGRICULTURE—EZRA TAFT BENSON, of Utah, continued from preceding administration.

SECRETARY OF COMMERCE—SINCLAIR WEEKS, of Massachusetts, continued from preceding administration. LEWIS L. STRAUSS, of New York, ad interim, November 13, 1958, to June 27, 1959. FREDERICK H. MUELLER, of Michigan (Under Secretary), ad interim, July 21, 1959, to August 6, 1959. FREDERICK H. MUELLER, of Michigan, August 6, 1959.

SECRETARY OF LABOR—JAMES P. MITCHELL, of New Jersey, continued from preceding administration.

SECRETARY OF HEALTH, EDUCATION, AND WELFARE—MARION B. FOLSOM, of New York, continued from preceding administration. ARTHUR S. FLEMMING, of Ohio, July 9, 1958; entered upon duties August 1, 1958.

———

## Administration of JOHN F. KENNEDY

### JANUARY 20, 1961, TO NOVEMBER 22, 1963

PRESIDENT OF THE UNITED STATES—JOHN F. KENNEDY, of Massachusetts. (Died November 22, 1963.)

VICE PRESIDENT OF THE UNITED STATES—LYNDON B. JOHNSON, of Texas.

SECRETARY OF STATE—DEAN RUSK, of New York, January 21, 1961.

SECRETARY OF THE TREASURY—DOUGLAS DILLON, of New Jersey, January 21, 1961.

SECRETARY OF DEFENSE—ROBERT S. McNAMARA, of Michigan, January 21, 1961.

ATTORNEY GENERAL—ROBERT F. KENNEDY, of Massachusetts, January 21, 1961.

POSTMASTER GENERAL—J. EDWARD DAY, of California, January 21, 1961. JOHN A. GRONOUSKI, of Wisconsin, September 24, 1963; entered upon duties September 30, 1963.

SECRETARY OF THE INTERIOR—STEWART L. UDALL, of Arizona, January 21, 1961.

SECRETARY OF AGRICULTURE—ORVILLE L. FREEMAN, of Minnesota, January 21, 1961.

SECRETARY OF COMMERCE—LUTHER H. HODGES, of North Carolina, January 21, 1961.

SECRETARY OF LABOR—ARTHUR J. GOLDBERG, of Illinois, January 21, 1961. W. WILLARD WIRTZ, of Illinois, September 20, 1962; entered upon duties September 25, 1962.

SECRETARY OF HEALTH, EDUCATION, AND WELFARE—ABRAHAM A. RIBICOFF, of Connecticut, January 21, 1961. ANTHONY J. CELEBREZZE, of Ohio, July 20, 1962; entered upon duties July 31, 1962.

## First Administration of LYNDON B. JOHNSON
### NOVEMBER 22, 1963, TO JANUARY 20, 1965

PRESIDENT OF THE UNITED STATES—LYNDON B. JOHNSON, of Texas.

SPEAKER OF THE HOUSE OF REPRESENTATIVES—JOHN W. McCORMACK, of Massachusetts.

SECRETARY OF STATE—DEAN RUSK, of New York, continued from preceding administration.

SECRETARY OF THE TREASURY—DOUGLAS DILLON, of New Jersey, continued from preceding administration.

SECRETARY OF DEFENSE—ROBERT S. McNAMARA, of Michigan, continued from preceding administration.

ATTORNEY GENERAL—ROBERT F. KENNEDY, of Massachusetts, continued from preceding administration. NICHOLAS DEB. KATZENBACH, of Illinois (Deputy Attorney General), ad interim, September 4, 1964.

POSTMASTER GENERAL—JOHN A. GRONOUSKI, of Wisconsin, continued from preceding administration.

SECRETARY OF THE INTERIOR—STEWART L. UDALL, of Arizona, continued from preceding administration.

SECRETARY OF AGRICULTURE—ORVILLE L. FREEMAN, of Minnesota, continued from preceding administration.

SECRETARY OF COMMERCE—LUTHER H. HODGES, of North Carolina, continued from preceding administration. JOHN T. O'CONNOR, of New Jersey, January 15, 1965; entered upon duties January 18, 1965.

SECRETARY OF LABOR—W. WILLARD WIRTZ, of Illinois, continued from preceding administration.

SECRETARY OF HEALTH, EDUCATION, AND WELFARE—ANTHONY J. CELEBREZZE, of Ohio, continued from preceding administration.

---

## Second Administration of LYNDON B. JOHNSON
### JANUARY 20, 1965, TO JANUARY 20, 1969

PRESIDENT OF THE UNITED STATES—LYNDON B. JOHNSON, of Texas.

VICE PRESIDENT OF THE UNITED STATES—HUBERT H. HUMPHREY, of Minnesota.

SECRETARY OF STATE—DEAN RUSK, of New York, continued from preceding administration.

SECRETARY OF THE TREASURY—DOUGLAS DILLON, of New Jersey, continued from preceding administration. HARRY H. FOWLER, of Virginia, March 25, 1965; entered upon duties April 1, 1965. JOSEPH W. BARR, of Indiana, entered upon duties December 21, 1968 (recess appointment); confirmed January 9, 1969.

SECRETARY OF DEFENSE—ROBERT S. McNAMARA, of Michigan, continued from preceding administration. CLARK M. CLIFFORD, of Maryland, January 30, 1968; entered upon duties March 1, 1968.

ATTORNEY GENERAL—NICHOLAS DEB. KATZENBACH, of Illinois (Deputy Attorney General), ad interim, continued from preceding administration. NICHOLAS DEB. KATZENBACH, of Illinois, confirmed February 10, 1965; entered upon duties February 11, 1965. RAMSEY CLARK, of Texas, March 2, 1967.

POSTMASTER GENERAL—JOHN A. GRONOUSKI, of Wisconsin, continued from preceding administration. JOHN A. GRONOUSKI, of Wisconsin, recommissioned February 17, 1965. LAWRENCE F. O'BRIEN, of Massachusetts, September 1, 1965; entered upon duties November 3, 1965. W. MARVIN WATSON, of Texas, April 23, 1968; entered upon duties April 26, 1968.

SECRETARY OF THE INTERIOR—STEWART L. UDALL, of Arizona, continued from preceding administration.

SECRETARY OF AGRICULTURE—ORVILLE L. FREEMAN, of Minnesota, continued from preceding administration.

SECRETARY OF COMMERCE—JOHN T. O'CONNOR, of New Jersey, continued from preceding administration. ALEXANDER B. TROWBRIDGE, of New York, ad interim, February 1, 1967. ALEXANDER B. TROWBRIDGE, of New York, June 8, 1967; entered upon duties June 14, 1967. CYRUS R. SMITH, of New York, March 1, 1968; entered upon duties March 6, 1968.

SECRETARY OF LABOR—W. WILLARD WIRTZ, of Illinois, continued from preceding administration.

SECRETARY OF HEALTH, EDUCATION, AND WELFARE—ANTHONY J. CELEBREZZE, of Ohio, continued from preceding administration. JOHN W. GARDNER, of New York, August 11, 1965; entered upon duties August 18, 1965. WILBUR J. COHEN, of Michigan, ad interim, March 2, 1968. WILBUR J. COHEN, of Michigan, May 16, 1968.

SECRETARY OF HOUSING AND URBAN DEVELOPMENT—ROBERT C. WEAVER, of New York, January 17, 1966; entered upon duties January 18, 1966. ROBERT C. WOOD, of Florida, ad interim, January 2, 1969.

SECRETARY OF TRANSPORTATION—ALAN S. BOYD, of Florida, January 12, 1967; entered upon duties January 16, 1967.

Administration of RICHARD M. NIXON

JANUARY 20, 1969 TO JANUARY 20, 1973

PRESIDENT OF THE UNITED STATES--RICHARD M. NIXON, of
    California.

VICE PRESIDENT OF THE UNITED STATES--SPIRO T. AGNEW,
    of Maryland

SECRETARY OF STATE--WILLIAM P. Rogers, of Maryland,
    January 20, 1969; entered upon duties January 22,
    1969

SECRETARY OF THE TREASURY--DAVID M. KENNEDY, of Illi-
    nois, January 20, 1969; entered upon duties January
    22, 1969.  JOHN B. CONNALLY, of Texas, entered upon
    duties February 11, 1971.  GEORGE P. SHULTZ, of
    Illinois, May 16, 1972; entered upon duties June
    12, 1972.

SECRETARY OF DEFENSE--MELVIN R. LAIRD, of Wisconsin,
    January 20, 1969; entered upon duties January 22,
    1969

ATTORNEY GENERAL--JOHN N. MITCHELL, of New York, Janu-
    ary 20, 1969; entered upon duties January 21, 1969.
    RICHARD G. KLEINDIENST, of Arizona, February 15,
    1972; entered upon duties June 12, 1972.

POSTMASTER GENERAL--WINTON M. BLOUNT, of Alabama, Janu-
    ary 20, 1969, entered upon duties January 22, 1969

SECRETARY OF THE INTERIOR--WALTER J. HICKEL, of Alaska,
    January 23, 1969; entered upon duties January 24,
    1969.  FRED J. RUSSELL, of California, ad interim,
    November 26, 1970.  ROGERS C. B. MORTON, of Mary-
    land, entered upon duties January 29, 1971.

SECRETARY OF AGRICULTURE--CLIFFORD M. HARDIN, of Ne-
    braska, January 20, 1969; entered upon duties Janu-
    ary 21, 1969.  EARL L. BUTZ, of Indiana, November
    11, 1971; entered upon duties December 2, 1971.

SECRETARY OF COMMERCE--MAURICE H. STANS, of New York,
    January 20, 1969; entered upon duties January 21,
    1969.  PETER G. PETERSON, of Illinois, January 27,
    1972; entered upon duties February 21, 1972.
    FREDERICK B. DENT, of South Carolina, December 6,
    1972; entered upon duties January 18, 1973

SECRETARY OF LABOR--GEORGE P. SHULTZ, of Illinois,
    January 20, 1969; entered upon duties January 22,

1969.   JAMES D. HODGSON, of California, June 17, 1970;
   entered upon duties July 2, 1970.  PETER J. BRENNAN,
   of New York, November 29, 1972; entered upon duties
   January 17, 1973.

SECRETARY OF HEALTH, EDUCATION, AND WELFARE--ROBERT H.
   FINCH, of California, January 21, 1969.  ELLIOT L.
   RICHARDSON, of Massachusetts, June 15, 1970; en-
   tered upon duties June 24, 1970.  CASPAR W. WEINBER-
   GER, of California, nominated November 28, 1972.

SECRETARY OF HOUSING AND URBAN DEVELOPMENT--GEORGE
   ROMNEY, of Michigan, January 20, 1969; entered upon
   duties January 22, 1969.  JAMES T. LYNN, of Ohio,
   nominated December 5, 1972

SECRETARY OF TRANSPORTATION--JOHN A. VOLPE, of Massachusetts, January 20, 1969; entered upon duties
   January 21, 1969.  CLAUDE S. BRINEGAR, of California,
   December 7, 1972; entered upon duties, January 18,
   1973.

Second Administration of RICHARD M. NIXON

JANUARY 20, 1973 TO AUGUST 9, 1974

PRESIDENT OF THE UNITED STATES--RICHARD M. NIXON, of
   California

VICE PRESIDENT OF THE UNITED STATES--SPIRO T. AGNEW,
   of Maryland.  (Resigned October 10, 1973).

VICE PRESIDENT OF THE UNITED STATES--GERALD R. FORD,
   of Michigan.  (Nominated by President NIXON under
   provisions of the Twenty-fifth Amendment and approved by the Senate and House of Representatives.)
   Sworn in December 6, 1973.

SECRETARY OF STATE--WILLIAM P. ROGERS, of Maryland,
   continued from preceding administration.  HENRY
   A. KISSINGER, of New York, entered upon duties
   August 22, 1973.

SECRETARY OF THE TREASURY--GEORGE P. SHULTZ, of Illinois, continued from preceding administration.
   WILLIAM E, SIMON, of New York, April 17, 1974;
   entered upon duties April 30, 1974.

SECRETARY OF DEFENSE--ELLIOT L. RICHARDSON, of Massa-

chusetts, entered upon duties January 29, 1973.
JAMES RODNEY SCHLESINGER, of New York, May 10,
1973; entered upon duties June 28, 1973.

ATTORNEY GENERAL--RICHARD G. KLEINDIENST, of Arizona,
    continued from preceding administration.  ELLIOT L.
    RICHARDSON, of Massachusetts, April 30, 1973; en-
    tered upon duties May 25, 1973.  WILLIAM B. SAXBE,
    of Ohio, November 1, 1973; entered upon duties
    January 4, 1974.

SECRETARY OF THE INTERIOR--ROGERS C. B. MORTON, of
    Maryland, continued from preceding administration.

SECRETARY OF AGRICULTURE--EARL L. BUTZ, of Indiana
    continued from preceding administration.

SECRETARY OF COMMERCE--FREDERICK B. DENT, of South
    Carolina, continued from preceding administration.

SECRETARY OF LABOR--PETER J. BRENNAN, of New York, con-
    tinued from preceding administration.

SECRETARY OF HEALTH, EDUCATION, AND WELFARE--CASPAR W.
    WEINBERGER, of California, entered upon duties
    February 8, 1973.

SECRETARY OF HOUSING AND URBAN DEVELOPMENT--JAMES T.
    LYNN, of Ohio, entered upon duties January 31, 1973.

SECRETARY OF TRANSPORTATION--CLAUDE S. BRINEGAR, of
    California, continued from preceding administration.

———

Administration of GERALD R. FORD

AUGUST 9, 1974 TO JANUARY 20, 1977

VICE PRESIDENT OF THE UNITED STATES--NELSON A. ROCKE-
    FELLER, of New York. (Nominated by President FORD
    under provisions of the Twenty-fifth Amendment and
    approved by the Senate and House of Representatives.)
    Sworn in December 19, 1974

SECRETARY OF STATE--HENRY A. KISSINGER,  of New York,
    continued from preceding administration.

SECRETARY OF THE TREASURY--WILLIAM E. SIMON, of New
    York, continued from preceding administration.

SECRETARY OF DEFENSE--JAMES R. SCHLESINGER, of New
York, continued from preceding administration.

ATTORNEY GENERAL--WILLIAM B. SAXBE, of Ohio, continued
from preceding administration.

SECRETARY OF THE INTERIOR--ROGERS C. B. Morton, of
Maryland, continued from preceding administration.

SECRETARY OF AGRICULTURE--EARL L. BUTZ, of Indiana,
continued from preceding administration.

SECRETARY OF COMMERCE--FREDERICK B. DENT, of South
Carolina, continued from preceding administration.

SECRETARY OF LABOR--PETER J. BRENNAN, of New York,
continued from preceding administration.

SECRETARY OF HEALTH, EDUCATION, AND WELFARE--CASPAR W.
WEINBERGER, of California, entered upon duties
February 8, 1973.

SECRETARY OF HOUSING AND URBAN DEVELOPMENT--JAMES T.
LYNN, of Ohio, entered upon duties January 31, 1973.

SECRETARY OF TRANSPORTATION--CLAUDE S. BRINEGAR, of
California, continued from preceding administration.

NAME INDEX

Celebrezze, Dorothy Marcu-
gusieppe, 738
Celebrezze, Jean Anne, 738
Celebrezze, Rocco, 738
Celebrezze, Susan Marie,
738
Chamberlain, Austen, 537
Chambers, Whitaker, 667
Chamoun, President, 682
Chandler, Ann Caroline
(Gilmore), 338
Chandler, Margaret Orr,
295
Chandler, Mary Ann Tucker,
337
Chandler, Nathan S., 337
Chandler, Samuel, 295
Chandler, William E., 337,
338, 339
Chandler, Zachariah, 295,
296
Chapin, Daniel, 569
Chapin, Edward Cornelius,
569
Chapin, Ella King, 569
Chapin, Inez (Tiedeman),
569
Chapin, Joan King, 569
Chapin, John Carsten, 569
Chapin, Manning, 569
Chapin, Roy, 569
Chapin, Roy D., 568, 569
Chapin, Sara Ann, 569
Chapman, Ann (Kendrick),
654
Chapman, James Jackson,
653
Chapman, James Raleigh, 654
Chapman, Olga Pauline (Ed-
holm), 653
Chapman, Oscar L., 653,
654
Chapman, Rosa Archer Blant,
653
Chappell, Absalom, 355
Chase, Eliza Ann (Smith),
234
Chase, Ithmer, 234
Chase, Janette Ralston, 234
Chase, Jeremiah Townley,
150
Chase, Katherine Jane (Gar-
niss), 234

Chase, Philander, 234
Chase, Salmon P., 234, 235,
236, 237, 292, 238, 292
Chase, Samuel, 22, 33, 47,
67, 84, 172
Chauncey, Commodore, 66
Cherlick, Commissioner, 346
Chinan, Julia, 126
Christensen, Neils L., 588
Christiancy, Isaac P., 296
Church, Judge, 330
Churchill, Winston, 604,
624. 627, 660
Clairborne, Governor, 101
Clark, Champ, 471
Clark, Georgia (Welch), 748
Clark, Mary Jane (Ramsey),
645, 748
Clark, Mildred, 645
Clark, Ronda Kathleen, 748
Clark, Thomas C., 644, 645,
646, 647, 748
Clark, Thomas Campbell (son
of Thomas C.), 645
Clark, Thomas Campbell (son
of Ramsey), 748
Clark, Virginia Maxey
(Falls), 644
Clark, /William7 Ramsey,
645, 748, 749
Clay, Senator Alexander S.,
388
Clay, C. C., 227
Clay, Elizabeth Hudson, 90
Clay, Henry, 78, 79, 81, 82,
90, 91, 92, 93, 121, 143,
152, 153, 179, 189, 198
Clay, James B., 90
Clay, Rev. John, 90
Clay, Joseph, 116
Clay, Lucretia (Hart), 90
Clay, Thomas H., 90
Clayton, James, 179
Clayton, John M., 186
Clayton, Sara Middleton, 179
Clemens, Samuel (see also
Mark Twain), 476
Cleveland, Grover, 244, 254,
272, 317, 323, 331, 333,
340, 342, 343, 344, 345,
346, 347, 348, 349, 350,
351, 352, 353, 354, 355,
356, 357, 358, 374, 375